A BANK'S DUTY OF CARE

In recent years, an increasing number of clients and third parties have filed claims against banks such as for mis-selling financial products, poor financial advice, insufficient disclosure of and warning about financial risks. The scope of a bank's duty of care seems to expand, not only to include protection of consumers against unclear risks of complicated products but also protection of professional parties against more obvious risks of relatively straightforward products.

This topic raises many questions, both at a theoretical and practical level. This book provides a rich source of information about how various jurisdictions (Germany, Austria, France, Italy, Spain, the Netherlands, England and Wales, Ireland, and the United States of America) deal with these questions and how answers are found or embedded in their national legal systems. The book also contains a detailed chapter on the MiFID I and II conduct-of-business provisions. Finally, the book provides a thorough comparative analysis and perspective.

A Bank's Duty of Care

Edited by
Danny Busch and Cees van Dam

•HART•
OXFORD • LONDON • NEW YORK • NEW DELHI • SYDNEY

HART PUBLISHING
Bloomsbury Publishing Plc
Kemp House, Chawley Park, Cumnor Hill, Oxford, OX2 9PH, UK

HART PUBLISHING, the Hart/Stag logo, BLOOMSBURY and the Diana logo are trademarks of Bloomsbury Publishing Plc
First published in Great Britain 2017

First published in hardback, 2017
Paperback edition, 2019

A catalogue record for this book is available from the British Library.

Library of Congress Cataloging-in-Publication Data

Names: Busch, Danny, editor. | Dam, C. C. van, editor.

Title: A bank's duty of care / edited by Danny Busch and Cees van Dam.

Description: Oxford [UK] ; Portland, Oregon : Hart Publishing, 2017. | Includes bibliographical references and index. | Description based on print version record and CIP data provided by publisher; resource not viewed.

Identifiers: LCCN 2017013635 (print) | LCCN 2017014024 (ebook) | ISBN 9781509912612 (Epub) | ISBN 9781849468114 (hardback)

Subjects: LCSH: Financial institutions—Law and legislation. | Financial services industry—Law and legislation. | Banking law. | Consumer protection—Law and legislation. | Bank failures—Law and legislation. | Banks and banking, International—Law and legislation.

Classification: LCC K1066 (ebook) | LCC K1066 .B366 2017 (print) | DDC 346/.082—dc23

LC record available at https://lccn.loc.gov/2017013635

ISBN: HB: 978-1-84946-811-4
PB: 978-1-50993-570-3
ePDF: 978-1-50991-263-6
ePub: 978-1-50991-261-2

Typeset by Compuscript Ltd, Shannon

To find out more about our authors and books visit www.hartpublishing.co.uk. Here you will find extracts, author information, details of forthcoming events and the option to sign up for our newsletters.

TABLE OF CONTENTS

LIST OF CONTRIBUTORS

Kern Alexander is Professor of Banking and Financial Market Law at the University of Zurich and a Senior Research Fellow in Legal and Financial Risk at the Cambridge Judge Business School.

Jens-Hinrich Binder is Professor of Private Law, Commercial Law, Company and Securities Law at Eberhard Karls University, Tübingen, Germany.

Thierry Bonneau is Professor of law at University Panthéon-Assas (Paris, France).

Danny Busch is Professor of Financial Law and Director of the Institute for Financial Law (IFL), University of Nijmegen, the Netherlands, Visiting Professor at Università degli Studi di Genova, Visiting Professor at Università Cattolica del Sacro Cuore di Milano and Member of the Dutch Banking Disciplinary Committee (Tuchtcommissie Banken).

Blanaid Clarke holds the McCann FitzGerald Chair of Corporate Law, Trinity College Dublin.

Marco Garavelli is Senior Associate at Lombardi Segni Law Firm in Milan and Teaching Assistant of Company and Business Law at Bocconi University in Milan.

Eduardo Valpuesta Gastaminza is Professor of Commercial Law at University of Navarra.

Pedro-José Bueso Guillén is Professor of Commercial and Business Law at the University of Zaragoza.

George C Harris is Senior Counsel at Morrison & Foerster LLP in San Francisco, California.

Sabrina Larson is an associate at Morrison & Foerster LLP.

Jorge Noval Pato is Senior Lecturer of Commercial Law at University of Navarra.

Julian Ring is assistant lecturer at the chair of Martin Spitzer at the Wirtschaftsuniversität in Vienna.

Filippo Rossi is Partner at Lombardi Segni Law Firm in Milan.

Manuel Ángel López Sánchez is Professor of Commercial Law at University of Navarra.

Martin Spitzer is Professor of Civil Law and Civil Procedure Law at the Wirtschaftsuniversität in Vienna.

Hannibal Travis is Professor of Law at Florida International University College of Law.

Cees van Dam is Professor of European Tort Law at Maastricht University, Professor of International Business and Human Rights at the Rotterdam School of Management, Erasmus University, and Visiting Professor at King's College London.

Bart van der Wiel is advocaat in Amsterdam at Houthoff Buruma.

ABBREVIATIONS

ABF	*Arbitro Bancario Finanziario* (Banking-Financial Arbitrator)
ABGB	*Allgemeines Bürgerliches Gesetzbuch* (Austrian General Civil Code)
ABS	asset-backed securities
ACF	*Arbitro per le Controversie Finanziarie* (Financial Disputes Arbitrator)
ADR	alternative dispute resolution
AIFs	alternative investment funds
AktG	*Aktiengesetz* (Stock Corporations Act)
BaFin	*Bundesanstalt für Finanzdienstleistungsaufsicht*
BBA	British Bankers Association
BFA	*Banco Financiero de Ahorros*
BGH	*Bundesgerichtshof* (Federal Supreme Court)
BGHS	*Bezirksgericht für Handelssachen Wien* (Vienna Commercial District Court)
BörseG	*Börsegesetz* (Stock Exchange Act)
CCA	*Camera di Conciliazione e Arbitrato* (Conciliation and Arbitration Chamber)
CCA	Consumer Credit Act
CDO	structured finance notes
CDS	credit default swaps
CFPB	Consumer Financial Protection Bureau
CIBC	Canadian Imperial Bank of Commerce
CLNs	Credit Linked Notes
CMHC	Commission for Monitoring Hybrid Capital and Subordinated Debt Instruments
COBS	Conduct of Business Sourcebook
CPC	Ceylon Petroleum Corporation
CRD	Capital Requirements Directive
CRR	Capital Requirements Regulation
CRSM	*Cassa di Risparmio della Repubblica di San Marino*
CX	Catalunya Caixa
DCC	Dutch Civil Code (*Burgerlijk Wetboek*)
EBA	European Banking Authority
ECJ	European Court of Justice
EFTA	Electronic Fund Transfer Act
ESMA	European Securities and Markets Authority
EU	European Union

FCA	Financial Conduct Authority
FDIC	Federal Deposit Insurance Corporation
FinDAG	*Finanzdienstleistungs–Aufsichtsgesetz*
FINRA	Financial Industry Regulatory Authority
FMA	*Finanzmarktaufsicht*
FOS	Financial Ombudsman Service
FROB	*Fondo de Reestructuración Ordinaria Bancaria* (Fund for Orderly Bank Restructuring)
FSA	Financial Services Authority
FSMA	Financial Services and Markets Act
FTC	Federal Trade Commission
GLBA	Gramm-Leach-Bliley Act
GSI	Goldman Sachs International
HG	*Handelsgericht Wien* (Vienna Commercial Court)
HR	Hoge Raad
ICI	Investment Company Institute
ICOB rules	Insurance: Conduct of Business Rules
ICOBS	Insurance: Conduct of Business Source
IM	information memorandum
IMD	Insurance Mediation Directive
IPO	initial public offering
ISD	Investment Services Directive
ISPs	investment service providers
JN	*Jurisdiktionsnorm* (Court Jurisdiction Act)
KiFID	*Klachteninstituut Financiële Dienstverlening* (Complaint Institute Financial Services)
KMG	*Kapitalmarktgesetz* (Capital Market Act)
KSchG	*Konsumentenschutzgesetz* (Consumer Protection Act)
KYC	know your customer
LCCC	*Ley de Contratos de Crédito al Consumo* (Act on Credit Contracts for Consumers)
LCD	*Ley de Competencia Desleal* (Unfair Competition Act)
LCDSFDC	*Ley de Comercialización a Distancia de Servicios Financieros destinados a los Consumidores* (Act on Distance Selling to Consumers of Financial Services)
LCGC	*Ley de Condiciones Generales de la Contratación* (General Conditions of Contract Act)
LDIEC	*Ley de Disciplina e Intervención de las Entidades de Crédito* (Act on Discipline and Intervention of Credit Institutions)
LEC	*Ley de Enjuiciamiento Civil* (Civil Procedure Act)
LES	*Ley de Economía Sostenible* (Sustainable Economy Act)
LGP	*Ley General de Publicidad* (General Advertising Act)
LIA	Libyan Investment Authority

LMH	*Ley de Regulación del Mercado Hipotecario* (Mortgage Market Regulation Act)
LMPDH	*Ley de Medidas para Reforzar la Protección de los Deudores Hipotecarios* (Act on measures to reinforce protection of mortgage debtors, debt restructuring and social rental housing)
LOSSEC	*Ley de Ordenación, Supervisión y Solvencia de las Entidades de Crédito* (Act on Regulation, Supervision and Solvency of Credit Institutions)
LSC	*Ley de Sociedades de Capital* (Capital Companies Act)
LSP	*Ley de Servicios de Pago* (Payment Services Act)
LSSICE	*Ley de Servicios de la Sociedad de la Información y del Comercio Electrónico* (Information Services and Electronic Commerce Act)
MAR	Market Abuse Regulations
MEL	Meinl European Land
MiFID	Markets in Financial Instruments Directive
MiFIR	Markets in Financial Instruments Regulation
MTF	multilateral trading facility
NCAs	national competent authorities
OCC	Office of the Comptroller of the Currency
OECD	Organisation for Economic Cooperation and Development
OGH	*Oberster Gerichtshof* (Supreme Court)
OTF	organised trading facility
PD	probability of default
PPI	payment protection insurance
PSLRA	Private Securities Litigation Reform Act
SCB	Standard Chartered Bank
SCPI	*société civile de placements immobilier*
SEC	Securities Exchange Commission
SIM	syndication information memorandum
SMEs	small and medium-sized enterprises
SNB	Swiss National Bank
SPV	special purpose vehicle
SRBE	*Servicio de Reclamaciones del Banco de España* (Claims Service of Bank of Spain)
SRO	self-regulatory organisation
TILA	Truth in Lending Act
TISA	Truth in Savings Act
TRLGDCU	*Texto Refundido de la Ley General para la Defensa de los Consumidores y Usuarios y legislación Complementaria* (Consolidated text of the General Act for the Defence of Consumers and Users and other complementary laws)
TRLMV	*texto refundido de la Ley del Mercado de Valores* (consolidated text of the Securities Market Act)
UBIL	Ulster Bank Ireland Limited

UCC	Uniform Commercial Code
UCITS	undertakings for collective investment in transferable securities
UCL	Unfair Competition Law
UPIA	Uniform Prudent Investor Act
UWG	*Bundesgesetz gegen den unlauteren Wettbewerb* (Act against Unfair Competition)
VKrG	*Verbraucherkreditgesetz* (Consumer Credit Act)
WAG	*Wertpapieraufsichtsgesetz* (Securities Supervision Act)
WCAM	*Wet Collectieve Afwikkeling Massaschade* (Collective Settlement Mass Claims Act)
WestLB	WestLandesbank
Wft	*Wet op het financieel toezicht* (Dutch Financial Supervision Act)
WpHG	*Wertpapierhandelsgesetz* (Securities Trading Act)
ZPO	*Zivilprozessordnung* (Code of Civil Procedure)

Part I

Introduction

1

Introduction

DANNY BUSCH AND CEES VAN DAM

I. Introduction

In recent years, more and more clients and third parties have filed claims against banks such as for mis-selling financial products, poor financial advice, insufficient disclosure of and warning for financial risks. The scope of the duty of care of banks seems to expand: from protection of consumers against unclear risks of complicated products to protection of professional parties and against more obvious risks of relatively straightforward products.

The duty of care of banks raises many questions, both at a theoretical and practical level. The topic is relatively novel and in a state of flux. Many important questions are still in search of clear answers. Comparative law books on the topic are scarce. We therefore ventured to collect information about how various jurisdictions deal with a bank's duty of care and how answers are found or embedded in the national legal system. We also aimed to place a bank's duty of care in a European and comparative law perspective. We hope this book will facilitate cross-border discussion and exchange of ideas on the role and limitations of a bank's duty of care, both in theory and practice. The aim of this book is necessarily modest. Given the dynamic character of the topic, the best this book can offer is a snapshot in time.

II. Scope and Terminology

The book is principally concerned with the duty of care in the area of the provision of investment services, ie execution-only services, investment advice and asset management. However, as will be seen in the next chapters, in many jurisdictions the duty of care applies well beyond this scope.

In all jurisdictions covered, banks offer investment services on a large, if not massive, scale. Nevertheless, independent investment advisers and asset managers may also provide investment services, even though they do not qualify as a bank from the perspective of the applicable regulatory framework. Most of what is said in this book on the duty of care of banks providing investment services equally applies to non-bank entities providing such services, at least as far as the European jurisdictions covered by this book are concerned.

'Duty of care' is not the term of art in all jurisdictions. In common law jurisdictions in particular the term is bound to cause confusion. We essentially aimed to focus on duties to investigate, duties to disclose or warn, and—in exceptional cases—outright duties to refuse to render financial services or offer products, no matter the nature of their legal source. In view of this we adopted a functional approach and also included discussion on fiduciary duties, common law duties (other than duties of care), as well as all kinds of statutory duties. In this chapter and in Chapter 12, we will nevertheless use the term 'duty of care' as convenient shorthand.

III. MiFID

Banks providing investment services have been subject to the Markets in Financial Instruments Directive (MiFID I) since 1 November 2007.[1] On 3 January 2018—some 10 years later—the MiFID I regime will be replaced by MiFID II (in the remainder of this chapter, MiFID I and II are collectively referred to as MiFID).[2] MiFID contains a general duty of loyalty, which to some extent has been fleshed out in more specific conduct of business rules for banks (and others) providing investment services, including detailed duties to investigate (know your customer or KYC rules) and duties to inform.[3] In most of the EU jurisdictions included in this book, it is now commonly accepted that these regulatory rules, especially the conduct of business rules, help to define the pre-contractual and contractual duty of care of banks under private law. Moreover, in many jurisdictions, an infringement of national implementing provisions can constitute not only a breach of the civil duty of care but also a tort (unlawful act)

[1] The MiFID I regime at level 1 and 2 is composed of three measures: (1) Directive 2004/39/EC [2004] OJ L145/1; (2) Commission Regulation (EC) No1287/2006 [2006] OJ L241/1; (3) Commission Directive 2006/73/EC [2006] OJ L241/26. It should be noted that not all Member States of the European Union and countries forming part of the European Economic Area succeeded in implementing the MiFID regime as of 1 November 2007.

[2] The MiFID II regime at level 1 and 2 is composed of the following measures: (1) Directive 2014/65/EU [2014] OJ L 173/349 (MiFID II); (2) Regulation (EU) No. 600/2014 [2014] OJ L 173/84 (MiFIR); (3) a truly impressive number of implementing measures. Initially, MiFID II/MiFIR stipulated that the bulk of the new legislation would become binding on the financial sector as of 3 January 2017, but this has been postponed until 3 January 2018 by means of a directive and a regulation published in the Official Journal on 23 June 2016, see (1) Directive 2016/1034/EU [2016] OJ L 175/8; (2) Regulation (EU) No 2016/1033 [2016] OJ L 175/1.

[3] MiFID I, Art 19(1); MiFID II, Art 24(1).

for breach of a statutory duty. It should also be noted that duties of care under public law and other regulatory provisions are regularly explicitly incorporated into the contract, with all the contractual consequences this entails. This is why the book starts with a detailed chapter on the conduct of business rules pursuant to MiFID.

IV. The National Legal Systems Studied

As for our choice for the national legal systems included in this book, the following factors were leading: (1) a focus on Europe; (2) inclusion of jurisdictions with a major banking sector; (3) inclusion of the most important representatives of the civil and common law legal systems; (4) a fair balance between civil and common law legal systems; and (5) specific substantive law reasons.

It seemed only natural to include the civil law jurisdictions of Germany, France and Italy. They all have a large domestic banking sector and are important representatives of the civil law tradition. Austria, Spain and the Netherlands are less obvious choices, but the inclusion of these civil law jurisdictions is justified for specific substantive law reasons. In Spain and Austria disputes with banks are often resolved by reference to the doctrine of error or fraud. This divergent approach provides an interesting contrast with the other jurisdictions covered by this book, where the focal point is a damages claim for breach of a bank's duty of care. The Netherlands is an interesting jurisdiction for specific substantive law reasons as well, because the Dutch Supreme Court succeeded in developing a coherent and very consumer-friendly body of case-law on a bank's 'special' duty of care (*bijzondere zorgplicht*).

As for the common law jurisdictions in this book, we note the following. The UK has the fourth largest banking sector in the world and the largest in Europe. England and Wales is the most important common law jurisdiction in Europe. Inclusion of a chapter on England and Wales therefore goes without saying, although Brexit may well have an impact on its leadership in the banking sector. Common law jurisdictions are scarce in Europe so it seemed an obvious choice to include Ireland, which over the past few years has also emerged as a major international financial services centre. Both in Ireland and England and Wales the common law plays a more modest role with a stronger focus on statutory actions as compared to continental Europe. We completed the picture with a chapter on the US. The US is clearly outside of Europe, but its inclusion is justified because it is the most important common law jurisdiction outside of Europe and it has a large banking sector. Finally, the inclusion of a chapter on the US strikes a better balance between the civil law and common law jurisdictions included in the book. Moreover, the US and England and Wales are interesting because of the different balance between private and public enforcement and the active role of the regulators in forcing banks to provide remedies to investors.

V. Methodology

It was important to us to provide the authors of the national chapters with flexibility in the preparation of their chapters. The instructions they received were limited to a brief questionnaire with some fairly general questions. We did not seek to impose a certain structure or uniformity in approach in general. We considered it important to allow the contributors to emphasise the principles and remedies which they deemed important in their own legal system. At times, one of the national chapters may discuss an issue not covered in the other chapters. We were happy to include such features, provided that they covered material that was relevant. We saw it as our duty to create the overall picture in our comparative law evaluation (Chapter 12). As long as each chapter provided us with the main ingredients, uniformity of approach in the national chapters themselves was not necessary.

In this book we have used the so-called successive comparative law method, according to which material from national legal systems is analysed first, followed by the comparative law evaluation.[4] In our view, especially in view of the fact that no fewer than nine legal systems are taken into account, this method is the best way of ensuring that the research is clearly organised and can be easily consulted and checked.

VI. Structure of the Book

This book is structured as follows. Part I consists of the present introductory chapter. Part II contains a chapter on the EU regulatory framework: MiFID (Chapter 2). Part III contains the civil law jurisdictions covered by this book: Germany (Chapter 3), Austria (Chapter 4), France (Chapter 5), Italy (Chapter 6), Spain (Chapter 7) and The Netherlands (Chapter 8). Part IV covers the following common law jurisdictions: England and Wales (Chapter 9), Ireland (Chapter 10) and the United States of America (Chapter 11).

Part V contains a chapter on a bank's duty of care from a European and comparative law perspective (Chapter 12). In this final chapter, we focus on five topics which are hotly debated in theory and practice. The first topic is the scope and intensity of the essential duties which typically flow from a bank's duty of care: duties to investigate, duties to disclose or warn, and—in exceptional cases—outright duties to refuse to render financial services or offer products. In some jurisdictions (Spain and Austria), financial disputes between investors and banks

[4] On this subject, see D Kokkini-Iatridou et al, *Een inleiding tot het rechtsvergelijkende onderzoek* (Deventer: Kluwer, 1988) 187–88.

are not so much resolved by reference to a bank's duty of care, but by reference to the traditional doctrine of error or mistake, and fraud. That is the second topic we discuss in this chapter. The third topic is the impact of MiFID on a bank's duty of care. The fourth topic focuses on the role of the financial regulator in settling disputes between banks and clients. Under the heading of a fifth topic we highlight some recent reform proposals which enable us to put the bank's duty of care into a larger perspective.

This book purports to describe the law as it stood on 1 February 2017.

Part II

EU Law

2

Conduct-of-Business Rules under MiFID I and II

DANNY BUSCH

I. Introduction

As regulatory provisions are in most jurisdictions classified as public law, any failure by a bank or investment firm to comply with one or more regulatory provisions applicable to it will primarily affect its relationship with the competent financial regulator.[1] In other words, the relevant financial regulator can enforce these provisions under administrative law in the event of an infringement, for example by imposing an administrative fine on the firm.[2]

However, the regulatory provisions, in particular the conduct-of-business rules under MiFID I and MiFID II,[3] also have a major influence on relations

[1] Please note that in Germany a minority view in the legal literature qualifies the MiFID conduct-of-business rules (which most clearly pursue investor protection) as norms with a dual legal nature (*Doppelnatur*), with the effect that they not only qualify as regulatory rules, but also as private law norms. See inter alia M Casper and C Altgen, 'Chapter 4—Germany' in D Busch and DA DeMott (eds), *Liability of Asset Managers* (Oxford: Oxford University Press, 2012) § 4.23; R Veil, 'Anlageberatung im Zeitalter der MiFID—Inhalt und Konzeption der Pflichten und Grundlagen einer zivielrechlichen Haftung' (2007) 61 *Wertpapier-Mitteilungen* 1821, 1825–26; T Weichert and T Wenninger, 'Die Neuregelung der Erkundigungs-und Aufklärungspflichten von Wertpapierdienstleistungsundernehmen gem. Art. 19 RiL 2004/39/EG (MiFID) und Finanzmarkt-Richtlinie-Umsetzungsgesetz' (2007) 61 *Wertpapier-Mitteilungen* 627, 635. One German author even advances the view that the MiFID conduct-of-business rules qualify solely as private law norms because they place an obligation on a private firm towards its clients. See D Einsele, 'Anlegerschutz durch Information und Beratung—Verhaltens- und Schadenserzatzpflichten der Wertpapierdienstleistingsundernehmen nach Umsetzung der Finanzmarktrichtlinie (MiFID)' (2008) *JuristenZeitung* 477, 482. In Italy, the MiFID duties have a dual nature because they are considered both public and private law duties that an asset manager owes its clients. See P Giudici and M Bet, 'Chapter 5—Italy' in Busch and DeMott (eds), *Liability of Asset Managers* (above) § 5.42.

[2] The same applies if a regulated market infringes MiFID rules.

[3] Directive 2004/39/EC, OJ L 145, 30 April 2004, 1–47 (MiFID I); Commission Directive 2006/73/EC, OJ L 241, 2 September 2006, 26–58 (MiFID I Implementing Directive); Commission Regulation (EC) No 1287/2006, OJ L 241, 2 September 2006, 1–25 (MiFID I Implementing Regulation). MiFID

between the bank or investment firm and its clients under private law.[4] It is now commonly accepted in most European jurisdictions that the regulatory rules help to define the pre-contractual and contractual duty of care of banks and investment firms under private law. Moreover, in many jurisdictions, an infringement of national implementing provisions can constitute not only a breach of the civil duty of care but also a tort (unlawful act) for contravention of a statutory duty. It should also be noted that in the context of institutional portfolio management (for pensions funds, insurers and so forth) duties of care under public law and other regulatory provisions are regularly explicitly incorporated into the contract, with all the contractual consequences that this entails. Institutional portfolio management contracts routinely include a provision in which the portfolio manager declares that he has an authorisation from the competent financial supervisor and will at all times comply with the applicable regulatory law.[5]

Against this backdrop, the main conduct-of-business rules to be observed under MiFID I and II by banks (and others) providing investment services are examined below. In each case, the MiFID II regime is compared with the MiFID

I and the MiFID I Implementing Directive should have been transposed into national legislation in the various Member States of the European Union (EU) and the European Economic Area (EEA) by 1 November 2007 at the latest. In the Netherlands, eg, they have been transposed into the Financial Supervision Act (*Wet op het financieel toezicht*, Wft) and various implementing regulations such as the Market Conduct Supervision (Financial Institutions) Decree (*Besluit gedragstoezicht financiële ondernemingen*), in Germany into the *Wertpapierhandelsgesetz* (WpHG) and in the United Kingdom into the Financial Services and Markets Act 2000 (FSMA), the Financial Services and Markets Act 2000 (Carrying on Regulated Activities by way of Business) Order 2001 and, above all, the Financial Conduct Authority Handbook, which was known as the FSA Handbook before 1 April 2013. The name changed when the Financial Conduct Authority (FCA) succeeded the Financial Services Authority (FSA) on 1 April 2013. The MiFID II regime consists of (1) Directive 2014/65/EU, OJ L 173, 15 May 2014, 349–496 (MiFID II); (2) Regulation (EU) No 600/2014, OJ L 173, 15 May 2014, 84–148 (MiFIR); and (3) an impressive number of implementing measures. The relevant directives pertaining to MiFID II will, in a similar fashion to MiFID I, be transposed into national law (see above). Initially, MiFID II and MiFIR stipulated that the bulk of the new legislation would become binding on the financial sector as of 3 January 2017, but this has been extended to 3 January 2018. See Directive 2016/1034/EU OJ L 175, 23 June 2016, 8–11; (2) Regulation (EU) No 2016/1033 OJ L 175, 23 June 2016, 1–7. The reason for the extension lies in the complex technical infrastructure that needs to be set up for the MiFID II package to work effectively. The European Securities and Markets Authority (ESMA) has to collect data from about 300 trading venues on about 15 million financial instruments. To achieve this result, ESMA must work closely with national competent authorities and the trading venues themselves. However, the European Commission was informed by ESMA that neither competent authorities nor market participants would have the necessary systems ready by 3 January 2017. In light of these exceptional circumstances and in order to avoid legal uncertainty and potential market disruption, an extension was deemed necessary. See http://europa.eu/rapid/press-release_IP-16-265_en.htm?locale=en. See extensively on MiFID II, D Busch and G Ferrarini (eds), *Regulation of the EU Financial Markets: MiFID II and MiFIR* (Oxford: Oxford University Press, 2017).

[4] The same applies to the relationship between regulated markets and their participants.

[5] See for a comparative overview of the civil law effect of MiFID in several European jurisdictions, Ch 12, s IV of this book. See also Busch and DeMott (eds), *Liability of Asset Managers* (n 1); D Busch, 'Why MiFID Matters to Private Law—the Example of MiFID's Impact on an Asset Manager's Civil Liability' (2012) 7 *Capital Markets Law Journal* 386–413.

I regime. But before doing so, I will first provide a brief treatment of the central term 'investment firm'.

Below, MiFID I and MiFID II will be jointly referred to as 'MiFID'.

II. 'Investment Firm'

Under MiFID, an 'investment firm' is defined as an entity that provides investment services and/or performs investment activities. The distinction between the two is that investment services are always provided to third parties (clients), whereas investment activities are always performed on own account. Both the services and the activities relate by definition to financial instruments.[6] The investment services are (1) reception and transmission of orders in financial instruments; (2) execution of orders in financial instruments on behalf of clients (execution-only service); (3) portfolio management; (4) investment advice; and (5) underwriting or placing of financial instruments with and without a firm commitment basis.[7]

It should be realised in this connection that the categories of investment services listed above can overlap. When providing a service, an individual portfolio manager or an investment adviser may execute orders in financial instruments on behalf of the client (although there are also portfolio managers and investment advisers who leave the execution of orders on behalf of clients to other parties). In short, individual portfolio management and investment advice include the power to execute orders on behalf of clients.

The investment activities are (1) dealing on own account and (2) operation of a multilateral trading facility (MTF).[8] MIFID II adds an additional investment activity to the list, namely the operation of an organised trading facility (OTF).[9] For the sake of clarity, it should be noted that although the operator of a regulated market is not an investment firm, it is subject to MiFID, albeit to a different set of rules than those applicable to investment firms.[10]

If a given financial product is not a financial instrument, it cannot be the subject of an investment service or activity and the relevant entity is not an investment firm in relation to that product and is not subject to the MiFID regime for investment firms. It should be noted, incidentally, that the term 'financial instrument' is

[6] See MiFID I, Art 4(1) and (2) in conjunction with Annex I, ss A and C; MiFID II, Art 4(1) and (2) in conjunction with Annex I, ss A and C.

[7] See MiFID I, Annex I, s A (1), (2), (4), (5), (6) and (7), and MiFID II, Annex I, s A (1), (2), (4), (5), (6) and (7). Most investment services are defined in more detail.

[8] See MiFID I, Annex I, s A (3) and (8), and MiFID II, Annex I, s A (3) and (8). These activities are defined in more detail.

[9] See MiFID II, Annex I, s A (9). MiFID II, Art 4(1)(23) contains the following definition of 'organised trading facility': a multilateral system which is not a regulated market or an MTF and in which multiple third party buying and selling interests in bonds, structured finance products, emission allowances or derivatives are able to interact in the system in a way that results in a contract in accordance with Title II (Authorisation and operating conditions for investment firms).

[10] Title II of MiFID I and MiFID II sets out the rules for investment firms, and Title III of MiFID I and MiFID II the rules for regulated markets.

a fairly broad concept. It includes not only equities and bonds but also interest rate swaps and many other derivative products.[11]

Under MiFID II the definition of financial instrument has been broadened still further as it now also includes greenhouse gas emission allowances.[12] This is because in recent years a range of fraudulent practices has occurred in spot secondary markets in emission allowances. Although trading in emission allowances is admittedly already regulated within the EU by a specific directive,[13] it has been decided that in order to reinforce the integrity of these markets, greenhouse gas emission allowances should be classified under MiFID II as financial instruments, thereby bringing this trade within the scope of the strict MiFID II regime.[14]

Another important change introduced by MiFID II is that structured deposits are brought within the scope of MiFID II, although they are not treated as financial instruments. A structured deposit is a deposit on which the interest to be paid is not determined by reference to an interest rate (such as Euribor), but is instead dependent, for example, on the position of the AEX index.[15] Investment firms and credit institutions (banks) which sell structured deposits or advise clients about them are bound by the MiFID II rules on conflicts of interest, product governance, general principles of fair dealing, information to clients, fees, Know your Customer (KYC), client order handling and the provisions on supervision and enforcement.[16]

Insurance-based investment products are also brought within the scope of MiFID II, although they are not treated as financial instruments either. MiFID II applies certain conduct-of-business rules to insurance-based investment products, based on the rationale that they are comparable to MiFID II regulated investment products and that the client therefore deserves a similar level of investor protection.[17] For this purpose, MiFID II amends the Insurance Mediation Directive (IMD), incorporating a definition of insurance-based investment product. Based on this definition, such product is an insurance product offering a maturity of surrender value, such value being wholly or partially exposed to market fluctuations. Excluded from the definition are non-life products and life products providing for payable benefits only in the event of death or in respect of incapacity due to injury, sickness or infirmity as well as certain pension products. The additional rules in the IMD for insurance-based investment products include: (1) conflict of interest

[11] See MiFID I, Annex I, s C and MiFID II, Annex I, s C.

[12] See MiFID II, Annex I, s C (11).

[13] Directive 2003/87/EC [2003] OJ L 275, 32–46.

[14] MiFID II, Recital (11).

[15] See the definition of structured deposit in MiFID II, Art 4, para 1 (43) in conjunction with Art 2(1)(c) of Directive 2014/49/EU, OJ L 173/149, 12 June 2014 (Deposit Guarantee Schemes Directive).

[16] MiFID II, Art 1(4).

[17] See MiFID II, Recital (87).

rules; (2) general principles of fair dealing; and (3) rules on client information. Furthermore, Member States *may* prohibit or limit the acceptance or receipt of fees paid or provided to insurance intermediaries or insurers by any third party (ie other than the client itself).[18]

In any event, the basic rule is that an investment firm needs authorisation granted by the home Member State competent authority in order to act as such.[19] Once an investment firm has this authorisation, it can provide investment services and perform investment activities throughout the entire EU/EEA, in so far as these services and activities are covered by the authorisation (the so-called 'European passport').[20] To be eligible for an authorisation, an investment firm must fulfil extensive authorisation requirements.[21] These requirements also apply even after the investment firm has obtained authorisation. It follows that investment firms must comply with the conditions for initial authorisation at all times.[22] Moreover, they must also comply with any additional requirements that may be imposed.[23]

Many investment firms are banks. In practice, they are designated as investment banking companies and are largely subject to the same MiFID rules as investment firms that are not banks.[24] Naturally, banks are also subject to rules of supervision that apply specifically to them, as laid down in the Capital Requirements Directive (CRD IV) and the related Capital Requirements Regulation (CRR).[25]

[18] See MiFID II, Art 91. Please note that from 23 February 2018 onwards IMD, (OJ L 9/3, 15 June 2003) will be replaced by the Insurance Distribution Directive (IDD), 2016/97/EU, OJ L 26, 20 January 2016, 19–59 (see IDD, Arts 42–44). In relation to insurance-based investment products more elaborate conduct-of-business provisions will apply under IDD than pursuant to the MiFID II amendments to IMD. See IDD, Recital (10), ch V (Information requirements and conduct-of-business rules) and ch VI (Additional requirements in relation to investment-based insurance products).

[19] See MiFID I, Art 5(1); MiFID II, Art 5(1).

[20] See MiFID I, Art 6(3), (31) and (32); MiFID II, Art 6(3), (34) and (35).

[21] MiFID I, Arts 9–13; MiFID II, Arts 9–16.

[22] MiFID I, Art 16; MiFID II, Art 21.

[23] MiFID I, Art 18 et seq; MiFID II, Art 23 et seq.

[24] See MiFID I, Art 1(2); MiFID II, Art 1(3) and (4).

[25] CRD IV reads in full: Directive 2013/36/EU of the European Parliament and of the Council of 26 June 2013 on access to the activity of credit institutions and the prudential supervision of credit institutions and investment firms, amending Directive 2002/87/EC and repealing Directives 2006/48/EC and 2006/49/EC, OJ L 176, 338–436. CRR reads in full: Regulation (EU) No 575/2013 of the European Parliament and of the Council of 26 June 2013 on prudential requirements for credit institutions and investment firms and amending Regulation (EU) No 648/2012, OJ L 176, 1–337. Please note that on 23 November 2016 the European Commission proposed a comprehensive package of reforms to further strengthen the resilience of EU banks, including amendments to CRD IV (known as CRD V) and CRR (known as CRR II). See Press release 'EU Banking Reform: Strong banks to support growth and restore confidence' (available at: http://europa.eu/rapid/press-release_IP-16-3731_en.htm), and see (1) Proposal for a Directive of the European Parliament and of the Council amending Directive 2013/36/EU, COM(2016) 854 final, 23.11.2016 (CRD V); (2) Proposal for a Regulation of the European Parliament and the Council amending Regulation (EU) No 575/2013 and Regulation (EU) No 648/2012, COM(2016) 850 final, 23.11.2016 (CRR II).

III. Reclassification of Dealing on own Account to Dealing on Behalf of the Client

In order to get a clear picture of the scope of the MiFID II conduct-of-business rules, it is important to flag that MiFID II reclassifies certain cases of dealing on own account (an investment activity) as dealing on behalf of the client (an investment service). As a consequence, all kinds of MiFID II conduct-of-business rules will become applicable to cases of dealing on own account that are reclassified as dealing on behalf of the client. This reclassification has important consequences for investor protection. If an investment firm deals wholly or partly on behalf of the investor (as intermediary or representative), it is subjected to all kinds of conduct-of-business rules. If, on the other hand, an investment firm enters into a transaction with an investor solely as a contractual counterparty, it owes few if any conduct-of-business rules pursuant to MiFID. Once it has been established that the firm is acting on behalf of the client, the level of protection depends next on the classification of the client and the exact framework in which the transactions are carried out (ie whether the transactions involve execution-only, investment advice or portfolio management services). In any event, this reclassification concerns the following two situations.

First, the definition of 'execution of orders on behalf of clients' has been modified to such an extent that some instances of dealing on own account have been reclassified and brought within its ambit, with the result that the definition of 'dealing on own account' is now much narrower. Likewise, under MiFID II the phrase 'the conclusion of agreements to sell financial instruments issued by an investment firm or credit institution at the moment of their issuance' comes within the definition of 'execution of orders on behalf of clients'.[26] What is the exact scope of this change? Some examples may help to clarify this. If an investment firm sells an investor shares in its own capital at the time of issuance and the sale does not involve the provision of any form of investment service, the investment firm acts solely as the investor's contractual counterparty. Under MiFID I this is an instance of dealing on own account. Under MiFID II, however, it is reclassified as acting on behalf of the client and is suddenly treated as a form of investment service. Issuance is usually taken to mean the issuance of marketable shares and bonds, but in MiFID II it has a broader meaning. In the terminology of MiFID II the concept of issuance is linked to financial instruments. This means that where an investment firm acts as contractual counterparty in an interest rate swap this too is treated as the conclusion of an agreement for the sale, at the time of issuance, of a financial instrument issued by an investment firm. After all, an interest rate swap is a financial instrument, like many other derivatives. This interpretation also benefits investor protection, which is one of the key objectives of MiFID I and MiFID II.

[26] MIFID II, Art 4 lid 1 sub (5).

Recital (45) of the preamble to MiFID II explicitly states that this reclassification is intended 'to eliminate uncertainty and strengthen investor protection'.

Second, although this is not apparent from the broadening of the definition of 'execution of orders on behalf of clients' but rather from Recital (24) in the preamble to MiFID II, matched principal trading (back-to-back trading) is regarded, inter alia, as execution of orders on behalf of the client, although under MiFID I it was treated solely as dealing on own account. In Article 4(1), point (38), of MiFID II matched principal trading is defined as

> a transaction where the facilitator interposes itself between the buyer and the seller to the transaction in such a way that it is never exposed to market risk throughout the execution of the transaction, with both sides executed simultaneously, and where the transaction is concluded at a price where the facilitator makes no profit or loss, other than a previously disclosed commission, fee or charge for the transaction.

In terms of economic result, matched principal trading resembles the position in which the firm acts on both sides of a transaction for the client, ie matching opposite client orders (agency crosses).[27]

These two instances of reclassification enhance investor protection, but this is in my view not sufficient. If an investment firm sells a financial instrument that it has not issued itself, I cannot see any reason why the investor should not enjoy the protection of the MiFID conduct-of-business rules that apply to execution-only services. This approach is also in keeping with the reasonable expectations of the investor, certainly in the case of a retail investor. An investor may reasonably expect the investment firm used by him to look after his interests adequately and thus to observe certain conduct-of-business rules towards him. The investment firm is, after all, ideally placed to use its expertise. Its fund of knowledge is bound to be superior to that of an investor, particularly a retail investor.[28] Nor is this any different where the investment firm acts purely as the investor's contractual

[27] More precisely, Recital (24) in the preamble to MiFID II provides that 'dealing on own account when executing client orders [ie (systematic) internalisation] should include firms executing orders from different clients by matching them on a matched principal basis (back-to-back trading), which should be regarded as acting as principal and should be subject to the provisions of this Directive covering both the execution of orders on behalf of clients and dealing on own account'. Equating matched principal trading with (systematic) internalisation is in fact based on a fallacy. In economic terms, matched principal trading much more closely resembles agency crosses, as opposite client orders are in fact matched with one another.

[28] In fact, the European Commission acknowledges in its letter to the Committee of European Securities Regulators (CESR) of 19 March 2007 that the investor's reasonable expectations play a role of importance in answering the question of whether in a given case the investment firm transacts as agent or solely as principal. That is understandable, since whether or not the investment firm transacts as agent or solely as principal is a matter of interpretation of the legal relationship. But this approach has its limits. If it is absolutely clear on the facts that the investment firm transacted solely as principal, it is not possible to argue that the investment firm in fact transacted as agent. Preferably, therefore, the distinction between acting as agent and acting as principal should simply no longer be treated as relevant in determining the degree of investor protection. For the European Commission's letter, see: Working Document ESC-07-2007, Commission answers to CESR scope issues under MiFID and implementing directive (Appendix to CESR, Best Execution under MiFID, Questions & Answers, May 2007, CESR/07-320.

counterparty. In such cases, the investor is reasonably entitled to expect the investment firm to observe the same conduct-of-business rules that would apply if it were providing an execution-only service. Moreover, the distinction between dealing on own account (principal dealing) on the one hand and trading on behalf of the client (and other forms of investment service) on the other is tenuous, arbitrary and easy to manipulate. This is all the more so where a contractual clause providing that an investment firm acts solely as contractual counterparty is claimed to apply even where an employee of the investment firm advises the investor, contrary to the terms of the agreement.[29] Clearly, also MiFID II does not provide a practicable criterion. Indeed, to achieve an adequate level of investor protection, MiFID II resorts to the artifice of reclassifying certain types of dealing on own account as acting on behalf of the client. Moreover, the Dutch Supreme Court has already extended the special civil duty of care to dealing on own account. In a case involving the offering of risky and complex financial products to retail investors, it held that it followed from the special civil duty of care that there was a duty to warn investors of the risks involved and a duty to comply with KYC rules, even though the bank was only acting as contractual counterparty.[30] Finally, the UK government (in response to the Kay Review) takes the view that duties of care must also apply where an investment firm acts solely as an investor's contractual counterparty.[31] Under a future MiFID III, an investment firm which acts solely as contractual counterparty should be required to observe the same conduct-of-business rules as apply in the case of an execution-only service.[32]

IV. Client Classification

A. General

What rules of conduct an investment firm must comply with in relation to clients depends on two factors: (1) the category to which the client belongs

[29] This may be illustrated by the Scottish case *Grant Estates Ltd v The Royal Bank of Scotland plc* [2012] CSOH 133. In this case Lord Hodge (now one of the Justices of the UK Supreme Court) held that a clause providing that the investment firm acted solely as contractual counterparty was valid, despite the fact that an employee had advised the investor. See extensively on this case D Busch, 'Agency and Principal Dealing under MiFID I and MiFID II' in Busch and Ferrarini (eds), *Regulation of the EU Financial Markets: MiFID II and MiFIR* (n 3) 227–49; D Busch, 'Agency and Principal Dealing under the Markets in Financial Instruments Directive' in D Busch, L Macgregor and P Watts (eds), *Agency Law in Commercial Practice* (Oxford: Oxford University Press 2016) 141–75. See for similar cases in England & Wales: *Green & Rawley v RBS* [2013] EWCA Civ 1197; *Thornbridge v Barclays* [2015] EWHC 3430 (QB).

[30] See HR 5 June 2009, *JOR* 2009/199, annotated by Lieverse (*Treek v Dexia Bank Nederland*), ground 5.2.1.

[31] *Ensuring equity markets support long-term growth.* The government response to the Kay review (November 2012) para 2.8.

[32] For an in-depth analysis of this issue, see Busch, 'Agency and Principal Dealing under MiFID I and MiFID II' (n 29) 227–49; Busch, 'Agency and Principal Dealing under the Markets in Financial Instruments Directive' (n 29) 141–75.

(client classification or categorisation) and (2) the type of investment service. Investment firms are obliged to categorise their investment clients at the start of the relationship as retail clients, professional clients or—in some cases—eligible counterparty and must notify them of the classification.[33] This is the case under MiFID I and will be no different under MiFID II.

Fewer conduct-of-business rules apply to services to professional clients than to services to retail clients. In other words, professional clients enjoy less protection than retail clients. For example, the KYC rules are less strict in the case of professional clients and not all obligations to provide information apply.[34]

MIFID I and MiFID II give an exhaustive list of parties classified as professional clients. They include banks, investment firms and other authorised or regulated financial institutions such as undertakings for collective investment in transferable securities (UCITS) and alternative investment funds (AIFs). Undertakings that meet certain quantitative requirements ('large undertakings') are also classified as professional clients.[35] All clients not classified as professional clients are deemed to be retail clients. These include private clients and undertakings that do not meet the quantitative criteria for large undertakings.[36]

It should be noted that national and regional governments, including public bodies that manage public debt at national or regional level, are also classified as professional investors under MiFID I and MiFID II.[37] According to the Commission:

> [t]he reference to regional governments does not extend to public administrations at large and does not include e.g. local governments or municipalities or their respective administrations.[38]

In keeping with the Commission's clarification,[39] MiFID II explicitly provides that 'local public authorities' and 'municipalities' are treated as retail clients.[40] 'Local

[33] MiFID I Implementing Directive, Art 28; Draft Commission Delegated Regulation MiFID II, C(2016) 2398 final, 25 April 2016, Art 45.

[34] MiFID I Implementing Directive, Arts 30–34 and 35(2); Draft Commission Delegated Regulation MiFID II, C(2016) 2398 final, 25 April 2016, Arts 47–51, 54(3) and 56(1).

[35] An undertaking is categorised as large if it meets 2 of the following size requirements on a company basis: (1) a balance sheet total of €20 million; (2) net turnover of €40 million; (3) own funds of €2 million. For a complete list of parties categorised as professional clients, see Annex II to MiFID I and MiFID II.

[36] MiFID I, Art 4(4)(10); MiFID II, Art 4 (1)(11).

[37] MiFID I, Annex II, at I (3); MiFID II, Annex II, at I (3).

[38] See Questions & Answers (ID 249. Client classification, internal reference 83, meaning of 'regional governments). (http://ec.europa.eu/yqol/index.cfm?fuseaction=legislation.show&lexId=1.) The legislative history of the implementation of MiFID I in the Netherlands contains a comparable observation, namely that the Dutch term *regionaal overheidslichaam* (literally, regional government body, which is the term used in the Dutch implementing legislation for 'regional governments') should be taken as a reference to German *Länder* (states) and French and Belgian *régions*, and does not include Dutch provinces, municipalities or water boards. It follows that under the MiFID I system, Dutch provinces, municipalities and water boards are retail investors and qualify for the highest level of protection. See *Dutch Parliamentary Papers II* 2006/07, 31 086, no 3, 85.

[39] And Dutch legislative history, see previous footnote.

[40] See MiFID II, Annex II, at II.1, first para.

public authorities' and 'municipalities' have thus been added to 'public sector bodies'. However, it would have been clearer to talk about 'public sector bodies (other than national and regional governments and public bodies that manage public debt at national or regional level)'. This does not therefore involve a substantive change from MiFID I.

The correct classification of semi-public bodies such as housing associations, educational establishments and health care institutions is not entirely clear under either MiFID I or MiFID II. It could be argued that semi-public bodies must be equated in terms of their professional status with provinces, municipalities and water boards and, like them, cannot therefore be treated as national and regional governments and public bodies that manage public debt at national or regional level. For this reason, semi-public bodies would not qualify as professional investors. It can also be argued that semi-public bodies can also not be treated as professional investors in so far as they fulfil the quantitative requirements applicable to 'large undertakings' (see above). As public sector bodies are treated separately by MiFID I and MiFID II for the purpose of client classification, the category of 'large undertakings' appears to be reserved for commercial enterprises. This restrictive interpretation of the 'professional investor' category also benefits investor protection, which is one of the key objectives of MiFID I and MiFID II.[41] In my view, therefore, there are good grounds for assuming that semi-public bodies, as well as provinces, municipalities and water boards, are 'local public authorities', or are in any event public sector bodies which should be treated as retail investors.[42]

Finally, there is the eligible counterparty client category.[43] These are highly professional clients (a species of the genus professional client). Fewer conduct-of-business rules apply in relation to eligible counterparties than in relation to 'ordinary' professional clients. In other words, they enjoy even less protection than other professional clients.[44] The list of eligible counterparties is virtually identical to the list of professional clients, save for two exceptions (one of which is the large undertakings (see above)).[45] In brief, large undertakings can never be classified as eligible counterparties.

The category of eligible counterparty is applicable only in relation to the execution of orders on behalf of clients (execution-only service), dealing on own account and receiving and transmitting orders, or ancillary services directly relating to such transactions.[46] The category of eligible counterparty is therefore not relevant

[41] Recital (2) to MiFID I; Recital (70) to MiFID II.

[42] But Dutch Finance Minister Dijsselbloem has a different take on this (although he does not give reasons), namely that '[t]he question whether a semi-public body should be treated as a professional or a retail investor (…) is determined, in principle, by the size of the undertaking'. See his letter to the House of Representatives dated 26 April 2013 (reference BZ/2013/232M) 3.

[43] MiFID I Implementing Directive, Art 28(1); Draft Commission Delegated Regulation MiFID II, C(2016) 2398 final, 25 April 2016, Art 45(1).

[44] MiFID I, Art 24(1); MiFID II, Art 30(1).

[45] MiFID I, Art 24(2), first para; MiFID II, Art 30(2), first para.

[46] MiFID, Art 24(1); MiFID II, Art 30(1).

to portfolio management, investment advice and the underwriting or placing of financial instruments, whether on a firm commitment basis or otherwise. Here there are only two possibilities for the investment firm: it classifies the client either as a retail client or as a professional client. This analysis may cause some confusion. Portfolio managers and investment advisers will regularly execute orders on behalf of clients and/or transmit orders to another investment firm, in each case as part of their portfolio management or investment advice for the client. Nonetheless, according to the Commission, the category of eligible counterparty does not apply in relation to investment advice and portfolio management.[47]

B. Changing Client Category

Clients may switch to a different category either on a trade-by-trade basis or for the provision of the service in general. Such a request may be made for more protection (opting down) or for less protection (opting up). An investment firm should inform its clients of the possibility of opting up and opting down, and about how this will lower or raise the level of protection.[48]

An investment firm may, on request, classify a retail investor as a professional investor (*opting up*) if the investment firm considers that the investor has sufficient expertise, knowledge and experience to take investment decisions himself and correctly assess the related risks.[49] An agreement between the investment firm and the retail investor must specify for what investment services, types of financial instrument or transaction the latter is to be treated as a professional investor.[50] Even if the conditions for opting up have been fulfilled, an investment firm is not obliged to grant the request. This is apparent from the use of the words 'may also be allowed'.[51]

It is worth noting here that MiFID II makes it possible for Member States to adopt specific criteria for the assessment of the expertise and knowledge

[47] See Questions & Answers (ID 243. Client classification, internal reference 78). (http://ec.europa.eu/yqol/ index.cfm?fuseaction=legislation.show&lexId=1). This Q&A relates to MiFID I, but there is no reason to assume that things will be any different under MiFID II.

[48] MiFID I Implementing Directive, Art 28, MiFID I, Art 24(2), second para, MiFID I, Annex II at II and MiFID I Implementing Directive, Art 50; Draft Commission Delegated Regulation MiFID II, C(2016) 2398 final, 25 April 2016, Art 45, MiFID II, Art 30(2), second para, MiFID II, Annex II at II, Draft Commission Delegated Regulation MiFID II, C(2016) 2398 final, 25 April 2016, Art 71.

[49] A retail investor is deemed to have sufficient expertise, knowledge and experience if he meets at least 2 of the following criteria: (1) the client has carried out transactions, in significant size, on the relevant market at an average frequency of 10 per quarter over the previous 4 quarters; (2) the size of the client's financial instrument portfolio, defined as including cash deposits and financial instruments, exceeds €500,000, or (3) the client works or has worked in the financial sector for at least 1 year in a professional position, which requires knowledge of the transactions or services envisaged. See MiFID I, Annex II.II.1, fifth para; MiFID II, Annex II.II.1, fifth para.

[50] MiFID I, Annex II.II.2, first para, first indent; MiFID II, Annex II.II.2, first para, first indent.

[51] MiFID I Annex II.II.1, first para; MiFID II Annex II.II.1, first para.

of municipalities and local public authorities requesting to be treated as professional clients. These national criteria can be applied as an *alternative* to the requirements set by MiFID II itself in respect of the expertise, knowledge and experience in order to be able to grant a request for treatment as a professional investor. However, the national criteria can also be *additional* to the MiFID II requirements.[52]

A professional client can often request to be treated as an eligible counterparty.[53] Even a retail client that has opted up and been recognised as a professional client can request to be treated as an eligible counterparty. However, strict conditions have to be satisfied in such cases. For example, the client must be an *undertaking*, which shows that this second opt-up is not available for natural persons.[54] In line with the advice of the European Securities and Markets Authority (ESMA), the possibility of a second opt-up will be abolished under MiFID II.[55] At present, the existence of this possibility means that small undertakings can be treated as an eligible counterparty. ESMA previously argued that this is undesirable from the perspective of investor protection.[56]

An investment firm may, either on request or on its own initiative, treat an eligible counterparty or professional investor as a professional investor or eligible counterparty respectively. An eligible counterparty may also request to be treated as a retail investor. Just as in the case of opting up (see above), an investment firm is under no obligation to grant such a request.[57] In the literature some writers have pointed out that from a civil law perspective not granting an opt-down request would not always be without risk, since in making such a request a professional investor is in fact indicating that it needs more protection.[58] I am inclined to agree with this assessment.

[52] See MiFID II, Annex II, at II.1, last para. It seems from the Draft Bill to implement MiFID II that the Netherlands does not intend to exercise this option. The requirements which must be met in the Netherlands by retail clients opting up to become professional clients have been implemented in Wft, s 4:18c. This provision has not been altered in the Draft Bill to implement MiFID II and the accompanying Explanatory Memorandum makes no mention of this point. See *Dutch Parliamentary Papers II*, 2016/2017, 34 583, no 2 (Draft Bill) and no 3 (Explanatory Memorandum).

[53] MiFID I Implementing Directive, Art 50(1), first para in conjunction with MiFID, Annex II, s I, points 1, 2 and 3.

[54] MiFID I Implementing Directive, Art 50(1), second para in conjunction with s II of Annex II to MiFID.

[55] In Draft Commission Delegated Regulation MiFID II, C(2016) 2398 final, 25 April 2016, Art 71(1), an equivalent of MiFID I Implementing Directive, Art 50(1), second para has not been included.

[56] ESMA/2014/1569, *Final Report—ESMA's Technical Advice to the Commission on MiFID II and MiFIR* (19 December 2014) 185 (no 10 and no 1(i)).

[57] MiFID, Annex II.I, second para; MiFID II, Annex II.I, second para. For eligible counterparties, see MiFID I Implementing Directive, Art 50(2); Draft Commission Delegated Regulation MiFID II, C(2016) 2398 final, 25 April 2016, Art 71(2) and (4).

[58] See eg LJ Silverentand (ed), *Hoofdlijnen Wft* (Recht & Praktijk Financieel Recht No 6), 3rd edn (Aphen aan den Rijn: WoltersKluwer, 2015) 230.

V. General Duty of Loyalty

This concludes the section on the system of client classification under MiFID and MiFID II. Once a client has been classified, it is possible to determine (by reference to the type of service) what conduct-of-business rules must be observed by the investment firm in providing the service.

The investment firm must act honestly, fairly and professionally in accordance with the best interests of its clients (general duty of loyalty).[59] This obligation applies when providing an investment service to both retail and professional clients. However, it is noteworthy that it does not apply under MiFID I in relation to eligible counterparties.[60] The thinking behind this must have been that eligible counterparties do not need the protection of the law since they are in a sufficiently strong position to negotiate a comparable standard of protection contractually. Apparently this thinking changed during the negotiations on MiFID II. Under MiFID II the general duty of loyalty also applies in relation to eligible counterparties.[61]

The general duty of loyalty has to some extent been defined in more specific conduct-of-business rules for investment firms that provide investment services: (1) information obligations (section VI), (2) KYC rules (sections VII and § VIII), (3) best execution (section IX), (4) client order handling (section X), (5) conflicts of interest (section XI), (6) inducements (section XII), (7) obligations to record telephone conversations and electronic communications (section XIII). These are dealt with below.

VI. Information Obligations

A. General

This section deals with the information obligations to which investment firms are subject under MiFID II. The general information obligations dealt with below in subsection B apply in relation to both retail and professional clients. Subsection C gives separate consideration to the new distinction between independent and non-independent advice and the related obligations to provide information. These

[59] MiFID, Art 19(1); MiFID II, Art 24(1). See extensively on the general duty of loyalty: L Enriques and M Gargantini, 'The Overarching Duty to Act in the Best Interest of the Client in MiFID II' in Busch and Ferrarini (n 3) 85–122.

[60] MiFID, Art 24(1).

[61] MiFID II, Art 30(1). See also Recital (86) to MiFID II.

information obligations also apply in relation to both retail and professional clients. Subsection D examines the provision of information on bundled packages of services and products to professional and retail clients. Many of the general information obligations dealt with in subsection B have been elaborated in more specific obligations, particularly in relation to retail clients.[62] In consequence, retail clients must be given more extensive information than professional clients. The more specific rules on the general information obligations dealt with in subsection B in relation to retail and professional clients are dealt with separately in subsections E and F. The special position of eligible counterparties is addressed in subsection G. It should be noted in this connection that the information obligations under MiFID II apply not only where investment services are provided but also where an investment firm or bank sells or advises clients in relation to structured deposits.[63]

B. Professional and Retail Clients

The information addressed by an investment firm to clients or potential clients for whom it provides investment services must fulfil certain general requirements. Under MiFID I the rule is that all information, including marketing communications, must be fair, clear and not misleading. Marketing communications must also be clearly identifiable as such.[64]

MiFID I also provides that investment firms must provide appropriate information in a comprehensible form to clients or potential clients about: (1) the investment firm and its services; (2) financial instruments and proposed investment strategies (including appropriate guidance on and warnings of the risks associated with investments in those instruments or in respect of particular investment strategies); (3) execution venues and (4) costs and associated charges. The aim of providing this information is to ensure that clients and potential clients are reasonably able to understand the nature and risks of the investment service and of the specific type of financial instrument that is being offered and, consequently, to take investment decisions on an informed basis.[65]

Under MiFID II, the general information obligations referred to in the previous two paragraphs also apply where an investment firm provides investment services.[66] However, as there are also additional general obligations to provide information, more general information has to be provided under MiFID II than under MiFID I (see below at points 1–3). A new provision introduced in MiFID II

[62] MiFID I Implementing Directive, Arts 27–34; Draft Commission Delegated Regulation MiFID II, C(2016) 2398 final, 25 April 2016, Arts 44–53.

[63] MiFID II, Art 1(4)(b).

[64] MiFID I, Art 19(2).

[65] MiFID I, Art 19(3).

[66] MiFID II, Art 24(3), (4), opening words and (b) and (c), and (5).

is that these general information obligations also apply where an investment firm or bank sells or advises clients in relation to structured deposits.[67]

1. The investment firm must indicate whether the financial instrument/structured deposit is intended for retail or professional clients, taking account of the identified target market.[68] By requiring that the investment firm indicates whether the financial instrument/structured deposit is intended for retail or professional clients, taking account of the identified target market, MiFID II establishes a clear link with the new product governance requirements.[69]
2. The investment firm must provide more extensive information on all costs and associated charges, including aggregated information to allow the client to understand the overall cost as well as the cumulative effect on the return of the investment. At the client's request, an itemised breakdown must be provided. Where applicable, this information must be provided to the client on a regular basis, at least annually, during the life of the investment.[70]
3. Under MiFID investment firms may provide the information in a standardised format.[71] Under MiFID II this has become an option for the Member State: Member States *may* allow that information to be provided in a standardised format.[72] In short, if a Member State does not allow this, it seems that the information must always be provided in a personalised format.[73]

C. Independent and Non-independent Advice

The obligations to provide information in the case of investment advice have been strengthened in relation to both retail and professional clients. As I have already pointed out above (see section IV.A), the eligible counterparty category is not relevant to investment advice.

[67] MiFID II, Art 1(4)(b) in conjunction with Art 24(3) and (4), opening words and (b) and (c), and (5).

[68] MiFID II, Art 24(4)(b) (financial instruments) in conjunction with Art 1(4)(b) (structured deposits).

[69] See on the new product governance rules: D Busch, 'Product Governance and Product Intervention under MiFID II/MiFIR' in Busch and Ferrarini (n 3) 123–46.

[70] MiFID II, Art 24(4)(c) (financial instruments) in conjunction with Art 1(4)(b) (structured deposits).

[71] MiFID, Art 19(3), last sentence.

[72] MiFID II, Art 24(5), last sentence (financial instruments) in conjunction with Art 1(4)(b) (structured deposits).

[73] In eg the Netherlands this Member State option is exercised (implicitly). The relevant Dutch implementing provision (Wft, Art 4:20(6)) is not altered in the Draft Bill to implement MiFID II, and the accompanying Explanatory Memorandum is also silent on this point. See *Dutch Parliamentary Papers II*, 2016/2017, 34 583, no 2 (Draft Bill) and no 3 (Explanatory Memorandum). It will therefore remain possible in the Netherlands to provide information in standardised format. The situation will undoubtedly be different in at least a few other Member States. If the Member States had unanimously considered that information could be provided in standardised format, a compromise in the form of a Member State option would have been unnecessary.

Unlike MiFID I, MiFID II draws a distinction between independent and non-independent advice. This distinction and the corresponding information obligations also apply where an investment firm or a bank provides advice about a structured deposit.[74] Presumably, these rules do not apply where the transaction involves the sale of a structured deposit, not accompanied by the provision of advice. Although strictly speaking, the rules would appear to apply in such cases under Article 1(4) of MiFID II, I assume that this effect is unintended.

Firms providing investment advice on an *independent* basis must define and implement a selection process to assess and compare a sufficient range of financial instruments/structured deposits available on the market.[75] 'Financial instruments' and 'structured deposits' are in the remainder of this subsection C collectively referred to as 'financial products'. The selection process must include the following elements: (1) the number and variety of financial products considered must be (a) proportionate to the scope of investment advice services offered by the independent investment adviser and (b) adequately representative of financial products available in the market; (2) the quantity of financial products issued by the firm itself or by entities closely linked[76] to the firm itself must be proportionate to the total amount of financial products considered; and (3) the criteria for selecting the various financial products must include all relevant aspects such as risks, costs and complexity as well as the characteristics of the firm's clients, and must ensure that the selection of the financial products that may be recommended is not biased.[77] Where such comparison is not possible owing to the business model or the specific scope of the service provided, the firm providing investment advice may *not* present itself as independent.[78]

[74] MiFID II, Art 1(4)(b) in conjunction with Art 24(4), opening words and (a).

[75] Draft Commission Delegated Regulation MiFID II, C(2016) 2398 final, 25 April 2016, Art 53(1), first sentence (financial instruments), in conjunction with Art 1(2) (structured deposits).

[76] MiFID II, Art 4(1)(35) defines the term 'close links' as:

> A situation in which two or more natural or legal persons are linked by: (a) participation in the form of ownership, direct or by way of control, of 20% or more of the voting rights or capital of an undertaking; (b) 'control' which means the relationship between a parent undertaking and a subsidiary, in all the cases referred to in Article 22(1) and (2) of Directive 2013/34/EU, or a similar relationship between any natural or legal person and an undertaking, any subsidiary undertaking of a subsidiary undertaking also being considered to be a subsidiary of the parent undertaking which is at the head of those undertakings; (c) a permanent link of both or all of them to the same person by a control relationship.

[77] Draft Commission Delegated Regulation MiFID II, C(2016) 2398 final, 25 April 2016, Art 53(1), under (a)–(d) (financial instruments), in conjunction with Art 1(2) (structured deposits).

[78] Draft Commission Delegated Regulation MiFID II, C(2016) 2398 final, 25 April 2016, Art 53(1), *in fine* (financial instruments), in conjunction with Art 1(2) (structured deposits). A firm that provides advice on an independent basis and that focuses on certain categories or a specified range of financial instruments must comply with the following requirements: (1) the firm should market itself in a way that is intended only to attract clients with a preference for those categories or range of financial instruments; (2) the firm should require clients to indicate that they are only interested in investing in the specified category or range of financial instruments; and (3) prior to the provision of the service, the firm should ensure that its service is appropriate for each new client on the basis that its business model matches the client's needs and objectives, and the range of financial instruments that are suitable for the client. Where this is not the case the firm may not provide such a service to the client. See Draft Commission Delegated Regulation MiFID II, C(2016) 2398 final, 25 April 2016, Art 53(2) (financial instruments) in conjunction with Art 1(2) (structured deposits).

The concept of non-independent advice strikes me as strange. All forms of advice should surely meet certain basic requirements, because in the final analysis any advice that is given must be of a good standard. It would have been better if MiFID II had not distinguished between independent and non-independent advice and had instead provided that all forms of advice should meet certain basic requirements. Under the current definition of non-independent advice in MiFID II, there is a risk that an adviser may allow its own interests to prevail over those of the client and accordingly that the client may be saddled with bad advice. Although it could be argued that this should not be possible in practice because of the general duty of loyalty and the rules on conflicts of interest, the situation is still unsatisfactory. What basic requirements should advice therefore meet? It is submitted that all types of advice should in fact meet the above requirements of independent advice, although I realise that this is setting an exacting standard for advice.[79]

When providing advice, the investment firm must, in good time before it provides this advice, give the client the information described below. As already noted above, the distinction between independent and non-independent advice and the corresponding information obligations also apply where an investment firm or a bank provides advice on a structured deposit.[80]

1. The firm must inform the client whether or not the advice is provided on an independent basis.[81] Firms should explain in a clear and concise way whether and why investment advice qualifies as independent or non-independent and the type and nature of the restrictions that apply, including, when providing investment advice on an independent basis, the prohibition to receive and retain inducements.[82] Where advice is offered or provided to the same client on both an independent and non-independent basis, firms should explain the scope of both services to allow investors to understand the differences between them and not present themselves as an independent investment adviser for the overall activity. Firms may not give undue prominence to their independent investment advice services over non-independent investment services in their communications with clients.[83] Moreover, a firm may not hold itself out

[79] Also critical on the distinction between independent and non-independent advice: P Giudici, 'Independent Financial Advice' in Busch and Ferrarini (n 3) 147–63.

[80] MiFID II, Art 1(4)(b) in conjunction with Art 24(4), opening words and (a).

[81] MiFID II, Art 24(4)(a) (i) (financial instruments) in conjunction with Art 1(4)(b) (structured deposits); Draft Commission Delegated Regulation MiFID II, C(2016) 2398 final, 25 April 2016, Art 53(3) sub (a) (financial instruments) in conjunction with Art 1(2).

[82] Draft Commission Delegated Regulation MiFID II, C(2016) 2398 final, 25 April 2016, Art 52(1), first para (financial instruments), in conjunction with Art 1(2) (structured deposits). See further on inducements MiFID II, Art 24(7)(b), explained in more detail in section XII below.

[83] Draft Commission Delegated Regulation MiFID II, C(2016) 2398 final, 25 April 2016, Art 52(1), second para (financial instruments), in conjunction with Art 1(2) (structured deposits). Draft Commission Delegated Regulation MiFID II, C(2016) 2398 final, 25 April 2016, Art 53(3)(c) (financial instruments) in conjunction with Art 1(2) (structured deposits) also stipulates that a firm offering

as 'independent' for its business as a whole. However a firm may hold itself out as acting independently in respect of the services for which it provides independent advice.[84]

I wonder how effective this information obligation is. Private investors especially will often not read the information owing to its sheer quantity. As a result, there is a risk that clients will not realise until much later (once the service has long since started) that the information they are receiving is not provided on an independent basis and is therefore possibly biased. This is yet another reason why, in my view, it would be preferable if MiFID II were not to distinguish between independent and non-independent advice and were instead to prescribe certain basic requirements for good quality advice.

2. The firm must indicate whether the advice is based on a broad or on a more restricted analysis of different types of financial products and, in particular, whether the range is limited to financial products issued or provided by entities having close links with the firm (or any other legal or economic relationships, such as contractual relationships, so close as to pose a risk of impairing the independent basis of the advice provided).[85] The information provided on this subject is fairly detailed.

   Firms should provide a description of the types of financial products considered, the range of financial products and providers analysed per each type of product according to the scope of the service. When providing independent advice, the firm should also explain how the service provided satisfies the conditions for the provision of advice on an independent basis and the factors taken into consideration in the selection process used by the firm to recommend financial products, such as risks, costs and complexity of the financial products.[86]

   When the range of financial products assessed by the firm providing advice on an independent basis includes the firm's own financial products or those issued or provided by entities having close links or any other close legal or economic relationship with the firm as well as other issuers or providers which are not linked or related, the firm should distinguish, for each type of financial

investment advice on both an independent basis and on a non-independent basis has adequate organisational requirements and controls in place to ensure that both types of advice services and advisers are clearly separated from each other and that clients are not likely to be confused about the type of advice that they are receiving and are given the type of advice that is appropriate for them. The firm may not allow a natural person to provide both independent and non-independent advice.

[84] Draft Commission Delegated Regulation MiFID II, C(2016) 2398 final, 25 April 2016, Art 53(3) sub (c) (financial instruments) in conjunction with Art 1(2) (structured deposits).

[85] MiFID II, Art 24(4)(a) (ii) (financial instruments) in conjunction with Art 1(4)(b) (structured deposits); Draft Commission Delegated Regulation MiFID II, C(2016) 2398 final, 25 April 2016, Art 52(2) (financial instruments) in conjunction with Art 1(2) (structured deposits).

[86] Draft Commission Delegated Regulation MiFID II, C(2016) 2398 final, 25 April 2016, Art 52(3) (financial instruments) in conjunction with Art 1(2) (structured deposits).

product, the range of the financial products issued or provided by entities not having any links with the firm.[87]

3. The firm must indicate whether it will provide the client with a periodic assessment of the suitability of the financial products recommended to the client.[88] So, in other words, the adviser is not obliged to provide the client with a periodic assessment of suitability, but *may* provide this service. If the firm does provide the service, it must supply disclose all of the following: (1) the frequency and extent of the periodic suitability assessment and where relevant, the conditions that trigger that assessment; (2) the extent to which the information previously collected will be subject to reassessment; and (3) the way in which an updated recommendation will be communicated to the client.[89]

D. Bundled Packages of Services and Products

Another new feature introduced by MiFID II, besides the distinction between independent and non-independent advice, is the explicit focus on the provision of information to professional and retail clients on bundled packages of services and products. These provisions too apply not only where an investment service is provided but also where an investment firm or a bank sells a structured deposit or provides advice on this.[90]

MiFID II provides that when an investment service is offered together with another service or product as part of a package or as a condition for the same agreement or package, the investment firm must inform the client whether it is possible to buy the different components separately and must provide for a separate evidence of the costs and charges of each component.[91] One of the products covered by this provision will be interest rate swaps linked to an underlying loan at a variable rate of interest.

Where the risks resulting from an agreement or package are likely to be different from the risks associated with the components taken separately, the investment firm must provide an adequate description of the different components of the agreement or package and the way in which its interaction modifies the risk. It should be noted that this obligation applies only in relation to retail clients.[92]

[87] Draft Commission Delegated Regulation MiFID II, C(2016) 2398 final, 25 April 2016, Art 52(4) (financial instruments) in conjunction with Art 1(2) (structured deposits).

[88] Art 24(4)(a) (financial instruments) in conjunction with Art 1 (4)(b) (structured deposits).

[89] Draft Commission Delegated Regulation MiFID II, C(2016) 2398 final, 25 April 2016, Art 52(5) (financial instruments) in conjunction with Art 1(2) (structured deposits).

[90] MiFID II, Art 1 (4)(b) in conjunction with Art 24(11).

[91] MiFID II, Art 24(11), first para (financial instruments) in conjunction with Art 1(4)(b) (structured deposits). See also the definition of 'cross-selling practice': the offering of an investment service together with another service or product as part of a package or as a condition for the same agreement or package. On the subject of cross-selling, see also s VIII.E, below.

[92] MiFID II, Art 24(11), second para, (financial instruments) in conjunction with Art 1(4)(b) (structured deposits).

As SMEs must often be classified as retail investors, an investment firm will also have to comply with this information obligation in relation to them.

ESMA has published guidelines for the assessment and supervision of cross-selling practices indicating, in particular, situations in which cross-selling practices are contrary to the general duty of loyalty.[93]

E. Retail Clients

Under MiFID II, investment firms are required to satisfy a number of stricter and additional information obligations specifically in relation to retail clients. These provisions apply not only where investment services are provided but also where an investment firm or a bank sells a structured deposit or gives advice on this. In relation to MiFID II, 'financial instruments' and 'structured deposits' are in this subsection E collectively referred to as 'financial products'.

1. Under the MiFID I Implementing Directive, the information should not emphasise any potential benefits of an investment service or financial instrument without also giving a fair and prominent indication of any relevant risks.[94] In short, if an investment firm does not highlight the benefits, it need also not draw attention to the risks (although in practice an investment firm will naturally always wish to emphasise the benefits). Things are no different under MiFID II. However, the stricter nature of the rules lies in the fact that the manner of presentation should meet certain requirements: (1) a *prominent* indication should be given of the risks; (2) the font size used in indicating the risks should be at least equal to the predominant font size used throughout the information provided, as well as a layout ensuring such indication is prominent; (3) all information must be consistently presented in the same language, unless the client has accepted that it will receive information in more than one language; and (4) the information must always be up-to-date, taking account of the method of communication used (some time may elapse before the investment firm's website is updated).[95] The exception allowing for a situation in which information can be given in different languages strikes me as undesirable, particularly in relation to retail clients. In many cases retail clients will not read through the whole contract. If the contract contains a standard clause that the client agrees that information may be included in different languages, investor protection is largely nullified in this respect.

[93] ESMA/2015/1861, *Final Report—Guidelines on cross-selling practices* (22 December 2015) 35 et seq, based on MiFID II, Art 24(11), third para, in conjunction with Art 24(1).

[94] MiFID I Implementing Directive, Art 27(2), second para.

[95] Draft Commission Delegated Regulation MiFID II, C(2016) 2398 final, 25 April 2016, Art 44(2) sub (b), (c), (f) and (g) (financial instruments) in conjunction with Art 1(2) (structured deposits). *Cf* ESMA/2014/1569, *Final Report—ESMA's Technical Advice to the Commission on MiFID II and MiFIR* (19 December 2014) 103 (no 2).

2. Where information provided to retail clients contains information on future performance, MiFID I provides that a number of conditions must be fulfilled: (1) the information must not be based on or refer to simulated past performance; (2) it must be based on reasonable assumptions supported by objective data; (3) where the information is based on gross performance, the effect of commissions, fees or other charges must be disclosed; (4) it must contain a prominent warning that such forecasts are not a reliable indicator of future performance.[96] MiFID II adds that where the information contains information on future performance it (1) should be based on performance scenarios in different market conditions (both negative and positive scenarios), and (2) should reflect the nature and risks of the specific types of financial products included in the analysis.[97]
3. It has already been noted in subsection B, at point 2, that MiFID II requires the provision of more extensive information about costs and charges, including aggregated information allowing the client to understand the overall cost as well as the cumulative effect on the return on the investment (and, where the client so requests, an itemised breakdown; where applicable, this information must be provided to the client on a regular basis, at least annually, during the life of the investment).[98] MiFID II specifies in detail what information must be provided to retail investors about costs and charges.[99]

F. Professional Clients

Under MiFID II, the obligations to provide information specifically to professional clients are also tightened. These provisions apply not only where investment services are provided but also where an investment firm or a bank sells a structured deposit or gives advice on this. In relation to MiFID II, 'financial instruments' and 'structured deposits' are in this subsection F collectively referred to as 'financial products'.

1. Information addressed to or likely to be received by professional clients: (1) must not reference any potential benefits of a service or financial product without also giving a fair and prominent indication of any relevant risks; (2) must not disguise, diminish or obscure important items, statements or warnings; and (3) must be accurate and up-to-date, relevant to the method of communication used.[100] The requirements mentioned at (1) and (2) already

[96] MiFID I Implementing Directive, Art 27(6).

[97] Draft Commission Delegated Regulation MiFID II, C(2016) 2398 final, 25 April 2016, Art 44(6) sub (b) and (d) (financial instruments) in conjunction with Art 1(2) (structured deposits).

[98] MiFID II, Art 24(4)(c) (financial instruments) in conjunction with Art 1(4)(b) (structured deposits).

[99] Draft Commission Delegated Regulation MiFID II, C(2016) 2398 final, 25 April 2016, Art 50 (financial instruments) in conjunction with Art 1(2) (structured deposits).

[100] Draft Commission Delegated Regulation MiFID II, C(2016) 2398 final, 25 April 2016, Art 44(2) sub (b), (e) and (g) (financial instruments) in conjunction with Article 1(2) (structured deposits).

apply to retail clients under MiFID I (with the exception of the requirement that a *prominent* indication should be given of the risks),[101] but also apply to professional clients under MiFID II.

2. As noted above in subsection B, at point 2, MiFID II requires the provision of more extensive information about costs and charges, including aggregated information allowing the client to understand the overall cost as well as the cumulative effect on the return on the investment (and, where the client so requests, an itemised breakdown; where applicable, this information must be provided to the client on a regular basis, at least annually, during the life of the investment).[102] MiFID II specifies in detail what information about costs and charges must be provided to professional investors.[103] When providing services to professional clients (but not retail clients), an investment firm may *agree* a limited application of these detailed requirements, *except* (1) when the services of investment advice or portfolio management are provided; or (2) when, irrespective of the investment service provided, the financial instruments concerned embed a derivative.[104]

G. Eligible Counterparties

The information obligations under MiFID I do not apply at all in relation to eligible counterparties. The idea behind this was apparently that eligible counterparties do not need the protection of the law as they have a sufficiently strong negotiating position to stipulate contractually what information they need in order to make correct investment decisions. Ideas about this evidently changed during the negotiations on MiFID II, as this introduces various obligations to provide information to eligible counterparties as well. Strictly speaking, these provisions apply not only to the provision of investment services but also in cases where an investment firm or a bank sells a structured deposit or advises on this.[105] As the provision of investment advice is one of the services that is not relevant to the eligible counterparty category (see section IV.A above), it seems to me only logical that the provision of advice on a structured deposit is also not relevant to this category.[106]

1. Firms are obliged to ensure, even in their relationship with eligible counterparties, that they communicate in a way which is fair, clear and not misleading,

[101] MiFID I Implementing Directive, Art 27(2), first and third paras.

[102] MiFID II, Art 24(4)(b) and (c) (financial instruments) in conjunction with Art 1(4)(b) (structured deposits).

[103] Draft Commission Delegated Regulation MiFID II, C(2016) 2398 final, 25 April 2016, Art 50 (financial instruments) in conjunction with Art 1(2) (structured deposits).

[104] Draft Commission Delegated Regulation MiFID II, C(2016) 2398 final, 25 April 2016, Art 50(1), second para, (financial instruments) in conjunction with Art 1(2) (structured deposits).

[105] MiFID II, Art 1(4), opening words and (b), in conjunction with Art 30.

[106] For the meaning of the term 'sale', see the discussion in s VII.A, second para, of the main text below.

(although they may take into account the nature of the eligible counterparty and of its business).[107]

2. Firms must also provide appropriate information in good time to eligible counterparties about (1) the firm and its services; (2) financial instruments/structured deposits and proposed investment strategies (including appropriate guidance on and warnings of the risks associated with investments in those instruments or in respect of particular investment strategies); (3) execution venues; and (4) costs and associated charges (including aggregated information to allow the client to understand the overall cost as well as the cumulative effect on the return of the investment). All of this is to ensure that clients or potential clients are reasonably able to understand the nature and risks of the investment service and of the specific type of financial instrument/structured deposit that is being offered and, consequently, to take investment decisions on an informed basis.[108]
3. As noted above in subsection B, at point 2, MiFID II requires the provision of more extensive information on all costs and associated charges, including aggregated information, to allow the client to understand the overall cost as well as the cumulative effect on the return of the investment. (At the client's request, an itemised breakdown must be provided. Where applicable, this information must be provided to the client on a regular basis, at least annually, during the life of the investment.)[109] MiFID II specifies in detail what information about costs and charges must be provided.[110] When providing services to eligible counterparties (like professional clients but unlike retail clients), an investment firm may *agree* that less information will be provided about costs and charges, irrespective of the investment service provided, except where the financial instruments concerned embed a derivative.[111] The exception included in relation to professional clients in cases where the investment firm provides investment advice or portfolio management services is naturally not included for eligible counterparties, since advice and services of this kind are not relevant in the case of the eligible counterparty category (see subsection B above).
4. Under MiFID II the Member States *may* allow information to be provided in a standardised format, and this naturally also applies in relation to eligible counterparties.[112]

[107] MiFID II, Art 30, second para (financial instruments) in conjunction with Art 1(4)(b) (structured deposits).

[108] MiFID II, Art 30(1), first para, in conjunction with Art 24(4), opening words and (c) and last para, and (5), first sentence, (financial instruments) in conjunction with Art 1(4)(b) (structured deposits).

[109] MiFID II, Art 24(4)(b) and (c) (financial instruments) in conjunction with Art 1(4)(b) (structured deposits).

[110] Draft Commission Delegated Regulation MiFID II, C(2016) 2398 final, 25 April 2016, Art 50 (financial instruments) in conjunction with Art 1(2) (structured deposits).

[111] Draft Commission Delegated Regulation MiFID II, C(2016) 2398 final, 25 April 2016, Art 50(1), third para (financial instruments) in conjunction with Art 1(2) (structured deposits).

[112] MiFID II, Art 30(1), first para, in conjunction with Art 24(5), last sentence (financial instruments) in conjunction with Art 1(4)(b) (structured deposits). As noted in n 73, in eg The Netherlands

Article 24(4)(b) (in conjunction with Article 1(4)(b)) MiFID II contains the provision that the firm must indicate whether the financial instrument/structured deposit is intended for retail or professional clients, taking account of the identified target market. As the provision itself refers only to retail and professional clients, it clearly plays no role in relation to eligible counterparties. The information obligations that apply in the case of investment advice[113] do not in any event apply in relation to eligible counterparties since this is one of the services that is not relevant to this category (see section IV.A above)

VII. Know your Customer Rules: Appropriateness Assessment

A. General

If an investment firm provides investment services, it must comply with the Know your Customer (KYC) rules. The basic principle under both MiFID I and MiFID II is that the appropriateness assessment applies to: (1) the reception and transmission of orders in financial instruments, and (2) the execution of orders in financial instruments on behalf of clients (execution-only service).[114]

Does MiFID II extend the appropriateness assessment to (1) the reception and transmission of orders in structured deposits, and (2) the execution of orders in respect of a structured deposit on behalf of a client?[115] Strictly speaking, Article 1(4) MiFID II merely provides that the KYC rules must be complied with in *providing advice* on structured deposits and in their *sale*. The mere *sale* of a

this Member State option is exercised (implicitly). The relevant Dutch implementing provision (Wft, Art 4:20(6)) is not altered in the Draft Bill to implement MiFID II, and the accompanying Explanatory Memorandum is also silent on this point. See *Dutch Parliamentary Papers II*, 2016/2017, 34 583, no 2 (Draft Bill) and no 3 (Explanatory Memorandum). It will therefore remain possible in the Netherlands to provide information in standardised format. The situation will undoubtedly be different in at least a few other Member States. If the Member States had unanimously considered that information could be provided in standardised format, a compromise in the form of a Member State option would have been unnecessary.

[113] MiFID II, Art 24(4)(a).

[114] MiFID I, Art 19(5), first para; MiFID II, Art 25(3), first para. Both articles apply the assessment of appropriateness in relation to investment services other than: (1) the provision of investment advice, and (2) the provision of portfolio management. Besides the investment services referred to in the main text, namely (a) the reception and transmission of orders in relation to financial instruments, and (b) the execution of orders in financial instruments on behalf of clients (execution-only service), the appropriateness assessment therefore also applies, strictly speaking, to the investment services (c) the underwriting or placing of financial instruments whether on a firm commitment basis or otherwise. However, I cannot really envisage how an appropriateness assessment could be usefully applied to this last form of investment service.

[115] See MiFID II, Art 1(4).

structured deposit means, basically, that a credit institution or investment firm acts purely as the buyer's contractual counterparty (dealing on own account), and does not yet result in (1) the reception and transmission of orders in relation to structured deposits, and/or (2) the execution of orders in relation to a structured deposit on behalf of the client. On the other hand, it is perhaps conceivable that the European legislator would not wish to exclude the application of the appropriateness assessment to the reception and transmission of orders in structured deposits and the execution of orders in structured deposits on behalf of the client. The term 'sale' should therefore be broadly interpreted in relation to structured deposits. Another approach would be to reclassify the sale of a structured deposit as the execution of an order in a structured deposit on behalf of the client, by analogy with the manner in which this happens on the sale of a financial instrument issued by the credit institution or investment firm itself.[116] In one of these ways the appropriateness assessment could therefore also be applicable to the sale of structured deposits.

B. Retail Clients

Under both MiFID I and MiFID II, the appropriateness assessment in relation to retail clients means that the investment firm must obtain information about the client's knowledge and experience of the relevant financial instrument or the relevant service, so that it can assess whether the financial instrument or service is *appropriate* for the client.[117]

C. Professional Clients and Eligible Counterparties

Under MiFID I the appropriateness assessment need not be applied at all in relation to professional clients and eligible counterparties.[118] The position is no different under MiFID II.[119]

D. Non-complex Financial Instruments

In the case of (1) the reception and transmission of client orders in financial instruments, and (2) the execution of orders in financial instruments on behalf of a client (execution-only service), it is not always necessary to apply the

[116] See MiFID II, Art 4(1), at (5), about which see s III above.

[117] See MiFID I, Art 19(5), first para; MIFID II, Art 25(3), first para.

[118] See MiFID I Implementing Directive, Art 36, second para, (professional clients); MiFID, Art 24(1) in conjunction with Art 19(5) (eligible counterparties).

[119] See, Draft Commission Delegated Regulation MiFID II, C(2016) 2398 final, 25 April 2016 (professional clients) Art 56(1), second para; MiFID II, Art 30(1), first para, in conjunction with Art 25(3) (eligible counterparties).

appropriateness assessment in relation to retail clients under either MiFID I or MiFID II. Of particular importance here is the exception to the appropriateness assessment for non-complex financial instruments. For the sake of clarity, it should be noted that under both MiFID I and II this exception is important only in relation to retail clients, as the appropriateness assessment does not apply to professional clients and eligible counterparties (see section VII.C above).

The exception to the appropriateness assessment for non-complex financial instruments as included in MiFID I takes the following form. An investment firm that provides investment services consisting solely of execution of client orders in financial instruments (execution-only service) and/or the reception and transmission of client orders with or without ancillary services, may provide those investment services to its clients *without* the need to apply the appropriateness assessment, provided that all the following conditions are met: (1) the service relates to orders in non-complex financial instruments, (2) the service is provided at the initiative of the client, (3) the bank or investment firm has informed the client before the start of the service that it has not assessed whether the service is suitable for the client, *and* (4) the investment firm complies with its obligations under Article 18 MiFID I (conflicts of interest).[120] 'Suitability' (see point 3 above) is, by the way, an unfortunate choice of term. After all, this is about the application of the appropriateness assessment, not the application of the suitability assessment.

According to MiFID I, the following financial instruments are not complex: (a) shares admitted to trading on a regulated market or in an equivalent third country market, money market instruments, bonds or other forms of securitised debt (excluding those bonds or securitised debt that embed a derivative), (b) units in UCITS, and (c) other non-complex financial instruments.[121]

The category at (c) above is elaborated in the MiFID I Implementing Directive. An instrument constitutes a non-complex financial instrument other than those explicitly mentioned in MiFID I if it satisfies the following *cumulative* criteria: (1) the financial instrument may not be a *transferable security* that gives the right to acquire or sell shares, depositary receipts in respect of shares and bonds traded on capital markets, giving rise to a cash settlement determined by reference to transferable securities, currencies, interest rates or yields, commodities or other indices or measure (derivative-like securities) and the financial instrument may also not be a derivative; (2) there are frequent opportunities to dispose of, redeem, or otherwise realise that instrument at prices that are publicly available to market participants and that are either market prices or prices made available, or validated, by valuation systems independent of the issuer; (3) the financial instrument does not involve any actual or potential liability for the client that exceeds the cost of acquiring the instrument; and (4) adequately comprehensive information on its characteristics is publicly available and is likely to be readily understood so as

[120] See MiFID I, Art 19(6).
[121] MiFID I, Art 19(6), first indent.

to enable the average retail client to make an informed judgement as to whether to enter into a transaction in that instrument.[122]

MiFID II restricts the exception to the appropriateness assessment for non-complex financial instruments in various ways, but also expands and clarifies certain elements of the assessment.

1. Under MiFID II as well, an investment firm that exclusively executes client orders in financial instruments (execution-only service) and/or receives and transmits client orders with or without ancillary services may provide those investment services to its clients *without* the need to apply the appropriateness assessment, provided that certain conditions are fulfilled.[123] However, the exception to the appropriateness assessment no longer applies to the ancillary service of granting credits or loans to an investor to allow him to carry out transactions in financial instruments where the firm granting the credit or loan is involved in the transaction, in so far as the loan or credit does not come within existing credit limits of loans, current accounts and overdraft facilities of clients.[124] It is understandable that the scope of the exception has been narrowed. Although a transaction may involve a non-complex financial instrument, the transaction as a whole does qualify as complex if the instrument is acquired with money borrowed from the investment firm concerned. Applying an appropriateness assessment in such cases seems to me to be justified.
2. MiFID II, like MiFID I, provides that the assessment must always concern shares and bonds admitted to trading on a regulated market or on an equivalent third country market. However, MiFID II has expanded this to include shares and bonds admitted to trading on an MTF.[125] This expansion strikes me as justified since the economic function performed by an MTF is comparable to that of a regulated market and, like a regulated market, is regulated by MiFID I and MiFID II. For the time being, the expansion may perhaps add less to investor protection than might be expected. Shares and bonds traded on MTFs are, for the time being, nearly always also admitted to trading on a regulated market or on an equivalent third country market. Naturally, this may change if the species of the genus MTF—the SME growth market—included in MiFID II proves to be a success. After all, the financial instruments traded on that market will not be admitted to trading on a regulated market. A stock exchange listing is simply too expensive for SMEs, which is why the SME growth market has been introduced as an alternative for businesses of this kind.[126]

[122] MiFID I Implementing Directive, Art 38.
[123] MiFID II, Art 25(4).
[124] MiFID II, Art 25(4), first para.
[125] MiFID II, Art 25(4)(a), at (i) and (ii).
[126] On the subject of the SME growth market, see MiFID II, Art 33 and MiFID II, Recitals (132)–(135); Draft Commission Delegated Regulation MiFID II, C(2016) 2398 final, 25 April 2016, Art 77–79 and Recitals (111)–(115). MiFID II, Art 4(1)(13) defined 'small and medium-sized

3. MiFID II makes clear that shares qualify as non-complex only if they are shares in *companies*.[127] The European legislator has thus tried to stress that rights of participation in an alternative investment fund (AIF, ie a non-UCITS collective investment undertaking) are, by definition, complex financial instruments, even if the rights are issued in the form of shares admitted to trading on a regulated market (or on an equivalent third country market), which will be the case if the AIF has the legal form of a public limited liability company. MiFID I also intended to provide that rights of participation in non-UCITS collective investment undertakings were always complex financial instruments. However, it is apparent from a close reading of MiFID I that it has not been entirely successful in this, because, strictly speaking, rights of participation in the form of shares in non-UCITS collective investment undertakings which have been admitted to trading on a regulated market (or on an equivalent third country market) must be treated as non-complex.[128] Moreover, all shares that embed a derivative are treated by definition as complex financial instruments under MiFID II.[129] Under MiFID I, such shares could still be classified as non-complex financial instruments.
4. Under MiFID II it is a basic principle that not only bonds but also other forms of securitised debt are treated as non-complex financial instruments. To this extent the exception to the appropriateness assessment for non-complex financial instruments is expanded.[130] However, the exception to the appropriateness assessment is restricted at the same time because MiFID II provides that bonds or other forms of securitised debt that embed a derivative or incorporate a structure which makes it difficult for the client to understand the risk involved are designated as complex financial instruments.[131] As interest rate derivatives are used in practice to hedge the risk in the case of almost all securitisations, the exception to the appropriateness assessment for securitised debt seems to be of only limited value.
5. Under MiFID II *all* money market instruments no longer automatically qualify as non-complex financial instruments. Money market instruments that embed a derivative or incorporate a structure which makes it difficult for the client to understand the risk involved are treated as complex financial instruments under MiFID II.[132] The condition that the money market instruments must have been admitted to trading on a regulated market (or on an

enterprises' as: companies that had an average market capitalisation of less than €200,000,000 on the basis of end-year quotes for the previous 3 calendar years. See for a critical assessment of the new rules pertaining to SME growth markets: R Veil and C Di Noia, 'SME Growth Markets' in Busch and Ferrarini (n 3) 345–62.

[127] MiFID II, Art 25(4)(a), at (i).
[128] MiFID I, Art 19(6), first indent.
[129] MiFID II, Art 25(4)(a), at (i).
[130] MiFID II, Art 25(4)(a), at (ii).
[131] MiFID II, Art 25(4)(a), at (ii).
[132] MiFID II, Art 25(4)(a), at (iii).

equivalent third country market) in order to be treated as non-complex no longer applies under MiFID II.[133]

6. Under MiFID II *all* shares or units UCITS no longer automatically qualify as non-complex financial instruments. On the contrary, shares or units in structured UCITS are defined as complex financial instruments.[134]
7. MiFID II adds structured deposits to the list of non-complex products, *excluding* those that incorporate a structure which makes it difficult for the client to understand the risk of return or the cost of exiting the product before term.[135]
8. The requirements laid down in Article 38 of the MiFID I Implementing Directive for non-complex financial instruments not explicitly mentioned at level 1 is expanded under MiFID II.[136] MiFID II adds two criteria that financial instruments of this kind would need to meet to be considered non-complex, namely: (1) it does not incorporate a clause, condition or trigger that could fundamentally alter the nature or risk of the investment or pay out profile, such as investments that incorporate a right to convert the instrument into a different investment; (2) it does not include any explicit or implicit exit charges that have the effect of making the investment illiquid even though there are technically frequent opportunities to dispose of, redeem or otherwise realise it.[137]
9. Finally, the following requirements apply under MiFID II, just as under MiFID I, if the appropriateness assessment is not to be applied in relation to non-complex financial instruments: (1) the service is provided at the initiative of the client; (2) the bank or investment firm has informed the client before the start of the service that it has not assessed whether the service is appropriate for the client; *and* (3) the investment firm complies with its obligations in respect of conflicts of interest (regulated in MiFID II in Article 23).[138]

E. Records of Appropriateness Assessments

MiFID I does not contain an explicit provision on the manner in which records of an appropriateness assessment should be kept. Under MiFID II, however, the following records of an appropriateness assessment must be kept: (1) the result of the appropriateness assessment; (2) where the investment service or product purchase was assessed as potentially inappropriate for the client, the records should show (a) whether the investment firm warned the client about this, (b) whether the client asked to proceed with the purchase despite the warning, and (c) where

[133] MiFID II, Art 25(4)(a), at (iii).
[134] MiFID II, Art 25(4)(a), at (iv).
[135] MiFID II, Art 25(4)(a), at (v).
[136] For this category in MiFID II, see Art 25(4)(a), at (vi).
[137] Draft Commission Delegated Regulation MiFID II, C(2016) 2398 final, 25 April 2016, Art 57(d) and (e).
[138] MiFID II, Art 25(4)(b)–(d).

applicable, whether the firm accepted the client's request to proceed with the transaction; and (3)(a) whether the investment firm warned the client where the client did not provide sufficient information to enable the firm to undertake an appropriateness assessment, (b) whether the client asked to proceed with the transaction despite this warning, and (c) where applicable, whether the firm accepted the client's request to proceed with the transaction.[139] I take this to mean that the investment firm may grant an ill-advised request from the client and does not have a duty to refuse the request. It should also be remembered that under MiFID II the appropriateness assessment need not be applied in relation to professional clients and eligible counterparties and that the duty to keep records also therefore does not apply (see section VII.C above).

VIII. Know your Customer Rules: Suitability Assessment

A. General

If an investment firm provides investment advice or portfolio management, it should, in principle, apply not the *appropriateness assessment* but the more stringent *suitability assessment*. Under MiFID II the suitability assessment is extended to the provision of advice in relation to structured deposits.[140]

B. Retail Clients

Under both MiFID I and II the suitability assessment in relation to retail clients requires the investment firm to obtain the necessary information regarding (1) the client's or potential client's knowledge and experience in the investment field relevant to the specific type of product or service; (2) his financial situation (including his ability to bear losses); and (3) his investment objectives (including his risk tolerance), so as to enable the firm to recommend to the client or potential client the investment services and financial instruments that are suitable for him (and, in particular, are in accordance with his risk tolerance and ability to bear losses).[141]

Unlike the situation with the appropriateness assessment, an investment firm is therefore obliged not only to obtain information about knowledge and experience but also about the financial situation and investment objectives of a retail client. The information about the client's *financial situation* includes (where relevant)

[139] Draft Commission Delegated Regulation MiFID II, C(2016) 2398 final, 25 April 2016, Art 56(2).
[140] See MiFID II, Art 1(4).
[141] MiFID I, Art 19(4); MiFID II, Art 25(2), first para.

information on (1) the source and extent of his regular income; (2) his assets (including liquid assets, investments and real property); and (3) his regular financial commitments.[142] The information about the *investment objectives* includes (where relevant) information on (i) the length of time for which the client wishes to hold the investment (investment horizon); (ii) his preferences regarding risk taking (risk tolerance); (iii) his risk profile; and (iv) the purposes of the investment.[143] If the investment firm fails to obtain the specified information, it may not recommend investment services or financial instruments to the client or potential client.[144]

C. Professional Clients and Eligible Counterparties

Under both MiFID I and II, an investment firm which provides investment advice or portfolio management services to a professional client (including an opt-up professional client) is entitled to *assume* that the client has the necessary experience and knowledge to understand the risks involved in the transaction.[145] In providing investment advice (but not portfolio management services!) the investment firm is also entitled to assume that a professional client (but not an opt-up professional client!) is able financially to bear any losses that may occur.[146] This means therefore that information need be obtained only over the client's risk tolerance and investment objectives.[147]

Finally, I would point out once again that the eligible counterparty client category is not relevant in the case of portfolio management or investment advice. Only two client categories are relevant to such services, namely professional and retail clients.[148]

D. Stricter Suitability Assessment

Under MiFID II, the suitability assessment is clarified and tightened in relation to both retail and professional clients. A number of important changes are examined below.

1. Where (1) a client is a legal person or (2) a client consists of a group of two or more natural persons or (3) one or more natural persons are represented

[142] MiFID I Implementing Directive, Art 35(3); Draft Commission Delegated Regulation MiFID II, C(2016) 2398 final, 25 April 2016, Art 54(4).

[143] MiFID I Implementing Directive, Art 35(4); Draft Commission Delegated Regulation MiFID II, C(2016) 2398 final, 25 April 2016, Art 54(5).

[144] MiFID I Implementing Directive, Art 35(5); Draft Commission Delegated Regulation MiFID II, C(2016) 2398 final, 25 April 2016, Art 54(8).

[145] See MiFID I Implementing Directive, Art 35(2), first para; Draft Commission Delegated Regulation MiFID II, C(2016) 2398 final, 25 April 2016 Art 54(3), first para.

[146] See MiFID I Implementing Directive, Art 35(2), second para; Draft Commission Delegated Regulation MiFID II, C(2016) 2398 final, 25 April 2016, Art 54(3), second para.

[147] This is elaborated in MiFID I Implementing Directive, Art 35(1)(a) and (4).

[148] See s IV.A of this chapter.

by another natural person, the investment firm must establish and implement policy as to who should be subject to the suitability assessment and how this assessment will be done in practice, including from whom information about knowledge and experience, financial situation and investment objectives should be collected. The investment firm must record this policy. Where a natural person is represented by another natural person or where a legal person having requested treatment as professional client in accordance with section 2 of Annex II of MiFID II is to be considered for the suitability assessment, the financial situation and investment objectives must be those of the legal person or, in relation to the natural person, the underlying client rather than of the representative. The knowledge and experience must be that of the representative of the natural person or the person authorised to carry out transactions on behalf of the underlying client.[149]

2. An investment firm must take reasonable steps to ensure that the information collected about its clients is reliable. This includes (but is not limited to) (1) ensuring clients are aware of the importance of providing accurate and up-to-date information; (2) ensuring all tools, such as risk assessment profiling tools or tools to assess a client's knowledge and experience, employed in the suitability assessment process are fit for purpose and are appropriately designed for use with its clients, with any limitations identified and actively mitigated through the suitability assessment process; (3) ensuring questions used in the process are likely to be understood by clients, capture an accurate reflection of the client's objectives and needs, and the information necessary to undertake the suitability assessment; and (4) taking steps, as appropriate, to ensure the consistency of client information, such as by considering whether there are obvious inaccuracies in the information provided by clients.[150]
3. An investment firm must not recommend or decide to trade if none of the investments it offers is suitable for the client.[151]
4. When providing investment advice or portfolio management services that involve switching investments (either by selling an instrument and buying another or by exercising a right to make a change in regard to an existing instrument) it must collect the necessary information on the client's existing investments and the recommended new investments, and it must undertake an analysis of the costs and benefits of the switch, such that they are reasonably able to demonstrate that the benefits of switching are greater than the costs.[152]

However, some of the above tighter provisions and clarifications, including at (1) and (2) above, seem to me to be equally relevant to the appropriateness

[149] Draft Commission Delegated Regulation MiFID II, C(2016) 2398 final, 25 April 2016, Art 54(6).
[150] Draft Commission Delegated Regulation MiFID II, C(2016) 2398 final, 25 April 2016, Art 54(7).
[151] Draft Commission Delegated Regulation MiFID II, C(2016) 2398 final, 25 April 2016, Art 54(10).
[152] Draft Commission Delegated Regulation MiFID II, C(2016) 2398 final, 25 April 2016, Art 54(11).

assessment. It therefore seems inconsistent not to have similar changes and clarifications in relation to the appropriateness assessment.

E. Suitability Assessment and Bundled Packages of Services or Products

Unlike MiFID I, MiFID II provides that where an investment firm provides investment advice recommending a bundled package of services or products, the overall bundled package must be 'suitable'.[153] This assessment must be made in relation to both retail and professional clients, but not in relation to eligible counterparties.[154] A bundled package exists where an investment service is offered together with another service or product as part of a package or as a condition for the same agreement or package.[155]

F. Suitability Reports

Just as in the case of appropriateness assessments, MiFID I does not contain an explicit provision on the manner in which records of a suitability assessment should be kept. Under MiFID II, however, when providing investment advice, investment firms must provide a report to the *retail client* that includes an outline of the advice given and how the recommendation provided is suitable for the retail client, including how it meets the client's objectives and personal circumstances with reference to the investment term required, client's knowledge and experience and client's attitude to risk and capacity for loss.[156]

Investment firms must draw clients' attention to and must include in the suitability report information on whether the recommended services or instruments are likely to require the retail client to seek a periodic review of their arrangements.[157]

Where an investment firm provides a service that involves periodic suitability assessments and reports, the subsequent reports after the initial service is established may only cover changes in the services or instruments involved and/or the circumstances of the client and may not need to repeat all the details of the first report.[158]

[153] MiFID II, Art 25(2), second para.

[154] See MiFID II, Art 30(1), first para, in conjunction with Art 25(2), second para.

[155] MiFID II, Art 24(11), first para. See also the definition of 'cross-selling practice': the offering of an investment service together with another service or product as part of a package or as a condition for the same agreement or package. On the subject of cross-selling, see also s VI.D, above.

[156] Draft Commission Delegated Regulation MiFID II, C(2016) 2398 final, 25 April 2016, Art 54(12), first para.

[157] Draft Commission Delegated Regulation MiFID II, C(2016) 2398 final, 25 April 2016, Art 54(12), second para.

[158] Draft Commission Delegated Regulation MiFID II, C(2016) 2398 final, 25 April 2016, Art 54(12), third para.

Investment firms providing a periodic suitability assessment must review, in order to enhance the service, the suitability of the recommendations given at least annually. The frequency of this assessment must be increased depending on the risk profile of the client and the type of financial instruments recommended.[159]

Finally, as the obligation to keep records of the suitability assessment is limited to retail clients, it does not apply to professional clients. Moreover, the obligation to keep records does not apply to eligible counterparties at all, because this category does not exist in relation to investment advice and portfolio management.[160]

IX. Best Execution

A. MiFID

The MiFID I regime provides that investment firms are obliged to take all reasonable steps to obtain, when performing transactions on behalf of clients (executing orders), the best possible result for their clients.[161] The best execution obligation is intended not only to make a contribution to investor protection but also to promote free competition between trading venues (regulated markets, multilateral trading facilities (MTFs), systematic internalisers acting in that capacity, and, where appropriate, a system outside the Community with similar functions to a regulated market or MTF).[162] The obligation of an investment firm to execute an order at the venue where the best result can be achieved for the client may mean that the order is executed through the trading facility where this can be achieved on the most favourable terms, thereby ensuring that trading venues engage

159 Draft Commission Delegated Regulation MiFID II, C(2016) 2398 final, 25 April 2016, Art 54(13).

160 See s IV.A.

161 See MiFID I, Art 21(1). The best execution regime has been elaborated in several provisions; see MiFID I, Art 21 and MiFID I Implementing Directive, Arts 44–46.

162 See MiFID I Implementing Regulation, Art 2(8). NB The term 'trading venue' is also defined in MiFID II, Art 4(1), at (24). A new concept is that of the 'organised trading facility' (OTF), but terms that have been dropped are 'systematic internaliser' and 'system outside the Community with similar functions to a regulated market or MTF'. There is also a broader definition of 'execution venue'. This includes not only the trading venues but also market makers and other liquidity providers or an entity that performs a similar function in a third country to the functions performed by any of the foregoing. For the definition of 'execution venue' see MiFID I Implementing Directive, Art 44(1). According to the definition in MiFID I, Art 4(1) at (8), and MiFID II, Art 4(1) at (7), a 'market maker' is a person who holds himself out on the financial markets on a continuous basis as being willing to deal on own account by buying and selling financial instruments against his proprietary capital at prices defined by him. Liquidity provider is not a defined term. In general, a liquidity provider is someone who provides liquidity to the market by entering into buying and selling transactions on his own account, whether or not after quoting bid and/or offer prices. Most liquidity providers are obliged to issue quotes at certain times.

in actual and efficient competition with one another.[163] The free competition between trading venues and the accompanying abolition of the concentration rule[164] constituted one of the main innovations introduced by MiFID. It is now clear that this free competition has got off to a reasonably successful start.[165] The established regulated markets are now experiencing serious competition from various MTFs (although some of them have already been taken over by the operators of regulated markets). Whether the best execution rules have actually assisted in this process is naturally a moot point. In any event, it is apparent from a recent ESMA report that most national regulators give only a low priority to monitoring observance and enforcement of the best execution rules. At the same time, there are also few complaints from the sector about non-compliance with the best execution rules. ESMA notes that:

> This can likely be attributed to the low level of understanding of execution quality amongst investors as well as a certain 'opacity' of the best execution practices followed by the firms. The fact that several supervisory systems seem to be very 'reactive' in approach and heavily reliant on complaints before a further investigation is triggered, could also explain the low level of enforcement in this sector.[166]

The best execution obligation applies in relation to both the execution-only service and to the execution of client orders within the context of advice or portfolio management. A client need not have made a specific request to enter into a given transaction in order for the execution of a transaction to be treated as the execution of an order on behalf of the client.[167]

[163] See eg European Commission, Proposal for Directive of the European Parliament and the Council on Investment Services and Regulated Markets, and Amending Council Directives 85/611/EEC, Council Directive 93/6/EEC and European Parliament and Council Directive 2000/12/EC, COM(2002) 625 final (*Pb EU* C 71E of 25/03/2003, 62–125) 7, 11 and 26; European Commission, Draft Commission Directive implementing Directive 2004/39/EC of the European Parliament and of the Council as regards record-keeping obligations for investment firms, transaction reporting, market transparency, admission of financial instruments to trading, and defined terms for the purposes of the Directive. Background Note (ec.europa.eu/internal_market/securities/isd/MiFID2_en.htm) § 7.7. ('Best execution obligations not only form a fundamental element in investor protection, but are also necessary to mitigate possible problems associated with market fragmentation'.); CESR, *Best Execution under MiFID, Questions & Answers, May 2007*, CESR/07-320 (www.cesr-eu.org) 3. See on this point, G Ferrarini, 'Best Execution and Competition between Trading Venues—MiFID's Likely Impact (2007) *Capital Markets Law Journal* 404–13; D Frase, 'Conduct of Business Standards—Best Execution' in M Elderfield (ed), *A Practitioner's Guide to MiFID* (Surrey: City & Financial Publishing, 2007) 185–212, 191. For a discussion of the interaction between the 2 objectives of best execution (investor protection and promoting competition between trading venues), see the interesting monograph of S McCleskey, *Achieving Market Integration. Best Execution, Fragmentation and the Free Flow of Capital* (Oxford: Butterworth-Heinemann, 2004). Besides the best execution rules, the MiFID pre-trade and post-trade transparency obligations naturally also help to create efficient competition between trading venues.

[164] The abolition of the concentration rule means that it is up to the Member States themselves to determine whether it is necessary for retail orders relating to financial instruments to be executed by being forwarded to regulated markets.

[165] See European Commission, MiFID Impact Assessment (COM(2011) 656 final) 88 et seq.

[166] ESMA/2015/494, *Best Execution under MiFID—Peer Review report* (25 February 2015) 7 (no 20).

[167] Explicit provision in MiFID I Implementing Directive, Art 45(7) in conjunction with MiFID I, Art 21.

When taking 'all reasonable steps to obtain the best possible result' for the client, an investment firm must take into account: (1) the price of the financial instruments, (2) costs of execution, (3) speed, (4) likelihood of execution and settlement, (5) size, (6) nature and (7) any other consideration relevant to the execution of the order.[168] When determining the relative importance of these factors, the investment firm applies the following criteria: (1) the characteristics of the client, including the client's classification as retail or professional; (2) the characteristics of the client order; (3) the characteristics of financial instruments that are the subject of that order; and (4) the characteristics of the execution venues to which that order can be directed.[169]

The best execution obligation applies in relation to both retail and professional clients. Where an investment firm executes an order on behalf of a retail client, it determines the best possible result in terms of the total consideration, representing the price of the financial instrument and the costs of execution.[170] The best execution obligation does not apply in relation to eligible counterparties.[171]

Where there is a specific instruction from the client about an order or a specific aspect of an order, an investment firm executes the order following the specific instruction and thus acts in accordance with the best execution obligation.[172] In view of the discretionary nature of portfolio management, the execution of a client's order as part of such management will not generally involve specific instructions of the client.

Finally, investment firms are required to establish and implement an order execution policy to allow them to obtain, for their client orders, the best possible result.[173]

An investment firm which receives and transmits orders to another investment firm does not execute orders for the client and is consequently not bound by the best execution obligation as described above. In transmitting client orders to third parties for execution, however, it is bound by an obligation that can be regarded as a supplement to the best execution obligation. If an investment firm transmits orders for execution to a third party, it must, when involving that third party in the execution of the order, take all reasonable steps to achieve the best possible result for its clients.[174] The rationale for this provision is that an investment firm which transmits orders for execution to a third party has a major influence on the quality of the execution of that order through its selection of the third party.

[168] MIFID I, Art 21(1).
[169] MiFID I Implementing Directive, Art 44(1), first para.
[170] See MiFID I Implementing Directive, Art 44(3), first para.
[171] MiFID I, Art 24(1), in conjunction with Arts 19 and 21. As Arts 44–46 of the MiFID I Implementing Directive are based on Arts 19 and 21 MiFID I (or parts of them), these provisions too do not apply in relation to eligible counterparties.
[172] MiFID I, Art 21(1), second sentence.
[173] MiFID I, Art 21(2), second sentence,; MiFID II, Art 27(4), second sentence.
[174] MiFID I, Art 19 lid 1 in conjunction with MiFID II Implementing Directive, Art 45.

B. MiFID II

Under MIFID II the best execution rules are not fundamentally revised. MiFID's best execution rules as described above are maintained, although MiFID II talks of 'all sufficient steps' rather than 'all reasonable steps' to obtain the best possible result for clients, but this change is much more cosmetic than substantive.[175] Under MiFID II, the best execution rules are once again intended to help boost free competition between trading venues, but it should be noted here that under MiFID II a new member is added to the family of trading venues, namely the organised trading facility or OTF.

Nonetheless, MiFID II does change the best execution rules in a number of respects. The main changes are outlined below.

1. As noted in Recital (76) to the MiFID I Implementing Directive, the availability, comparability and consolidation of data related to execution quality provided by the various execution venues is crucial in enabling investment firms and investors to identify those execution venues that deliver the highest quality of execution. However, the MiFID I regime did not make it mandatory for execution venues to publish this information. Instead, the market was given the opportunity to develop its own solutions.[176] The market has evidently failed to take advantage of this opportunity, because MiFID II makes publication mandatory. For financial instruments that are subject to the trading obligation of Articles 23 (particularly listed shares) and 28 (standardised OTC derivatives) MiFIR, each trading venue and each systematic internaliser must make available to the public, without any charges, data relating to the quality of execution of transactions on that venue on at least an annual basis. The same obligation applies to other financial instruments for all execution venues. In addition, an investment firm that executes a transaction on behalf of a client must inform the client where the order was executed. The periodic reports must include details about price, costs, speed and likelihood of execution for individual financial instruments.[177]
2. The information which investment firms give their clients about the order execution policy is still too often of a generic and standard nature. As a result, it is often not possible for clients (1) to understand how an order will be

[175] For the best execution rules, see MiFID II, Art 27 and Draft Commission Delegated Regulation MiFID II, C(2016) 2398 final, 25 April 2016, Arts 64–66. As regards the non-applicability of the best execution rules in relation to eligible counterparties, see MiFID II, Art 30(1), first para, in conjunction with Art 27.

[176] See also Recital (76) to the MiFID I Implementing Directive.

[177] MiFID II, Art 27(3). See also Recital (96) to MiFID II. Under MiFID II, Art 27(10)(a), ESMA has developed draft regulatory technical standards to determine the specific content, format and periodicity of data relating to the quality of execution to be published, taking into account the type of execution venue and the type of financial instrument concerned. See Annex I to Draft Commission Delegated Regulation MiFID II, C(2016) 3333 final, 8 June 2016 (RTS 27).

executed, and (2) to verify firms' compliance with their obligation to execute orders on terms most favourable to their client. To enhance investor protection, MiFID II therefore provides that clients must be given more specific information about the order execution policy.[178]

3. Another measure to enhance investor protection in MiFID II is the introduction of an obligation for investment firms that execute client orders to summarise and make public on an annual basis, for each class of financial instruments, the top five execution venues in terms of trading volumes where they executed client orders in the preceding year. They must also publish information on the quality of execution.[179] This information must then be taken into account by the investment firm in its order execution policy.[180] Under MiFID II a comparable obligation applies to investment firms that receive orders and transmit them to other investment firms.[181] The periodic reports should indicate the top five execution venues in terms of trading volumes where firms have executed client orders in the preceding year and include information on the quality of execution.[182]

X. Client Order Handling

Under both MiFID I and II investment firms are bound not only by the best execution obligation but also by rules on client order handling.[183] An investment firm must implement procedures and arrangements which provide for the prompt, fair and expeditious execution of client orders relating to financial instruments (1) relative to other client orders, or (2) the trading interests of the investment firm itself. These procedures and arrangements enable the investment firm to execute otherwise comparable client orders in accordance with the time of their reception.[184] And these rules are naturally also applicable to portfolio managers and advisers who execute orders on behalf of clients in that context. The client

[178] In a general sense, see Recital (97) to MiFID II. See also MiFID II, Art 27(5), second para, as well as Draft Commission Delegated Regulation MiFID II, C(2016) 2398 final, 25 April 2016, Art 66.

[179] MiFID II, Art 27(6).

[180] See Recital (97) to MiFID II.

[181] Draft Commission Delegated Regulation MiFID II, C(2016) 2398 final, 25 April 2016, Art 65(6).

[182] MiFID II, Art 27(6); Draft Commission Delegated Regulation MiFID II, C(2016) 2398 final, 25 April 2016, Art 65(6). Under MiFID II, Art 27(10)(b), ESMA has developed draft regulatory technical standards which determine the content and format of information to be published by investment firms. See Annex II to Draft Commission Delegated Regulation MiFID II, C(2016) 3337 final, 8 June 2016 (RTS 28).

[183] MiFID I, Art 22; MiFID II, Art 28.

[184] See MiFID I, Art 22 and MiFID I Implementing Directive, Arts 47–49. MiFID I Implementing Regulation, Arts 31 and 32 are also important. As regards MiFID II, see MiFID II, Art 28 and Draft Commission Delegated Regulation MiFID II, C(2016) 2398 final, 25 April 2016, Arts 67–70.

order handling rules apply in relation to both retail and professional clients. Once again, they do not apply in relation to eligible counterparties.[185]

However, an important change introduced by MiFID II is that the client order handling rules will also apply in relation to selling or advising clients in relation to structured deposits.[186]

The distinction between the best execution rules and the client order handling rules can best be explained as follows. The best execution rules are intended to ensure that an investment firm, when executing orders for the purchase and sale of financial instruments, achieves the best possible result available in the marketplace for the client. By contrast, the client order handling rules are intended to guarantee the client's position *within the investment firm*, in particular relative to other clients and the firm itself.[187]

XI. Conflicts of Interest

A. General

Conflicts of interest frequently occur in the financial services industry. An example would be where an investment firm that acts as portfolio manager also underwrites an initial public offering (IPO). To ensure the success of the IPO, the investment firm might be tempted to arrange for the financial instruments offered in the flotation to be included in the investment portfolios of its clients (and thus perform a purchase transaction on behalf of the client), although this need not necessarily be in the client's best interests.[188]

The conflicts of interest rules have not been radically revised in MiFID II. The following rules apply under both MiFID I and MiFID II. An investment firm must have in place procedures and measures to prevent conflicts of interest between the investment firm and its clients and between one client and another. The use of the term 'clients' makes clear that the conflicts of interest rules are only intended to protect clients. Investors with whom an investment firm acts purely as contractual counterparty (dealing on own account) therefore do not enjoy the protection of these rules. The aim of the policy must be to prevent and manage conflicts of

[185] MiFID I, Art 24(1) in conjunction with Art 19 and 22(1). As MiFID I Implementing Directive, Arts 47–49 are once again based on MiFID I, Arts 19 and 22 (or parts of them), these provisions too do not apply in relation to eligible counterparties. As regards MiFID II, see Art 30(1), first para, in conjunction with MiFID II, Art 28(1).

[186] MiFID II, Art 1(4)(b).

[187] European Commission, Proposal for Directive of the European Parliament and the Council on Investment Services and Regulated Markets, and Amending Council Directives 85/611/EEC, Council Directive 93/6/EEC and European Parliament and Council Directive 2000/12/EC, COM(2002) 625 final (*Pb EU* C 71E of 25/03/2003, 62–125) 27.

[188] *Cf* Recital (56) to MiFID II.

interest. If a conflict of interest proves inevitable, the investment firm must treat its clients fairly and, before transacting business, disclose the conflict to its clients.[189] These rules are generic (ie they apply regardless of the client classification).

An important change introduced by MiFID II is once again that the conflicts of interest rules will apply in relation to the provision of advice on structured deposits.[190]

Although the conflicts of interest rules may not have been radically overhauled in MiFID II, they are tightened and clarified in various respects (set out below).

1. The disclosure of a conflict of interest is a measure of last resort and may be used only where the effective organisational and administrative arrangements put in place by the investment firm to prevent or manage conflicts of interest are not sufficient to ensure, with reasonable confidence, that the risks of damage to the interests of the client will be prevented.[191] This stricter criterion can be seen as a reaction to the fact that, in practice, investment firms tend to put undue reliance on disclosure of conflicts of interest, without having made reasonable efforts to prevent or manage such conflicts.
2. If disclosure of specific conflicts of interest is required, it must be made clear that the organisational and administrative arrangements established by the investment firm to prevent or manage conflicts of interest are not sufficient to ensure, with reasonable confidence, that the risks of damage to the interests of the client will be prevented. The disclosure to clients must be made in a durable medium[192] and must provide a detailed description of the conflict of interest that arises in the provision of investment and/or ancillary services, taking into account the nature of the client to whom the disclosure is being made. The description must explain the general nature and/or sources of conflict of interest, as well as the risks to the client that arise as a result of the conflict and the steps undertaken to mitigate these risks. Moreover, the description must be sufficiently detailed to enable the client to make an informed investment decision.[193] This tightening of the rule is a reaction to the fact that the provision of information by investment firms on conflicts of interest is often of a very generic and standard nature and therefore, in fact, largely meaningless.

[189] MiFID I, Art 13(3) and 18 and MiFID I Implementing Directive, Arts 21–25. See also MiFID II, Arts 23 and 16(3) and Draft Commission Delegated Regulation MiFID II, C(2016) 2398 final, 25 April 2016, Arts 33–43. See extensively on the conflicts of interest rules under MiFID I and II: S Grundmann and P Hacker, 'Conflicts of Interest' in Busch and Ferrarini (n 3) 165–204.

[190] MiFID II, Art 1(4)(b).

[191] Draft Commission Delegated Regulation MiFID II, C(2016) 2398 final, 25 April 2016, Art 34(4), first para.

[192] A 'durable medium' is defined as 'any instrument which: (a) enables a client to store information addressed personally to that client in a way accessible for future reference and for a period of time adequate for the purposes of the information; and (b) allows the unchanged reproduction of the information stored' (MiFID II, Art 4(1), at (62)).

[193] Draft Commission Delegated Regulation MiFID II, C(2016) 2398 final, 25 April 2016, Art 34(4), second para.

3. Investment firms must assess and periodically review—at least annually—their conflicts of interest policy and take all appropriate measures to address any deficiencies. Over-reliance on disclosure of conflicts of interest must be considered a deficiency in an investment firm's conflicts of interest policy.[194]
4. The conflicts of interest rules that apply in relation to reports of financial analysts are tightened in various respects.[195]

B. UCITS IV and AIFMD

It should be noted here that both UCITS IV and the AIFMD also have a specific conflicts of interest rule relevant to investments firms that not only provide portfolio management services but also manage undertakings for collective investment in transferable securities (UCITS) and/or alternative investment funds (AIFs) (in-house funds). In such a situation, the portfolio manager is not permitted to invest all or part of the investor's portfolio in units of collective investment undertakings or units or shares of the AIFs it manages, unless it receives prior (written) approval from the client.[196] In short, the portfolio manager may not execute buying transactions in these shares or units on behalf of the client without prior (written) approval. Strangely enough, this conflicts of interest rule does not appear to extend to other entities within the portfolio manager's group.

C. Best Execution

Finally, the following rule is important. As already noted above, an investment firm is required to establish and implement an order execution policy that enables it to comply with its best execution obligation.[197] MiFID I provides that when an order execution policy provides for the possibility that client orders may be executed outside a regulated market or an MTF, the investment firm must, *in particular*, inform its clients about this possibility. This means that investment firms must obtain the prior express consent of their clients before proceeding to execute their orders outside a regulated market or an MTF. Investment firms may obtain this consent either in the form of a general agreement or in respect of individual transactions.[198] It follows that the client (1) must be expressly informed of the possibility that orders may be executed for them by means of (systematic) internalisation or agency crosses; (2) must give express prior consent for the execution of the

194 Draft Commission Delegated Regulation MiFID II, C(2016) 2398 final, 25 April 2016, Art 34(5).

195 Draft Commission Delegated Regulation MiFID II, C(2016) 2398 final, 25 April 2016, Arts 36 et seq.

196 See UCITS IV, Art 12(2); AIFMD, Art 12(2)(a).

197 MiFID I, Art 21(2), second sentence; MiFID II, Art 27(4), second sentence.

198 MiFID I, Art 21(3), third para.

order by means of (systematic) internalisation or agency crosses. This is because the risk of a conflict of interest exists where client orders are executed in either of these ways. In the former case, because the investment firm acts not only as the client's representative but also as contractual counterparty in the transaction. Suppose that a client instructs an investment firm to buy 100 Shell shares for him and the transaction is handled by means of (systematic) internalisation. This creates a conflict for the investment firm since as the client's representative its interest is to obtain the lowest possible price, but as the client's contractual counterparty (ie as the seller of the 100 Shell shares) its interest is to achieve the highest possible price. Although the firm is naturally bound by its best execution obligation, there is still a risk that it will allow its own interests to take precedence over those of the client. This risk of a conflict of interest must be disclosed and the client must expressly indicate beforehand that he accepts this risk. Naturally, it is debatable whether a client will be sufficiently aware of the risk of a conflict of interest if he is merely informed in the order execution policy *in particular* of the possibility that orders may be executed outside the regulated market or an MTF and is required to give his express consent beforehand to this manner of executing client orders. Whatever the case, the risk of a conflict of interest also occurs in the case of agency crosses (matching of opposing client orders), since here the investment firm acts on behalf of both the buying and the selling client. As the representative of the seller, the investment firm has a duty to achieve the highest possible price, but as representative of the buyer its duty is to keep the price as low as possible.

MiFID II contains conflicts of interest rules comparable to those discussed in the previous paragraph, but nonetheless does make a major change. Instead of talking about executing orders 'outside a regulated market or an MTF', MiFID II refers (more broadly) to the execution of orders 'outside a trading venue'.[199] A 'trading venue' is 'every regulated market, an MTF or an OTF'.[200] In other words, MiFID II expands the MiFID I list to include the concept of the organised trading facility (OTF). Opposing client orders in non-equity products (such as derivatives and bonds) can be matched with each other through an OTF (agency crossing systems).[201] Under MiFID I the conflicts of interest rules described in the previous paragraph apply to all transactions involving agency crosses. Under MiFID II, however, this is no longer the case if opposing client orders are matched with each other through an OTF, because settlement through an OTF constitutes settlement on a trading venue and hence not settlement outside a trading venue for which the conflicts of interest rules described in the previous paragraph apply. This is noteworthy, because the risk of a conflict of interest still exists in such cases. After all, the investment firm operating the OTF acts on behalf of both the buyer and the seller in the same transaction and, since it applies discretionary rules, can influence what orders are or are not matched together. This means that there is

[199] MiFID II, Art 27(5), third para.
[200] MiFID II, Art 4(1), at (24).
[201] See eg MiFID II, Art 20(6), second para.

unequal treatment between client orders matched on an OTF (non-equity) and client orders matched outside a trading venue (equity). In the latter case, the conflicts of interest rules dealt with in the previous paragraph continue to apply in full.

XII. Inducements

MiFID I contains rules on inducements which investment firms pay or are paid for their services.[202] The idea behind these rules is to prevent conflicts of interest where an investment firm allows itself to be swayed by interests other than the client's interests (eg by its own interests). In MiFID I the rules on inducements are seen as implementing the general duty of loyalty: an investment firm is not regarded as acting honestly, fairly and professionally in accordance with the best interests of a client if it fails to observe the rules on inducements.[203] MiFID II contains a comparable provision, but also indicates that if the rules on inducements are not complied with, this also constitutes a violation of the general conflict of interest rules.[204] The basic principle of the rules on inducements is that they are not permitted. This is the case in both MiFID I and MiFID II, although the rules have been tightened in MiFID II in relation to independent investment advice and portfolio management. The rules on inducements apply in relation to both retail and professional clients. They are not applicable in relation to eligible counterparties.[205]

Various exceptions to the basic principle that inducements are not permitted exist under MiFID I and MiFID II. *First*, the prohibition on inducements does not apply under MiFID I and MiFID II if the inducement is paid by or to the client.[206] The rationale for this exception is that in such cases influence is no longer exercised by a third party and the investment firm therefore no longer has an incentive not to put the client's interests first. Moreover, the client himself is aware of the inducement and thus determines in part whether and, if so, to what extent it serves as an incentive. *Second*, if the inducement is provided by or to a third party, the prohibition on inducements under MiFID I and MiFID II does not apply if: (1) the existence, nature and amount of the payment or benefit, or, where the amount cannot be ascertained, the method of calculating that amount, is clearly disclosed to the client, in a manner that is comprehensive, accurate and

[202] MiFID I Implementing Directive, Art 26.

[203] MiFID I Implementing Directive, Art 26, first para.

[204] MiFID II, Art 24(9), first para, in conjunction with Arts 23 and 24(1).

[205] MiFID I, Art 24(1); MiFID II, Art 30(1). See extensively on inducements under MiFID I and II, as well as in the UK and the Netherlands: L Silverentand, J Sprecher and L Simons, 'Inducements' in Busch & Ferrarini (n 3) 205–25.

[206] MiFID I Implementing Directive, Art 26, opening words and (a); MiFID II, Art 24(9), opening words.

understandable, prior to the provision of the relevant investment or ancillary service;[207] *and* (2) the payment of the inducement enhances the quality of the relevant service and does not impair compliance with the investment firm's duty to act in the client's best interests.[208] And, *third*, payments or benefits which 'enable' or 'are necessary for' the provision of investment services are not covered by the prohibition on inducements.[209] Examples of necessary payments include custody costs, settlement and exchange fees, regulatory levies and legal fees.[210]

Under MiFID II the rules on inducements paid by a third party to a portfolio manager or independent investment adviser (or vice versa) are stricter than under MiFID I. Under MiFID I the rules described in the previous paragraph apply, but under MiFID II the following rules apply both to retail and professional clients. An independent investment adviser or a portfolio manager may not accept and *retain* inducements paid by a third party in relation to the provision of services to clients. Minor non-monetary benefits that are capable of enhancing the quality of service provided to a client and are of such a scale and nature that they could not be judged to impair compliance with the investment firm's duty to act in the best interest of the client must be clearly disclosed and are excluded from this prohibition.[211] It should be noted that the prohibition does not in any event apply if the inducements are not retained by the independent investment adviser or portfolio manager, but are instead remitted to the client. Nor does the prohibition apply to a non-independent investment adviser. In the latter case, however, the general rules on inducements dealt with in the previous paragraph do apply.[212]

Finally, MiFID II provides that an investment firm must not receive any inducements for routing client orders to a particular trading venue or execution venue *in so far as* this would infringe the general requirements on conflicts of interest or inducements.[213] Although MiFID I does not contain a provision of this kind, it in fact follows from the general rules on conflicts of interest and, above all, the rules on inducements.

The new rules will have a major impact on the most common business models in the financial services industry. For example, a distribution fee (also known as a kick-back fee, trailer fee or rebate) is a payment which, say, a portfolio manager

[207] MiFID II adds that, where applicable, the investment firm must also inform the client about mechanisms for transferring to the client the fee, commission, monetary or non-monetary benefit received in relation to the provision of the investment or ancillary service. See MiFID II, Art 24(9), third para, second sentence.

[208] MiFID I Implementing Directive, Art 26, opening words and (b); MiFID II, Art 24(9), opening words and (a) and (b).

[209] MiFID I Implementing Directive, Art 26, opening words and (c); MiFID II, Art 24(9), opening words fourth para.

[210] See MiFID I Implementing Directive, Art 26(c).

[211] MiFID II, Art 24(7)(b) (independent investment advice); MiFID II, Art 24(8) (portfolio management).

[212] The MiFID II rules on inducements are elaborated in Draft Commission Delegated Directive MiFID II, C(2016) 2031 final, 7 April 2016, Arts 11–13.

[213] MiFID II, Art 27(2).

receives from the manager of a collective investment scheme (a 'fund operator') for making available its 'distribution channel'. Payments of this kind may mean that shares or units in collective investment schemes are included by the portfolio manager in investment portfolios of clients only if the manager receives an attractive distribution fee. Such investments are not necessarily the best choice for the client. Under MiFID I, fees of this kind do not appear to be prohibited outright. Under MiFID II, however, distribution fees paid to an independent investment adviser or portfolio manager are prohibited by definition if the adviser or manager concerned does *not* remit the payment to the client.[214]

XIII. Obligations to Record Conversations and Electronic Communications

MiFID II obliges investment firms to record relevant telephone conversations and electronic communications. Such communications relate, at least, to transactions concluded when dealing on own account and the provision of client order services that relate to the reception, transmission and execution of client orders.[215] Each communication intended to result in a transaction must be recorded, even if the communication does not actually result in the conclusion of a transaction.[216] Face-to-face conversations with a client must be recorded, for example by using written minutes or notes.[217] The records kept in this manner must be provided to the client upon request.[218] The records must be kept for five years and, where requested by the competent authority, for seven years.[219] Such records should ensure that there is evidence to prove the terms of any orders given by clients and its correspondence with transactions executed by the investment firms, as well as to detect any behaviour that may have relevance in terms of market abuse.[220]

[214] Inducement rules analogous to those resulting from MiFID II have been in force in the UK since May 2014. See FCA, *Policy Statement—Changes to the Use of Dealing Commission Rules: Feedback to CP13717 and Final Rules* (May 2014). More stringent rules on inducements than those resulting from MiFID and MiFID II have also applied in the Netherlands since 1 January 2014. See Market Conduct Supervision (Financial Institutions) Decree (*Besluit gedragstoezicht financiële ondernemingen*) Art 168a. The Netherlands has based this provision on Art 4 of the MiFID Implementing Directive and Art 24(12) of MiFID II. See also Recital (76) to MiFID II. See extensively Silverentand, Sprecher and Simons, 'Inducements' (n 205) 205–25.

[215] MiFID II, Art 16(7), first para.

[216] MiFID II, Art 16(7), second para.

[217] Recital (57), second para, to MiFID II.

[218] MiFID II, Art 16(7), ninth para.

[219] MiFID II, Art 16(7), ninth para.

[220] Recital (57), first para, to MiFID II. For more detail on record-keeping, see Draft Commission Delegated Regulation MiFID II, C(2016) 2398 final, 25 April 2016, Arts 72–76.

XIV. Conclusion

The picture that emerges from all this is that the conduct-of-business rules for investment firms will not undergo any fundamental change under MiFID II. The information paradigm is still predominant. Investor protection is therefore still about providing investors with the information that will enable them to make an informed investment decision. Under MiFID II the amount of information that must be provided to investors is set to increase rather than decrease and the information will also have to be more detailed. This is despite the fact that many people doubt whether the huge volume of information provided really helps investors to make informed and well-considered decisions.[221]

The strict and detailed conduct-of-business rules which MiFID II imposes on investment firms will also put pressure on the staff of these firms. If they are unable to comply with these rules in their day-to-day contacts with clients, the rules will remain a dead letter and MiFID II will have overreached itself. It is not for nothing that MiFID II explicitly provides that investment firms must ensure and demonstrate to the competent authorities on request that natural persons giving investment advice or information about financial instruments, investment services or ancillary services to clients on behalf of the investment firm possess the necessary knowledge and competence to comply with the conduct-of-business rules.[222] This is no easy matter because compliance presupposes a given standard of education and training, and it is still debatable whether the supply of candidates and the relevant cost tag would even permit the right staff to be recruited. In a broader sense, it may be doubted whether compliance is even possible with the torrent of new supervisory rules.[223]

Whatever the case, the conduct-of-business rules are tightened, clarified and expanded in certain respects. For investment firms and their advisers, the devil is well and truly in the detail. The stricter rules will in any event make it necessary to modify many aspects of the standard contracts and other documentation used in contacts with clients.

[221] See eg N Moloney, *How to Protect Investors—Lessons from the EC and the UK* (Cambridge, Cambridge University Press, 2010) 288 et seq; L Enriques and S Gilotta, 'Disclosure & Financial Markets Regulation' in N Moloney, E Ferran and J Payne, *The Oxford Handbook of Financial Regulation* (Oxford: Oxford University Press 2015) 511–36; V Colaert, 'Building Blocks of Investor Protection—All-embracing Regulation Tightens its Grip' (draft paper, to be published); K Broekhuizen, 'Klantbelang, belangenconflict en zorgplicht' (The Hague: Boom juridische uitgevers, 2017).

[222] MiFID II, Art 25(1). ESMA has adopted guidelines for the requisite assessment of knowledge and competence. See ESMA/2015/753, *Consultation Paper—Draft Guidelines for the Assessment of Knowledge and Competence* (23 April 2015).

[223] For a recent commentary, see V Colaert, *Normvlucht en systeemdwang in de financiële sector—Wetsnaleving in tijden van normatieve expansie* (Acta Falconis VI) (inaugural lecture KU Leuven) (Antwerp/Cambridge: Intersentia, 2015).

MiFID II also introduces a number of interesting or in any event noteworthy new concepts and provisions. One of them is the distinction between independent and non-independent advice. The concept of non-independent advice strikes me as strange. It would have been better if MiFID II had not distinguished between independent and non-independent advice and had instead provided that all forms of advice should meet certain basic requirements. Under the current definition of non-independent advice in MiFID II, there is a risk that an adviser may allow its own interests to prevail over those of the client and that the client may therefore be saddled with bad advice. Also new is the explicit attention paid by MiFID II to the provision of information to professional and retail clients on bundled packages or services and products. Moreover, although structured deposits are not financial instruments, they are subjected to the KYC rules, conflicts of interest rules and rules on information provision, inducements and client order handling. As we have also seen, the rules on inducements in relation to independent advice and portfolio management are being tightened and an obligation to record relevant telephone conversations and electronic communications is being introduced.

Part III

Civil Law Legal Systems

3

Germany

JENS-HINRICH BINDER

I. Introduction

The provision of financial advice traditionally forms a core part of German banking business. To date, most German banks operate as universal banks and, in addition to current accounts, payment services and traditional forms of deposit-based saving facilities, usually offer a considerable range of investment-related products and services to retail clients, including the execution of acquisitions or sales of securities on a commission basis, brokerage and/or the provision of investment-related advice. As of the end of 2015, a total of 1,740 authorised banks held a banking licence within the country, including 179 ('private') commercial banks in the form of public limited companies or partnerships, 422 savings banks owned by municipalities or counties, eight *Landesbanken* owned by one or more federal states, and 1,027 cooperative banks.[1] A 'one–stop' approach, whereby clients make and receive payments, maintain savings accounts, receive investment-related advice and, finally, execute investment transactions with the assistance of a single intermediary is thus characteristic for traditional bank–client relationships within the country. More recently, however, this trend has weakened somewhat as, fostered by the integration of markets in financial services across the European Union and the harmonisation of the relevant regulatory frameworks under EU law, non-bank financial services providers have gained an increasing market share and established themselves as an alternative to traditional forms of comprehensive, universal banking activities. By the end of 2015, a total of 674 financial services institutions and 86 German branches of foreign institutions were authorised to

[1] See Bundesanstalt für Finanzdienstleistungsaufsicht (BaFin), *Annual Report 2015*, www.bafin.de, 130. For a useful introduction to the German banking system (with special emphasis on the consequences of the global financial crisis), see generally F Hüfner, 'The German Banking System: Lessons from the Financial Crisis' (2010) OECD Economics Department Working Papers, No 788, http://dx.doi.org/10.1787/5kmbm80pjkd6–en. See also H Schneider et al, *The German Banking System*, 4th edn (Frankfurt am Main: Fritz Knapp Verlag, 1986) (outdated on the facts but still valid with regard to concepts and basic structures).

provide financial services other than activities classified as banking business under the Banking Act (*Kreditwesengesetz*).[2]

Specific duties of care towards clients may arise, albeit in different forms and to a different extent, in any of these different settings and the respective contractual relationships between financial intermediaries and their customers. Leaving aside insurance-related financial advice, for which an explicit, comprehensive duty to advise and to inform has been enacted in section 6 of the Law on Insurance Contracts (*Versicherungsvertragsgesetz*) (not to be covered in detail in the present chapter),[3] the relevant duties, as well as the corresponding remedies in private law, have been developed more or less exclusively on the basis of general principles of breach of contractual (or indeed pre-contractual) duties and tort law.

In the field of bank loans (section II), courts have generally been very reluctant to recognise duties to inform, or warn, towards borrowers in conjunction with loan contracts, holding borrowers to be fully responsible for both the decision to take out a loan *and* for the decision how to invest it. With regard to investment advice (section III), the picture is far more complex. While Germany has, of course, transposed Community or Union law requirements for the provision of financial services into national securities trading legislation, both civil (as opposed to administrative) courts and the predominant academic literature continue to prefer a strict approach to the legal construction of the relationship between intermediaries and their clients by reference to regulatory requirements. In their interpretation, the contractual relationship is genuinely private in nature, governed almost exclusively by principles of general contract law, whereas regulatory duties have little if any bearing on the scope and substantive content of the relevant intermediaries' duties towards their clients. As a result, notwithstanding the natural links between regulatory requirements after the transposition of the relevant EU legislation on the one hand and the private law obligations with regard to the provision of investment advice and related services on the other, the provision of such services continues to be subject to two independent regimes, namely (1) a purely public administrative law body of requirements which reflects the harmonised Union law (with legislation underway to effect transposition of the MiFID II/MiFIR regime), and (2) an increasingly complex set of general principles and specific requirements as defined by a vast body of legal precedents over the years (see section III.A below). Conceptually, the latter have been developed by the courts on the basis of general principles of contract law. Duties to protect clients against uninformed or otherwise unsound investment decisions, only incompletely described by the term 'duties of care', are generally based on the concept of

[2] BaFin, *Annual Report 2015* (n 1) 131.

[3] For an overview of the relevant provisions and legal principles, see eg P Reiff, 'Versicherungsvertrieb' in RM Beckmann and A Matusche-Beckmann (eds), *Versicherungsrechts-Handbuch*, 3rd edn (Munich: CH Beck, 2015).

contracts for advice or contracts for information, with similar principles applying to loan-related advice (see section III.B below).

In principle, such duties are owed towards both commercial clients and consumers (although courts usually recognise the different backgrounds when determining the level of protection in each particular case), while third parties would not normally be included. In this context, also the avoidance or limitation of liability on the grounds of contributory negligence will follow general principles of contract law, but plays a limited role (see section IV below). Finally, the role of the Bundesanstalt für Finanzdienstleistungsaufsicht (BaFin) as the (single) authority responsible for the supervision of securities markets and the provision of financial services can be characterised as limited. While BaFin presents itself as open to hear individual complaints on a case-by-case basis, there is no obligation for it to react and no formal right of clients to seek legal redress if it refuses to do so (see section V below).

II. Duties Related to Loan Contracts

A. General Basis in Contract Law

For loan contracts, the legal basis is to be found in sections 488–490 of the Civil Code (*Bürgerliches Gesetzbuch*), which are the general basis for the core duties of the parties and termination rights. None of these provisions lays down any specific duties of information towards the borrower, however. Such duties therefore can be derived only from general principles of contract law, which do recognise, in an abstract form, general duties of care towards the other party both before and after formation of the contract (sections 311(2) in conjunction with 241(2) and 241(2) of the Civil Code, respectively). Only in the area of consumer loans, addressed in sections 491–505d of the Civil Code, is the lender expressly required to provide the borrower prior to the formation of the contract with adequate information on the basis of which the borrower can assess whether the loan conforms with his individual objectives and financial circumstances. This regime has recently undergone a substantial reform as a result of the transposition of the EU Mortgage Credit Directive,[4] in which context the duties for pre-contractual disclosure and information (section 491a Civil Code) were expanded and restated and a new provision for the duties of mortgage-related credit advice (section 511 Civil Code) was introduced.

[4] Directive 2014/17/EU of the European Parliament and of the Council of 4 February 2014 on credit agreements for consumers relating to residential immovable property and amending Directives 2008/48/EC and 2013/36/EU and Regulation (EU) No 1093/2010, OJ L 60 of 28 February 2016, 34.

Outside the scope of the special regime for consumer loans, the general rules on pre-contractual duties of information set out in sections 311(2) and 241(2) of the Civil Code have to be construed with regard to the particular circumstances of individual types of contract, however. In this context, a considerable body of precedents in case-law has always stressed that, within a loan contract, the lender does not assume any responsibility towards the borrower for the ultimate viability of either the loan itself in view of its conditions, or the investment to be funded with it.[5] Consequently, the lender is under no obligation in private law to explore either the borrower's financial capability or the commercial viability of the planned investment. Unless the borrower has entered, in addition to the loan contract as such, into a contract for investment advice with the lender (as to which, see section III below), duties to inform the borrower, let alone to warn against specific commercial risks associated with the loan or the intended use of it, have only been recognised in exceptional circumstances. The relevant cases typically involve a number of specific scenarios developed in available precedents (discussed below).

B. Relevant Scenarios

Notwithstanding the general reluctance to recognise duties of care towards the borrower, past case-law has formulated a number of conditions under which such duties, and corresponding liability to the borrower may nonetheless arise. In abstract terms, this may be the case if it can be established that the lender, when granting the loan, (1) had significantly superior knowledge of risks associated with the loan-funded investment than the borrower; (2) was under a conflict of interest; and/or (3) went beyond the typical role of a lender when promoting the loan.[6] The distinction between the relevant criteria is not clear-cut. Indeed, in many cases, more than one of the criteria will be met.

[5] eg Bundesgerichtshof (Federal Supreme Court), 29 October 1952—II ZR 283/51, reported in Amtliche Sammlung des Bundesgerichtshofs in Zivilsachen (BGHZ) 7, 371, at 374 et seq; Bundesgerichtshof, 8 June 1978—III ZR 136/76, reported in BGHZ 72, 92, at 104; Bundesgerichtshof, 28 February 1989—IX ZR 130/88, reported in BGHZ 107, 92, at 101; Bundesgerichtshof, 3 December 1991—XI ZR 300/90, reported in BGHZ 116, 209, at 213; Bundesgerichtshof, 14 June 2004—II ZR 393/02, reported in BGHZ 159, 294, at 316; Bundesgerichtshof, 26 October 2004—XI ZR 255/03, reported in BGHZ 161, 15, at 20; Bundesgerichtshof, 16 May 2006—XI ZR 6/04, reported in BGHZ 168, 1, at 19–20. And see, for further discussion and an overview of the relevant case-law, J-H Binder, '§ 488 BGB' in B Gsell et al (eds), *Beck'scher Online Großkommentar zum BGB* (Munich: CH Beck, 2017) paras 6, 167.

[6] eg Oberlandesgericht (Regional Court of Appeals) Hamm, 11 November 1996—31 U 25/96, reported in ZIP Zeitschrift für Wirtschaftsrecht 1997, 360, at 361, involving a bank that had provided the borrower on his request with a specific funding proposal for a construction project. Cf, discussing similar cases, J Köndgen, 'Die Entwicklung des Bankkreditrechts in den Jahren 1995–1999' (2000) *Neue Juristische Wochenschrift* 468, 469; P Buck-Heeb, 'Kreditberatung, Finanzierungsberatung' (2014) *Zeitschrift für Bank- und Kapitalmarktrecht* 221, 228–36.

i. *Superior Knowledge of Risks*

Under the first criterion, banks have been held liable in damages if they positively knew, or grossly negligently failed to recognise in the light of strong evidence, that the loan-funded investment, or project, came with substantial risks to the borrower, who himself did not have the relevant information.[7] Effectively, there is thus a duty to warn the borrower and disclose relevant information prior to the formation of the loan contract if the bank has strong reasons to believe that the borrower himself fails to realise the relevant risks. As the bank itself is under no obligation to explore the commercial viability of the proposed investment, however,[8] and as liability will occur only in cases of positive knowledge or, at least, gross negligence with regard to the bank's lack of information, the duty will apply only in exceptional circumstances. These have frequently been established in cases of cooperation between the bank, on the one hand, and the initiator or sponsor of the loan-funded investment, on the other, in particular where both had been collaborating in a systematic, institutionalised way. In such cases, the bank will be held liable on the basis of implied knowledge of facts attributable to the initiator or sponsor.[9]

ii. *Conflicts of Interest*

Similarly, banks have been held to be under a duty to inform the borrower if they had their own commercial interest in the loan-funded investment or project. This will not be the case merely if the bank has funded not just the loan to the prospective investor but also, previously, the investment itself, however.[10] By contrast, if the bank actively solicits the granting of new loans in order to protect its earlier engagement in the funding of the investment as such, it has to disclose this interest to the prospective borrower.[11]

iii. *Bank Exceeding the Typical Role of a Lender*

Relevant cases usually include circumstances that meet either, or both, of the first two criteria. Within this category, banks have been held to be under a duty to

[7] eg Bundesgerichtshof, 16 May 2006—XI ZR 6/04, reported in BGHZ 168, 1, at 19–20; Bundesgerichtshof, 19 September 2006—XI ZR 204/04, reported in BGHZ 169, 109, at 115; Bundesgerichtshof, 29 June 2010—XI ZR 104/08, reported in BGHZ 186, 96, at 102.

[8] Cf, in the present context, Bundesgerichtshof, 18 November 2003—XI ZR 322/01, reported in BKR—Zeitschrift für Bank- und Kapitalmarktrecht 2004, 108, at 109–10; Bundesgerichtshof, 27 January 2004—XI ZR 37/03, reported in NJW—Neue Juristische Wochenschrift 2004, 1376, at 1378.

[9] eg Bundesgerichtshof, 19 September 2006—XI ZR 204/04, reported in BGHZ 169, 109, at 115; Bundesgerichtshof, 29 June 2010—XI ZR 104/08, reported in BGHZ 186, 96, at p. 102. See also, for further discussion, Binder, '§ 488 BGB' (n 5) paras 173–74.

[10] eg Bundesgerichtshof, 5 May 2011—XI ZR 365/09, reported in NJW-RR—Neue Juristische Wochenschrift—Rechtsprechungsreport 2011, 1064, at 1066.

[11] eg Bundesgerichtshof, 29 May 1978—II ZR 173/77, reported in NJW 1978, 2547–48; Bundesgerichtshof, 20 March 2007—XI ZR 414/04, reported in NJW 2007, 2396, at 2398; Bundesgerichtshof, 3 June 2008—XI ZR 131/07, reported in NJW 2008, 2572, at 2574.

inform their borrowers if their relationship to the initiator or sponsor of the loan-funded investment goes beyond mere cooperation, for example when the bank itself acts as co-sponsor and, in this capacity, has exercised an influence on the design of the relevant prospectus.[12]

III. Duties Related to Investment Advice

A. The Contractual and Regulatory Setting

i. The Contractual Setting

Investment services in general, and investment-related advice in particular, have never been addressed explicitly in the Civil Code, leaving it for market practice and courts to develop the relevant principles.[13] Over time, different types of contracts have evolved in this process, each associated with distinctive rights and obligations. Under German doctrine, the mere execution of transactions for the account, or on behalf of clients, is classified as legally distinct from the provision of investment-related advice. Consequently, the following types of contracts have to be distinguished:

a. Execution of Purchase and/or Sale Transactions on a Commission Basis or through Sales Contracts

Where an intermediary merely buys or sells securities or other financial products on behalf of a client, the contract is either on a commission basis (pursuant to sections 383–406 of the German Commercial Code (*Handelsgesetzbuch*)) or structured as a sales transaction. In the former alternative, the intermediary takes and accepts the obligation to execute the transaction in its own name but for the account of the client at a market price and to credit and/or debit his account accordingly (*Finanzkommissionsgeschäft*). In the latter form, which amounts to proprietary trading, the intermediary itself becomes a party to the transaction which is not executed at a previously agreed price (*Festpreisgeschäft*).[14]

[12] Cf eg Bundesgerichtshof, 8 June 1978—III ZR 136/76, reported in BGHZ 72, 92, at 101; Bundesgerichtshof, 16 June 1992—XI ZR 166/91, reported in NJW 1992, 2148, at 2149; Bundesgerichtshof, 6 November 2007—XI ZR 322/03, reported in NJW 2008, 644, at 646.

[13] See also, discussing the legal basis for asset management under German law, M Casper and C Altgen, 'Germany' in D Busch and DA DeMott (eds), *Liability of Asset Managers* (Oxford: Oxford University Press 2012) Ch 4, paras 4.08–4.10.

[14] See generally eg H Bergmann, 'Effekten und Effektengeschäfte' in K Langenbucher, D Bliesener and G Spindler (eds), *Bankrechts-Kommentar* (Munich: CH Beck, 2013) para 8. And, for more detailed discussions, see D Einsele, *Bank- und Kapitalmarktrecht*, 2nd edn (Tübingen: Mohr Siebeck, 2010) s 8, paras 6 et seq, 24 et seq; J Ekkenga, 'Effektengeschäft' in K Schmidt (ed), *Münchener Kommentar*

In addition to general principles of commission or sales law, the respective contracts are governed by harmonised standard terms of contract that have been developed in the industry and are generally used as contractual basis for any securities business (*Sonderbedingungen für Wertpapiergeschäfte*).[15]

In either case, the intermediary may, in principle, become liable for breach of contractual obligations under general rules of contract law, including for misrepresentation (sections 280(1) and 241(2) of the German Civil Code (*Bürgerliches Gesetzbuch*)). The practical scope and relevance for such liability, however, are considerably restricted by the fact that the provision of specific advice is not part of the intermediary's obligations. Intermediaries engaging in both types of transactions may, however, be held liable for information-related breaches of duty if they are found to have provided investment-related advice or information other than advice on the basis of a separate 'contract for advice' in connection with, and prior to, placing the specific purchase or sale order in question (see section III.A.iii below).

b. Execution of Transactions as Agent

Alternatively, the intermediary may offer to execute the sale or purchase of securities openly as a proxy (pursuant to section 164 of the German Civil Code) on behalf of a client (*Abschlussvermittlung*) or alternatively undertake merely to broker transactions in securities between the client and an interested third party purchaser or seller (*Anlagevermittlung*).[16] While brokers continue to play a role in modern markets, the execution of business by intermediaries is rare. Neither type comes itself with obligations to inform the clients of investment-related circumstances that may be of relevance to the envisaged investment decision, but may be deemed to be supplemented by a separate 'contract for information' if advice is sought by the client ahead of entering into the purchase or sale (see section III.A.i.d below).

c. Contracts for Investment Advice

If and to the extent that, an intermediary provides explicit investment-related advice to a client, this is generally deemed to have been done on the basis of what has evolved as a special form of contract for advice, with complex and

zum Handelsgesetzbuch (Munich: CH Beck 2009) vol 5, paras 82–104 and 105–09, respectively. For an excellent overview on the applicable case-law from which this chapter has benefited considerably, see P Buck-Heeb and V Lang, 'Anlageberatung' in Gsell et al (eds), *Beck'scher Online–Großkommentar zum BGB* (n 5). See also Ekkenga (n 14) paras 318 et seq.

[15] Reprinted eg in R Fischer and Th Klanten (eds), *Bankrecht*, 4th edn (Cologne: RWS, 2010) 1171 et seq.

[16] See generally eg D Starke, 'Effektengeschäft' in S Kümpel and A Wittig (eds), *Bank– und Kapitalmarktrecht*, 4th edn (Cologne: Otto Schmidt, 2011) paras 17.11–17.13.

differentiated distinct features developed in case-law (*Anlageberatungsvertrag*).[17] At its core, the contractual relationship is recognised to be a contract *sui generis*, with elements of contracts for services or agency contracts, respectively. Sections 611 et seq of the German Civil Code (agency contracts whereby the debtor owes an agreed activity but not a specific outcome) and sections 631 et seq of the German Civil Code (contract for services where the debtor owes a specific success) thus form the statutory basis where advice is granted for consideration and section 662 does so for non-gratuitous agency contracts where no fee is paid. However, these provisions, in combination with the general statutory principles for contractual obligations, merely provide a starting point for the development of an increasingly specialised framework in case-law, which is only loosely connected with more traditional forms of either agency or services agreements (see section III.B. below).

In practice, it may be difficult to determine whether, on the facts, the parties have actually entered into a contract for investment advice or, alternatively, the intermediary is merely acting as a securities broker (*Anlagevermittlungsvertrag*, see section III.A.i.b above). This is a matter of the construction of the respective declarations leading up to the contract which, under general contract law (sections 133, 157 of the German Civil Code), must take into account how a neutral recipient in the person of the actual party would have understood what was offered to him. If, therefore, the client realised that the intermediary provided information of an advertising rather than objective character, this could be construed as the basis for a transaction by way of brokerage.[18]

The practical relevance of contracts for investment advice thus defined can hardly be underestimated. Even where advice is provided, usually against a fee, outside ongoing contractual relationships between intermediaries and clients, courts have generally held such principles to be applicable in view of the clients' reliance placed on the advisers' expertise. Where a client seeks investment advice, the adviser's obligations will be determined in accordance with such principles even where the parties have not expressly agreed the contract to be governed by the principles of *Anlageberatungsvertrag*.[19] The same applies where clients, as part

[17] See generally eg G Spindler, 'Wertpapier– und Anlagegeschäft, Grundlagen' in Langenbucher, Bliesener and Spindler (eds), *Bankrechts–Kommentar* (n 14) para 53–9; P Buck-Heeb, 'Der Anlageberatungsvertrag—Die Doppelrolle der Bank zwischen Fremd– und Eigeninteresse' (2012) *Wertpapiermitteilungen—Zeitschrift für Wirtschafts– und Bankrecht* 625; M–Ph Weller, 'Die Dogmatik des Anlageberatungsvertrags—Legitimation der strengen Rechtsprechungslinie von Bond bis Ille/ Deutsche Bank' (2011) *ZBB—Zeitschrift für Bankrecht und Bankwirtschaft* 191.

[18] Cf eg Bundesgerichtshof, 6 December 2012—III ZR 307/11, reported in NJW–RR 2013, 293, at 294.

[19] For early examples of this, see, again, Bundesgerichtshof, 25 November 1981—IVa ZR 286/80, reported in NJW 1982, 1095, at 1095–96. See also esp Bundesgerichtshof, 4 March 1997—IVa ZR 122/85, reported in BGHZ 100, 117, at 118–19; Bundesgerichtshof, 6 July 1993—XI ZR 12/93, reported in BGHZ 123, 126, at 128.

of their ongoing contractual relationship with an intermediary, usually a bank, which keeps their investment accounts, seek advice prior to the placement of a specific purchase or sale of securities.[20]

In both circumstances, the client's request for information as such has been held as sufficient grounds for the conclusion of a contract for investment advice, provided that the intermediary should, on the facts, have been aware that the client would place particular trust on the requested advice in view of the intermediary's superior experience and market expertise.[21] Generally, it has been held irrelevant whether the client first approached the intermediary with a specific request or whether the intermediary took the initiative first, whereupon the client then asked for further information.[22] The same principles apply where, having purchased securities on the advice, the client later returns to the bank with a request for further information, for example in view of a deteriorating market price.[23]

Likewise, it has been held irrelevant whether the parties expressly agreed a fee for the advice or not.[24] Lastly, the qualification of advice does not depend on whether the client finally enters into a transaction on a commission basis or by way of a sales contract with the intermediary.[25]

Essentially, the doctrine pertaining to contracts for advice amounts to supplementing the contractual relationship between intermediaries and clients with a set of implied terms that become applicable by virtue of the clients' reliance on the professional advice received. It should be noted, though, that the relevant principles, as defined by case-law, are not derived from general duties of care arising out of the specific purchase or sale of securities, for example the law of commissions, sales law or the law of service contracts. This is so even though general German contract law provides for a duty to protect the other party's rights and interests before and during the performance of the relevant contractual obligations (sections 241(2) and 311(2) of the German Civil Code), a breach of which can

[20] Bundesgerichtshof, 4 March 1997—IVa ZR 122/85, reported in BGHZ 100, 117, at 119.

[21] See again Bundesgerichtshof, 4 March 1997—IVa ZR 122/85, reported in BGHZ 100, 117, at 118–19. And see further Bundesgerichtshof, 17 October 1989—XI ZR 39/89, reported in WM Wertpapiermitteilungen—Zeitschrift für Wirtschafts– und Bankrecht 1989, 1836, at 1837; Bundesgerichtshof, 13 May 1993—III ZR 25/92, reported in WM 1993, 1238, at 1239; Bundesgerichtshof, 15 June 2000—III ZR 305/98, reported in WM 2000, 1548, at 1549; Bundesgerichtshof, 11 September 2003—III ZR 381/02, reported in WM 2003, 2064, at 2065; Bundesgerichtshof, 19 October 2006—III ZR 122/05, reported in WM 2006, 2301, at 2302. But see also Bundesgerichtshof, 14 March 1996—XI ZR 188/95, reported in NJW–RR 1996, 947, at 948 (no contractual duty to inform client who has expressly described himself as experienced investor); Bundesgerichtshof, 5 October 1999—XI ZR 296/98, reported in BGHZ 142, 345, at 355 (no contract for advice where bank expressly advises that it does not have sufficient expertise to give informed recommendations and client places order regardless).

[22] Bundesgerichtshof, 4 March 1997—IVa ZR 122/85, reported in BGHZ 100, 117, at 118; Bundesgerichtshof, 6 July 1993—XI ZR 12/93, reported in BGHZ 123, 126, at 128.

[23] Bundesgerichtshof, 21 March 2006—XI ZR 63/05, reported in NJW 2006, 2041, at 2041.

[24] Bundesgerichtshof, 4 March 1997—IVa ZR 122/85, reported in BGHZ 100, 117, at 119.

[25] Cf Bundesgerichtshof, 6 April 1981—II ZR 84/80, reported in NJW 1981, 1440, at 1441. See also Spindler, 'Wertpapier– und Anlagegeschäft, Grundlagen' (n 17) para 54; Buck-Heeb, 'Kreditberatung, Finanzierungsberatung' (n 6) 628.

give rise to liability in damages pursuant to section 280(1) of the German Civil Code. The concept of separation of the obligation to advise from the (subsequent) obligation to execute the client's order can be explained on the grounds that the contractual basis for both forms of execution focuses on the execution as such, whereas the provision of information or indeed proper advice is not part of the core obligations characteristic for any of the underlying types of contract. If, in addition and in advance of the execution of a specific order, the intermediary gives advice or merely informs the client of certain facts pertaining to the envisaged investment, the attribution of its duty of care to a specific type of contract which is legally separate from the contractual basis of the transaction as such thus facilitates a flexible construction of the contractual relationship that can be tailored to the parties' needs and to the content of their agreement in each particular case, and it underlines the character of the intermediary's duties as independent and non-accessory to the transaction. On this basis, the intermediary owes correct information as a core obligation, failing which its liability will be assessed in relation to what the client was entitled to have received if proper advice had been given.[26] The contractual relationship between intermediary and client can be restricted to the mere execution of the latter's orders in one form or another, or it can take the form of a complex set of rights and obligations involving both comprehensive investment advice and, ultimately, the arrangements for the execution of the investment decisions. As a result, such duties can arise even in cases where the client, having received information from one intermediary, ultimately decides to pursue the transaction with the aid of a different intermediary.

However, as such duties—as indicated above—are deemed to have been agreed irrespective of whether the parties themselves have expressly negotiated the conditions for the provision of advice, the concept has been criticised by some as resting on doctrinal fiction rather than a sound analysis of the parties' actual agreement, running counter to their own perception when contracting.[27] Proposals have been made to classify the intermediary's duties as pre-contractual and/or accessory to the main duties arising in connection with the client's orders,[28] but have been rejected by the courts to date. In fact, there are good reasons to doubt the viability of the concept as such, which seems rather technical, artificial and not entirely reconcilable with the parties' perception that their relationship is subject to *one* contract rather than a building block combination. Given the undisputed application

[26] See further section IV.A below.

[27] See eg B Mertens, 'Culpa in contrahendo beim zustande gekommenen Kaufvertrag nach der Schuldrechtsreform' (2003) 203 *AcP—Archiv für civilistische Praxis* 818, 851; R Schaub, 'Beratungsvertrag und Sachmängelgewährleistung nach der Schuldrechtsmodernisierung' (2002) 202 *AcP* 757, 788–93, 806; K-R Wagner, 'Der stillschweigende Anlagevermittlungs–/–beratungsvertrag' (2003) *DStR—Deutsches Steuerrecht* 1757, 1760.

[28] For an overview, see Buck-Heeb (n 6) 228.

of the doctrine in case-law, however, the search for alternatives continues to be of academic interest only and will therefore not be discussed further in this chapter.

d. Contracts for Information

Conceptually similar to contracts of advice in the sense described above, contracts for information have been held to be the basis for the information provided to clients in cases where the client could not reasonably expect comprehensive advice. The relevant case-law typically involves the purchase of securities from a broker acting for the issuer (ie *Anlageberatung* in the meaning described above in section III.A.i.b). In such situations, the clients were held not to be entitled to the full range of tailored information they could expect under a contract for advice, but could expect correct and full information as to all facts and risks that are material for the promoted investment.[29] In contrast to a contract for advice, the intermediary thus owes information but no evaluation of the client's needs and no recommendation based on such an assessment.[30] As with contracts for advice, contracts for information with this scope are deemed to have been agreed implicitly if it was foreseeable for the intermediary that the client would base his decision on the information thus received.[31] The doctrine thus supplements the contractual basis for the transactions with yet another specific contract and is subject to similar objections as the doctrine for contracts for advice discussed above.

ii. The Regulatory Framework

The MiFID[32] and, previously, the Investment Services Directive (ISD)[33] have been transposed in Germany as part of the Securities Trading Act (*Wertpapierhandelsgesetz, WpHG*),[34] which lays out the general basis for all aspects of securities trading, except the organisation of securities exchanges, prospectus requirements and takeover law. The Act was first introduced in 1994/95, not least in order to transpose parts of the ISD into German law,[35] and was significantly amended so

[29] Cf eg Bundesgerichtshof, 11 September 2003—III ZR 381/02, reported in ZIP –2003, 1928, at 1929; Bundesgerichtshof, 17 September 2013—XI ZR 332/12, reported in BKR 2002, 645, at 645; Bundesgerichtshof, 13 May 1993—III ZR 25/92, reported in WM 1993, 1238, at 1239; Spindler (n 17) para 60.

[30] Spindler, ibid.

[31] Bundesgerichtshof, 13 January 2000—III ZR 62/99, reported in NJW–RR 2000, 998, at 998; Bundesgerichtshof, 22 March 1979—VII ZR 259/77, reported in NJW 1979, 1449, at 1449.

[32] Directive 2004/39/EC of the European Parliament and of the Council of 21 April 2004 on markets in financial instruments, OJ L 145 of 30 April 2004, 1.

[33] Council Directive 93/22/EC of 10 May 1993 on investment services in the securities field, OJ L 141 of 11 June 1993, 27.

[34] The Act was first introduced on 26 July 1994 (BGBl. I 1794) and re-introduced on 9 September 1998 (BGBl I 2708). For an introduction, see eg Casper and Altgen, 'Germany' (n 13) paras 4.11–4.36.

[35] For an account of the developments leading to its introduction and subsequent reforms, see eg H Hirte and T Heinrich, 'Einleitung' in H Hirte and Th Möllers (eds), *Kölner Kommentar zum WpHG*, 2nd edn (2014) paras 57 et seq; H-D Assmann, 'Einleitung' in H-D Assmann and UH Schneider (eds), *WpHG*, 6th edn (2012) paras 12 et seq.

as to accommodate the revised European framework set out by MiFID in 2007.[36] The relevant provisions can now be found mainly in sections 31–31e of the WpHG, while sections 33–34a stipulate governance and organisational requirements for securities firms which are, to a large extent, outside the scope of this chapter. Section 31 of the WpHG first lays out general rules of conduct (transposing Article 19 of MiFID) for all providers of investment services in subsections 1, 2 and 3. Special requirements for investment advice are then set out in subsection 3a, 4, 4a–d (parts of which have only recently been added; see section III.E below). Subsections 4 (transposing Article 19(4) of MiFID) and, to a lesser extent, also subsection 5 (transposing Article 19(5) of MiFID) require intermediaries to investigate the clients' past investment experience in order to be able to provide clients with adequate advice. Subsection 8 (transposing Article 19(8) of MiFID) lays down reporting duties vis–à–vis clients. Subsection 9 (cf Article 35(2) of the Implementing Directive 2006/73/EC) finally lowers the requirements for transactions with 'professional clients'. The different categories of clients are defined in section 31a WpHG. Section 31b WpHG then exempts transactions with 'eligible counterparties'[37] from requirements arising, inter alia, under section 31(2), (3) and (5). Section 31c WpHG (transposing Article 22 of MiFID) stipulates requirements for the execution of client orders, section 31d (transposing Article 26 of the Implementing Directive 2006/73/EC, which in turn specifies the provisions on conflicts of interest in Articles 18 and 19 of MiFID) restricts the intermediaries' rights to accept commissions from third parties. Section 31e (transposing Article 20 of MiFID) finally extends the regime to organisational requirements for the execution of client orders. As part of the firms' organisational obligations, section 33a (transposing Articles 19 and 21 of MiFID and Articles 44–46 of Directive 2007/73/EC) finally requires the firms to ensure the best execution of client orders.

iii. The Relationship between the Legal Frameworks; Implications for Enforcement

The relationship between regulatory requirements on the one hand and contractual duties on the other has been debated controversially in German legal doctrine ever since the transposition of the Investment Services Directive 1993 (see section ii above), while the courts have been reluctant to recognise any implication of the regulatory regime for the construction of the contractual relationship between intermediaries and their clients.[38]

[36] Act Transposing the MiFID (*Gesetz zur Umsetzung der Richtlinie über Märkte für Finanzinstrumente und der Durchführungsrichtlinie der Kommission* [*Finanzmarktrichtlinie–Umsetzungsgesetz*] of 16 July 2007 (BGBl. I 1330)).

[37] ie mainly corporate clients and clients with similar expertise; see for details WpHG, s 31a(4).

[38] See generally Casper and Altgen (n 13) paras 4.37–4.41; Buck-Heeb and Lang, 'Anlageberatung' (n 14) paras 159–64 and 167–70.

This is not to say, however, that regulatory requirements have not been considered by courts when developing the contractual duties of intermediaries over time, especially under contracts for investment advice as defined above. In a few judgments prior to the transposition of MiFID into the German Securities Trading Act, the Federal Supreme Court did acknowledge, albeit somewhat imprecisely, that sections 31 et seq of the WpHG could have a bearing on contractual duties to the extent that their objective was to protect the clients, but that this would not be sufficient to construe duties of care independent from those established under general contract law.[39] In a few decisions, the Federal Supreme Court and other courts have also referred to provisions of earlier versions of the WpHG as a basis for a duty to avoid adverse consequences of conflicts of interests for clients.[40] The intention may have been to allow for a flexible development of the private law regime in the future, which would allow the courts to take the intermediaries' public law duties into account but nonetheless leave intact the system of protective principles that had evolved in case-law already prior to the implementation of EU law. The practical consequences of this approach, however, remained obscure, and the courts certainly did not use subsequent cases to spell them out in more detail. Indeed, in a more recent decision the Federal Supreme Court expressly rejected the argument that section 31d of the WpHG, stipulating restrictions on the acceptance of inducements from third parties in connection with the provision of investment services or ancillary services, should be construed as binding with regard to the contractual relationship between intermediaries and clients.[41] More generally, the Court held that German law transposing MiFID requirements intentionally refused to acknowledge any contractual duties of care on which clients could rely as a basis for contractual claims.[42] Likewise, in the Court's reading, sections 31 et seq WpHG cannot be construed as a statutory duty intended to protect investors within the meaning of section 823(2) of the German Civil Code, negligent or wilful violation of which would make the intermediary liable in damages under general tort law pursuant to that provision.[43] Neither have the courts yet developed the relevant case-law by way of cross-references to other regulated services. It is perhaps noteworthy that this judgment—controversially[44]—has been released *after* the ECJ's ruling in the *Bankinter* case (on which, see section IV

[39] Cf eg Bundesgerichtshof, 19 December 2006—XI ZR 56/05, reported in BGHZ 170, 226, at 232; Bundesgerichtshof, 24 July 2011—XI ZR 329/00, reported in NJW–RR 2002, 405, at 406. See also Bundesgerichtshof, 17 September 2013—XI ZR 332/12, reported in BKR 2014, 32, at 33–36.

[40] Cf eg Bundesgerichtshof, 19 December 2006—XI ZR 56/05, reported in BGHZ 170, 226, at 234. See also Kammergericht (Regional Court of Appeals) Berlin, 16 May 2013—8 U 258/11, reported in WM 2013, 1601, at 1603.

[41] Bundesgerichtshof, 19 December 2013—XI ZR 332/12, reported in BKR 2014, 32, at 33–36.

[42] Bundesgerichtshof, 27 September 2011—XI ZR 182/10, reported in BGHZ 191, 119, at 133–36; see also Bundesgerichtshof, 17 September 2013—XI ZR 332/12, reported in BKR 2014, 32, at 33–34.

[43] Bundesgerichtshof, 19 December 2013—XI ZR 332/12, reported in BKR 2014, 32, at 34. In this regard, see also (referring to earlier versions of ss 31 et seq WpHG) Bundesgerichtshof, 19 December 2006—XI ZR 56/05, reported in BGHZ 170, 226, at 232.

[44] For a critical assessment of the German doctrine, see eg C Herresthal, case note on ECJ C-604/11 (*Genil 48 SL e.a./Bankinter SA e.a.*), ZIP 2013, 1417, 1420–22.

of Chapter 12 of the present volume). Upon the completion of the present manuscript and irrespective of the recent critique in the academic literature, the Federal Supreme Court has not changed its position in any way. Even before the 2013 decision, an increasing number of academic authors had been calling for a revision over the years, arguing for either the recognition of sections 31 et seq WpHG as semi–contractual provisions setting out both regulatory *and* contractual requirements,[45] or as protective duties under section 823(2) of the German Civil Code.[46] Some authors have indeed claimed that the refusal to recognise contractual implications of the relevant regulatory requirements should be regarded as a violation of EU law, given the roots of sections 31 et seq WpHG in MiFID provisions.[47] Yet while their arguments were considered in the relevant decisions, they have not persuaded the courts to alter their stance and cannot therefore be classified as representative of the law as it presently stands. Whether or not this will change merely as a consequence of the transposition of MiFID II into German law is open to doubt,[48] in particular since leading commentaries have refused to interpret the ECJ's ruling to the effect that EU law *would* require private law implications.[49] Very likely, only a further clarification by the ECJ can eventually accomplish a review of the present position. From a practical point of view, therefore, the regulatory and contractual obligations of intermediaries vis-à-vis their clients are subject to two separate regimes, each associated with separate enforcement regimes (on which see also section V below).

B. The Scope and Content of Contractual Duties of Care

i. The General Standard in Contract Law: Advice Commensurate with the Investor's Profile and Investment Risk

The general standard of care that will be applied in all cases of contracts for investment advice was first established by the Federal Supreme Court in a landmark

[45] eg I Koller, 'Commentary to section Vor 31 WpHG' in Assmann and Schneider (eds), *WpHG* (n 35) paras 3, 5; E Schwark, 'Commentary to section Vor 31 WpHG' in E Schwark and D Zimmer (eds), *Kapitalmarktrechts–Kommentar*, 4th edn (Munich: CH Beck, 2010) paras 16 et seq; C Herresthal, 'Die Pflicht zur Aufklärung über Rückvergütungen und die Folgen ihrer Verletzung' (2009) *ZBB—Zeitschrift für Bankrecht und Bankwirtschaft* 348, 350; N Lang, 'Doppelnormen im Recht der Finanzdienstleistungen' (2003) *ZBB* 289, 294.

[46] eg J Ekkenga, 'Effektengeschäft' (n 14) para 283; A Fuchs, 'Commentary to section Vor §§ 31–37a' in A Fuchs (ed), *Wertpapierhandelsgesetz*, 2nd edn (2014) paras 80 et seq; G Spindler, 'Grundlagen' in Langenbucher, Bliesener and Spindler (n 14) para 67; N Horn, 'Die Aufklärungs– und Beratungspflichten der Banken' (1997) *ZBB* 139, 150.

[47] For a forceful exposition of this argument, see PO Mülbert, 'Anlegerschutz bei Zertifikaten—Beratungspflichten, Offenlegungspflichten bei Interessenkonflikten und die Änderungen durch das Finanzmarkt–Richtlinie–Umsetzungsgesetz (Frug)' (2007) *WM* 1149, 1156.

[48] Cf, arguing for a closer integration of regulatory and contractual requirements, S Grundmann, 'Wohlverhaltenspflichten, interessenkonfliktfreie Aufklärung und MIFID II—Jüngere höchstrichterliche Rechtsprechung und Reformschritte in Europa' (2012) *WM* 1745, 1751–53.

[49] Buck-Heeb and Lang (n 14) para 156.

decision in 1993, known as the '*Bond*' case (named after an Australian issuer whose bonds were the subject matter).[50] According to that decision, a provider of investment advice has to investigate the individual client's expertise and past investment experience, as well as his individual risk preferences prior to offering specific advice ('*anlegergerechte Beratung*', ie advice commensurate with the client's profile), and the proposed investment must itself be adequate in view of these circumstances ('*objektgerechte Beratung*', ie proposed object commensurate with the client's needs).[51] This must be fulfilled with regard to each provision of advice individually.[52] If the intermediary has not investigated the relevant facts prior to giving the advice sought, it will have to explore whether the client has fully understood the risk associated with an investment before the execution of the respective order.[53] In terms of the quality of advice, the general standard is that any advice given must be appropriate given the available information at the time; the courts will determine whether the advice given was justifiable in these circumstances and not second-guess with the benefit of hindsight which information may have provided the best possible results at the time.[54]

Thus specified, intermediaries are required to align any advice with the needs of the client in each particular case, a standard that cannot be met merely by the provision of standardised information. In this context, the differentiation between retail and commercial clients is meaningless for the determination of the scope and intensity of care, as each provision of advice has to be tailored individually.[55] Consequently, in a prominent decision of 2011, the Federal Supreme Court assessed the provision of information to a corporate client on the basis of the principles enunciated in *Bond* just as it would apply those principles in cases of retail clients. In that decision, a bank was held liable in damages after having sold a highly complex structured interest rate swap to a corporate customer, who in the negotiations was represented by an economist who, in principle, could arguably be deemed to have the necessary methodological skills at least to comprehend the underlying formula.[56]

[50] Bundesgerichtshof, 6 July 1993—XI ZR 12/93, reported in BGHZ 123, 126.

[51] ibid, first headnote.

[52] Oberlandesgericht Bamberg, 22 October 2001—4 U 62/01, reported in BKR 2002, 185, at 186. But see Bundesgerichtshof, 27 September 2011—XI ZR 178/10, reported in NJW–RR 2012, 43, at 44–45 (no duty to inform client of issuer-specific risk if the client has been alerted to such risk in the course of earlier investments in products of the same class).

[53] Bundesgerichtshof, 22 March 2011—XI ZR 33/10, reported in BGHZ 189, 13, at 19.

[54] Bundesgerichtshof, 21 March 2006—XI ZR 63/05, reported in BKR 256, at 257.

[55] See, for further discussion in this regard, PO Mülbert, 'Anlegerschutz und Finanzmarktregulierung' (2013) 177 *ZHR—Zeitschrift für das gesamte Handelsrecht und Wirtschaftsrecht* 160, at 179–80.

[56] See Bundesgerichtshof, 22 March 2011—XI ZR 33/10, reported in BGHZ 189, 13. For discussions of that case, see eg case notes by AA Lange, 'BGH: Beratungspflichten einer Bank bei Abschluss eines Zinssatz–Swap–Vertrags' (2011) *BB—Betriebs-Berater* 1674; C Schmitt, 'Aktuelle Rechtsprechung zur Anlageberatung bei OTC–Derivaten' (2011) *BB* 2824. And see Weller, 'Die Dogmatik des Anlageberatungsvertrags—Legitimation der strengen Rechtsprechungslinie von Bond bis Ille/Deutsche Bank' (n 17) 191–1.

Pursuant to this standard, advice has to be provided (only) to the extent necessary in view of the client's background and risk appetite. Therefore, an intermediary may refrain from providing advice if the client has placed a specific order without a request for any information, in which case a contract for investment advice cannot be deemed to exist.[57] Similarly, the intermediary cannot be held liable where it knows the client has the relevant knowledge and expertise prior to the relevant transaction, except in special circumstances where the intermediary has specific information of circumstances that come with a higher than usual risk.[58] Intermediaries are not, however, required to investigate whether a client who professes to possess sufficient expertise actually meets that standard.[59] If the client requests specific information on an investment for which the intermediary does not have significant experience, it may refuse to provide the requested advice on these grounds and will not be held liable if the client nonetheless engages in the relevant transaction.[60]

ii. Investigation of the Client's Expertise, Financial Position and Risk Preferences

Under the first aspect of the general principle ('*anlegergerechte Beratung*', see section III.B.i above), intermediaries are required to investigate carefully the individual client's expertise, his risk preferences and the purpose pursued with the envisaged investment. As explained before (see section B.i. above), this standard has been developed without reference to the regulatory requirements arising from sections 31 et seq WpHG. Nonetheless, the contractual duties arising in this respect are broadly in line with the requirements under section 31(4) WpHG.[61] In this context, the intermediary is also required to investigate the client's financial position, which will be considered as an important factor to determine whether the recommended investment was actually commensurate with the client's profile under the second principle enunciated in *Bond* ('*objektgerechte Beratung*',

[57] Bundesgerichtshof, 19 March 2013—XI ZR 431/11, reported in BGHZ 196, 370, at 377; Bundesgerichtshof, 12 November 2013—XI ZR 312/12, reported in BKR 2014, 77, at 79. On this and the following, see generally Buck-Heeb and Lang (n 14) paras 194 et seq.

[58] Cf Bundesgerichtshof, 28 June 2005—XI ZR 363/04, reported in BGHZ 163, 311, at 320. See also Oberlandesgericht Düsseldorf, 30 July 2010—9 U 236/09, reported in WM 2010, 1943, at 1944–45. See further Oberlandesgericht Braunschweig, 13 September 1993—3 U 175/92, reported in WM 1994, 59, at 60–61; Oberlandesgericht Celle, 25 November 1992—3 U 303/91, reported in NJW–RR 1993, 500, at 501 (increased level of information required where bank knows client to be inexperienced with regard to a specific type of investment).

[59] Cf Bundesgerichtshof, 11 November 2003—XI ZR 21/03, reported in BKR 2004, 124, at 125; Bundesgerichtshof, 19 May 1998—XI ZR 286/97, reported in NJW 1998, 2675, at 2676.

[60] Bundesgerichtshof, 11 November 2003—XI ZR 21/03, reported in BKR 2004, 124, at 126.

[61] Cf Bundesgerichtshof, 22 March 2011—XI ZR 33/10, reported in BGHZ 189, 13, at 22. See generally Buck-Heeb and Lang (n 14) paras 245–80. Cf also M Hannöver, 'Beratungs– und Informationspflichten im Effektengeschäft' in H Schimansky, H-J Bunte and H-J Lwowski (eds), *Bankrechts–Handbuch*, 4th edn (Munich: CH Beck, 2011) s 110, para 47.

see section III.B.i above).[62] As a rule, the intermediary may rely on the client's information and, if provided with information requested by the client, is required to pursue further explorations only if and to the extent he has reason to doubt their correctness.[63] However, if the client, upon a request by the intermediary, responds in an ambiguous way, the intermediary has to explore this further and may not simply proceed on the basis of the given response.[64] Risks pertaining to the proposed investment must be described in a realistic way, so as to facilitate an unbiased, informed decision on the part of the client.[65]

iii. Duties to Inform Clients

As part of their duties spelled out in the landmark *Bond* case (see section III.B.i above), intermediaries engaging in contracts for investment advice have a duty to inform their clients of all aspects that are material for their investment decision. All information given has to be accurate, prompt and prior to the execution of the client's order, complete and comprehensible given the individual client's profile.[66] In giving the advice, the intermediary may, as explained above, rely on information provided by issuers of securities, but its duty to inform typically requires more than merely passing on information material provided by the issuer.[67] If the intermediary is aware of adverse information concerning the respective issuer or the investment itself, it must not conceal it.[68]

As explained above, the nature and content of information will be deemed to be dependent on the client's expertise and needs in each particular case, so that it is almost impossible to define generalised standards in this context.[69] As a rule, however, intermediaries are required to inform the client both of general risks associated with any type of investment in given market circumstances and specific

[62] Cf Bundesgerichtshof (Federal Supreme Court), 12 November 2013—XI ZR 312/12, reported in BKR 2014, 77, at 79; Oberlandesgericht Saarbrücken, 18 December 2012—4 U 234/11, reported in MdR—Monatsschrift für deutsches Recht 2013, 612, at 612. See generally Buck–Heeb and Lang (n 14) paras 281–347. See also Hannöver, 'Beratungs– und Informationspflichten im Effektengeschäft' (n 61).

[63] Cf Bundesgerichtshof, 11 November 2003—XI ZR 21/03, reported in BKR 2004, 124, at 125; I Koller, 'Commentary to section 31 WpHG' in Assmann and Schneider (eds), *WpHG* (n 35) para 149.

[64] Bundesgerichtshof, 25 October 2007—III ZR 100/06, reported in WM 2007, 2228, at 2230.

[65] Cf Bundesgerichtshof, 17 March 1992—XI ZR 204/91, reported in NJW 1992, 1879, at 1880; Oberlandesgericht Stuttgart, 31 March 2011—3 U 148/10, reported in VuR—Verbraucher und Recht 2013, 231, at 232–33.

[66] Bundesgerichtshof, 6 July 1993—XI ZR 12/93, reported in BGHZ 123, 126, at 129; Bundesgerichtshof, 9 May 2000—XI ZR 159/99, reported in NJW–RR 2000, 1497, at 1498; Bundesgerichtshof, 21 March 2006—XI ZR 63/05, reported in BKR 2006, 256, at 257; Bundesgerichtshof, 22 March 2011—XI ZR 33/10, reported in BGHZ 189, 13, at 21. See generally Buck-Heeb and Lang (n 14) paras 297–337.

[67] Bundesgerichtshof, 18 April 2013—III ZR 83/12, unreported.

[68] Bundesgerichtshof, 13 January 2004—XI ZR 355/02, reported in NJW 2004, 1868, at 1869.

[69] See Bundesgerichtshof, 11 June 1996—XI ZR 172/95, reported in BGHZ 123, 126, at 128; Bundesgerichtshof, 14 May 1996—XI ZR 188/95, reported in NJW–RR 1996, 947, at 947; Bundesgerichtshof, 4 April 2002—III ZR 237/01, reported in BKR 2002, 397, at 398. See also Bundesgerichtshof, 27 October 2009—XI ZR 337/08, reported in BKR 2010, 35, at 36.

types of risk associated with the proposed investment.[70] The more complex the structure of the recommended investment is, the higher the required standard of information will be in this context.[71] Likewise, intermediaries will generally be required to inform their client if the proposed investment entails the risk of full loss of the invested capital.[72]

Last but not least, the advice given has to be commensurate with the client's individual investment purposes and risk appetite. In this regard, a given investment product may be deemed suitable for particular investors but unsuitable for others.[73] Details in this regard are still being worked out in recent and ongoing litigation. For example, the Federal Supreme Court has not yet finally decided whether a declared objective to invest money for retirement arrangements per se rules out any recommendation that would expose the client to a risk of loss.[74] As a rule, clients must be made aware of the speculative nature of an investment.[75]

As a rule, intermediaries have to inform their clients of conflicts of interest that may affect their advice and have a bearing on the clients' return on investment. As to the doctrinal basis, a few decisions have derived the duty from general principles of contract law, specifically section 241(2) of the German Civil Code (which codifies a general, unspecified duty of care towards the counterparty's rights and interest).[76] The predominant view seems to interpret the duty merely as a special emanation of the general principles arising under *Bond*.[77] A conflict of interest in this sense does not exist merely because of the intermediary's profit motive as such. Accordingly, no duty to inform has been held to exist with regard to the intermediary's profit or trade margins, as it would be entirely unrealistic and inappropriate for the client to assume that the intermediary's services are offered pro bono.[78] However,

[70] eg Bundesgerichtshof, 6 July 1993—XI 1993, reported in BGHZ 123, 126, at 129; Bundesgerichtshof, 9 May 2000—XI ZR 159/99, reported in NJW–RR Rechtsprechungsreport 2000, 1497, at 1498; Bundesgerichtshof, 7 October 2008—XI ZR 89/07, reported in BGHZ 178, 149, at 153; Bundesgerichtshof, 14 July 2009—XI ZR 152/08, reported in NJW 2009, 3429, at 3433.

[71] See, again, the recent landmark case Bundesgerichtshof, 22 March 2011—XI ZR 33/10, reported in BGHZ 189, 13, at 25–26.

[72] Cf eg Bundesgerichtshof, 6 March 2008—III ZR 298/05, reported in NJW 2008, 1365, at 1368; Bundesgerichtshof, 27 September 2011—XI ZR 182/109, reported in BGHZ 191, 119, at 128; Oberlandesgericht Frankfurt, 21 September 2010—9 U 151/09, reported in WM 2010, 2111, at 2113; Oberlandesgericht Munich, 28 May 2010—19 U 1932/10, reported in WM 2010, 1945, at 1945; Oberlandesgericht Nuremberg, 19 December 2001—12 U 1297/01, reported in BKR 2002, 738, at 739.

[73] Cf eg Bundesgerichtshof, 9 May 2000—XI ZR 159/99, reported in NJW–RR 2000, 1497, at 1498. See generally Buck-Heeb and Lang (n 14) paras 257–77.

[74] Cf Bundesgerichtshof, 14 July 2009—XI ZR 152/08, reported in NJW 2009, 3429, at 3433; Bundesgerichtshof, 27 September 2011—XI ZR 182/10, reported in BGHZ 191, 119, at 129–30; Bundesgerichtshof, 6 December 2012—III ZR 66/12, reported in BKR 2013, 70, at 72.

[75] eg Bundesgerichtshof, 27 September 2011—XI ZR 182/10, reported in BGHZ 191, 119, at 138.

[76] eg Oberlandesgericht Düsseldorf, 7 October 2013—9 U 101/12, reported in WM 2013, 2026, at p. 2027.

[77] eg Bundesgerichtshof, 22 March 2011—XI ZR 33/10, reported in BGHZ 189, 13, at 27.

[78] eg Bundesgerichtshof, 22 March 2011—XI ZR 33/10, reported in BGHZ 189, 13, at 30; Bundesgerichtshof, 27 September 2011—XI ZR 182/10, reported in BGHZ 191, 119, at 122–23; Bundesgerichtshof, 26 June 2012—XI ZR 355/U11, reported in BKR 2013, 17, at 21.

if the intermediary, when giving the advice, is driven by commercial interests that are incompatible with the client's, it has to disclose this to the client, who may then decide whether or not to trust the advice. For example, the intermediary has to inform the client if it has structured the recommended product in a way that facilitates a hidden profit to itself, which the client has no reason to suspect ex ante.[79] In particular, the intermediary has to disclose kickbacks received from the issuers of securities which are then marketed to clients against an additional fee paid by them.[80] This aspect of the contractual duties of intermediaries has been decided in a vast body of case-law in recent years, with many aspects still unsettled and debated controversially in the academic literature.[81] In this context, courts have differentiated between advice given by banks, which have to disclose kickbacks received when giving advice in the course of a normal banker–customer relationship,[82] and freelance investment advisers who do not, as clients realistically would have to expect them to be paid by issuers or promoters of financial products.[83] Banks are required to disclose kickbacks even if these are mentioned in the prospectus on the recommended investment, except where the prospectus itself also specifies the size of the kickback that will be payable to the bank.[84] By contrast, hidden commissions paid to intermediaries out of the specified asset costs of an investment do not have to be disclosed to the client, unless they substantially reduce the profitability of the investment, which may be the case if the commissions amount to 15 per cent or more of the asset costs.[85]

[79] See Bundesgerichtshof, 22 March 2011—XI ZR 33/10, reported in BGHZ 189, 13, at 27 (complex currency swap whose formula includes a negative market price to the advantage of the bank); Oberlandesgericht Düsseldorf, 7 October 2013—I-9 U 101/12, reported in BKR 2014, 80, at 81 (same).

[80] eg Bundesgerichtshof, 24 September 2013—XI ZR 204/12, reported in NJW 2013, 3574, at 3575.

[81] See, for further discussion and detailed analysis of the recent case-law, H Edelmann, 'Die Kick-back–Rechtsprechung—ein Irrweg?' (2010) *BB* 1163; R Harnos, 'Die Reichweite und zivilrechtliche Bedeutung des § 31d WpHG' (2014) *BKR* 1; M Zoller, 'Das Ende des Kick–Back–Jokers im Kapitalanlagerecht' (2013) *BB* 520; P Buck-Heeb, 'Vom Kapitalanleger– bis zum Verbraucherschutz—Befund und Auswirkungen auf das Recht der Anlageberatung' (2012) *ZHR* 66; K-O Knops/L Brocker, 'Die Pflicht zur Aufklärung über Bonifikationen im Effektengeschäft—ein Rechtsirrtum (bei Banken)?' (2010) *WM* 1101; V Lang/S Bausch, 'Aufklärungspflicht über Gewinnmargen und Handelsspannen?' (2010) *WM* 2101; C Herresthal, 'Kritik der aktuellen Ausdifferenzierungen in der höchstrichterlichen Kick–Back–Rechtsprechung' (2010) *ZBB—Zeitschrift für Bankrecht und Bankwirtschaft* 305; H-D Assmann, 'Die Pflicht von Anlageberatern und Anlagevermittlern zur Offenlegung von Innenprovisionen' (2009) *ZIP—Zeitschrift für Wirtschaftsrecht* 2125; T Brocker/U Klebeck, 'Rückvergütungen an "unabhängige" Anlageberater und Haftung beteiligter Dritter' (2010) *ZIP* 1369; M Habersack, 'Die Pflicht zur Aufklärung über Rückvergütungen und Innenprovisionen und ihre Grenzen' (2010) *WM* 1245. See generally Buck-Heeb and Lang (n 14) paras 355–62.

[82] eg Bundesgerichtshof, 19 December 2006—XI ZR 56/05, reported in BGHZ 170, 226, at 234; Bundesgerichtshof, 9 March 2011—XI ZR 191/10, reported in BKR 2011, 299, at 301; Bundesgerichtshof, 8 May 2012—XI ZR 262/10, reported in BGHZ 193, 159, at 164.

[83] eg Bundesgerichtshof, 19 July 2011—XI ZR 191/10, reported in BKR –2011, 433, at 434; Bundesgerichtshof, 19 July 12—III ZR 308/11, reported in NJW 2012, 2952, at 2953; Bundesgerichtshof, 18 April 2013—III ZR 225/12, reported in BKR 2013, 288, at 289.

[84] Bundesgerichtshof, 9 March 2011—XI ZR 70/91, reported in BKR 2011, 299, at 300.

[85] eg Bundesgerichtshof, 12 February 2004—III ZR 359/02, reported in BGHZ 158, 110, at 121; Bundesgerichtshof, 22 March 2007—III ZR 218/06, reported in BKR 2007, 254, at 255.

iv. Investigation of Information Pertaining to Proposed Investments

As part of their duty to ensure that the advice is commensurate with the client's individual profile (see section III.B.i above), as a rule intermediaries may only recommend investments whose characteristics and risk they understand. If and to what extent they themselves are obliged to make investigations, however, depends on the facts of each particular case and also on whether the client has reason to assume that the intermediary's advice relies on its own research and expertise, given the representations made by the intermediary in the course of its dealings with the client.[86] Generally, intermediaries may rely on trustworthy information, especially information corroborated by third party opinions or testified by chartered accountants.[87] To the extent that intermediaries are responsible for providing the clients with information under the criteria described above, they have also been held responsible for following and considering relevant media coverage, in particular in financial newspapers. Specifically, they have to inform their client on adverse information reported in the media, if it could have a bearing on the client's investment decision.[88] This does not extend to mere rumours, however.[89] Intermediaries also have to consider the issuer's rating when preparing the advice[90] and have to inform clients of a deterioration in the ratings prior to the advice.[91]

v. Duty to Warn Clients

Under the principles enunciated in the *Bond* case, intermediaries are generally required to warn clients if, on the basis of the necessary exploration of their individual expertise and risk profile, they perceive the client to be unaware of specific risks arising in the context of a proposed investment.[92] Likewise, an intermediary has been held to be under an obligation to warn the client against the risk that potential losses from a certain (credit-funded) investment may exhaust the client's financial resources.[93] This is also consistent with the general principle, mentioned above, that investment advice will not be considered to be commensurate with the client's profile if it does not properly take into account his financial means.[94] If the

[86] Cf eg Oberlandesgericht Stuttgart, 31 March 2011—3 U 148/10, reported in VuR 2013, 231, at 232. See generally Buck-Heeb and Lang (n 14) paras 281–89.

[87] J Vortmann, *Aufklärungs- und Beratungspflichten der Banken*, 10th edn (2013) 203, para 872.

[88] Cf Bundesgerichtshof, 6 July 1993—XI ZR 12/93, reported in NJW 1993, 2433, at 2434; Bundesgerichtshof, 7 October 2008—XI ZR 89/07, reported in BGHZ 178, 149, at 156; Bundesgerichtshof, 15 March 2009—III ZR 302/07, reported in BKR 2009, 199, at 200.

[89] Oberlandesgericht Hamburg, 16 May 2012—14 U 291/10, reported in VuR 2012, 484, at 485.

[90] See Oberlandesgericht Hamburg, 16 May 2012—14 U 291/10, reported in VuR 2012, 484, at 484–85.

[91] Oberlandesgericht Frankfurt, 15 December 2004—23 U 281/03, reported in VersR—Versicherungsrecht 2005, 797, at 797.

[92] Vortmann, *Aufklärungs- und Beratungspflichten der Banken* (n 87) 183, para 784.

[93] Oberlandesgericht Celle, 15 August 2002—11 U 291/01, reported in VersR 2003, 61, at 64.

[94] See text accompanying n 62. See generally Buck-Heeb and Lang (n 14) paras 342–44.

intermediary is aware of financial irregularities or criminal conduct on the part of the issuer or sponsor of financial products, it must also inform the client accordingly.[95] By contrast, no duty to warn clients has been held to exist if, as a rule, the intermediary recommends only its own financial products.[96]

No duty to warn exists once the advice has been given and the client has placed an order accordingly. While this would be arguable in special circumstances under general principles of contract law,[97] the courts have so far denied that such duties exist in cases where the market price of a proposed investment deteriorated later[98] and held that the intermediary was under no obligation to continually monitor market developments with regard to recommended securities after the advice was given.[99]

IV. Liability to Clients and Third Parties

A. Liability to Clients

Intermediaries acting at least negligently in breach of the duties set out above will be held liable in damages to their clients for breach of contractual duty. In principle, their liability follows general principles of contract law (in particular, sections 280 and 276 of the German Civil Code), but with some exceptions developed in case-law. In particular, over time the courts have come to lower the burden of proof to be met by claimants in investment-related liability cases with regard to the link of causation between the (alleged) breach of duty and the ensuing loss arising out of a recommended investment. If a claimant can establish that an intermediary has not performed its duties arising under the *Bond* doctrine (see section III above), it will be presumed that he would have acted in his best interest if he had received correct information (known as '*Vermutung beratungsrichtigen Verhaltens*', or '*Vermutung aufklärungsrichtigen Verhaltens*'). The intermediary then has to prove that this was *not* the case, which usually it will be unable to do.[100]

[95] Cf Bundesgerichtshof, 10 November 2011—III ZR 81/11, reported in NJW–RR 2012, 283, at 284.

[96] Bundesgerichtshof, 19 December 2006—XI ZR 56/05, reported in NJW 2007, 1876, at 1878.

[97] See, for detailed discussion, J-H Binder, 'Nachsorgende Vertragspflichten? Begründung und Reichweite fortdauernder Schutzpflichten nach Leistungsaustausch in Schuldverhältnissen' (2011) *AcP* 211, 587.

[98] Bundesgerichtshof, 8 March 2005—XI 170/04, reported in BGHZ 162, 306, at 311.

[99] Bundesgerichtshof, 21 March 2006—XI ZR 63/05, reported in BKR 2006, 256, at 257.

[100] See also for discussion of potential evidence that could be relied upon in order to refute the presumption, Bundesgerichtshof, 13 January 2004—XI ZR 355/02, reported in NJW 2004, 1868, at 1869; Bundesgerichtshof, 21 October 2003—XI ZR 453/02, reported in NJW–RR 2004, 203, at 205; Bundesgerichtshof, 12 May 2009—XI ZR 586/07, reported in BKR 2009, 342, at 344; Bundesgerichtshof, 22 March 2011—XI ZR 33/10, reported in BGHZ 189, 13, at 31; Bundesgerichtshof, 8 May 2012—XI

Pursuant to sections 280(1) and 249 of the German Civil Code, the intermediary will have to compensate the client for all losses arising out of the client's reliance on the advice (broadly, reliance interest). Usually, therefore, this would amount to full indemnification for the costs of the investment plus interest and, if the client can prove that he would have chosen an alternative investment with a higher return, even compensation for the difference to the existing contract.[101] The damages will be adjusted for returns from the investment, if any,[102] whereas tax advantages realised by the client will not be considered in calculating the amount of damages.[103] In extreme cases of wilful breach of the standards set out above, the intermediary may also be held liable in tort (section 826 of the German Civil Code), which may be attractive for the client if liability in contract is subject to statutory limitation.[104]

B. Third Party Liability

While liability would normally be restricted to the intermediary's counterparty, in exceptional circumstances the intermediary may also be held liable for losses incurred by third parties who do not themselves become party to the contract. Under general principles of contract law, this may be the case where a client informs the intermediary that its advice will be relied upon by that third party, and where the intermediary consents to it.[105]

ZR 262/10, reported in BKR 2012, 368, at 371; Bundesgerichtshof, 8 May 2012—XI ZR 262/10, reported in BGHZ 193, 159, at 167–72; Bundesgerichtshof, 26 February 2013—XI ZR 498/11, reported in BGHZ 196, 233, at 237; Bundesgerichtshof, 9 April 2013—XI ZR 337/10, reported in BKR –2013, 260, at 261. For further discussion, see eg M Bassler, 'Die Vermutung aufklärungsrichtigen Verhaltens—kritische Würdigung der richterrechtlichen Beweislastumkehr im Kapitalanlageberatungsrecht' (2013) *WM Wertpapiermitteilungen* 544; A Piekenbrock, 'Der Kausalitätsbeweis im Kapitalanlegerprozess: ein Beitrag zur Dogmatik der "ungesetzlichen" tatsächlichen Vermutungen' (2012) *WM* 429; A Dieckmann, 'Die Vermutung aufklärungsrichtigen Verhaltens bei Beratungsfehlern von Banken' (2011) *WM* 1153; J Oechsler, 'Commentary to section 826 BGB' in J Hager (ed), *Staudinger BGB* (Berlin: De Gruyter, 2013) para 380f; Spindler (n 17) paras 209–10.

[101] See eg Bundesgerichtshof, 26 September 1991—VII ZR 376/89, reported in NJW 1992, 228, at 230; Bundesgerichtshof, 22 January 1991—XI ZR 151/89, reported in NJW 1991, 1108, at 1109; Bundesgerichtshof, 13 January 2004—XI ZR 355/02, reported in BKR 2004, 152, at 155; Bundesgerichtshof, 13 November 2012—XI ZR 334/11, reported in BKR 2013, 154, at 155–56. For a detailed assessment, see Buck-Heeb and Lang (n 14) paras 384–481.

[102] eg Bundesgerichtshof, 15 January 2009—III ZR 27/08, reported in NJW–RR 2009, 603, at 604; Bundesgerichtshof 13 November 2012—XI ZR 334/11, reported in BKR 2013, 154, at 156. See also *Oberlandesgericht* Düsseldorf 10 October 2002—6 U 9/02, reported in WM 2003, 1263, at 1264.

[103] Bundesgerichtshof, 15 July 2010—III ZR 336/08, reported in BGHZ 186, 205, at 213–14.

[104] eg Bundesgerichtshof, 19 February 2008—XI ZR 170/07, reported in BGHZ 175, 275, at 283. For further discussion, see Buck-Heeb and Lang (n 14) paras 485–89.

[105] Cf Oberlandesgericht Munich, 27 July 2010—5 U 2100/10, reported in BKR 2010, 385, at 387; Spindler (n 17) para 53.

C. Contributory Negligence

Under general principles of contract law, contributory negligence will, as a rule, be admissible as a potential defence. Given the characteristic information asymmetry between intermediaries and clients, however, courts will usually be very reluctant to hold clients responsible for an omission to analyse critically the received advice.[106] If the client, on the facts of the individual case, had serious reason to doubt the correctness of the advice even given his limited expertise, contributory liability may be accepted and lead to a reduction of damages awarded.[107]

V. The Role of the Supervisor in Enforcement

To date, the role of Bundesanstalt für Finanzdienstleistungsaufsicht (BaFin), the single federal authority for financial markets supervision, with regard to the enforcement of the relevant duties has been somewhat ambiguous. On the one hand, pursuant to section 4(4) of the statute establishing the authority (*Finanzdienstleistungs–Aufsichtsgesetz* (*FinDAG*) of 2002, as amended), the authority performs its obligations solely in the public interest. This provision is intended to preclude claims for state liability for misfeasance against the Federal State under section 839(1) of the German Civil Code and Article 34 of the German Constitution (*Grundgesetz*).[108] As a result, individuals, as a rule, have no enforceable right to apply to BaFin for protection in the event that an intermediary is in breach of obligations arising under either contract law or, indeed, the regulations stipulated in the Securities Trading Act.[109]

These restrictions notwithstanding, however, BaFin as a regulator may take up, investigate and sanction individual complaints using its general supervisory

[106] Cf eg, Bundesgerichtshof, 9 April 1987—III ZR 126/85, reported in WM 1987, 1546, at 1547–48; Bundesgerichtshof, 24 July 2001—XI ZR 164/00, reported in BKR 2001, 92, at 93; Bundesgerichtshof, 22 March 2011—XI ZR 33/10, reported in BGHZ 198, 13, at 31–32; Bundesgerichtshof, 13 November 2012—334/11, reported in BKR 2013, 154, at 156. See also Bundesgerichtshof, 22 March 1979—VII ZR 259/77, reported in BGHZ 74, 102, at 112 (obiter, expressing doubts as to admissibility of defence in general).

[107] Cf eg Bundesgerichtshof, 13 January 2000—III ZR 62/99, reported in NJW–RR 2000, 998, at 1000; Oberlandesgericht Braunschweig 12 June 1996—3 U 78/95, reported in WM 1996, 1484, at 1486–87; Cologne, 18 June 1999—3 U 106/98, reported in NZG—Neue Zeitschrift für Gesellschaftsrecht 2000, 51, at 52; Oberlandesgericht Karlsruhe, 24 October 2002—9 U 94/02, reported in BKR 2003, 382, at 384–85. For further discussion, see generally Buck–Heeb and Lang (n 5) 403–09.

[108] Cf eg Bundesgerichtshof, 20 January 2005—III ZR 48/01, reported in BGHZ 162, 48, at 58–66 (discussing the constitutionality of the provision and its compatibility with EU law in the context of banking regulation).

[109] For further discussion (including of possible exceptions under general principles of public law), see L Giesberts, 'Commentary to section 4 WpHG' in Hirte and Möllers (eds), *Kölner Kommentar zum WpHG* (n 35) paras 64–100.

powers arising out of section 4 of the WpHG. In fact, it invites individual complaints on its website and undertakes to act accordingly.[110] In 2013, an Act for the Protection of Small Investors (*Kleinanlegerschutzgesetz*) introduced a new section 4b to the FinDAG, which now expressly provides for a procedure for handling consumer complaints within BaFin. Even prior to this amendment of the legal framework, the number of consumer complaints appears to have been quite substantial.[111] Compared with the overall number of court decisions (and ongoing litigation) at all levels of the judicature, however, the relevance of BaFin in terms of the effective enforcement of contractual (as opposed to regulatory) duties and requirements still appears to be considerably lower than the relevance of private enforcement by means of lawsuits for liability.

VI. Summary

Under German law, the provision of investment advice over time has come to be governed by an ever more detailed body of case-law, which is based on general principles of contract law but has grown into an increasingly distinct field of the law. Courts are rather generous to assume that 'contracts for investment advice' have been concluded in a situation where the client seeks specific advice before making his investment decision. In such circumstances, the intermediary is faced with a number of specific duties, starting with the detailed investigation of the client's individual profile. Any information given will have to be commensurate with the client's past expertise, his financial position and individual risk appetite. In specific circumstances, intermediaries will have to warn their clients of specific risks. If these duties are not complied with, intermediaries will be held liable (mainly to their clients) on rather generous conditions, with the clients facing a reduced burden of proof. Contributory negligence generally will not be admissible as a defence. Generally, the contractual regime has been developed with little, if any, meaningful reference to the regulatory framework. Consequently, its enforcement mainly rests on private litigation rather than supervisory intervention.

[110] See (in English) www.bafin.de/EN/Verbraucher/verbraucher_node_en.html.

[111] In 2015, BaFin has received, and dealt with, a total of 5,636 written complaints and 254 enquiries. See BaFin (n 1) 58–60.

4

Austria

JULIAN RING AND MARTIN SPITZER

I. Jurisdiction

A. Introduction: A Flood of Cases Concerning Investment Products

Since 2008, a vast number of legal actions against banks and other financial companies have been brought before Austrian courts. These cases concern miscellaneous financial products, ranging from investment products to credit agreements. They are based on various kinds of (alleged or in some cases actually confirmed) wrongdoings by the defendants and they have been filed by both private and business investors alike.

Since there is a special jurisdiction over specific claims against businesses (arising from contracts the defendant entered into in the course of his commercial or professional activities, §§ 51, 52 JN)[1] and since most financial institutions are domiciled in Austria's capital city Vienna, most cases are pending before only two courts of first instance: the Vienna Commercial District Court (BGHS),[2] which has jurisdiction in cases with an amount in dispute of up to €15,000 (§§ 52, 65, 75 JN), and the Vienna Commercial Court (HG),[3] which has jurisdiction in cases involving claims with even higher values (§§ 51, 65, 75 JN).

In November 2012, more than 8,700 of such proceedings were pending before the Vienna Commercial District Court and the Commercial Court of Vienna. In total, these proceedings deal with around 22,000 claims, around half of which are part of so-called 'Austrian class actions'. Many of these claims are directed against only a handful of financial companies, the most prominent being Meinl European Land Ltd (now 'Atrium European Real Estate'; around 3,200 actions),

[1] *Jurisdiktionsnorm*, Court Jurisdiction Act; Federal statutes are available at: http://ris.bka.gv.at/Bund.

[2] Bezirksgericht für Handelssachen Wien.

[3] Handelsgericht Wien.

Constantia Privatbank AG (now 'Aviso Zeta'; around 2,000 actions) and Immofinanz/Immoeast (around 1,300 claims).[4]

B. Constantia

The cases against Constantia result from the aftermath of the bankruptcy of Lehman Brothers. They all deal with a financial product called 'Dragon FX Garant'.[5] Constantia Privatbank AG (Constantia) promoted Dragon FX, which was a certificate based on a basket of various Asian currencies[6] issued by Lehman Brothers Treasury Co. In order to advertise their product, Constantia produced a brochure which eye-catchingly stated that the buyer of the certificate would enjoy 'enormous potential and 100% security' by means of a '100% capital guarantee', boasting three excellent ratings (A1/A+/A+). The investment would have no risk of loss whatsoever.

The brochure, however, did not reveal that the guarantor for the certificate was not a company independent from Lehman Brothers Treasury Co but the Lehman Brothers Holding Inc, a grandparent company of the former. When advertising Dragon FX in 2006, Constantia deemed the risk of default by Lehman to be of a merely theoretical nature. In late 2008, however, theory turned into practice: as commonly known, the Lehman Brothers group filed for bankruptcy. Subsequently, the value of Dragon FX dropped, rendering the capital guarantee worthless.

The first Supreme Court procedure[7] concerning this case was not initiated by investors seeking damages or contract avoidance, but by a non-profit consumer protection organisation[8] which filed a lawsuit against Constantia requesting to prohibit the use of such, or similar, brochures. The claimant argued that the wording of Constantia's brochure violated competition law since, first, it was capable of misleading an average reader of the target group to believe that Constantia itself was giving a guarantee for the product.[9] Secondly, the close connection between the issuer (Lehman Brothers Treasury Co) and the guarantor (Lehman Brothers Holding Inc) was not disclosed. Therefore, investors had at least reason to believe that the guarantor was an entity independent from the issuer.

[4] All previous numbers taken from: S Kalss, 'Der zivilrechtliche Schutz der Anleger in Österreich—ein Überblick über die große Verfahrenswelle' (2013) *ZBB* 126.

[5] For an overview of the Dragon FX cases see also: J Baier, 'Die Rechtsprechung des OGH zum Dragon FX Garant—Ein Überblick' (2012) *ZFR* 113.

[6] Concerned countries were China, India, Malaysia, Indonesia and the Philippines.

[7] 4 Ob 176/10a ÖBA 2011, 265 = ZFR 2011/42 = ÖBl-LS 2011/51 = ecolex 2011, 343 (*Horak*) = RdW 2011, 219; decisions of the OGH can be found at: www.ris.bka.gv.at/Jus.

[8] Verein für Konsumenteninformation (VKI); the VKI is one of the entities entitled by law to file competition law suits even though they are not affected by the respondent's actions: UWG (*Bundesgesetz gegen den unlauteren Wettbewerb*, Act against Unfair Competition) § 14(1) and KSchG (*Konsumentenschutzgesetz*, Consumer Protection Act) § 29(1).

[9] For such claims it is not necessary to prove that the respondent actually misled certain customers, but only that his actions are likely to do so.

The claim was rejected by the Supreme Court, the OGH,[10] which argued that the brochure could not evoke wrong assumptions concerning the guarantor, since it did not contain any information regarding its identity. Moreover, the OGH emphasised that, when Dragon FX was sold, the risk of insolvency of the Lehman Brothers Holding Inc was indeed only of theoretical nature; therefore, the statements concerning the risk of the certificate at hand were not misleading.

Only three months after this judgment, the OGH had to deal with the first claim by *private investors* concerning Dragon FX.[11] Their claim—substantially they reclaimed their lost money—was primarily based on avoidance of the contract due to mistake. For such claim, three main requirements must be met:[12] first, the mistake must be relevant, meaning that it concerns the (subject of the) contract itself[13] and not only the mere motives for its conclusion. Secondly, the mistake must have led to the conclusion of the contract. Finally, the mistake must have either been caused by the contractual partner, or have been obvious to the latter or been clarified in good time.[14] Here, the claimant argued that the mistake (which led to conclusion of the contract) was caused by the defendant by violating duties to inform, thereby invoking regulatory duties set forth in §§ 11 et seq WAG[15] 1997, which provide for duties of care and good conduct.[16]

Of course, the above-cited judgment rejecting the brochure's general capacity to mislead an average member of Dragon FX's target group made it difficult to prove that the claimants in this case were misled unduly. The OGH therefore dismissed the claim for reasons similar to the ones brought forward in the first Dragon FX case: it was not to be assumed that the respondent caused any mistake concerning the identity of the guarantor since he did not give any misleading information at all. Also, the respondent did not violate any duties to inform according to § 871 (2) ABGB[17] by refraining from warning about the general risk of insolvency of the issuer respectively the guarantor. After this decision, the OGH decided on substantive and procedural aspects of numerous comparable cases, all with the same outcome: no avoidance of the contract shall be granted.[18]

[10] Oberster Gerichtshof.

[11] 4 Ob 20/11m, EvBl 2011, 825 (*Klausberger*) = RdW 2011, 474 = JBl 2011, 708; see also: G Graf, 'Sind Drachen wirklich so harmlose Tiere?' (2011) *ecolex* 506.

[12] S Perner, M Spitzer and G Kodek, *Bürgerliches Recht*, 3rd edn (2012) 86 et seq.

[13] This, according to ABGB, § 871(2), is always the case when a duty to inform has been violated.

[14] Perner, Spitzer and Kodek, *Bürgerliches Recht* (n 12) 90.

[15] *Wertpapieraufsichtsgesetz*, Securities Supervision Act. The WAG was revised in 2007 in order to implement the MiFID (Markets in Financial Instruments Directive, 2004/39/EG) into national law.

[16] Contrary to the WAG 2007, the duties in the WAG 1997 were broadly phrased and much less detailed. Of interest in this case was (1) WAG 1997, § 11, providing that a financial institution shall act in the best interest of its customers, and § 14 No 1 providing that a bank may not advise its customers to buy products which do not comply with the customers' interests.

[17] *Allgemeines Bürgerliches Gesetzbuch*, Austrian General Civil Code.

[18] eg 8 Ob 148/10p, 9 Ob 87/10z, 4 Ob 20/11m, 8 Ob 38/11p, 7 Ob 29/11g, 7 Ob 79/11k, 8 Ob 47/11m, 1 Ob 71/11i, 1 Ob 108/11f, 1 Ob 109/11b, 1 Ob 135/11a, 7 Ob 107/11b.

i. Constantia: 6 Ob 116/11v (Avoidance of Contract if Bank Fails to Name Issuer and Guarantor)

An exception to this was the decision 6 Ob 116/11v:[19] here, the claimant was not given the respective brochure, but only had a brief telephone conversation about Dragon FX with one of Constantia's employees. The employee, however, mentioned neither the issuer nor the guarantor of the investment product, causing the claimant to believe that Constantia was the issuer of Dragon FX. The OGH found this to be a violation of duties to inform arising from regulatory provisions applicable to this contract (§ 13 No 4 WAG in the version of BGBl No 753/1996, which provides that investors are to be given all material information concerning the intended transaction). Therefore, Constantia had caused a relevant mistake and claimant was entitled to avoid the contract. The price of the investment papers was to be paid back.

The points of interest in this ruling are, first, the line the OGH draws between solely failing to name the guarantor (which had not been reason enough to avoid the contract in the past; see above) and failing to name both guarantor and issuer of the security (which led to voidability of the contract). Secondly, this case gives a good example for obligations deriving from regulatory law and their impact on civil law.

ii. Constantia: 4 Ob 129/12t (Financial Adviser Can Be Vicarious Agent of Bank)

In 4 Ob 129/12t,[20] the claimants were advised by a third party (AWD), while Constantia solely carried out transactions as customers ordered. Here, the claimants tried to reclaim their money not by avoiding the contract based on mistake, but rather by claiming damages[21] for wrong information provided by AWD, which had—according to the claimants—claimed that Constantia, rather than Lehman, was acting as guarantor for Dragon FX. The harm done, they argued, consisted of the fact that due to AWD's wrong advice they now possessed securities they never wanted, namely securities without the promised guarantee by Constantia.[22] As compensation, they requested the price of the securities in exchange for returning them.[23]

[19] 6 Ob 116/11v; ÖBA 2012, 67.

[20] 4 Ob 129/12t, EvBl 2013, 316 (*Foglar-Deinhardstein*) = ZFR 2013, 85 (*Steinmair*) = wbl 2013, 230 = ÖBA 2013/1921 (*Rabl*) = RZ 2013, 140 EÜ120; see also P Bydlinski, 'Haftung der Bank für Fehlberatung durch den Vertriebspartner?' (2013) *ÖBA* 463; G Graf, 'Bank haftet für ständig betrauten Vertriebspartner' (2013) *ecolex* 762.

[21] For an English introduction into the Austrian tort law as well as law of contractual damages, see H Koziol, *Basic Questions of Tort Law from a Germanic Perspective*; the main requirements for claims for damages are: (1) damage, (2) causation, (3) unlawfulness and (4) fault.

[22] This view is in accordance with settled case-law; see RIS-Justiz RS0022537.

[23] Of course, damages due to wrong advice can never be granted amounting to the theoretical maximum value of the bought securities; see RIS-Justiz RS0108267.

As this suit was not filed against AWD, but against Constantia, the main question here was whether AWD was acting as a vicarious agent for Constantia. In more general terms: under which conditions can a bank be held responsible for actions of a third party financial adviser? Doctrine had discussed this problem thoroughly before the case was decided, but was divided on this question.[24] The OGH clarified these issues as follows: when clients are advised by a third party securities service company, banks may exclude their own duties to inform. If it must be obvious for a bank that, for some reason, the third party adviser will not fulfil his duties properly, however, such exclusion will be null and void. The obligation then still rests upon the bank.[25] If the bank nevertheless assigns this third party to inform clients on the basis of a permanent business relationship, it will be assumed that the bank uses the adviser to fulfil its own duties, which will make it reliable for its actions according to § 1313a ABGB.

Here, the OGH found that this was exactly the case. Therefore, any wrongful acts of AWD concerning advising Constantia's customers will be seen as undertaken by Constantia itself. The OGH emphasised that the bank does not have to bear the damages ultimately since it has the right to take recourse against the financial adviser. The OGH did not decide on the merits here, but sent the case back to the court of first instance to verify whether AWD had indeed claimed that Constantia was guarantor of Dragon FX. More recently, in a case very much comparable to this one (also with Constantia as respondent, but not concerning Dragon FX), the OGH continued this reasoning and granted damages to investors.[26]

C. Meinl Bank

Maybe the most emotionally debated cases concerning a bank's duty of care are the Meinl Bank cases. The respondents were the Austrian-based bank Meinl Bank AG (Meinl Bank) and its daughter company Meinl Success Finanz AG, which specialised in advising investors about Meinl Bank's financial products. The product of interest here was a share certificate of a real estate company, called Meinl European Land (MEL), based on Jersey. Since MEL is not Austrian, its shares could not be traded 'directly' on the Austrian stock market. Instead, Meinl Bank sold certificates which represented the value of the actual MEL shares.

Until mid-2007, MEL did not make public that it had bought back a number of its own certificates worth around €1.8 billion. While Austrian courts are still investigating whether this act constituted illegal price manipulation,[27] the Jersey

[24] See references in the decision.

[25] See also 1 Ob 48/12h ZfRV-LS 2013/23 (*Ofner*) = ecolex 2013, 323 = ÖBA 2013, 506 (*Thiede*) = Jus-Extra OGH-Z 5369 = RdW 2013, 334 = ZVR 2013, 76.

[26] 2 Ob 24/13p, ecolex 2013/310 (*Wilhelm*), VbR 2013/10.

[27] The opinion approving this found support in a report of an expert appointed by the public prosecutor; see A Möchel, 'Ein fragwürdiger Market-Maker' *Wiener Zeitung* (27 August 2012).

Financial Services Commission found this to be permissible under Jersey law.[28] Nonetheless, holders of MEL certificates lost trust in the company and started selling their securities; the stock price dropped drastically, giving investors reason to find legal grounds to reverse the deal they had made.[29] Again, it was a brochure—issued by both Meinl Bank and Meinl Success Finanz AG to advertise the MEL certificates—that gave rise to claims by investors that they had been misinformed and/or misled. In this brochure the respective securities were inaccurately called 'shares'; in fact they were, as stated above, certificates representing shares. Also, the risk of the securities was downplayed in the brochure (it did, however, refer to the official prospectus of the security for further information).

Just like in the Dragon FX case series, the first MEL case before the OGH concerned the bank's compliance with *competition law*. The OGH ruled that the respondents could no longer use the term 'shares', if they did not disclose that the certificates in question were in fact share-representing certificates. In respect of the brochure's statements about the risk of the paper, the OGH admitted that it is not a bank's duty to inform about all possible risks in advertising brochures, for such detailed information is to be communicated in the prospectus of the respective security. If a bank decides to inform about such risks in advertising material, however, the given information must not be misleading. Since this was the case, further use of the respective statements was to be refrained from.

i. Meinl Bank: 4 Ob 65/10b and 8 Ob 25/10z (Contract Avoidance Due to Mistake Caused by Bank)

After the above-cited competition law judgment, public attention focused on the fourth senate of the OGH, which had to give its first, highly anticipated judgment concerning a customer who claimed to have been misled by Meinl Bank's brochure and, therefore, that he had the right to avoid the contract over the certificates in question.[30] Of course, the fact that there already had been a competition law judgment against the respondent did not mean that the claimant would succeed in his claim to avoid the contract due to mistake: as mentioned above, for this purpose, it is necessary to prove that the claimant was actually misled and, furthermore,

[28] Press Release of the Jersey Financial Services Commission in February 2012, available at: www.jerseyfsc.org/the_commission/general_information/press_releases/release279.asp.

[29] Meinl claims that this was only due to the global economic crisis; see www.meinlbank.com/.

[30] As examples for media attention in the daily press, see: P Aichinger, *Die Presse* (27 October 2009) 11; C Höller, *Die Presse* (18 November 2009) 15; J Urschitz, *Die Presse* (19 November 2009) 1; J Hierländer, *Die Presse* (27 November 2009); doctrine also discussed the outcome of such case beforehand; see: G Wilhelm, 'Irreführende Werbung und ihre rechtsgeschäftlichen und Haftungsfolgen' (2009) *ecolex* 92; H Krejci, 'Zur Anfechtung von Wertpapierkäufen wegen irreführender Werbung und Beratung' (2010) *ÖJZ* 10.

that his misconception led to the conclusion of the contract. Proving the general capacity to mislead an average member of the security's target group is not sufficient for such claim.[31]

Still, the OGH decided in favour of claimant: although the Court admitted that wrong assumptions about future price developments are naturally always to be seen as mere motives for investing in certain securities, and thus do not constitute a relevant mistake,[32] it found that the claimant thought that he would be investing in low-risk securities while he actually received high-risk investments.[33] Therefore, the mistake concerned the subject matter of the contract; furthermore, the respondent had caused the mistake by stating wrong information in the brochure[34] which, in turn, led to the agreement. These requirements being met, the contract could be avoided.

Shortly after this decision, the eighth senate of the OGH decided on an almost identical case: here, the claimant was certain that he had actually bought MEL shares, not share-representing certificates. Again, the OGH decided in favour of claimant.[35]

ii. Meinl Bank: Addendum

In several decisions that followed, the OGH determined investors' rights in this context more precisely. Among scholars, special attention was paid to the judgments concerning the so called '*aliud* problem'. Whereas 4 Ob 65/10b and 8 Ob 25/10z were decided upon the assertion of mistake during completion of contract, in 4 Ob 93/11x[36] the claimant based his argument not on avoidance of contract due to mistake. Instead, he claimed that the contract he had entered into was concluded over shares, and not certificates. What was delivered

[31] As most recently emphasised in 2 Ob 19/13b, factors like expertise and/or general education of the claimant, on the other hand, cannot preclude him from claims based on contract avoidance due to mistake. Of course, it will make it harder to furnish proof of the necessary requirements.

[32] Mistakes concerning only motives for the conclusion of the contract generally do not make contracts voidable.

[33] 4 Ob 65/10b = ecolex 2010, 952 (*Wilhelm*) = EvBl 2011, 28 = ZFR 2011, 25 (*Pletzer*) = RdW 2010, 767 = ÖBA 2011, 582; see also: G Graf, 'Zur Schadenersatzhaftung des schuldhaft Irrenden' (2010) *ecolex* 1131; P Leupold and M Ramharter, 'Ausgewählte Aspekte der Irrtumsanfechtung beim Wertpapierkauf' (2011) *ÖJZ* 107; M Oppitz, 'Zur irrtumsrechtlichen "MEL"-Judikatur des OGH' (2011) *ÖBA* 534; A Riedler, 'Schadenersatzpflicht irregeführter Anleger?' (2011) *ecolex* 194; A Vonkilch, 'Von Geschäftsirrtümern und Sollbeschaffenheiten beim Wertpapierkauf, irrtumsrechtlichen Kausalitätsbeweisen und Mitverantwortlichkeiten von Irrenden' (2011) *JBl* 2.

[34] Again, the reference to the accurate prospectus in the brochure could not prevent this fact.

[35] 8 Ob 25/10z Zak 2010, 377 = EvBl 2011, 31.

[36] 4 Ob 93/11x Zak 2012, 15 = RdW 2012, 16 = ÖBA 2012, 114/1776 = ecolex 2012, 27 (*Wilhelm*); = JBl 2012, 175 (*Geroldinger/Radler*) = JAP 2011/2012/20 (*Liedermann/Philadelphy*) = ZFR 2012, 88 (*Rabl*) = ZIK 2012, 76; see also P Leupold, 'Aktien vs Zertifikate—zur aliud-Problematik—Zugleich eine Besprechung von OGH 22. 11. 2011, 4 Ob 93/11x' (2012) *Zak* 23; A Riedler, 'Aktien erklärt, Zertifikate gekauft—"(k)ein Zweifel"?' (2012) *ecolex* 20; G Wilhelm, 'Das unbekannte Qualifikations-Aliud—Eine Kritik zu 4 Ob 93/11x' (2011) *ecolex* 1073.

afterwards—MEL certificates—was, according to the claimant, something entirely different, which had to be considered a so-called 'aliud'. Hence, this case was not decided as a case of vitiation of consent but rather a case of breach of contract. Granting claims for breach of contract would result in markedly different rules on the respective limitation periods: while the latter prescribe only three years after the conclusion of the contract (§ 1487 ABGB) or after the damage becomes evident (§ 1489 ABGB), such claim can be enforced within 30 years after conclusion of the contract (§ 1478 ABGB). For many investors who had waited too long to sue Meinl Bank this line of argument now somewhat constituted their 'last resort'—for banks, of course, it was a serious threat.[37] The OGH decided in favour of respondent: since the certificates at hand had almost *identical functions* as shares, they were not to be considered an aliud; the claim was dismissed.

In 2014, the OGH decided over a case comparable to the above cited 4 Ob 65/10b and 8 Ob 25/10z. Here, a customer claimed inter alia that he had been purposely misled (*List*), a line of argument that also leads to the long period of limitation of 30 years (§§ 1487, 1478). The OGH granted the claim,[38] which lead to the assumption that MEL will continue to be subject of a vast number of disputes in the future.[39]

D. Immofinanz

Immofinanz is a listed real estate company based in Austria, which was tightly connected with Constantia, which provided the entire management, infrastructure as well as personnel for Immofinanz.[40] Since the former CEO of both Constantia and Immofinanz is suspected of having taken part in several financial offences,[41] Immofinanz has been subject to intensive media attention. Before this, in the course of several increases of capital stock, optimistic shareholders invested billions in Immofinanz shares. Thereby, Constantia worked as the issuing bank. In the course of the global economic crisis, Immofinanz' shares dropped in value in 2008 and investors took legal steps against Immofinanz. Inter alia, they claimed that the capital they invested was not used as the company claimed, namely for investment in real estate, but rather to support associated companies.

[37] M Schauer, 'Zertifikate statt Aktien: Das Aliud als Ausweg?' (2011) *RdW* 3; G Schima, 'OGH: Aktienzertifikate kein "Aliud" gegenüber Aktien' (2012) *RdW* 3.

[38] 6 Ob 203/13s.

[39] O Jaindl, 'Anwalt: Bahnbrechende OGH-Entscheidung im Fall MEL' *Wirtschaftsblatt* (4 April 2014).

[40] Geschäftsbericht 2002/2003, 17, available at: http://www.immofinanz.com/de/investor-relations/berichte/.

[41] See eg APA, 'Immofinanz will Buwog-Provision zurück' *Der Standard* (7 July 2013).

i. *Immofinanz: 7 Ob 77/10i (Protection of Investors Has Priority Over Prohibition of Investment Reimbursement; Investor Carries Burden of Proof Concerning Alternative Investments)*

In this very thoroughly discussed decision[42] the claimant sued Immofinanz, Constantia as the issuing bank as well as their CEO. The claims against the first and second respondent were based on liability for the prospectus of the issue of the respective shares according to § 11 KMG.[43] According to this provision, the issuer shall be liable for damages caused by culpably communicating wrong information in the prospectus. The same applies according to § 11(1) No 3 KMG to the issuing bank if it had acted with gross negligence. In case both entities violate the respective stipulations, § 11(3) KMG provides for a joint and several liability.

This case gave the OGH the chance to deal with a much disputed question: the relationship between the *prohibition of repayment of contributions* to shareholders according to § 52 AktG[44] and claims of shareholders concerning contracts over shares. The OGH had to balance the interests of the stock company's creditors (which § 52 AktG seeks to protect from diminishing the capital) and the interests of shareholders. The OGH decided in favour of the claimant: § 52 AktG does not prevent claims for damages of shareholders—a decision that caused great controversy.[45]

The second topic the OGH had to deal with—although not for the first time[46]—was the *burden of proof* for the *causation* of damages due to 'wrong investments'. In other words: who is it to prove that, if respondent had acted rightfully (here: if he had not stated wrong information in the respective prospectus), the claimant would not have suffered damage (for example by investing in similar securities which also subsequently lose value)? The OGH held that—not only in cases concerning wrong advice, but also for example prospectus liability—the burden of proof lies with the claimant; he has to furnish evidence that he would have invested in securities

[42] 7 Ob 77/10i GES 2011, 223 = GesRZ 2011, 251 (*Diregger*) = ÖBA 2011, 501 = wbl 2011, 500 = AnwBl 2011, 355 = ZFR 2011, 238 (*Gruber*) = ecolex 2011, 609 (*Wilhelm*) = RdW 2011, 401 = AnwBl 2011, 407 = JAP 2011, 181 (*Jaindl*) = ZVR 2012, 75 = SZ 2011/40; see also A Auer, 'Naturalrestitution für geschädigte Wertpapieranleger' (2011) *RdW* 725; G Graf, 'OGH verteidigt Prospekthaftung' (2011) *ecolex* 599; M Karollus, 'Neues zur Prospekthaftung (Konkurrenz zum Verbot der Einlagenrückgewähr und zur "fehlerhaften Gesellschaft", Kausalität des Prospektfehlers für die Disposition des Anlegers, Schadensberechnung und Schadensnachweis)' (2011) *ÖBA* 450; H Krejci, 'Anlegerschutz des Aktionärs, Kapitalerhaltung und fehlerhafte AG' (2011) *GesRZ* 193; C Völkl, 'Anlegerschutz: OGH macht's einfach(er)' (2011) *wbl* 474; U Torggler, 'Emittentenhaftung: roma locuta und alle Fragen offen' (2011) *ecolex* 1121; W Sindelar, 'Durchbrechung des Grundsatzes der Kapitalerhaltung auch bei Geltendmachung von Schadenersatzansprüchen aufgrund des Aktienerwerbs am Sekundärmarkt' (2012) *ÖBA* 763; J Told, 'Noch offene Fragen zur Geltendmachung von Prospekthaftungsansprüchen nach 6 Ob 28/12d?' (2012) *GES* 333; M Trenker, 'Kapitalmarktrechtliche Ansprüche von Genussrechtsinhabern in der Insolvenz' (2013) *VbR* 16.

[43] *Kapitalmarktgesetz*, Capital Market Act.

[44] *Aktiengesetz*, Stock Corporations Act.

[45] See esp Karollus, 'Neues zur Prospekthaftung' (n 42); Krejci, 'Anlegerschutz des Aktionärs, Kapitalerhaltung und fehlerhafte AG' (n 42).

[46] See RIS-Justiz RS0106890 (T9).

which are still of value now, if the information in the prospectus had been correct. Since this means proving a hypothetical course of events, a lower standard of proof than usual is to be applied:[47] in general, claimants must prove that the facts asserted in their claim took place with a 'high probability';[48] when proving a hypothetical course of events, however, a preponderance of evidence is sufficient.[49]

E. General Relevance of Past Jurisprudence

The vast majority of cases regarding a bank's duty of care have been decided in the context of the sale of investment products. This gives rise to the question of whether and to what degree this jurisprudence is relevant in other case, such as for example credit agreements. Recently, the OGH has shown a tendency towards facilitating the extensive jurisprudence in similar circumstances. In a recent case concerning credit agreements, the OGH explicitly referred to its jurisprudence regarding investment products:[50] the rule stating that a financial product with an unwanted level of risk in itself constitutes damage regardless of the value of the investment product (see below at section V.B) was accordingly applied here. Also, the OGH referred to the above-cited jurisprudence concerning a bank's vicarious agent in regard to duties to warn.

II. Legal Nature of a Bank's Duties

A. Duties Based on Supervision Law

i. General Part

In its centrepiece, the WAG 2007,[51] which was revised in order to implement the MiFID[52] into national law, imposes various rules of good conduct on—to use the

[47] RIS-Justiz RS0106890 (T27).

[48] W Rechberger in H Fasching and A Konecny (2004) Vor § 266 ZPO, Rz 11 et seq.

[49] RIS-Justiz RS0022900; authors rejecting this opinion explicitly named in the decision: BC Steininger, discussing 7 Ob 220/04k, ÖBA 2006, 61; P Bydlinski, 'Haftung für fehlerhafte Anlageberatung: Schaden und Schadenersatz' (2008) *ÖBA* 159; H Koziol, 'Zum Ersatzanspruch unzulänglich aufgeklärter Anleger—Eine angeregte österreichische Diskussion als Anregung für das deutsche Recht?' (2010) *FS Picker* 539 et seq; G Wilhelm, 'Zu Haftungsbegründung und Haftungsausfüllung beim Anlegerschaden' (2010) *ecolex* 232. See also (with further references) P Bydlinski, 'Anlageberaterhaftung: Beweislast, Beweismaß, Beweiswürdigung und Non liquet hinsichtlich Schaden(shöhe) und Kausalität' (2012) *ÖBA* 797.

[50] 8 Ob 66/12g EvBl 2013,922 (*Cach*); see also: G Graf, 'Der zu Unrecht empfohlene Fremdwährungskredit' (2013) *VbR* 3.

[51] Hereinafter WAG.

[52] Effective 2018 MiFID will be substituted by MiFID II and MiFIR, which seek to find solutions to institutional problems that were revealed during the financial crisis; see eg W Sindelar, 'Quo vadis MiFID II—Welche Neurungen und Herausforderungen bringt die neue Finanzmarktrichtlinie?' (2014) *ÖBA* 478.

words of the law—'legal entities';[53] such being investment services enterprises, certain insurance companies and especially credit institutions, and their branch companies. As its predecessor, the WAG 1997, the WAG 2007 contains supervisory and regulatory provisions and is therefore to be considered public law. As will be shown below, however, the WAG has a great impact on the law of (pre-)contractual damages as well as tort law.

§ 38 WAG contains a general clause of good conduct, stating that a legal entity shall act 'honestly, fairly and professionally in accordance with the best interests of its clients'. The following provisions define this duty more closely. Thereby, these rules of good conduct are generally owed to both *professional* and *private customers*, but vary in their intensity depending on whether the customer is a professional or not. In some aspects, the WAG also differentiates between the different types of services provided by the financial institution (see duties to investigate discussed below, which vary from an obligatory 'appropriateness test', to a 'suitability test' or no such duty, depending on which financial service is offered).

ii. Duties to Warn/Inform

§ 40 WAG provides for a 'basic' *duty to inform*. This information is to be provided regardless of the kind of service offered. The information provided may be communicated in a standardised way[54] and only has to concern the form of investment in general rather than the specific financial product. In this 'basic information', according to § 40(1) No 5 and (2) WAG, customers also have to be *warned* about the risks inherent to the respective investment instruments and strategies. The content of these warnings is specified in annex No 3 of § 40 WAG, which refers to the customers' 'level of knowledge' implying that in regard to *business customers* a lower standard of such duties is to be applied.

iii. Duties to Investigate

In two provisions, §§ 44 and 45, WAG also provides for duties to *investigate*, ie to obtain information from the client.[55] § 44 WAG concerns entities that manage portfolios of their clients or advise[56] them on their investments. Here, the highest standard of such duties to investigate is to be applied. In order to ensure that the entity has a reasonable basis of information about its customers, it must inquire about the investor's knowledge and skills in respect of the securities of interest,

[53] See WAG, § 15 ('*Rechtsträger*'); in the following, the terms 'financial institution' and 'investment firm' are used with the same (broad) meaning.

[54] Under MIFID II, which is to be effective from 3 January 2018, Member States are free to choose if they want to allow financial institutions to use such standardised information; see MiFID II, Art 24(5). If a Member State chooses not to offer this possibility, financial institutions providing only standardised information violate supervision law. For the relationship between supervision law and private law, see below, section II.B.

[55] These provisions are supplemented with WAG, § 43.

[56] 'Advising' means specifically suggesting certain investment instruments; see eg G Graf in M Gruber and N Raschauer (2011), WAG § 44 Mn 3.

his financial situation and his goals concerning the investment (*suitability test*).[57] If the financial institution finds that the specific product is not suitable for the customer, it must warn him accordingly. For *professional clients*, § 44(6) WAG provides that it may be presumed that they have sufficient skills in respect of their professional activity. Also, professional clients who obtain financial advice are presumed to have sufficient financial resources for the investment of interest.

§ 45 WAG deals with legal entities that offer any financial services not mentioned in § 44 WAG and therefore applies to all financial services apart from portfolio management or financial advice. Especially order execution without financial advice is typically subsumed under § 35 WAG.[58] For these transactions, a lower standard for such duties to investigate applies: the entity must take into account the client's experience and knowledge about the respective security and evaluate if the security is suitable for the customer. The financial situation and the goals concerning the investment, however, do not have to be taken into account (*appropriateness test*). An occurring inappropriateness of the specific product must, again, be warned of. In respect of *professional customers*, there is no duty to investigate for such transactions.[59]

According to § 27 WAG, an investment firm is released from its obligation to investigate about the client's skills, experience and (when § 44 is applicable) goals and financial situation, if a *different licensed entity* according to § 15 WAG has already fulfilled these duties. According to the OGH, this also applies to the subsequent assessment of appropriateness/suitability,[60] since a 'duplication' of these duties is not reasonable. Furthermore, the entity may trust in the correctness of advice given by such third party. The legal relationship between the third party and the investment firm (eg vicarious agent, carrier or agent) is generally of no relevance.[61]

Furthermore, according to § 46 WAG, under certain circumstances, entities may offer *execution-only* services to both professional and private clients without giving rise to any obligations to investigate for themselves or third parties.[62] This requires, first, that these services concern non-complex financial instruments,[63]

[57] Terminology taken from Recital (56) of the MiFID Implementing Directive.

[58] M Gruber, 'Die Wohlverhaltensregeln' in P Braumüller, D Ennöckl, M Gruber and N Raschauer (Hrsg), *Von der MiFID zum WAG 2007* (2008) 83 (138).

[59] Graf in Gruber and Raschauer, WAG § 45 Mn 16.

[60] OGH explicitly following *Knobl/Gasser*, 'Aufklärungspflichten und irrtumsrechtliche Gehilfenzurechnung bei Einschaltung einer kundennäheren Wertpapierfirma' (2012) *ÖBA* 352; in 1 Ob 48/12h ZfRV-LS 2013/23 (*Ofner*) = ecolex 2013, 323 = ÖBA 2013, 506 (*Thiede*) = Jus-Extra OGH-Z 5369 = RdW 2013, 334 = ZVR 2013, 76; contrary: G Graf, 'Zur Aufklärungspflicht der Bank bei Einschaltung eines weiteren Finanzdienstleisters' (2012) *ÖBA* 229;

[61] 1 Ob 48/12h ZfRV-LS 2013/23 (*Ofner*) = ecolex 2013, 323 = ÖBA 2013, 506 (*Thiede*) = Jus-Extra OGH-Z 5369 = RdW 2013, 334 = ZVR 2013, 76.

[62] To execution-only deals in general, see M Oppitz, 'Das "Execution-only-Geschäft neu" Zur Befugnis für die Geschäftstätigkeit nach § 46 WAG 2007' (2007) *ÖBA* 953.

[63] As defined in WAG, § 1 Nr 7, eg shares.

secondly, that the service is provided at the initiative of the client or potential client, and thirdly, that the customer has been informed that the service he ordered will be executed without giving rise to duties to investigate.[64] The general information according to § 40 WAG (including warnings) is still to be provided.

Finally, the law exempts entities offering transmission of orders and executing orders on behalf of the customer from all obligations laid down in §§ 38–57 WAG when a customer qualifies as an '*eligible counterparty*'. This is only the case when the client is a financial institution, investment firm, insurance company etc itself.[65]

B. Duties Based on Contractual Relationships

The relationship between the rules of the WAG (which are, as stated above, primarily public law) and private law (foremost the law of contractual damages or tort law) has drawn a considerable amount of interest and attention among legal scholars.[66] While it is commonly accepted that the WAG does have an impact on civil law,[67] different positions have been taken in respect of the degree as well as the reasoning for this influence. One opinion claims that the rules of good conduct of the WAG *directly affect* the contractual relationship between the financial institution and its customer. The WAG, they argue, lays down previously unwritten (pre-)contractual duties.[68] A violation of WAG rules of good conduct therefore 'automatically' constitutes unlawfulness within the system of contractual damages.[69] A different opinion claims that, on the contrary, the WAG rules are only to be used for the interpretation of contractual duties without necessarily being in complete accordance with the former and thus assume a non-obligatory *indirect effect* on civil law.[70] So far, the OGH has not decided in favour of one opinion or the other.

[64] Also, the obligations provided in WAG, §§ 34 and 35 concerning conflicts of interest must be complied with.

[65] The qualifying entities are listed in WAG, § 58 (2) Nr 1–4. For eligible counterparties in general, see also MiFID, Art 24, which WAG, § 60 is based on.

[66] eg H Baum, 'Das Spannungsverhältnis zwischen dem funktionalen Zivilrecht der "Wohlverhaltensregeln" des WpHG und dem allgemeinem Zivilrecht' (2013) *ÖBA* 396; Brandl and Klausberger, '"Ausstrahlungstheorie"—Zum Verhältnis zwischen Aufsichtsrecht und Zivilrecht nach MiFID und WAG' (2009) *ZFR* 131; P Knobl and K Grafenhofer, 'Haftung einer Bank für allfälliges Fehlverhalten von externen Anlageberatern oder Vermittlern' (2010) *GesRZ* 27.

[67] E Brandl and P Klausberger in E Brandl and G Saria (2015), *WAG Kommentar*, § 38 Mn 7; Graf in Gruber and Raschauer, WAG § 38 Mn 44; S Kalss, M Oppitz and J Zollner, *Kapitalmarktrecht* (2015) § 6 Mn 5 figuratively speak of the 'janus-faced' character of supervision rules.

[68] M Gruber in P Braumüller, D Ennöckl, M Gruber and N Raschauer, *MiFID* (2008) 153 et seq; G Graf, 'Anlageberatung—quo vadis?' (2009) *ZFR* 82.

[69] Naturally, the further requirements—mainly: damage, causation and fault—for such claim must also be met in order to warrant recovery of damages; see n 21.

[70] With references to German literature, see: Brandl and Klausberger in Brandl and Saria (n 67) § 38 Mn 9; Brandl and Klausberger, 'Ausstrahlungstheorie' (n 66) 131; P Knobl and G Janovsky, discussing 6 Ob 110/07f, (2008) *ZFR* 70; C Wendehorst, 'Anlageberatung, Risikoaufklärung und Rechtswidrigkeitszusammenhang' (2010) *ÖBA* 562.

A lower limit for the degree of this influence is rendered by EU law. Since the WAG implements an EU directive, the principle of *effet utile* may not be violated. Naturally, the assumption of an only indirect effect of the WAG (and therefore the MiFID) on civil law does not per se lead to a violation of the principle of effectiveness. Instead, for each single provision of the WAG, it must be evaluated to what extent its violation must also affect civil law in order to ensure the provision's effectiveness.[71]

On the other side, it has been argued that duties deriving from contractual relationships may reach *further* than those provided by the WAG. If, for example, an entity has provided sufficient information according to § 40 WAG, but must notice that in this particular case further information is needed, a failure to provide such shall cause civil law unlawfulness without violating the WAG.[72] The same should apply when an entity does not give financial advice in terms of suggesting a certain security and therefore is only subject to a duty to investigate according to § 45 WAG, which does not include investigations about the client's financial situation and his goals in respect of the investment instrument. If, in such case, an entity must notice that a certain investment instrument may be in conflict with the client's goals/financial situation, but nevertheless fails to warn its customer, a breach of duties deriving from the contract is to be assumed. This—according to the cited opinion—is owing to the fact that the inflexible, formalistic character of the WAG cannot completely represent the duties of care deriving from a contract, which have to be construed on a case-to-case basis.[73] These arguments are convincing; the OGH, however, has explicitly left open this question so far.[74]

The WAG is not applicable to *credit agreements*. Where *private customers* are concerned, the VKrG[75] is to be applied, which provides for a duty to investigate in respect of client's funds, a duty to inform before entering into a contract and a duty to inform in the contract itself.[76] The VKrG, however, neither contains a general clause comparable to § 38 WAG, providing that financial institutes must act in accordance with 'the best interests of their clients', nor a suitability or appropriateness test, as stipulated in the WAG. Therefore, when a credit agreement is not suitable for a customer for reasons other than his personal funds or in cases where professional clients are concerned, further (unwritten) (pre-)contractual duties to warn, inform etc, may derive from general contractual law.[77] In 2013, the

[71] So far, the ECJ has also refrained from a more general statement in this question; see ECJ, 30 May 2013, C-604/11 *Genil 48 SL e.a./Bankinter SA e.a.* at [57].

[72] Graf in Gruber and Raschauer, WAG § 40 Mn 8.

[73] Graf, 'Anlageberatung—quo vadis?' (n 68) 82.

[74] Most recently: 6 Ob 179/12k.

[75] The VKrG (*Verbraucherkreditgesetz*, Consumer Credit Act) implements Directive 2008/48/EG into national law.

[76] On contracts within the scope of the VKrG in general, see R Pesek, *Der Verbraucherkreditvertrag* (2012).

[77] G Graf, 'Der zu Unrecht empfohlene Fremdwährungskredit' (2013) *VbR* 3.

OGH assumed a breach of such duties in a case in which a bank must have noticed that a certain foreign currency loan was not suitable for its customer, but failed to warn accordingly.[78]

C. Duties Based on Pre-contractual Relationships

Any kind of wrong information communicated to customers by financial institutes—eg in advertisement material—before entering into a contract may induce liability according to the general principle of *culpa in contrahendo*, given the fact that the error has caused damage and the tortfeasor has acted culpably. Whenever duties laid down in the WAG apply—see especially the duty to inform according to § 40 WAG—the pre-contractual relationship between customer and bank may be specified by these obligations.

In case of wrong information in prospectuses, the legal consequences are explicitly laid down by law: According to § 11 (1) No 1 KMG,[79] the *issuer* of a financial product is liable for damages arising out of wrong or missing information communicated in prospectuses provided the other requirements for such claim[80] are met. *Entities professionally trading financial products*, and other intermediaries accepting investors' contract declarations, however, are only liable if they know of the error or incompleteness or are unaware of this owing to gross negligence. Owing to these explicitly laid down legal consequences, the OGH refers to prospectus liability as a further development of the *culpa in contrahendo*.[81]

D. Duties Based on Tort Law

A claim in Austrian tort law is based on the same main requirements as a claim for contractual damages.[82] In tort law the requirement of 'unlawfulness' is induced mainly either by a behaviour that violates 'absolutely protected interests'[83] and not just pure economic interests, or 'protective laws'. In order to qualify as such a protective law, it must be the law's intent to protect a victim against damages typically caused by the forbidden behaviour. The OGH has generally denied that § 15 of the WAG 1997, which explicitly stated that a violation of the respective duties to inform causes liability, constitutes such a protective law.[84] The Court argued that

[78] 8 Ob 66/12g, EvBl 2013, 922 (*Cach*).

[79] § 11 KMG implements Directive 2003/71/EC, Art 6 into national law.

[80] See n 21.

[81] RIS-Justiz RS0108218 (T2).

[82] See n 21.

[83] Like property, life, health etc. Pure economic interests (which are of interest here) are not absolutely protected. Such damages are only to be compensated if 'protective laws' or contractual obligations have been violated. See Koziol, *Basic Questions of Tort Law from a Germanic Perspective* (n 21), Mn 1/24.

[84] RIS-Justiz RS0120998.

this rule laid down (pre-)contractual duties. So far, the OGH has not held that any rules of good conduct of the WAG 2007 are to be considered protective laws.

The Court stated, however, that § 48a(1) No 2 lit c BörseG,[85] which prohibits market manipulation through communication of wrong information, is to be seen as a protective law.[86] This was of relevance in a case in which customers were given the (poor) advice by a third party, AWD, not to sell their Immofinanz and Immoeast shares, but to keep them and wait until their value would rise again. It is undisputed that Constantia did not violate any duties laid down in the WAG 1997 in this case, since these duties mostly apply at the time of sale of the products to the customer.[87] Here, however, Constantia is alleged to have communicated wrong information to AWD, which then, in turn, gave wrong advice. The OGH sent the case back to the courts of first instance in order to decide whether § 48a (1) No 2 lit c BörseG was violated and, therefore, the claimants could claim damages not only against AWD, but also against Constantia.

Since damages caused by banks by wrong advice etc typically occur within contractual or pre-contractual relationships, tort law generally plays a minor role in this aspect.

E. Duties towards Third Parties

The WAG typically governs the relationship between financial institutions and their customers. Hence, duties towards third parties are not explicitly laid down in the WAG. The doctrine of *Vertrag mit Schutzwirkung zugunsten Dritter* (contracts having protective effect on third parties), however, may be applied in cases in which a bank violates duties of care.[88] According to this principle, a third party may claim damages resulting from a breach of contractual duties between two other parties. Thereby, this third party may base their claim on contractual damages, having the benefit that the burden of proof concerning the tortfeasor's fault lies with the latter and purely economic damages are to be compensated.[89] Furthermore, the doctrine of vicarious agents applies. Requirement for the applicability of this doctrine is the fact that the third party is foreseeably affected by the fulfilment of the contract and has no other possibility to claim contractual damages.[90]

A prominent example of a bank's duties towards persons other than their customer is § 25 KSchG, which applies whenever a consumer guarantees (or provides

[85] *Börsegesetz 1989*, Stock Exchange Act.

[86] 8 Ob 104/12w ZFR 2013, 89 = Jus-Extra OGH-Z 5326 = ÖBA 2013, 438 = RdW 2013, 395 = RZ 2013 EÜ130 = Graf, ecolex 2013, 864 = ecolex 2013, 871.

[87] This also is the case in regard to the current WAG. In the absence of duties of bank to inform etc, a third party adviser cannot be a vicarious agent according to § 1313a ABGB.

[88] Graf in Gruber and Raschauer WAG § 38 Mn 53.

[89] This is disputed; see Reischauer in P Rummel, 3rd edn (2007) § 1295 Mn 33.

[90] Perner, Spitzer and Kodek (n 12) 319.

other personal securities) for someone else's loan granted by a financial institution.[91] In such cases, the creditor must warn this third party accordingly, if it knows, or has reason to know, that its customer, the credit recipient, may not be able to pay back the loan. If the creditor fails to do so, the third party is not obliged to pay back the loan despite having given the guarantee.[92]

Another example is the liability of a bank working as *intermediary* between the customers and another financial institution, as laid down in § 11 KMG. Even though the contract of sale concerning the investment products is concluded between the customer and the other financial institution, the bank may be held liable for damages caused by wrong information in the product's prospectus, if the bank has acted with at least gross negligence. If both financial institutions violate § 11 KMG, they can be held liable jointly and severally (§ 11 (3) *leg cit*).

III. Specific Duties

A. Information about Financial Products

The 'basic' *duty to inform* according to § 40 WAG includes, as stated above, a duty to warn about risks inherent to the respective type of investment product. This information is to be given to both private and professional customers. Annex No 3 of § 40 WAG[93] specifies these obligations to warn; in regard to *business customers*, a lower standard of these duties is to be applied ('level of knowledge of the client').

> The description of risks shall include, where relevant to the specific type of instrument concerned and the status and level of knowledge of the client, the following elements:
>
> (a) the risks associated with that type of financial instrument including an explanation of leverage and its effects and the risk of losing the entire investment;
> (b) the volatility of the price of such instruments and any limitations on the available market for such instruments;
> (c) the fact that an investor might assume, as a result of transactions in such instruments, financial commitments and other additional obligations, including contingent liabilities, additional to the cost of acquiring the instruments;
> (d) any margin requirements or similar obligations, applicable to instruments of that type.

[91] Of course, the guarantor for the loan does have a contractual relationship with the bank and, therefore, is not a 'third party' in a strict sense.

[92] Unless the creditor proves that the third party would have guaranteed for its customer anyway; see Perner, Spitzer and Kodek (n 12) 630.

[93] The following citation is taken from the English version of the identical Art 31 (2) of the MiFID Implementing Directive.

The information the financial institution has to provide is defined in great detail in §§ 40, 41 WAG and annex No 1 and 2 of § 40 WAG. As stated above, standardised information about respective financial instruments is generally sufficient. The most important pieces of information which have to be provided according to these stipulations are set out below.

B. Information about the Financial Institution and its Services

This includes the name and address, communication media etc.[94] When providing the service of portfolio management, an appropriate method of evaluation such as a benchmark is to be established.[95] Furthermore, the financial institution has to inform its client where and under which legal conditions his funds may be held by a third party.[96] Moreover, the institute has to give notice if the client's funds may be held in an omnibus account by a third party and if it is not possible under the respective foreign national law to hold the client's financial instruments separately from the third party's funds.[97] Finally, before entering into securities financing transactions in relation to the client's financial instruments, the investment firm has to inform about the customer's obligations and rights.[98]

C. Duty to Refuse to Carry out Customer's Instructions

Generally, it is agreed upon that an investment firm is subject to a duty to warn if a product is not suitable/appropriate for the customer, but there is no prohibition to sell these products, if a customer insists on buying such despite any warnings. Interestingly, one author has argued that in certain cases within the scope of § 45 WAG (appropriateness test in regard to financial instruments other than portfolio management and financial advice) a financial institute must indeed *refuse to carry out the customer's instructions*. According to this opinion, the investment firm may not sell certain securities if, first, it finds that such are inappropriate and, secondly, this conclusion is based on information investigated by another financial institution.[99] This view surprises insofar as the same author agreed that, when the investment firm has investigated about clients' skills itself and subsequently considers the product as inappropriate, it is only obliged to *warn the customer* about this fact.[100]

[94] WAG, Annex No 1 of § 40.
[95] WAG, § 40 (1) Nr 1; see also the MiFID Implementing Directive, Art 30 (2).
[96] WAG, Annex No 2 of § 40; See also the MiFID Implementing Directive, Art 32 (2).
[97] WAG, Annex No 2 of § 40; See also the MiFID Implementing Directive, Art 32 (3).
[98] WAG, Annex No 2 of § 40; See also the MiFID Implementing Directive, Art 32 (7).
[99] G Graf, 'Zur Aufklärungspflicht der Bank bei Einschaltung eines weiteren Finanzdienstleisters' (2012) *ÖBA* 229; according to this opinion, the investment firm may sell the product if it informs the client so that he can understand its risks. The OGH generally assumes that one assessment of appropriateness conducted by the first entity suffices.
[100] Graf in Gruber and Raschauer WAG § 45 Mn 7 ff.

IV. Standard of Care

Generally, the standard of care expected of a person is based on the fiction of a reasonable, averagely careful person of the same profession.[101] If the tortfeasor does not act accordingly, his behaviour will be considered a culpable act, unless he proves that he did not possess the necessary abilities to act diligently.[102] Whenever the tortfeasor and the claimant are in a *contractual relationship*, the tortfeasor is assumed to have acted objectively culpably and carries the burden of proof that he has not.[103]

Furthermore, just like medical doctors, auditors, notaries etc, banks are to be seen as *experts* according to § 1299 ABGB. Under this rule, experts have to meet an especially high standard of care. Also, when considered an expert, the tortfeasor is subject to an objective standard of fault: the—already mostly theoretical[104]—possibility of proving absence of fault due to a lack of abilities precludes.[105]

When the tortfeasor gives *advice in return for payment*, he is liable for any damage caused by wrong or insufficient advice according to § 1300 ABGB, regardless of whether he and the claimant are in a contractual relationship or not.[106] The phrase 'in return for payment' is construed in a very broad sense and includes every legal relationship that the tortfeasor has entered into for not entirely altruistic reasons (eg commissions paid by third parties and free advice that leads to a contract concluded for pecuniary interest).[107]

V. Legal Consequences of Violation of Duties

A. Supervision Law

A violation of the duties to investigate and to warn deriving from the WAG may have legal consequences in different fields of law. The FMA[108] is responsible for monitoring the compliance of financial institutions with *supervision law* as laid down in the WAG. In order to do so, the FMA is entitled to gain access to documents of financial institutions and to take copies thereof. Violation of the rules of

[101] M Harrer in F Schwimann, *ABGP Praxiskommentar*, 3rd edn (2006) §§ 1297, 1298 Mn 11.

[102] This possibility, however, is hardly ever applied by the courts, which tend to apply objective standards of diligence; see Harrer (n 101) §§ 1297, 1298 Mn 11.

[103] See eg G Kodek in *ABGB-ON* (2010) § 1298; the further requirements (see n 21) for a claim for damages are to be proven by claimant.

[104] Harrer (n 101).

[105] Perner, Spitzer and Kodek (n 12) 306.

[106] Reischauer (n 89) § 1300 Mn 4.

[107] J Schacherreiter in *ABGB-ON* § 1299 Mn 62.

[108] Finanzmarktaufsicht.

good conduct (including duties to investigate and the duties to warn) constitutes an *administrative offence*, which, according to § 95(2) No 1 WAG, is to be sanctioned with fines up to €100,000. In cases of serious, systematic breaches of supervision law, the financial institution's licence may be withdrawn according to § 5(2) No 3 WAG.

The FMA also acts as deciding authority of first instance in cases of administrative offences laid down in the WAG. In this function, notices from private parties are seen as a valuable source of information;[109] clients, however, are not recognised as parties in such proceedings. Also, the FMA does not decide on claims by private parties, eg seeking damages etc.

B. Civil Law

As stated above, a violation of the rules of good conduct in the WAG not only causes *unlawfulness* in the field of (pre-)contractual damages, but also indicates the relevance of a mistake according to § 871(2) ABGB, which may lead to an avoidance of the contract.

Whenever damages were caused in relation to contracts over securities, the typical volatility of their value made it a challenging topic for courts as well as doctrine[110] to *assess* the respective *damages*. Closely connected to this problem is the question of *what kind of compensation* is to be granted. Thereby, the OGH established that if a security was sold that was not actually wanted by the client, the unwanted contract itself constitutes damage, regardless of the current value of the sold security.[111] Hence, primarily, the price the securities were sold at can be claimed as compensation in exchange for the respective securities, which are to be transferred back to the financial institution. If the client has sold the securities already, however, he may subsidiarily claim the difference between his current assets and the assets he would have had, had the financial institute acted rightfully.[112] As mentioned above, in any case the claimant must prove that, without the respondent's misbehaviour, he would have invested in a security that is still of value or would not have bought any securities.[113] Furthermore, it is established that declaratory actions are to be dismissed, if a claim for satisfaction is reasonable.[114] The reasoning behind this is that declaratory actions make it possible for the claimant to wait and speculate whether the securities he (unwillingly) bought turn

[109] See the website of the FMA; available at: www.fma.gv.at/de/ueber-die-fma/kompetenzen/aufgaben-der-fma.html.

[110] On this and assessment of such damages in general see G Kodek, 'Ausgewählte Fragen der Schadenshöhe bei Anlegerschäden' (2012) *ÖBA* 11.

[111] RIS-Justiz RS0120784.

[112] RIS-Justiz RS0120784.

[113] RIS-Justiz RS0106890 (T26 and 27).

[114] See explicitly in: 8 Ob 39/12m, AnwBl 2013,107 = ÖBA 2013,209 = ecolex 2013,120 = RdW 2013,136 = -ZVR 2013, 76.

out to be profitable after all. Such completely risk-free speculations at the expense of the respondent are to be refused.

Since the claimant must prove that, first, if he had been advised correctly, he would not have bought the respective high-risk securities[115] and, secondly, he would have invested in (lower-risk) securities which are still of value now, cases of hardship might occur. In particular, the secondly-mentioned aspect typically causes difficulties for the claimant: if there are multiple alternative investment products matching the client's risk profile, it is very hard for the claimant to furnish evidence supporting the fact that he would have bought the profitable ones amongst them.

In order to solve this problem, some authors suggest that in such cases courts may *estimate* the damage according to § 273 ZPO.[116] When applied, this rule provides that the claimant does not have to prove that he would have invested in a specific compound of certain products and, therefore, has suffered a certain amount of damage. The average value of the investment alternatives may rather be granted.[117] Some authors, however, argue that this provision may only be applied by courts if the claimant can prove that all investment alternatives are at least more profitable than the unwanted high-risk products.[118] So far, the OGH has explicitly agreed that § 273 ZPO may be used by courts in such cases but has left open which exact requirements have to be met.[119]

In cases where *many clients* were affected by the same misconduct of a certain financial institution, a legal construction often referred to as 'Austrian class action' has been facilitated,[120] which—though not used for the first time[121]—has caused lively discussion.[122] Such class action is not specifically provided for in statutory law, but simply describes the fact that many claims are transferred to one party—like the abovementioned VKI—which subsequently sues the respondent. Different

[115] On the standard of proof see text at n 49 et seq.

[116] M Trenker, 'Die hypothetische Alternativveranlagung' (2013) *ÖJZ* 5; See also C Völkl, 'Anlegerschutz: OGH macht's einfach(er)' (2011) *wbl* 474; Kodek, 'Ausgewählte Fragen der Schadenshöhe bei Anlegerschäden' (n 110) 11.

[117] The chance of each alternative to be chosen is also to be taken into consideration; see P Leupold and M Ramharter, 'Anlegerschaden und Kausalitätsbeweis bei risikoträchtiger hypothetischer Alternativanalge' (2010) *ÖBA* 718 (726).

[118] ibid.

[119] 9 Ob 44/13f; 9 Ob 85/09d ÖBA 2010, 533 = ecolex 2010, 749 = ZFR 2010, 179 = EvBl 2010, 914 = RZ 2010, 237 = JBl 2010, 713 (*Bydlinski*) = RdW 2010, 573 = ZIK 2011, 35 = ZVR 2011, 75 (Danzl) = SZ 2010/53.

[120] 6 Ob 224/12b Zak 2013, 119 = ZFR 2013, 147 = RdW 2013, 268 = AnwBl 2013, 331 = EvBl-LS 2013/94 = ecolex 2013, 533 = ÖBA 2013, 682.

[121] See 4 Ob 116/05w ÖBA 2011/1705 = ZFR 2011, 89 = ÖBl-LS 2011/51 = ecolex 2011, 343 (*Horak*) = RdW 2011, 219.

[122] eg P Oberhammer, '"Österreichische Sammelkage" und § 227 ZPO' (2010) *Jahrbuch Zivilverfahrensrecht* 247; A Klauser, 'Prozessfinanzierung, Rechtsfreunde, quota litis und Sammelklage' (2013) 5 *VbR*; G Kodek and O Jaindl, 'Sammelklage stammt nicht aus DDR—Sommergespräch' *Wirtschaftsblatt* (25 July 2013); with further references: A Klauser, 'Sammelklagen von Verbraucherorganisationen' in M Reiffenstein and B Blaschek (Hrsg), *Konsumentenpolitisches Jahrbuch 2009—2010* (2011).

from class actions in the American legal culture, here, courts decide over singular, although bundled, claims independently. Also, persons who decide not to transfer their claim will formally not be affected by the judgment.[123] Generally, however, the same principles of *assessment of damages* as mentioned above apply here as well as in cases of only one claimant.

VI. Client's Contributory Negligence

It is disputed whether negligence on the side of the claimant may lead to a preclusion of the right to avoid a contract based on *mistake*. Negligence in that context means that the claimant would not have been mistaken if he had acted diligently (by carefully reading the prospectus, for example). While some argue that at least gross negligence must make the respondent more worthy of legal protection than the claimant,[124] others claim that fault is simply not part of the law of mistake and, therefore, may not be taken into consideration.[125] The OGH differentiates between two situations: in (extraordinary) cases in which it must have been 'entirely obvious' to the claimant that the respondent has communicated wrong or insufficient information and the claimant has had the possibility to validate the given information, no avoidance of the contract is to be granted. This is owing to the fact that the contract is to be seen as concluded based on correct and sufficient information. In any other case, the OGH agrees that fault is no parameter of the law of mistake; therefore, the contract may be avoided, regardless of the claimant's fault. The OGH, however, stated obiter that the claim for the price of the investment products may be reduced or even precluded on basis of the doctrine of *culpa in contrahendo* (see next paragraph).[126]

According to § 1304 ABGB, *contributory negligence* reduces—in extreme cases even precludes—a claim based on (pre-)contractual damages or tort law. Since a client may trust the expertise of a financial institute, courts tend to be reluctant in granting such reductions in context with wrong advice.[127] If, for example, after investigating information about the skills, goals etc of a client, a financial institution advises its client to buy a certain security which, in fact, is not suitable for him,

[123] For these differences and Austrian class action in general, see G E Kodek, 'Die "Sammelklage" nach österreichischem Recht, Ein neues prozeßrechtliches Institut auf dem Prüfstand' (2004) *ÖBA* 615.

[124] Krejci, 'Zur Anfechtung von Wertpapierkäufen wegen irreführender Werbung und Beratung' (n 30) 58.

[125] A Vonkilch, 'Rechtsfragen der Irrtumsanfechtung von Wertpapierkäufen—Zugleich ein Beitrag zum Irrtumsrecht des ABGB' (2010) *ÖBA* 579.

[126] 8Ob25/10z Zak 2010, 377 = EvBl 2011, 31 = JBl 2011, 32 = ecolex 2010, 1039 (Wilhelm) = ZFR 2011, 25 (Pletzer) = ZIK 2011, 34 = Riedler, ecolex 2011, 194 = Oppitz, ÖBA 2011, 534 = RZ 2011, 46 EÜ49 = MietSlg 62.091 = SZ 2010/113.

[127] S Dullinger, 'Aktuelle Fragen der Haftung wegen Beratungsfehlern bei der Vermögensanlage' (2011) *JBl* 693.

ignoring written warnings will not reduce the client's claim for damages.[128] In cases in which a client with profound financial knowledge must have noticed that the respective advice is not correct, however, the OGH assumed such negligence on the claimant's side.[129]

Also based on § 1304 ABGB is the victim's *duty to minimise damages*. This has been of relevance for the question of how long a client, who was advised wrongly, has to keep the respective securities: selling such papers too early (before their value rises) or keeping them too long (until after their value has dropped) may constitute a violation of this duty causing a reduction of the claim for damages. In this context, the OGH has also assumed that such reduction is only to be granted in exceptional cases, since it is hard—even for experienced investors—to determine the best moment to sell.[130] According to general principles, the burden of proving such negligence lies upon the respondent.[131]

VII. Conclusion

The increase of claims against banks and other financial institutions in the last years has given doctrine and jurisdiction reason to focus on civil law problems in various fields ranging from tort law (eg concerning the assessment of damages, causation, contributory negligence, vicarious agency etc), contract law (eg concerning the law of mistake, the 'aliud' problem), company law (eg concerning the prohibition of investment reimbursement) to civil procedure (eg concerning rules of burden of proof, the so-called 'Austrian class actions' and the relationship between declaratory actions and claims for satisfaction). While in some of these topics, a broad consensus seems to have been reached, other questions are still left open by courts and are disputed in doctrine. Above all, the relationship between the WAG (respectively the MiFID) and civil law will continue to give rise to discussion.

[128] Most recently: 7 Ob 178/11v ÖBA 2013, 526 = ZFR 2013, 183.

[129] RIS-Justiz RS0102779.

[130] RIS-Justiz RS0120785; the OGH has rejected this argument in more recent cases: 4 Ob 62/11p, 1 Ob 188/12x, 2 Ob 74/12i.

[131] Explicitly so in: 1 Ob 188/12x ecolex 2013, 320 (Wilhelm) = RdW 2013, 199.

5

France

THIERRY BONNEAU

I. Introduction

There are a lot of court rulings that have held financial institutions civilly responsible for mis-selling financial products, poor financial advice, and insufficient disclosure of and warning of financial risks. The number of rulings is much higher than it was 20 years ago. However, it remains difficult to state the precise number, even if I only take into account the rulings handed down by the Cour de Cassation (French Supreme Court).

The decisions from the French Supreme Court do not contain many facts. The Court's role is not to a take position on the facts. The Court only assesses the decision as regards the law. It says if the Court of Appeal has correctly applied the legislation to the facts and/or has correctly interpreted the legislation.

Financial institutions are more often than not held civilly responsible to their clients; they are not civilly responsible to third parties. This assertion is, in my opinion, not debatable in French legislation since the subject matter of the study implies necessarily a relationship between a client and a professional or at least the start of the process that culminates in establishing such a relationship. People could nevertheless retort that a responsibility towards third parties (who are not potential clients) is not inconceivable. That is right:[1] according to the French Supreme Court,[2] third parties to a contract may take action, on the basis of tort, for a breach of contract where that breach caused him harm. However, such decisions are infrequent: the decisions handed down by the French Supreme Court bear out this point.

For a French lawyer, the main cases are less connected to the facts or circumstances of the case than to the rules or principles mentioned by the French

[1] On liability vis-à-vis third parties, see A Couret, Ph Goutay and B Zabala, 'France' in D Busch and De DeMott (eds), *Liability of Asset Managers* (Oxford: Oxford University Press, 2012) esp 3.64 and 3.103 et seq.

[2] Cass Ass Plenary, 6 October 2006, D 2006, 2826, note G Viney; JCP 2006, éd G, 10181, avis A Gariazzo et note M Billau.

Supreme Court in its decisions. Therefore, I would like to highlight the decisions that can be labelled important, because they originate new rules or principles in the existing French legal framework.

II. Major Cases

A. Financial Products and Investment Services

i. Cass Com 5 November 1991, Buon[3]

A retail client, Mr Jacques Buon, resorted to a financial intermediary, Banque populaire de Bretagne-Atlantique, to speculate on futures markets. He speculated as to the fluctuations in gold prices by performing uncovered operations. The result was a loss for the client. Because of the negative balance on the bank account, the financial intermediary took legal proceedings against its client. To defend himself, the client claimed that the financial intermediary was the origin of his damage and had to be declared responsible for it.

The Court of Appeal dismissed the claim because the contract concluded between the parties was not a portfolio management contract but a securities deposit contract (*contrat de dépôt de titres*), which does not impose any duty of advice on professionals. Its decision was overturned by the French Supreme Court—its commercial chamber—which decided, in its ruling handed down on 5 November 1991, that *whatever the contractual relationship between the client and the bank, the bank has the duty to inform the client about the risks incurred owing to speculative financial operations on futures markets unless the client knows the risks.*

ii. Cass Com 12 February 2008, Société Dubus[4]

A retail client, Miss Chênefront, concluded an agreement with the company Dubus that enabled her to perform short sales. The balance of her account became negative. The financial intermediary asked her to cover her debt position, but without success, and therefore decided to liquidate the position. Miss Chênefront took legal action against Dubus in order to secure payment of the debt. Then, the client claimed that the professional had made some errors at the beginning of the relationship.

The Court of Appeal dismissed the claim. The French Supreme Court overturned the decision. While the Court of Appeal had decided that the financial intermediary was not required, in the absence of a portfolio management contract,

[3] Bull Joly bourse mai-juin 1993 § 56 292.
[4] Droit des sociétés Juillet 2008, n° 162, obs Th Bonneau.

to assess the wealth of the clients, the Supreme Court decided that *whatever the contractual relationship between the client and the bank, the financial institution has the duty to assess the financial situation of the client.*

iii. Cass com 26 February 2008, Société Cortal consorts[5]

A retail client, Mr C, held a securities account with the bank called Société Cortal consorts. He carried out several naked short-selling operations and the balance of his account became negative. The bank asked him to cover his debt position without success, and therefore decided to liquidate it. The client claimed that the bank infringed the legislation about the cover required by the legislation concerning short selling and consequently that the bank had to be declared responsible for his damages.

The Court of Appeal dismissed the claim because clients are not authorised to take advantage of a rule that is laid down only to protect markets and professionals. The French Supreme Court overturned the decision in its ruling handed down on 28 February 2008 for the following reason: *professionals have to act with due skill, care and diligence in the best interests of their clients and the integrity of the market as well as complying with all the rules applicable to their activities in a way which enables them to promote the interests of their clients and the integrity of the market.*

iv. Cass Com 24 June 2008, Caisse d'épargne et de prévoyance Ile-de-France[6]

A retail client, Miss Aubin, bought units of UCITS. The commercial advertising mentioned only the potential profit and didn't underline the risk of loss. At maturity, the value of the units was below the value of the subscription. Therefore, Miss Aubin accused her financial intermediary, la caisse d'épargne et de prévoyance Ile-de-France, of not fulfilling its obligation to inform her of the risk and took legal proceedings against the credit institution in order to obtain damages.

The Court of Appeal dismissed her claims because the client was informed of the risk by reading the prospectus approved by the financial authority. The French Supreme Court overturned the decision for the following reason: *the commercial advertising given out by the professional that offers the clients the option to purchase units of UCITS must be consistent with the financial product and mention the negative characteristics as well as the potential risks that can be the counterparts of the advantages listed; this obligation of information cannot be regarded as fulfilled by the delivery of the prospectus approved by the financial authority.*

[5] Droit des sociétés Juillet 2008, n° 161, obs Th Bonneau.
[6] Droit des sociétés January 2009, n° 12, observations Th Bonneau.

v. Cass Com 26 June 2012, Société Dubus[7]

A retail client, Mr X, held a securities account with a financial institution called Société Dubus. He carried out several naked short-selling operations that caused losses and an inadequate margin. The financial intermediary asked him to cover his debt position without success and took legal proceedings against him. In response, the client claimed that the professional infringed his obligation to liquidate the uncovered position.

The Court of Appeal decided to exonerate the financial intermediary in part as regards the inadequate margin because the client, informed of the situation and asked several times by the professional to cover his debt position, decided voluntarily to postpone the liquidation of his position in the hope of a more favourable market environment. The French Supreme Court overturned the decision for the following reason: *the professional acting on behalf of a client on a futures market has, even without a client's liquidation order and despite any contrary order, to close out the client's position when the client does not cover his position in time.*

B. Credits and Ancillary Services

i. Cass civ 1, 27 June 1995, Crédit Foncier de France[8]

A couple obtained loans from banks in order to finance the building of a house. For some reasons not disclosed by the ruling, the debtors wanted to nullify the contracts. The claim was dismissed, but the Court of Appeal upheld the liability of the banks that granted the credits. The French Supreme Court confirmed the decision. According to the Court, *the fact of presenting a proposal of credit compliant with the existing legislation is not a dispensation from the obligation to warn clients against the risks resulting from their financial debt and the disproportion of their loans compared to their limited resources.*

ii. Cass Assemblée plénière, 2 March 2007, Epoux Dailler v Caisse régionale de crédit agricole mutuel de la Touraine et du Poitou[9]

A client had taken out an insurance policy proposed by the bank that gave him the loan. Although the insurance covered the total disability, it did not cover the

[7] JCP 2012, éd E, 1486, obs Th Bonneau; Bull Joly Bourse octobre 2012 § 183 421, note L Ruet; Revue droit bancaire et financier novembre-décembre 2012, com n° 199, obs A-C Muller; Banque et droit n° 145 septembre-octobre 2012 33, obs H de Vauplane, J-J Daigre, B de Saint-Mars et J-P Bornet; Droit des sociétés mars 2013, com n° 51, obs S. Torck.

[8] D 1995 J 621, note S Piedelièvre; Rev dr bancaire et bourse n° 51, septembre-octobre 1995 185, obs F-J Crédot et Y Gérard; Quotidien juridique n° 91, 14 novembre 1995 6; RJDA 12/95 n° 1400; Defrénois 1995 art 36210, n° 149, p1416, obs D Mazeaud; Contrats, Concurrence, Consommation, décembre 1995, n° 211, note H Raymond.

[9] Banque et droit n° 114, juillet-août 2007 20, obs Th Bonneau; JCP 2007, éd G, II, 10098, note A Gourio et éd E, 1375, note D Legeais; Rev trim dr com 2007 433, obs D Legeais; D 2007, p 985, note S Piedelièvre; Rev dr bancaire et financier, mai-juin 2007 11, obs F-J Crédot et Th Samin.

partial inability to perform the farming activity. The judge refused to condemn the bank to redress the client's damage. The decision was set aside by the French Supreme Court: according to the Court, *a bank that proposes an insurance policy to the client to whom it gives a loan must enlighten the client about the adequacy of the cover for his personal situation.*

iii. Cass Com 20 October 2009, Caisse de crédit agricole mutuel Laval v Jouvin[10]

A credit granted in line with a business activity was guaranteed by a person that was sued by the bank due to the default of the debtor. The guarantor claimed that the bank did not warn him against the risks resulting from the financial debt. The judge ordered the bank to redress the damage that was equivalent, according to him, to the amount of the debt. The French Supreme Court overturned this decision because *the damage resulting from the infringement of the duty to warn only consists of a loss of opportunity.*

III. Legal Basis of a Bank's Duty of Care

A. Financial Products and Investment Services

There was a period of time during which it was really difficult to take legal action against financial institutions. The reason is easy to understand. When a client accused such professionals of wrongdoing on the basis of a rule laid down in legal text, the issue on the table was about interests covered by the rule. More often than not, rules were regarded only as securing market's and professionals' interests. They were not considered as protecting clients. Consequently, the infringement of these rules was not a civil fault and clients could not put forward this infringement in order to secure a conviction. However, this solution was ruled out when contracts provided for the duties. On the basis of these contracts, clients could secure the conviction of financial institutions.

The situation started to change when the French Supreme Court decided, in 1993,[11] to set out the duty to warn irrespective of any legal text and despite the content of contracts. People could retort that the Court based its decision for imposing the duty to warn on Article 1147 of the Civil Code. However, this text is irrelevant to justify such a duty. It is only about contractual liability in general. This comment equally applies to Article 1231-1 of the Civil Code,

[10] Banque et droit n° 129, janvier-février 2010 20, obs Th Bonneau; JCP 2009, éd G, 422, obs L Dumoulin, éd G, 482, note S Piedelièvre et éd E, 2053, note D Legeais; Rev dr bancaire et financier janvier-février 2010 39, obs D Legeais D 2009, 2607, obs X Delpech et 2971, note D Houtcieff.

[11] See section II.A.i.

which has replaced Article 1147 since the French reform concerning contractual law.[12]

There was a further development in 2008, when the French Supreme Court decided that any infringement of professional duties is a civil fault. The change was crucial because previously such infringements could only trigger a disciplinary or administrative sanction.

To our knowledge, the first decision is the ruling handed down on 12 February 2008 (section II.A.ii). One commentator[13] thinks that the first decision with this scope is a decision dated 24 June 2008. However, the decision handed down on 12 February 2008 refers to Article 1147 of the Code Civil and the former Article L 533-3 of the Monetary and Financial Code. There is no doubt about its importance.

The ruling handed down on 26 February 2008[14] is also crucial because, regarding the obligation to cover positions on financial markets, the French Supreme Court put an end to a traditional case-law. Before this decision, the Court had held that clients were not authorised to take advantage of the infringement of the legislation concerning the coverage. By contrast, according to this decision, financial institutions are to blame if they do not call their clients for the margins required by legal texts.

These decisions are indicative of an important change because it is now easier to challenge the liability of financial institutions. However, the consequences must be well understood. The new case-law does not imply that it is not possible to base a legal action on the contract concluded between the parties or on classical notions of contract law such as error and good faith. These kinds of claims can still be grounds for the conviction of financial institutions. Even so, they are of less importance since the texts—monetary and financial code and AMF general regulations—laid down detailed rules.

B. Credits and Ancillary Services

If there were some difficulties in challenging the liability of financial institutions in the financial field, difficulties were of less importance as regards credits and insurance. That is not to imply that there has not been any change over time. The creation of the duty to warn the debtor and the guarantor against the risk resulting from their financial debt shows the opposite.

This duty, which is distinct from the duty laid down in the Consumer Code,[15] was set out irrespective of any legal text and despite the content of contracts. One could retort that the Court based its decision for imposing the duty to warn

[12] Ordonnance n° 2016-131 du 10 février 2016 portant réforme du droit des contrats, du régime général et de la preuve des obligations.

[13] M Cohen-Branche, 'La Cour de cassation, la finalité de la loi et la nouvelle protection de l'investisseur' (January 2011) *Bull Joly bourse* § 1, 55.

[14] See section II.A.iii.

[15] See n 12 above.

on Article 1147 of the Civil Code. However, this text is irrelevant when justifying such a duty. It is only about contractual liability in general. This comment equally applies to Article 1231-1 of the Civil Code, which has replaced Article 1147 since the French reform concerning contract law.[16]

Finally, information and warning are not specific to financial institutions. For instance, medical doctors have to inform their patients about their illness, any possible treatment and the risks and the consequences of the treatment that should be administrated. This duty is currently laid down in Article L 1111-2 of the Code of Public Health.[17] Likewise, a garden centre has to warn the client about the disease risks that they may face when buying a domestic rat. This solution results from a decision handed down the 14 May 2009[18] in a case in which a rat bit a child who became heavily ill.

These decisions are only examples. Some commentators[19] have underlined that they illustrate a classical principle whose objective is to enlighten the client's consent.[20]

IV. Duties to Investigate and to Warn

A. Financial Products and Investment Services

Case-law and legislation impose on financial institutions a duty to warn their clients: neither of these sources of duties have exactly the same extent. In addition, the duty to warn imposed by case-law is firmer than the duty to warn laid down in legal texts. How to articulate both these duties is not crystal clear.

The abovementioned decision dated from 5 November 1991[21] is the decision that originated the duty to warn in France. After this ruling, there have been a lot of other decisions that decide that *whatever the contractual relationship between the client and the bank, the bank has the duty to inform the client about the risks incurred due to speculative financial operations on futures markets, unless the client knows the risks.*[22]

[16] Ordonnance n° 2016-131 du 10 février 2016 portant réforme du droit des contrats, du régime général et de la preuve des obligations.

[17] See F Terré, Ph Simler and Y Lequette, *Droit civil, Les obligations*, 10° éd (Paris: Dalloz, 2009) n° 1005 et seq.

[18] Cass Civ 1, 14 May 2009, JCP 2009, éd G, 285, obs M Brusono-Aillaud.

[19] J-M Moulin, 'Responsabilité des banques en matière de commercialisation de produits financiers' (mars-avril 2010) *Rev dr bancaire et financier*, Etudes 7, esp n° 16.

[20] On the duty to warn imposed on real estate agents, see Cass Civ 1, 2 October 2013, Rev trim dr civ 2013 855, obs P-Y Gautier.

[21] See section II.A.i. Also see Couret, Goutay and Zabala, 'France' (n 1) esp n° 3.68.

[22] Cass Com 13 July 2010, arrêt n° 772 F-D, pourvoi n° E 09-69.638, *Bayle v Caisse d'épargne et de prévoyance d'Auverge et du Limousin*; Cass Com 9 November 2010, arrêt n° 1110 F-D, pourvoi n° F 09-71.065, *Perrin v Société Georget courtage européen (GCE)*; Cass Com 12 June 2012, arrêt n° 666 F-D, pourvoi n° X 11-21.661, *Bayle v Caisse d'épargne et de prévoyance d'Auverge et du Limousin*.

The duty resulting from these decisions is a judicial creation of the French Supreme Court. If the Court refers to Article 1147 of the Civil Code, this text is about the liability in general and doesn't lay down such a duty. Therefore, it is crystal clear that this duty to warn is a judicial creation.

The rule, as expressed by the French Supreme Court, is not general.

On the one hand, the duty to warn is closely linked to the performance of speculative financial operations. If the operation that causes losses is not speculative, financial institutions have no duty to warn.[23] The French Supreme Court regularly recalls that financial institutions, in such a hypothesis, do not have to warn their clients about the risks connected to the unpredictable variability of financial markets.[24]

On the other hand, the duty to warn is ruled out if the client knows the risk.[25] By contrast, clients who do not know have to be warned. These clients are labelled casual investors while clients who know the risks are qualified as properly informed investors.

The notion of speculative operation is not crystal clear.[26] It all depends on the circumstances. More often than not, such operations are short-selling operations or futures. However, they are not the only type of speculative operation. Operations on units or shares of UCITS as well as subscriptions for units of a real estate investment company (*société civile de placements immobilier, SCPI*) can also be regarded as speculative. However such a qualification has not been adopted for formula-based funds although they implied losses for the client and had been the subject of a warning from the French financial authority, l'Autorité des marchés financiers.[27]

[23] Cass com 12 February 2013, arrêt n° 135 F-D, pourvoi n° X 11-28.400, *Durand v société HSBC Hervet et other*; Cass com 14 May 2013, arrêt n° 470 F-D, pourvoi n° D 12-17.554, *Armand v Société Financière Meeschaert*; Rev dr bancaire et financier juillet-août 2013, com n° 141, obs M Storck; Cass com 28 January 2014, arrêt n° 107 F-D, pourvoi n° S 12-29.204, *Mortreux v BNP Paribas*; Cass Com 24 June 2014, arrêt n° 628 F-D, pourvoi n° T 13-16.812, *Gaulier v Société Financière Uzès*; Cass Com 10 February 2015, arrêt n° 129 F-D, pourvoi n° D 13-28.483, *Ney and alii v société CIC Est.*

[24] Cass Com, 19 September 2006, Dr sociétés janvier 2007, n° 13, note Th Bonneau; JCP 2006, éd G, II, 10201, note A Gourio; D 2007, pan 761, obs H Synvet; Cass com 12 June 2012, arrêt n° 662 F-P+B, pourvoi n° D 11-12.513, *Dupeyrat v Banque Neuflize Obc.*

[25] Cass com, 10 May 1994 et 2 November 1994, RJDA 1/95, n° 31 (1re et 3e esp); Cass com, 18 February 1997, Bull civ IV, n° 51, 45; Banque, n° 581, mai 1997 91, obs J-L Guillot; Cass com, 27 January 1998, Bull civ IV, n° 41, 31; Banque et droit, mars-avril 1998, n° 58, 31, obs de H Vauplane; Cass com, 8 July 2003 (aff Vantrou), Dr sociétés, janvier 2004, n° 13, note Th Bonneau; Cass Com 1 October 2013, pourvoi n° P 12-24 118, arrêt n° 885 F-D, *Baudesson v Société Générale*; Cass Com 13 May 2014, arrêt n° 489 FS-P+B, pourvoi n° S 09-13.805, *Talibi and alii v société Dubus.*

[26] See A-C Muller, 'Dernières décisions relatives à la responsabilité des professionnels' (mars-avril 2010) *Rev dr bancaire et financier*, com n° 74, esp 76.

[27] Cass Com 19 September 2006, case *Bénéfic*; Cass Com 15 février 2011, case *Bénéfic*, arrêt n° 124 F-D, pourvoi n° B 10-12.185, *Bru v La Banque Postale*; see Moulin, 'Responsabilité des banques en matière de commercialisation de produits financiers' (n 19) esp n° 25. See also Cass Com 30 November 2010, arrêt n° 1203 F-P+B, *Société Farrucci constructions v Société JP Morgan and other*; Bull Joly bourse March 2011, § 89, 185, obs I Riassetto; in this decision, the Court underlined that the subscription for units of a real estate investment company (*société civile de placements immobilier*, SCPI) was not a speculative operation.

According to a commentator,[28] the notion of speculative operation is based on the idea of risk: the operation is speculative if the risk is higher than the amount invested in the financial product.

Consumer clients as well as commercial clients can be considered as casual investors or as properly informed investors. The distinction made by the French Supreme Court only depends on client's knowledge and awareness, whatever its category, natural person or legal entity. In a decision handed down by the French Supreme Court on 30 September 2010,[29] the client was a company and qualified as a casual investor benefiting from the duty to warn.

To know whether clients are or not properly informed is not so easy. Some elements like the profession can be taken into consideration. The courts can only regard a client as a properly informed investor if he or she is sufficiently informed and experienced to be capable of assessing the profits and risks of the financial product.

The burden of proof lies with financial institutions. They have to assess the client's aptitudes and situation in order to determine whether the client is a casual investor or a properly informed investor. At the same time, they have to keep any evidence of this assessment, as they have to keep any evidence of the performance of their duty to warn if the client is a casual client.

The duty to warn laid down by legislation dates from the Ordinance n° 2007-544 of 12 April 2007: this text is currently Article L 533-13, of the Monetary and Financial code. This text was rewritten by Ordinance n° 2016-827 of 23 June 2016,[30] which will enter into force on 3 January 2018.[31]

Article L 533-13, in its current version as well as in its future version, does not lay down the duty to warn for all the investment services. There is not, indeed, such a duty in case of investment advice and portfolio management. For these services, financial institutions have only to be able to make recommendations: pointing the client towards the investment services or financial instruments that are suitable for them. By contrast, as far as the other services are concerned, financial institutions have to assess whether the investment services or products that are recommended are appropriate for the client, and to give a warning if the service or the product is not appropriate.

This warning has to be issued for all retail and professional clients. Only eligible counterparties are not concerned by this duty.

The text does not distinguish between casual investors and properly informed investors. In addition, it does not address speculative operations differently from ordinary operations. The notion of speculative operations is not a criterion that would trigger the duty to warn.

[28] Muller, 'Dernières décisions relatives à la responsabilité des professionnels' (n 26).

[29] Arrêt n° 1203 F-P+B, *Société Farrucci constructions* (n 27).

[30] Ordonnance n° 2016-827 du 23 juin 2016 relative aux marchés d'instruments financiers.

[31] ibid, Art 28.

The duty to warn laid down in Article L 533-13 of the Monetary and Financial code seems to be the main obligation: one might even think that it should be the sole obligation. This opinion is based on the fact that the legal text implements Article 19 of the Directive of 21 April 2004[32] and does not allow the Member States to keep the previous framework. However, this opinion is debatable and some commentators point out that the legal text does not mean the end of the duty to warn as a judiciary creation.[33] If one thinks, like these commentators, that the judicial duty to warn is still legal because it concerns matters that are not covered by the European text, it seems that this duty should remain in force after the Directive and the Regulation of 15 May 2014, commonly called MiFID II[34] and MiFIR[35,36] whose provisions were implemented by the Ordinance of 23 June 2016.

B. Credits and Ancillary Services

The duty to warn the debtor and the guarantor against the risk resulting from their financial debt is a judicial creation of the French Supreme Court. In the ruling handed down on 27 June 1995, the Court even referred to the duty to advise clients. However, the notion of advice is different from the concept of warning. In the decisions handed down subsequently, the Court only mentions the duty to warn; it has not mentioned again the duty to advise.[37]

The duty to warn only imposes on credit institutions a duty to check the clients' financial situation and to warn them if the credit seems disproportionate to this situation.[38] Clients must be warned only if there is an excessive risk. Once this

[32] Directive 2004/39/EC of the European Parliament and of the Council of 21 April 2004 on markets in financial instruments amending Council directive 85/611/EEC and 93/6/EEC and Directive 2000/12/EC of the European Parliament and of the Council and repealing Council Directive 93/22/EEC, OJ L 145, 30 April 2004.

[33] See Th Bonneau, *Droit bancaire*, 11° éd (Paris: LGJD, 2016) n° 947; J-J Daigre, 'L'obligation prétorienne de mise en garde a-t-elle vocation à survivre ?' (2009) 4 *RTDF* 108; I Tchotourian, 'La loyauté à travers la contrainte de la transparence: retour sur les évolutions jurisprudentielles de la responsabilité bancaire en matière d'investissements boursiers' (mars-avril 2011) 116 *Actes pratiques et ingénierie sociétaire* 25; M Cohen-Branche, note sous Com, 22 mars 2011, Bull Joly bourse juillet-août 2011 § 209, 435, esp 436.

[34] OJ L 173/349, 12 June 2014.

[35] OJ L 173/84, 12 June 2014.

[36] Directive 2014/65/EU of the European Parliament and of the Council of 15 May 2014 on markets in financial instruments and amending Directive 2002/92/EC and directive 2011/61/EU (recast), OJ L 173, 15 May 2014; Regulation (EU) n° 600/2014 of the European Parliament and of the Council of 15 May 2014 on markets in financial instruments and amending Regulation (EU) n° 648/2012, OJ L 173, 15 May 2014.

[37] Cass com, 24 September 2003 (aff Hélias), Bull civ IV, n° 137, 157; Banque et droit n° 93, janvier-février 2004 57, obs Th Bonneau; Rev trim dr com 2004. 142, obs D Legeais Cass civ 1re, 8 juin 2004, Bull civ I, n° 166, 138; Banque et droit n° 98, novembre-décembre 2004 56, obs Th Bonneau; D 2004, act jurisp 1897; Rev dr bancaire et financier n° 4, juillet-août 2004 245, obs F-J Crédot et Y Gérard; Rev trim dr com 2004. 581, obs D Legeais; JCP 2004, éd E, 1442, note D Legeais.

[38] See Bonneau, *Droit bancaire* (n 33) n° 907.

warning is carried out and despite the risk, the credit may be granted. If there is no excessive risk, banks do not have to warn the client.[39]

The duty to warn does not benefit all clients. Only unwary clients are covered by the duty. It is ruled out if clients are sophisticated.[40] Consumer clients as well as commercial clients can be considered as unwary clients or as sophisticated clients. The distinction made by the French Supreme Court depends only on the client's knowledge and awareness, whatever its legal nature, natural person or legal entity. The distinction is not so easy to implement. Some factors like the profession can be taken into consideration. The courts can only regard a client as a sophisticated client if he or she is sufficiently informed and experienced to be capable of assessing the risks resulting from the credit.

In line with the Consumer Code, the provisions of which take into account the Consumer Directive of 23 April 2008,[41] and which was reformed in 2016,[42] banks have many obligations whose infringement is source of civil liability. For instance, banks are to blame if they do not explain sufficiently why the credit offered is appropriate to the client's situation.[43] They are also to blame if they do not check clients' credit-worthiness[44] or if they do not draw the client's attention to the main features of credit offered and on the potential consequences of that credit on the client's situation.[45]

This legislation only benefits natural persons acting for purposes which are outside their trade, business or profession. On the other hand, it does not matter that clients are unwary or sophisticated. All are protected by the consumer legislation.

[39] Com, 7 July 2009, Banque et droit, n° 127, septembre-octobre 2009 26, obs Th Bonneau; JCP 2009, éd E, 1948, note D Legeais et 2010, éd E, 1496, n° 14, obs N Mathey; Rev trim dr com 2009 795, obs D Legeais; D 2009, p 2318, note J Lasserre Capdeville; Cass civ 1re, 19 November 2009, Banque et droit n° 129, janvier-février 2010 21, obs Th Bonneau; JCP 2009, éd E, 2140, note D Legeais; Rev dr bancaire et financier janvier-février 2010 38, obs D Legeais et mars-avril 2010 46, obs F-J Crédot et Th Samin; Cass com, 30 November 2010, Banque et droit n° 135, janvier-février 2011 33, obs Th Bonneau; Cass com, 2 October 2012, Banque et droit, n° 146, novembre-décembre 2012. 29, obs Th Bonneau; Cass com, 12 mars 2013, arrêt n° 233 F-D, pourvoi n° E 10-30335; Cass com. 29 avril 2004, arrêt n° 397 F-D, pourvoi n° F 13-15.789; Cass civ 1, 4 June 2014, arrêt n° 668 F-P+B, pourvoi n° Y 13-10.975; Cass com 23 September 2014, arrêt n° 830 F-D, pourvoi n° Y 13-22.475; Cass civ 1, 13 November 2014, arrêt n° 1345 F-D, pourvoi n° A 13-26.295; Cass com 13 January 2015, arrêt n° 20 F-D, pourvoi n° H 13-24.875, *Société Générale v Gourgeau*.

[40] Cass civ 1re, 12 July 2005, Bull civ I, n° 324, 325, 326 et 327, 268 et seq; Banque et droit n° 104, novembre-décembre 2005 80, obs Th Bonneau; D 2005, act jurisp 2276, obs X Delpech; JCP 2005, éd E, 1359, note Legeais et éd G, II, 10140, note A Gourio; Rev dr bancaire et financier n° 6, novembre-décembre 2005 n° 203, note F-J Crédot et Y Gérard; Rev trim dr com 2005 820, obs D Legeais; D 2006, pan 167, obs D- Martin; Cass civ 1re, 2 novembre 2005, Banque et droit, mai-juin 2006, obs Th Bonneau.

[41] Directive 2008/48/EC of the European Parliament and of the Council of 23 April 2008 on credit agreements for consumers and repealing Council Directive 87/102/EEC, OJ L 133/66, 22 May 2008.

[42] Ordonnance n° 2016-301 du 14 mars 2016 relative à la partie législative du Code de la consommation.

[43] Consumer Code, Art L 312-14 (former L 311-8).

[44] Consumer Code, Art L 312-16 (former L 311-9).

[45] Consumer Code, Art L 312-14 (former L 311-8).

In addition, a bank that proposes an insurance policy to the client to whom it gives a loan must enlighten the client about the adequacy of the cover for his or her personal situation. This duty is a judicial creation of the French Supreme Court. The decision handed down on 2 March 2007[46] is important because, according to the Court,[47] the fact of giving the information notice in accordance with the legislation is not sufficient to be compliant with this duty.

V. The Impact of the Regulatory Framework on a Bank's Duty of Care

A. Financial Products and Investment Services

French texts require financial participants to cover their positions on financial markets. This obligation is a condition to be satisfied before any performance of orders by professionals. After this execution, financial institutions have to require complementary margins if the changes on the markets are not in favour of clients.

Monitoring of margin requirements brings up several questions.

Are clients authorised to take advantage of the infringement of texts obliging professionals to call their clients for covering their positions?

For a long time, the answer was negative.[48] However, in its decision handed down on 26 February 2008,[49] the French Supreme Court revisited this rule. Since

[46] See section II.B.ii.

[47] See also in the same direction: Cass civ 2e, 20 March 2008, Banque et droit n° 120 juillet-août 2008 17, obs Th Bonneau; Cass civ 2e, 2 October 2008 (2 arrêts), Banque et droit n° 122, novembre-décembre 2008 22, obs Th Bonneau; JCP 2008, éd E, 2425, note D Legeais; Civ 1re, 22 January 2009, Banque et droit n° 125, mai-juin 2009 24, obs Th Bonneau; Cass civ 2e, 3 September 2009 et Cass com, 22 September 2009, Banque et droit n° 128, novembre-décembre 2009 39, obs Th Bonneau; Cass civ 2e, 13 January 2011, Banque et droit n° 136 mars-avril 2011 27, obs Th Bonneau; Cass com, 13 September 2011, Banque et droit n° 140, novembre-décembre 2011 20, obs Th Bonneau; Cass com 16 September 2014, arrêt n° 702 F-D, pourvoi n° V 13-19.459, *Caise de crédit mutuel d'Avranches v Jouenne*. Adde, G Courtieu, 'Assurance des emprunteurs: la Cour suprême met les banques en demeure' (avril 2007) *Responsabilité civile et assurances*, Étude 8; J-M Moulin, 'Les obligations d'information et de conseil du banquier souscripteur d'une assurance groupe (à propos de Cass civ 1re, 12 janvier 1999 et 23 novembre 1999)' (janvier/février 2000) 1 *Rev dr bancaire et financier* 50; I Rivière, 'L'obligation d'information et de conseil du banquier souscripteur en assurance de groupe' (22 juin 2001) 124 *Les Petites Affiches* 4; D Legeais, 'Les obligations et la responsabilité d'un banquier souscripteur d'une assurance de groupe' (septembre-octobre 2001) 5 *Rev dr bancaire et financier* 316; S Gossou, 'La distribution de l'assurance par les banques' *Thèse Poitiers* dact 2005, sous la direction du Professeur C Ophele, n° 364; F Sauvage, 'Le devoir d'information et de conseil du banquier intermédiaire en assurance emprunteurs (à propos de Cass Ass plén, 2 mars 2007)' (mai-juin 2007) *Rev dr bancaire et financier* 57; N Dupont, 'Retour sur le devoir de conseil du banquier en matière d'assurance de groupe' (2009) *JCP* 511.

[48] See Th Bonneau and F Drummond, *Droit des marchés financiers*, 3° éd (Paris: Economica 2010) n° 909.

[49] See section II.A.iii.

then, it has regularly recalled that financial institutions are to blame if they do not call their clients for the margins required by texts. For example, in two decisions handed down on 5 April 2010,[50] the Court decided that the professional, having the duty to ensure that the obligation to cover the operation carried out on behalf of clients is fulfilled, must call for a complementary coverage, whatever the origin of this shortfall[51]

If professionals are sanctioned when they do not call for the margins laid down in the texts, they are also liable when they require an amount of margins that is not proportionate to the risks linked to the variability of financial markets. This solution results from a decision dated 18 May 2010.[52]

When clients have to cover their positions and they do not cover them despite the call from the professionals, the professionals have to close out the clients' position even without a client's liquidation order and notwithstanding any contrary order. If they do not liquidate, they are liable for the damages borne by their clients.[53] This solution implies that the texts lay down the obligation for professionals to close out the client's position when clients do not cover their positions. Otherwise, the professionals are not liable.

Clients may have assets held by their financial institutions irrespective of the debit positions to cover. Therefore the latter might be tempted to sell these assets if the clients do not deliberately cover the debit positions or do not respond to its call. This sale is authorised only if the agreement concluded between the parties authorise the financial institution to sell, at any moment and at its initiative, clients' assets in order to cover the debit positions. If not, the professional is liable.[54]

Many texts—legal texts and AMF general regulations—impose on professionals a duty to provide detailed information to the client ('informed consent'). If financial institutions fail to give the pieces of information laid down in texts, they infringe the rules applicable to them and are ordered to repair the damage borne by clients.

The Monetary and Financial Code provides information especially in its Article L 533-12.[55] According to the text (in its current version and whose provisions were

[50] Cass Com 5 April 2011, arrêt n° 353 F-D, pourvoi n° W 10-14.917, *de Nicolay v Société Banque Transatlantique*; Cass Com 5 avril 2011, arrêt n° 352 F-D, pourvoi n° V 10-14.916, *société Camboun Finance v Société Banque Transatlantique*.

[51] See also Cass Com 13 October 2009, Droit des sociétés February 2010, n° 31, obs Th Bonneau; Cass Com 13 September 2011, arrêt n° 819 F-S, pourvoi n° T 10.19 008, *Ueberschlag v Caisse de crédit mutuel de Hagenthal-Neuwiller*.

[52] Cass Com 18 May 2010, arrêt n° 525 F-D, pourvoi n° Y 09-67.102, *Epoux Bernard v Société Fimatex*.

[53] Cass Com 13 October 2009 (n 51); Cass Com 9 July 2013, arrêt n° 742 F-D, pourvoi n° A 12-21 415, *Couturier v Société Aurel BGC*; Cass Com 9 July 2013, arrêt n° 741 F-D, pourvoi n° P 12-20 691, *Catalan v Société Dubus*; see also Cass Com 7 April 2010, arrêt n° 406 F-D, pourvoi n° C 09-14.022, *Jaeger v société Banque CIC*; Cass 14 December 2010, arrêt n° 1303 F-D, pourvoi n° P 09-72.521, *Couturier v Société Aurel BGC*.

[54] Cass Com 25 September 2012, arrêt n° 913 F-D, pourvoi n° W 11-22.143, *Devaux v BNP Paribas*.

[55] See Cass Com 15 February 2011, arrêt n° 124 F-D, pourvoi n° B 10-12 185, *Bru v société La Banque postale*.

reproduced and complemented in the new version resulting from the Ordinance of 23 June 2016):

> I—All the information, including communications of a promotional nature, that is sent to clients, including potential clients, by an investment service provider, shall have a content which is accurate, clear and not misleading. Communications of a promotional nature shall be clearly identifiable as such.
>
> II—Investment service providers shall communicate to their clients, including their potential clients, information that enables them to have a reasonable understanding of the nature of the investment service, and the specific type of financial instrument proposed, as well as the risks associated therewith, thus enabling them to make their investment decisions in full knowledge of the facts.

There are many texts, in the AMF general regulations, concerning information.

Some of them lay down some general rules. Article 314-11 is an example. According to the text,

> The information shall include the name of the investment services provider.
>
> It shall be accurate and in particular shall not emphasise any potential benefits of an investment service or financial instrument without also giving a fair and prominent indication of any relevant risks.
>
> It shall be sufficient for, and presented in a way that is likely to be understood by, an average investor in the category at which it addressed or by which it is likely to be received.
>
> It shall not disguise, diminish or obscure important items, statements or warnings.

Another example is Article 314-18:

> Appropriate information presented in an understandable form shall be addressed to clients concerning:
>
> 1° The investment services provider and its services;
> 2° The proposed financial instruments and investment strategies, which must include appropriate guidelines and warnings about the inherent risks of investing in such instruments or of certain investment strategies;
> 3° Execution systems, if appropriate;
> 4° Costs and associated charges.
>
> The purpose of providing this information is to enable clients to understand the nature of the proposed investment service and the specific type of financial instrument, along with the associated risks, and, consequently, to make informed investment decisions. This information may be provided in a standardised format.

Other texts address questions that are common in practice such as those concerning comparisons, as well as past and future performance.

Article 314-12

> Where the information compares investment or ancillary services, financial instruments, or persons providing investment or ancillary services, the following conditions shall be satisfied:
>
> 1° The comparison must be meaningful and presented in a fair and balanced way.

2° The sources of the information used for the comparison must be specified.
3° The key facts and assumptions used to make the comparison must be included.

Article 314-13

Where the information contains an indication of past performance of a financial instrument, a financial index or an investment service, the following conditions shall be satisfied:

1° That indication must not be the most prominent feature of the communication.
2° The information must include appropriate performance information which covers the immediately preceding 5 years, or the whole period for which the financial instrument has been offered, the financial index has been established, or the investment service has been provided if less than five years, or such longer period as the investment services provider may decide. In every case that performance information must be based on complete 12-month periods.
3° The reference period and the source of information must be clearly stated.
4° The information must contain a prominent warning that the figures refer to the past and that past performance is not a reliable indicator of future results.
5° Where the indication relies on figures denominated in a currency other than that of the Member State in which the retail client is resident, the currency must be clearly stated, together with a warning that the return may increase or decrease as a result of currency fluctuations.
6° Where the indication is based on gross performance, the effect of commissions, fees or other charges must be disclosed.

Article 314-14

Where the information includes or refers to simulated past performance, it must relate to a financial instrument or a financial index, and the following conditions shall be satisfied:

1° The simulated past performance must be based on the actual past performance of one or more financial instruments or financial indices which are the same as, or underlie, the financial instrument concerned.
2° In respect of the actual past performance referred to in Point 1° of this Article, the conditions set out in Points 1°, 2°, 3°, 5° and 6° of Article 314-13 must be complied with.
3° The information must contain a prominent warning that the figures refer to simulated past performance and that past performance is not a reliable indicator of future performance.

Article 314-15

Where the information contains information on future performance, the following conditions shall be satisfied:

1° The information must not be based on or refer to simulated past performance.
2° It must be based on reasonable assumptions supported by objective data.
3° Where the information is based on gross performance, the effect of commissions, fees or other charges must be disclosed.
4° The information must contain a prominent warning that such forecasts are not a reliable indicator of future performance.

All these texts come from the transposition of MiFID of 21 April 2004. They have amplified the obligations incumbent on financial institutions according to the French Supreme Court. Some recent decisions have underlined that the marketing material must be consistent with the financial product offered to clients and mention, should this happen, the worst characteristics and risks connected to it.[56]

Financial institutions have to conduct an investigation into the financial position of the client. The 'know-your-customer' principle is not new. It was already set out in the previous Article L 533-4 of the Monetary and Financial Code, which was connected to the Directive of 10 May 1993 (Investment Services Directive or ISD), and taken into account by the French Supreme Court. Its role has increased since the MiFID Directive of 21 April 2004 and is given importance in the texts that transposed this directive. This importance has been confirmed by MiFID II.

According to former Article L 533-4, financial institutions have to obtain information from clients about their financial situation, their experience in the field of financial markets and their objectives as regards the services asked. On the basis of this text, the French Supreme Court decided that financial institutions, whatever the contractual relationships with the client, have to inquire about the client's financial situation,[57] to assess the competence of their clients and to provide suitable information.[58] If not, they are at fault and are responsible for damages incurred by the clients.

By the same token, financial institutions are liable if they do not inform their clients about the suitability of financial products with their financial situation and their expectations.[59] In the original case of the decision handed down on 12 January 2010,[60] a credit institution granted a loan secured by a pledge on a saving plan in

[56] Cass Com 19 January 2010, arrêt n° 79 F-D, pourvoi n° N 09-10.027, *Fellah v société Banque postale*; Cass Com 14 December 2010, arrêt n° 1279 F-D, pourvoi n° F10-10.165, *Bertrand v BNP Paribas*; Cass Com 8 March 2011, arrêt n° 211 F-S, pourvoi n° V 10-14.456, *Houlbracq v Société générale*. See also Cass Com 11 February 2014, arrêt n° 195 F-D, pourvoi n° Z 12-26.083, *Bertrand v BNP Paribas*; Cass Com 4 March 2014, arrêt n° 220 F-D, pourvoi n° X 12-35.350, *Bouvier v Société Caixa Bank France*.

[57] Cass Com 12 February 2008, Droit des sociétés July 2008, n° 162, obs Th Bonneau; Cass Com 2 February 2010, arrêt n° 147 F-D, pourvoi n° T 08-20.150, *Gouarec v Société Dubus*; Cass Com 13 May 2014, arrêt n° 489 FS-P+B, pourvoi n° S 09-13.805, *Talibi and alii v société Dubus*.

[58] Cass Com 16 December 2008, First decision, Droit des sociétés May 2009, n° 98, obs Th Bonneau; Cass Com 13 October 2009, Droit des sociétés February 2010, n° 32, obs Th Bonneau; Cass Com 3 May 2011, arrêt n° 436 F-D, pourvoi n° Q 10-14 865, *Soria v société Monte Paschi banque*; Cass Com 15 June 2011, arrêt n° 606 F-D, pourvoi n° J 10-18 517, *Tonfoni v société Lyonnaise de banque*; Cass Com 5 juin 2012, arrêt n° 653 F-D, pourvoi n° N 10-27.536, *Herscovici and other v société Barclays Bank*; Cass Civ 1, 11 September 2013, arrêt n° 915 F-D, pourvoi n° C 12-18.864, *Buzzini v Société Banque CIC Est*, Bull Joly bourse novembre 2013, 529, note J Lasserre-Capdeville; Banque et droit n° 152 novembre-décembre 2013 23, obs J-J Daigre. See also Cass Com 11 March 2014, arrêt n° 246 F-D, pourvoi n° U 13-10.465, *Fellah v La Banque Postale*.

[59] Cass Com 14 December 2010, arrêt n° 1275 F-D, pourvoi n° X 09-17.306, *Greboval v Société Axa banque and other*; Cass Com 4 March 2014, arrêt n° 200 F-D, pourvoi n° Q 12-29.501, *Godard v Banque populaire Val de France*; Cass Com 11 March 2014, arrêt n° 246 F-D, pourvoi n° U 13-10.465, *Fellah v La Banque Postale*.

[60] Cass Com 12 January 2010, arrêt n° 10 F-D, pourvoi n° J 09-11.015, *Cathala v société Banque Chaix*.

shares (*Plan d'épargne en actions, PEA*) invested in parts of collective funds. Due to the losses borne by him, the client took legal proceedings against the bank. The Court of Appeal denied any responsibility on the part of the bank. The French Supreme Court overturned the ruling because the Court of Appeal did not look into whether the bank, which advised the client to subscribe for the financial product, had assessed his family and professional situation.

The burden of proof lies with financial institutions. The French Supreme Court also decided that they have to prove that they have assessed the clients' competence and provided some information based on this assessment.[61]

The 'know-your-customer' principle is also taken into account by existing texts that oblige financial institutions to obtain information from their clients. If the principle is applicable, whatever the investment service provided, French legislation[62] distinguishes, according to MiFID,[63] whose provisions haven been taken over by MiFID II of 15 May 2014,[64] between, on the one hand, investment advice and portfolio management, and on the other hand, other investment services. Regarding the former, financial institutions have to get information concerning clients' knowledge and experience as well as their financial situation and their investment's objectives. Only information about clients' knowledge and experience is required as far as the latter are concerned. All this information must be given by clients in order to assess the appropriateness of the services to their situation (investment advice or portfolio management)[65] or to check (other services)[66] that the service or the financial instrument offered to clients suits them.

Are there hypotheses where financial institutions have to refuse to carry out the client's instructions? The answer is traditionally negative, even when the financial risks are especially high. Financial institutions have, in certain cases, a duty to warn. They do not have to turn down. The answer remains the same currently. I would like to recall that only, according to MiFID, Article L 533-13 of the Monetary and Financial Code lays down the following rule: 'Where the clients, including potential clients, fail to provide the information requested, the service providers shall refrain from recommending financial instruments to them or from providing the third-party portfolio management service on their behalf'. This provision disappeared for the version resulting from the Ordinance of 23 June 2016.

B. Credits and Ancillary Services

Information is a vital means of protection of clients. It can be general or specific. General information is given when professionals want to promote the credits that

61 Cass Com 12 February 2008 (n 57).
62 Monetary and Financial Code, Art L 533-13.
63 MiFID, Art 19(4) and (5).
64 MiFID II, Art 25(2) and (3).
65 See AMF general regulations Art 314-43.
66 AMF general regulations, Art 314-48.

they can offer to their clients. Specific information is connected to the conclusion of contracts. Some pieces of information must be given before the closing of the contract. Other must be included in the contract.

The Consumer Code,[67] the provisions of which take into account the Consumer Directive of 23 April 2008, and which was reformed in 2016,[68] targets any advertising material, whatever it is, in particular on the internet and in email messages. It also addresses the content of advertisements, notably as regards the borrowing rate and the annual percentage rate of charge. All the pieces of information must be mentioned in a clear, concise and prominent way.[69] The following mention is mandatory: a credit is a commitment and must be repaid. Check your creditworthiness before concluding the credit agreement.[70]

In good time before the consumer is bound by any credit agreement or offer, the bank creditor provides the consumer with the information needed to compare different offers in order to take an informed decision on whether to conclude a credit agreement.[71] In addition, if the bank agrees to grant the credit, the borrower may obtain a copy of the credit offer on request.[72] The pre-contractual information is the object of a document that is distinct from other pieces of information connected to the credit offer.[73]

The credit agreement is a document distinct from any advertising material and any pre-contractual information document. At the top of the contract, there is a summary box, which sets out the key features of the credit agreement.[74] Furthermore, the consumer must be informed of any change in the borrowing rate, on paper or another durable medium, before the change becomes applicable.[75]

VI. Liability for Breach of Duty of Care

Two aspects must be addressed. The first is substantive; it is about the amount of compensation and the fault on the part of the customer. The second concerns the way investors may take legal proceedings against financial institutions.

[67] Consumer Code, Art L 311-4, L 311-4-1 and L 311-5.

[68] Ordonnance n° 2016-301 du 14 mars 2016 relative à la partie législative du Code de la consommation.

[69] Consumer Code, Art L 312-6 (former L 311-4).

[70] Consumer Code, Art L 312-8 to L 312-11 (former L 311-5).

[71] Consumer Code, Art L 312-12 (former L 311-6, I).

[72] Consumer Code, Art L 312-13 (former L 311-7).

[73] Consumer Code, Art L 312-13 (former L 311-7).

[74] Consumer Code, Art L 312-28 (former L 311-18) and R 311-5.

[75] Consumer Code, Art L 312-31 (former L 311-21).

A. Full or Partial Compensation

A financial institution that fails to comply with its duties is ordered to pay damages to its clients. This rule is not different from the rule generally applicable. There is no specific rule for the compensation payable by financial institutions because of infringement of their duties.

The main question is about the amount of damages for the loss suffered by clients. The principle of full compensation for the damage suffered is, in this field as in others, applicable.[76]

However, the French Supreme Court[77] considers that the damage resulting from the infringement of the duty to warn and the duty to inform consists of a loss of opportunity; it is the loss of opportunity[78] to invest funds better. This solution is not specific to the financial field. There is the same solution as regards credits as the decision handed down on 20 October 2009[79] demonstrates.

By the same token, according to the Court, the damage resulting from the infringement of the duty to dispense advice on the adequacy of the operation to the client's personal situation consists of a loss of opportunity not to enter into an agreement;[80] according to the Court, the damage resulting from the infringement of the duty to obtain information from clients about their financial situation, their experience in the field of financial markets and their objectives as regards the services requested, consists of the loss of opportunity to escape through a clever investment decision from a risk that eventually materialised.[81]

This approach does not concern financial institutions' duties alone; this analysis is common. The consequence is important because clients cannot obtain full compensation for their loss; they only can get partial compensation. As the Court pointed it out in its ruling handed down on 15 February 2011,[82] the loss of opportunity is not equivalent to the lost opportunity and cannot equate to a potential gain.

B. Client's Negligence

What is the effect of the client's negligence on his or her compensation? There are two alternatives: either we consider that this fault should be taken into

[76] The full compensation is the rule as regards the culpable order execution: see Cass Com 24 June 2014, arrêt n° 614 F-D, pourvoi n° M 13-17.772, *Bendali v CRCAM Brie Picardie.*

[77] Cass Com 9 November 2010, arrêt n° 1109 F-D, pourvoi n° V 09-69.997, *Campan v Banque de gestion privée Indosuez*; Cass Com 4 February 2014, arrêt n° 153 F-P+B, pourvoi n° Y 13-10.630, *Société Banque privée v Emmanuelli*; Cass Com 9 December 2014, arrêt n° 1083 F-D, pourvoi n° A 13-23.673, *Houiller v société Oddo et compagnie and alii*; Cass Com 31 March 2015, arrêt n° 340 F-D, pourvoi n° J 14-11.012, *Bayle v Caisse d'épargne et de prévoyance d'Auvergne et du Limousin.*

[78] On the theory of loss of chance, see Couret, Goutay and Zabala (n 1) esp n° 3 121.

[79] See section II.B.iii.

[80] Cass Com 15 February 2011, arrêt n° 123 F-D, pourvoi n° Z 09-16.779, *Caisse régionale de crédit agricole mutuel Sud Rhône-Alpes v Bergeron.*

[81] Cass Com 12 June 2012, arrêt n° 664 F-D, pourvoi n° W 11-20.303, *Robin v Société Crédit du Nord.*

[82] Cass Com 15 February 2011 (n 80).

consideration with the result that the compensation is only partial or we decide that the fault is irrelevant so that the client has the right to full compensation.

The first position implies that the fault on the part of the client is seen as one of the causes of the damage and this cause must be taken into consideration together with the financial institution's negligence.[83] If so, we consider that the damage results from several causes and that the financial institution is not the only one to blame. Therefore the client must bear responsibility for a part of the damage and their compensation may only be partial.

According to the second approach,[84] the client's negligence is unimportant and cannot be considered as a cause for the damage because his or her error would not have occurred without the error by the financial institution. Consequently, only the latter is relevant; the former is irrelevant. It implies that the sole person responsible for the damage is the financial institution and that the client may get a full compensation for the losses suffered.

The question about the effect of the client's negligence is raised as an answer to the financial intermediary's claim. More often than not, the client's fault is taken into consideration together with the financial institution's negligence.[85] However, it is not systematic.

It is common that clients, who perform operations on financial markets, cover their positions too late or do not answer the professional's claims. Afterwards, the financial intermediary decides to liquidate the client's position and takes legal proceedings against their client to procure payment of the debit position. In response, the client claims that the professional infringed their professional obligation to liquidate his or her debit position in time and wants to recover compensation for the prejudice suffered.

For the French Supreme Court, the client has the right to full compensation. According to the Court, the client's negligence is unimportant because professionals must close out the client's position even without a client's liquidation order and despite any contrary order. This solution results from the decision handed down on 26 June 2012: it has been confirmed by other decisions.[86]

Several commentators[87] have criticised the decisions because the client must cover, according to the law, all their positions so that the first fault is attributable to them. Consequently, even if the professional is to blame because of the infringement of their duties, it is not fair to consider them as solely responsible for the damage suffered by the client.

[83] On the doctrine of equivalent causes, see Couret, Goutay and Zabala (n 1) esp n° 3 110.

[84] On the doctrine of adequate causation, see Couret, Goutay and Zabala (n 1) esp n° 3 110.

[85] See eg Cass Com 4 November 2014, arrêt n° 971 F-P+B, pourvoi n° U 13-24.196, *Moufounda v société Lyonnaise de banque*.

[86] Cass Com 26 March 2013, arrêt n° 293 F-P+B, *Lanes v Société Dubus*, Bull Joly Bourse juin 2013 § 104, 285, note L Ruet; Droit des sociétés juin 2013, com n° 107, note S Torck; Banque et droit n° 149 mai-juin 2013 3, obs J-J Daigre and J-P Bornet; *Revue Banque* n° 763 septembre 2013. 79, obs J-L Guillot and P-Y Bérard; RTDF n° 3-2013 108, obs A-C Rouaud; Cass Com 11 June 2013, arrêt n° 597 F-D. pourvois n° N 12-12 180 and Q 12-18 507, *Société CIC v Jeager*.

[87] See Bonneau, Torck as well as Daigre and Bornet.

C. Individual Action, Representative Action and Class Action

Investors may take legal proceedings against financial institutions on their own. They may also mandate an association in order to get compensation for individual damage. This kind of action is a representative action and not a class action. Such an action has been recently introduced in French legislation. However, the question whether investors may benefit from this action is controversial.

The representative action[88] is strictly regulated. There are several categories of conditions. Some of them concern associations authorised to perform such actions—in particular, their explicit purpose must be the defence of investors—and one category consists of approved associations.[89] Other conditions concern the performance of the representative action. First, investors must have suffered individual damage having a common origin through the actions of the same entity. Secondly, the association has to be instructed by at least two investors:[90] according to Article L 452-2:

> The power so to act cannot be solicited via a public appeal on television or radio, nor via a poster campaign, leaflets or personalised letters. It must be given in writing by each investor.
>
> However, if an association approved according to the third paragraph of Article L 452-1 brings an action for damages before the civil or commercial courts, the presiding judge of the regional court or the Commercial Court, as applicable, may issue a summary order authorising it to seek a power of attorney from the shareholders empowering it to act on their behalf and, at its own expense, to have recourse to the means of publication referred to in the previous paragraph.

This set of provisions explains that the representative action is not frequently used and that it would be better if the French legislation encompassed legislation about class actions.

Such a class action has been introduced by the law n° 2014-344 of 17 March 2014 concerning the Consumer Code.[91] This action, which is reserved for the compensation of individual losses suffered by consumers and resulting from the infringement of professional duties, is a genuine class action because an association may carry it out without a mandate from consumers; as observed, the system

[88] Monetary and Financial Code, Art L 452-2.
[89] Monetary and Financial Code, Art L 452-1.
[90] Monetary and Financial Code, Art L 452-2.
[91] Law of 17 March 2014, Art 1; Consumer Code, Art L 423-1 et seq. See D Roskis and S Jaffar, 'L'introduction de l'action de groupe à la française' (juillet-août 2013) n° 4 *cahiers de droit de l'entreprise*, 22; D Mainguy and M Depincé, 'L'introduction de l'action de groupe en droit français' (2014) *JCP* éd E, 1144; M Bacache, 'Introduction de l'action de groupe en droit français. A propos de la loi n° 2014-344 du 17 mars 2014' (2014) *JCP* éd G, 377; V 'Rebeyrol, La nouvelle action de groupe' (2014) *D* 941; N Molfessis, 'L'exorbitance de l'action de groupe à la française' (2014) *D* 947; E Jouffin, 'Les actions de groupe à la française: un rendez-vous manqué?' (mai-juin 2014) n° 155 *Banque et droit* 3; J-J Daigre, 'Quelques observations sur l'action de groupe dans le secteur bancaire et financier' (Novembre 2014) *Banque et droit—Hors série* 46.

chosen by the French lawmaker is the 'opt in' and not the 'opt out' system and the action is only possible in order to get compensation for material damage; it is not authorised for non-pecuniary harm. These conditions show clearly that the class action is strictly regulated. The objective is to avoid excess, as may exist in some countries.[92]

We should underline that only consumer associations are authorised to carry out such an action. The main consequence is, according to some authors,[93] that class actions only concern the consumer field; class actions are not authorised to recover compensation for financial damage. However, for other people,[94] a class action is open for financial damage resulting from the infringement of professional duties. Their position seems to be based on the fact that the definition of the consumer in the law is wide and may include [professional?] investors.[95]

D. Limitation and Exclusion of Liability

There is no specific rule in the Monetary and Financial Code and the AMF general regulations.[96] Therefore the validity of clauses that limit financial institutions' liability is subject to common rules. The French Supreme Court makes a distinction between two categories of clauses: the clauses that rule out any responsibility and the exemption clauses.[97]

According to clauses of the first category, financial institutions are not responsible and cannot be ordered to pay damages in case of infringement of any of their duties. These disclaimers are valid except in the event of intent or gross negligence. The French Supreme Court decides that there is such negligence when the breach is about an essential contractual obligation.[98]

The second category of clauses encompasses the clauses that suppose the evidence of the contractual fault and set out the maximum amount of damages. This kind of clause is valid except in the event of a breach of an essential contractual obligation or a breach of an essential contractual condition.[99]

[92] R Hammadi and A Le Loch, *Rapport au nom de la commission des affaires économiques sur le projet de loi relatif à la consommation*, rapport n° 1156, 13 Juin 2013, esp 58.

[93] ibid, 57.

[94] G Rameix, 'Lettre à Monsieur le Président de la République', *Rapport annuel AMF pour 2012*, esp 5; V Magnier, 'Droit boursier et financier' (16 mai 2013) 136, *Gazette du Palais* 21; D Mainguy and M Depincé, 'L'introduction de l'action de groupe en droit français' (2014) n° 6 *JCP*, éd E, 1144.

[95] Preliminary article, Consumer Code: for the present code, any natural person acting for purposes, which may be regarded as being outside his professional capacity, is considered as a consumer.

[96] On limitation and exclusion of liability, see also Couret, Goutay and Zabala (n 1) esp n° 3 132 et seq.

[97] See F Terré, Ph Simler and Y Lequette, *Droit civil, Les obligations*, 10° éd (Paris: Dalloz, 2009) n° 612 et seq.

[98] ibid, n° 615.

[99] ibid, n° 615.

Therefore the main question is about the notion of essential contractual obligation. In our opinion, we may consider such obligations as the duty to assess, to inform and to warn the clients. Consequently, in the event of breaches of such duties, the court should rule out all the clauses that would limit the financial institutions' liability. However, to our knowledge, there is no judicial decision that bears out this point.

However, under MIFID II, this approach seems vital. Indeed, according to the end of its Article 69,

> Member States shall ensure that mechanisms are in place to ensure that compensation may be paid or other remedial action be taken in accordance with national law for any financial loss or damage suffered as a result of an infringement of this Directive or of Regulation (EU) n° 600/2014.

The fact of considering that duties laid down in EU law constitute essential contractual obligations will be a means of enabling France to be compliant to this provision.

VII. Acting on Behalf of Clients versus Dealing on own Account

When professionals act on behalf of clients and provide them with services, they are subject to some obligations in order to protect their clients. However, in some circumstances, if clients are in relation with professionals, the latter would seem to be dealing on their own account. Therefore the question is whether one can consider that they act only on their own behalf or if they also act on behalf of clients.

The question is not easy because it implies knowing if, beyond a deal on their own account, professionals provide a service for their clients. According to some rulings[100] the criterion consists of a client's order. If there is such an order, professionals clearly act on behalf of clients and the fact that professionals also act on their own behalf has no consequence for their duties. By contrast, if there is no order from a client, one might consider that professionals only act on their own account with the result that they do not have any obligations vis-à-vis parties with whom they have concluded an agreement.

[100] See CE, 13 July 2006, n° 259231 and n° 259232, Case *Dokhan*, Banque et droit n° 109, septembre-octobre 2006, obs H de Vauplane, J-J Daigre, B de Saint-Mars et J-P Bornet; AMF, Commission des sanctions, 4 September 2008, *Banque d'Orsay et others*, Banque et droit n° 122, novembre-décembre 2008, obs H de Vauplane, J-J Daigre, B de Saint-Mars et J-P Bornet; CA Paris, pôle 5, chambre 6, répertoire général: 11/19539, *SARL Société minière Georges Montagnat (SMGM) v Société Générale*. On this point, see Bonneau and Drummond, *Droit des marchés financiers* (n 48) n° 217-1.

VIII. The Role of the Regulator in Settling Disputes

The French financial regulator—formerly the Commission des opérations de bourse, now the Autorité des marchés financiers—has played an active role in settling disputes between financial institutions and clients since 1991. However, it was only in 2003[101] that the French lawmaker passed a law that has given it legal support. According to Article L 621-19 of the Monetary and Financial Code,

> The Autorité des Marchés Financiers is authorised to deal with claims from any interested party relating to matters within its competence and to resolve them appropriately. Where the conditions so permit, it proposes a friendly settlement of the disputes submitted to it, via arbitration or mediation.
>
> A referral to the Autorité des Marchés Financiers seeking extrajudicial settlement of a dispute shall suspend limitation of any civil or administrative action. Said limitation shall resume when the Autorité des Marchés Financiers announces the close of the mediation procedure.
>
> The Autorité des Marchés Financiers cooperates with its foreign counterparts to facilitate the extra-judicial settlement of cross-border disputes.
>
> It may formulate proposals for amendments to the laws and regulations concerning the information provided to the holders of financial instruments and to the public, the markets in financial instruments and in assets referred to in paragraph II of Article 421-1 and the status of the investment service providers. Said report presents, in particular, the changes to the regulatory framework of the European Union applicable to the financial markets and reviews the cooperation with the regulatory authorities of the European Union and of the other Member States.
>
> Each year, it draws up a report to the President of the Republic and to Parliament which is published in the Official Journal of the French Republic.

In addition to this text, there is a Charter[102] that describes the role of the mediator and the mediatory proceeding.

The mediation procedure has several features:[103]

— free of charge;
— confidential: neither the pieces of information communicated during the mediation process nor the parties' names nor the final recommendation can be made public;
— impartial: the ombudsman addresses the files in an independent way;
— fast: the mediation's time period is, in principle, three months from the day on which all the elements of the file haven been communicated to the mediator by the parties;

[101] Law n° 2003-707, 1er August 2003, de sécurité financière.
[102] See *Rapport du médiateur de l'AMF 2012*, annexe 3, 23.
[103] See: Le médiateur de l'AMF on the site www.amf.france.org.

- non-mandatory: the ombudsman hands down a recommendation that the parties are free to turn down;
- assessed as regards all the rules applicable and in equity (fair, equal and equitable treatment).

In 2012,[104] there were 747 requests for mediation; in 2013,[105] there were 907 requests for mediation; in 2014,[106] there were 1,001 requests for mediation; and in 2015, there were 1,406 requests for mediation.[107] In 2012, there was a mass claim that concerned 143 investors who accused 20 financial institutions of breaching their duty to inform them about the acquisition of a listed company's shares and which had then since been subjected to collective insolvency proceedings: investors lost all the value of their investment.[108] The subjects of the other files concerned: the commercialisation of financial instruments that were not adequate for the situation and objectives of clients; the time required for the transfer of securities accounts; the bad execution of orders on the financial markets; the investors' misunderstanding after the dissolution of UCITS and some difficulties in line with portfolio management; and investors claiming that their portfolio was not managed in their best interests.[109] In 2013,[110] some new items, such as trading of warrants and certificates, smartphone applications and structures funds, were addressed by the mediator. In 2014,[111] many difficulties with the Forex and trading binary options were handled.

The role of the financial authority as a mediator is specific to AMF. The French banking authority, l'Autorité de contrôle prudentiel et de résolution (ACPR), which is competent for credits and insurance does not play such a role. However, on the other hand, credit institutions have to appoint one or several mediators with to the assignment of making recommendations concerning the disputes with clients defined as natural persons acting for purposes that are outside their trade, business or profession.[112] On the other hand, there is a public body, le comité de la médiation bancaire, which is responsible for supervising the way credit institutions carry out the mediation.[113]

[104] Rapport du médiateur de l'AMF 2012, 4.
[105] Rapport du médiateur de l'AMF 2013, 5.
[106] Rapport du médiateur de l'AMF 2014, 5.
[107] Rapport du médiateur de l'AMF 2015 11.
[108] Rapport du médiateur de l'AMF 2012, 4. On this case, see also Rapport du médiateur de l'AMF 2013, 12.
[109] Rapport du médiateur de l'AMF 2012, 4.
[110] Rapport du médiateur de l'AMF 2013, 13.
[111] Rapport du médiateur de l'AMF 2014, 14.
[112] Monetary and Financial Code, Art L 316-1.
[113] Monetary and Financial Code, Art L 615-2. On 'le comité de la médiation bancaire', see Comité consultatif du secteur financier (CCSF), Rapport pour 2013, 85. See also Rapport d'activité 2014 de la médiation du crédit, mars 2015.

IX. Concluding Remarks

In conclusion, the tendency, in French legislation and case-law, is to increase all the duties imposed on financial institutions. Therefore the level of the client's protection has been increasing over time. This is true for financial products as well as banking products. The distinction concerning the categories of products is vital because the same legal framework does not cover financial and banking products. However, the distinction must be put into perspective because the objective is the same—the client's protection—and duties are similar. Professionals have to know their clients, to inform them and warn them if needs be. This fact is not surprising because more and more provisions derive from the EU law.

EU law is effective in France. One could have some reservations because the French Supreme Court created some obligations that are still applicable and which seem to go further than MiFID. The duty to inform the client about the risks incurred owing to speculative financial operations on futures markets is the striking example. However, this special duty does not prevent the judges from applying the EU legislation in a way that is compliant with EU objectives and there is no obstacle that prevents the client's protection, as required under EU law, from being effective. One might think that this point should be confirmed under MiFID II.

The same observation is true as regards the Consumer Directive of 23 April 2008, whose provisions may be interpreted on request of the French judge: the decision handed down on 18 December 2014[114] is an example because it is partly based on the principle of effectiveness that is explicitly mentioned in Article 69 lid 1, in fine, of MIFID II.

[114] CJEU, 18 December 2014, C-449/13, *CA Consumer Finance SA v Bakkaus*, D 2015, 715, note G Poissonnier; Revue banque février 2015 n° 781, 83, obs P-Y Bérard.

6

Italy

FILIPPO ROSSI AND MARCO GARAVELLI

I. Introduction

In Italy the identification of the content of investment firms' duty of care towards their clients is a topic that, in recent years, has attracted much attention in Courts and by academics. As of 2002–03, a vast number of cases have been brought against investment firms by private investors seeking compensation of damages suffered in connection with the default of some securities issuers.

This flood of lawsuits originated from the dot-com bubble burst of 2001, as well as from the default of the State of Argentina in 2001 and the well-known corporate scandals of Cirio in 2002 and of Parmalat in 2003.

To provide a hint of the magnitude of the phenomenon, one should consider that, on one side, the Argentine scandal alone affected around 450,000 Italian investors[1] and, on the other side, until 2010 in Italy class-actions were not admitted.[2] This, in turn, opened the floodgate of litigation against intermediaries, who were blamed for having breached their duties towards investors. As a consequence of the structure of the Italian financial markets, the majority of such intermediaries were universal banks.

In particular, some banks were accused of having been aware of the serious indebtedness of the relevant issuers well before their customers and for having exploited such information asymmetry in order to place securities they held in

[1] See L Pera, 'Rischio prescrizione? Allora vai col tango' (18 October 2006) *Economy* 65.

[2] The 'class action' governed by para 140-bis of Legislative Decree no 206 of 6 September 2005 (the so-called 'Consumer Code'), introduced by Law of 23 July 2009, no 99, has been, since 1 January 2010, a possible tool with which to seek compensation for the damage suffered in connection with wrongdoings committed after 15 August 2009. This is a procedural tool that can be used against companies to protect (for compensation purposes only) the 'homogeneous rights' of a plurality of consumers or users. In such context, the terms 'consumer' or 'user' mean individuals who act for purposes unrelated to the entrepreneurial, professional, commercial or handicraft activity possibly performed.

their proprietary portfolios to private clients, thus transferring to the latter the insolvency risk of those issuers.[3]

In such a context, starting from the beginning of the 2000s, investors have filed lawsuits allegedly based upon different grounds, claiming (often jointly in the same lawsuit) for the declaration of nullity and voidness of the contract, its annulment for error or fraud, the compensation of damages on a contractual basis and/or in tort.

As we will see below, Italian law—consistent with EU law—provides for quite a detailed set of rules of conduct and of organisational rules that investment firms must comply with in providing investment services to clients, but it does not establish a statutory regime governing the liability of financial intermediaries towards their clients.

As a consequence of this, in the immediate aftermath of the abovementioned state defaults and corporate scandals, the 'early' case-law (the first decisions were issued in 2004) developed different doctrines for identifying the remedies available for the aggrieved customers.

However, examining the first instance decisions issued in the years between 2004 and 2006, it is fairly easy to recognise an attempt by Italian tribunals to find legal solutions which could provide adequate protection to clients' interests, despite the systematic consequences of such rulings on the legal system. This is particularly so with reference to those cases in which the investor appeared to be unsophisticated or in which the investment under dispute involved a material portion of the client's global assets.

This trend has been detected in Italian case-law also by some empirical studies, which focused on decisions regarding alleged breaches of the rules of conduct applicable to the provision of investment services.[4] In particular, research published

[3] See G Ferrarini and P Giudici, 'Financial Scandals and the Role of Private Enforcement: The Parmalat Case' (May 2005) European Corporate Governance Institute (ECGI), Law Working Paper no 40, where the authors summarise this pattern as follows:

> In the recent Italian financial scandals banks have been under attack, in the media and in the courts, for the breach of rules of conduct governing their activity as investment brokers. Allegedly, banks advised their clients to buy Cirio bonds, knowing that the proceeds would be used, as agreed with the issuer, to repay the food group's bank loans. Moreover, many banks advised their clients to buy high interest bonds, such as those issued by Argentina, Cirio or Parmalat, which were not suitable to their clients' portfolios. The public uproar, the activism of consumer associations that fuelled investors' litigation (even though not comparable to US class-action litigation), and investigations carried out by the capital markets supervisor and criminal prosecutors forced the most exposed banks to open settlement discussions with their clients. This situation shows another typical pattern of the Italian (and probably European) enforcement system. When great cases explode, criminal prosecutors step in and investigations end up in the hands of criminal judges. The Ferruzzi case created a huge criminal investigation at the beginning of the 1990s. The Cirio and the Parmalat cases did the same in the new decade. As we have noted, no significant civil litigation lies in the middle of the cyclical explosion of criminal scandals and the ensuing response on the part of the politicians.

[4] See A Perrone and M Musitelli, 'La giurisprudenza milanese sul "risparmio tradito": un'analisi quantitativa' (2014) I *Giur comm* 158 et seq, which focused on decisions issued between 15 January 2007 and 31 December 2009. See also A Perrone, A Voiello and V Dragone, 'La giurisprudenza sul c.d. risparmio tradito: un'analisi quantitativa' in A Perrone (ed), *I soldi degli altri. Servizi di investimento e regole di comportamento degli intermediari* (Milan: Giuffrè, 2008) 83 et seq, which in turn examined decisions issued in the period 2005–06.

in 2014 confirms that a claim brought by an unsophisticated investor has more probability of being upheld: the probability of having such a claim upheld equals to 94.3 per cent, while the probability for a claim by an expert investor to be rejected is 77.8 per cent.[5]

The results of this research are meaningful particularly because they were conducted on the archive of decisions issued by the Sixth Division of the Tribunal of Milan, which is the specialised division of the Tribunal, which, in turn, most probably enjoys the highest familiarity with financial and banking disputes in Italy.

The fact that, in particular in the period 2004–06, the average chances for investors to see their claims upheld by tribunals were probably higher than what would have been correct on a merely technical basis, in turn, encouraged many of them to bring their claims to court.[6]

Finally, in 2007 the United Chambers of the Italian Supreme Court issued an important judgment,[7] setting a clear indication of the nature of intermediaries' liability and, thus, of the remedies available for customers. However, such decision also left several issues unresolved.

Subsequently, several disputes reached appellate courts and, in some cases, the Supreme Court. Therefore, the Supreme Court in recent years has issued decisions concerning some specific issues related to the litigation between banks and investors, such as the quantification of awardable damages or possible contributory negligence on the part of the client.[8]

At the same time, a significant number of new claims have been brought against investment firms. To name just the most widely known cases, the following could be mentioned: (1) various forms of investments which have been negatively affected by the Lehman Brothers default (eg Lehman Brothers' bonds and index-linked policies); (2) unit-linked policies whose internal funds were somehow connected with Madoff-feeder funds; and (3) derivative financial instruments. Furthermore, another litigation trend concerns small and local banks, blamed for having suggested (if not forced) their clients to purchase their own shares or subordinated bonds, often to be pledged as security for loans granted by the same banks, subsequently the value of such shares and bonds dropped, causing damages to such clients.

Still in 2015–16 the attention of the Italian public was drawn to the issue of banks' duty of care because of the default (or at least the serious crisis) of some

[5] Perrone and Musitelli, 'La giurisprudenza milanese sul "risparmio tradito": un'analisi quantitativa' (n 4) 162.

[6] It has also to be taken into account that, generally speaking, alternative dispute resolution (ADR) systems have never had a wide success in Italy; therefore, the litigation over the provision of investment services was concentrated in courts. See section IV below for an outline of the most recent legislative developments in the field of ADR in the financial law sphere.

[7] United Chambers of the Italian Supreme Court, decision no 26724 of 19 December 2007 (*San Paolo IMI v FinCom Valori*).

[8] In this regard, it has to be pointed out that in the Italian legal system the *stare decisis* principle does not apply; nonetheless, the Supreme Court decisions, especially if adopted by its United Chambers, although not binding, do exercise a strong influence on lower courts.

local banks,[9] whose high-risk bonds and shares were placed with uninformed retail customers and often with those who were clients of the same banks for traditional banking services.[10]

This chapter is structured as follows. In section II we will discuss the content and extension of the duties and standards of behaviour imposed by Italian law upon intermediaries while providing investment and non-core services and activities. Section III identifies the consequences deriving from intermediaries' breach of duty of care towards their customers, as well as the remedies available for such customers. Section IV will provide an overview of the alternative dispute resolution schemes implemented in Italy with reference to the disputes between financial intermediaries and their customers. Finally, section V will contain some concluding remarks.

II. Defining Intermediaries' Duty of Care under Italian Law

In Italy the first relevant step towards a 'modern' regulation of financial markets was taken in 1974, with the institution of the Commissione Nazionale per le Società e la Borsa (the Italian securities regulator and supervisory agency: Consob).[11]

In 1991, with the enactment of Law no 1 of 2 January 1991 (the so-called '*Legge SIM*'), the first organic regulation of the provision of investment services was introduced.[12] Law no 1/1991 remained in force until 1996; and it is worth

[9] eg Banca Popolare dell'Etruria e del Lazio, Banca delle Marche, Cassa di Risparmio di Ferrara, CariChieti, Veneto Banca and Banca Popolare di Vicenza.

[10] eg in September 2016 it was ascertained that Banca Popolare di Vicenza put in place a scheme under which clients who turned to the bank for obtaining traditional mortgage loans were forced to purchase also a certain number of the bank's shares. This has led, so far, to the imposition on the bank of a fine of €4.5 million by the Autorità Garante della Concorrenza e del Mercato (the Italian Antitrust Authority), owing to the breach of regulation on unfair commercial practices, but since such shares' value dropped, it is likely that the same facts will cause the clients to bring further litigation against the same bank in court. The decision issued by the Autorità Garante della Concorrenza e del Mercato is available at: www.agcm.it/component/joomdoc/allegati-news/PS10363 _scorr_sanz.pdf/download.html.

[11] Consob was originally established by Legislative Decree of 8 April 1974, no 95 and Law of 7 June 1974, no 216 as a mere branch within the structure of the Ministry of Treasury, to supervise companies listed on the Italian Stock Exchange. However, in 1985 Consob was severed from the governmental structure and provided with full operational independence (Law of 4 June 1985, no 281). A further step in this direction was taken in 1995, when it was decided that the Commission would have been funded not only through a specific allocation from the central governmental budget, but also through fees collected by supervised undertakings. See Art 40 of Law of 23 December 1994, no 724: 'Misure di razionalizzazione della finanza pubblica'. See E Cardi and P Valentino, *L'istituzione CONSOB* (Milan: Giuffrè, 1993); S Cassese, 'La Commissione Nazionale per le Società e la Borsa—Consob e i poteri indipendenti' (1994) I *Riv soc* 412; N Marzona, 'Il regolamento sull'organizzazione e sul funzionamento della CONSOB' (1995) *Giorn dir amm* 522.

[12] See F Annunziata, *Regole di comportamento degli intermediari e riforme dei mercati mobiliari, L'esperienza francese, inglese e italiana* (Milan: Egea, 1993) throughout.

mentioning that some cases decided in recent years by the Supreme Court applied such piece of legislation, whose fundamental guidelines remained in their essence unchanged even after subsequent legislative reforms.

In 1996 Italy implemented the Investment Services Directive, no 93/22/CEE,[13] replacing the *Legge SIM* with Legislative Decree no 415 of 23 July 1996 (the so-called '*Decreto Eurosim*'), which, however—in short—modified the provisions contained in Law no 1/1991 only with reference to mutual recognition of intermediaries and markets among EU Member States.

In the same year the Italian government instituted a commission, headed by Mario Draghi and in which prominent scholars as well as representatives of Consob and the Bank of Italy took part, with the task of drafting a consolidated law on financial markets and investment services regulation. The result of the work of such commission was the Legislative Decree no 58 of 24 February 1998 (the 'Consolidated Law', also known as '*Legge Draghi*').[14]

At present, the Consolidated Law is the main source of law regulating the provision of investment services, having been amended in 2007 in order to implement in Italy the Market in Financial Instruments Directive, no 2004/39/CE[15] (the so-called MiFID Directive), as well as the second level Directive no 2006/73/CE.[16]

The general provisions of the Consolidated Law were at first detailed—as regards the rules of conduct that investment firms have to follow in providing investment services—by Consob regulation no 11522/1998, later replaced—in the MiFID implementation process—by Consob regulation no 16190 of 29 October 2007 ('Consob Regulation 16190').

Both the Consolidated Law and Consob Regulation 16190 strictly reflect the MiFID provisions concerning the rules of conduct applicable to investment firms, consistently with MiFID's objective of maximum harmonisation.

In such context, the content and extent of the duties imposed by Italian law upon intermediaries is provided for by (1) the general contract law principles prescribed by the Italian Civil Code, and (2) the Consolidated Law and its implementing Consob regulations, principally Consob Regulation 16190.

In decision no 17340 of 25 June 2008, the Italian Supreme Court clarified that the rules of the Consolidated Law governing the provision of investment services provide for a 'different and more intense' regime, compared to the

[13] OJ L 141, 11 June 1993, 0027—0046.

[14] On the Consolidated Law, see in general G Alpa and F Capriglione (eds), *Commentario al Testo Unico delle disposizioni in materia di intermediazione finanziaria* (Padua: Cedam, 1998); G Ferrarini and P Marchetti (eds), *La riforma dei mercati finanziari dal decreto Eurosim al testo unico della finanza* (Rome: Bancaria Editrice, 1998); A Patroni Griffi, M Sandulli and V Santoro (eds), *Intermediari finanziari, mercati e società quotate* (Turin: Giappichelli, 1999); G Alpa, 'L'armonizzazione del diritto comunitario dei mercati finanziari nella prospettiva della tutela del consumatore' (2002) II *NGCC* 391.

[15] OJ L 145, 30 April 2004 0001–0044.

[16] OJ L 241, 2 September 2006 26–58.

ordinary one set forth by the Civil Code.[17] With this judgment the Italian Supreme Court further stated that the provisions established by the Consolidated Law have to be construed taking into account their specific purpose, commonly identified in protection of clients and of the integrity of the market. This ruling is important since it makes clear that there is a fundamental difference between the 'common' contract law principles and the relevant 'special' provisions: the former are supposed to apply to relationships between peers; the latter, instead, were issued to regulate relationships in which there is usually a material information asymmetry between the parties (in favour, of course, of the investment firm).

In a subsequent decision (no 1094, 15 April 2009) the Court of Appeal of Milan held that the rules of the Consolidated Law

> represent a specification of the general principle of good faith set by Article 1337 of the Civil Code, in order to raise the standard of fairness of the qualified operator, which has a simplified access to all investment information and data.

Therefore, it is necessary to go through the 'special' rules applicable to the provision of investment services, which the Consolidated Law and the implementing regulations impose in pursuing investors' protection.

The 'general criteria' with which intermediaries must comply are set forth in Article 21 of the Consolidated Law; it states that, 'in providing investment and non-core services and activities', such authorised intermediaries shall:

(a) act diligently, fairly and transparently in the interest of customers and the integrity of the market;
(b) acquire the necessary information from customers and operate in such a way that they are always adequately informed;
(c) use publicity and promotional communications which are correct, clear and not misleading; and
(d) have resources and procedures, including internal control mechanisms, suitable for ensuring the efficient provision of services and activities.

In the following paragraphs we will address those duties in detail.

[17] Many authors underline that the discipline established by the Consolidated Law sets up more pervasive duties compared to those arising from the principle of good faith as provided for in Arts 1175 and 1337 of the Italian Civil Code (see, *ex multis*, G Gobbo, 'comment to art. 21' in F Vella, *Commentario T.U.F.* (Turin: Giappichelli, 2012); F Sartori, *Regole di condotta degli intermediari finanziari. Disciplina e forme di tutela* (Milan: Giuffrè, 2004) 151; A Di Majo, 'La correttezza nell'attività di intermediazione mobiliare' (1993) I *Banca, Borsa, Tit Cred* 292; G Castronovo, 'Il diritto civile della legislazione nuova. La legge sulla intermediazione immobiliare' (1993) *Banca Borsa, Tit Cred* 318; C Gandini, 'La nozione di intermediazione mobiliare' (1992) *Contratto e impresa* 152; F Realmonte, 'Dovere di informazione e responsabilità contrattuale nell'attività di intermediazione mobiliare' (1994) *Banca, Borsa, Tit Cred* 617.

The Court of Appeal of Milan, in a decision of 15 April 2009, stated that the rules of conduct that investment firms must comply with '*add to the discipline established by the Civil Code and cover the entire duration of the contract*'. See also Supreme Court, decision no 3773, 17 February 2009, (2009) *Danno e Resp* 503.

A. The Duty to Act Diligently, Fairly and Transparently in the Interest of Customers and the Integrity of the Market

As stated above, Article 21(a) of the Consolidated Law states that, 'in providing investment and non-core services and activities', authorised intermediaries shall act diligently, fairly and transparently in the interest of customers and of the integrity of the market.[18]

The *duty to act diligently* has to be interpreted in accordance with Article 1176, subsection 2, of the Civil Code, which sets forth the threshold of due care and diligence referring to the care and diligence expected from professionals (ie lawyers, accountants, doctors, consultants, etc). This standard requires a higher level of care, proportionate to the special knowledge of professionals and to the nature of the activity as well as its social implications.

In this perspective, it has also been held that banks, due to the common consideration which provokes clients to rely on their professionalism, must act in accordance with the social expectation of a high standard of care.[19] For this reason, banks are expected (also independently from their specific regulatory duties) to provide clients with all the information that is appropriate under the circumstances; for instance, the Supreme Court has stated that a bank cannot omit (under sanction of liability for damages) to provide certain information to clients only because the latter could easily have access otherwise to the same information by other means, eg through the press.[20]

The *duty to act fairly* refers to the duty to perform the contract in good faith, as provided for in Article 1175 of the Civil Code and, in specific contexts, in Articles 1337, 1366 and 1375 of the Civil Code. Here good faith implies a duty on the contracting parties to behave correctly and loyally.

Finally, intermediaries have *to act transparently*, with a view to overcoming the informational gap existing in the relationship with customers. This concept of 'transparency' has been interpreted extensively, imposing on the intermediary the duty to provide the customer with information which is correct, full and adequate as reasonably possible.[21]

[18] It is commonly observed that the breach of these rules of conduct undermines investors' confidence and their propensity to invest, so leading to unsatisfying allocation of resources: this is the reason why Art 21 of the Consolidated Law expressly requires intermediaries to behave in such a way as to preserve the integrity of the markets (Gobbo, 'comment to art. 21' (n 17)).

[19] See M Franzoni, 'La responsabilità nell'intermediazione finanziaria' (2014) *Danno e resp* 785.

[20] See Supreme Court no 7922, 17 April 2015.

[21] See B Inzitari and V Piccinini, *La tutela del cliente nella negoziazione di strumenti finanziari*, (Padua: Cedam, 2008) 38.

B. The Duty to Acquire Information ('Know your Customer Rule' and 'Know your Merchandise Rule')

Article 21(b) of the Consolidated Law states that, 'in providing investment and non-core services and activities', such authorised intermediaries shall acquire the necessary information from customers and operate in such a way that they are always adequately informed.

As clearly pointed out by the Supreme Court in its decision no 18039 of 19 October 2012,

> the agent has the duty to get information about the customer profile (he should ask him about his experience, financial situation, investment objectives, risk appetite) and to acquire all necessary and appropriate information on the characteristics of any investment proposed to or requested by the customer

The *know your customer rule* is set in Article 39 of Consob Regulation 16190; it states that the intermediaries shall obtain the 'necessary details' from the customer, or potential customer, 'in order to recommend the investment services and financial instruments suited to the customer or potential customer, in the provision of investment consultancy or portfolio management services'. Such details concern:

1. *awareness and experience of the investment sector relevant to the type of financial product or service*: to the extent to which they take into account the customer characteristics, the nature and importance of the service to be provided, and the type of product or transaction concerned, together with the complexity and risks of such service, product or transaction, these details shall include the following elements:
   i. the type of service, transaction and financial instruments with which the customer is familiar;
   ii. the nature, volume and frequency of financial instrument transactions performed by the customer and the period in which such transactions were executed; and
   iii. the level of education, profession or, if relevant, the former profession of the customer;
2. *financial position*, which shall include, where appropriate, data on the source and consistency of the customer's incomes, overall assets and financial commitments;
3. *investment objectives*, which shall include data on the period for which the customer wishes to retain the investment, his preferences in relation to risk, his own risk profile and investment aims, where relevant.[22]

It is further established that intermediaries shall not encourage a customer or potential customer to withhold information required for the purposes of

[22] See also Trib Terni, 10 June 2005; Trib Roma, 8 October 2004; Trib Lecce, 29 October 2004; Trib Firenze, 18 February 2005.

Article 39; in addition, they may rely on the information provided by the customer or potential customer unless such information proves to be 'clearly exaggerated, incorrect or incomplete'.

The Court of Florence (with a decision on 18 April 2006) held that, even where

> the client denies to provide such information, still the financial intermediary has the duty to investigate and obtain, from the size and the type of operations actually carried out by the client, his investments experience and his risk appetite. The further absence of this information points out the client's lack of knowledge of financial instruments, his minimum risk appetite and, consequently, investment objectives oriented to the preservation of invested capital.

In case the client refuses to provide such information, or when the information provided is insufficient, a distinction has to be made depending upon the kind of investment services to be provided to the client.

With reference to investment consultancy or portfolio management services, Article 39, paragraph 6 of Consob Regulation 16190 provides that, when intermediaries are unable to obtain the information concerning the client's financial position and investments objectives, they shall abstain from providing the said services.

This rule does not expressly regulate the case in which the pieces of information lacking are those related to the client's awareness and experience; nonetheless, it has been held that in such a case too a diligent investment firm should abstain from providing investment consultancy or portfolio management services.[23]

With reference to services other than consultancy or portfolio management, Article 41 of Consob Regulation 16190 imposes on intermediaries the duty to request from the customer, or potential customer, information concerning 'his awareness and experience in the investment sector relevant to the type of instrument or service proposed or requested'.

Should such information not be provided, the investment firm shall advise the customer or potential customer that such refusal inhibits any assessment of the appropriateness of the relevant service or financial product. After such warning—usually given in writing[24]—the investment firm may nonetheless carry out the service requested by the client.

There are two main exceptions to the regime described above, namely the case of 'execution-only' services and of professional clients.

[23] See D Spreafico and D Pennati, 'L'adeguatezza e l'appropriatezza' in L Zitiello (ed), *La MiFID in Italia* (Turin: Itaedizioni, 2009) 349.

[24] Italian practice is in line with the remarks expressed in CESR, *Questions and answers on MiFID: Common positions agreed by CESR Members*, Ref CESR/08-266, 11 April 2008 (available at: www.esma.europa.eu/system/files/08_266.pdf), according to which: 'If a client wishes to proceed with a transaction after the client has been given a warning, it is for the investment firm to decide whether to do so, having regard to the circumstances of the case. But in such cases it may be prudent for the investment firm to ask the client or potential client to confirm in a durable medium his intention to proceed with the service'.

In short, Article 43 of Consob Regulation 16190 sets out the condition which shall be satisfied to provide order execution of services on behalf of customers, or the receipt and transmission of orders, 'without the need to obtain information or to perform the assessment' seen above.[25] In case the investment firm is dealing with a 'professional customer', it may presume that it has 'the necessary level of experience and awareness to understand risks relating to the investment service or transactions or type of transaction or instruments according to which the customer was classified as professional' (Article 42 of Consob Regulation 16190).

As far as the *know your merchandise rule* is concerned, it was initially set by Article 26, subsection 1(e) of Regulation 11522/98, which stated the duty of intermediaries to 'acquire a knowledge of own and third-party financial instruments, services and products other than investment services they provide that is adequate in relation to the type of service to be performed'.[26] The same principle is established also by Consob Regulation 16190.

With reference to the *know your merchandise rule*, in some cases Italian courts have deemed that, when a customer claims that she has not been provided with the necessary information related to an investment decision, investment firms should give evidence that the relevant pieces of information were available within the firm

[25] The following are the requirements prescribed by Art 43: (a) the aforementioned services are linked to shares admitted for trading on a regulated market, or equivalent market in another country, money market instruments, bonds or other debt securities (excluding bonds or debt securities with an underlying derivative), harmonised UCITS and other simple financial instruments; (b) the service is provided on the initiative of the customer or potential customer; (c) the customer or potential customer has been clearly informed that, in providing the said service, the intermediary is not obliged to assess appropriateness and therefore that the investor shall not benefit from the protection offered by related measures. Such advice may be provided in a standardised format; (d) the intermediary complies with conflict of interest obligations.

Art 44 states that any financial instrument not mentioned under Art 43(1)(a) shall be considered simple if the following criteria are met: (a) it does not find definition under the terms of Article 1 (1-bis)(c) and (d) of the Consolidated Law, or in the definitions provided by Art 1(2)(d), (e), (f), (g), (h), (i) and (j) of the said Consolidated Law; (b) there are frequent opportunities to sell, redeem or otherwise obtain repayment of such a financial instrument at prices openly available to market operators. Such prices must be those of the market or those made available, or confirmed, by assessment systems other than those adopted by the issuer; (c) no actual or potential liability for the customer is implied which exceeds the cost of purchase of the instrument; and (d) sufficient complete information is openly available and the characteristics are sufficiently simple to understand that the average retail customer may make an informed decision regarding whether or not to execute a transaction in relation to such instrument.

[26] Trib Cuneo, 31 May 2012, which states that the financial intermediary has the duty to acquire all the necessary information about the securities being offered (Consob Regulation 11522/1998, Art 28(2)) so as to provide for the investor, before recommending or carrying out any operation, adequate information on the nature, implications and risks, knowledge of which is necessary for the client to make informed choices. The intermediary also has the burden of proving that all necessary pieces of information have been provided to investors about the nature of the securities purchased, the rating recognised by international agencies and the risks associated with it, so that the customer can come to their own decision in an informed way. On the same matter, see Trib Lecco, 12 January 2010; Trib Forlì, 21 March 2009; Trib Cuneo, 22 May 2008; Trib Roma, 8 October 2004, which states that the *know your merchandise rule* imposes a duty of knowledge on intermediaries that encompasses the issuer, the situation of the relevant markets and their destination among investors.

and to the employees liaising with the client. For example, the Court of Appeal of Turin held a bank liable with reference to an investment in Cirio bonds essentially because no evidence was provided that the bank itself had gathered sufficient information about such financial instrument. In particular, the Court deemed that the mere fact that the bank acquired the Offering Circular of the relevant bond issuance was not sufficient to prove the correct performance of the duty at stake.[27]

C. The Duty to Inform

Article 21(c) of the Consolidated Law states that, 'in providing investment and non-core services and activities', investment firms shall provide clients with information which is correct, clear and not misleading.[28]

Also Consob Regulation 16190 regulates the duties imposed on intermediaries with reference to 'information, advertising and promotion notices, contract' and, at Article 27, establishes that all of them must be 'correct, clear and not misleading'; in addition, advertising and promotional notices shall be 'clearly identifiable as such'.

The conditions for information to be considered 'correct, clear and not misleading', are set forth in Article 28;[29] a detailed prescription is then provided with reference to the information concerning 'the intermediary and his services' (Article 29), 'the safeguarding of financial instruments and sums of money of the customer' (Article 30), 'financial instruments' (Article 31), 'costs and charges' (Article 32) and 'open-end UCITS' (Article 33).

[27] Court of Appeal of Turin, decision no 1245 of 30 July 2007.

[28] *Ex multis*, Supreme Court no 18140, 26 July 2013; Supreme Court no 22147, 28 September 2010, which states that

> The financial intermediary, pursuant to art. 29 of CONSOB Resolution no. 11522, July 1, 1998, before executing an order, has the duty to provide appropriate information to investors, in order to meet their specific needs, regarding both personal and financial situation. Should the operation results not adequate, it can execute the order only if the client signs a document in which he make explicit reference to the warnings received.

Court of Appeal of Milan, no 3908, 20 October 2013; Court of Appeal of Lecce, no 787, 4 November 2013; Court of Appeal of Milan, no 1094, 15 April 2009; Trib Ravenna, 2 September 2011; Trib Firenze, 18 February 2005; Trib Roma, 8 October 2004; Trib Firenze, 30 May 2004.

[29] Art 28 states that all information that are issued to retail consumers (or potential retail consumer) or that may be received by such persons must: (a) include the name of the intermediary; (b) not emphasise any potential advantage of an investment service or financial instrument unless a correct and clear indication is given of any significant risks; (c) have a content and presentation that in all probability will be comprehensible to the average investor in the population to which it is addressed or is likely to be received; and (d) not conceal, minimise or withhold important elements or warnings.

There are further detailed conditions to be met in case of information that: (1) 'compares investment or accessory services, financial instruments or persons providing the investment or accessory services'; (ii) 'contains an indication of past results of a financial instrument, financial index or investment service'; (iii) 'includes or makes reference to historic data processing, such information must relate to a financial instrument or financial index'; (iv) 'contains estimated future results' or 'makes reference to a specific tax treatment'. In any case the information provided shall not indicate or suggest that the competent authority guarantees or approves the products and services specified in the information (see Art 28).

Article 27, subsection 2 of Consob Regulation 16190 further establishes that intermediaries shall provide customers and potential customers with

> *appropriate information*, in a *comprehensible format*, in order that the nature of the investment service, the specific types of financial instruments involved and related risks are *easily understandable* and, consequently, the customer shall be able to make informed decisions regarding investments.[30]

In order to satisfy such requirement, intermediaries are requested to provide the retail customer (or the potential retail customer) with all information relating to the terms of the contract, as well as, subsequently, any significant amendment of the information provided 'in good time prior to any binding contract for the provision of investment or accessory services'.[31]

The exact scope of application of the banks' duty to inform is debated. In particular, it is not settled whether a bank providing investment services different from investment advice and portfolio management owes a duty of information vis-à-vis the client also after the execution of a purchase order of financial instruments.[32] The issue is widely discussed since it relates to the very common case in which the client purchases corporate or state bonds through an execution-only service and, afterwards, the economic conditions of the relevant issuer worsen. In such cases, banks could be blamed for not having reported to the client the worsening of the risk profile of the investment.

Some authors maintain that investment firms have to (continue to) provide to investors a so-called '*consulenza strumentale*' ('incidental investment advice'), which is not expressly contemplated by law.[33] The Supreme Court in 2013, in line with the applicable statutory provisions, excluded that investment firms' duty to inform actually stretches to include also the period after the purchase of the financial instruments.[34] Nonetheless, some authors have continued to maintain the existence of such an (implicit) obligation on investment firms.[35]

The Italian Supreme Court, with the decision no 7776 of 3 April 2014, specified that, since the duty to inform implies a specific obligation of the investment firm

[30] See Supreme Court no 22147, 19 October 2010; Court of Appeal of Milano, 8 October 2013, which states that 'the bank, as a professional trader, is burdened with a duty to inform, which consists in collecting data and giving them to the customer, in order to enable a conscious choice of investment under d. lgs. No. 58 of 1998'; Supreme Court no 11412, 6 July 2012, which states that 'the content of the duty to inform is characterized by dynamism, since it has to be performed in relation to the single need of each investor'.

[31] It is further established that such information shall be provided 'in hard copy or through the intermediary's web site', in accordance with the additional requirement set by the Regulation (see Art 34(5)).

[32] Such a duty occurs, eg according to the Court of Rome, 25 May 2005 in *ilcaso.it*.

[33] See L Zitiello, 'La consulenza in materia di investimenti' in Zitiellio *La MiFID in Italia* (n 23) 443; A Sciarrone Alibrandi, 'La "consulenza in materia di investimenti": profili di novità della fattispecie' in L Frediani and V Santoro (eds), *L'attuazione della direttiva MIFID* (Milan: Giuffrè, 2009) 94.

[34] Supreme Court 2185, 30 January 2013. Accordingly, see Court of Turin, 22 December 2010 (2010) *Resp civ Prev* 1350; Court of Turin, 30 April 2012 (2013) II *Giur Comm* 462.

[35] See GM Uda, 'L'informativa alla clientela in relazione ai servizi di investimento' in V Troiano and R Motroni (eds), *La MiFID II. Rapporti con la clientela—regole di governance—mercati* (Padua: Cedam, 2016) 50.

to put the client in a position to easily understand the relevant information, contractual documents also have to be written in plain language.[36]

Article 37 provides a detailed description of the form and content of the investment contract. It states that 'Intermediaries shall provide retail customers with their own investment services, other than investment consultancy, on the basis of a specific contract in writing'; in addition, 'a copy of said contract shall be provided to the customer'.

Such contract shall inter alia: (a) specify the services provided and their characteristics, indicate the content of the services provided and the type of financial instruments and transactions involved; (b) establish the period of validity and renewal method for the contract, together with the terms to be adopted for any amendment to the said contract; (c) indicate the methods by which the customer may issue orders and instructions; (d) indicate the frequency, type and content of documentation to be provided to the customer as statements on the activities performed; (e) indicate, with reference to execution of orders on behalf of clients, receipt and transmission of orders and portfolio management, the applicable loss threshold in cases where there is an uncovered open position in a contingent liability transaction, that could lead to losses greater than the purchase cost of the relevant financial instruments, above which the customer must be notified; (f) indicate the fees payable to the intermediary or objective criteria for their calculation, specifying how such fees are accrued and, unless otherwise communicated, regarding incentives received in compliance with Article 52; (g) indicate if and by what method and content, in relation to the investment service, investment consultancy services may be provided; (h) indicate other contractual terms agreed with the investor for provision of the service; (i) indicate any settlement and arbitration procedures for the out-of-court settlement of any dispute, as defined in Article 32-ter of the Consolidated Law. Additional requirements are prescribed for '*portfolio management contracts*'.[37]

[36] Also the Bank of Italy, on 20 June 2012 issued specific instructions for the banks concerning how documents and contracts related to banking services should be drafted to ensure they are sufficiently clear, even establishing guidelines on lay-out of the documents and grammar.

[37] Such additional requirements are listed by Art 38; it states that:

> In addition to the terms established under art. 37, the contract with retail customers relating to portfolio management shall: a) indicate the types of financial instruments that may be included in the customer portfolio and the types of operation that could be performed on such instruments, including any limits; b) indicate the management objectives, the level of risk within which the manager may exercise his discretion and any specific restrictions to said discretion; c) indicate whether the customer portfolio may be characterised by a leverage effect; d) provide the description of the reference parameter against which the customer portfolio yield shall be compared; e) indicate whether the intermediary delegates execution of the assignment to third parties, specifying details of the relevant powers delegated; f) indicate the method and frequency of assessment of the financial instruments contained in the customer portfolio. 2. For the purposes of subsection 1a), the contract shall specify the intermediary options to invest in financial instruments not admitted for trading on a regulated market, in derivatives or illiquid or highly volatile instruments; or to proceed with short sales, purchases using borrowed sums of money, financial transactions through securities or any transaction involving the payment of margins, guarantee deposits or exchange risk.

Furthermore, Article 31 of Consob Regulation 16190 (Information on financial instruments) provides that intermediaries shall provide customers or potential customers with 'a general description of the nature of risks involved with the financial instruments concerned'.[38] Such description, in practice, is provided through a standard form delivered to clients. In this regard, considering the standard content of the warnings directed to clients, some Italian case-law deems that the delivery of such document is per se insufficient and the investment firm would be in default of its duty to inform.[39] On the other hand, it cannot be excluded that an omission to provide the document containing the 'general description of the nature of the risks' could lead to a declaration of liability on the part of the investment firm.

The implementation of the EU Directive No 2014/65[40] (the so-called MiFID II), that will take place in 2017 (with effect as of 3 January 2018), could have an impact on the possibility for investment firms to provide information to clients in a standardised form. In particular, Article 24, paragraph 5 of MiFID II establishes that each Member State will have to exercise an option related to the possibility to allow investment firms to provide to clients in a standardised manner the information concerning the nature of the investment service provided and of the specific kind of securities offered.

It is not possible, at the time of writing, to predict how the Italian legislator will exercise such option. Nonetheless, it is reasonable to expect that any choice by the legislator in this respect would not per se materially affect the abovementioned case-law position, according to which investment firms have to assess whether their customer is actually in a position to understand (and not only to physically receive) the information needed.

[38] Art 31(2) of Regulation 16190/2007 further prescribes that, the description of the risks shall include, where relevant to the specific type of instrument, and the status and level of awareness of the customer, the following elements: (a) the risks related to the type of financial instrument, including an explanation of its effect and impact, together with the risk of total loss of the investment; (b) the price volatility of such instruments and any related liquidability limits; (c) the fact that an investor might assume, as a result of transactions on such instruments, financial commitments and other additional obligations, including potential liabilities, further to those relating to the purchase cost of the instruments; and (d) any marginal requirements or similar obligations applicable to such instruments.

The following are further prescription provided by Art 31: where it is likely that the risks relating to a financial instrument or combined financial transaction involving 2 or more different financial instruments are greater than the risks relating to the individual components, the intermediary shall provide an adequate description of the individual components and the manner in which their interaction increases risk. In a case in which financial instruments incorporate a third party guarantee, information relating to such guarantee shall include sufficient detail regarding both the guarantor and the guarantee, in order that the retail customer or potential retail customer may correctly evaluate the guarantee.

[39] See Court of Novara, 23 June 2011.

[40] OJ L 173, 12 June 2014, 349–496.

D. The Assessment of 'Appropriateness' or 'Suitability'

As an effect of the implementation in Italy of the MiFID Directives, a principle of graduation of regimes of investor protection has been introduced. In particular, a distinction has been drawn between different types of investment services.

In the case of provision of investment advice and portfolio management, the investment firm is requested to assess the 'suitability' of any single advice and/or investment for the client. In case of unsuitability, the investment firm has to refrain from carrying out the transactions on behalf of the client.[41]

In particular, the analysis required should take into account the following criteria: (1) the correspondence of the relevant transaction with the customer's investment objectives; (2) the financial ability of the customer to bear the risks related to the relevant investment; and (3) the fact that the customer has the necessary experience and suitable awareness of the nature of the transaction to understand the risks involved.[42]

With reference to services other than investment advice or portfolio management, Article 42 of Consob Regulation 16190 requires the investment firm to carry out a more limited analysis, aimed at verifying that the client has the necessary level of 'awareness and experience' in order to understand the risks connected to the transaction at stake.

In case the analysis conducted by the investment firm leads to the conclusion that the transaction would not be appropriate for the customer, the latter has to be informed of such circumstance. The law deems that such warning is sufficient to 'protect' the client; therefore, provided that the client confirms his willingness that the relevant investment is carried out by the investment firm, the transaction can be legitimately executed.

An examination of Italian case-law allows an appreciation that the allegation of the breach of suitability or appropriateness rules is one of the most frequent complaints brought against investment firms. At the same time, it has to be noted that decisions in this regard are usually taken on a case-by-case basis; therefore, it is quite difficult to infer general principles from such case-law.

[41] The Supreme Court (as well as some lower courts) have held that banks have to follow the same standard of conduct already before the implementation of MiFID Directives, when statutory law did not expressly forbid investment firms to carry out investment services in relation to transactions that are unsuitable for the client, but did provide (only) for a duty to warn the client of such unsuitability. See Supreme Court no 16828, 9 August 2016, which decided a case initially brought in 2005.

[42] See Supreme Court no 29864, 29 December 2011, in (2012) I *Foro It* 2120, which states that 'the duty to assist the client in the best possible way (art. TUF 21), reinforced by the specific regulations of the second level [...], implies that the intermediary, before performing trading orders, has to verify the client level of risk awareness and the adequacy of the transaction in relation to its financial condition, its investment objectives and its risk appetite'; Trib Palermo, 17 January 2005; Trib Genova, no 1230, 15 March 2005; Trib Roma, 8 October 2004; Trib Taranto, 27 October 2004; Trib Mantova, 18 March 2004; Trib Mantova, 12 November 2004; Trib Roma, 15 December 2004.

E. Internal Control Mechanisms, the Prevention and Management of Conflict of Interests and the 'Best Execution'

Banks and, in general, investment firms have almost always been requested to adopt a sound organisation of their own business. Nonetheless, with specific regard to the activities related to investment services provision, the implementation of MiFID brought a material increase to the number (and complexity) of internal procedures investment firms have to put in place.

As an example, since the enactment of Law no 1/1991 investment firms have been requested to avoid carrying out investment services where they had a conflicting interest. At the same time, it was left to investment firms to decide how to comply with such principle.

Now, Article 21(d) of the Consolidated Law states that, 'in providing investment and non-core services and activities', investment firms shall arrange resources and procedures, including internal control mechanisms, suitable for ensuring the efficient provision of services and activities. On the basis of such holding, the Consolidated Law further rules out the criteria that investment firms have to follow in order to identify and manage any conflict of interest which may arise in the provision of financial services. In other words, investment firms are now not prevented from carrying out investment services where they have a conflicting interest. This, however, only applies when the investment banks have adopted internal procedures that ensure that such situation will not negatively affects the counterparty (ie the client).[43]

Consob Regulation 16190 has also introduced the principle of 'best execution' by the intermediary of orders on behalf of customers. Pursuant to Article 45 (measures for the execution of orders under the best conditions for the customer) intermediaries shall adopt

> all reasonable measures and, for this purpose, implement effective mechanisms to achieve, where orders are to be executed, *the best possible result for their customers*, with due regard to the price, cost, speed and probability of execution and settlement, to the size and nature of the order, or any other consideration relevant to its execution.[44]

[43] In particular Art 21(1-bis) states that in the provision of investment services and activities and accessory services, investment firms:

(a) shall adopt all reasonable measures to identify and manage conflict of interest which may arise with the customer or between customers, also by the adoption of appropriate organisational measures, in order to avoid a negative impact on the interests of the customer;
(b) shall clearly inform customers, prior to acting on their behalf, of the general nature and/or sources of conflict of interest where measures taken pursuant to paragraph (a) are not sufficient to ensure, with reasonable certainty, that the risk of damaging the interests of the customer is avoided;
(c) shall perform independent, sound and prudent management and take measures to safeguard the rights of customers with regard to their assets.

[44] The *best execution rule* is the principle according to which the intermediary must ensure customers that orders are executed at the best possible conditions in a situation where there are alternative trading venues. On this matter see Trib Roma, no 7154, 3 April, 2008; Trib Roma, no 6376, 25 May 2008; Trib di Rimini, no 442, 21 April 2007.

It is a specific duty of the intermediary to adopt 'an order execution strategy' that: (1) for each financial instrument category, identifies at least the execution venues that in the long term offer the best possible result in relation to the execution of customer orders; and (2) steers the decision towards an execution venue identified under the previous paragraph.[45]

It goes without saying that whenever the customer issues specific instructions, the intermediary shall execute the order, only in relation to the elements for which indications are received, in accordance with said instructions.

Finally, Article 47 imposes on intermediaries the duty to verify and update the execution measures and strategy. It states that intermediaries shall monitor the efficacy of their order execution measures and execution strategy in order to identify and, if necessary, correct any failings. Such execution measures and strategy shall be revised at least on an annual basis, and at the time of occurrence of significant circumstances that could influence the ability to achieve the best long-term results possible in the execution of customer orders through venues included in the execution strategy.

In Italian case-law, as per our knowledge, there has been no significant litigation specifically concerning the compliance by an investment firm with the duty to adopt proper internal procedures (apart from cases in which Consob or the Bank of Italy imposed administrative fines on investment firms or banks for organisational failings and the latter challenged such sanctions before courts).

F. Banks' Duties to Third Parties (not being Potential Customers) and/or while Acting other than in their Capacity as Intermediary

As already reported, the greatest part of Italian case-law involving banks' duties of care is connected to the provision of investment services.

According to case-law, the scope of application of such standard of care encompasses also cases of scams committed by bank's tied agents, even when it is clear that the latter acted in the absence—or beyond the limits—of a proxy to represent the banks.

The most common case is that of the tied agent unduly receiving money from the clients and diverting it to its own personal accounts. In fact, in such

[45] Art 46 ('information on order execution strategy') imposes on intermediaries the duty to: (a) provide information appropriate to their customers with regard to the order execution strategy adopted pursuant to Art 45(3); (b) specifically inform customers whether or not the strategy may involve the execution of orders outside a regulated market or multilateral trading facility. In addition they shall: (a) obtain the preliminary consent of the customer regarding the order execution strategy; (b) obtain specific preliminary consent of the customer prior to the execution of orders outside a regulated market or multilateral trading facility. Such consent may be expressed in general terms or in relation to individual transactions. Finally, intermediaries must be able to demonstrate to customers, on request, that orders have been executed in compliance with the execution strategy.

cases banks could not be deemed to be providing any service at all to clients, but the mere fact that the tied agent received a mandate by the bank to act in its interest is deemed sufficient to ground a vicarious liability on the bank itself pursuant to Article 2049 of the Italian Civil Code (establishing the liability of employer for damages caused by its employees to third parties).[46] The main consequence of this trend in the case-law is that the sole effective defence for a bank in these cases is related to a possible contributory negligence by clients, considering that usually tied agents are not entitled at all to directly receive money from clients.

Furthermore, clients have invoked the application of the standard of care (along with the connected liability rules) elaborated by case-law with reference to investment services provision also to different, quite peculiar cases.

For example, some lawsuits were brought against a bank which acted, in fact, as a 'depositary' in relation to management contracts entered into by clients with another investment firm. In particular, clients entered into deposit and check account contracts with the bank at issue, while entering also into contracts with a different investment firm for the management of the sums deposited with the bank through investments in the forex market. In such context, the clients provided the management company with a proxy in order to dispose of the sums deposited with the bank. It was then discovered that some executives of the management company deceived clients with false reports of investments and, moreover, illicitly diverted the sums at issue to certain accounts abroad which they could dispose of. The management company was then declared bankrupt and some clients brought actions against the 'depositary' bank alleging, among other things, that it should have monitored the conduct of the management company; failure to do so would have amounted to a breach of the duty of care allegedly owed by the bank owing to its professional qualification.

The decisions rendered by the Courts of Milan and Rome[47] on such cases rejected the clients' claims, affirming that the bank was not a party to management contracts and, therefore, it could not be blamed for the breach by the management company. Moreover, it has been established that the bank had no duty of care vis-à-vis the clients other than those strictly connected to the deposit and check account contracts.

Such decisions, in our view, are worth mentioning because they set limits to the potential expansion of the scope of application of a particularly severe standard of care on the banks that, otherwise, could turn out to be an undue hindrance in the ordinary activity of banks and other investment firms.

[46] See eg Supreme Court, decision no 6091 of 20 March 2006; Supreme Court decision no 19166 of 29 September 2005.

[47] See Court of Milan, decision 20 June 2014 (Justice F Ferrari); Court of Rome, decision 10 September 2014 (Justice G Romano).

III. Remedies for Breach of Intermediaries' Duty of Care

A. The Development of Italian Case-law and Future Perspectives

As seen in section II, Italian law provides quite a detailed framework of duties imposed on intermediaries while providing an investment service. However, there is no specific statutory regulation of the nature and extent of the liability regime applicable to intermediaries.

As anticipated earlier, for many years the lack of a statutory regime lead investors to sue their respective intermediary under different bases; this, in turn, allowed the case-law to develop different doctrines in identifying the remedies available for the aggrieved customers affected by the corporate scandals Cirio, Parmalat and Argentine bonds.

A clear indication of the nature of intermediaries' liability and, thus, of the remedies available for customers has been established by the Italian Supreme Court in the leading case no 26724, issued on 19 December 2007.

We will now briefly present the different models developed over time by Italian lower courts, to finally present the current state of Italian case-law.

Initially lower courts facing the litigation arising from the abovementioned financial scandals, held financial contracts *null and void*.[48]

The basis for this doctrine is that the execution of a financial contract in breach of the information and transparency duties imposed on the intermediary, amounts to a breach of mandatory rules and public policy. Therefore, such contract cannot be enforced pursuant to Article 1418 of the Civil Code, which in turn states that, unless otherwise provided by the law, contracts contrary to mandatory rules are null and void.

This early case-law stressed the fact that the rules prescribed by the Consolidated Law and by the implementing Consob Regulations pursue general objectives, such as the interest of customers and the integrity of the market. Therefore, a contract breaching such rules should be considered null and void.

[48] This doctrine has been held by several decisions from Italian lower courts; see amongst the others Trib Mantova, 18 March 2004 (2004) II *Banca Borsa e Titoli di Credito* 440; Trib Firenze, 30 May 2004; Trib Venezia, 22 November 2004; Trib Palermo, 17 January 2005; Trib Firenze, 18 February 2005; Trib Brindisi 21 February 2005; Trib Ferrara, 25 February 2005; Trib Santa Maria Capua Vetere, 1 March 2005; Trib Parma 16 June 2005; Trib Parma 6 July 2005; Trib Marsala 12 July 2005; Trib Brindisi 22 July 2005; Trib Brindisi 26 December 2005; Trib Treviso 10 October 2005; Trib Parma, 21 December 2005; Trib Torino, 7 November 2005; Trib Catania 25 November 2005; Trib Cagliari 2 January 2006; Trib Cagliari 11 January 2006 (2007) *Resp civ prev* 1442; Trib Foggia 15 May 2006; Trib Teramo 18 May 1006; Trib Trani, 30 May 2006; Trib Brindisi, 18 August 2006; Trib Firenze 4 December 2006; Trib Trento 1 February 2007; Trib Modena 10 January 2008.

Whenever the financial contract is considered null and void by the court, the *restitutio in integrum* principle applies (Article 2033 of the Italian Civil Code); therefore, parties should be returned to the same position they would have been in had no contract been entered into (the principle applies also in the case of contracts held void for lack of the prescribed form: Article 37 of Consob Regulation 16190).

Therefore, the intermediary is obliged to return the sums received from the customer, and also to pay interest at a legal rate from the date of the payment.[49]

Some other decisions held that financial contract entered into by the customer on the base of false or erroneous information provided by the intermediary can be annulled, under the doctrine of *mistake* pursuant to Article 1428 of the Italian Civil Code or under the doctrine of *fraud* pursuant to Article 1439 of the Italian Civil Code.[50]

The vast majority of decisions from lower courts, instead, have recalled the traditional distinction between rules prescribed for the validity of a contract and behavioural rules. According to this doctrine, only the breach of the first rules leads to the invalidity of the financial contract; on the contrary, a breach of the behavioural rules may lead to termination of such contract and compensation of damages. The liability of the firm is based on Article 1218 of the Italian Civil Code. It establishes that 'the debtor who does not exactly render due performance is liable for damages unless he proves that the non-performance or delay was due to impossibility of performance for a cause not imputable to him'.[51]

[49] See S Swann and C von Bar, *Unjustified Enrichment: (PEL Unj Enr)* (Munich: Sellier European Law Publishers, Brussels: Bruylant, and Berne: Stampfli Publishers Ltd, 2010) 104–05.

[50] See Trib Pinerolo, 14 October 2005; Trib Lanciano, 30 April 2007; Trib Ancona, 12 April 2007; Trib Parma, 6 December 2006; Trib Napoli, 7 November 2006; Trib Parma 17 November 2005.

[51] See Art 1218 of the Civil Code. A dual regime is then provided in case of partial performance of the contract according to the nature of the contractual obligation. First, a contracting party may promise to achieve a certain result (so-called '*obbligazioni di risultato*'): in this case, the party in breach will still have to prove that non-performance (or delay) was due to impossibility of performance for a cause not imputable to her. Second, a contracting party may promise to perform the contract with due diligence (so-called '*obbligazioni di mezzi*'): in this case, the innocent party will have to prove both non-performance and that the party in breach did not perform the contract with due care. This can be either ordinary diligence (ie the diligence of a reasonable man, the *bonus pater familias*) or professional diligence. An instructive definition of the former standard has been provided by the Supreme Court (Supreme Court, 23 December 2003, no 19778). It held that of the *bonus pater familias* the diligence is that which is reasonably to be expected from every person of average carefulness and shrewdness, mindful of her undertaking, and conscious of her responsibilities). The standard of professional diligence is evaluated taking into account the nature of the activity (ie taking into account all the practices, rules and precautions commonly adopted in the relevant profession). Art 1176(2) of the Civil Code establishes that 'in the performance of obligations inherent in the exercise of a professional activity, diligence shall be evaluated with respect to the nature of that activity'. However, Art 2236 of the Civil Code recognises that, in cases where the professional services involve the solution of technical problems of a particular difficulty, the person who renders such services is not liable for damages, except in case of fraud, malice or gross negligence.

This different approach has been adopted by several decisions issued by lower courts.[52] Such doctrine has been upheld by the by the Italian Supreme Court in the first judgment on the matter, issued on 29 September 2005 (decision no 19024), where it stated that the lack of information useful for evaluating the convenience of a transaction or the breach of the duties imposed on the financial intermediary by the Consolidated Law and by the Civil Code cannot lead the financial contract to be held null and void, pursuant to Article 1418 of the Civil Code. Such breach may lead to the termination of the investment contract, and to the compensation of damages.

B. The Leading Case by the United Chambers of Italian Supreme Court no 26724/2007

This approach has been further developed by the United Chambers of the Italian Supreme Court in the leading case no 26724 of 19 December 2007, which stated the current regime for the financial institutions' duty of care.

i. Nature of the Liability

With reference to the nature of the liability of intermediaries for having breached the duty of care towards their investors, the United Chambers of the Italian Supreme Court excluded that it leads to the invalidity of the investment contract.

Such a breach, instead, can produce effects only as regards the liability of the investment firm vis-à-vis the investors, for the damage they suffered as a consequence thereof.

Secondly, the United Chambers drew a relevant distinction, stating that, according to the circumstances, the liability of the firm could be pleaded under the doctrine of the *pre-contractual liability* (*culpa in contrahendo*) provided by Article 1337

[52] See Trib Roma, 8 October 2004, Trib Taranto 27 October 2004; Trib Monza, 16 December 2004; Trib Lodi, 22 February 2005; Trib Milano, 9 March 2005; Trib Roma, 11 March 2005; Trib Genoa, 15 March 2005; Trib Mantova, 15 March 2005; Trib Torino, 21 March 2005; Trib Rimini, 11 May 2005; Trib Roma, 25 May 2005; Trib Bologna, 31 May 2005; Trib Parma, 16 June 2005; Trib Alba, 4 July 2005; Trib Milano, 25 July 2005; Trib Genoa, 2 August 2005; Trib Biella 30 September 2005; Trib Modena, 14 October 2005; Trib Firenze, 18 October 2005; Trib Catania, 21 October 2005; Trib Milano, 9 November 2005; Trib Padova, 13 January 2006; Trib Rovereto, 18 January 2006; Trib Firenze, 21 Febraury 2006; Trib Cosenza, 1 March 2006; Trib Milano, 20 March 2006; Trib Rimini, 22 March 2006; Trib Foggia, 21 April 2006; Trib Milano, 26 April 2006; Trib Venezia, 4 May 2006; Trib Modena, 10 May 2006; Trib Padova, 17 May 2006; Trib Firenze, 29 May 2006; Trib Lecce, 12 June 2006; Trib Lodi, 12 January 2007; Trib Catania, 23 January 2007; Trib Modena, 14 February 2007; Trib Udine, 21 March 2007; Trib Oristano, 12 June 2007; App Brescia, 20 June 2007; App Torino, 19 October 2007; Trib Padova, 31 October 2007.

of the Civil Code or as a contractual liability, on the basis of the *breach of the investment contract* pursuant to Article 1453 of the Italian Civil Code.[53]

In general, a claim under the heading of pre-contractual liability may arise whenever one of the contracting parties does not act in good faith during either the negotiations leading to or the formation of the contract. The relevant provision here is Article 1337 of the Civil Code. Such provision has traditionally been interpreted as a tool to prevent unfair breaking-off of contractual negotiations or the conclusion of invalid contracts when one of the parties was already aware of the reasons for the invalidity of the prospective contract.[54]

Since the pre-contractual liability under Article 1337 of the Italian Civil Code is usually considered a form of liability in tort (as opposed to contractual liability),[55] the traditional doctrine held that a breach of such duty to act in good faith could be invoked only until a valid contract has been entered into. The Supreme Court, with its decision of 29 September 2005, no 19024 overruled this traditional principle, stating that the party to a contract, which has been damaged by the unfair conduct of the other party during the negotiations, is entitled to claim damages also after the conclusion of the contract itself.[56] In other words, pre-contractual liability may arise also when the contract is valid but 'disadvantageous' for a party, as a result of a behaviour contrary to good faith by the other party during the relevant negotiations.

Adhering to this principle, the United Chambers of the Supreme Court in 2007 reaffirmed that an action under Article 1337 of the Civil Code might be brought also when the contract has been entered into.

On the basis of such holding, the United Chambers stated that if the investor's claim against an investment firm is based upon the alleged breach of obligations

[53] See also Supreme Court no 8462, 10 April 2014, which states that:

> The breach of the duties of customer information and proper execution of the operations, that the law imposes on the agents authorized to provide services in financial investment, can lead to pre-contractual liability, with consequences for compensation, in case of violations occurring in the period preceding or coincident with the signing of the contract [...]; may give rise, however, to the breach of contract, and eventually lead to resolution, in the case of violations relating to the acquisition or divestment carried out after the contract was entered into.

On the same matter Trib Monza, no 605, 24 February 2014 in www.dirittobancario.it; Supreme Court no 3773, 17 February 2009 (2009) 5 *Danno e Resp* 503; Supreme Court no 17340, 25 June 2008 (2009) I *Nuova giur civ comm* 24; Supreme Court nos 26745 e 26725, 19 December 2007 (2008) *Danno e Resp* 526; Court of Appeal of Lecce, no 787, 4 November 2013 in www.dirittobancario.it.

[54] See V Roppo, *Il Contratto* (Milan: Giuffré, 2001) 180.

[55] In fact, the legal nature of the pre-contractual liability is disputed under Italian law, but the majority of decisions by the Supreme Court affirm its tortious nature, with the consequence that the tort law regime applies (the issue is relevant with reference to the applicable statute of limitation for example, the term applicable to tort law being 5 years and the term applicable to contract law being 10 years). See Supreme Court, 29 April 1999, no 4299; Supreme Court, United Chambers, 16 July 2001, no 9645; Supreme Court, 4 March 2002, no 3103; Supreme Court, United Chambers, 26 June 2003, no 10160.

[56] Such decision was considered a 'brave reversal' by M Franzoni, 'La responsabilità nell' intermediaizone finanziaria' (2014) *Danno e resp* 785 et seq, esp 789.

that should have been performed *before* the contract was entered into, such claim should be assessed under Article 1337 of the Civil Code. Conversely, if the claim referred to the violation of duties arising from the contract itself, the action should be assessed under the rules governing the contractual liability.

In the picture drawn by the United Chambers, therefore, the most common cases of investment services litigation, in which investors blame banks for not having provided them with sufficient information on certain investments, would fall within the scheme of contractual liability pursuant to Article 1453 of the Civil Code.

ii. Burden of Proof

Article 23, subparagraph 6 of the Consolidated Law states that '[i]n actions for damages in respect of injury caused to the customer in the performance of investment services or non-core services, *the burden of proof of having acted with the due diligence required shall be on the intermediaries*'.

Thus, an investment firm summoned before court by a client in connection with the provision of investment services has the burden of proving that it acted with the 'due diligence required'.[57] In this respect it has to be stressed that Article 23(6) of the Consolidated Law has been interpreted to require the higher standard of professional diligence. This interpretation—at first proposed by academics[58] and later upheld by some decisions[59]—derives from the wording of Article 23(6) itself, which refers to the '*due* diligence required'.[60] The standard of professional diligence is evaluated taking into account the nature of the activity (ie taking into account all the practices, rules and precautions commonly adopted in the relevant profession),[61] and it is breached by simple negligence.[62]

In this regard, MiFID does not provide for a rule similar to the abovementioned Article 23(6) of the Consolidated Law. Therefore, insofar it was considered a rule causing a disadvantage for intermediaries, it could be considered to be in contrast with the aim of MiFID of ensuring a level playing field.[63]

[57] It is worth noting that the current system has raised the standard of care imposed on intermediaries, including underwriters. The standard of diligence previously applied under Art 13(10) of Law 2 January 1991, no 1, was that 'of a mandatary', which is the diligence of an ordinary person (the *bonus pater familias*).

[58] G Alpa, 'Nuovi aspetti della tutela del risparmiatore' (1998) *Vita notarile* 665–700.

[59] Among others, see Tribunal of Venice, 22 November 2004 (dealing with the placement of Argentine bonds).

[60] See Consolidated Law, Art 23(6).

[61] The Civil Code, Art 1176(2) establishes that 'in the performance of obligations inherent in the exercise of a professional activity, diligence shall be evaluated with respect to the nature of that activity'.

[62] However, Art 2236 of the Civil Code recognises that, in case the professional services involve the solution of technical problems of a particular difficulty, the person who renders such services is not liable for damages, except in the case of fraud, malice or gross negligence.

[63] See F Civale, *Il contenzioso bancario e finanziario* (Rome: Aracne, 2014) 214.

Nonetheless, Article 23(6) of the Consolidated Law does not depart from the common standard of the burden of proof in contract law (Article 1218 of the Civil Code), under which it is the defendant who has to prove that the non-performance is not due to his fault. In other words, the non-breaching party has to prove merely the existence and enforceability of a contract, its breach by the other party and the amount of damages claimed. The party who allegedly has not rendered due performance is liable for damages unless she proves that she has acted with the due diligence requested.[64]

Therefore, the abovementioned provision affects the burden of proof in cases under tort law, where, typically, it is the (alleged) victim of the tort that has the burden of proving the defendant's fault, pursuant to the principle *actore incumbit probatio*.

In short, in investment services lawsuits, irrespective of the qualification of the action in tort or in contract, the plaintiff has merely to prove the damage she suffered and the existence of a causal link between the intermediary's action (or omission) and the damage.[65] Conversely, the burden is on the intermediary to prove that it complied with the required standard of diligence. Therefore, if the customer claims that the bank failed to provide all the information required by law, according to the nature of the investment service provided, it will be up to the firm to provide evidence to the contrary. Typically, such bank will have to show a written declaration by which the client, at the moment of the relevant transaction, confirmed that she has received all appropriate warnings.[66]

An unresolved issue concerning Article 23(6) of the Consolidated Law is its scope of application. In particular, the Italian Supreme Court still has to clarify whether such provision applies also to claims for the annulment of contract for mistake or fraud. Considering that the rule at stake expressly refers to the '*proof of having acted with the due diligence*', we believe that such provision does not derogate from common principles of the burden of proof; therefore, the burden of giving evidence of the alleged mistake or fraudulent conduct should be on the plaintiff.

Another issue arises in cases in which the investment firm is blamed for having acted in a situation of a conflict of interests. In fact, the duty imposed by MiFID-implementing rules upon intermediaries to act so as to prevent the possible interference of conflict of interests may well fall within the scope of application of Article 23(6), ie the 'proof of having acted with the due diligence'.

However, Italian case-law excluded that Article 23(6) of the Consolidated Law is applicable to claims based upon the alleged conflict of interests of the investment

[64] See F Galgano, *Diritto Privato*, 3rd edn (Padua: Cedam, 1985) 198.

[65] On this matter, see Supreme Court no 3773, 17 February 2009 (2009) *Danno e Resp* 503; Supreme Court no 18039, 19 October 2012 (2012) *Giust civ Mass* 1232; Supreme Court no 22147, 29 October 2010 (2010) *Giust civ Mass* 1386; Tribunal of Bari, no 1020, 3 May 2001, no 1020 (2001) *Contr* 90–95 (*Benvestito v Banca Popolare di Bari*).

[66] See Supreme Court no 5089, 15 March 2016; Supreme Court no 17356, 26 August 2016.

firm; therefore, under Italian case-law as it currently stands, it is on the investor to prove the existence of the conflict of interest of the intermediary, as well as of the causal link between the same and the alleged damage.[67]

iii. Damages and Contributory Negligence

Italian courts have stated that in case of pre-contractual liability damages shall not be limited, as traditionally held, to the expenses and losses strictly connected with the negotiations and the advantages that the party acting in good faith would have achieved with others (the so-called reliance or negative interest).[68] On the contrary, damages encompass the 'decrease of profitability' and the 'increase of economic burden' caused by the intermediary, in addition to further damages, where proved by the aggrieved investor.[69]

In case of contractual liability the measure of damages arising from non-performance shall include the loss suffered by the creditor as well as lost profits (Article 1224(1) of the Civil Code).

In both cases (pre-contractual or contractual liability) only damages that are a direct and immediate consequence of the breach will be awarded (Article 1223 of the Civil Code). The general criterion here is that the investor should be put in the same situation in which he or she would have been, had no breach of the investment contract (or no wrongdoing) being committed by the financial intermediary.

It follows that compensation for losses should be proportionate to the value of the initial investment less the residual value of the securities collected during the period of detention.[70] However, if in the meantime the securities have been sold, the compensation for losses should be proportionate to the value of the initial investment less the value of the amount earned with the subsequent sale;[71] in the same way, possible sums received by the issuer's bankruptcy proceedings must be deducted from the amount due for compensation.

This is the so-called principle of *compensatio lucri cum damno*, whose legal basis is set in Article 1223 of the Civil Code, which expresses the principle of equivalence between damage and repair. Therefore, whenever a financial advantage is an immediate and direct consequence of the event of damage it appears fair to deduct

[67] Court of Appeal of Brescia, 10 January 2007 in *ilcaso.it*.

[68] See Supreme Court, 14 February 2000, no 1632 (2000) I 1 *Giur it* 2250. See further GL Certoma, *The Italian Legal System* (London: Butterworths, 1985) 357.

[69] On this matter, see T Febbrajo, 'Pre-contractual Liability in Italy toward the European Pattern' (2010) 1–4 *Le Corti Pugliesi* 133–43. See also Supreme Court no 29864, 29 December 2011 (2012) I *Foro it* 2120 which states that 'giving the fact that investments always incorporate themselves a risk of future loss of the capital, the damage consists in this: the well-informed customer would not presumably assume it, or at least not to that extent [...]. The consequences of undue assumption of risk cease—or at least are no longer directly related to the violation by the intermediary of the information duty—from the moment in which the costumer, using the ordinary diligence has been able to perceive himself the existence of such risks'; Supreme Court no 19024, 29 September 2005 (2006) *Danno e Resp* 25.

[70] Trib Udine, 21 March 2007; Trib Alba, 3 October 2007; Trib Padova, 17 March 2008.

[71] Trib Velletri, 26 October 2007.

a proportional decrease from the amount due for compensation: on the contrary, in fact, the victim would be in a better position than the one he would have been in if the damage had never occurred.

However, whenever the breach is not caused by the fraud or malice of the debtor, compensation is limited to the damages that could have been foreseen at the time the obligation arose (Article 1225 of the Civil Code). If damages cannot be proved in their exact amount, they can be equitably assessed by the judge (Article 1226 of the Civil Code).

Compensation is not due for damages that the creditor could have avoided by using ordinary diligence (Article 1227(2) of the Civil Code). Thus, depending on the concrete factual circumstances, contributory negligence may be a useful device to control the expansion also of tort liability of the financial intermediary. Article 1227 of the Civil Code, applicable to tort law by virtue of Article 2056 of the Civil Code, provides that if the creditor's negligence has contributed to cause the damage, the compensation is reduced according to the seriousness of the negligence and the extent of the consequences arising from it. Furthermore, compensation is not due for damages that the creditor could have avoided by using ordinary diligence.

Therefore, Italian law imposes on investors the duty to mitigate the damages suffered in connection with the breach (or the wrongdoing) committed by the financial intermediary.

Finally it should be noted that, since rules of conduct imposed on investment firms are deemed as a specification of the general rules of correctness and good faith established by the Civil Code for any contractual relationship, the Italian legal system might be considered as already complying with the principle of effectiveness expressly set forth in Article 69 of MiFId II.[72]

IV. Alternative Dispute Resolution Mechanisms

Following the corporate scandals of the beginning of 2000s (namely Cirio and Parmalat) and the connected litigation against financial intermediaries, the Italian legislator took an initiative of reform of statutory discipline of financial markets. Meaningfully, such initiative substantiated in the issuance of the so-called 'savings protection law' (*legge per la tutela del risparmio* of 28 December 2005, no 262).

[72] According to which 'Member States shall ensure that mechanisms are in place to ensure that compensation may be paid or other remedial action be taken in accordance with national law for any financial loss or damage suffered as a result of an infringement of this Directive or of Regulation (EU) No 600/2014'. As is known, the principle of effectiveness was already affirmed in the EU Court of Justice case-law (see ECJ 30 May 2013, C-604/11 *Genil 48 SL and Comercial Hostelera de Grandes Vinos SL v Bankinter SA and Banco Bilbao Vizcaya Argentaria SA*; ECJ 19 July 2012, C-591/10 *Littlewoods Retail Ltd and Others v Her Majesty's Commissioners of Revenue and Customs*).

The express aim of such intervention was to address the request from society for a more intense regulatory protection of investors.[73]

Among other measures, on such occasion the Italian legislator introduced some alternative dispute resolutions systems intended to attract at least a portion of banks-clients litigation, with a view to ease their out-of-court settlement.[74]

In particular, the 'savings protection law' set up the Banking-Financial Arbitrator (Arbitro Bancario Finanziario; also ABF), which is seated with the offices of the Bank of Italy, and the Conciliation and Arbitration Chamber (Camera di Conciliazione e Arbitrato; also CCA), at Consob.

The Banking-Financial Arbitrator was established through the introduction of the new Article 128-bis in Legislative Decree no 385 of 1 September 1993 (ie the Consolidated Banking Act), subsequently implemented by Resolution no 275 of the Inter-ministerial Committee of Credit and Savings (Comitato Interministeriale per il Credito e il Risparmio) of 29 July 2008 and the Implementing Provisions issued by the Bank of Italy on 18 June 2009.

ABF is an adjudicating system, meaning that the parties submit their pleadings in writing and the ABF panel renders its decision (without holding a hearing at which the parties are present). ABF may rule only on claims not exceeding €100,000 regarding banking and financial transactions and services implemented by brokers, excluding those related to investment services and activities or placement of financial products pursuant to the Consolidated Financial Law.[75]

The Conciliation and Arbitration Chamber, instead, was established by Article 27 of the 'savings protection law', then specified by Legislative Decree no 179 of 8 October 2007 and by Consob's Regulation no 16763 of 29 December 2008. CCA was set up for the resolution of the disputes between retail investors and investment firms in case of alleged breach by the latter of contractual obligations to provide notices and information and to act fairly and transparently. The abovementioned Regulation no 16763 governs mediation procedures and two distinct forms of administered arbitration (ordinary or 'simplified').

As regards mediation procedure, the CCA, after the filing of an application by a client, shall appoint the mediator and, after receiving the investment firm's

[73] It could be said that the political purposes of Law no 262/2005 were quite similar to those that accompanied the introduction of the Sarbanes-Oxley Act in the US, even if the impact of the Italian new regulation was definitely softer.

[74] Previously, other ADR systems existed in Italy for the settlement of banking and financial disputes (eg the Ombudsman), but they never met with great success.

[75] Even if this procedure falls out of the scope of this chapter, it is nonetheless interesting to mention that, according to Art 128-bis (3) of the Consolidated Banking Act, the possibility to have recourse to ABF 'do[es] not exclude *the customer's* right to use any other tool contemplated in the legal system'. This means that the customer may still resort to ordinary courts regardless of the decision of the ABF. In addition, Resolution no 275 adopted by the Credit and Finance Committee (*Comitato Interministeriale per il Credito ed il Risparmio* or CICR) on 29 July 2008 (Art 6(6)) provides that: '*Both parties* are entitled to resort to ordinary courts or have recourse to any other tool provided for by the legal system to assert and protect their rights and interests'. As a matter of fact, ABF's decisions do not affect the parties' legal positions.

acceptance, shall notify such appointment to the mediator and the parties. There are no procedural formalities during the hearing, and there is no obligation to record the hearing in minutes; the conciliator may hear the parties separately, with them having the possibility to reply to each other's arguments, and he or she may, with the parties' agreement and at their expense, order the intervention of third parties. The proceedings shall end within 60 days of the filing of the application for conciliation.

The administered arbitration before the CCA, instead, is a ritual arbitration and has the same legal effects stated by Article 824-bis of the Italian Code of Civil Procedure for any other kind of arbitration: in particular, it has the same force as a judicial decision.[76]

While ABF had good success in practice (in 2015 it received 13,575 claims),[77] CCA in 2014 administered only 121 conciliation procedures and no arbitration proceedings.[78]

The experience of recent years led the Italian legislator to replace the CCA with an adjudicating system competent over disputes related to the provision of investment services. Therefore, Legislative Decree no 130 of 6 August no 130 and Law no 208 of 28 December 2015 introduced a new ADR institution, the Financial Disputes Arbitrator (Arbitro per le Controversie Finanziarie; ACF), seated with Consob. ACF was then established with Consob decision no 19602, issued on 4 May 2016 and became operative on 9 January 2017.

In particular, ACF is competent to decide disputes between investors and investment firms, whose value does not exceed €500,000, related to alleged breaches of diligence, correctness, information and transparency duties vis-à-vis investors in the provision of investment services and asset management services.

Furthermore, it has to be pointed out that previously, in 2010, the Italian legislator had taken a further initiative affecting ADRs (also) in financial law matters, by enacting Legislative Decree 4 March 2010, no 28.

In fact, the occasion for such intervention occurred when European Directive on Mediation 2008/52/EC[79] of 21 May 2008 was to be implemented in Italy. This directive is part of an EU-wide initiative to promote mediation throughout the EU, in particular with reference to cross-border disputes in civil or commercial matters.

In light of the fact that, for many years, Italian Courts have been experiencing great workloads, whose main effect is that, on average, first instance civil proceedings take not less than three years, the legislator decided to introduce a regulation

[76] Art 824 bis of the Civil Procedure Code states that 'the award has, from the date of its signing, the same effects of a judgment' rendered by an ordinary court.

[77] See the Annual Report on ABF's activities for 2015, available at: www.arbitrobancariofinanziario.it/pubblicazioni/relazioniAnnuali.

[78] See the ISDACI Report on ADRs in Italy for 2014, available at: www.camera-arbitrale.it/Documenti/Ottavo-rapporto-ISDACI.pdf.

[79] OJ L 136, 24 May 2008, 3–8.

of mediation in civil and commercial matters whose scope of application is wider than that provided for by the directive.

In particular Legislative Decree no 28 of 4 March 2010, with reference to 'internal' (ie non-transnational) disputes in certain matters, introduced the necessity of proceeding with an attempt to reach an out-of-court settlement before resorting to ordinary courts.[80] In fact, failure to proceed with this attempt shall result in the preclusion of the claim before ordinary courts.[81] 'Insurance, banking and financial agreements' are included in the list of matters to which such obligation is imposed.[82]

It is further provided that the attempt for conciliation under Legislative Decree no 28/2010 shall take place before a body entered in the register kept by the Ministry of Justice. As regards disputes concerning 'Insurance, banking and financial agreements', it has been established that this condition could be satisfied also by using proceedings before the ABF or before the CCA/ACF.

As expressly stated in Legislative Decree no 28/2010, mediation is an activity carried out by a neutral and impartial third party—the mediator—with the goal of assisting two or more parties in reaching an amicable agreement and the resolution of the dispute.

In particular, after the submission of a request to start a mediation procedure, the Institution designates a mediator and arranges for an initial meeting between the parties in order to evaluate the possibility to reach an amicable agreement.

In case of successful outcome, a conciliation report (*processo verbale*) is signed by the parties and by the conciliator; in the case of non-performance of the provisions of the conciliation agreement, the report may be certified by the court and thus become enforceable for the purpose of execution (*espropriazione forzata*), the specific execution process (*esecuzione in forma specifica*) and the registration of judicial mortgage.

[80] Legislative Decree no 28/2010 provided for 3 different types of mediation: (1) voluntary mediation, when mediation is freely chosen by the parties; (2) judicial mediation, when the judge invites, at any stage but before the last hearing, the parties to attempt to resolve the disputed issue through mediation; and (3) mandatory mediation, when it is imposed by law. Of course, the last one is the most relevant novelty introduced.

[81] The provision for the compulsory nature of carrying out an attempt to settle the dispute through mediation, before resorting to court, was challenged by some associations (mainly by some Bars) due to its alleged unconstitutionality. In fact, such provision was declared unconstitutional by the Constitutional Court decision of 6 December 2012, no 272, but the reason for such decision was that the Law no 69/2009, enabling the government to introduce a regulation for mediation, did not provide for the possibility to establish the compulsory nature of mediation in certain matters. However, the legislator reintroduced the same obligation, even though partially amended, with Legislative Decree of 21 June 2013, no 69. Under the current regulation, the mediation procedure will be mandatory for an experimental period of 4 years.

[82] However, the claim preclusion is 'relative', in that the judge, after having ascertained the failed attempt at conciliation (which may be found ex officio by the date of the first hearing or may be claimed by the opposing party by the date of filing of the statement of appearance, which shall take place 20 days prior to the first hearing), must order the stay of court proceedings for no less than 4 months, so as to enable the parties to make an attempt at conciliation. After that, if the term granted by the judge has lapsed without any conciliation having been reached, the proceedings shall continue.

It has to be noted that, in order to set up an incentive to parties to reach reasonable out-of-court settlements, it is provided that, at the end of ordinary court proceedings, the court can refuse to award costs and expenses to the winning party, if this party had previously rejected a mediator's proposal of settlement which had the same content as the judicial decision. In such circumstances, the court may even order the winning party to pay the losing party's costs and court fees.

V. Concluding Remarks

Current Italian statutory discipline of 'banks' duty of care' concerning the provision of investment services largely follows the patterns set forth by EU legislation, namely the MiFID Directives.

Although such statutory regulation is quite detailed, in legal literature it is still debated whether it forms a 'closed' or an 'open' area of law, ie whether the relevant regulation is per se complete or, on the contrary, it has to be integrated with the general principles of Italian civil law. If the regulation applicable to the provision of investment services was a 'closed' system, any issue should be addressed in light of the contents of MiFID Directives and Regulations (and, therefore, within the related implementing statutes and Consob regulations). An argument in favour of this thesis is that, in this way, the maximum harmonisation goal of the MiFID Directives is met.[83] On the other hand, it has been noted that the complete lack of a statutory discipline of remedies applicable in case of breach of the investment firms' rules of conduct speak of the correctness of the opposite thesis, since such statutory gap needs to be filled through the general principles of civil law.[84]

Such issue seems to be confined to academia, since Italian case-law took—usually implicitly, sometimes expressly—a steady stance according to which the rules of conduct deriving from MiFID have to be applied along with the general rules of good faith in contractual relationships (Article 1375 of the Italian Civil Code), correctness (Article 1175 of the Italian Civil Code) and, even though to a lesser extent, due diligence in performing obligations (Article 1176 of the Italian Civil Code).

Such principles are usually applied by case-law in order to complete and, often, to construe the exact scope of statutory rules of conduct, in light of the common assumption that 'the special relationship for the provision of investment services necessarily implies a certain degree of reliance on the professionalism of the investment firm'.[85]

[83] See R Lener and P Lucantoni, 'comment to art. 21', in M Fratini and G Gasparri (eds), *Il testo unico della finanza* (Turin: UTET, 2012) 380.

[84] See Uda, 'L'informativa alla clientela in relazione ai servizi di investimento' (n 35) 38.

[85] Supreme Court no 8394, 27 April 2016.

Starting from the leading decision rendered by the Supreme Court on 19 December 2007, it is settled that the breach of banks' duty of care leads, according to the circumstances of each case, to pre-contractual liability (in case of breach of duties before the conclusion of investment contract) or to contractual liability for compensation of damages (in case of breach of rules applicable after the conclusion of the contract).

Nonetheless, the common feeling in Italy is that the risk for investment firms of being held liable—ex post—in civil proceedings brought by clients is not per se a sufficient incentive to behave correctly.[86]

Indeed, considering the contents of MiFID II (in particular with reference to the so-called 'product intervention' discipline),[87] as well as some intervention taken by the European Banking Authority,[88] it could be argued that the same need is sensed also at the European level. It seems likely, therefore, that also the further evolution of the Italian legal system in this respect will strictly follow European sources and trends.

[86] The issue is not only relevant for the purposes of single investors' protection, but also for the public interest in enhancing markets and financial stability. See GJ Schinasi, 'Defining Financial Stability' (2004) International Monetary Fund Working Paper no 187. See also Ferrarini and Giudici, 'Financial Scandals and the Role of Private Enforcement: The Parmalat Case' (n 3).

[87] See M De Mari, 'Product governance e product intervention nella MiFID 2: dalle regole di comportamento al controllo sui prodotti finanziari?' (2015) *Riv dir impr* 671; V Ricciuto, 'La tutela dell'investitore finanziario. Prime riflessioni su contratto, vigilanza e regolazione del mercato nella c.d. MiFID II' in Troiano and Motroni (eds), *La MiFID II. Rapporti con la clientela—regole di governance—mercati* (n 35) 7; F Capriglione, *Prime riflessioni sulla MiFID II (tra aspettative degli investitori e realtà normativa)* (2015) *Riv trim dir Economia* 72.

[88] See European Banking Authority's Guidelines on remuneration of sales staff, published on 28 September 2016. According to the related EBA's final report (available at: www.eba.europa.eu/regulation-and-policy/consumer-protection-and-financial-innovation/guidelines-on-remuneration-policies-for-sales-staff), 'developments in recent years have shown significant cases of misconduct and mis-selling by staff in financial institutions, with poor remuneration policies and practices having been identified as a key underlying driver' (see p 3 of the report).

7

Spain

MANUEL ÁNGEL LÓPEZ SÁNCHEZ,
EDUARDO VALPUESTA GASTAMINZA,
PEDRO JOSÉ BUESO GUILLÉN AND JORGE NOVAL PATO

I. Introduction

For a long time, the Spanish legal framework has featured a significant regulatory toolset for the protection of customers of credit and investment institutions. Indeed, many provisions have been issued since the 1980s, targeting the preservation of the economic interests of financial services customers. To a great extent, this happened because of European Union action, pushing for a consumer-friendly orientation and for strengthening the fairness, transparency and efficacy of the markets for credit and shares.

The present chapter aims to give an overview of the Spanish law regarding the duties of transparency, information and advice that financial institutions have to fulfil in order for their customers to take thoughtful and consistent decisions in the related markets. The largest part of this study is devoted to the analysis of the most relevant provisions that contribute to achieving this target. This analysis includes references to the most important court decisions, especially the decisions taken in the last five years. These are a very significant component of the legal framework, owing to the high level of litigiousness caused by the massive commercialisation of complex and high-risk-level financial products.

II. Major Cases

A. Floor Clause Agreements with Consumers in Mortgage Contracts

In cases of loans or credit at variable interest rates, the 'floor clause' is one that establishes a minimum interest rate that must be paid even when the applicable variable interest rate formula is lower. By doing so, the customer does not benefit from a major drop in benchmark interest rates. The 'floor' is sometimes accompanied by a 'cap', giving the customer a maximum interest rate; the customer benefits from this if the benchmark interest rate rises markedly. These clauses are referred to as 'collar clauses'.

A consumers' association proposed an injunction to protect collective consumers' interests against three credit institutions that had marketed mortgage loans to consumers with floor clauses (in every case there were also cap clauses, although these were not the reason for the lawsuit). The basic reasoning behind the claim was that there was a lack of information and clarity with regard to the content and consequences of these clauses. In a decision that was extremely important, not only because it affected three banking institutions, but also because it set a precedent applicable to floor clauses in any bank financing contract, the Spanish Supreme Court declared such clauses to be void. In its decision of 9 May 2013,[1] the Supreme Court ruled that floor clauses are legal as long as they are transparent enough to enable the consumer: (1) to identify the clause as a defining feature of the main subject matter of the contract; and (2) to know the real distribution of risks in the variability of rates. If both conditions are satisfied, the consumer may clearly appreciate that what is stipulated is a loan with a fixed minimum interest rate. In this particular case the Court considered that the floor clauses were not transparent. The clauses were found to be not transparent for several reasons: (1) sufficiently clear information that would indicate that the clauses were a defining feature of the main subject matter of the contract was lacking; (2) the clauses were inserted together with the cap clauses and as an apparently additional consideration to them; (3), there were no simulations of different scenarios regarding the reasonably predictable behaviour of the interest rate at the time of entering into the contract; (4) there was no clear and understandable information about the comparable costs of other loan modalities offered by the same institution; and (5) in the case of one of the three respondents, the clauses were inside a bewildering amount of data that distracted the consumer's attention and where they were disguised.

This decision was also the subject of clarification in a subsequent ruling of the Court, dated 3 June 2013. According to the ruling, the abovementioned circumstances do not constitute an exhaustive list of circumstances to be considered to the exclusion of others, and the isolated presence of one or more of them is not enough for the clause to be considered to be not transparent for the purposes of controlling its abusive nature. Neither was the nullity prevented by the fact that the consumer would have benefited from the decrease in benchmark interest rates for a period of time.

[1] This decision was the subject of numerous doctrinal comments, which are referred to in A Carrasco Perera and Ma C González Carrasco, 'La doctrina casacional sobre transparencia de las cláusulas suelo conculca la garantía constitucional de la tutela judicial efectiva' (2013) 7 *Revista CESCO de Derecho de Consumo* 125 et seq (https://cesco.revista.uclm.es/index.php/cesco/article/view/356/309). See also F Pertíñez Vílchez, 'Falta de transparencia y carácter abusivo de la cláusula suelo en los contratos de préstamo hipotecario' (2013) 3 *Indret Revista para el análisis del derecho* (www.indret.com/pdf/995.pdf).

As can be seen, the decision bases the nullity of the clauses on a lack of 'transparency' with regard to their existence and the consequences of their being fixed. No assessment was made as to whether the content of the clauses themselves could be abusive for a consumer.

The floor clause is considered to be part of the object of the contract, an essential element, but in this particular case the issue was not one of 'control of content' of the clause, but rather control of its clarity and transparency within the terms and conditions (the so-called 'control of inclusion'). The floor clause failed to pass the control of inclusion and was not a stipulation of the contract at all.

The same criterion of nullity of the floor clause for lack of transparency has been followed in other judgments of the same court (decisions of 9 May 2013, 8 September 2014, 24 March 2015, 25 March 2015 and 29 April 2015). Furthermore, the decision of 25 March 2015 has declared that the nullity of the clause does not have retroactive effects, so that the floor clauses were effective until publication of the judgment of 9 May 2013, and did not apply, however, from the time of such publication. If a floor clause is declared void for lack of transparency, the interest paid from the publication of the judgment of 2013 would have to be returned. This issue has generated an intense discussion and gave rise to several requests for a preliminary ruling from the European Court of Justice, asking if it is in line with Directive 93/13/EEC[2] to not recognise full retroactive effects of the nullity

The judgment of the European Court of Justice was delivered on 21 December 2016, and the Court held that Article 6(1) of Council Directive on Unfair Clauses

> must be interpreted as precluding national case-law that temporally limits the restitutionary effects connected with a finding of unfairness by a court, in accordance with Article 3(1) of that directive, in respect of a clause contained in a contract concluded between a consumer and a seller or supplier, to amounts overpaid under such a clause after the delivery of the decision in which the finding of unfairness is made.

In accordance with this decision, the Spanish government approved the Royal-Decree-Law (Real Decreto-Ley) 1/2017, of 20 January, concerning urgent measures to protect consumers in terms of floor clauses. According to the same, credit institutions must set up a Prior Claim System, so that the consumer may request a calculation of amounts to be returned, and an agreement can be reached between the bank and the consumer. If the consumer does not accept the amount offered by the bank, and files a claim in court, legal costs will only be imposed on the bank if the judgment is more favourable than the final offer made by the bank.[3]

[2] OJ L 95, 21 April 1993, 29–34.

[3] For detailed information and further references, see F Pertíñez Vílchez, *La Nulidad de las Cláusulas Suelo en Préstamos Hipotecarios* (Valencia: Tirant Lo Blanch, 2016).

B. Interest Rate Swaps

On a number of occasions the Supreme Court has had the opportunity to pass judgment on interest rate swaps agreed with customers of credit institutions.[4] Speculative swaps were involved in every case, not linked to a particular loan of the customer. As a general rule the Court considered that there was no error caused to the customer's part if the customer was a company with knowledge about this type of product, but on the other hand an error was deemed to exist when the contracting party was a retail investor (an investor who does not have specific knowledge of the risks involved in the financial market).

In a decision of 21 November 2012, a swap contracted with a company was studied where the company requested an annulment on the grounds of an error for not having been informed of the consequences of the swap.[5]

In the decision under appeal the contract was annulled on the grounds of an error, but the Supreme Court revoked the decision and considered that no mistake had in fact been proven. According to the Court, the company was aware of the nature of the operation not only because of the underlying structure of the agreed regulations, but also because it was expressly notified by the credit institution as to the essential risks, as it declared in the decision under appeal. Besides, the company could not allege that it was unaware of the fact that the fluctuations of the Euribor could give rise to payment settlements that went against it, given that in these types of contract the parties assume this very risk of losing against the possibility of making a profit.

A decision of 29 October 2013 considered a swap agreed with a company, which had received several positive payment settlements, but which then claimed the contract was void when it received the first payment against itself. The decision

[4] For decisions deriving from lower courts see, amongst others, the studies by F Mercadal Vidal and G Hernández Paulsen, *La comercialización de swaps de tipos de interés por las entidades de crédito. Estudio sobre la jurisprudencia de las Audiencias Provinciales* (Barcelona: Bosch, 2012) and I Raluca Stroie, 'Deberes de información en los contratos de permuta financiera: un recorrido por la jurisprudencia civil de 2012 (2013) 5 *Revista CESCO de Derecho de Consumo* 123 et seq (https://cesco.revista.uclm.es/index.php/cesco/article/view/264/229); A Caba, 'El contrato de permuta financiera (swap), modalidad de tipos de intereses, en las sentencias de las Audiencias Provinciales' (2013) 290 *Revista de Derecho Mercantil* 503 et seq; S Baz Barrios, 'La problemática de los *swaps* o contratos de permuta financiera' (2013) 8 *Revista CESCO de Derecho de Consumo* 146 et seq (www.revista.uclm.es/index.php/cesco/article/view/428/370).

[5] This decision was the subject of a number of doctrinal comments; esp those by JMa Garrido, 'Permutas financieras de tipos de interés y obligaciones informativas de las empresas de servicios de inversión (Comentario a la STS de 21 de noviembre de 2012)' (2013) 288 *Revista de Derecho Mercantil* 429 et seq; AM Morales Moreno, 'Permuta financiera de intereses (swap), deberes de información, error e indemnización. Reflexiones sobre la STS de 21-11-2012' (2013) 289 *Revista de Derecho Mercantil* 407 et seq; and JM Bustos Lago 'Sentencia de 21 noviembre 2012 (RJ 2012, 11052). Acción de nulidad de contrato de permuta financiera de tipos de interés (swap) fundada en error en el consentimiento derivado de pretendidos defectos en la información precontractual. Inexistencia. La incertidumbre de la ganancia y el riesgo de pérdida es propio de los contratos con componentes aleatorios' (2013) 92 *Cuadernos Cívitas de Jurisprudencia Civil* 561 et seq.

under appeal also considered that there was an error by the contracting party, but the Supreme Court revoked this decision on the ground that the account of factual evidence of the decision showed no basis for understanding that there had been an error.[6] The very nature of the contract involved a considerable degree of uncertainty and the company assumed the risk of making a loss that correlated with the hope of making a profit. A company with experience in the market and in relations with banking institutions could not allege an error in this type of contract, and there was no change to the unforeseeable circumstances, given that in this type of contract uncertainty is the basis for determining contractual regulations.

In a decision of 17 February 2014,[7] a company that had contracted a swap also attempted to claim an annulment, and at the same time alleged that an attempt at early cancellation of the contract had been met with an excessive demand for payment for such cancellation. In this case, as with the others, the Court of Appeal had annulled that contract on the grounds of a mistake. The Supreme Court considered that no such error could be demonstrated, and that the alleged lack of information does not always give rise to an error, or, in other words, the person informed may have fallen into an error—the fact that it is excusable is another matter—while on the other hand there are those who are not informed and who do not suffer any error as a result of that lack of information. In this particular case, the lack of information about the cost of early termination of the contract had not been shown to be essential for the client:

> a lack of due information about the cost of early termination of the financial operation should not be regarded as the cause of an essential error, or at least in the manner demonstrated here, and therefore does not provide the institution with sufficient motives to bring about the annulment of the entire contract.

Finally, a decision of 20 January 2014 did, by contrast, consider that there was a mistake in a case where the contracting party to the swap was also a company.[8] It had not been demonstrated that the company had special financial knowledge and that suitability or convenience tests had been conducted. The only pre-contractual information was two email letters, in which the bank (which offered the product)

[6] On this and the other decisions of the Supreme Court on swaps, see the comments of MC Juan Gómez, 'Interest Rate Sawps. A vueltas con el error vicio' (May-June 2014) 55 *El Notario del Siglo XXI* 38 et seq (www.elnotario.es/index.php/opinion/opinion/3759-interest-rate-swaps-a-vueltas-con-el-error-vicio).

[7] A brief note on this decision can be seen in P Franquet, 'Swaps: de lo visible a lo invisible (Comentario a la STS 46/2014, de 17 de febrero de 2014)' *Revista de Derecho del Mercado Financiero* (23 April 2014) (www.jausaslegal.com/resources/doc/140424-pablo-franquet-swaps-de-lo-visible-a-lo-invisible-8231842439527539206.pdf).

[8] As regard this decision, see amongst others the comments of J Alfaro Águila-Real, 'La sentencia sobre swaps del Tribunal Supremo' http://derechomercantilespana.blogspot.com.es/2014/02/la-sentencia-sobre-swaps-del-tribunal.html (20 March 2014); L Sanz Acosta, 'La evolución de la jurisprudencia del TS en materia de swaps y su culminación en la sentencia de 20 de enero de 2014' (2014) 2 *La Ley mercantil* 92 et seq; and E Valpuesta, 'Incumplimiento de la normativa comunitaria MiFID en cuanto a los deberes de información y evaluación del cliente: consecuencias en el ámbito contractual según la jurisprudencia española' (March 2016) 8(1) *Cuadernos de Derecho Transnacional* 271–99 (http://e-revistas.uc3m.es/index.php/CDT/article/viewFile/3030/1736).

presented it as insurance against inflation. The decision defined the company as a 'retail investor', and considered that there was an error because the information given to the contracting party was minimal (the two emails mentioned above), and using this data as a basis, the company could not have known of the risk associated with the contracted product. It could only be aware of this when it received the first settlement, which was a payment obligation. The credit institution should also have performed the suitability and convenience tests, and although not doing so does not necessarily imply an error (as there may be an error even though the tests are completed, and there may be full knowledge even if they are not), the Court considered that the absence of the tests and information does in fact make the error probable: 'that is why the absence of the test does not determine in itself if the procedural error exists, but it does allow for its possible existence'. The consequence of that decision was the annulment of the swap agreement.

In all these rulings, the clients' claims were based on an error in contracting, basically caused by a lack of information. The decision of 20 January 2014 was the first to state expressly the consequences of not complying with the requirements regarding information and tests of the MiFID Directives package, and affirms that this breach may not be the cause of the error, but does enable the error to be a presumable option.

The subsequent decisions of the Supreme Court have followed along these lines. Among others, in its decisions of 13 October 2015, 10 November 2015, 30 November 2015 and 4 December 2015, the Court has condemned the financial intermediary who sold swaps to non-expert customers. However, the Court has dismissed a claim where the investor had been regarded as an expert, as in the decision of 17 February 2014.

C. Lehman Brothers Bond Underwriting by Retail Clients

The Spanish Supreme Court has passed judgment on many occasions on situations where Lehman Brothers bonds were acquired. On several occasions it has passed rulings against the investor because he was an investor with financial knowledge who was aware of the risks involved in the investment. In the decision of 18 April 2013 (no 243/2013), the investors were a group of families that had expressly requested a bank to present them with a bond they could underwrite, similar to those offered to them by other financial institutions. The bank offered Lehman Brothers bonds to them, and the group underwrote them. After the bankruptcy of the issuer, the families claimed that the bank had breached its obligations as agent by not providing information and claimed compensation for damages. The Supreme Court upheld the rejection of the claim because the person who acted on behalf of the group of families was an expert investor, who had established the characteristics of the bond, and therefore lack of information could not be alleged. The case was not one of an investment consultancy but rather of the performance of an acquisition order given by the client. Besides, at the time of acquisition there was no information indicating that the subsequent insolvency of Lehman Brothers was in any way likely to occur.

In a decision of 20 February 2014 an investor with considerable experience—'with full knowledge of the financial market, with a great deal of experience in investments that most people find hard to understand, who was duly consulted in the investment'—had acquired Lehman Brothers bonds, and after the collapse of the institution claimed that the bank that had acted as intermediary in the underwriting was a guarantor for the process. The Supreme Court considered that there was no guarantee whatsoever on the bank's part and that the investor could only count on the solvency of the issuer of the bonds, Lehman Brothers.[9]

Finally in a decision of 18 April 2013 (no 244/2013, the same date as the previously mentioned decision—both decisions are plenary sessions of the court), the case consisted of a married couple with a conservative investment profile, who had contracted the management of a securities portfolio to a credit institution.[10] The institution acquired Lehman Brothers bonds, Lehman Brothers then went bankrupt, and the couple presented a claim demanding damages for negligence in compliance with the commission agreement. According to the Supreme Court, the bank did not comply with the standards of diligence, good faith and the provision of complete, clear and precise information required of it, by proposing the acquisition of high risk and complex securities, without explaining to the clients that they did not match the extremely low-risk profile that they had selected when entering into the discretional securities portfolio contract. The challenged ruling was revoked and the contract was annulled.[11] In the same sense, considering that there was a lack of information to investors who were not experts in financial investment.[12]

[9] In the same sense, considering that there was no lack of information, because the investor was a professional who knew the risks taken, see the decisions of 26 June 2014, 2 July 2014, 8 September 2014 (in plenary session), 18 December 2014, 23 April 2015 or 21 July 2015.

[10] See comments by F Juan y Mateu on this ruling in 'Responsabilidad del banco gestor de una cartera de inversión por la compra de participaciones preferentes de Lehman Brothers. (Comentario a la STS [Sala 1ª Pleno] de 18 de abril de 2013 [ponente: Rafael Sarazá Jimena])' (2013) 290 *Revista de Derecho Mercantil* 455 et seq; and K Lyczkowska, 'Responsabilidad del gestor de la cartera de valores por las pérdidas derivadas de la evolución de los productos financieros adquiridos' (2013) 6 *Revista CESCO de Derecho de Consumo* 197 et seq (: www.revista.uclm.es/index.php/cesco/article/view/305/282).

[11] In the 2 decisions of 18 April 2013 the action taken was for compensation for damages for negligent breach of the commission agreement. The events had taken place prior to the entry into force of the MiFID Directives. The claims were based on a breach of contract. However, the Court considered that such a breach of duties by the financial institution caused the annulment of the contract because of lack of consent, and ordered restitution by the financial institution of the invested sums and compensation of the damages suffered by the customers; see section V.A for further details.

[12] See also decisions of 10 September 2014, 18 December 2014, and 30 December 2014, 7 July 2015, 10 July 2015 or 20 November 2015.

D. Claims on 'Preferred Stock' Issued by Credit Institutions

There is currently a great deal of litigation in Spain on the underwriting of debt instruments that have the name of 'preferred stock' or 'subordinated debt' by credit institutions. These debt instruments have the following general characteristics: they are 'perpetual', so that the invested capital is not returned (although sometimes the issuing institution may cancel the product and return the capital in a particular period); interest is paid, but with the condition that benefits be obtained by the issuer; in cases of bankruptcy, the holders are subordinate creditors; and the instruments can be sold on the secondary market. A large number of investors acquired these instruments, sometimes cancelling bank deposit contracts to invest the money in underwriting them. Many of the issuers have been unable to comply with their payment obligations because of the financial crisis (in fact, some issuers have been subject to public intervention). This had led to an enormous number of claims, some of which shall be settled by arbitration established specifically for these cases.[13]

The decisions of courts of first instance or appeal take widely differing positions on the issue.[14] In some cases the bank has been held liable for misleading advertising, because the advertisement highlighted the rate of interest of the instruments without making reference to characteristics that might be less attractive (although these were included in the leaflet given to the client): this is the case with the decision given in the Provincial Court of Palma de Mallorca on 2 June 2005.

In most cases where the person acquiring the instruments was a retail investor, the contract was annulled owing to the existence of an error. See the decision of the Provincial Courts of Palma de Mallorca of 21 March 2011 (error due to lack of information), Murcia of 1 April 2011 (error due to lack of information: it was not made clear that the capital could be lost), Zaragoza of 17 April 2012 (sale of preferred stocks to senior citizens: lack of information and product unsuitable for the investor's profile), Pontevedra of 25 April 2012 (the purchaser wanted to have the money available in a period of two years, while the product sold was perpetual: the error was based on the lack of information about the product characteristics), Madrid of 26 June 2012 (the sale of preferred stock was drawn up in a contract whose heading was 'Fixed-term deposit agreement' and the training of the investor in financial products was not accredited), Cordoba of 30 January 2013

[13] See section VI for further details about the stock issued by institutions that is subject to intervention by the state.

[14] For further details about these decisions, see M Fernández Benavides, 'Participaciones preferentes: aproximación al problema y primeras respuestas de la jurisprudencia civil' (2012) 4 *Revista CESCO de Derecho de Consumo* 25 et seq (available at: www.revista.uclm.es/index.php/cesco/article/view/134/116); and F Caballero García, 'Doctrina jurisprudencial sobre las participaciones preferentes' in A Caba Tena and E Sanjuán y Muñoz (eds), *Reclamaciones frente a la comercialización de las participaciones preferentes* (Barcelona: Bosch, 2013) 149 et seq.

(error in the type of product purchased and lack of information), Pontevedra of 4 April 2013 (which distinguished between the legal system existing before and after the entry into force of the MiFID Directives and noted the existence of an error in consent).

In other cases, what was requested was not an annulment as a result of an error, but rather the termination of the contract for breach of the agent's obligations. This was the situation in both decisions of the Provincial Court of Palma de Mallorca of 2 September 2011 and 16 February 2012, because after the investor purchased Lehman Brothers bonds he was not subsequently informed of the situation of the institution, or the decision of the Provincial Court of Asturias of 26 September 2011 (the error was not grave or relevant, and the contract was not annulled for this reason, but there was a lack of information prior to and after the contract that determined the breach of the obligations of the credit institution), or that of Murcia of 21 February 2012 (the underwriter was a professional investor).

However, at the same time, decisions have been given against the investor, basically when it was proven that he had financial knowledge. This was the case in the decisions of the Provincial Court of Zaragoza of 3 February 2012 (investor with certain previous experience, and lack of information was not demonstrated), or that of Valladolid of 20 February 2012 (there was sufficient information, and the lack of payment of the bonds was not attributable to the bank).

Decisions have also been passed against the investor in cases where the acquisition of these instruments was due to an express order from the consumer, with no assessment from the bank (as was the case in the decision of the Provincial Court of Madrid of 6 April 2011).

In its decisions of 16 September 2015 and 25 February 2016, the Supreme Court ruled in favour of non-expert customers when contracting for financial products. The Court was of the view that the information the financial institution provided to the claimants neither could be regarded as being sufficient nor satisfied the standards required by the regulation in force at the time of the claim. Furthermore, the fact that customers had entered into contracts for similar products before did not imply that they had investment experience in complex financial products, if at the time of entering such prior contacts they had not received the information required by the regulation in force. However, the Supreme Court dismissed claims brought by an investor who bought preferred stock and who did have financial expertise and was properly informed (decisions of 8 September 2014 and 30 September 2015). These decisions insisted that preferred stocks were fully lawful financial products; hence the act of selling these product supported with proper information could not be annulled. In doing so, the Supreme Court followed the path established in arbitration claims against the commercialisation of preferred stocks.[15]

[15] See section VI below.

E. Misrepresentation in the Issue of Prospectus of Shares of Bankia

In two decisions of 3 February 2016 (plenary session) the Supreme Court has decided claims against the sale of shares of Bankia. Bankia is a bank resulting from the merger of several saving banks that had entered financial difficulties during the financial crisis. At the time of its incorporation, all shares were owned by the Banco Financiero de Ahorros (BFA). In 2011, in order to raise funds, BFA sold 55 per cent of its Bankia shares to the public by means of a placement and flotation operation on the stock exchange. Shares were sold for €3.75 per share. In the middle of 2012, the value of Bankia's shares slumped owing to the publication of data about the negative asset value of the institution. Even the nominal value of the shares had to be reduced from €2 to 10 cents. Dealing with claims of retail investors, the Supreme Court accepted misrepresentation in the issuing the prospectus and ordered Bankia to reimburse the sums paid for the shares. In order to stop the pending litigation and to avoid new litigation (with savings of around €400 million in litigation costs), Bankia offered to reimburse the investment to all retail investors adding an annual 1 per cent interest rate. It can be estimated that 200,000 retail investors bought shares against a total value of €1.5 million. At the time of writing, it is not clear whether also institutional investors can benefit from an annulment of the share acquisition contracts, because the Supreme Court is of the view that the misrepresentation in the issue prospectus was indeed enough to mislead retail investors, whereas institutional investors were able to know and should have done further and more extensive investigations with respect to the solvency of the institution.

F. The Execution of a Collective Action against Unfair Contractual Terms and Conditions Does not Prevent the Execution of an Individual Action to Establish the Unfair Character of such Clauses

Terms and conditions of financial and banking products are a frequent target of collective actions by consumer associations. If such a collective action against a concrete clause is pending, it was not clear whether a single consumer could execute an individual action for a declaration that the clause is *lis pendens*, by virtue of Article 43 of the Civil Procedure Act. If the exemption is given, the judge can suspend the proceeding until a decision on the collective action has been given. Several courts requested a preliminary ruling from the European Court of Justice on whether such suspension was automatic. The Court, in its decision of 14 April 2016, ruled that Article 7 of Directive 93/13/EEC must be interpreted as precluding a provision of national law, such as that at issue in the main proceedings, which requires a court, before which an individual action has been brought by a consumer seeking a declaration that a contractual term binding him to a seller or supplier is unfair, automatically to suspend such an action pending a final judgment concerning an ongoing collective action brought by a consumer association. The judge shall not automatically suspend the individual action, but he shall take into consideration if such a suspension is accurate from the point of view of the protection of the consumer.

III. Preferred Legal Basis: Error

Although in doctrinal terms a framework does exist of a general duty of financial institutions towards the correct guidance of the free will of its customers, this is not an autonomous duty, different from the one provided in Article 7 of the Civil Code or Article 1258 of the Civil Code. The same can be said of the duties to inform that Articles 209 to 217 of the consolidated text of the Securities Market Act (TRLMV)[16] set for institutions that provide investment services: such duties are framed as specifications of the general duty, with regard to the legal situation they are applied to. This explains why judges have resorted to duties arising from the MiFID Directives, incorporated into Spanish law by the abovementioned Articles 209–217 TRLMV, to integrate and specify the duty of general diligence applicable to financial institutions, in the understanding that an infraction by these institutions of duties to inform consists of a breach of the duty of due diligence, and as a result of this is either the deficient guidance in forming the consent of the customer, with the subsequent voiding of the signed contract, or there is a grave breach of its contractual duties.[17]

[16] Texto refundido de la Ley del Mercado de Valores (Royal Legislative Decree 4/2015, of 23 October).

[17] As required by MiFID, Art 19(3), the Spanish legislator has established that the information which financial institutions have to provide to their clients 'may be provided in a standardised format' (TRLMV, Art 210(2)). This stance of the Spanish legislator may change when introducing MiFID II (Directive 2014/65/EU on 15 May 2014), whose Art 24(5) provides that 'Member States may allow that information to be provided in a standardised format'. Pending the corresponding legislation to adapt the TRLMV to the requirements stated in MiFID II, it is not clear how a possible no-option normative decision of the Spanish legislator in the sense of MiFID II shall be interpreted. However, taking into account (1) on the one hand, the protective aim of the provision, and (2) on the other hand, the wording in force at the present time (precedent of the future provision), it is plausible that, in such a case, the provision of information 'in a personalised manner' can be regarded as compulsory; if the financial institution acts in a different manner, both an administrative sanction because of infringement of the provision and the private-law effect already described may arise, except for in the case that the financial institution is able to bring evidence that the clients were 'reasonably able to understand the nature and risks of the investment service and of the specific type of financial instrument' offered 'and, consequently, to take investment decisions on an informed basis'.

In short, as may be gleaned from the major cases mentioned in section II above, it is clear that the courts, in response to claims by customers against financial institutions, usually set about resolving them by means of the error as an invalidation of consent or the breach of duties arising from the commission or portfolio management contract, or a combination of the two. Nevertheless, in cases where the contract has been executed while the MiFID regulations are in force, the breach of this regulation is not irrelevant: thus, if the intermediary did not comply with the duties to perform the suitability or convenience tests, or performed tests that were incomplete or too general, there is an infraction that can be punished with a fine, and the breach of this regulation can also be used to underline the fact that there was a lack of information, error in the investor's part or a breach of due diligence by the bank. As indicated above,[18] the decision of the Supreme Court of 20 January 2014 considered this very same issue, affirming that the lack of testing does not necessarily bring about an error in the investor, but it does permit said error to be assumed by rebuttable presumption.

That said, compliance by financial institutions with the MiFID regulations does not seem to be sufficient to bring about the understanding that they have worked with due diligence. On the one hand, because the duties established in the TRLMV do not replace the duties for any contracting party that derive from the general law on contracts, these duties are additional to the 'general' duties and besides, in some cases, specify or put into practice the content of the general duties; therefore, they should never be interpreted as an 'exemption' from the general duties, because that would go against a purposive interpretation of the regulations (Civil Code, Article 3.1) and would contradict the requirements of good faith, both pre-contractual (with consequences in the system of invalid consent (Civil Code, Articles 1266, 1269 and 1270)) and contractual (Civil Code, Article 1258). On the other hand, case-law has, until recently, maintained the opinion that a merely formal observance of the requirements arising from these regulations is not sufficient (eg documentary evidence), but that there should be results arising from what the 'spirit' of the regulations sets out to provide, without the possibility of behaviour in sales activity that might pervert this (eg the financial institution has documentary proof that it has complied with the pre-contractual duties to warn, but in reality the customer was not duly assessed so that he could provide informed consent, as he was told not to worry, that it was a safe investment, etc).

It cannot be said that there is a specific standard of diligence for financial institutions as there is for certain professionals (doctors, lawyers, auditors, etc) in the context of the requirement for liability under private law. The result is that case-law does not resolve issues raised by the observance or breach of due diligence by financial institutions by resorting to a set of standards belonging to a professional activity that are assessed by experts in the profession or skill concerned. This is owing to the fact that financial institutions do not have the status of professionals in Spanish law, but rather that of traders or commercial entrepreneurs

[18] See section II.

(Article 1.2° of the Code of Commerce[19] and Article 2 of the Capital Companies Act (LSC))[20] and so lack a specific formalised *lex artis* that can be compared to the *lex artis* of the professions of medicine, law, etc.

Nevertheless, financial institutions have to observe a standard or model of diligence when practising their activities that is different from the one governing general legal-private relations. Indeed, while the reference standard in the latter group is that of the 'orderly paterfamilias', although 'the nature of the obligation' is also relevant in this case as is 'the circumstances of the persons, the time and the place' (Civil Code, Article 1104), the main factor in the model of conduct for financial institutions is that of the 'orderly businessman'—and when applicable, the 'loyal representative'—coined in case-law (and adopted in statutory law for members of boards of directors of capital companies (see LSC, Article 225)). However, although it is undisputed that the level or degree of diligence required by the model of 'orderly businessman' is superior to that of the 'orderly paterfamilias', it is unclear what the level or degree of diligence should be in a particular case, since it continues to be a vague legal concept.

The notion of 'best practices' of financial institutions is especially interesting. This was established in Article 2.4 of Order ECC/2502/2012, of 16 November, regulating the procedures for the presentation of claims at the Claims Services of the Bank of Spain, the National Securities Market Commission and the General Directorate of Insurance and Pension Funds. 'Best practices' is understood by the above provision as referring to

> those that are not imposed by contract law or rules of supervision and do not constitute a financial usage, and they are reasonably enforceable to responsible, diligent and respectful management of financial business dealings with customers.

This 'concept', which has its natural base in the administrative regulation of the protection of clients of financial institutions, has been the subject of specifications, for a large number of banking products and services, in the opinions given and reports issued by the Claims Service of the Bank of Spain (SRBE)[21] in its annual reports published since it was created in 1987;[22] and more recently, for the operators and products themselves of the securities markets, in the Communication of the General Directorate of Institutions of the National Securities Market Commission on the commercialisation of complex financial instruments, of 10 April 2014. This report has its own best practices and also makes use of the ones

[19] Código de Comercio of 22 August 1885, with subsequent modifications.

[20] Ley de Sociedades de Capital (Royal Legislative Decree 1/2010, of 12 July, with subsequent modifications).

[21] Servicio de Reclamaciones del Banco de España.

[22] For further information about the Claims Service of the Bank of Spain and of the National Securities Market Commission, the annual Memoranda are available at www.bde.es/bde/es/secciones/informes/Publicaciones_an/Memoria_del_Serv/ and at www.cnmv.es/portal/Publicaciones/PublicacionesGN.aspx?id=23.

established in the Opinions of the ESMA[23] on MiFID practices for the sale of complex financial instruments of 7 February 2014 and on best practices for the design, issue and sale of structured products of 27 March 2014, both of which were issued under Article 29 of Regulation (EU) No 1095/2010 of the European Parliament and the Council, of 24 November 2010.[24]

It should be pointed out that the concept of 'best practices' is a broad and complex one, as it covers the content of advertising, the terms and conditions that form a part of the contractual document, the mode of conduct and action for credit institutions with regard to their customers and even the agreements, collective decisions or recommendations and organised or consciously parallel practices between financial institutions. It should likewise be borne in mind that the concept goes beyond compliance with legal and regulatory obligations: it represents an added diligence, or to put it another way, a reinforced diligence, that financial institutions should observe in their dealings with their customers. In this respect, it could be said that 'best practices' set out a standard of special diligence, such as those used by certain professionals,[25] although the regulations and the praxis that establish it make it by no means certain that it can be compared to the notion of *lex artis* because of its peculiar nature. Thus, notwithstanding the direct effects of the infraction of these standards—which are not just legal-public in nature (see section V below)—, it is arguable whether it is worthwhile making use of this standard of reinforced diligence and its specifications by supervisory authorities when setting out to integrate the content of the contract using the provisions of Articles 7 and 1258 of the Civil Code or Articles 80 et seq of the Consolidated text of the General Act for the Defence of Consumers and Users and other complementary laws (TRLGDCU),[26] in their application to relations between financial institutions and their customers, at least, when they are consumers, too.

The legal and administrative provisions regulating the activities of financial institutions with regard to their customers have the principal objective of increasing transparency in the supply of financial products and services. However, such provisions do not require financial institutions to meet the claims of their customers by the fact that according to the Claims Service in question such claims are justified (Article 12.6 of Order ECC/2502/2012). The likelihood therefore exists that, despite the favourable report issued by the relevant Claims Service, the financial institution may not rectify its conduct, and the customer may be obliged to go to the courts to seek satisfaction for his legitimate interests. In a judicial context, a likely case in this situation would therefore be that the lack of observance of

[23] European Securities and Markets Authority (www.esma.europa.eu/).

[24] OJ L 331, 15 December 2010, 84–119.

[25] G Hernández Paulsen, *La obligación precontractual de la entidad de crédito de informar al cliente en los servicios bancarios y de inversión* (Madrid/Barcelona/Buenos Aires/Sao Paulo: Marcial Pons, 2014) 424–25.

[26] Texto Refundido de la Ley General para la Defensa de los Consumidores y Usuarios y legislación complementaria (Royal Legislative Decree 1/2007, 16 November, with subsequent modifications).

due diligence by the financial institution would be noted, based on the criteria arising from administrative or even informational practices in which the Service or supervisory body has demonstrated the existence of malpractice. In this regard, the SRBE has affirmed on numerous occasions that its reports constitute 'authorised opinions' on the observance or infraction of standards of discipline, best banking practice and customs by the bank in question. They could therefore be considered to be documentary or expert proof of a conduct that accords or not with generally observed banking practices,[27] from which the deduction of a particular breach by the financial institution can be drawn. Even so, the Supreme Court has stated that the opinions maintained by the SRBE are not binding for the judge, either as proof or as an evaluation of the behaviour of the parties, and should in any case be considered as evidentiary material to be left to the court's discretion.[28]

Nevertheless, the SRBE report may be taken into account when interpreting the conduct of the parties to the contract, 'when it verifies or confirms a business practice or use that should be observed in banking activities' (decision of the Provincial Court of Madrid of 4 February 1993). However, the decision of the Provincial Court of Seville, of 29 October 2004, goes further, as it makes use of the comments of the SRBE on the non-observance of best banking practice and customs by a credit institution and infers that there is a contractual breach by the credit institution as a result of the violation of best banking practice and customs 'by delaying several days, without justification or powers to do so, the payment of the loan funds to the borrower'. This malpractice, admitted to by the respondent itself, according to the decision, 'unmistakably constitutes a contractual breach provided for in article 1101 and corroborating part of the Civil Code and the bank shall be subject to payment of compensation for any loss or damages caused'.[29]

Besides this, it should be borne in mind, on the one hand, that there may be standards of special diligence for investment services companies included in

[27] For further information about this point, see MA López Sánchez, 'Disciplina bancaria y protección del consumidor' (1997) 42 *Estudios sobre consumo* 19–21.

[28] In other words, the Supreme Court limits the legal-private effectiveness of the reports of the SRBE:

> As regards the report of the Bank of Spain and the claim formulated by the plaintiff. … although it affirms that the Bank responding to the claim has acted against best banking practices and with manifest abuse of a dominant position by drawing up terms and conditions different from those it declared to have agreed, thereby enabling the creation of discrepancies and breach of the contract, said declarations are not binding to the jurisdiction; this is understood as such by the Claims Service of the Bank of Spain when it recognises the powers of the courts in determining the value of the documents as evidentiary material for establishing facts and intentions and affirming in the first of its conclusions that 'it does not correspond to this Service to determine the scope and content of the loan contract entered into between the claimant and the institution'. The facts declared and proven do not enable the conduct of the Bank responding to the claim to be qualified as contrary to one of good faith (decision of 21 December 2003).

[29] See the decisions of the Provincial Court of Madrid, of 21 July 2005, and that of the Provincial Court of Tenerife, of 18 July 2005 for similar cases.

the 'internal rules of conduct' (Article 202.1.c) TRLMV); and on the other, that Article 202.1.b) of the TRLMV makes provision for the approval of specific codes of conduct for the government or for the Ministry of the Economy and Inland Revenue, but this approval has not been given so far.

In addition to the abovementioned regulatory provisions, recent years have seen a consolidation in the doctrinal and jurisprudential position postulating the existence of a *general duty* of credit institutions, which is not explicitly stated, to ensure the correct formation of the contractual consent of their customers, even when they are professionals. This conception arises from the attempt to provide adequate protection to the interests of bank customers as a whole, above and beyond the protection granted by the legal framework currently in force.

As was highlighted above, legal protection of bank customers in the Spanish legal system, despite the profusion of regulations mentioned above, is unsatisfactory and requires improvement. In particular, any reform requires greater coordination of the duties placed on credit institutions to prevent overlapping as well as gaps, more complete and homogenous regulations from the viewpoint of customers, which in the same way as those established for investment services can act to guide the interests of customer protection in credit institutions as a whole, although with a different degree of intensity.

At present, banking discipline focuses essentially on customer protection for consumers and natural persons. However, there are other subjects, especially small and medium-sized companies, who frequently find themselves in similar situations of informational asymmetry in their relations with credit institutions, and who therefore, despite their status as companies, occupy a weaker position against them, since they do not have the knowledge, experience or qualifications required to adequately understand the contracts they enter into with credit institutions, especially where highly complex, sophisticated or risky products or services are concerned.

To counteract the effects of this unequal situation, rather than the traditional thesis defending the prevalence of the principle of the freedom of contract, and the tendency to place the burden of informing oneself on the shoulders of the company prior to executing a contract due to the company's nature as a professional body, it should be considered that credit institutions have the duty to provide their customers with the relevant background and circumstances, which are fundamental if they are to give suitable consent, above all when it can be seen that such customers have insufficient knowledge, experience or qualifications to enable them to be aware of, or to assess correctly, the information.

By way of summary, credit institutions should provide customers with any information that once adequately known and assessed by the customer, may lead him to withdraw from the intention to enter into a contract, or which at least become subject to the existence of other conditions.

The imposition of such an obligation of special diligence on credit institutions does not lack regulatory support. The duty of loyalty and cooperation is based mainly on the principle of good faith that presides over the preparation of any contract (Article 1258 of the Civil Code)[30] and in general over the exercise of any law (Article 7 of the Civil Code) and which ultimately obliges credit institutions not to take advantage of bank customers who act in good faith and without gross misconduct. At the same time, any specification in a given situation of the scope of good faith and the consequent duty of loyalty is not simple or exempt from uncertainties. Consequently, this principle does not represent a secure foundation and should always be a last resort when setting out to protect the interests of bank customers.

Despite the above, an as previously mentioned, present disputes between credit institutions and their customers continue to be resolved mostly by resorting to traditional remedies: the existence of lack of consent (Articles 1265 to 1270 of the Civil Code), either from an error or due to misconduct. In this regard, it should be pointed out that Spanish law requires that for the error to be relevant there should be a concurrence of two qualified requirements: it should be essential and it should be excusable on the part of the customer. That is why the customer's claim that his consent is invalid is only justified, on the one hand, when the error is applicable to substantial elements of the contract or on the terms of the contract that led to its execution; and on the other hand, when the error cannot be attributed to the customer. This last requirement should be handled with tremendous care. The customer is the person who is most responsible for coming to an adequate statement of his own free will, and therefore should bear the consequences of the errors of his own lack of diligence when gathering the information. However, on some occasions the customer's error can be deemed to be excusable when, as a result of his personal circumstances (age, cultural and professional position), he does not have the knowledge, experience or qualifications required to understand the contract being executed. It should be remembered in this line of reasoning that the customer's negligence is not relevant when evaluating the excusability of the error, when the credit institution is aware at the time of executing the contract (or should have known) of the essential error that the customer is committing and does not warn him appropriately. On the other hand, ignorance of or inaccurate representation to the customer and the consequent invalidity of the customer's consent may have been caused by the credit institution itself, either as wilful misconduct or through mere negligence, for having provided inaccurate information, for its ignorance of the essential nature of the error or for its reticence or omission when warning the customer about the substantial features and risks of the contracted operation or product.

30 Código civil of 24 July 1889, with subsequent modifications.

IV. Duties to Investigate and to Warn

Spanish credit institutions are subject to a large number of duties to inform.[31] From a private law perspective, the duties to inform are of a general nature, non-specific for financial services and products, and, because of this and the complexity of such services and products, integration by means of the more specific regulatory public law is required. The varied nature of the regulatory provisions establishing these duties not only makes it difficult to know about them but also to systematise them.

On the one hand there are the *duties to inform established by general standards*, which are not specifically directed towards regulating banking activities, but are applicable to credit institutions.

Thus, when a credit institution establishes a relationship with a *consumer*, the duties to inform established in the TRLGDCU should be borne in mind. This consolidated text recasts the Spanish legal provisions of transposition of the Community directives established for consumer and user protection (in particular those featured in the annex of Directive 98/27/EC).[32] The determining criteria to qualify a bank customer as a consumer, either natural person or legal entity, is that he should act for a purpose which is outside his trade, business or profession; in addition, in the case where the consumer is a legal entity, it is necessary that he acts without speculative ends in mind (Article 3 TRLGDCU). Amongst the provisions contained in these consolidated text are: the right to information of consumers (Article 8 TRLGDCU); the characteristics and content of the information that should be supplied when making services available (Article 18 TRLGDCU); the information required for commercial offers (Article 20(1) TRLGDCU); and especially the scope of pre-contractual information that should be supplied to customers (Article 60 TRLGDCU).

In so far as it is habitual banking practice to use forms with general conditions, as well as the use of conditions that are not individually negotiated in contracts, credit institutions should also comply with the protection standards for subscribers established in the General Conditions of Contract Act (LCGC)[33] and in the TRLGDCU. These regulations represent in terms of the issues referred to here the Spanish transposition of Directive 93/13/EEC, on unfair terms in contracts entered into with consumers. From a subjective point of view, it is not essential for the bank customer to be qualified as a consumer to enable the LCGC to apply: what is relevant in this case is that the subscriber is made subject to the standard contract

[31] For a more detailed explanation of these duties, see Hernández Paulsen, *La obligación precontractual de la entidad de crédito de informar al cliente en los servicios bancarios y de inversión* (n 25), which also contains an exhaustive bibliography.

[32] OJ L 166, 11 June 1998, 51–55.

[33] Ley de Condiciones Generales de la Contratación (Act 7/1998, 13 April, with subsequent modifications).

terms used by credit institutions in a wide range of contracts. In such situations, the standard contract terms only form part of the contract when they comply with the legal requirements of incorporation; that is to say when the subscriber has had a real opportunity to know the terms and accept them when entering into the contract, when these terms are clear and their regulatory content is understandable, and when they are in accordance with the legitimate expectations of the customers (which excludes surprising terms) (Articles 5 and 7 LCGC). Moreover, if the subscriber is a consumer, the protection is extended to contracts that include terms that are not individually negotiated—even when they are not standard terms—, because in this case the content of these contract terms may be subject to control in accordance with the requirements of good faith and fair balance between the rights and obligations of the parties. Such requirements naturally exclude any potential validity of the unfair terms (Articles 80 to 91 TRLGDCU).

At present, a notable percentage of bank contracts are entered into without the simultaneous physical presence of the contracting parties, that is, through long distance communication media. In situations such as these, the activities of credit institutions should adapt to the acceptance requirements laid down in Article 5.4 LCGC. This requirement is also set out for distance contracts with consumers in Article 80.1.b-II TRLGDCU. For issues relating to distance contracts, especially when made electronically, the Information Services and Electronic Commerce Act (LSSICE)[34] and the Act on Distance Selling of Financial Services to Consumers (LCDSFDC)[35] apply. These Acts have respectively been enacted to incorporate into Spanish law Directive 2000/31/EC, concerning certain aspects of the information society and electronic commerce,[36] and Directive 2002/65/EC on the distance marketing of financial services to consumers.[37] In particular, the application of Article 27.4 of the LSSICE requires credit institutions, prior to the contracting procedure, to make the general conditions available to the customer, so that he may store them and reproduce them, and by virtue of Article 9.1 of the LCDSFDC, when the credit institution enters into a distance contract with a consumer, it must inform the customer of all the contractual conditions before he should assume any obligations as a result of a distance offer or contract.

Alongside these general provisions, there are other *specific provisions geared at guaranteeing transparency and information to the customers of banking services.* Order EHA/2899/2011, of 28 October, on transparency and consumer protection in banking services, and Circular of the Bank of Spain[38] 5/2012, of 27 June, of the

[34] Ley de Servicios de la Sociedad de la Información y del Comercio Electrónico (Act 34/2002, of 11 July, with subsequent modifications).

[35] Ley de Comercialización a Distancia de Servicios Financieros destinados a los Consumidores (Act 22/2007, 11 July, with subsequent modifications).

[36] OJ L 178, 17 July 2000, 1–16.

[37] OJ L 271, 9 October 2002, 16–24.

[38] A Circular of the Bank of Spain is a binding norm addressed to credit institutions; the Bank of Spain issues such norms because it is the supervisory authority of the credit institutions in Spain. It has its own normative empowerment to do so. Not fulfilling the duties established in a Circular might be an administrative offence.

Bank of Spain, are noteworthy in this respect as they are directed towards credit institutions and payment service providers for issues of transparency of banking services and responsibility in granting loans. These administrative provisions currently recapitulate the wide variety of regulations that have been established for more than 20 years as regards the discipline and intervention of credit institutions by virtue of the enablement provided in Article 48.2 of the Act on Discipline and Intervention of Credit Institutions (LDIEC),[39] recently repealed by the Act on Regulation, Supervision and Solvency of Credit Institutions (LOSSEC).[40] However, Article 5 of the second Act has renewed the mandate of regulatory development of the protection of clients of institutions such as these.

At this point, it is interesting to emphasise the fact that the protection deriving from these regulations only benefits *natural persons*, independent of the fact that they may be regarded as consumers, neither on their considerations as retail investors or customers; that means, a sole trader who may be a professional investor or customer is protected by these regulations, too. Likewise, the activities of credit institutions with regard to specific banking contracts (mortgage loans, consumer credit and payment services) are also specifically regulated by the abovementioned Order EHA/2899/2011, the Act on Credit Contracts for Consumers (LCCC),[41] and the Payment Services Act (LSP)[42] and Order EHA/1608/2010, of 14 June, on transparency of contractual conditions and information requirements for payment services (the duties to inform that derive from this set of regulations will be indicated in greater detail below in this section). Another factor that should be remembered in this case is the duty imposed on credit institutions by the Sustainable Economy Act (LES),[43] to perform an adequate assessment of the solvency of consumers, as well as the need to actively encourage a series of practices geared towards guaranteeing responsible loan concession.

Credit institutions can also act as investment service providers (ISPs) and so are subject to regulations protecting the investor, as established in the TRLMV. This Act underwent a profound change with the amplification of the duties to inform and transparency brought about by the incorporation into the Spanish law of Directives 2004/39 (MiFID),[44] 2006/73[45] and Regulation 1287/2006.[46] In accordance with the provisions of these regulations and with no special characteristics with regard to Community law, the level and intensity of the duties of ISPs varies according to the type of customer. *Professional customers* are those that claim to have sufficient experience, knowledge and qualifications to enable them to

[39] Ley de Disciplina e Intervención de las Entidades de Crédito (Act 26/1988, of 29 July).
[40] Ley de Ordenación, Supervisión y Solvencia de las Entidades de Crédito (Act 10/2014, of 26 June).
[41] Ley de Contratos de Crédito al Consumo (Act 16/2011, of 24 June).
[42] Ley de Servicios de Pago (Act 16/2009, of 13 November, with subsequent modifications).
[43] Ley de Economía Sostenible (Act 2/2011, of 4 March, with subsequent modifications).
[44] OJ L 145, 30 April 2004, 1–44.
[45] OJ L 241, 2 September 2006, 26–58.
[46] OJ L 241, 2 September 2006, 1–25.

make their own investment decisions and to correctly assess the risks, while '*retail customers*' is the term used for the remainder (Article 202 TRLMV). Fulfilment of the duties to inform is conditioned by the extent and nature of the knowledge the ISPs have of their customers beforehand. Therefore, as an application of the principle of 'know your customer', the ISPs should 'get informed in order to inform' (Article 212 TRLMV, Articles 72 to 74 Royal Decree 217/2008, of 15 February, on the legal regulation of investment companies and other institutions that provide investment services, and Circular 3/2013, of the National Securities Market Commission, of 12 June) and are obliged to perform suitability and convenience tests on their customers. However, at the same time there is nothing that impedes the customer from entering into the contract, even though he has not passed the tests or has refused to take it or has received the warning by the ISP that the product or service is not suitable for him. The Order ECC/2316/2015, of 4 November, has specified the information duties and the classification of financial products.

Furthermore, all this regulatory network geared towards protecting the bank customer should be complemented by provisions that regulate advertising: of a general nature (contained in the General Advertising Act (LGP),[47] and the Unfair Competition Act (LCD))[48] and those applicable to consumers (Article 19.4 TRLGDCU), as well as administrative provisions that specifically cover financial services advertising: Order EHA/1718/2010, of 11 June, on regulation and control of advertising of banking products and services; and Circular 6/2010, of the Bank of Spain, of 28 September, directed towards credit and payment institutions on the advertising of banking products and services.

In addition to an explanation of the regulatory framework set out to protect the bank customer in the Spanish legal system, in what follows we will address the specific provisions, again mostly administrative in nature, that directly and specifically aspire to guarantee transparency and information for the recipients of banking and investment services.

This set of regulations has undergone significant growth in recent years as a result of the growing desire by Spanish legislators to strengthen the protection of bank customers and investors in their relations with financial institutions. This special concern is a notable feature of the LES, which introduces a novel legal principle that specifically regulates 'the responsibility in credit and protection of users of financial services' (Article 29). This legal principle, besides setting out to improve transparency in credit contracts, establishes in general terms that credit institutions are obliged to adequately inform their customers. However, to achieve this objective, the duty is not imposed on institutions to gather personal information on each potential client—in order to establish to what extent the product on offer is suitable for him—, but rather it is enough to provide adequate explanations so that he shall be the one, in the light of the information received,

[47] Ley General de Publicidad (Act 34/1988, of 11 November, with subsequent modifications).
[48] Ley de Competencia Desleal (Act 3/1991, of 10 January, with subsequent modifications).

to consider whether the bank product matches his interests, needs and financial situation. Nevertheless, from a subjective point of view, the scope of application of this duty is limited, since it only governs credit institutions when they relate to consumers (Article 29.2.a) 5º LES).

To develop this legal principle, and with the simultaneous aim of updating and concentrating the set of provisions concerning the protection of bank customers, the Ministry of the Economy and Inland Revenue promulgated Order EHA/2899/2011, of 28 October. As mentioned above,[49] this regulatory development mandate was renewed by Article 5.1 of the recent LOSSEC. At the same time, Order EHA/2899/2011 enabled the Bank of Spain to specify the development and performance of the Order. To comply with this mandate, the Bank of Spain approved Circular 5/2012, of 27 June.

Both the Order and the Circular provide for a sizeable number of general duties to warn. Thus, credit institutions should facilitate the customer of the banking services by providing all the *pre-contractual information* that the customer is legally entitled to demand. The duty sets out to ensure that the customer is in a condition to make an informed decision about a banking service and to compare similar offers (Article 6 of Order EHA/2899/2011). To do this, the information should be governed by a set of commitments to clarity, timeliness, sufficiency, objectivity and it should not be misleading. In terms of time, the customer should also receive this information before being bound, and the specific period in which the information should be provided in advance depends on the type of contract or offer. The minimum content of the pre-contractual obligation has been standardised by the Bank of Spain, which has provided a detailed description of the essential elements of each contract that should be provided to customers (sixth standard of Circular 5/2012). A specification of the this general duty to inform is that credit institutions, when selling *linked banking services*, should indicate to their customers expressly and in an understandable manner to what extent both services are only offered in a linked form or if they can be contracted independently under certain conditions (Article 12 of Order EHA/2899/2011).

Likewise, both the Order and the Circular set out to guarantee adequate *contractual information* for bank customers. Credit institutions should provide the customer with a suitable copy of the contract, without the customer being obliged to request one (Article 7 of Order EHA/2899/2011). The Bank of Spain has developed and systematised in detail the issues that contracts should explicitly and clearly explain (sixth standard of Circular 5/2012). The same standard specifies that, in any case, contracts should be drafted to be clear and understandable. To do this, the measures include the duty of credit institutions to avoid the use of technical jargon, or when this is unavoidable, to explain its meaning properly.

On the other hand, another point of interest is the regulatory provisions concerning the characteristics that should govern *communications* between credit

[49] See section IV.

institutions and their customers during the valid period of the contract in question. In particular, the communications should: (1) faithfully and clearly reflect the terms under which the services are performed; (2) not highlight any potential benefit of the service while expressly concealing the inherent risks thereof; (3) be sufficient so that the habitual recipient of the communication may adequately understand the essential terms of the service; and (4) not omit or distort any relevant information (Article 8.1 of Order EHA/2899/2011).

In accordance with the provisions of Article 29 LES, the Order EHA/2899/2011 and the Circular 5/2012 complete the general regulatory framework by establishing a duty to warn that is highly relevant. The legislator, aware of the difficulties of understanding and assimilation that recipients of information and communications might have, imposes a series of parameters that should guide the activities of credit institutions when they provide *explanations* to their customers. To demarcate the scope of these obligations, it is emphasised that the explanations should be adequate and sufficient to understand the essential terms of the contract in order to make an informed decision (Article 9 of Order EHA/2899/2011). What is more, the same legal principle establishes that credit institutions should take the needs and financial situation of their customers into account when providing the clarifications. Therefore, diligent compliance with this duty, which is incompatible with the idea of offering a simple, general and undifferentiated reply, requires credit institutions to ascertain and inform themselves about the personal circumstances of each customer.

In this respect, the Bank of Spain has developed this regulatory provision by underlining the *special diligence* that banks should assume for banking products and services in a number of situations: (1) when they imply special risks, such as that of zero remuneration in structured or hybrid deposits with capital guarantee, or one where there is a potentially significant increase of the cost of the loan as a result of its specific characteristics; (2) when the evaluation of a number of aspects is required such as the evolution (past or future) of benchmarks or the price of linked products that need to be contracted to enable the customer to make a correct assessment; (3) when as a result of the amount and duration, they imply obligations for the customer that might be especially onerous; (4) when their sale is accompanied by a personal recommendation, especially in the case of massive distribution campaigns for products or services mentioned above. In all these situations, banks should increase the diligence in explanations that have to be provided to customers receiving the offer when informing themselves and informing them, so that they can understand the features of the product and be able to make an informed decision and assess, in accordance with their knowledge and experience, the suitability of the product for their interests. To this end, they should collect adequate information about the customer as regards his needs and financial situation, and adapt the information they provide him in accordance with the gathered data (sixth standard of Circular 5/2012). It should be highlighted that this special duty is applicable to *structured or hybrid deposits*, in other words, to fixed term deposits with a performance partly or totally linked to the evolution of a given market index or benchmark or to an interest rate.[50]

On the other hand, it should be underlined that the pre-contractual informational duty that credit institutions should comply with, within the framework of marketing their own banking services, should be clearly differentiated from that of the provision of information and advice where a credit institution, by virtue of a specific contract, personally and justifiably makes recommendations about the institution or institutions offering the banking service sought by the customer which best meets the customer's needs. This contract, called a *consulting agreement*, is generally onerous and the credit institution should inform itself in order to be in a position to advise in the best interests of the customer. In particular, the credit institution is obliged to consider both the personal and financial situation of the customer, and his preferences and objectives (Article 10 of Order EHA/2899/2011), and to perform an objective and sufficiently wide-ranging analysis of the banking services available in the market. For this reason, the credit institution should exclusively safeguard the interests of its customer in the consultancy process and should under no circumstance transform the contract into a privileged opportunity to market its own banking services.

In relation to the general duties to inform, the provisions introduced by the recent LOSSEC should be mentioned. Article 5 of this Act, which simply enables the Ministry of the Economy and Competiveness to dictate regulations that it deems appropriate for the protection of clients of credit institutions, at the same time establishes the criteria that should govern these potential regulations. It states that both pre-contractual and contractual information, along with any notifications it provides, should reflect

> explicitly and with the maximum clarity the rights and obligations of the parties, the risks deriving from the service or product to the client, and other circumstances required to guarantee transparency of the most relevant conditions of the services or products and to enable the client to assess if they adapt to his needs and financial situation.

Along with the abovementioned general regulations, there is another group of provisions that impose specific obligations of information and transparency on credit institutions for certain banking contracts. In the case of *loan contracts*, credit institutions are required before granting a loan to perform an adequate assessment of the capacity of the potential borrower to comply with his future obligations. To this end, the institutions have to possess adequate internal procedures, specifically developed to assess the solvency of the customer, which should respect certain minimum regulatory guidelines (Article 18 of Order EHA/2899/2011 and tenth standard of Circular 5/2012). Use of this assessment not only sets out to protect the customer, but also promotes the idea that credit institutions should grant

[50] See Bank of Spain, *Memoria del SRBE—2012* (Madrid, 2013) 237–38 (www.bde.es/f/webbde/Secciones/Publicaciones/PublicacionesAnuales/MemoriaServicioReclamaciones/12/MSB_2012.pdf).

loans responsibly and therefore reduce the risks of default and over-indebtedness. Throughout this process of informing, and beforehand, informing themselves to inform, credit institutions should act 'honestly, impartially and professionally', attending to the personal and financial situation and preferences and objectives of their customers. They should highlight any condition or characteristic of the contract that does not respond to this objective and should 'appropriately inform their customers about the characteristics of those products that match what is requested, to enable them to reflect, compare and make an informed, rational and prudent decision' (tenth standard of Circular 5/2012). It does not appear that enactment of the LOSSEC will change this policy for responsible loan granting, given that although it has left invalid part of the legal principle that set out to regulate this issue (in particular no 2 of Article 29 LSE), it has included the same derogated provisions in its Article 5.1.

Customer protection is significantly amplified when the purpose of the contract is to grant a *mortgage loan*. On the one hand, the pre-contractual information of the customer is increased via the following three instruments: the 'Guide to Access to a Mortgage Loan', drawn up by the Bank of Spain; the 'Pre-Contractual Information Sheet', in which every credit institution provides generalised, but clear and sufficient, guidance as to the different loans it offers; and the 'Personalised Information Sheet', in which the credit institution provides individualised information in response to a specific credit request by a potential customer, according to the information it has gathered about his financing needs, his financial situation and his preferences. Once again therefore the credit institution is expressly obliged *to inform itself to inform* (Articles 20 to 23 Order EHA/2899/2011). On the other hand, transparency with regard to the interest rate risk coverage mechanisms is strengthened (Article 24 of Order EHA/2899/2011), and with regard to floor or cap clauses, which establish limits on variations in interest rates (Article 25 of Order EHA/2899/2011).

In the case of a *reverse mortgage*, the provision of an independent consultancy service is required in favour of the applicants for this product. When performing this service, the adviser has to take into consideration the financial situation of the applicant and the financial risks arising from subscribing to this product (first additional provision to Law 41/2007, of 7 December, thereby modifying the Mortgage Market Regulation Act, or LMH[51] by its Spanish acronym, and Article 32 of Order EHA/2899/2011).

As regards *consumer loans* that fall within the scope of application of the LCCC, credit institutions, like other natural or legal persons that can act as lenders, are subject to the detailed duties of pre-contractual and contractual information provided in this Act. In this respect, it is important to remember that, in accordance with the provisions of Article 8 of Directive 2008/48/EC,[52] on consumer credit,

[51] Ley de Regulación del Mercado Hipotecario (Act 2/1981, of 25 March, with subsequent modifications).

[52] OJ L 133, 22 May 2008, 66–92.

the lender is obliged to evaluate the credit-worthiness of the borrower prior to executing the loan contract. To this end, the lender may make use of information obtained by his own means and that facilitated by the potential borrower, even on the basis of a consultation of the relevant database (Article 14 LCCC).

Finally, it is important to highlight the fundamental role played by the public notary, who can intervene in the loan operation in question, in terms of *verification of compliance* with the above regulations. Thus, when granting the notarial instruments that formalise the loans, the notary should not only inform and warn the customers of the most relevant points of the contract, but also check as to what extent the credit institution has respected its duties to warn. What is more, the notary should refuse the authorisation of the loan when he considers that the credit institution has not respected these duties (Article 30.3 of Order EHA/2899/2011).

The number of guarantees increases when the subject matter of the contract consists of a mortgage loan. In cases such as these, proof of *informed consent* is required, so that the notarial instrument has to include a handwritten declaration alongside the customer's signature in which the borrower states that he has been fully warned as to the possible risks deriving from the contract (Article 6 of the Act on measures to reinforce protection of mortgage debtors, debt restructuring and social rental housing, or LMPDH[53] by its Spanish acronym).

V. Liability

A. Remedies

Without prejudice to the consequences that may arise, in the field of law against unfair competition, any misconduct by financial institutions that might constitute misleading advertising (eg from a lack of pre-contractual transparency) and that as such might lead to decisions ordering the cessation of the conduct and the compensation for losses and damages that it has caused (Articles 6.1 LGP and 32 LCD), the pre-contractual and contractual fields are where the greatest possibilities are presented, from a theoretical and practical perspective, to protect customers from institutions of this nature. Here, according to the decision of the European Court of Justice of 30 May 2013,[54] it shall be kept in mind: first, that MiFID has not dealt with the contractual consequences or effects of a violation by the financial

[53] Ley de Medidas para Reforzar la Protección de los Deudores Hipotecarios (Law 1/2013, of 14 May).

[54] This decision of the ECJ addresses the preliminary questions submitted by the civil Court of First Instance No 12 of Madrid by writ issued on 14 November 2011 in C-604/11 *Genil 48, SL v Bankinter, SA*; more precisely, the questions addressed were: (1) if the omission of the suitability test provided for in Art 19(4) of that directive for a retail investor causes the contract entered into between the

institutions of the duties imposed by the directive (particularly, the duties imposed in Article 19.4 and 5);[55] second, that the task of establishing such contractual consequences or effects is a matter for the national legislators of each Member State;[56] third, that in performing the abovementioned task, Member States are subject to the observance of the principles of equivalence and effectiveness. Thus, in the case of Spain, the following points are relevant in this regard:

— If the existence of errors in consent can be proven by the customer (eg from lack of sufficient information, unsuitable product in terms of customer's knowledge and preferences or even misconduct by the financial institution), then the contract can be rendered null and void (Article 1300 of the Civil Code), by taking the appropriate action within a period of four years dating from the execution of the contract (Article 1301(5) of the Civil Code), unless there is express or tacit confirmation of the contract by acts of the party entitled to take the action (by means of acts that necessarily imply a wish to waive the right (Article 1311 of the Civil Code)). The annulment of the contract in any case determines the reciprocal restitution between the parties of the affected benefits, increased by the application of the appropriate interest rate (Article 1303 of the Civil Code), and possible compensation for damages to be paid to the contracting party that suffered as a result of the error, which may consist of the costs and specific investments made to execute the contract (consequential damages) as long as they can be proven and also, at least in the case of wilful misconduct, the damages caused by the loss of better contractual opportunities. In practice, however, judicial decisions that have annulled the contract as a result of error or wilful misconduct have rarely decided on compensation for damages, owing to the fact that compensation was not requested and/or the damages suffered by the client were not proven.

— A similar case may arise in those cases where the contract is declared void by the courts, by application of Article 6.3 of the Civil Code as a result of the infringement by the financial institution of duties established in the interests of their customers, with regard to the phase of conclusion of the contract, by a legal regulation (or by a regulation enacted using a legal empowerment as

investor and the investment institution to be void ab initio; and (2) if, in the event that the service is not regarded as investment advice, the mere fact of purchasing a complex financial instrument, into which category falls an interest-rate swap agreement, without the appropriateness test provided for in Art 19(5) of MiFID being carried out, for reasons imputable to the investment institution, causes the contract to be void ab initio (see no 22, questions 2 and 3, ECJ 30 May 2013).

This decision of ECJ has been considered by the Spanish Supreme Court in its decision of 20 January 2014, referred to in sections II and III.

[55] Such duties, mentioned in section IV, have been included in TRLMV, Arts 213 and 214.

[56] *Bankinter* (n 54). Unlike MiFID, MiFID II (Article 69.2, final para of Directive 2014/65/EU, 25 May 2014) establishes that 'Member States shall ensure that mechanisms are in place to ensure that compensation may be paid or other remedial action be taken in accordance with national law for any financial loss or damage suffered as a result of an infringement of this Directive or of Regulation (EU) No 600/2014'.

its basis).[57] However, the contract can still be kept in force and be integrated in accordance with the requirements of good faith, usage and the law (Article 1258 of the Civil Code, relating to Articles 10.2 LCGC and 83 TRLGDCU). This may be the case where the contract was based on general terms and conditions or, when the signatory is a consumer, on terms or conditions that are not individually negotiated. In such a case, the judge may decide either the non-inclusion of the terms or conditions that do not pass the inclusion check (in accordance with Articles 5 and 7 of the LCGC and 80.1, letters (a) and (b) TRLGDCU, respectively) or to declare void one or more terms or conditions for being against good faith in situations where there is a contract with consumers (Articles 8.2 LCGC and 80.1.c) and 82 et seq of the TRLGDCU).[58] However, the contract shall be kept in force if there is no basic element declared as non-included or void.

— In the field of contractual and associated pre-contractual breaches, provided that they have sufficient weight, or rather are severe/relevant/essential in nature, the legal consequences that might arise are those that interact with the termination of the contract, based on Article 1124 of the Civil Code, except when the option is selected of demanding correct fulfilment of the contract in some specific way. Affairs should therefore proceed in the case of termination for breach of contractual obligations (or assimilated pre-contractual breaches) towards the restitution of benefits incurred since execution of the contract, unless it is permanent or for continuous performance—because then the restitution should not affect those benefits that have already been respectively consumed—, with compensation for the losses and damages caused to the party that terminates the contract. The compensation should cover consequential damages and loss of earnings, and should not only include the lost profit, but also lost opportunities, as long as these are not speculative, uncertain or imaginary (and therefore can be proven), referring solely to those that were foreseeable at the time of executing the contract and are a necessary consequence of the breach, in cases of involuntary breaches, or that have derived knowingly from the breach when this was wilful (Articles 1106 and 1107 of the Civil Code). In practice, the courts have specified the compensation for damages in a heterogeneous manner: in cases of breach of duties to inform or to advise, within the context of a commission contract or a portfolio management agreement relating to bonds and preferred shares, the compensation has sometimes been set at the full value of

[57] As would or could be the case with the supervisory and disciplinary regulation of credit institutions and the conduct-of-business rules for investment service companies on the basis of a number of proposals of a doctrinal (referred to by López Sánchez, 'Disciplina bancaria y protección del consumidor' (n 27) 13–14) and case-law nature (see I Moralejo, 'Las normas de actuación en los mercados de valores' in AB Campuzano et al, *Los mercados financieros* (Valencia: Tirant Lo Blanch, 2013) 375–78), also with the additional support represented by Art 2.5 of Order ECC/2502/2012 (according to Hernández Paulsen (n 25) 295–99 and 382–89).

[58] See Hernández Paulsen (n 25) 247–382.

the investment, sometimes with the already received benefits discounted; in other cases, at the percentage of the investment that the customer would have received by selling the product if he had been informed in time of the adverse circumstances of the issuer; in cases of interest rate swaps, the compensation has consisted in some cases of repaying the customer with the sum paid by the early termination of the contract, as a consideration for the infringement by the financial institution of its duties to warn about the cost of the cancellation.[59]

Furthermore, Spanish law has specific routes to enable a wide variety of injured parties to obtain compensation for losses suffered from one and the same and contracting party or party causing the damage. The possible outcomes of the cases below are given as an example:

— As the exercise of an injunction to protect collective consumer interests claiming against the general conditions of a contract that go against mandatory provisions or which are abusive in nature (Article 12.1 LCGC). In such a situation it is possible that such a remedy—which can be exercised by certain institutions and organisations (including consumer associations that fulfil the requirements established in the TRLGDCU (Article 16 LCGC)) and whose purpose is to obtain a decision that declares the general conditions being claimed against to be void and to oblige whosoever benefits from them to delete them from the contracts of which they form a part and to abstain from using them in future—may find accumulated an action to return the sums that would have been collected by virtue of the general condition contested in court and another of compensation for the losses and damages that application of the terms declared to be void would have caused (Article 12.2 LCGC). The consequence in this case is that the possible penalty would have to specify the individual identity of the consumers that are considered to benefit from the decision, and if this is impossible, the details, characteristics and requirements to be in a position to require payment (Articles 221.1 and 519 of the Civil Procedure Act (LEC)).[60]
— In cases of causation of damages to the collective interests of consumers. In this situation the *locus standi* that sets out to defend the abovementioned interests is legally recognised; the groups of consumers made up of those who have been prejudiced by a harmful event, with the proviso that the consumers should be precisely defined or definable, with a similar proviso being applicable to legally constituted consumer associations (Articles 6 and 11.2 LEC), which should also have legitimate powers to defend the interests of their members, the association itself, the general interests of consumers and those

[59] For further information about the cases resolved by courts and the penalties set in the decisions, see Hernández Paulsen (n 25) 437–45.

[60] Ley de Enjuiciamiento Civil (Act 1/2000, of 7 January, with subsequent modifications).

of consumers prejudiced by a harmful event when their identity is undefined or difficult to define (Articles 11.1 and 3 LEC).

— In the area of arbitral resolution of disputes between traders or professionals and their customers. Here on the one hand, Royal Decree 231/2008, of 15 February, includes the option of a so-called 'collective consumer arbitration', which aims to resolve disputes based on one particular de facto premise that may have injured the collective interests of consumers in one single arbitral proceeding, when the consumers concerned are defined or definable (Article 56 et seq). On the other hand, a special arbitral solution has been driven in practice to try to resolve the claims made against financial institutions by those affected by the sale of most preferred stocks and subordinated debt in recent years (mentioned in section VI).

B. Limitation and Exclusion of Liability

According to Spanish law, a financial institution can reduce or exclude its liability for breach of contract with its customers by providing terms that modify it. Clauses of this nature are effectively admissible, with the provisos deriving from legislation on consumer protection (Articles 82 et seq TRLGDCU), so as to exclude that limit liability, unless there is a wilful breach of contract (Article 1102 of the Civil Code). When the clause concerned has the function of a penalty, it is understood *ex lege*, if there is no clear agreement to the contrary and no wilful breach exists, that the amount established as a penalty replaces the compensation that the claimant could have demanded if the most severe damage caused can be proven (Articles 1152 et seq of the Civil Code).

C. Contributory Negligence and Waiver

Besides this situation, the financial institution may have its liability for breach of contract reduced if there is a contributory negligence by the customer, as was generally accepted by the Supreme Court in situations of breach of contract where the subsequent damages were not exclusively caused by the conduct of the party in breach but also by the other contracting party;[61] and it can even be released from liability in cases where the customer waives the right to bring an action against it, which is admissible as long as the waiver is not prejudicial to third parties (Article 6.2 of the Civil Code), or allows the action that would have enabled it to be claimed to expire (Article 1961 of the Civil Code).

[61] See amongst others the decisions of the Supreme Court of 15 January 2000, 6 November 2003 and 20 May 2004.

D. Burden of Proof

To add to the above comments, it would be appropriate to refer to the problem of proving compliance/breach of the duties that financial institutions have towards their customers. In principle, the latter has the burden of proving the facts that might act as a basis for a claim when they set out to make a claim against a financial institution for breaching its obligations. This proof, however, may be very difficult in one particular case, when what they have to demonstrate is the existence of a negative event (eg omission or defect of pre-contractual information on the part of the financial institution). Thus, it is understandable that courts resort to the principle of the availability of evidence and locate the burden of proof on the party who is in a better position to provide it, as enshrined in Article 217.7 LEC, to charge the financial institution with the burden of proving compliance with their duties. Furthermore, it should not be forgotten that, as mentioned in sections II and III, the Supreme Court has shown a bias towards rebuttable presumptions, in situations where correct compliance cannot be proven of the duties to inform and the tests of suitability and convenience, in the understanding that although lack of compliance does not necessarily have to be the cause of error for the customer, the same error can in principle be presumed.[62]

VI. The Role of the Regulator in Settling Disputes

In Spain, there are two supervisory authorities in the field of financial products: the Bank of Spain, with powers in banking operations and the credit market; and the National Securities Market Commission, with supervisory powers over securities markets. Both authorities issue reports and recommendations about the activities of operators in each market, and have powers to sanction in situations where there is a breach of public regulations[63] (eg in a situation where an investment services company breaches the obligation to perform tests of suitability and convenience). But they do not have binding powers over disputes between customers and credit institutions or between customers and investment services companies. For example, as mentioned in section III, the Claims Service of the Bank of Spain draws up an annual report with the claims received and determines what in its opinion are reasonable banking practices; however, it cannot oblige a bank to modify its behaviour, nor may it decide on disputes between customers and banks.

Nevertheless, a system to resolve disputes has been established for claims concerning the sale of preferred stock and subordinated debt issued by credit

[62] Decision of Supreme Court of 20 January 2014.
[63] See section III.

institutions that have been intervened by public powers (ie credit institutions in financial difficulties where, in the public interest, the state has decided to replace the administrators in order to rationalise and restructure the institution). The public body responsible for the intervention is called the 'Fund for Orderly Bank Restructuring' (or FROB[64] by its Spanish acronym), regulated by Act 9/2012, of 14 November 2012 (Act on restructuring and resolution of credit institutions. Currently, the regulation is contained in the Act 11/2015, of 18 June 2015, which has replaced the Act 9/2012). This Act of 2012 regulated so-called 'management of hybrid capital instruments and subordinated debts', since in many cases the credit institution is obliged to recognise the partial or total loss of the value of the instruments, and may proceed to offer or force their exchange for other financial instruments.

As the problem of selling preferred stock was very severe, and the volume of shares issued was a very high one,[65] it was made the subject matter of a specific regulation via Real Decreto-ley 6/2013, of 22 March, on 'protection of holders of certain savings and investment products and other measures of a financial nature'.[66] This regulation created the figure of a special arbitral process and constituted the 'Commission for Monitoring Hybrid Capital and Subordinated Debt Instruments' (CMHC), which has set the basic criteria in accordance with which arbitrations are to be decided (although not as criteria that are binding for the arbitrator, but rather to guide the investor with regard to whether his claim will be upheld).[67] The basic characteristics of such arbitral process are as follows:

- Natural persons may bring cases (with the exclusion of professionals and business people), and not-for-profit legal entities, if in both cases they are retail investors.
- The arbitral process does not paralyse any exchange of shares that might have been established by the credit institution at the prompting of the FROB.
- The arbitrator is the National Arbitration Board, a public body attached to the National Consumers Association, and recorded in the European Commission as an extrajudicial body that fulfils the requirements of quality, independence and impartiality
- There is a prior phase in which the investor requests the arbitration, and a body acting as 'independent expert' dictates if, in its opinion, the claim is a viable one. If it decides that it is, the independent expert sets the amount that

[64] Fondo de Reestructuración Ordinaria Bancaria.

[65] See Defensor del Pueblo, 'Informe sobre participaciones preferentes' (Madrid: March 2013) (www.defensordelpueblo.es/es/Documentacion/Publicaciones/monografico/Documentacion/Informe_Preferentes.pdf).

[66] The Real Decreto-ley 6/2013 has been considered under the Spanish Constitution by the Constitutional Court (decision 12/2015 of 5 February 2015, available at: http://www.boe.es/diario_boe/txt.php?id=BOE-A-2015-2258).

[67] The criteria involved were made public by press release from the FROB, on 17 April 2013 (available at: www.frob.es/es/Lists/Contenidos/Attachments/319/20130417_PREFERENTES.pdf).

the investor can claim, and if he can bring the claim to arbitration or not; if it decides that it is not, the investor cannot bring the case to specific arbitration and may take it the courts of law.

— As a result of the legal regulation of the arbitration, whosoever brings a case to arbitration may not then take it to the law courts. Besides, the decision of the arbitrator (arbitration award) can only be appealed for certain specific reasons relating to procedural issues, but not for the success, reasonableness or correctness of the arbitrator's decision (what in Spanish terminology is called the '*fondo del asunto*' or the merits of the case).

According to data included in the last and definitive Report of the CMHC,[68] the number of customers of Bankia and Catalunya Caixa (CX), financial institutions in which the state intervened with the option of requesting arbitration,[69] was 417,490, with a total sum of €7,940 million. Of that amount, 78 per cent requested arbitration (327,391 affected persons, who had hybrids to the value of €5,168 million). 75 per cent of the arbitration requests were accepted by the independent expert, at a sum of €2,761 million. Up to 31 March 2015, 240,207 awards had been given in favour of the customer (73 per cent of the total) at the amount of €2,630 million. To assess the volume that this arbitration implies, it should be highlighted that judicial claims for products issued by the same institutions were in the region of 28,924 claims, for the amount of €1,811 million. Therefore, the vast majority of those affected opted for arbitration, although those that chose recourse to law had been affected by larger sums to be claimed.

— As regards Bankia, 229,931 customers requested arbitration, which means 78 per cent of the holders, for the amount of €4,043 million. 77 per cent of the total number of requests had been accepted (176,723), which represents 57 per cent of the amount, and 171,854 positive awards were given.
— As regards Catalunya Caixa (CX), the independent expert accepted the claims of 68,356 holders, 70 per cent of the total, equivalent to 41 per cent of the amount analysed. 34,378 of these received a positive award.
— As regards Novagalicia, of a total number of 116,660 customers, 93,899 customers decided to enter into arbitration. 60 per cent of these claims were awarded, hence 58,017 holders recovered €496 million.

[68] It is the 8th Report issued by the mentioned Commission (on March 2015), available at: www.adabankia.com/wp-content/uploads/2014/01/2015-03-01-Informe-Comisi%C3%B3n-Seguimiento-CNMV-BE-CCU.pdf.

[69] The first reports of the CMHC also included data on NGC Banco. In early 2014, such arbitrations had already been concluded, with the following results: 93,898 claims were requested, 58,017 (34 per cent of the amount claimed) were accepted by the independent expert, and the latter were all successful apart from one (see: http://86.109.123.178/es/Lists/Contenidos/Attachments/280/20140205_comparecencia.pdf, as well as A Missé, 'Los juicios con la banca colapasan los juzgados' *Alternativas Económicas*, no 16 (June 2015) www.jausaslegal.com/wp-content/uploads/2015/06/Alternativas-econ%C3%B3micas.pdf).

As can be seen, these were arbitrations under private law by private arbitrators, and not a resolution of disputes by public supervisory authorities. But they were established by law and are controlled, or controlled to some extent, by supervisory bodies.

VII. Concluding Remarks

This chapter has shown that the regulation in force today in Spain on the protection of customers of credit and investment institutions possesses specific legal tools designed to achieve such protection from a preventive perspective (duties of transparency, information and advice of the financial institutions). At the same time, this regulatory framework has evidenced, from the perspective of traditional private law, that these instruments are also effective to deal with bad practices on the part of financial institutions, by annulling or terminating a defective or unfulfilled contract because of the incorrect behaviour of the financial institution. This may lead to the award of reimbursement or compensation of the damage caused by such behaviour. Finally, courts have used the doctrine of misrepresentation—the non-fulfilment of the duties to inform and advise by the financial institutions—to establish lack of consent on the part of the customer and to nullify a significant number of contracts for financial products.

8

Netherlands

DANNY BUSCH, CEES VAN DAM AND BART VAN DER WIEL

I. Introduction

The increase in the offering of financial products to consumers has driven developments in Dutch case-law pertaining to a bank's duty of care. In view of this, it seems only natural to begin with an overview of the major cases in this area (section II), followed by a treatment of the legal basis of a bank's duty of care (section III), and the essential duties typically flowing from it (section IV). The hotly debated topic of the impact of MiFID on a bank's duty of care is dealt with in section V. In section VI, in view of the fact that a claim based on a breach of a bank's duty of care is in Dutch law generally based on tort or breach of contract, we will focus on the requirements which must be fulfilled in order to institute a successful damages claim based on tort or breach of contract. Then we move on to the relation between a bank's duty of care and more traditional doctrines, including reasonableness and fairness, mistake and other defects of consent, unfair contract terms, and voidability or avoidance based on breach of mandatory law or the violation of public morals or public policy (section VII). We continue this chapter with some remarks on group actions and mass claims (section VIII), a proposal of the Ministry of Finance to concentrate civil litigation on the provision of investment services, investment activities and prospectus liability at the Amsterdam District Court (section IX), alternative dispute settlement at the Complaint Institute Financial Services (section X) and the role of the regulator in settling disputes (section XI). Section XII contains some concluding observations.

II. Major Cases

A. Option Trades

In 1997, in the matter of *Rabobank v Everaars*, the Hoge Raad (the Dutch Supreme Court) adopted a 'special duty of care' (*bijzondere zorgplicht*) of banks towards private, non-professional clients in a case about option trading.[1]

Everaars suffered considerable losses by trading in options over a period of two years using Rabobank as his broker. The applicable Trade Rules of the European Options Exchange put Rabobank under the obligation to require Everaars to provide 'margin' that would cover Everaars' losses on his trades. Everaars however traded almost continuously without providing the required margin. After suffering heavy losses, Everaars claimed damages from Rabobank, arguing that Rabobank had failed to keep him to his margin obligations and for that reason should have refused to execute Everaars' orders. The Hoge Raad ruled that owing to the potentially very large risks to which investors are exposed while trading options, a bank—being pre-eminently professional and knowledgeable in this area—has to observe a special duty of care towards its private, non-professional clients. This duty of care follows from the requirements of reasonableness and fairness (*redelijkheid en billijkheid*) as they relate to the nature of the contractual relationship with this type of client and aims to protect the client against his own rashness or lack of insight, and, in this case, entails the obligation for the bank to act in compliance with the applicable trade rules. The warnings that were extended to Everaars did not suffice for meeting this duty of care because enforcing the margin requirement would have been more effective. Moreover, the seriousness of these warnings was put in doubt because Rabobank continued executing option orders notwithstanding Everaars' negligence in providing the required margin.

After the *Rabobank v Everaars* ruling, which was very much tailored to the specific circumstances in that case, in the matter of *Kouwenberg v Rabobank*, the Hoge Raad laid down the rule that a bank, in principle, breaches its duty if it executes a client's orders for option trades while the client does not meet the margin requirement.[2]

B. Share Leases

The development of a second line of case-law was prompted by the offering of so-called 'share leases' to consumers, starting from the late 1990s up to and including the first years of the twenty-first century. These products consisted

[1] HR 23 May 1997, *NJ* 1998/192 (*Rabobank/Everaars*).

[2] HR 11 July 2003, *NJ* 2005/103 (*Kouwenberg/Rabobank*). Soon after *Rabobank/Everaars*, in *Van de Klundert/Rabobank* (HR 26 June 1998, *NJ* 1998/660) the Hoge Raad still suggested a case-by-case approach by stressing the relevant circumstances of the matter. In later cases, the bank's duty with respect to the enforcement of the margin requirement seems to have been relaxed somewhat. See HR 23 March 2007 *NJ* 2007/333 (*ABN AMRO/Van Velzen*) and HR 4 December 2009, *NJ* 2010/67 (*Nabbe/Staalbankiers*).

of a loan providing the funds to buy shares. The consumer paid interest on the loan. The principal amount either had to be repaid in instalments or at maturity. This type of leveraged product had a potentially huge upside (if the shares did well) but also carried the risk of substantial losses (if the value of the shares decreased) potentially resulting in a net debt that the consumer had to repay. Unfavourable developments in the financial markets triggered a flood of claims against the financial institutions that had offered these share leasing products. In 2009, in three key judgments,[3] the Hoge Raad confirmed the special duty of care towards private clients which had been developed in the margin requirement cases (mentioned above). The Hoge Raad added that the scope of such duty depends on the particular circumstances of each case. Relevant circumstances to take into account, according to the Hoge Raad, are the expertise and experience of the bank's counterparty, the product's complexity, the risks involved and the applicable regulatory framework. The Hoge Raad found that since a share leasing contract comprises periodical payment obligations and a risk of a net debt remaining due at maturity, the seller of share leasing products has a pre-contractual obligation to explicitly and unequivocally warn its counterparty of the risk of such a debt remaining due at maturity. The seller also has to review the consumer's level of income and wealth. When the outcome of this review leads to the conclusion that the consumer's income and wealth are insufficient to bear the obligations the agreement would entail, the seller has to disadvise the consumer entering into the agreement.

C. Investment Advice and Asset Management

A third line of case-law concerns advice and asset management for private clients. The Hoge Raad found that a bank, being pre-eminently professional and knowledgeable in the field of asset management, in accordance with the nature of the asset management agreement with its client, has a special duty of care that may lead to a specific duty to explicitly and unequivocally warn of the risks in relation to the asset portfolio that is being managed by the bank. Again, this duty of care is based on the requirements of reasonableness and fairness (*redelijkheid en billijkheid*) as they relate to the nature of the contractual relationship between the bank and this type of client and aims to protect the client against his own rashness or lack of insight.[4] Furthermore, the Hoge Raad found that the duty of care entails that the bank has to diligently review the financial prospects, expertise and goals of the client before entering into an advisory relationship. Also, the bank has a duty to warn its client of the special risk involved with entering into derivative

[3] HR 5 June 2009, *NJ* 2012/182 (*De Treek/Dexia*); HR 5 June 2009, *NJ* 2012/183 (*Levob/Bolle*); HR 5 June 2009, *NJ* 2012/184 (*Stichting Gesp/Aegon*).

[4] HR 24 December 2010, *NJ* 2011/251 (*Fortis/Bourgonje*).

transactions. Furthermore, when the strategy envisaged by the client is not in line with his financial prospects, expertise and goals, the bank has a duty to warn the client as well. The special duty of care may entail that the bank is only allowed to continue a certain strategy when the bank has confronted the client with its risks, has made sure that the client is actually aware of these risks, and the client has agreed to continuing the strategy.[5]

D. Third Parties

A fourth line of case-law concerns banks' liability towards third parties. In 1998, in *Mees Pierson/Ten Bos*, the Hoge Raad held that the role that banks have within society causes banks to have a special duty of care, not only towards clients on the basis of contractual relationships, but also towards third parties whose interests the bank has to take into account on the basis of the requirements of unwritten law. The scope of this duty of care depends on the circumstances of the case.[6] The cases *Fortis/Stichting Volendam*[7] and *ABN AMRO/SBGB*[8] concerned fraudulent investment services; the banks' only involvement in these matters was that the fraudulent 'investment services provider' used bank accounts held with these banks. In both cases, the Hoge Raad upheld the Court of Appeal's finding that the banks are liable for the investors' losses (in *ABN AMRO* this was only a conditional finding).[9] In the *Fortis* matter, the bank's liability was grounded on the fact that the bank had at some point in time realised that the services were possibly being provided without the required regulatory licence, but had failed to investigate this further. In the *ABN AMRO* case, the (presumed) liability of the bank was based on the fact that the payments to and from the fraudster's private bank account were unusual in quantity and nature, which should have prompted the bank to further investigate these transactions. In *ABN AMRO*, the Hoge Raad held that the special duty of care towards third parties also aims to protect these third parties against their own rashness or lack of insight. In the *Befra* case,[10] Rabobank and other institutions were not held liable vis-à-vis third parties for their purported failure to investigate, because in those matters the consumers had invested to become a limited partner in a limited partnership (and the fraudulent service provider was the general partner). The Hoge Raad

[5] HR 2 February 2012, *NJ* 2012/95 (*Rabobank/X.*); HR 14 August 2015, *NJ* 2016/107 (*Brouwer/ABN AMRO*).

[6] HR 9 January 1998, *NJ* 1999/285 (*Mees Pierson/Ten Bos*).

[7] HR 23 December 2005, *NJ* 2006/289 (*Fortis/Stichting Volendam*).

[8] HR 27 November 2015, *RvdW* 2016/88 (*ABN AMRO/SBGB*).

[9] The Court of Appeal allowed the bank to rebut the assumption of its knowledge of unusual payment transactions.

[10] HR 8 April 2011, *NJ* 2012/361 (*Befra/Rabobank*).

held that these consumers had acted as entrepreneurs and not as investors, meaning that no regulatory licence had been required for the services. Consequently, according to the Hoge Raad, there had effectively been no reason for the bank to start an investigation prompted by a suspicion that services were being rendered without the required licence.

A final important judgment on a bank's liability towards third parties concerns World Online's IPO.[11] The Hoge Raad held as being relevant aspects for ABN AMRO and Goldman Sachs' duty of care towards investors of World Online, the fact that these banks were the (joint) global coordinators, lead managers and bookrunners to the IPO. According to the Hoge Raad, this meant that they had been engaged by World Online as issuer to lead the syndicate of banks involved in the IPO and that they were responsible for the determination of the price, for the due diligence investigation and for drafting and distributing the prospectus. As a syndicate leader, a bank has the responsibility to prevent potential investors from getting a false impression of the issuer, as far as is possible within the syndicate leader's sphere of influence—for example within the scope of the due diligence investigation and when drafting the prospectus.

E. Interest Rate Swaps

A fifth line of cases concerns lower case-law on interest rate swaps which accepts that banks are also subject to a special duty of care towards SMEs, resulting in the usual duties to investigate and warn.[12] In some of these cases, instead of claiming damages based on infringement of the bank's duty of care,[13] clients have successfully sought nullification of interest rate swaps on the basis of mistake.[14] Judgments by the Hoge Raad on these interest rate swap cases are expected to be rendered over the next couple of years.

The question whether SMEs and other inexperienced commercial parties are sufficiently protected by the law when obtaining financial services and products is a hotly debated issue in the Netherlands. Largely triggered by the massive mis-selling of interest rate swaps to SMEs, the Dutch Ministry of Finance recently

[11] HR 27 November 2009, *NJ* 2014/201 (*VEB c.s./World Online c.s.*).

[12] See esp Court of Appeal Den Bosch 15 April 2014, *JOR* 2014/168, with annotation Van der Wiel en Wijnberg; *Ondernemingsrecht* 2014/92, with annotation Arons (*Holding Westkant BV, in liquidatie/ABN AMRO Bank NV*), and Court of Appeal Den Haag 14 February 2017, ECLI:NL:GHDHA:2017:255, concerning a relatively large company. Please also note that the open norms in the Dutch Civil Code could in any event facilitate the development of any such special duty of care towards commercial parties. See Dutch Civil Code (DCC), Art 6:2, Art 6:248 and Art 7:401, on which see sections III and VII.B.

[13] eg Court of Appeal Den Bosch 15 April 2014, *JOR* 2014/168 (*Holding Westkant/ABN AMRO*).

[14] eg Court of Appeal Amsterdam 15 September 2015, *JOR* 2015/334 (*X./ING*); Court of Appeal Amsterdam 10 November 2015, *JOR* 2016/37 (*X./ABN AMRO*); Court of Appeal Amsterdam 11 October 2016, case no 200.153.823/01 (*X./ABN AMRO*).

published a consultation document, soliciting stakeholder views on possible law reform to increase protection.[15]

F. Suretyship

A recurring case in which duties to warn and investigate are accepted by the Dutch courts beyond the scope of investment services, is the situation where a consumer acts as the guarantor of a debtor of a bank loan. In the Netherlands the bank has a duty to warn such guarantor for the risks involved.[16]

III. Legal Basis of a Bank's Duty of Care

Banks are generally held to have a duty of care that results in pre-contractual duties and duties during the term of the contract. In the pre-contractual stage the duty of care follows from the general private law principle of reasonableness and fairness (*redelijkheid en billijkheid*).[17] During the term of the contract this duty can be based on either (1) Article 7:401 DCC, which applies to services contracts generally and requires service providers to observe the care of a prudent service provider, or (2) the general private law principle of reasonableness and fairness.[18] A bank's the duty of care also follows from Article 2 of the General Banking Conditions 2009 and 2017 to the extent that they apply to the relevant contract; the Conditions provide that a bank must exercise due care when providing services and must take the client's interests into account to the best of its ability.[19]

[15] See Dutch Ministry of Finance, *Consultatiedocument—Effectivitieit en gewenste mate van bescherming voor zzp-ers en mkb-ers bij financiële diensten en producten* (1 September 2016) (available at: www.internetconsultatie.nl/consultatiebeschermingkleinzakelijk).

[16] See HR 1 April 2016, ECLI:NL:HR:2016:543, *NJ* 2016/190 (*Aruba Bank c.s./Hardeveld*), consideration 3.4.1. See for similar reasoning in the context of avoidance of the guarantee on the basis of mistake (*dwaling*): HR 1 June 1990, *NJ* 1991/759 with annotation Brunner (*Van Lanschot/Bink*).

[17] Flowing from the Dutch system of private law as such.

[18] See explicitly on reasonableness and fairness during the term of the relevant legal relationship (eg an asset management contract) DCC, Arts 6:2(1) and 6:248(1). DCC, Art 6:2 reads: 'A creditor and debtor must, as between themselves, act in accordance with the requirements of reasonableness and fairness'. Art 6:248(1) reads: 'A contract has not only the legal effects agreed upon by the parties, but also those which, according to the nature of the contract result from the law, usages or the requirements of reasonableness and fairness'. Apart from these provisions, reasonableness and fairness also flow from the Dutch system of private law as such during the term of the relevant legal relationship (eg an asset management contract).

[19] Cf also the General Banking Conditions 1995, Art 2. The General Banking Conditions 2017 entered into force on 1 March 2017. The General Banking Conditions 1995, 2009 and 2017 are available at: www.nvb.nl/publicaties-standpunten/publicaties/619/algemene-bankvoorwaarden-general-banking-conditins.html.

The duty of care, an open-ended norm, is made more specific through either legislation or judicial interpretation. The Dutch Civil Code (*Burgerlijk Wetboek* or DCC) does not impose specific pre-contractual duties on banks, while imposing some, but not many, specific duties during the term of the relationship. In contrast, the *Wet op het financieel toezicht* (Dutch Financial Supervision Act, Wft) and subordinate legislation issued pursuant thereto set out in detail the acts that a bank must perform (or refrain from performing) to comply with the general norm. In addition, as we have seen above, a fair amount of case-law helps clarify a bank's obligations.

According to the Hoge Raad, the position of banks in society brings with it a 'special' duty of care towards both private, non-professional clients and private, non-professional third parties whose interests banks must take into account. In the Hoge Raad's view, a bank's special duty is also based on the fact that it is a professional service provider that must be deemed to have the necessary expertise. The scope and intensity of this duty of care depends on the circumstances of the case. These circumstances may include the client's expertise, if any, its financial position, and the regulatory rules to which the particular bank is subject.[20]

Under Dutch law, the special duty of care owed by a bank is a counterpart to the duties of care that have been developed in the context of the professional liability of professional service providers (such as medical doctors, civil law notaries, attorneys-at-law and auditors).[21] The position of both banks and professional service providers in society brings with it that they owe clients and to a certain extent third parties a special duty of care. In both cases, the duty of care is also based on the fact that they are professional parties that are deemed to have the necessary expertise. They all perform essential functions in society. If they fail to comply with their duty of care, this has a severe impact on the financial markets, health and justice.

IV. Duties to Investigate, Warn and Refuse

A. General

As expressed in the previous paragraph, the scope and intensity of a bank's duty of care depends on the circumstances of the case. However, based on this

[20] See the cases mentioned in section II above.

[21] See HR 9 November 1990, *NJ* 1991/26 (*Speeckaert v Gradener*); HR 12 July 2002, *NJ* 2003/151 (both on the duty of care of medical doctors); HR 13 June 2003, *NJ* 2004/196 (*Beatrixziekenhuis v ProCall*) (attorneys-at-law and civil law notaries); HR 13 October 2006, *NJ* 2008/528 (*X, Y, Z & Q v Stichting Vie d'Or*) with annotation CC van Dam under *NJ* 2008/529 (auditors). See generally on the liability of professional service providers Asser/Tjong Tjin Tai, 7-IV* 2014/66, 191 et seq, 406 et seq (with further references).

theoretical starting point, the Hoge Raad has developed specific duties to investigate and to warn, and, in exceptional circumstances, outright duties to refuse to provide a product or service.

B. Duties to Investigate

Before entering into a credit agreement with a consumer, a lender has to investigate the consumer's credit-worthiness. Furthermore, the case-law on share leasing (see section II.B above) implies that when a financial product comprises periodical payments and may result in a net debt remaining due at maturity, the bank has to review the product's suitability for the consumer before entering into a contract.

C. Duties to Warn

The share leasing cases also imply that there is an obligation to explicitly and unequivocally warn a consumer of the risk of a debt remaining due at maturity and, when such a product is not deemed suitable for the consumer, to advise the consumer against entering into an agreement. The third line of cases, pertaining to advice and asset management for private clients (see section II.C above), implies a duty to explicitly and unequivocally warn of the special risks of particular transactions and of any potential mismatch between the chosen investment strategy and the financial prospects, expertise and goals of the client. The special duty of care furthermore may entail that the bank is only allowed to continue a certain strategy when the bank has confronted the client with its risks, has made sure that the client is actually aware of these risks, and the client has agreed to continuing the strategy.

The fourth line of case-law (on liability vis-à-vis third parties, see section II.D above) implies that when a bank becomes aware of any unusual transactions, it has a duty to further investigate the matter in order to protect third parties.

D. Duty to Refuse

Apart from duties to investigate and duties to warn, there are instances in which a bank has a duty to act or a duty to refuse to act. In cases on option trading, the infringement of margin requirements results in an obligation for the bank to refuse to execute any further transactions for the client and to liquidate the client's asset portfolio to prevent further losses from occurring.

Such a duty to refuse to enter into an agreement may also arise with respect to credit agreements between banks and consumers, when a bank concludes that a particular consumer is insufficiently creditworthy. This obligation is in line with Article 4:34, section 2 Wft.

V. The Impact of MiFID on a Bank's Duty of Care

A. General

As regulatory provisions are classified as public law, any failure by a bank to comply with one or more regulatory provisions applicable to it will primarily affect its relationship with the relevant financial regulator.[22] In other words, the financial regulator can enforce these provisions under administrative law in the event of an infringement, for example by imposing an administrative fine on the firm.

However, the regulatory provisions, in particular the conduct-of-business rules under MiFID/MiFID II, also have a major influence on relations between the bank and its clients under private law. It is now commonly accepted in Dutch case-law and literature that the regulatory rules help to define the pre-contractual and contractual (special) duty of care of banks (and other financial undertakings as well) under private law.[23] Moreover, an infringement of provisions of the Wft and subordinate legislation can constitute not only a breach of the civil duty of care but also a tort (unlawful act) for contravention of a statutory duty. In addition, the rules on unfair commercial practices explicitly provide in relation to retail clients (consumers) that a breach of a contractual or pre-contractual obligation to provide information under or pursuant to section 4:20 Wft (including an obligation under MiFID and, in due course, MiFID II) in commercial communications (including advertising and marketing) constitutes, by definition,

[22] In the Netherlands, the Stichting Autoriteit Financiële Markten (AFM) is the conduct-of-business regulator for financial institutions, including banks and investment firms. De Nederlandsche Bank NV (DNB) is the prudential regulator for financial institutions, including banks and investment firms (subject to some exceptions, such as the granting of a banking licence, in which case the European Central Bank (ECB) is competent). But if a bank is 'significant' within the meaning of the SSM Regulation the ECB instead of DNB is the prudential regulator. See on the SSM Regulation eg D Busch and G Ferrarini (eds), *European Banking Union* (Oxford: Oxford University Press, 2015).

[23] See eg HR 23 March 2007, *NJ* 2007/333, with annotation by Mok (*ABN AMRO v Van Velzen*) (breach of special duty of care due to non-compliance with margin requirement on a trade in options); HR 3 February 2012, *NJ* 2012/95; *AA* (2012) 752, with annotation by Busch; *JOR* 2012/116, with annotation by Van Baalen (*Coöperatieve Rabobank Vaart en Vecht UA v X*) (breach of special duty of care due to non-compliance with KYC rules when providing investment advice); HR 8 February 2013, *NJ* 2013/105; *JOR* 2013/105 (*Daelmans v Dexia*) (breach of special duty of care due to non-compliance with KYC rules in relation to portfolio management). See also inter alia the following authors: SB van Baalen, 'Aansprakelijkheid als gevolg van een schending van de Wft-regels' in D Busch et al (eds), *Onderneming en financieel toezicht* (Onderneming en Recht nr 57), 2nd edn (Deventer: Kluwer, 2010) 1013–38, 1015; B Bierens, 'Het waarheen en waarvoor van de bancaire zorgplicht. De ontwikkeling van een weerbarstig leerstuk op het snijvlak van financieel publiek- en privaatrecht' (2013) *NTBR* 15–27, 3.3; D Busch and LJ Silverentand, 'Chapter 7: The Netherlands' in D Busch and DA DeMott (eds), *Liability of Asset Managers* (Oxford: Oxford University Press, 2012) 7.56 et seq; OO Cherednychenko, 'European Securities Regulaion, Private Law and the Firm-Client Relationship' (2009) *ERPL* 925–52.

an unfair commercial practice and hence also a tort.[24] It should also be noted that in the context of institutional asset management (for pensions funds, insurers and so forth) duties of care under public law and other regulatory provisions are regularly explicitly incorporated into the contract, with all the contractual consequences that this entails. Institutional asset management contracts routinely include a provision in which the portfolio manager declares that he has an authorisation from the AFM and will at all times comply with the Wft and subordinate legislation.

B. May the Dutch Civil Courts be Stricter than MiFID?

In the Netherlands it is unclear whether civil courts may be stricter than MiFID. In 2009, in the *Dexia* case and in two other decisions handed down on the same date, the Hoge Raad ruled that, in the circumstances of the case, the private law duty of care could be stricter than the public law duties of care contained in the conduct-of-business rules.[25] However, these decisions did not concern the conduct-of-business rules implementing the *maximum* harmonisation regime of MiFID, but rather the conduct-of-business rules implementing the *minimum* harmonisation regime of its predecessor, the Investment Services Directive (ISD). In view of this, it is an open question in the Netherlands whether the civil courts can impose a private law duty of care that is stricter than the regulatory rules implementing the current MiFID regime.

[24] See DCC, Art 6:193b(1) and (3)(a), Art 6:193d(1) and (2) and Art 6:193f, opening words and (f). Since 13 June 2014 a contract concluded as a consequence of an unfair commercial practice may also be rescinded (DCC, Art 6:193j(3) (*Stb* 2014, 40). As regards the application of the legislation on unfair commercial practices to investment services, see AA Ettema, 'De Wet oneerlijke handelspraktijken in de praktijk' (2010) *Bb* 111–13. There is some discussion about whether the unfair commercial practices legislation can also relate to the duty to provide information during the term of a contract. From the history of the Dutch implementing legislation, this would indeed seem to be the case because the Unfair Commercial Practices Directive is said to apply to unfair business-to-consumer commercial practices before, during and after a commercial transaction in relation to a product (*Dutch Parliamentary Papers II* 2006/07, 30 928, no 3, 1). See also Rotterdam District Court 24 June 2010, *JOR* 2010/237, with note by Grundmann-van de Krol. This is also the view we have taken in the main text above. For a different view, at any rate in relation to the duty of a bond-issuing institution to provide information during the maturity of the bonds, see TMC Arons, JBS Hijink and ACW Pijls, 'Oneerlijke handelspraktijken bij aanbiedingen van obligaties: een never ending story?' (2009) *WPNR* 6821 953–57; JBS Hijink, 'Enige ontwikkelingen rondom de financiële verslaggeving van obligatie-uitgevende instellingen: toepasselijkheid van het "403-regime" en het toezicht van de AFM op "oneerlijke handelspraktijken"' (2010) *TvJ* 74–81, 80. Possibly likewise, see WH van Boom, *Handhaving consumentenbescherming. Een toelichting op de Wet handhaving consumentenbescherming* (Amsterdam: Uitgeverij Paris, Amsterdam 2010) 77 note 233. To date, there has been no discussion of this question in relation to the duties to provide information under MiFID, as implemented in Wft, s 4:20 and the more detailed rules, let alone in relation to the corresponding duties under MiFID II.

[25] HR 5 June 2009, *NJ* 2012/182; *JOR* 2009/199 with annotation by Lieverse (*De Treek/Dexia Bank Nederland*) consideration 4.11.5; HR 5 June 2009, *NJ* 2012/183; *JA* 2009/116 (*Levob Bank/Bolle*) consideration 4.5.8; HR 5 June 2009, *NJ* 2012/184 with annotation by Vranken; *JOR* 2009/200 (*Stichting Gedupeerden Spaarconstructie/Aegon Bank*) consideration 4.6.10.

The Dutch legal literature is divided on this issue. Some Dutch authors argue that for the sake of legal certainty, and in view of MiFID's purpose a European level playing field and the idea of maximum harmonisation, it should not be possible for civil courts to impose a higher or stricter standard than the conduct-of-business rules contained in MiFID.[26] Other Dutch authors argue that the civil courts can impose a higher or stricter standard, based on an alleged autonomy of private law. After all, these authors argue, MiFID only harmonises regulatory law, not private law. This autonomous position of private law is important, they argue, because the ex ante application of regulatory law may lead to ex post solutions that are unacceptable in the circumstances of a specific case. According to these authors, the *Dexia* case would provide an excellent illustration.[27] The argument that the European civil courts cannot render justice in individual cases because the MiFID duties are inflexible, has been rejected as unconvincing by some authors, because important MiFID duties are principle-based. A well-known example is Article 19 of MiFID, providing that a bank must act honestly, fairly and professionally in accordance with the best interests of its clients. It is argued in the legal literature that this and other principles-based provisions give the civil courts sufficient latitude to render justice in individual cases, although, these authors claim, for the sake of legal certainty, that the principles-based duties under MiFID should be used with caution.[28]

In any event, one cannot rule out that the civil courts would feel free to subject banks to private law duties which are stricter or more demanding than the MiFID duties. This can be illustrated by the *Fortis Bank/Bourgonje* judgment rendered by the Hoge Raad in 2010. The case came before the Court prior to the implementation of MiFID, but it cannot be ruled out that that the Hoge Raad would have rendered the same decision under MiFID. In any event, in *Fortis Bank/Bourgonje* it was held that Fortis was subject to a special duty of care towards its non-professional client Bourgonje. This special duty of care was based on the fact that Fortis was a professional provider of asset management services with the necessary expertise par excellence. According to the Hoge Raad, this special duty may encompass a duty to explicitly and unequivocally warn the client of the risk of considerable financial loss posed by the composition of the portfolio (excessive concentration of the portfolio in a particular asset). Whether and to what extent such duty to warn exists, and whether it is breached, depends on the relevant circumstances of the case.[29] Those circumstances may result in a duty to warn that is more or less

[26] Lieverse in her annotation No 12 under HR 5 June, *JOR* 2009/199 (*Treek/Dexia Bank Nederland*); in a similar vein Van Baalen, 'Aansprakelijkheid als gevolg van een schending van de Wft-regels' (n 23) 1013–38, 1024.

[27] See esp Cherednychenko, 'European Securities Regulation, Private Law and the Firm-Client Relationship' (n 23) 945–46 (2009); OO Cherednychenko, 'De bijzondere zorgplicht van de bank in het spanningsveld tussen publiek- en privaatrecht' (2010) *NTBR* 66–77, 74.

[28] See D Busch, 'Why MiFID Matters to Private Law—The Example of MiFID's Impact on an Asset Manager's Civil Liability' (2012) *CMLJ* 386–413, 395–96.

[29] HR 24 December 2010, *NJ* 2011/251 with annotation by Tjong Tjin Tai; *JOR* 2011/54 with annotation by Pijls (*Fortis Bank/Bourgonje*), consideration 3.4.

intense. The circumstances may even lead to the conclusion that there is no duty to warn at all.

In view of the above, it is submitted that a duty to warn explicitly and unequivocally based on the circumstances of the case goes further than to warn appropriately in a standardised format, as is allowed under Article 19(3), third dash of MiFID.[30] Also it should be borne in mind that more recent case-law from the Hoge Raad (but still pertaining to the pre-MiFID era) even requires that the bank should verify whether the consumer actually understood the warning.[31]

VI. Liability for Breach of Duty of Care

A. General

In relation to a breach of a bank's duty of care the most important remedy in practice is a claim for damages. As we have seen, such a claim is normally based on the general tort provision (*onrechtmatige daad*)[32] or breach of contract (*toerekenbare tekortkoming*).[33] Under Dutch law, a contractual claim does not preclude a damages claim based on tort, if an action or failure to act amounts to a tort independent from an imputable non-performance of a contractual obligation. Thus, a client may institute a general tort claim against the bank during the term of the contract, for example, with respect to a violation of regulatory duties to furnish information during that term. In practice, clients often base claims both on tort and breach of contract. In the absence of a contractual relationship with a bank, parties other than the bank's clients (third parties) must base their claim on tort.[34]

[30] Please note that the provision of information in a standardised format becomes a Member State option under MIFID II: the Member States *may* allow the information to be provided in a standardised format (see Art 24(5), last sentence, MIFID II). In short, if a Member State does not allow this, it seems as though the information must always be provided in a personalised format. In the Netherlands this Member State option is exercised (implicitly). The relevant Dutch implementing provision (Wft, Art 4:20(6)) is not altered in the Draft Bill to implement MiFID II, and the accompanying Explanatory Memorandum is also silent on this point. See *Dutch Parliamentary Papers II*, 2016/2017, 34 583, no 2 (Draft Bill) and no 3 (Explanatory Memorandum). It will therefore remain possible in the Netherlands to provide information in standardised format. The situation will undoubtedly be different in at least a few other Member States. If the Member States had unanimously considered that information could be provided in standardised format, a compromise in the form of a Member State option would have been unnecessary.

[31] See HR 3 February 2012, *NJ* 2012/95; *AA* (2012) 752, with note by Busch; *JOR* 2012/116, with note by Van Baalen (*Coöperatieve Rabobank Vaart en Vecht UA v X*) (duty of care in relation to the provision of investment advice), consideration 3.6.2. See also HR 14 August 2015, *NJ* 2016/107 (*Brouwer/ ABN AMRO*) (duty of care in relation to the provision of investment advice).

[32] DCC, Art 6:162.

[33] DCC, Arts 6:74 et seq.

[34] See D Busch, *Vermogensbeheer* (Mon BW no B8) (Deventer: Kluwer, 2014) § 21.1 (109).

In the case of misleading information, a claim for damages may also be based on special tort provisions regarding unfair commercial practices[35] or misleading advertising.[36] In the case of a bank's breach of contract, alternative remedies are (1) specific performance if proper performance is still possible, either instead of or in addition to damages for late performance;[37] and (2) dissolving the contract, either instead of or in addition to damages.[38] These alternative remedies have limited practical relevance in the case of liability of banks.

In view of the above we will now look in more detail at the requirements for a successful damages claim based on the general tort provision, the special tort provisions mentioned above and breach of contract.

B. Tort Liability

i. General

A client or third party claiming damages on the basis of the general tort provision must meet the following requirements: (1) unlawful behaviour (*onrechtmatigheid*); (2) attributability (*toerekening*); (3) loss (*schade*); (4) causation between the loss and the tort committed;[39] and (5) 'proximity' or 'relativity' (*relativiteit*).[40] As a general rule, the (potential) client or third party has the burden of proof on these requirements,[41] subject to exceptions, in particular concerning proof of causation.

ii. Unlawful Behaviour

Except where there are grounds for justification, unlawful behaviour may be based on (1) the violation of a right; (2) the breach of a statutory duty; or (3) the breach of an unwritten rule pertaining to proper social conduct.[42] In the context of liability of banks, tortious behaviour normally consists of an act or omission under (2) and/or (3) above.

In the case of *non-professional* clients and *non-professional* third parties whose interests the bank is required to take into account, the Hoge Raad refers to a 'special' duty of care; see sections II and III above. A violation of this duty amounts

[35] DCC, Arts 6:193a through 6:193j.
[36] DCC, Arts 6:194 and 6:195.
[37] DCC, Art 3:296(1).
[38] DCC, Art 6:265.
[39] DCC, Art 6:162(1).
[40] DCC, Art 6:163.
[41] Rv (DCCP: Dutch Code of Civil Procedure, *Wetboek van Burgerlijke Rechtsvordering*), Art 150. Explicitly in relation to the burden of proof of a breach of duty of care by an asset manager: HR 15 December 2006, *NJ* 2007, 203 with annotation by Mok; HR 11 July 2008, *JOR* 2008/272 with annotation by Voerman (*Noordnederlands Effektenkantoor BV/Mourik*).
[42] DCC, Art 6:162(2).

to a tort because it constitutes an act or omission breaching a rule of unwritten law pertaining to proper social conduct.

The duty of care is frequently specified by reference to regulatory duties contained in the Wft (and its predecessors) and the regulations pursuant thereto, particularly the conduct-of-business rules. In such cases, a tort claim based on the violation of regulatory rules amounts to an unlawful act for breaching a statutory duty. However, such an approach is not always an option. Some cases took place prior to the enactment of detailed regulatory duties, in which cases a tort claim could only be based on breach of a duty of care. It transpires from recent decisions from the Hoge Raad that the position prior to the enactment of detailed regulatory rules is sometimes not materially different from the position after their enactment, especially after the enactment of the MiFID.[43]

iii. Attributability, Causation, Loss

Liability in tort also requires that the tortious act be attributable to the bank. This is the case if the act is due to the bank's fault (*schuld*) or a cause for which the bank is accountable by statutory provision (*wet*), or pursuant to generally accepted principles (*in het verkeer geldende opvattingen*).[44] In reported cases on the liability of banks, the requirement of attributability has not been the object of much litigation. On requirements of causation and loss, which are regularly the object of litigation in relation to liability of banks, see sections VI.D and VI.E, respectively.

iv. Proximity

'Proximity' or 'relativity' (*relativiteit*) means that the violation of a standard leads to liability towards persons who allege damages as a consequence of such violation only when and to the extent that the standard is intended to protect the claimant's patrimonial interests.[45] For the liability of banks, this means that only the breach of a written or unwritten rule that aims to protect the claimant's patrimonial interest can serve as a basis for a claim for unlawful conduct.

According to the legislative history of the Wft, the requirement in Article 6:163 DCC will be met when a financial institution's client suffers loss as a consequence of a violation of the Wft. These prudential rules and the conduct-of-business rules not only serve the general interest, but also the client's individual interests.[46]

[43] HR 5 June 2009, *JA* 2009/116 (*Levob Bank/Bolle*), considerations 4.5.6 and 4.5.7; HR 5 June 2009, *JOR* 2009/199 with annotation by Lieverse; *JA* 2009/117 (*Treek/Dexia Bank Nederland*), considerations 4.11.4 and 4.11.5; HR 5 June 2009, *JOR* 2009/200; *JA* 2009/118 with annotation by Van Boom (*Stichting Gedupeerden Spaarconstructie/Aegon Bank*) considerations 4.6.4 and 4.6.8.

[44] DCC, Art 6:162(3).

[45] DCC, Art 6:163. See further Busch, *Vermogensbeheer* (n 34) § 21.4.4.

[46] *Dutch Parliamentary Papers II*, 2003/04, 29 708, No 3, 28–9; *Dutch Parliamentary Papers II*, 2005/06, 29 708, No 19, 393. This view accords with HR 13 October 2006, *NJ* 2008, 529 with annotation by Van Dam; *JOR* 2006/295 with annotation by Busch (*DNB/Stichting Vie d'Or*) consideration 4.2.2, where it was held that the patrimonial interests of policyholders are protected by the prudential rules to which life insurance companies were subject pursuant to the Wtv, one of the predecessors of the Wft.

This approach also seems to apply in relation to non-compliance with MiFID/MiFID II rules, since they have been (or, as the case may be, will be) transposed into Dutch law in the Wft and subordinate legislation. Nevertheless, some Dutch authors doubt whether this is the correct approach and argue that in fact only (some) conduct-of-business rules are drafted to protect the interests of individual clients, and that prudential rules in principle are not so drafted.[47]

The proximity test may also have a bearing on the recoverable amount of damages. The Hoge Raad has held that the specific regulatory provisions on margin requirements, which banks must observe, only aim to protect clients against relatively large losses, not against any loss suffered as a result of a violation.[48]

v. *Unfair Commercial Practices*

The implementation[49] of the Unfair Commercial Practices Directive[50] has been in effect since 15 October 2008.[51] These rules also apply to financial products and services.

A trader who engages in an unfair commercial practice acts unlawfully towards the consumer.[52] A trader is defined as any natural person acting in the conduct of his/her profession or business.[53] A consumer is defined as any natural person not acting in the conduct of his/her profession or business.[54] The point of departure in the rules on unfair commercial practices is the 'average consumer'. The European Court of Justice has held that the average consumer is informed, cautious and prudent.[55] According to the rules on unfair commercial practices the average consumer also includes the average member of a particular group addressed by the trader or an average member of a specific group when the trader could reasonably be expected to foresee that such group, owing to their mental or physical infirmity, age or credulity, will be especially vulnerable to the commercial practice or the underlying product.[56]

The rules on unfair commercial practices are particularly relevant to a bank's liability in relation to a violation of Article 4:20 Wft (and the further regulations

[47] See eg Van Baalen (n 23) 1014–1021.

[48] HR 4 December 2009, *NJ* 2010, 67 with annotation by Mok; *JOR* 2010/19 with annotation by Frielink (*Nabbe/Staalbankiers BV*) consideration 3.7. The case concerned Art 28(2)–(4) of the Further Regulation on Supervision of the Securities Trade (*Nadere Regeling toezicht effectenverkeer 1999*) a predecessor of BGfo, Arts 85 and 86, but the decision is generally held to apply *mutatis mutandis* to BGfo, Arts 85 and 86. See eg Frielink in his annotation No 7 under the decision as published in *JOR*. See also on this case Van Baalen (n 23) 1015–16.

[49] DCC, Arts 6:193a through 6:193j.

[50] Directive 2005/29/EC, OJ L149/22, 11 June 2005.

[51] *Stb* 2008, 398.

[52] DCC, Art 6:193b(1) DCC.

[53] DCC, Art 6:193a(1)(b).

[54] DCC, Art 6:193a(1)(a).

[55] ECJ, 16 July 1998, C-210/96 *Gut Springenheide GmbH and Rudolf Tusky/Oberkreisdirektor des Kreises Steinfurt*, *NJ* 2000, 374.

[56] DCC, Art 6:193a(2).

pursuant thereto) on pre-contractual duties of information and duties of information during the term of the contract. The rules on unfair commercial practices explicitly provide that a violation of these provisions automatically amounts to a misleading and therefore unfair commercial practice to the extent that the provisions apply in relation to non-professional clients/consumers.[57] Thus, clients who are consumers can base their damages claim against the bank on the rules on unfair commercial practices when the bank violates these provisions.[58]

In case of a violation of Article 4:20 Wft (and the further regulations pursuant thereto) non-professional clients can also base their damages claim on the general tort provision of Article 6:162 DCC or, to the extent the claim concerns inadequate information during the term of the contract, also on breach of contract. However, a damages claim based on the rules on unfair commercial practices is more advantageous for the consumer. First, as a general rule, the bank has the burden of proof with respect to the material correctness and completeness of the information provided to the consumer.[59] He only needs to state that the information is incorrect and/or incomplete. Secondly, attribution of the tortious act is assumed, unless the bank proves that the tort was not due to its fault and that it cannot be held accountable for the fault on any other ground.[60]

Finally, since 13 June 2014 a contract concluded as a consequence of an unfair commercial practice may also be rescinded (Article 6:193j(3) DCC).[61]

vi. Misleading Advertisements

Like the rules on unfair commercial practices, the rules on misleading advertisements[62] are special tort provisions. Although the rules on misleading advertisements entered into force in 1975, they are considered to incorporate the provisions of the 1984 Misleading Advertisements Directive.[63] Before 15 October 2008, the rules on misleading advertisements applied in relation to both consumers and professionals. Since the entry into force of the rules on unfair commercial practices, the rules on misleading advertisements apply only to professionals. Since then, Article 6:194 DCC states that a person who makes public or causes to be made public information regarding goods or services which he, or the person for whom he acts, offers in the conduct of a profession or business, acts unlawfully towards another person acting in the conduct of its business if this information

[57] DCC, Art 6:193b(1) and (3)(a), Art 6:193d(1) and (2) and Art 6:193f, opening words and sub(f).

[58] See on the application of the rules on unfair commercial practices in relation to the provision of information by investment services providers: Ettema, 'De Wet oneerlijke handelspraktijken in de praktijk' (n 24).

[59] DCC, Art 6:193j(1).

[60] DCC, Art 6:193j(2).

[61] *Stb*, 2014, 40.

[62] DCC, Arts 6:194 and 6:195.

[63] Directive 1984/450/EEC, OJ L 250, 19 September 1984, 17. Cf Busch, *Vermogensbeheer* (n 34) § 21.7.1.

is misleading in one or more respects. 'Goods' is interpreted broadly to include securities such as shares.[64] 'Services' includes financial services.

The rules on misleading advertisements often serve as the basis for misleading-prospectus claims against issuers and banks, for example, in connection with initial public offerings. Prior to the entry into force of the rules on unfair commercial practices, the misleading character of a prospectus had to be established with reference to the average informed, cautious and prudent ordinary investor,[65] a reference derived from the case-law of the European Court of Justice.[66] The 'average investor' may be expected to be prepared to dive into the information offered, but not to have specialised or special knowledge and experience at his/her disposal, unless the advertising is directed solely to persons with such knowledge and experience.[67] Since the entry into force of the unfair commercial practices rules, the rules on misleading advertisements apply only in relation to professionals.

In relation to a bank's liability, the rules on misleading advertisements are (like the rules on unfair commercial practices) particularly relevant in relation to a violation of Article 4:20 Wft on pre-contractual duties of information and duties of information during the term of the contract. It is submitted that a violation of these provisions, to the extent that they concern professional clients, automatically amounts to a misleading statement within the meaning of Article 6:194 DCC. Thus, when a bank violates Article 4:20 Wft a professional client can base a damages claim on the rules on misleading advertisements.

In case of a violation of Article 4:20 Wft (and the further regulations pursuant thereto) a client can also base a damages claim on the general tort provision of Article 6:162 DCC or, as far as it concerns inadequate information during the term of the contract, on breach of contract. However, a damages claim based on the rules on misleading advertisements has some advantages in comparison to a claim based on the general tort provision or breach of contract. First, the bank has the burden of proof with respect to the material correctness and completeness of the information that the bank provided.[68] The client must merely state that the information was incorrect and/or incomplete. Secondly, attribution of the tortious act is assumed, unless the bank proves that the tort committed was not due to its fault and that it cannot be held accountable for the tort on any other ground.[69]

[64] *Dutch Parliamentary Papers II*, 1975/76, 13 611, No 3, 9.

[65] See eg HR 27 November 2009, *JOR* 2010/43 with annotation by Frielink (*Vereniging van Effectenbezitters c.s./World Online International NV c.s.*) consideration 4.10.3.

[66] ECJ, 16 July 1998, C-210/96 *Gut Springenheide GmbH and Rudolf Tusky/Oberkreisdirektor des Kreises Steinfurt*, *NJ* 2000, 374, confirmed in ECJ, 19 September 2006, C-356/04 *Lidl Belgium GmbH & Co KG/Etablissementen Franz Colruyt NV*, *NJ* 2007, 18.

[67] HR 27 November 2009, *JOR* 2010/43 with annotation by Frielink (*Vereniging van Effectenbezitters c.s./World Online International NV c.s.*) consideration 4.10.3.

[68] DCC, Art 6:195(1).

[69] DCC, Art 6:195(2).

C. Breach of Contract

i. General

A damages claim based on breach of contract[70] may, amongst other things, concern (1) an alleged breach of the investment guidelines; (2) underperformance; (3) breach of margin requirements in relation to options transactions; (4) breach of duties of information during the term of the contract; and (5) breach of contractual representations and warranties.

A client claiming damages on the basis of breach of contract must establish the following requirements: (1) failure in the performance of a contractual obligation; (2) attributability (*toerekening*); (3) loss (*schade*); (4) causation between the loss and failure in the performance of the relevant contractual obligation.[71] Unless proper performance is permanently impossible, the client is entitled only to damages when the bank is in default under Articles 6:81 et seq DCC. As a general rule, the burden of proof with regard to these requirements is with the client.[72] However, there are some important exceptions to this rule, particularly in relation to proof of causation. In addition, the client has a duty of prompt protest against defects in the performance of a contract; failure bars the client's ability to base a claim on this defect.[73]

ii. Failure in the Performance of a Contractual Obligation

If a bank violates his duty of care,[74] this amounts to a failure in the performance of a contractual obligation in the sense of Article 6:74 (1) DCC.[75]

The contractual duty of care is frequently specified by the civil courts by reference to regulatory duties imposed on a bank contained in or pursuant to the Wft (and its predecessors), including the conduct-of-business rules. In principle, the violation of such regulatory rules amounts to a breach of the contractual duty of care.

iii. Attributability, Causation, Loss

The failure in the performance of the bank's contractual obligation must be attributable to the bank, on the basis of fault (*schuld*), a statutory provision (*wet*),

[70] DCC, Art 6:74 et seq.

[71] DCC, Art 6:74(1).

[72] Rv, Art 150. Thus explicitly in relation to the burden of proof of a breach of duty of care by an asset manager: HR 15 December 2006, *NJ* 2007, 203 with annotation by Mok; HR 11 July 2008, *JOR* 2008/272 with annotation by Voerman (*Noordnederlands Effektenkantoor BV/Mourik*).

[73] DCC, Art 6:89.

[74] In the case of private, non-professional clients and private, non-professional third parties whose interests the bank is required to take into account, the Hoge Raad refers to a 'special' duty of care.

[75] In the pre-contractual stage and during the term of the contract, a violation of the duty of care can also amount to a tort.

a juridical act (*rechtshandeling*) or generally accepted principles (*in het verkeer geldende opvattingen*) (Article 6:75 DCC). An example of a failure in performance that is attributable to the bank on the basis of a juridical act (here the contract) is the breach of a contractual representation or warranty. In reported cases on the liability of banks, the requirement of attributability has not been the object of much litigation. On requirements of causation and loss, which are regularly the object of litigation in relation to liability of banks, see sections VI.D and VI.E, respectively.

iv. Duty to Protest

Under Article 6:89 DCC, a creditor may not invoke a defect in the performance of an obligation in the absence of prompt protest after the creditor has discovered, or should reasonably have discovered, the defect. The purpose of this rule is to protect the debtor against claims that are difficult to dispute owing to the passage of time. Whether the creditor is considered to have protested promptly enough depends on the circumstances of the case. The court does not apply Article 6:89 DCC on its own initiative; the creditor must invoke the provision[76] and has the burden of proving that protest was timely made and in a manner apparent to the debtor.[77] If the creditor does not manage to prove that it protested in time, its claim will be rejected. The duty to protest also applies if the creditor bases its claim concerning defective performance on tort.[78]

Article 6:89 DCC applies to claims against financial services providers. Non-compliance with the duty to protest is regularly invoked in court proceedings in relation to alleged losses on investments in financial instruments. The loss on investments in financial instruments (unlike many other losses) is often difficult to determine. As long as the client does not sell an investment, its value may fluctuate owing to market developments. It is argued that it is undesirable that a client can just wait and see how the markets develop, filing a claim only when an investment turns into a loss, for example, on the basis that the investment policy was too risky in the light of the client's investment objectives.[79] If the client protests, he must clearly specify in which ways the bank's performance is defective. Most of the time the bank's defence of non-compliance with the duty to protest is unsuccessful.[80]

[76] See HR 20 January 2006, *NJ* 2006, 80 (*Robinson/Molenaar v o. f.*).

[77] See HR 23 November 2007, *RvdW* 2007, 996.

[78] HR 23 November 2007, *RvdW* 2007, 996. See on Art 6:89 DCC in connection with investment services Busch, *Vermogensbeheer* (n 34) § 21.5.5.

[79] Cf AA Ettema, 'Protesteerplicht bij klachten over effectendienstverlening' (HR 11 juni 2010, LJN: BL8297) (2010) *Bb* 161–64, 161.

[80] See eg HR 11 June 2010, *JOR* 2010/199 with annotation by Lieverse; HR 8 October 2010, *NJ* 2010/545 (*Tan c.s./Forward Business Parks 2000 NV & Chipshol 2000 B.V.*); HR 8 February 2013, *RvdW* 2013/253; *AA* (2013) 755 with annotation Van Boom; *JOR* 2013/106, with annotation Van der Wiel (*Van de Steeg c.s./Rabobank*); HR 8 February 2013, *RvdW* 2013/250; *JOR* 2013/107, with annotation Van der Wiel (*Kramer/Van Lanschot*).

D. Causation

i. General

The loss suffered by a (potential) client or third party must be caused by the bank's unlawful behaviour or imputable non-performance. The decisive test is whether, without the tortious behaviour or imputable non-performance, the loss would not have occurred (the *condicio-sine-qua-non* or but-for test).[81] As a rule, the burden of proof for causation is on the client or the third party claiming damages.[82] Especially in cases of a failure to provide information or to adequately warn a non-professional client about financial risks), proof of this requirement is often problematic. In such cases, banks usually argue that there is no causal connection between the breach and the loss suffered because the non-professional client would have made the same investment decision had the bank complied with its duty to provide information.[83]

ii. Proportionate Liability

Recently, an attempt has been made to divide the risk of uncertainty about the *condicio-sine-qua-non* requirement between a bank and its client in a case concerning a violation of a duty to provide information. The Amsterdam Court of Appeal held that the bank providing asset management services breached its duty of care because it did not explicitly and unequivocally warn its non-professional client about the risk of considerable financial loss to the portfolio due to excessive concentration in a particular asset. The Court held that it was not entirely clear whether the client would have followed the bank's warning to sell the investment that constituted a disproportionately large portion of the portfolio as soon as possible. The Court held that there was a 50 per cent chance that the client would have followed the bank's explicit warning and ruled that the bank was liable for 50 per cent of the loss.[84]

[81] DCC, Art 6:162(1) and DCC, Art 6:74(1).

[82] Rv, Art 150.

[83] Given that the client keeps his investment after the moment that he knew or should have known that it is too risky, the courts sometimes infer that the client would not have opposed the relevant investment had he been adequately informed about the risks from the very start, with the effect that there is no *condicio-sine-qua-non* connection between the bank's breach of its duty of care and the damage suffered by the client. See eg Court of Appeal Amsterdam 2 November 2010, *JOR* 2011/80 (concerning an advisory relationship). See also n 144. In addition, it is sometimes reasoned that the causal chain between the bank's unlawful act or breach of contract and the damage suffered is broken from the moment that the client was or should have been aware of the risks, with the effect that any loss suffered thereafter cannot be attributed to the bank. See GCHB 1 July 2010–394, consideration 4.8.3 (concerning an advisory relationship). Similar results can be achieved through an application of the duty to mitigate damages because as soon as the client is or should have been aware of the risks he can instruct the bank to sell the relevant investment. See further section VI.F.ii below. See on GCHB, section X below.

[84] Court of Appeal Amsterdam 4 November 2008, *JOR* 2009/51 with annotation by Voerman.

The Hoge Raad quashed the decision. In a previous judgment, it had accepted proportionate liability in relation to damage to health,[85] considering that proportionate liability would also be conceivable in other types of cases, in particular if (1) the violation of the relevant standard is clear; (2) there is a fair chance that there is *condicio-sine-qua-non* connection between the violated standard and the loss suffered and (3) application of proportionate liability is justified by the purpose and nature of the violated standard. In its decision to quash the decision of the Amsterdam Court of Appeal, it considered that the nature of the violated standard was the bank's duty to warn its client and the purpose of the violated standard was preventing patrimonial loss. It also considered that the Court of Appeal had held that the chance that the client would have followed the bank's advice to sell the relevant investment as soon as possible was not particularly large.[86] In other words, it is not likely that proportionate liability will be applied when a bank breaches its duties to inform or to warn, as the claim will normally concern financial loss rather than personal injury.

iii. Loss of Chance

A second possibility is the theory of the loss of a chance, which is related to, yet distinct from, proportionate liability. Loss of a chance puts the focus on the damage rather than causation. Unlike with proportionate liability, the *condicio sine qua non*-test or but-for test is passed and the discussion only concerns how to translate into damages the chance that the client would have refrained from contracting, had he been properly informed or warned of the risks of the investment.

The Hoge Raad and the lower courts have applied this theory of the loss of a chance outside the area of liability for investment damage, with respect to the liability of attorneys-at-law (*advocaten*), tax advisers and medical doctors.[87] It cannot be excluded that at some point the courts may be asked to apply the theory to banks that have failed to inform or warn their client. It is, however, unlikely

[85] HR 31 March 2006, *RvdW* 2006, 328 (*Nefalit/Karamus*).

[86] HR 24 December 2010, *JOR* 2011/54 with annotation by Pijls (*Fortis Bank/Bourgonje*), considerations 3.8–3.10.

[87] Liability of attorneys-at-law: HR 24 October 1997, *NJ* 1998, 257, m.nt. Stein (*Baijings/Mr. H*); HR 19 January 2007, *NJ* 2007, 63 (*C Kranendonk Holding BV/Maatschap A*); HR 16 February 2007, *NJ* 2007, 256, m.nt. Maeijer; *JOR* 2007/112, m.nt. Van Veen en Van Wechem (*Gebroeders Tuin Beheer/Houthoff Buruma c.s.*). Liability of tax advisers: HR 21 december 2012, *NJ* 2013, 237, m.nt. Lindenbergh; *JA* 2013, 41, m.nt. Akkermans en Van Dijk (*Deloitte Belastingadviseurs/H&H Beheer*). Liability of medical doctors: Hof Amsterdam 4 januari 1996, *NJ* 1997, 213 (*Wever/De Kraker c.s.*); Rb Middelburg 11 maart 1998, *NJ* 1999, 41; Rb Amsterdam 28 oktober 1998, *NJ* 1999, 406 (*Brinkman/Stork*); 28 oktober Hof Arnhem 24 juni en 14 december 1999, *NJ* 2000, 742; Rb Zwolle 31 mei 2000, *NJkort* 2000, 89; Rb Den Haag 12 juli 2000, *VR* 2001, 20; Rb Leeuwarden 12 juli 2000, *TvGr* 2001, 13; Hof Den Haag 10 oktober 2002, *NJ* 2003, 99; Rb Amsterdam 23 mei 2003, *NJ* 2004, 45; Rb Maastricht 13 juli 2005, *JA* 2006, 44, m.nt. Zaadhof; Hof Arnhem 17 januari 2006, *JA* 2006, 37, m.nt. Giard; Rb Zwolle 1 februari 2006, ECLI:NL:RBZLY:2006:AW6459.

that this theory would lead to a different outcome from that when the doctrine of proportionate liability is applied.[88]

iv. Reversal Rule and Related Techniques

a. Reversal Rule

The Hoge Raad also regularly applies the so-called 'reversal rule'. The rule applies when: (1) an act or inaction violates a duty that aims to protect against the risk of suffering specific losses; and (2) the person who invokes the breach of duty makes it plausible that in its case this specific risk materialised. If the reversal rule applies, there is a rebuttable presumption of a *condicio-sine-qua-non* connection between the breach of the relevant duty and the loss suffered, unless the defendant makes it plausible that the loss is not due to its act or inaction.[89]

The reversal rule may apply when a bank violates duties to furnish information (including duties to warn). For example, it is arguable that a duty to warn the client against the risks of investing with borrowed funds specifically aims to protect the client against the risk of suffering losses as a result of investing in financial instruments with borrowed funds. If such risk materialises, the reversal rule may apply. Depending on the circumstances of the case, the bank's duty to pay damages may be mitigated by the client's contributory negligence.[90] Thus, the reversal rule, combined with the doctrine of contributory negligence, may in application result in outcomes largely similar to the technique of proportionate liability discussed above.

However, case-law from the Hoge Raad suggests that the reversal rule does not apply to 'informed consent' cases because duties to furnish information aim to enhance well-informed decisions and not to protect against the risk of suffering specific losses, as the reversal rule requires.[91] If so, the reversal rule probably has no role to play when a bank breaches its duties to furnish information, including duties to warn.[92]

[88] In this sense, inter alia, Akkermans and Van Dijk in their annotation no 15 under HR 21 December 2012, *JA* 2013, 41 (*Deloitte Belastingadviseurs/H&H Beheer*).

[89] HR 29 November 2002, *NJ* 2004, 404 (*TFS/NS*); HR 29 November 2002, *NJ* 2004, 305 with annotation by Asser (*Kastelein/Achterkarspelen*).

[90] DCC, Art 6:101 (*eigen schuld*). See for an example KCHB 31 March 2009, No 369. See on KCHB, section X below.

[91] HR 23 November 2001, *NJ* 2002, 386; HR 23 November 2001, *NJ* 2002, 387, with annotation by Brunner (both concerning medical liability); HR 2 February 2007, *NJ* 2007, 92 (*Juresta Nederland BV*) (concerning the liability of an attorney-at-law).

[92] See ACW Pijls, 'Het bewijs van causaal verband bij informatieverzuimen in de beleggingspraktijk' (2009) *NTBR* 170–81, 174; AJP Schild, 'Het "condicio sine qua non"-verband bij de schending van een zorgvuldigheidsverplichting: enige wegen naar Rome' (2009) *RMTh* 254–64, 257–59; see also the conclusion of the substitute Procurator-General De Vriesch Lentsch-Kostense, in No 3.36 before HR 5 June 2009, *JA* 2009/116 (*Levob Bank/Bolle*); HR 5 June 2009, *JOR* 2009/199 with annotation by Lieverse; *JA* 2009/117 (*Treek/Dexia Bank Nederland*); HR 5 June 2009, *JOR* 2009/200; *JA* 2009/118 with annotation by Van Boom (*Stichting Gedupeerden Spaarconstructie/Aegon Bank*).

b. Related Techniques

General

Recent case-law from the Hoge Raad suggests that more informal, ad hoc techniques are available that yield results similar to the reversal rule.[93] Although formally the Court did not apply the reversal rule in these cases, considerations of reasonableness apparently dictated that the risk of uncertainty about the *condicio-sine-qua-non* connection should shift to the party that violated a duty to furnish information. To the extent appropriate, damages may be reduced by the investor's contributory negligence.[94]

World Online

The reason to shift the risk of uncertainty about the *condicio-sine-qua-non* connection to the party violating the relevant duty of information, articulated in the *World Online* judgment on prospectus liability, may be relevant to liability of a bank for breach of duty of care. The European Prospectus Directive provides detailed rules about the content and layout of a prospectus but does not harmonise national regimes on prospectus liability.[95] Nevertheless, the Hoge Raad held that it follows from the directive's objectives that rules of national law must offer effective legal protection. Thus, the Court held that it may serve as a 'point of departure' that the *condicio-sine-qua-non* connection between the misleading statement and the investment decision is present. In principle it must be assumed that, but for the misleading statement, the investor would not have bought the securities; or, in a secondary market transaction, would not have bought them on the same terms. However, taking into account the nature of the misleading information and the other available information, a court might instead arrive at the conclusion that this point of departure should be displaced, for example, in the case of a professional investor, who in view of its experience and knowledge may not have been influenced by the misleading prospectus in making its decision to invest.[96]

[93] HR 5 June 2009, *JA* 2009/116 (*Levob Bank/Bolle*) considerations 4.7.8–4.7.10; HR 5 June 2009, *JOR* 2009/199 with annotation by Lieverse; *JA* 2009/117 (*Treek/Dexia Bank Nederland*) considerations 5.5.1–5.5.3 (both concerning liability for complex financial products); HR 27 November 2009, *JOR* 2010/43 (*Vereniging van Effectenbezitters c.s./World Online International NV*) (concerning prospectus liability), considerations 4.11.1 and 4.11.2.

[94] See eg HR 5 June 2009, *JA* 2009/116 (*Levob Bank/Bolle*) considerations 4.9.1–4.9.4; HR 5 June 2009, *JOR* 2009/199 with annotation by Lieverse; *JA* 2009/117 (*Treek/Dexia Bank Nederland*) considerations 4.13.1–4.14.4.

[95] The European Prospectus Directive merely indicates that the Member States are under an obligation to ensure that the national statutory provisions regarding civil law liability apply to those who are responsible for the information referred to in the prospectus (Directive 2003/71/EC, OJ L 345, 31 December 2003, 64, Art 6(2)).

[96] HR 27 November 2009, *JOR* 2010/43 with annotation by Frielink (*Vereniging van Effectenbezitters c.s./World Online International NV*) considerations 4.11.1 and 4.11.2.

Share Lease

The assessment of causation is strongly connected with the scope of the breached duty. The Hoge Raad emphasised this in three judgments handed down in 2009. The cases were about an investment in securities with money borrowed from the financial service provider or a third party (see section II.B above). The Hoge Raad held that the banks had breached their duties to warn the client in no unclear terms about the risk of the investment (here: a remaining debt) and to advise the client not to conclude the contract. The clients generally argued they would not have concluded the contract if the bank had warned them of the remaining debt or had advised them against concluding the contract.

In such a situation, according to the Hoge Raad, the question whether there is a causal connection between the bank's breach of duty and the client's damage (the remaining debt and the already paid interest and instalments), the court has to compare the client's actual situation and the hypothetical situation in which he would have found himself had the bank not breached its duty. The Hoge Raad held that the duties breached by the bank aim to prevent a private client from rashly or without sufficient insight concluding an investment contract. Concluding the contract can therefore be considered to be the consequence of the bank's breach of its duty of care. This means that the remaining debt, the paid interest, the instalments and the costs can be considered to be the client's damage caused by the bank's breach.[97]

More particularly, the Hoge Raad distinguished two situations. First, the causation test is supposed to be passed if the service provider should have understood that when offering the product, considering the client's financial position, payment of the lease instalments and the possible (maximum) remaining debt, would supposedly have put an unacceptably heavy financial burden on the client. In such a situation the chance that this client would not have concluded is so considerable that, had he realised the specific risks to which he would have been exposed, it can be assumed that without the bank's breach he would not have concluded the contract, unless there are strong indications of the opposite.[98]

Secondly, if at the time of concluding the contract, the client's financial situation was sufficient to meet his obligations flowing from the contract, including the possible remaining debt, the financial service provider has to specifically underpin its defence that the client would also have concluded the contract if the provider had not breached its duty, particularly its duty to warn. If this underpinning is insufficient, a causal connection can, in principle, be assumed.[99]

[97] HR 5 June 2009, ECLI:NL:HR:2009:BH2809 (*De Treek/Dexia*); in the same sense HR 5 June 2009, ECLI:NL:HR:2009:BH2811 (Levob/Bolle).

[98] HR 5 June 2009, ECLI:NL:HR:2009:BH2811 (*Levob/Bolle*), para 4.7.9.

[99] ibid, para 4.7.10.

These Hoge Raad judgments provide the guidance for the decisions of the lower courts with respect to causation.[100]

v. Rv, Art 149

Finally, there may sometimes be an easier way to establish causation. Consumer X argued that he would not have concluded certain contracts, including option contracts, had the bank complied with its duty to warn him, as he wanted to keep his capital, considering it was aimed at being a financial retirement provision. The bank did not dispute this statement but argued that the warnings would not have had affected the client's decision. However, the Court of Appeal rejected this statement, as not being sufficiently substantiated, the consequence of which was that the client's statement was considered to be insufficiently disputed and, hence, upheld. The Hoge Raad dismissed the appeal, considering that the Court of Appeal had correctly applied the rules on evidence and causation.[101]

E. Damages

i. General

The Dutch Civil Code contains a separate section on damages,[102] applicable to all legal obligations to repair damage, including liability arising from non-performance of a contractual obligation and from tort. It does not apply to damages that are the object of contractual provisions, such as liquidated damages and insurance.[103]

In case of the breach of a bank's duty of care, the damage will generally be pure economic loss (that is loss unrelated to property loss or personal injury). This loss may be related to:

— *investment losses*: the loss an investor suffers because of misleading information by or about securities issuing institutions;
— *inadequate financial services*: the loss someone suffers because his financial service provider does not carry out asset management in a proper way (eg by not following the client's risk profile);

[100] Court of Appeal Den Bosch 15 April 2014, ECLI:NL:GHSHE:2014:1052 (*Westkant/ABN. AMRO*); District Court Oost-Brabant 26 March 2014 (ECLI:NL: RBOBR:2014:1415, *JOR* 2014/167) (*X/Rabobank Peel*).

[101] HR 3 February 2012, *NJ* 2012, 95; *AA* (2012) 752, with annotation Busch; *JOR* 2012/116, with annotation Van Baalen (*Coöperatieve Rabobank Vaart en Vecht UA/X*). See in the same sense HR 8 February 2013, *RvdW* 2013, 249; *JOR* 2013/108, annotation Van der Wiel (*Van Lanschot Bankiers/ Grove c.s.*).

[102] DCC, Arts 6:95–110.

[103] Busch (n 34) § 24.1, 152.

— *investment losses*: the investor has invested in a product about which a financial service provider has given incorrect information with respect to a product, provided they would not have invested in the product if they had been given correct and complete information but in a different product.[104]

The basic principle is that the injured party must be placed as much as possible in the situation he would have been in had the event that caused the damage not occurred.[105] As a general rule, pecuniary loss is eligible for compensation[106] and may consist of sustained losses (*damnum emergens*) and lost profits (*lucrum cessans*).[107] The court evaluates the damage in a manner that is best suited to its nature.[108] When the extent of the damage cannot be precisely determined, it will estimate it.[109] The court may apply abstract calculations by quantifying damages on the basis of the difference between the purchase price and the market price.[110]

The duty to repair damage presupposes that the failure in the performance of a contractual obligation or the tortious act is the *condicio-sine-qua-non* of the damage.[111] In addition, damages under the DCC are recoverable only to the extent that they can be imputed to the bank as a consequence of its non-performance or tortious act.[112] All relevant circumstances of the case are taken into account. For patrimonial damage, normally the kind of damage suffered in the context of investment services, the concept of foreseeability plays an important part in legal practice.[113]

ii. Calculation of Losses

Usually the damage consists of the loss which would have been avoided had the bank not breached its duty. For example, if a disproportionate part of the portfolio is invested in a particular industry, often not all the loss suffered on investment in that particular industry will qualify as loss. An assessment must be made of the

[104] See eg District Court Utrecht 30 January 2013, ECLI:NL:RBMNE:LJN:BY9836 (*Stichting Claim SNS/SNS Bank c.s.*).

[105] Busch (n 34) § 24.1, 153.

[106] DCC, Art 6:95. Other harm may be eligible for repair as well, but only to the extent that statute law grants a right to reparation thereof (DCC, Art 6:95). In that connection, DCC, Art 6:106 provides in certain instances for the recovery of moral damage. However, in view of the strict criteria for recovery of moral damage (HR 22 February 2002, *NJ* 2002, 240 with annotation by Vranken (*Kindertaxi*)) such recovery will only in highly exceptional cases be possible in cases of liability of financial services providers. See Busch (n 34) § 24.1, 153; M van Luyn and E Du Perron, *Effecten van de zorgplicht: Klachten over effectendienstverlening in de praktijk* (Deventer: Kluwer, 2004) 276.

[107] DCC, Art 6:96(1).

[108] DCC, Art 6:97, first sentence.

[109] DCC, Art 6:97, second sentence.

[110] Busch (n 34) § 24.1, 153.

[111] See section VI.D.

[112] DCC, Art 6:98.

[113] Busch (n 34) § 24.2.

percentage that would have been acceptable in that industry in the light of the client's profile, plus the investment guidelines and restrictions. If 90 per cent of the portfolio is invested in one relevant industry where 45 per cent would have been acceptable, only half of the loss (ie 50 per cent of the 90 per cent) on the investment in that industry qualifies as loss. The remainder of the damage is considered not to have been caused by the bank. A similar reasoning may be followed if the client's (or third party's) assets are invested in too risky a manner owing to the bank's fault when it is plausible that, but for the fault, the assets would still be invested in a risky manner (albeit less risky), which would also have caused loss.[114] In many such cases, the amount of loss that is due to the bank's fault can only be estimated.[115] Often a comparison with a relevant benchmark is made to render the estimate more realistic.[116]

iii. Calculation of Lost Profits

Damage may also consist of the lost profits the client or third party would likely have made had he not breached its duty.[117] To take a similar example: if 70 per cent of a portfolio is invested in shares and 30 per cent in fixed income financial instruments, but the opposite allocation was warranted by the client's risk profile, the profits of which the client has been deprived (assuming a market in which the value of fixed income financial instruments moved favourably relative to the value of shares) consists of the difference in market value between shares and fixed income securities for the 40 per cent of the portfolio that should have been invested in fixed income financial instruments, not in shares. As is the case when calculating loss due to the bank's fault, the profits of which the client or third party has been deprived can often only be estimated.[118] Again, a comparison with a relevant benchmark may render the estimate more realistic.

iv. Deduction of Benefits Received by the Client or Third Party

If a breach of contract or a tort results in benefits as well as damage, those benefits must be deducted from the total amount of damage.[119] This is particularly

[114] KCHB 8 January 2004, *JOR* 2004/52; KCD 23 July 2004, 04-112. Cf Van Luyn and Du Perron, *Effecten van de zorgplicht: Klachten over effectendienstverlening in de praktijk* (n 106) 10, 271. See on KCD and KCHB, section X below.

[115] On the basis of DCC, Art 6:97, second sentence.

[116] KCD 27 August 2002, 02-153 (AEX index); KCD 3 June 2004, 04-81 (AEX index); KCD 7 June 2004, 04-96 (MSCI (Europe) index); KCD 14 July 2004 (CBS bond index); KCD 10 January 2007, 07-1, *JOR* 2007/92 with annotation by Voerman (Euronext 100 index); District Court Amsterdam 24 January 2007, *JOR* 2007/94 with annotation by 't Hart (*Laan c.s./Wijs & Van Oostveen*) (AEX-index); GC 6 July 2010, 10-132 (Robeco Solid Mix Fund). Cf Luyn and Du Perron (n 106) 272. See on KCD and GC section X below.

[117] DCC, Art 6:96(1).

[118] On the basis of DCC, Art 6:97, second sentence. See eg KCD 10 June 2004, 04-93. Cf Van Luyn and Du Perron (n 106) 273. See on KCD section X below.

[119] DCC, Art 6:100.

relevant in cases of incorrect asset allocation. In such cases, the correction must be made from the moment that the incorrect asset allocation took place. Thus, if 70 per cent instead of 30 per cent of a portfolio has been invested in shares, not only the loss suffered in the years of declining share prices should be taken into account but also the profits made in the years of rising share prices.[120] In addition, benefits to a client may also include tax benefits realised due to the bank's breach of contract or tort.[121]

v. Benefits Enjoyed by the Bank

The damage suffered by the client or third party does not include the benefit enjoyed by the bank as a result of its breach of contract or tortious act. Nevertheless, Article 6:104 DCC provides that when someone is liable to someone else on the basis of a breach of contract or a tort, the court may, upon the claimant's request, determine the damage according to the amount of that profit or a part thereof. For this rule to apply the claimant must prove that he suffered damage, but he does not need to prove its extent. The court may not apply this rule if the bank makes it plausible that the claimant cannot have suffered any damages due to the act for which the bank is held liable.[122]

vi. Statutory Interest and Reference Date

A bank is obliged to pay statutory interest on the amount of damages if it is liable in tort or contract.[123] Statutory interest is due from the reference date for the assessment of damages until the date on which the bank has satisfied its obligation to pay damages. The reference date is usually considered to be the date as closely as possible to the moment of the breach of contract or the unlawful act that caused the damage.[124] However, it may also be the date when the client discovered the breach of contract or tortious act or should have discovered it, as from then on he could have avoided further damage.[125] Finally, the reference date may be based on the parties' procedural positions.[126]

[120] Cf Van Luyn and Du Perron (n 106) 273, 274.

[121] Cf 't Hart in his annotation No 11 under District Court Amsterdam 24 January 2007, *JOR* 2007/94 (*Laan c.s./Wijs & Van Oostveen*).

[122] HR 24 December 1993, *NJ* 1995, 421 with annotation by Brunner (*Waeyen-Scheers/Naus*); HR 16 June 2006, *NJ* 2006, 585 with annotation by Snijders (*Kecofa/Lancme*); HR 18 June 2010, *LJN:* BM0893; HR 18 June 2010, *LJN:* BL9662. See Busch, *Vermogensbeheer* (n 34) § 24.7.

[123] DCC, Art 6:119.

[124] KCHB 22 November 2001, No 9; Amsterdam District Court 23 December 2009, *JOR* 2010/110 with annotation by Van Setten; *AA* 372-82 (2011) with annotation by Busch (*Stichting Pensioenfonds OPG/State Street Global Advisors Ltd*) consideration 5.9. Cf Van Luyn and Du Perron (n 106) 274. See on KCHB section X below.

[125] See further § VI.F.ii, below.

[126] KCHB 22 November 2001, No 9. Cf Van Luyn and Du Perron (n 106). 274. See on KCHB section X below.

F. Contributory Negligence and Duty to Mitigate Damages

i. General

The amount of damages payable by a bank may be reduced owing to the claimant's contributory negligence or his failure to mitigate the damage.[127]

When circumstances that can be attributed to the client (or third party) have contributed to the damage, the duty to pay damages is reduced by apportioning the damage between the client (or third party) and the bank, in proportion to the degree to which the circumstances attributable to each have contributed to the damage (primary apportionment on the basis of *condicio-sine-qua-non* causation,[128] supplemented by a reasonable imputation of damages in the sense of Article 6:98 DCC (*causaliteitsafweging*)).[129] However, a different apportionment is made, or the duty to pay damages may be considered nil, as a consequence of different degrees of seriousness in the faults committed or any other circumstances of the case (so-called correction based on considerations of equity, *billijkheidscorrectie*).[130] Article 6:101(1) DCC concerns not only situations of contributory negligence with respect to the initial occurrence of the damage, but also the failure to comply with a duty to mitigate damage once it has occurred.[131]

The Hoge Raad has held several times that faults by a non-professional client resulting from his/her rashness or lack of understanding in principle weigh less heavily than do faults committed by a financial institution.[132] Although it is not entirely clear, these considerations seem to refer not to the primary apportionment based on causation, but rather to the secondary apportionment based on equity. If so, the Hoge Raad provided a rule of thumb, ie that a non-professional client's faults weigh less heavily than faults committed by a financial institution, for cases in which the damage is also due to a non-professional client's faults resulting from rashness or lack of understanding.[133]

[127] In addition, the court may reduce a legal obligation to pay damages if a full award of damages would lead to clearly unacceptable results in the given circumstances, including the nature of the liability, the parties' existing legal relationship, and their financial resources (DCC, Art 6:109(1)). The reduction may not be made if it reduces the amount below that for which the debtor has covered his liability by insurance or was obliged to do so (DCC, Art 6:109(2)). Any stipulation in breach of DCC, Art 6:109(1) is null and void (DCC, Art 6:109(3)). We are not aware of any cases in which this provision has been applied in the context of liability of financial services providers. In view of this, the possibility of judicial reduction seems to be a largely theoretical possibility.

[128] See section VI.D, above.

[129] See section VI.E.i, above.

[130] DCC, Art 6:101(1).

[131] Busch (n 34) § 25.1, 160.

[132] HR 23 May 1997, *NJ* 1998, 192 with annotation by Van Zeben (*Rabo/Everaars*) consideration 3.3; HR 11 July 2003, *NJ* 2005, 103 with annotation by Du Perron (*Kouwenberg/Rabobank*) consideration 3.6.3; HR 5 June 2009, *JA* 2009/116 (*Levob Bank/Bolle*) consideration 4.7.12; HR 5 June 2009, *JOR* 2009/199 with annotation by Lieverse; *JA* 2009/117 (*Treek/Dexia Bank Nederland*) consideration 5.6.2.

[133] See Du Perron in his annotation under HR 11 July 2003, *NJ* 2005, 103 (*Kouwenberg/Rabobank*); WH van Boom, 'Bancaire zorgplicht en eigen verantwoordelijkheid van de belegger. Enige opmerkingen

In the share lease cases (see section II.B), the Hoge Raad held that the starting point is that paid interest, instalments and costs as well as the remaining debt are circumstances that can also be attributed to the claimant because the lease contract made sufficiently clear that the investment was made with borrowed money, that the contract included a loan and that interest had to be paid over this loan regardless of the value of the securities at the moment of selling them. In this respect it can be expected from the client that, before concluding the contract, he make a reasonable effort to understand the security lease contract.[134] Under these circumstances the court may reduce the amount of damages to be paid by the bank.

Subsequently, the court needs to assess whether equity justifies a higher percentage to be paid by the bank. In this assessment, errors made by the client because of rashness or lack of insight weigh in principle less heavily than errors on the side of the financial service provider when it breached its duty of care. If the financial position of the client was sufficient to pay interest and instalments, these heads of damage will in principle have to be borne by the client as this damage can be entirely contributed to the circumstance that the investment took place with borrowed money. If, however, the financial position of the client was such that he could not have reasonably continued meeting the obligations flowing from the contract, in principle part of the paid interest and instalments will be eligible for compensation. Part of the remaining debt will always partially have to remain for the account of the client.[135]

Generally speaking, a higher percentage of contributory negligence will be imputed on the claimant in case of an advisory relationship than in case of asset management. Some examples may illustrate this.

A bank advised a professional client to conclude an interest rate swap without advising him about the specific risk of high costs in case of premature termination of the contract. The Court considered this a breach of the bank's duty of care. However, it could have been expected from the client that he, before concluding the contract, made a reasonable effort to understand the interest rate swap and, if need be, ask questions. For this reason the damage was partially caused by circumstances that could be attributed to the client. The Court held that the bank had to compensate 60 per cent of the damage.[136]

Another example concerned a bank that had advised a client to take out a loan with a variable interest rate combined with an interest rate swap. The Court held that the bank's advice was flawed and that it had breached its duty. The client

naar aanleiding van HR 11 juli 2003, C01/257 (Erven Kouwenberg/Rabobank Schaijk-Reek)' (2003) *NTBR* 555–64, 562–64; FMA' t Hart, 'De maat van eigen schuld' (2005) *Ondernemingsrecht* 125–33, 128. Critical about such rule of thumb: SB van Baalen, 'Rien ne va plus. Over opties, zorg en aansprakelijkheid' (2004) *VrA* 46–79, 61–62.

134 HR 5 June 2009, ECLI:NL:HR:2009:BH2811 (*Levob/Bolle*), consideration 4.7.12.

135 HR 5 June 2009, ECLI:NL:HR:2009:BH2811 (*Levob/Bolle*), par. 4.7.13.

136 District Court Oost-Brabant 26 March 2014, ECLI:NL:RBOBR:2014:1415.

subsequently and undisputedly stated that if the bank would not have breached its duty, he would have taken out a loan with a fixed interest rate for a period of 10 years. The Court of Appeal held that the client should be brought into the situation in which he would have been had the breach not occurred. This means that a comparison had to be made between the costs of a loan with a fixed interest rate for 10 years and the arrangement as concluded in the contract. The Court did not accept contributory negligence of the client.[137]

In a case of breach of duty of care in advisory relationships, the Hoge Raad did not agree with applying the same apportioning of the damage between the client and the seller as in 'standard' share lease cases (see above). The Hoge Raad found that the client may assume that a professional adviser meets its duty of care, meaning that the client does not have to suspect and go into non-disclosed risks in the manner that is to be expected from someone who turns to a seller of share leases.[138]

On 2 September 2016, the Hoge Raad decided two cases in which share leases were sold to clients that were brought in by an intermediary. The seller of the share leases knew or ought to have known that the intermediary had advised these clients without having the required regulatory licence. Engagement with clients bought in by an unlicensed intermediary qualified as an infringement of regulatory law.[139] The Hoge Raad found that these circumstances give cause for a different apportioning of the damage between the client and the seller than in 'standard' share lease cases (see above), and that a secondary apportionment based on equity should in principle result in omitting any reduction of the amount of damages payable.[140]

ii. Duty to Mitigate Damages

Reported cases also address the duty to mitigate damages in the context of investment services after the damage has occurred. One case concerned asset management based on the risky *Premselaar*-method. In 1999 and 2000, the clients complained several times about disappointing investment results, which did not lead to termination of the asset management agreement because the asset manager convinced the clients that the results would improve. Based on correspondence between the clients and the asset manager, it should have been clear to the clients in February 2001 that the application of the *Premselaar*-method would not lead to

[137] Court of Appeal Den Bosch 15 April 2014, ECLI:NL:GHSHE:2014:1052, (*Westkant/ABN AMRO*).

[138] HR 6 September 2013, ECLI:NL:HR:2013:CA1725, NJ 2014/176 with annotation by Tjong Tjin Tai, consideration 3.4.2.

[139] More precisely of Art 41 of the Further Regulation on Supervision of the Securities Trade (now repealed).

[140] HR 2 September 2016 ECLI:NL:HR:2016:2012, consideration 5.7; HR 2 September 2016 ECLI:NL:HR:2016:2015, consideration 3.17.

the desired result, despite the asset manager's reassurances. They nevertheless consented to a continuation of the asset management agreement and even transferred additional funds to the asset manager. The Court held that the clients were fully responsible for the consequences; only damage suffered up to 31 January 2001 was recoverable.[141] Alternatively, one might reason that the causal chain between the tortious act or breach of contract by the asset manager and the damage suffered was broken from the moment that the clients were or should have been aware of the risks, with the effect that any loss suffered thereafter cannot be attributed to the manager.[142]

G. Limitation and Exclusion of Liability

i. Limitation and Exclusion of Liability contrary to Good Morals

A limitation or exclusion of liability for damage caused by the wilful default (*opzet*) or gross negligence (*grove schuld*) of the bank or its executives (*leidinggevenden*) is in principle contrary to public morals (*goede zeden*) in the sense of Article 3:40(1) DCC and thus null and void.[143] Hence, exemption clauses in, for example, asset management contracts do not exclude liability, at least to the extent that the damage is *directly* caused by the wilful default or gross negligence of the asset manager or its executives.

A limitation or exclusion of liability for damage caused by the wilful default or gross negligence of delegates (third parties, ie non-employees) is in principle permitted.[144] In line with this, the liability of the bank for damage caused by delegates is often limited to observing due diligence and care in selecting and monitoring delegates.[145] However, depending on the circumstances of the case, such clauses may be unreasonably onerous or contrary to reasonableness and fairness.

[141] KCD 17 June 2003, 03-98 (confirmed in KCHB 22 June 2004, No 70). Cf also District Court Zutphen 26 March 2003, *JOR* 2003/147; KCHB 18 November 2003, *JOR* 2004/16; KCD 9 February 2004, 04-19 (confirmed in KCHB 26 January 2005, No 100); District Court Leeuwarden 25 October 2006, *JOR* 2007/16 with annotation by Frielink under *JOR* 2007/19. See on the duty to mitigate damages in the case of liability for financial services: SE van Baalen, *Zorgplichten in de effectenhandel*, (Deventer: Kluwer, 2006) 419–25; see Van Luyn and Du Perron (n 106) 280–87. See on KCD and KCHB section X below.

[142] GCHB 1 July 2010, 2010-394, consideration 4.8.3 (concerning an advisory relationship). See on this case MBC Kloppenburg and EJ van Praag, 'Een vergissing van de bank in uw voordeel' (2011) *MvV* 93–99. From the fact that the client keeps his investment after the moment that he knew or should have known that it is too risky, it is sometimes inferred that the client would not have been opposed to the relevant investment if he would have been adequately informed about the risks from the very start, with the effect that there is no *condicio-sine-qua-non* connection between the breach of duty of care by the bank and the damage suffered by the client. See eg Court of Appeal Amsterdam 2 November 2010, *JOR* 2011/80 (concerning an advisory relationship). See also n 83. See on GCHB section X below.

[143] Busch (n 34) § 26.2. Cf HR 12 December 1997, *NJ* 1998, 208 (*Gemeente Stein/Driessen*).

[144] Busch (n 34) § 26.2.

[145] General Banking Conditions 1995, Art 3. Cf General Banking Conditions 2009 and 2017, Art 5(3).

Liability for damage caused by delegates that are group companies of the bank is often explicitly accepted in institutional asset management contracts on the same footing as liability for the bank's own acts.

Article 1:23 Wft explicitly provides that a juridical act is not invalid solely because it has been performed in violation of a rule laid down by or pursuant to the Wft (except where otherwise provided by the Wft). In view of this, it is submitted that clauses limiting or excluding the bank's liability for damage caused by a violation of such a rule cannot be void or voidable on the basis that they are contrary to mandatory law.[146] In theory, clauses excluding or limiting the bank's liability for damage caused by a violation of a rule laid down by or pursuant to the Wft can still be null and void on the basis that they are contrary to public morals (*goede zeden*) or public policy (*openbare orde*).[147] However, it seems highly unlikely that a court would render such a clause null and void, except of course to the extent that it concerns a violation by the bank or its executives caused by wilful conduct or gross negligence, or when, depending on the circumstances of the case, such clauses are considered to be unreasonably onerous or contrary to reasonableness and fairness.

ii. Unreasonably Onerous Limitation and Exclusion of Liability

To the extent that a clause limiting or excluding liability is included in standard terms, it may be unreasonably onerous and therefore voidable. Contract clauses qualify as standard terms to the extent that they are drafted to be included in a number of contracts.[148]

In institutional asset management, exclusion and limitation clauses are often heavily negotiated and tailored to the circumstances of a specific mandate. As a consequence, these clauses in institutional asset management contracts will not normally qualify as clauses included in standard terms. However, in consumer contracts limitation and exclusion clauses will by default qualify as such.

The general provision applicable to unreasonably onerous conditions is Article 6:233(a) DCC, which states that a stipulation in standard terms may be voidable if it is unreasonably onerous to the other party, taking into consideration the contract's nature and the further content, the manner in which the conditions have arisen, the parties' mutually apparent interest and the other circumstances of the case. Article 6:233(a) DCC protects only consumers and 'small-sized' businesses.[149]

It is questionable whether a bank may contractually limit or exclude the (special) duty of care. Given that exercising the care of a prudent service provider

[146] DCC, Art 3:40(2) and (3).

[147] Wft, Art 3:40(1).

[148] DCC, Art 6:231(a). DCC, Art 6:231(a) also stipulates that standard terms do not include clauses that constitute the essence of the mutual obligations. In the case of, eg, asset management, these obligations are the duty to manage the assets in a diligent and professional manner and the duty to pay the agreed fee.

[149] DCC, Art 6:235(1).

is a central duty of the bank, relying on a clause limiting its liability to wilful default and gross negligence is probably unreasonably onerous on the basis of Article 6:233(a) DCC and therefore voidable.

It follows from the Wft that banks that delegate activities to third parties must ensure that they comply with the MiFID implementation rules to which banks are subject with respect to the outsourced activities.[150] In other words, notwithstanding the outsourcing of activities, the bank remains responsible for compliance with the relevant MiFID implementation rules. In view of this, if the party to whom activities are outsourced (eg a more specialised asset manager) violates conduct-of-business rules pursuant to MiFID and thereby causes damage to the client, it is questionable whether the bank can successfully invoke a clause included in standard terms that limits its liability for third parties to observing due diligence and care in the selection (and monitoring) of such third parties. It is arguable that such a limitation clause is unreasonably onerous on the basis of Article 6:233(a) DCC and therefore voidable.

Inter alia in the cases described in the previous two paragraphs,[151] if the bank's client is a consumer, he/she can directly invoke Article 6:237(f) DCC, on the basis that stipulations freeing the user of the standard terms (the bank) or a third party (eg a delegate of the bank) in whole or in part from a legal obligation to repair damages, are presumed to be unreasonably onerous.[152] The bank may rebut this presumption. In one case, an asset manager limited its liability in the applicable standard terms to damage directly caused by wilful default or gross negligence. The Court ruled that the asset manager did not observe the care of a prudent asset manager and committed an imputable non-performance of its obligations under the asset management contract, inter alia because the asset manager omitted to draw up an adequate client profile. The Court also held that the clause limiting the asset manager's liability was included in standard terms and was unreasonably onerous on the basis of Article 6:237(f) DCC, which rendered the clause voidable.[153]

iii. Limitation and Exclusion of Liability contrary to Reasonableness and Fairness

Invoking an exemption clause may also be contrary to reasonableness and fairness. Whether this is so depends on the circumstances of the case. Relevant

[150] Wft, Arts 3:18(1), 3:22, and 4:16(1).

[151] Cf Van Baalen, *Zorgplichten in de effectenhandel* (n 141) 311–12.

[152] In the case described in the previous paragraph of the main text, the client who is a consumer may also invoke DCC, Art 6:237(b), stating that a clause that materially limits the scope of the obligations of the user of the standard terms (here: the bank) with respect to what the consumer could reasonably expect without such stipulation, taking into account the rules of law which pertain to the contract, is presumed to be unreasonably onerous. See Van Baalen (n 141) 311.

[153] District Court Amsterdam 24 January 2007, *JOR* 2007/94 with annotation by 't Hart (*Laan c.s./ Wijs & Van Oostveen*).

circumstances may include the gravity of the debtor's fault, the nature and the importance of the interests involved, the contract's nature and object, how the exemption clause was formed, the (dis)proportion between the exemption and the damage suffered, and the parties' degree of professionalisation and the relations between them.[154] However, when a bank or its executives have committed a wilful default or gross negligence, invoking an exemption clause will generally be contrary to reasonableness and fairness.[155]

In a case concerning asset management with a view to generating a pension, the Rotterdam District Court ruled that the asset manager did not observe the care of a prudent asset manager because the portfolio was invested disproportionately in shares. In view of the fact that observing the care of a prudent asset manager is such a central duty of the asset manager, reliance on a clause limiting its liability to gross negligence was held contrary to reasonableness and fairness.[156]

iv. Limitation and Exclusion of Liability and Contractual Interpretation

Unreasonable limitation and exclusion clauses can also be challenged through contractual interpretation of the relevant clause in the light of the contract's other provisions. Through reasonable interpretation of the contract, it may be concluded that the limitation or exclusion clause does not cover the imputable non-performance.[157] For example, Article 2(1) of the General Banking Conditions 2009 and 2017 provides that none of the provisions of the General Banking Conditions 2009 and 2017 or of any special conditions used by the bank may detract from the duty of care laid down in Article 2(1) of the General Banking Conditions 2009 and 2017. This can be read to mean that a bank may not, irrespective of any applicable limitation or exclusion clause, contractually deviate from the duty of care laid down in the General Banking Conditions.

Furthermore, if a limitation or exclusion clause is unclear it should be interpreted against the person invoking the clause (*contra proferentem*). Finally, the contractual clause that is breached may be a special clause that prevails in relation to the more general limitation or exclusion clause.[158]

[154] HR 19 May 1967, *NJ* 1967, 261 with annotation by Scholten (*Saladin/HBU*); HR 18 June 2004, *NJ* 2004, 585; Busch (n 34) § 26.4, 169.

[155] HR 12 December 1997, *NJ* 1998, 208. Busch (n 34) § 26.4; JH Duyvensz, 'Exoneratie en bewuste roekeloosheid' (2011) *WPNR* 225–31, 225–26.

[156] DCC, Art 6:2. See District Court Rotterdam, 18 July 2002, *JOR* 2002/167. Similarly KCD 23 July 2004, 04-112; KCD 26 June 2006, 06-120. See on the first 2 cases also Van Baalen (n 141) 398–99. See on KCD section X below.

[157] See Busch (n 34) § 26.5; Van Luyn and Du Perron (n 106) 288.

[158] See Busch (n 34) § 26.5; Van Luyn and Du Perron (n 106) 288.

VII. Relationship with Traditional Doctrines

A. General

In section III it was noted that a claim for a breach of duty of care may be based on contract, tort, or both. In general, the Hoge Raad has been hesitant to apply remedies that would lead to partial or total annulment of the contract, or that would render the contract partially unenforceable. Notably, the Hoge Raad has declined pleas that share leasing agreements are void or can be nullified on the basis of mistake (Article 6:228 DCC) or on the basis of an infringement of public law rules.

B. Reasonableness and Fairness

However, more recent case-law provides examples of the application of contractual remedies. For instance, the Hoge Raad upheld a Court of Appeal decision in which the termination of loans was deemed to be unacceptable according to standards of reasonableness and fairness (Article 6:248(2) DCC), rendering the penalties triggered by that termination unenforceable. In upholding the Court of Appeal's decision, the Hoge Raad pointed out that in determining whether the termination had been acceptable, the Court of Appeal was allowed to deem the duty of care mentioned in Article 2 of the General Banking Conditions relevant.[159]

The test of unacceptability as referred to in Article 6:248(2) DCC was also applied in a decision of the Amsterdam District Court. In this case the bank had provided a loan to a health care institution. The interest due consisted of a floating interest rate and a spread. Furthermore, the parties had entered into an interest rate swap agreement, swapping the floating interest due on the loan with a fixed interest rate. A year after these transactions, the bank raised the spread on the basis of a provision in the loan agreement. The Court found this unacceptable, holding that the bank had breached its duty of care by not warning the client of the fact that the swap did not cover the risk of the spread being raised, effectively raising the total interest due in spite of the swap.[160] The court's decision resulted in the unenforceability of the contractual terms rather than a damages award.

[159] HR 28 oktober 2014, *NJ* 2015/70 (*ING/De Keijzer c.s.*).
[160] District Court Amsterdam 4 November 2015, ECLI:NL:RBAMS:2015:7586.

C. Mistake and other Defects of Consent

The case-law also shows examples of attempts to avoid contracts with banks on the basis of mistake (*dwaling*).[161] In theory, avoidance of the contract is also possible on the basis of other defects of consent, ie threat (*bedreiging*), fraud (*bedrog*) or abuse of circumstances (*misbruik van omstandigheden*).[162] Avoidance of a contract (or of any other juridical act) has retroactive effect.[163] This means, that from the moment of avoidance onwards, the contract (or other juridical act) is deemed void *ab initio*. After avoidance, both the client and the bank have mutual claims to restore the position that existed prior to the conclusion of the contract (*restitutio in integrum*), based on undue payment.[164]

The provision of information plays an important role in actions brought by a client for mistake (*dwaling*). The Hoge Raad has held that a client must ensure that he does not conclude an agreement based on an incorrect understanding of its terms. This means that a client in principle has an obligation to investigate. This obligation entails, among other things, that he must review any documentation provided by the contracting party (such as the agreement itself and any brochures) and, if the documentation is unclear, ask questions to clarify the relevant points. On the other hand, the service provider has an obligation to provide appropriate information about the characteristics and risks of the relevant service or product. If the client does not meet his obligation to investigate and the service provider meets its obligation to provide sufficient information, the client has to bear the consequences of a mistake.[165]

It also follows from the Hoge Raad's case-law that a bank, although having provided sufficient information under the rules of mistake, may breach its special duty of care towards non-professional clients to warn them explicitly and unequivocally about financial risks.[166] This approach has been criticised in the legal literature.[167]

[161] DCC, Art 6:228.

[162] DCC, Art 3:44(2), (3), and (4), respectively.

[163] DCC, Art 3:53(1).

[164] DCC, Art 6:203. See Busch (n 34) § 27.1.

[165] HR 5 June 2009, *JA* 2009/116 (*Levob Bank/Bolle*) considerations 4.4.1–4.4.10; HR 5 June 2009, *JOR* 2009/199 with annotation by Lieverse; *JA* 2009/117 (*Treek/Dexia Bank Nederland*) considerations 4.4.1–4.4.6.

[166] HR 5 June 2009, *JA* 2009/116 (*Levob Bank/Bolle*) considerations 4.5.6–4.5.7; HR 5 June 2009, *JOR* 2009/199 with annotation by Lieverse; *JA* 2009/117 (*Treek/Dexia Bank Nederland*) considerations 4.10.1–4.10.4; HR 5 June 2009, *JOR* 2009/200; *JA* 2009/118 with annotation by Van Boom (*Stichting Gedupeerden Spaarconstructie/Aegon Bank*) considerations 4.6.4–4.6.13.

[167] See WL Valk, 'Dwaling, tekortkoming en effectenlease' (2009) *NTBR* 237; Lieverse in her annotation under *JOR* 2009/199; Van Boom in his annotation under *JA* 2009/116–18. For a more positive account, see AJP Schild, 'Mededelingsplichten komen van Venus, waarschuwingsplichten van Mars' (2009) *WPNR* 939–40.

Despite this Hoge Raad case-law, the Amsterdam Court of Appeal held in two cases that an interest rate swap was void on the basis of mistake.[168] The Court found that the bank had led the client, a real estate property trader, to believe that the interest rate swap would ensure that there would not be any floating interest rate costs due for the client's credit facility. However, the credit agreement contained a floating interest component that was not covered by the swap.

D. Violation of Regulatory Law

Pursuant to Article 1:23 Wft, a juridical act is not invalid solely because it has been performed in violation of a rule laid down by or pursuant to the Wft (except where otherwise provided by the Wft). Thus, a contract concluded by, for example an asset manager who lacks the licence required by regulatory law is not, for that sole reason, void or voidable. Of course, juridical acts can still be void or voidable if they are performed in violation of public morals (*goede zeden*) or public policy (*openbare orde*);[169] however, this seems highly unlikely in the context of an asset management contract.

VIII. Group Actions and Mass Claims

A. Group Actions

The Netherlands does not know class actions and public interest litigation as is known in common law jurisdictions. However, it is possible to file collective claims. Such collective actions are subject to three important limitations.[170]

First, a collective claim can only be filed by a foundation or an association that has full legal capacity and a clearly defined interest that it actually pursues. See Article 3:305a(1) Dutch Civil Code: 'A foundation or association with full legal capacity can institute an action intended to protect similar interests of other persons to the extent that its articles promote such interests'.[171]

[168] eg Court of Appeal Amsterdam 15 September 2015, *JOR* 2015/334 (*X./ING*); Court of Appeal Amsterdam 10 November 2015, *JOR* 2016/37 (*X./ABN AMRO*); Court of Appeal Amsterdam 11 October 2016, case number 200.153.823/01 (*X./ABN AMRO*).

[169] DCC, Art 3:40(1).

[170] See, inter alia, I Tzankova and H van Lith, 'Class Actions and Class Settlements Going Global: The Netherlands' in D Fairgrieve and E Lein (eds), *Extraterritoriality and Collective Redress* (Oxford: Oxford University Press, 2012) 67 et seq; M-J van der Heijden, 'Class Actions' (2010) 14 *Electronic Journal of Comparative Law* 3: www.ejcl.org/143/abs143-18.html; N Frenk, *Kollektieve akties in het privaatrecht* (PhD Utrecht) (Deventer: Kluwer, 1994).

[171] 'Een stichting of vereniging met volledige rechtsbevoegdheid kan een rechtsvordering instellen die strekt tot bescherming van gelijksoortige belangen van andere personen, voorzover zij deze belangen ingevolge haar statuten behartigt'.

Secondly, a collective action is only possible after prior consultation with the defendant. This follows from Article 3:305a(2) Civil Code:

> A legal person referred to in paragraph 1 shall have no *locus standi* if, in the given circumstances, it has not made a sufficient attempt to achieve the objective of the action through consultations with the defendant.[172]

Thirdly, a collective claim cannot serve to obtain damages:

> The right of action referred to in paragraph 1 may have as its object that an order against the defendant to publish or cause publication of the decision in a manner to be determined by the court and at the expense of the party or parties, as directed by the court. Its object may not be to seek monetary compensation.[173]

Abolishing the latter limitation is the subject of a Bill pending in the Dutch Parliament. If this Bill is adopted, collective redress may also include a claim for damages.[174]

The main aim of a collective claim is therefore to obtain a court order that the defendant committed a tort or breached a contractual duty. Such an order often serves as an important basis to reach an out-of-court settlement. The ban on seeking damages may be and is circumvented by combining the collective claim with individual claims by one or more (legal) persons. Such a combination of claims will be heard jointly by the court.

The fact that it is not possible to file a claim for damages means that questions of causation, damages and contributory negligence cannot be addressed. In the framework of the duty of care of the bank this has repercussions if clients have acted rashly or negligently when concluding a contract with respect to financial products. According to the Hoge Raad, the court has to decide the claim for a court order by not looking into specific circumstances on the side of the claimants. Those circumstances can only be relevant with respect to damage, causation and contributory negligence. Otherwise, the application of Article 3:305a Dutch Civil Code would be unduly limited.[175]

[172] 'Een rechtspersoon als bedoeld in lid 1 is niet ontvankelijk, indien hij in de gegeven omstandigheden onvoldoende heeft getracht het gevorderde door het voeren van overleg met de gedaagde te bereiken. Een termijn van twee weken na de ontvangst door de gedaagde van een verzoek tot overleg onder vermelding van het gevorderde, is daartoe in elk geval voldoende'.

[173] 'Een rechtsvordering als bedoeld in lid 1 kan strekken tot veroordeling van de gedaagde tot het openbaar maken of laten openbaar maken van de uitspraak, zulks op een door de rechter te bepalen wijze en op kosten van de door de rechter aan te geven partij of partijen. Zij kan niet strekken tot schadevergoeding te voldoen in geld'.

[174] IN Tzankova, 'Everything You Wanted to Know about Dutch Foundations but Never Dared to Ask: A Check List for Investors' (2015) 5 and 6 *Zeitschrift für Verbraucherrecht* also available at: http://papers.ssrn.com/sol3/papers.cfm?abstract_id=2730618. See *Dutch Parliamentary Papers II*, 2016/17, 34 608, no 2 (Draft Bill) and no 3 (Explanatory Memorandum).

[175] HR 23 December 2005, ECLI:NL:HR:2005:AU3713, NJ 2006/289 (*Safe Haven*); HR 27 November 2009, ECLI:NL:HR:2009:BH2162, *NJ* 2014/201 (*World Online*); HR 27 November 2015, ECLI:NL:HR:2015:3399, *RvdW* 2016/88 (*Ponzi scheme*).

B. Collective Settlement Mass Claims Act (WCAM)

A second important feature of Dutch law in this respect is the 'Collective Settlement Mass Claims Act (*Wet Collectieve Afwikkeling Massaschade* or WCAM), entering into force in 2005 and amended in 2013.[176] Whereas the collective action forms the basis for negotiations about an out-of-court settlement with respect to a mass claim for damages, the 'WCAM' enables a court to legally bind the entire group of claimants, represented by a foundation or an association to this out-of-court settlement. At the same time, this court order provides the claimants with the title to pursue payment for their claim by the responsible party or parties.

If the negotiations have led to an out-of-court settlement, the association or foundation with full legal capacity representing the claimants on one hand and the defendants on the other may submit a joint request to ask the court for an order to declare the agreement binding.

The binding character of the court order has been laid down in Article 7:907(1) DCC:

> An agreement concerning the payment of compensation for damage caused by an event or similar events concluded between a foundation or association with full legal competence and one or more other parties who have committed themselves by this agreement to pay compensation for this damage may, at the joint request of the parties that concluded the agreement, be declared binding by the court on persons to whom the damage was caused so long as the foundation or association represents the interests of these persons pursuant to its articles of association.

A court order to declare the agreement binding can only be justified if the interests of the victims are adequately safeguarded. Article 7:907(2) DCC lists the minimum provisions that must be included in the agreement,[177] whilst Article 7:907(3) DCC

[176] See W van Boom and T Arons, 'Beyond Tulips and Cheese: Exporting Mass Security Claim Settlements from The Netherlands (2010) 6 *European Business Law Review* 857–83; R Polak and R Hermans, 'International Class Actions Settlements in The Netherlands after Morrison and Ahold Decisions (2011) *International Comparative Legal Guides, Class & Group Actions* (www.iclg.co.uk); FB Falkena and MFJ Haak, 'De nieuwe wettelijke regeling afwikkeling massaschade' (2004) 37 *AV& S* 198–206; IN Tzankova, *Toegang tot het recht bij massaschade* (diss Tilburg) (Deventer: Kluwer 2007); CJM Klaassen, 'De rol van de (gewijzigde) WCAM bij de collectieve afwikkeling van massaschade "en nog wat van die dingen"' (2013) 9 *Ars Aequi* 627–39.

[177] '2. The agreement shall in any case include:

a. description of the group or groups of persons on whose behalf the agreement was concluded, according to the nature and the seriousness of their loss;
b. the most accurate possible indication of the number of persons belonging to the group or groups;
c. the compensation that will be awarded to these persons;
d. the conditions these persons must meet to qualify for the compensation;
e. the procedure by which the compensation will be established and can be obtained;
f. the name and place of residence of the person to whom the written notification referred to in Article 908 (2) and (3) can be sent.'

lists the circumstances under which the court will reject the request.[178] The Court of Appeal in Amsterdam has sole jurisdiction to deal with a request to declare an agreement binding.

Once the court has issued its order to make the agreement binding, a claimant cannot obtain compensation beyond the scope of the agreement. However, a claimant can 'opt out' of the agreement by notifying the representing foundation or association within a specified period of at least three months that he does not wish to be bound: see Article 7:908(2) DCC. They are then entitled to lodge their own claim and go to court if need be.

A relevant case under the WCAM for our purposes was the 'Dexia' share lease case (see section II.B). Dexia was held to have breached its duty of care by not sufficiently warning the consumers of the risks attached to these products. A number of collective actions were initiated and in 2004 a settlement was successfully concluded between Dexia on one hand and the Lease Loss Foundation, the Eegalease Foundation, the Dutch Consumers' Association and the Dutch Equity Holders' Association on the other hand. This arrangement implied that claimants would be paid out all or part of their residual claims at the end of the duration of the contract, a settlement that amounted to around one billion Euros. The foundations and associations and Dexia requested the Court of Appeal in Amsterdam to declare this agreement binding, which it did in January 2007.[179]

Another important case under the WCAM was the 'DSB' case. DSB Bank was declared bankrupt on 19 October 2009. Many consumers and several collective claim entities took the position that DSB Bank was liable for a breach of its duty of care on a number of grounds. In 2013, agreement was reached between DSB Bank and several of its subsidiaries on the one hand and three collective claim entities on a collective settlement, providing compensation for the alleged breaches of the duty of care. The parties requested the Court of Appeal in Amsterdam to declare

[178] '3. The court shall reject the request if:

a. the agreement does not comply with the provisions of paragraph 2;
b. the amount of the compensation awarded is not reasonable having regard, inter alia, to the extent of the damage, the ease and speed with which the compensation can be obtained and the possible causes of the damage;
c. insufficient security is provided for the payment of the claims of persons on whose behalf the agreement was concluded;
d. the agreement does not provide for the independent determination of the compensation to be paid pursuant to the agreement;
e. the interests of the persons on whose behalf the agreement was concluded are otherwise not adequately safeguarded;
f. foundation or association referred to in paragraph 1 is not sufficiently representative of the interests of persons on whose behalf the agreement was concluded;
g. the group of persons on whose behalf the agreement was concluded is not large enough to justify a declaration that the agreement is binding;
h. there is a legal entity which will provide the compensation pursuant to the agreement and it is not a party to the agreement'.

[179] Court of Appeal Amsterdam 25 January 2007, ECLI:NL:GHAMS:2007:AZ7033, NJ 2007/427 (Duisenberg-settlement).

this agreement binding. In an interim decision the Court questioned the reasonableness of several aspects of the compensation awarded, finding that its objections stood in the way of declaring the agreement binding.[180] After the parties had adjusted the agreement in light of the objections of the Court, the Court declared the agreement binding.[181]

IX. Concentration of Dispute Settlement in Amsterdam?

It is notable that the Dutch Ministry of Finance recently solicited stakeholder views on a new Article 1:23a Wft, stipulating that civil litigation on the provision of investment services, investment activities and prospectus liability should be concentrated at the Amsterdam District Court. The Ministry of Finance expressed the view that it expected that concentration of these cases would contribute to the quality and efficiency of justice, as well as to the establishment and preservation of knowledge and expertise at the Amsterdam District Court.[182] The Ministry of Finance envisages the entry into force of Article 1:23a Wft on 1 July 2018. However, at the time of completion of this chapter it is still undecided whether or not this provision will become law. In any event, the judiciary is severely split on the usefulness of Article 1:23a Wft.

X. Complaint Institute Financial Services

Financial services providers, including providers of investment services holding a Dutch investment firm or banking licence, must be affiliated with a dispute settlement authority that has been recognised by the Dutch Minister of Finance.[183] Currently, only the Complaint Institute Financial Services (*Klachteninstituut*

[180] Court of Appeal Amsterdam 13 May 2014, ECLI:NL:GHAMS:2014:1690, JOR 2015/9 with annotation IN Tzankova (DSB).

[181] Court of Appeal Amsterdam 4 November 2014, ECLI:NL:GHAMS:2014:4560, JOR 2015/10 with annotation IN Tzankova (DSB).

[182] See www.internetconsultatie.nl/wijzigingswetfm2018. See on this provision: D Busch and A Lenaerts, 'Naar een gespecialiseerde overheidsrechter voor civiele beleggingsgeschillen. Een kritische bespreking van art. 1:23a Wft mede in het licht van de gespecialiseerde geschilbeslechting door de OK, het Kifid, de Financial List en de Netherlands Commercial Court' in AM van Amsterdam, M Jurgens, GC Makkink and JWM Tromp (eds), *Fraude—Financieel recht—Ondernemingskamer* (Deventer: Kluwer 2016) 151–89; D Busch and A Lenaerts, 'Naar een gespecialiseerde overheidsrechter voor civiele beleggingsgeschillen—Het conceptvoorstel van art. 1:23a Wijzigingswet financiële markten kritisch belicht' (2016) *TREMA* 284–93.

[183] Wft, Art. 4:17(1)(b).

Financiële Dienstverlening, KiFID) has been recognised as such an authority.[184] Consequently, all financial services providers must become members of KiFID. KiFID is a self-regulatory organisation that provides consumers with mediation services and other facilities for the extrajudicial settlement of complaints and disputes. Since 26 January 2015 it has also provided extrajudicial settlement services to SMEs who entered into interest rate swap agreements with banks (albeit for the time being on a temporary basis only).[185] KiFID has no powers of regulation, except that its proceedings are governed by KiFID's own (procedural) rules. KiFID began its activities on 1 April 2007. From that date, KiFID's Complaints Board (*Geschillencommissie*, GC) and Appeal Committee (Commissie van Beroep, GCHB) took over the dispute settlement tasks of inter alia the Dutch Securities Institute Complaints Board (*Klachtencommissie* DSI, KCD) and the Appeal Committee of the Dutch Securities Institute (*Commissie van Beroep*, KCHB), which previously provided consumers with facilities for the extrajudicial settlement of complaints against inter alia asset managers. The decisions of the GC and the GCHB (and previously of the KCD and the KCHB) are binding on both parties on the basis of binding advice (*bindend advies*).[186]

The decisions of the GC and GCHB are binding on both parties on the basis of binding advice (*bindend advies*). Binding advice is a *species* of a contract of settlement (*vaststellingsovereenkomst*). Thus, the content of a binding advice is binding on the parties on the basis of contract. Binding advice resembles arbitration, but is more informal (statutory procedural rules are lacking). A binding advice clause in standard terms in a consumer contract is considered unreasonably onerous if the consumer is not offered the possibility of settling a dispute in a state court.[187]

XI. The Role of the Regulator in Settling Disputes

Finally, in the Netherlands, neither the conduct-of-business regulator AFM, nor prudential regulator DNB, have formal powers to settle disputes between banks and their clients. The same is true for the Dutch Ministry of Finance. Nevertheless, both the AFM and the Ministry of Finance have played an active role in settling the massive mis-selling of interest rate swaps to SMEs. In a first stage, the AFM investigated interest rate swap contracts with SMEs and concluded that in many cases the MiFID rules pertaining to interest rate swaps had not been complied with. In many cases the client had been insufficiently informed about the mechanics of interest rate swaps in general, and the benefits and risks of any such product for their individual situation. The AFM requested the banks concerned to re-evaluate

184 Since 1 January 2007, see *Stcrt* 2007, 5, 22.
185 See www.kifid.nl/rentederivaten.
186 See Busch (n 34) § 12.9.
187 See DCC Art. 6:236, opening words, and sub (n); Busch (n 34) § 29.3.

individual interest rate swap contracts and to the extent necessary compensate their clients. However, the process was badly managed by the AFM and the banks did not fully cooperate. In an unprecedented attempt to reach a solution, and in line with the advice of the AFM, the Minister of Finance appointed a Derivatives Committee (Derivatencommissie), consisting of three independent experts to (1) draw up a uniform settlement framework for derivatives with SMEs (*Uniform Herstelkader Rentederivaten MKB*); and if possible (2) reach agreement on implementation of the framework with the banks involved. On 5 July 2016, the committee published the framework, which has been accepted by the relevant banks.[188] In the view of many commentators, the whole process was far too lengthy and the role of the Minister of Finance—believed to have exerted intense pressure on the banks involved—crucial to the outcome. In view of this, some commentators propose a law reform to the effect that the AFM obtains true powers to settle disputes between banks and clients, very much like the UK Financial Conduct Authority (FCA).[189] The Dutch Ministry of Finance recently solicited stakeholder views on whether the AFM should have formal powers to settle disputes between banks and their clients.[190]

XII. Conclusion

In the Netherlands, the contours of a bank's duty of care are relatively clear. The Hoge Raad has developed a coherent and very consumer-friendly body of case-law with respect to the existence and scope of a bank's 'special' duty of care (*bijzondere zorgplicht*) towards consumers. The essential duties which typically flow from a bank's duty of care are duties to investigate, duties to disclose or warn, and—in exceptional cases—outright duties to refuse to render financial services or products.

In the Netherlands, the question whether banks also owe a special duty of care to SMEs and other commercial clients is hotly debated, largely triggered by the massive mis-selling of interest rate swaps to SMEs. There is some lower court case-law on interest rate swaps which accepts that banks are also subject to a special duty of care towards SMEs, resulting in the usual duties to investigate and warn. However, the Hoge Raad has not yet had the chance to confirm or reject this view.

[188] See for further information: www.derivatencommissie.nl/.

[189] See *Financieele Dagblad*, 'Juridisch gat bij swaps moet dicht' (6 July 2016) 2.

[190] See p 12 of the consultation document mentioned in § II.E, last para: Ministerie van Financiën, *Consultatiedocument—Effectiviteit en gewenste mate van bescherming voor zzp-ers en mkb-ers bij financiële diensten en producten* (1 September 2016) (available at: www.internetconsultatie.nl/consultatiebeschermingkleinzakelijk).

Duties to warn are a prominent feature of the bank's duty of care in the Netherlands. But recently the Amsterdam Court of Appeal revived the doctrine of mistake in connection with interest rate swaps. At the time of writing it is not clear whether the Dutch Supreme Court agrees with this approach. In another prominent case regarding the bank's duty of care, the argument of mistake was rejected and the Dutch Supreme Court took recourse to a breach of duty of care for not warning the client explicitly enough of the special risks involved.

It transpires from the case-law of the Hoge Raad that the public law duties set out in the Wft and in the subordinate legislation pursuant thereto—including the Dutch implementation of MiFID—influence both the pre-contractual and contractual duty of care to which banks (and other financial institutions) are subject.

The legislator intervened and eliminated uncertainty as to whether juridical acts performed in violation of the Wft can be void or voidable. Article 1:23 Wft makes it clear that a juridical act is not invalid solely because it has been performed in violation of a rule laid down by or pursuant to the Wft (except where otherwise provided by the Wft). Thus, a contract concluded by for example an asset manager who lacks the licence required by regulatory law is not void or voidable.

This does not mean, however, that no questions are left. First and foremost, it is an open question, contested in legal literature, whether the civil courts may, on the basis of private law, subject banks to duties that are stricter or more demanding than the regulatory duties implementing the current MiFID regime, particularly the conduct-of-business rules, in the absence of an express contractual provision imposing stricter duties. Also, the massive mis-selling of interest rate swaps to SMEs sparked a debate on whether the Dutch conduct-of-business regulator AFM should obtain powers to settle disputes between banks and clients, very much like the UK FCA.

Part IV

Common Law Legal Systems

9

England and Wales

KERN ALEXANDER*

I. Bank Civil Liability for Mis-selling and Advice

A. Introduction

The financial crisis of 2007–08 and ensuing economic slowdown have resulted in many legal and regulatory claims against UK banking institutions by their customers and third parties for mis-selling financial products and rendering inadequate advice and disclosure regarding their risks. Generally, English law liability rules tend to favour banks and impose a heavy burden on investors and customers to prove breach of any statutory, common law or fiduciary duties. A major hurdle for a claimant bank customer to overcome is to show that the bank owed it a duty of care in the sale of a product or the rendering of advice regarding the risks associated with the bank's products and investments. English common law generally allows a bank and its customer to contract out of the duty of care, resulting in an arm's length relationship between the bank and the customer in which the bank has no obligation to inform or advise its client, nor to reveal any of the risks associated with its product or to assess the suitability of its customer for the products it sells. Without a duty of care, the bank merely has an obligation not to make explicit material misrepresentations to its customers regarding its products.

As a result, claims against banks for breach of a duty of care or fiduciary duties under English law have rarely succeeded. Nevertheless, the impact of the financial crisis resulted in unexpected and crippling losses for millions of individuals and small businesses in addition to substantial losses for professional investors, all of which have resulted in an unprecedented number of civil lawsuits against banks for breach of the duty of care, in particular claims for misrepresentation, negligent advice, failure of the duty to warn and investigate. Moreover, several million complaints have been filed with the UK financial regulator—the Financial Conduct

* I would like to thank Dr Francesco De Pascalis and Dr Alexandra Balmer for comments on the chapter, and Katrine Narkiewicz for research assistance. All errors are solely the author's responsibility. I would also like to thank the editors Professors Busch and Van Dam for their comments and support.

Authority and its predecessor the Financial Services Authority—against banks for failing to treat their customers fairly and for breach of other regulatory principles in the sale of financial products.

In addition, the harshness for bank customers of the common law's *caveat emptor* approach to bank sales has been limited to some extent by the English courts in several recent rulings following the financial crisis.[1] Moreover, European Union law has sought to make it more difficult for banks to dispense with the duty of care obligation by contracting and to guarantee certain minimum rights for bank customers—especially small business customers—to recover compensation from banks who have mis-sold financial products. This chapter attempts to understand the nature and scope of a bank's duty of care under English common law and UK statutory and regulatory law. In doing so, it reviews the basic principles of English contract law and related areas of tort and fiduciary duties law. UK regulatory law will be discussed to show how it attempts to reverse the erosion of the duty of care under the common law by requiring banks to treat all of their customers fairly and to adopt governance and organisational structures so that the development of financial products takes due account of the interests of bank customers. Finally, European Union law in the form of the Market in Financial Instruments Directive II will be discussed to show how banks will be required to undertake further reforms in governance and trading practices so that banks will have an obligation to recognise a duty of care for their customers in a far greater number of transactions.

B. The Duty of Care and Freedom of Contract

A fundamental principle of English law, which militates against successful claims against banks, is freedom of contract, whereby parties negotiate their own terms which are generally upheld by the courts pursuant to the doctrine of contractual estoppel to ensure commercial certainty and that a bank does not generally owe a duty of care to its customers to advise on the merits of transactions unless the bank has expressly undertaken to do so in which case the bank would be required to advise with reasonable care and skill.[2] Despite the growth of statutory and regulatory obligations for banks, 'party autonomy is at the heart of English commercial law'.[3] In the absence of statutory or regulatory intervention, the courts give effect

[1] See *Rubenstein v HSBC* [2011] EWHC 2304 (QB) at [83] (discussed below). See also *Crestsign v The Royal Bank of Scotland* [2014] EWHC 3043 (Ch) at [88]–[89], [108].

[2] *Thornbridge Limited v Barclays Bank Plc* [2015] EWHC 3430 (QB) at [6], per Moulder J, upholding that a bank does not have a duty of care to advise a customer on the merits of a transaction unless the bank has undertaken to do so. *Thornbridge* also reaffirms a strict application of the doctrine of contractual estoppel that a bank customer that has signed an undertaking that it has not received advice from a bank on a particular transaction cannot later sue the bank for negligent advice even if the bank in fact had rendered erroneous advice or information about the transaction.

[3] See *Belmont Park Investments Pty Ltd v BNY Corporate Trustee Service Ltd (Revenue and Customs Commissioners intervening)* [2011] UKSC 38; [2012] 1 AC 383, per Lord Collins at [103].

to the contractual terms which the parties have freely agreed in writing and are reluctant to imply terms into a contract.[4] The courts respect the freedom of the parties to agree terms of their own choosing as expressed by the 'plain words' of the contract, and they are reluctant to interpret the words by using assumptions as to what they were purportedly intended to achieve without clear support from the natural and ordinary meaning of the words themselves.[5] This is particularly so for banks involved in the sale of complex financial instruments.[6] Moreover, the absence of any principle of good faith or unconscionability in English law further protects banks from a high volume of claims.[7]

A crucial case in recent years that reaffirms the principle of freedom of contract in litigation involving banks was *Bankers Trust International plc v PT Dharmala Sakti Sejahtera*,[8] involving the sale of interest rate swaps to an Indonesian company, which suffered a loss of US $45 million after the US Federal Reserve raised interest rates. The bank sued the Indonesian company for US $65 million in English court. The defendant company argued that the bank was guilty of misrepresentation, breach of contract and breach of duty of care. The Court rejected these claims on the grounds that commercial parties engaged in business are presumed to understand or seek advice about their area of operation and documentation. Moreover, the Court accepted that the bank staff believed the company's personnel had a sophisticated understanding of the nature and risks of the interest rate swaps sold. The Court was not satisfied that the plaintiff bank had made any representations as to profitability, suitability and safety of the financial products or that a full and fair presentation as to the products would have resulted in a different outcome for the defendant company. Nevertheless, the Court affirmed the bank's duty not

[4] The court's primary emphasis on giving effect to what the parties have freely agreed in writing without reference to the principles of good faith and unconscionability, has been attributed to the fundamental change in English contract law doctrine in the 19th century in which a communitarian and paternalistic approach to interpreting contracts was replaced by a market-oriented ideology that emphasised party autonomy and freedom of contract. See M Lobban, 'Contractual Fraud in Law and Equity' (1997) 17(3) *Oxford Journal of Legal Studies* 441–76, citing PS Atiyah, *The Rise and Fall of Freedom of Contract* (Oxford: Oxford University Press, 1979) discussing the orthodox view of the transformation of English contract law, while citing other commentators (eg AWB Simpson, 'The Horwitz Thesis and the History of Contracts' (1979) *University of Chicago Law Review* 533) who argued that contract law in the 18th century was not so paternalistic as merchants and traders were allowed to set their own terms by, inter alia, evading the law of usury for certain transactions. Lobban, however, provides a more nuanced view of this transition from a communitarian to party autonomy approach for interpreting contractual terms in the case of fraud.

[5] See *Anthracite Rtade Investments (Jersey) Ltd v Lehman Brothers Finance SA (In Liquidation)* [2011] EWHC 1822 (Ch); [2011] 2 Lloyd's Rep 538 (the Court determined the meaning and effect of early close-out provisions in 2 cash settled put options incorporating the 1992 ISDA Master Agreement, which were part of larger investment structures devised and marketed by Lehman Brothers).

[6] See *Belmont Park Investments Pty Ltd* (n 3) per Lord Collins at [104].

[7] Sir Ross Cranston QC, 'The (non)-liability of Banks under English Law' (International legal symposium in honour of the 50th anniversary of the Marianne and Marcus Wallenberg Foundation, 'Functional or Dysfunctional—the Law as a Cure? Risks and Liability in the Financial Markets' (Stockholm Centre for Commercial Law, 29 and 30 August 2013) 1 (on file with author).

[8] [1996] CLC 518.

to carelessly misstate facts but to state them fairly and accurately, and that there was a duty to present the financial implications of the products by a comprehensive graph and letter with disclosure about the downside and upside risks of the investment. Despite the court's recognition of the bank's duty not to act carelessly and to present the financial risks of investment products in a transparent manner, the defendant did not prevail on the merits of the bank's claim for enforcement of the contract.

i. Doctrine of Contractual Estoppel

British banks rely on the principle of freedom of contract to prevent their customers from relying on facts and occurrences that are extrinsic to the written terms of the contract. English common law permits this through the doctrine of contractual estoppel whereby parties are estopped from denying contractual terms expressed in writing, even if these are contrary to the real facts or give rise to unjust results.[9] For example, the courts have upheld an entire agreement clause where the parties acknowledge they have not been induced to enter the contract by representations other than in the contract such that a party cannot subsequently assert a misrepresentation that occurred outside the written contract.[10] As discussed above, the courts interpret contracts according to their natural and ordinary meaning[11] to achieve commercial common sense. The courts therefore can exclude any reference to facts—despite their truthfulness—that contradict the terms and undertakings entered into by parties to the contract. The courts however will set aside the doctrine if its strict application would be unreasonable under the circumstances where, for instance, there was unequal bargaining power and understanding of the nature of the risks between the parties, or that the bank had sold a complex product that it knew or should have known was unsuitable to a retail or unsophisticated commercial customer. Banks are permitted however to require retail customers who in fact suffer from unequal bargaining power to agree to undertakings in the written contract that they understand the nature of the risks in the financial product and that they are suitable customers to purchase the product, even though the bank may suspect that they are not suitable. The courts presume that such customers and larger commercial parties and professional investors do not suffer unequal bargaining power in commercial transactions and therefore do not warrant special protection.[12] In considering whether there is unequal bargaining power between the parties, the courts look to the disclosures of the parties

[9] See *Barclays Bank Plc v Svizera Holdings BV* [2014] EWHC 1020 (Comm), per Flaux J at [58]. See also *Springwell Navigation Corporation v JP Morgan Chase Bank & Ors* [2010] EWCA Civ 1221 and *Cassa Di Risparmio Della Repubblica Di San Marino Spa v Barclays Bank Ltd* [2011] EWHC 484 (Comm) at 505, per Hamblen J.

[10] *Cassa di Risparmio della Repubblica di San Marino v Barclays Bank Ltd* (n 9) at 525, per Hamblen J.

[11] *Re Lehman Brothers International (Europe) (In Administration)* [2013] EWCA Civ 188.

[12] See *Thornbridge Limited v Barclays Bank Plc* (n 2) per Moulder J at [79]–[83].

at the time the contract is entered into or at the relevant times as set forth in the contract.[13]

The doctrine of contractual estoppel was first developed in the case of *Peekay Intermark Ltd v Australia and New Zealand Banking Group Ltd*[14] which involved an investment product being sold by the bank to an Isle of Man company (an investment vehicle for United Arab Emirate investors) with repayment linked to the performance of Russian government bonds. A bank employee had mis-described the product as yielding an interest in those bonds. The investor signed the documentation which contained risk warnings and terms that the customer understood the true nature of the contract and determined its suitability, had taken independent advice and was not relying on the bank. The Court ruled that the contract gave rise to an estoppel.

The doctrine was later confirmed in *Springwell Navigation Corp v JP Morgan Chase Bank and others*,[15] which involved the bank selling US $87 million of notes linked to Russian bonds to Springwell, the investment vehicle of the Polemis shipping group. Springwell claimed the bank was in breach of contractual, tortious and fiduciary duties for misrepresentation when it advised that the products were conservative, liquid and without currency risk. The Court of Appeal rejected this claim on the basis that these were mere statements of opinion, not even implied representations, and that the bank had objective and reasonable grounds for its views. The notes also contained terms and conditions which provided that the bank had not made any representations or warranties claimed by Springwell and various terms stating that the claimant had the knowledge and experience to assess suitability of the investment, to understand the risks, had obtained independent advice and been provided with all the information it requested.[16] The Court held that Springwell was contractually estopped from claiming misrepresentation.

Contractual estoppel, particularly in commercial transactions where it has the purpose of promoting certainty, has also been confirmed in various first instance decisions. In *Titan Steel Wheels Ltd v Royal Bank of Scotland plc*,[17] the Court upheld the validity of the mandate issued by the investor claimant to the bank for execution of transactions involving foreign exchange and currency options, which

[13] See *Grupo Hotelero Urvasco SA v Carey Value Added SL* [2013] EWHC 1039 (Comm), per Blair J, a case involving an investment firm that had agreed to loan funds to a developer. Blair J interpreted a material adverse change clause in terms of the financial information of the borrower at the relevant times as set forth in the contract and whether any change in financial information provided by the borrower at a time not specified by the contract could be considered as material so as to affect significantly their ability to repay the loan and disadvantage the lender and awarded the borrower the benefit of the doubt regarding their access to and action upon financial information at the time of entering into the contract with the lender.

[14] [2006] EWCA Civ 386; see also Cranston, 'The (non)-liability of Banks under English Law' (n 7) 5.

[15] [2010] EWCA Civ 1221.

[16] ibid, [45], [49], [52], [141], [170]–[172], [182], available at: www.bailii.org/ew/cases/EWCA/Civ/2010/1221.html#back230.

[17] [2010] EWHC 211 (Comm).

stated the investor would not rely on the skill or expertise of the bank when entering any transactions and the bank's terms of business expressly excluded advisory services and provided for execution-only services. The Court disagreed with the claimant's assertion that the resources available to the bank to assess the suitability of the products were greater than those of the investor and found that there was no inequality of bargaining power.

Further, in *Raiffeisen Zentralbank Österreich AG v Royal Bank of Scotland Plc*,[18] the claimant bank sought to recover part of a syndicated loan it had lost owing to the collapse of Enron and alleged misrepresentation against the defendant bank, which arranged and syndicated the loan.[19] The Court held that the representations were not misleading or fraudulent and observed that the claimant bank was experienced in the syndicated loan market, had previously participated in syndications with Enron and that it was an arm's length transaction entered after mature deliberations and the contractual provisions were in a form habitually used in the market. Further, the information memorandum and confidentiality agreement were disclosed and signed by the claimant.

In addition, the courts have recognised statutory exceptions to the doctrine of contractual estoppel in the form of the Misrepresentation Act 1967,[20] which aims to prevent exemptions from liability for misrepresentations (test of reasonableness, which includes inequality of bargaining power) and the Unfair Contract Terms Act 1977, which aims to prevent standard form contracts rendering a contractual performance substantially different from what was reasonably expected.[21]

ii. Good Faith and Fiduciary Duties

There is no general duty of good faith in English contract law.[22] Lord Ackner in *Walford v Miles*[23] observed that a duty of good faith is 'inherently repugnant' in commercial negotiations. However, in some circumstances, it may be possible to imply a duty on the parties not to act in a manner that is commercially unacceptable to reasonable and honest people.[24] Even where a contract contains an express clause of good faith it will be interpreted to focus specifically on the purposes stated and that the parties will work together honestly to achieve those purposes.[25]

Fiduciary duties involve the fiduciary subordinating its own interests to those of its principal. Examples of recognised fiduciary relationships include: trustee-beneficiary, agent-principal and director-company. English courts are reluctant

[18] [2010] EWHC 1392 (Comm).
[19] ibid.
[20] *IFE Fund SA v Goldman Sachs International* [2007] All ER (D) 476.
[21] Unfair Contract Terms Act 1977, s 17(1)(a).
[22] See discussion in Cranston (n 7) 15.
[23] [1992] 2 AC 128.
[24] *Yam Seng Pte Ltd v International Trade Corporation Ltd* [2013] EWHC 111 (QB).
[25] *Compass Group UK and Ireland Ltd (t/a Medirest) v Mid Essex Hospital Services NHS Trust* [2013] EWCA Civ 200.

to recognise fiduciary relationships in commercial contexts, unless analogies are drawn with existing categories.[26]

An unsuccessful claim for breach of fiduciary duties was raised in *Saltri III Ltd v MD Mezzanine SA SICAR (t/a Mezzanine Facility Agent)*.[27] The case involved an acquisition of the Stabilus group by a private equity fund and involved an intercreditor agreement that subordinated mezzanine lenders to senior lenders. The business experienced severe financial problems and was transferred to an investment fund, subject to liabilities to the senior lenders; however, the mezzanine lenders received losses on principal ('haircuts') and received nothing in the restructuring. The mezzanine lenders accused the security trustee who accepted the transfer of breach of trust and fiduciary duty. The Court held that a person can act as a fiduciary in regards to some but not all of their activities. The duty alleged to be breached was in relation to enforcement, which was set out in the intercreditor agreement and superseded any fiduciary duties. The Court cited with approval the principle that the duties of parties governed by arm's length commercial contracts will be determined by the terms of the contract.[28] The Court held that the duties of the security trustee were not those of a fiduciary but of a mortgagee who is entitled to act in its own interests even if this is detrimental to the interests of the mortgagor as to the timing and manner of enforcement. Therefore the Court found that the bank was not in breach of its duty.[29]

More recently, in October 2016, the High Court ruled that the investment bank Goldman Sachs had not exercised undue influence on the Libyan Investment Authority (LIA) when encouraging it to undertake risky derivatives trades.[30] The judge also refused to set aside trades that the Libyan wealth fund wanted declared as unconscionable. The ruling does not mention the duty of care per se, but constitutes an illustration of the *caveat emptor*/buyer beware principle in English law, as even despite lavish gifts from the bank to the LIA, 'their relationship did not go beyond the normal cordial and mutually beneficial relationship that grows up between a bank and a client'.[31]

C. Statutory and Regulatory Claims

Customer complaints against UK banks and financial services firms have received much attention in recent years, especially following the British banking crisis of 2007–08. The UK statutory and financial regulatory regimes have created new

[26] *Ross River Ltd v Waveley Commercial Ltd* [2013] EWCA Civ 910.
[27] [2012] EWHC 3025.
[28] *Hospital Products Ltd v United States Surgical Corporation* (1984) 156 CLR 41; *Halton v Guernroy* [2005] EWHC 1968; *Kelly v Cooper* [1993] AC 205; *Henderson v Merrett Syndicates Ltd* [1995] 2 AC 145; *Belmont Park Investments Pty Ltd v BNY Corporate Trustee Services Ltd* [2012] 1 AC 383.
[29] ibid.
[30] *The Libyan Investment Authority v Goldman Sachs International* [2016] EWHC 2530 (Ch).
[31] ibid, [427 b].

avenues of redress in cases involving vulnerable retail customers—including individuals and small businesses—who are bank customers. The Financial Conduct Authority and the former Financial Services Authority have both played an active role in utilising the Financial Ombudsman Service to settle disputes between banks and retail clients and small business customers.[32] The Financial Services Markets Act 2000 established the Financial Ombudsman Service (FOS) that provides a scheme to allow customer complaints to be adjudicated against financial services firms in cases involving general insurance, banking and credit, and investment.[33] Consumer credit later came under its remit on 6 April 2007 based on the Consumer Credit Act 2006.[34]

The Ombudsman regime has been extensively utilised to file millions of claims against banks for mis-selling financial products, including payment protection insurance (PPI) and derivative products such as interest rate swaps. Since the early 2000s, borrowers who purchased PPI to insure against the risk that they may be unable to maintain loan repayments have sought redress for mis-selling through the FOS and the courts. The courts have clarified the law on PPI mis-selling in several decisions assessing the lawfulness of PPI mis-selling regulations[35] and on the unfair relationship between a lender and borrower.

The case of *Harrison & Harrison v Black Horse Limited*[36] involved the legal question of whether a lender's failure to disclose the existence or amount of commission from an insurer on their sale of PPI to a customer amounts to unfairness in the relationship between the parties pursuant to section 140A of the Consumer Credit Act 1974 (CCA). Both the High Court[37] and Court of Appeal decided the claim against the borrower claimants and their appeal to the Supreme Court was subsequently withdrawn by consent.

The borrowers had also claimed that an unfair relationship was created by the lender's[38] breach of the regulator's intermediary conduct of business rules (ICOB rules) and the PPI policy was unsuitable owing to the length of the cover and its cost.[39] The facts of the case involved two loans obtained by the borrower from the lender, both taken out with PPI. The second loan was then discharged by refinance

[32] The Financial Services Act 2012 abolished the Financial Services Authority and replaced it with a newly established Financial Conduct Authority. The FSA's prudential oversight function for banks, insurance firms and large investment banks was assumed by a newly created Prudential Regulation Authority. See Joint Committee on the draft Financial Services Bill, *Draft Financial Services Bill* (2010–12, HL 236, HC 1447).

[33] See Financial Services and Markets Act 2000, types of complaints: www.financial-ombudsman.org.uk/publications/technical.htm).

[34] See Consumer Credit Act 2006, s 59, www.legislation.gov.uk/ukpga/2006/14/section/59.

[35] See *R (on application of the British Bankers Association) v Financial Services Authority and Financial Ombudsman Service* [2011] EWHC 999.

[36] [2011] EWCA Civ 1128.

[37] Per Waksman J.

[38] The lender was part of the Lloyds TSB Group.

[39] The applicability of the ICOB rules to the bank's duty of care in the sale of PPI and other regulated financial products to commercial and individual customers has been reaffirmed in *Saville v Central Capital Ltd* [2014] EWCA Civ 337.

in 2009 and the PPI was cancelled. The PPI was sold by the lender to the borrower as agent for the actual insurer, Lloyds TSB General Insurance Limited; therefore, it was an insurance intermediary acting on an advised basis in relation to the specific PPI offered. The lender earned 87 per cent of the premium in commission from the insurer on the sale of the PPI, which was not at all disclosed to the borrowers.

In the County Court, the claim was dismissed on the grounds that the borrowers were not advised that PPI was compulsory, they had taken PPI before and understood what they were buying and had had the opportunity to understand the terms and freely accept them. In the High Court, Waksman J dismissed the appeal and held there was no breach in relation to cost and policy length and that there was no proof of unfair relationship.

On further appeal, Tomlinson LJ gave the judgment in the Court of Appeal and made the following rulings:

1. There was no breach of ICOB (Insurance: Conduct of Business Rules) rules (and the corresponding statutory duty under section 150 of the Financial Services and Markets Act 2000 (FSMA)).
2. A claim that the PPI was expensive will not be valid. A lender is not required to advise a borrower that a cheaper alternative with the same cover is available elsewhere or on the suitability of the PPI in terms of the cost as the borrowers did not indicate this was relevant to them.
3. If a lender complies with ICOB or ICOBS (Insurance: Conduct of Business Source) it will be very difficult to prove unfairness under section 140A of the Consumer Contract Act (CCA). The level of the commission, at 87 per cent was high; however it did not render the relationship unfair as ICOB did not require its disclosure.[40] Further, the regulator's (then the Financial Services Authority) list of 15 common failings in its Policy Statement of August 2010 did not include non-disclosure of commission as a failure in PPI selling practices. This ruling therefore prevents a court from considering non-disclosure of commission when assessing fairness between the parties under section 140A.
4. If there is a claim of unfairness under section 140A CCA, the court must consider whether the relationship between the parties is unfair and matters relating to both the lender and borrower.
5. A lender subject to either ICOB or ICOBS is required only to advise on the products it sells, not on whether other cheaper policies are available in the market.
6. Claims of PPI mis-selling must prove the alleged breach of ICOB or ICOBS has caused the borrower actual loss, which is not too remote and that the borrower has mitigated their loss. Claiming a refund of the PPI costs paid is not enough.

[40] Various FSA consultations concluded disclosure of commissions would not add to consumer protection.

7. The amount of compensation will be reduced where the borrower has been contributorily negligent, which will be significant if they fail to exercise their right to cancel.

This decision has raised the bar of proof even higher for borrowers seeking compensation for alleged PPI mis-selling—in particular, it cannot be argued that a lender's failure to disclose their commission created an unfair relationship under section 140A of the CCA. Alternatively, borrowers can seek redress through the FOS which applies a fairness test to decide cases and tends to result in a more favourable outcome for borrowers.[41]

Subsequent claims have been brought, however, in the courts on the basis of distinguishing the case on the facts. For example, the claimants in *Langley v Paragon Personal Finance Limited* (unreported) argued the case was different as it involved a broker, but the Court rejected this claim and awarded the lender Paragon indemnity costs. Arguably, the receipt of a high commission for selling PPI is relevant to a borrower as disclosure of this fact could result in the borrower seeking advice or products from another PPI seller or even a loan from another lender. Despite *Langley v Paragon*, the High Court judgment in 2011 upholding the PPI mis-selling regulatory scheme against a challenge by the British Bankers Association (BBA) had the effect of increasing the number of successful claims.

The cumulative effect on PPI mis-selling claims of these High Court judgments appears prima facie to be overall neutral. The slightly later 2011 decision in *Harrison* (see above), which found in favour of the lender, had the potentially opposite effect of discouraging and limiting claims. A future case with a new factual scenario may challenge the current status quo on PPI mis-selling.

In summary, all banks that sell financial products and services to UK clients and customers are generally subject to a duty of care in the sale of these products and services. The duty of care, however, is subject to limitations imposed by the principle of freedom of contract and the contractual estoppel doctrine. A bank has a duty of care not carelessly to misstate facts—which is breached to the extent that its representations or statements are inaccurate or false. However, a duty of care to advise its clients of the risks or on the suitability of a product 'should not be readily inferred in a commercial relationship'.[42] As discussed in section II below, depending on the financial product or investment sold, the duty of care could entail a duty to investigate the suitability of the products sold to customers and, if appropriate, a duty to warn customers of the risks of investing in these products.

[41] The vast bulk of mis-selling claims against British banks have been decided by the FOS in favour of customer claimants based on the UK regulatory principle of treating customers fairly. See FOS, 'consumer factsheet on payment protection insurance' www.financial-ombudsman.org.uk/publications/factsheets/payment-protection-insurance.pdf. See also 'How does the Ombudsman approach redress where a PPI policy has been mis-sold?': 'What we consider to be fair and reasonable redress will depend on the individual circumstances of the complaint', www.financial-ombudsman.org.uk/publications/technical_notes/ppi/redress.html.

[42] See *Bankers Trust International plc v PT Dharmala Sakti Sejahtera* [1996] CLC 518 at 531, per Mance J.

II. The Tests for Determining the Bank's Duty of Care and to Investigate and Warn

As implied in the previous section, a bank's duty of care could entail a duty to investigate the suitability of the products sold to customers and a duty to warn customers of the risks of investing in the products. As discussed above, however, these duties are subject to limitations imposed by the principle of freedom of contract and the contractual estoppel doctrine.

A. Commercial and Consumer Clients

Under English law, establishing a bank's duty of care in a tort claim for pure economic loss is the first—and possibly most important step—in holding the bank liable for its duty to investigate the suitability of the product for its customer and duty to warn its customers of the risks related to the financial products and services it provides. The duty of care arises if one of three tests are met for establishing a duty of care:[43] (1) assumption of responsibility; (2) a threefold test showing whether the loss to the claimant was a reasonably foreseeable consequence of what the defendant did or failed to do; whether the parties' relationship was sufficiently proximate; and whether it was fair, just and reasonable to impose a duty of care; and (3) the incremental or policy test: that the law should develop novel categories of negligence incrementally and by analogy with established categories.[44]

The first test assesses whether the defendant, objectively, assumed responsibility for their statements or conduct in relation to the claimant, or can be treated as having done so. Alternatively, the second test consists of three elements that the claimant must show to demonstrate a duty of care in negligence:

— the harm must be reasonably foreseeable as a result of the defendant's conduct;
— the parties must be in a relationship of proximity; and
— it must be fair, just and reasonable to impose liability.

This three-limbed test is known as the *Caparo Industries*[45] test to establish the existence of a duty of care. It was applied by the Court of Appeal in a 2009 case[46] to show whether a duty of care had been created by a bank to professional investors

[43] Lord Bingham cited the 3 tests in an important House of Lords decision, *Commissioners of Customs and Excise v Barclays Bank plc* Times Law Reports, 22 June 2006; [2006] UKHL 28.

[44] This third condition is addressed in greater detail in *Sutherland Shire Council v Heyman* (1985) 157 CLR 424, 481.

[45] See *Caparo Industries plc v Dickman* [1990] 2 AC 605.

[46] *So v HSBC Bank plc* [2009] EWCA Civ 296.

for alleged misrepresentations in the offer document. The Court held that for the duty of care to be established the *Caparo Industries* test required that the investor show whether the loss was a reasonably foreseeable consequence of the bank's conduct, whether the relationship between the parties was of sufficient proximity, and whether it was fair, just and reasonable to impose a duty of care on the bank towards the investor. Alternatively, the third test is known as the incremental test, which provides that new categories of negligence should be developed incrementally and by analogy with established categories.[47] This test has been criticised, however, for providing limited assistance in determining whether a duty of care has arisen because it does not provide any measurable criteria, and some observers refer to it as a policy catch-all test.[48]

In the context of a bank's potential liability for breaching its duty of care, Lord Bingham made the following general observations:

1. These were cases where one party could accurately be said to have *assumed responsibility* for what was said or done to another: the paradigm situation being a relationship having *all the indicia of contract save consideration*.
2. An assumption of responsibility was to be regarded as a sufficient but not a necessary condition of liability, a first test which, if answered positively, might obviate the need for further inquiry; if answered negatively, further consideration was called for.
3. The assumption of responsibility test was to be *applied objectively* and was not answered by what the defendant thought or intended.
4. The problem here was that the further the test was removed from the actions and intentions of the actual defendant, and the more notional the assumption of responsibility became, the less difference there was between that test and the threefold test.
5. The threefold test itself provided no straightforward answer to the vexed question whether or not in a novel situation a party owed a duty of care: see *Caparo*.
6. The incremental test was of little value in itself and was only helpful when used in combination with a test or principle which identified the legally significant features of a situation.
7. The closer the facts of the case in issue to a case in which a duty of care had been held to exist, the readier a court would be, on the approach adopted in *Caparo*, to find that there had been an assumption of responsibility or that the proximity and policy conditions of the threefold test were satisfied. The converse was also true.
8. The outcomes of the leading cases were in almost every instance sensible and just, irrespective of the test applied.

[47] *Customs & Excise Commissioners v Barclays Bank plc* (n 43) [32]–[33], 43, discussing application of *Caparo* test to the facts in *Customs*.

[48] *Customs & Excise Commissioners v Barclays Bank plc* (n 43) [32], per Lord Bingham, [49] per Lord Rodger, [72] per Lord Rodger.

9. That was not to disparage the value of and need for a test of liability in tortious negligence, which any law of tort must propound if it was not to become a morass of single instances. But it concentrated attention on the detailed circumstances of the particular case and the particular relationship between the parties in the context of their legal and factual situation as a whole.[49]

Despite the *Caparo* limitations in establishing a duty of care between a bank *and* commercial or individual clients, which make it difficult to prevail in a claim against the bank, the duty of care issue is the most frequently invoked issue in financial litigation regarding the bank's rendering of advice, or failing to give advice. Commercial or consumer investors who claim that there has been a breach of the duty of care at common law may also assert an additional claim for breach of regulatory requirement for the provision of suitable and adequate advice in the sale of financial products or investments. Section 138D (previously section 150) of FSMA provides a statutory right of action where breach of UK regulatory requirements cause loss to a private investor. As with claims for negligence or misrepresentation at common law, however, the claimant still has a high bar to surmount under section 138D to establish liability of the bank.

B. Causation and the Bank's Duties to Consumer Clients and Commercial Customers

Even if the bank's customer can establish that the bank owed it a duty of care, it additionally must show that the breach caused the loss in question and that the loss was foreseeable. As discussed in the previous section, the nature and scope of the bank's duty of care to its retail clients or consumer customers is defined by the *Caparo Industries* three-step test for establishing a duty of care (see above). The causation issue has arisen in several prominent cases where investor claims against banks have failed as they were unable to prove the reasonable foreseeability of loss. In *So v HSBC Bank plc*,[50] the Court applied the *Caparo Industries* three-limbed test to ascertain whether a duty of care had been established.[51] whether loss was a reasonably foreseeable consequence of the bank's conduct, whether the relationship between the parties was of sufficient proximity and whether it was fair, just and reasonable to impose a duty of care on the bank towards the investor. In this case, the investors transferred US $30 million into the bank account of a fraudster and the bank issued to the investors a letter of instruction which stated that the bank would act only on the instructions of investors to pay out the funds in the account; however, the letter was issued negligently. The Court held the investors' loss was

[49] See Lord Bingham, *Customs & Excise Commissioners v Barclays Bank plc* (n 43) at [192].

[50] [2009] EWCA Civ 296.

[51] *Caparo Industries plc v Dickman* (n 45); *Customs & Excise Commissioners v Barclays Bank plc* (n 43).

not caused by the bank's breach of duty but because there was no joint account giving them direct control over their money with HSBC.[52]

Another case, *Camerata Property Inc v Credit Suisse Securities (Europe) Ltd (No 2)*,[53] involved both the common law and statutory duties regarding a bank providing negligent advice on the riskiness of an investment product. In this case, the bank advised an investor to buy a note betting on the dollar weakening against the euro. The investor lost the investment when the US investment bank Lehman Brothers collapsed in 2008; however, if this collapse had not happened, the note would have paid off substantially. The Court found that even if the bank would have advised to sell the note, the investor would have retained the note, therefore there was no reliance and causation. Further, the investor claimed that they were negligently advised to buy the note, that it was an unsuitable investment and that therefore there was a breach of section 150 of FSMA. The claims failed; however, even if fault by the bank had been established, the 2008 collapse of Lehman Brothers was reasonably unforeseeable in 2007 when the note was purchased.

Similarly, causation was an issue in *Al Sulaiman v Credit Suisse Securities (Europe) Ltd*,[54] where the investor claimed that the risks of leveraged investments in structured notes had not been adequately explained to her. The Court found that any explanation would not have affected her desire to achieve higher returns and she would have invested in the notes in any event. Moreover, she was advised to sell the notes or put up margin; however, she refused and this broke any chain of causation.

Rubenstein v HSBC Bank plc,[55] however, is an example of a successful claim against a bank, where a solicitor sought advice about investing the proceeds of the sale of his home. The bank advised him to invest in AIG bonds and said that the bond was the same as a cash deposit, however the solicitor's money was invested in an enhanced variable rate fund in which the investor was entitled only to its value at the time of requesting withdrawal, which depended on the underlying assets in the fund, including derivatives. The trial judge held that the bank was negligent in its advice, on which the solicitor had relied and breached various statutory duties. However, the solicitor received only nominal damages at first instance as the Court found that the loss was caused by unprecedented market turmoil which was unforeseeable and too remote. However, on appeal, the Court disagreed and found that the loss was not too remote, and that 'what had caused Mr Rubenstein to suffer a loss might be said to be the very thing which he had wished to avoid: the risk of loss to his capital'.[56]

[52] *So v HSBC Bank plc* (n 46) [71] and [73], available at: www.bailii.org/ew/cases/EWCA/Civ/2009/296.html.

[53] [2012] EWHC 7 (Comm).

[54] [2013] EWHC 400 (Comm).

[55] [2012] EWCA Civ 1184, available at: www.bailii.org/ew/cases/EWCA/Civ/2012/1184.html.

[56] ibid, [70]–[71]. The Court discusses its reasoning further at [94], [95], [103], [115], [121], and discusses the facts of the case at [85]–[93].

C. UK Regulatory Law

The competent UK regulatory authorities have adopted legally binding regulatory rules and standards to ensure that banks treat their customers fairly and afford them adequate redress for violations of statute and regulation. This has had the effect of expanding the scope of the banks' potential liability. As discussed in section I, the most prominent application of UK regulatory rules to banks' mis-selling of financial products came in respect of the sale of payment protection insurance (PPI). The Financial Services Authority adopted regulatory guidelines and a policy statement on PPI complaints handling.[57] The FSA Statement on PPI mis-selling included amendments to the Handbook rules, guidance on how PPI sales complaints should be decided, an open letter to the BBA and others including a list of 'common failings' in PPI sales and guidance on a redress mechanism and a root cause analysis for customers who had not complained.

The lawfulness of the FSA's PPI mis-selling policy statement and guidelines were upheld by the High Court against a legal challenge by the BBA.[58] The main legal issue raised by the BBA was whether the FSA had the authority to issue a policy that included a statement that the FSA's main Principles (general statements by the FSA of conduct required of financial services firms)[59] would be taken into account when the Financial Ombudsman Service made decisions on whether compensation would be 'fair and reasonable' under section 228(2) of FSMA.

The judgment was a setback for the banks, as PPI sales have been a notorious source of customer complaints for years. The judgment upheld the validity of PPI mis-selling complaints that were filed against banks for conduct that preceded the FSA's adoption of the PPI mis-selling policy statement in 2010. The decision allows PPI claims to be judged by reference to the new rules and guidance of the 2010 policy statement, even if the sale complied with the applicable rules in effect at the date of sale. Moreover, the policy statement adopted a 'root cause analysis' of systemic but historical failings of bank mis-selling practices in which banks would be advised by the regulator to contact customers who may never have made a complaint and to offer them compensation if there was something sufficiently questionable about the bank's PPI policy or practice. The decision has had an important impact on the banking industry's liability to compensate customers for PPI mis-selling. In 2015, though PPI claims have fallen, the FOS has upheld over 60 per cent of mis-selling claims.

[57] See the FSA's Policy Statement 10/12 of 10 August 2010: '*The Assessment and Redress of Payment Protection Insurance Complaints*' (the Statement, available on http://www.fsa.gov.uk/library/policy/policy/2010/10_12.shtml).

[58] See *R (on application of the British Bankers Association) v Financial Services Authority and Financial Ombudsman Service* (n 35) (per Ouseley J).

[59] Contained in Ch 2 of 'Principles for Business' (PRIN) in the FSA Handbook, include: Integrity; Skill, care and diligence; Customers' interests; Communications with clients; and Customers: relationships of trust.

The effect of the 2011 High Court judgment was to facilitate the initiation and continuation of thousands of complaints and claims against banks that are still being heard by the FOS and the courts.

D. European Legislation—MiFID II

European Union legislation substantially impacts UK financial regulatory law. The Market in Financial Instruments Directive (Directive 2004/39/EC) (MiFID I) was regarded as a milestone in the European Union's regulation of financial markets. MiFID I sets out specific provisions for harmonising the regulation of investment services across the EU and guaranteeing an adequate level of investor protection. The UK implemented MiFID I in 2007. Following the regulatory reforms which took place worldwide after the 2007–08 financial crisis, the European Commission issued legislative proposals to repeal MiFID I through the adoption of Directive 2014/65/EU (MiFID II) and Regulation No 600/2014 (MiFIR).[60] The European Commission has issued a number of delegated acts further specifying the rules under MiFID II[61] and MiFIR.[62] Recently, under a regulation and a directive issued on 23 June 2016 the application of MiFID II and MiFIR has been postponed until 3 January 2018.[63] Moreover, MiFID II is expected to be transposed into national laws by 3 July 2017. In the wake of the 2016 Brexit referendum, the MiFID legislation will continue to apply until the UK starts the withdrawal procedure pursuant to Article 50 of the 2007 Lisbon Treaty and officially leaves the EU.[64]

[60] See Directive 2014/65/EU of the European Parliament and of the Council of 15 May 2014 on markets in financial instruments and amending Directive 2002/92/EC and Directive 2011/61/EU (recast) (2014) OJ L 173/349; see Regulation (EU) No 600/2014 of the European Parliament and of the Council of 15 May 2014 on markets in financial instruments and amending Regulation (EU) No 648/2012 (2014) OJ L 173/84.

[61] See Commission Delegated Regulation of 25.04.2016 supplementing Directive 2014/65/EU of the European Parliament and of the Council as regards organisational requirements and operating conditions for investments firms and defined terms for the purposes of that Directive; see Commission Delegated Directive of 07.04.2016 supplementing Directive 2014/65/EU of the European Parliament and of the Council with regard to safeguarding of financial instruments and funds belonging to clients, products governance obligations and the rules applicable to the provision or reception of fees, commissions or any monetary or non-monetary benefits.

[62] See Commission Delegated Regulation of 18.05.2016 supplementing Regulation (EU) No 600/2014 of the European Parliament and of the Council with regard to definitions, transparency, portfolio compression and supervisory measures on product intervention and positions; see also, 'Overview and state of play of RTS and ITS relating to MiFID/MiFIR (last updated: 01.02.2017) <http://ec.europa.eu/finance/securities/docs/isd/mifid/its-rts-overview-table_en.pdf>.

[63] See Regulation (EU) 2016/1033 of the European Parliament and of the Council of 23 June 2016 amending Regulation (EU) No 600/2014 on markets in financial instruments, Regulation (EU) No 596/2014 on market abuse and Regulation (EU) No 909/2014 on improving securities settlement in the European Union and on central securities depositories (2016) OJ L175/1; see also Directive (EU) 2016/1034 of the European Parliament and of the Council of 23 June 2016 amending Directive 2014/65/EU on markets in financial instruments (2016) OJ L175/8.

[64] Under Art 50(2): 'A Member State which decides to withdraw shall notify the European Council of its intention. In the light of the guidelines provided by the European Council, the Union shall negotiate and conclude an agreement with that State, setting out the arrangements for its withdrawal, taking

This means that the UK will have to comply with the current MiFID's application and transposition dates, unless the terms of withdrawal are agreed before.

In relation to the banks' duty of care, it is worth mentioning those rules of the revised legislation that set out organisational requirements and conduct of business provisions. As to the investment firms' organisational requirements, reference is made to the new provisions on product governance arrangements relating to firms which develop financial products and to those which sell them. The purpose of such provisions is to enhance the firms' understanding of the products they develop or sell and to ensure that they are suitable to the clients to whom they are being sold.[65] To this end, investment firms are required to maintain, operate and review the process for approval of each financial instrument and significant adaptations of existing financial instruments before it is marketed or distributed to clients.[66] Moreover, specific record-keeping provisions have been laid down in the context of the organisational requirements. In particular, records shall include the recording of telephone conversations or electronic communications relating to, at least, transactions concluded when dealing on own account and the provision of client order services that relate to the reception, transmission and execution of client orders. Investment firms must also notify new and existing clients that telephone communications or conversations between the investment firm and its clients that result, or may result, in transactions will be recorded.[67]

Sales targets and remuneration rules are also relevant in the context of a bank's duty of care. Indeed, such rules are based on the European Securities and Markets Authority's Guidelines on Remuneration Policies and Practices and aim at ensuring that staff incentives do not result in conflict of interests or impinge upon the firm's obligation to act in the best interest of the client.[68] Finally, as to conduct of business, Articles 25 and 27 of MiFID II narrow the list of execution-only products and widen the list of information investment firms have to provide with regard to best execution.[69]

Compared to MiFID I, MiFID II aims to enhance the level of protection of different categories of clients. However, there will be room for further analysis once the implementation process is completed in accordance with the Commission's ongoing level 2 rule-making process and the final level 3 compliance and enforcement stage. Before the Brexit referendum, the UK competent authorities

account of the framework for its future relationship with the Union. That agreement shall be negotiated in accordance with Article 218(3) of the Treaty on the Functioning of the European Union. It shall be concluded on behalf of the Union by the Council, acting by a qualified majority, after obtaining the consent of the European Parliament'.

[65] See Art 16 of Directive 2014/65/EU of the European Parliament and of the Council of 15 May 2014 on markets in financial instruments and amending Directive 2002/92/EC and Directive 2011/61/EU (recast) OJ L 173/349.

[66] Directive 2014/65/EU, Art 16(3).

[67] Directive 2014/65/EU, Art 16(6) and (7).

[68] Directive 2014/65/EU, Art 24(10).

[69] Directive 2014/65/EU, Arts 25 and 27.

were considering the necessary changes for transposing MiFID II and MiFIR into domestic legislation.[70] In particular, they were assessing the impact that the new EU legislation may have on the ability of UK credit institutions and investment firms to contract out of their duty of care to retail and wholesale customers and to use the doctrine of contractual estoppel to limit their liability to both consumer and commercial customers.[71] As mentioned above, the extent and scope of the EU legislation will not be known until 2018. The UK vote for 'leave' has triggered a period of uncertainty. Nonetheless, 'firms must continue to abide by their obligations under UK law, including those derived from EU law and continue with implementation plans for legislation that is still to come into effect'.[72]

III. The Bank's Duty to Professional Investors

English courts have generally followed the doctrine of *Hedley Byrne*[73] and *Caparo Industries*[74] in holding that a claimant does not have a legal claim against a third party with whom the claimant does not have a direct relationship (ie privity of contract), unless there are facts to show that the third party has made some representations to, or established some type of direct relationship with, the claimant in respect of its claim. Following the financial crisis of 2007–08, a growing number of legal claims were filed by professional and other sophisticated investors against third party banks who acted as arrangers or managers in the sale of structured finance and other complex financial products. For example, a professional investor holding a structured debt instrument issued as part of a securitisation who suffered losses as a result of negligent statements or misrepresentations in the sale of that product might look for redress to those parties who made the statements and promoted the products (the 'managers') or to those parties who structured the investment (the 'arrangers'). A preliminary issue would be whether the managers/arrangers acted *reasonably* and, if they did not, whether they are *liable* in negligence for making a false statement about the product or rendering negligent advice to its customer in deciding whether to purchase the product. If they did not act reasonably or acted deceitfully, to prove liability the investor must first show

[70] The Financial Services and Markets Act 2000 (Qualifying EU Provisions) (Amendment) Order 2016. This Order applies some amendments to the Financial Services and Markets Act 2000 (Qualifying EU Provisions) Order 2013. The purpose of these amendments is twofold: (1) to make the Markets in Financial Instruments Regulation (MiFIR) a qualifying EU provision for various parts of FMSA; and (2) to ensure that the FCA and PRA have the appropriate powers to perform their roles under MiFIR.

[71] See HM Treasury, 'Transposition of the Market in Financial Instruments Directive II' (March 2015) HMT Consultation Paper www.gov.uk/government/uploads/system/uploads/attachment_data/file/418281/PU_1750_MiFID_II_26.03.15.pdf.

[72] FCA, 'Statement on European Union referendum result' (2016) www.fca.org.uk/news/statements/statement-european-union-referendum-result.

[73] *Hedley Byrne & Co Ltd v Heller & Partners Ltd* [1963] 2 All ER 575; [1964] AC 465.

[74] *Caparo Industries plc v Dickman* (n 45).

whether the bank—as a manager or arranger of the product—owed a duty of care to the investor.

In these cases, the English courts have generally resisted expanding the scope of liability to third party banks because, as arrangers or managers of the sale of the complex financial product, they were not the issuers or the sellers of the product or securities in question. Instead, a special purpose vehicle (SPV) that was a separate legal entity was the seller or the issuer. Therefore, the banks were not parties to the contract with the claimant investors who purchased the investment products. Moreover, the investment contract entered into by the investors with the SPV expressly stated that the investors did not rely on any representations that were not stated in writing in the contract. In other words, any marketing statements or promotions provided by the bank as arranger or manager had no legal effect with respect to liability in the issuance or sale of the investment product.

A. The Bank's Duty of Care as Manager or Arranger in Offering Circulars and other Marketing Documents for Securities

The UK regulatory regime reinforces this market practice by not attributing responsibility for false statements or misrepresentations to managers or arrangers in an offering circular for debt instruments issued in a securitisation.[75] This is because the issuance of such debt instruments in a securitisation is typically an exempt transaction under FSMA. Even if listed on a regulated market, they will be 'specialist securities' that are dealt with in a 'professionals-only market' where sophisticated investors can be expected to assess the risks and protect their own interests. In this type of market, the regulatory standards will at most place responsibility only on those who expressly state that they accept responsibility for misstatements in the offering circular. Moreover, the UK regulations require that at least one person be named on the offering circular as accepting responsibility for its content; this will almost always be the issuer, and not the manager or arranger.

A bank's liability as a manager or arranger for misstatements in an offering circular for *exempt* or *specialist* debt instruments issued in a securitisation,

[75] Many of the securitisation litigation cases arising from the financial crisis relate to residential mortgage-backed securities (RMBS). RMBS are structured in the following way: loans are made to a current or potential homeowner by a loan originator, who often funds the loans through a warehouse line of credit supplied by a sponsor. The originator then transfers the loans to the sponsor, who pools thousands of them and then transfers the pool to a depositor, a bankruptcy remote entity affiliated with the sponsor that is created solely to receive and transfer the rights to the loans. The depositor transfers the pools to an issuing trust, and securitises the pool by dividing it into several tranches, corresponding to a different level of risk and reward. In exchange for the mortgages, the trust provides the depositor with certificates that represent interests in the trust. The depositor issues the certificates to underwriters, who then sell them to investors. See K Alexander and SL Schwarcz, *Macroprudential Regulation—A Conceptual Approach* (Oxford: Oxford University Press, 2017).

therefore, is highly questionable, as it is unlikely that a duty of care will arise by virtue of the offering circular itself. There must be an express statement that the manager/arranger has accepted responsibility for representations made in the offering circular; otherwise, the issuer will likely be the named party on the document to be held liable for any misrepresentations. In contrast, regarding *non-exempt* or *non-specialist* securities, it can be argued under English law that those who have authorised the contents of the document (ie prospectus or offering circular), such as the managers/arrangers, are responsible for its contents, and responsibility can be demonstrated merely by appending the bank's name to the bottom (or top) of the first page of the circular or offering document. This is not the case, however, regarding debt instruments issued in a securitisation, as it is unlikely that a duty of care will arise between the manager/arranger and investor merely on the basis of the contents of the offering circular itself. For example, a bank may be the lead 'manager' or 'co-lead manager' of an issuance of debt securities based on a securitisation, and the bank's name may be listed on the first page of the offering circular. In the London market, practitioners would presume that the bank's name listed prominently on the circular would be done for the bank's own marketing purposes, and not as a representation of the truthfulness of the document's contents. As a matter of law and practice, therefore, it will rarely be enough, without more, to show that the bank's role as manager or arranger of a particular issue is enough to create a duty of care between the bank and the potential investor in the issue.

Nevertheless, as discussed in the cases above, a duty of care can arise by a manager or arranger by voluntarily assuming responsibility for the truthfulness or correctness of what is stated in an offering document for the issue of debt securities based on a securitisation. The English courts have held that a duty of care can arise between the manager/arranger and investor in debt securities of a securitisation where the offering document does not contain an express disclaimer of responsibility for the manager/arranger. In such a case, English courts will look to the facts of each case to determine whether a manager or arranger did in fact assume responsibility for any representations contained in the offering document and additionally will look to extrinsic communications between the manager/arranger and investor to see if the manager/arranger provided specific answers to a particular investor's questions that the manager/arranger knew—or should have known—would induce that specific investor to invest in the issue. This factual situation arose in a 2008 case known as the *Boxclever* litigation that took place in the London Commercial Court. In this case, the French bank Natixis brought a claim against the Canadian bank (CIBC) and the German bank WestLandesbank (WestLB) for losses based on a note it purchased in a securitisation of the Boxclever group. Natixis alleged, amongst other things, that CIBC, as co-lead manager of the issue, and WestLB, as arranger of the issue, owed it a duty of care in respect of representations made in the offering circular and based on extrinsic communications. The case settled, however, and no judicial opinion was issued.

A subsequent case, *IFE v Goldman Sachs*,[76] stands for the above proposition that where there is an express disclaimer of responsibility for the manager/arranger in the offering documents there will be no duty of care and therefore no liability for the manager/arranger for unreasonable or false statements made in the offering documents on which the investor may have relied. In this case, IFE had purchased from Goldman Sachs (GSI), bonds and warrants issued by a French company, Autodis SA, for €20 million, which formed part of syndicated credit facilities provided to Autodis for the acquisition of an English company, Finelist Group plc. The credit facilities were provided in tiers, IFE financed the mezzanine facility, which was arranged by GSI, who also underwrote the mezzanine facility. Autodis' acquisition was unsuccessful, it was revealed that Finelist's financial position was misrepresented and it was placed into receivership. IFE brought an action against GSI for its losses, on the grounds of misrepresentation, pursuant to section 2(1) of the Misrepresentation Act 1967,[77] and common law negligence. IFE claimed it was induced to enter into the transaction by information provided by GSI in the syndication information memorandum (SIM), which presented a picture that was in fact misleading and which was not corrected or qualified after they had cause to doubt its reliability as a result of receiving two reports from accountants. GSI had made an express disclaimer in the SIM as to the accuracy or completeness of the SIM: that the information in it had been derived from many sources and was not to form the basis of any contract; that GSI had not independently verified the information and gave no representation, warranty or undertaking, express or implied, and did not accept responsibility for its accuracy; and that the information was not to be assumed to have been updated and did not constitute a representation by any person that the information would be updated. The court dismissed the claim and made the following rulings:

1. A reasonable person would not have understood that GSI was making any implied representations as alleged by IFE.[78]
2. There was a difference between actual knowledge that information previously supplied was misleading and acquiring information which merely gave rise to a possibility that the information previously supplied was misleading, which did not give rise to a duty to investigate the matter further, or advise the participant.

[76] *IFE Fund SA v Goldman Sachs International* (n 20).

[77] 'Where a person has entered into a contract after a misrepresentation has been made to him by another party thereto and as a result thereof he has suffered loss, then, if the person making the misrepresentation would be liable to damages in respect thereof had the misrepresentation been made fraudulently, that person shall be so liable notwithstanding that the misrepresentation was not made fraudulently, unless he proves that he had reasonable ground to believe and did believe up to the time the contract was made that the facts represented were true'.

[78] Goldman argued that its representations stated, among other things, that it was not aware of any facts which showed that the statements about Finelist's financial performance made in the Memorandum were or might be incorrect in any material way; and/or which showed that the opinions expressed in the Memorandum Reports were not or might not be reasonable.

3. GSI was not acting as an adviser to IFE or purporting to carry out any professional service, it was acting for the sponsors, therefore it did not owe the duty of care which IFE alleged.
4. Contractual disclaimer terms between the parties ruled out any representation that the information would be reviewed at any stage before the recipient acquired the bonds.
5. The only implied representation was one of good faith.
6. The extensive disclaimer, which negatived any assumption of responsibility, meant that no duty of care arose.

The *IFE v Goldman Sachs* case also clarifies the application of a statutory remedy for misrepresentation under the Misrepresentation Act 1967 by holding that the effect of an express disclaimer in an offering circular is to prevent a representation from having been made in the first place, thereby precluding an allegation of misrepresentation under the Misrepresentation Act 1967.

In *Raiffeisen Zentralbank Österreich AG v Royal Bank of Scotland plc*,[79] the Court cited with approval the *IFE* test for the express statement test: 'the court has to consider what a reasonable person would have understood from the words used in the context in which they were used;. The Court in this case further elaborated on this test in relation to the relevant factors in construing the express statement: 'nature and content of the statement, the context in which it was made, the characteristics of the maker and of the person to whom it was made, and the relationship between them'.[80]

The Court also cited *IFE* as authority for the rule that whether any representations were made has to be decided by reference to the provisions of the information memorandum (IM) and the confidentiality agreement as they are an important part of the context in which the representations are said to have been made, and are thus relevant to any inquiry as to what representation a reasonable reader of the IM would regard as having been made.[81] Further, the Court approved the finding in *IFE* of 'an implied representation that, in supplying the information memorandum, Goldman Sachs was acting in good faith, ie was not knowingly putting forward information likely to mislead'.[82] Moreover, the Court cited[83] with approval a passage from *IFE* on the nature of the 'disclaimers' in the SIM:

> The relevant paragraphs of the SIM are not in my view to be characterised in substance as a notice excluding or restricting a liability for negligence, but more fundamentally as going to the issue *whether there was a relationship between the parties* (amounting to or equivalent to that of professional adviser and advisee).[84]

[79] [2010] All ER (D) 111. The facts of the case were summarised in section I.B.i.
[80] ibid, [82].
[81] ibid, [97].
[82] ibid, [264].
[83] ibid, [294].
[84] *IFE Fund SA v Goldman Sachs International* (n 20) [70]–[71] per Toulson J, approved by Court of Appeal per Waller J at [28].

Following the *Raiffeisen Zentralbank* and *IFE* cases, the classic English judicial formulation of the narrowness of the bank duty of care doctrine in the structured financial product market occurred in *Cassa di Risparmio della Repubblica di San Marino SpA v Barclays Bank Ltd*,[85] also a case involving the mis-selling of complex structured financial products. This important case is now viewed as a test case for other potential cases involving the mis-selling of complex structured finance investments. The claim related to a series of structured finance notes (CDO^2) with a total nominal value of €406 million which were structured by Barclays and sold to Cassa di Risparmio della Repubblica di San Marino SpA (CRSM) in 2004 and 2005 and to a subsequent restructuring of the transactions. CRSM issued proceedings, alleging fraudulent misrepresentation, and claimed damages for deceit, or alternatively under section 2(1) of the Misrepresentation Act 1967, or alternatively for a breach of an implied term of the contracts of sale or restructure. However, all claims brought by CRSM against Barclays were dismissed by Hamblen J of the Commercial Court in a judgment delivered on 9 March 2011.

The total amount lent by Barclays to CRSM's subsidiaries, the Delta Companies, was €700m, spread over several tranches and over a period of eight months, and supported by five Credit Linked Notes (CLNs) transactions with aggregate principal of €450m. The four disputed CLNs were comprised of €176m credit default swaps (CDS) on the Delta Companies, and €230m in CDO^2. The CDO^2 were all single tranche synthetic transactions, where CRSM purchased a bespoke mezzanine tranche and Barclays effectively held the equity and senior tranches. Each CDO consisted of six inner CDOs and AAA-rate asset-backed securities (ABS) such that the overall rating of each Note was AAA. CRSM intended to hold the Notes until maturity; the key risk for CRSM was the 'credit risk' of the CDO^{2}s—that is, the risk that CRSM would cease to receive the full coupon and would not get back the full principal amount when the Notes matured, if a sufficient number and combination of 'credit events' (eg insolvency or default on a debt) occurred in relation to entities named in the portfolios underlying the CDO^{2}s. In March 2005, CRSM expressed concern about the presence of certain names in the reference portfolios, following which Barclays implemented on 14 June 2005 a restructuring of the four CDOs, with two components: (1) replacing some of the reference entities and (2) adding 'cross-subordination' to the CDO structures. In late 2005 the quality of the CDO began to deteriorate as defaults in the underlying reference entities began to occur. In April 2006, Barclays agreed to repurchase the various CDOs and in February 2010 Barclays formally notified CRSM that the principal of some of the Notes had been reduced to zero. The Court made the following rulings:

1. The use of ratings in representations to clients; a statement by an arranging bank about a AAA rating was not a general statement about risk or probability of default, but only a statement about the rating agency's opinion.[86]

[85] [2011] EWHC 484 (Comm).
[86] ibid, [264].

2. Historical default data, gathered over long periods covering all phases of the business cycle, are a reliable source for estimating expected future default rates.[87]
3. Hamblen J rejected CRSM's claim that the model used to compute Barclays' expected P&L could also be used to estimate the probability of default (PDs) expected over the life of the Notes.[88]
4. A contractual term in the sales contracts (similar to an ISDA non-reliance clause) would in any event have precluded the claim under contractual estoppel, with no finding of fraud. By the term, CRSM warranted that it understood and accepted the terms, conditions and risk of purchasing the notes.[89]

The Court affirmed the following principles of law:

1. It was established law that the tort of deceit involved the making of a false representation by a defendant, knowing it to be untrue, or being reckless as to whether it was true, and intending the claimant should act in reliance on it.[90]
2. Section 2(1) of the Misrepresentation Act, required proof of: (1) a representation made by the defendant; (2) which was false; (3) which induced the claimant to enter into the relevant contract; and (4) as a result of which the claimant suffered loss.[91]
3. A representation was a statement of fact made by the representor to the representee on which the representee was intended and entitled to rely as a positive assertion that the fact was true. In order to determine whether or what representation was made by a statement required: (1) construing the statement in the context in which it had been made; and (2) interpreting the statement objectively according to the impact it might be expected to have on a reasonable respresentee in the position and with the known characteristics of the actual representee. In order to be actionable, a representation had to be as to a matter of fact. A statement of opinion was therefore not in itself actionable. Where, however, the facts were not equally well known to both sides, a statement of opinion by one who knew the facts best might carry with it a further implication of fact, namely that the representor by expressing that opinion had impliedly stated that he believed that facts existed which reasonably justified it. A statement as to the future might imply a statement as to present intention. By itself, silence could not found a claim in misrepresentation. However, an express statement which was literally true might nevertheless involve a misrepresentation because of matters which the representor omitted to mention. In a deceit case, it was also necessary that the representor should

[87] ibid, [296].

[88] ibid, [302].

[89] ibid, [525].

[90] ibid, [210]. *AIC Ltd v ITS Testing Services (UK) Ltd; The Kriti Palm* [2006] All ER (D) 381 (Nov).

[91] ibid, [212]–[213] and [232]–[233]. *Raiffeisen Zentralbank Österreich AG v Royal Bank of Scotland plc* [2010] All ER (D) 111 (Jun) applied; *County NatWest Bank Ltd v Barton* [1999] All ER (D) 782 applied; *Dadourian Group International Inc v Simms* [2009] All ER (D) 175 (Mar) applied.

understand that he was making the implied representation and that it had the misleading sense alleged.[92]

4. It was established that the mental element to prove a claim in deceit was proof of fraud: that a false representation had been made knowingly, without belief in its truth, or recklessly, careless whether it be true or false. The unreasonableness of the grounds of the belief, though not of itself supporting an action for deceit, would be evidence from which fraud might be inferred.[93]
5. It was established law that parties can agree that one party had not made any pre-contract representations, or that any such representations had not been relied on, even if this occurred and that such an agreement might give rise to a contractual estoppel. Clear words were necessary; however, it did not apply where there had been a misrepresentation as to the effect of the contractual documents which gave rise to the estoppel.[94]
6. The statement by Barclays that a CDO had been rated AAA by a credit rating agency had not implied anything more than that the note had been given that rating by an agency, based on its expert opinion; it was not a statement by Barclays about default probabilities or risk.[95] Therefore, the purchase misrepresentations had not been made.[96] Even if a representation that the notes would have had a very low risk of default had been made by Barclays such a representation was a matter of opinion and/or expectation, made on reasonable grounds.[97] Further, CRSM had not proved that it had in fact relied on the purchase representations, had they been made.[98] Moreover, Barclays had not in fact made any representation that it would not profit from the restructuring.[99]
7. To prove deceit, CRSM would have to establish that the relevant employees of the defendant individually had the necessary subjective understanding and intention for fraud. On the evidence, the relevant employees of the defendant had no intention to mislead the claimant.[100]

[92] ibid, [215]–[223] and [232]–[233]. *Smith v Land and House Property Corpn* 28 Ch D 7 applied; *Clydesdale Bank Ltd v Paton* [1895–99] All ER Rep 1136 applied; *Brown v Raphael* [1958] Ch 636 applied; *Goose v Wilson Sandford & Co* [2000] All ER (D) 324 applied; *Kyle Bay Ltd v Underwriters subscribing to policy no 019057/08/01* [2007] All ER (D) 93 (Feb) applied; *Raiffeisen Zentralbank Österreich AG v Royal Bank of Scotland plc* (n 91) applied.

[93] ibid, [225]–[230]. *Derry v Peek* [1886–90] All ER Rep 1 applied; *Bradford Third Equitable Benefit Building Society v Borders* [1941] 2 All ER 205 applied; *Standard Chartered Bank v Pakistan National Shipping Corp (No 2)* [2000] 1 All ER (Comm) 1 applied; *AIC Ltd v ITS Testing Services (UK) Ltd; The Kriti Palm* (n 90) applied.

[94] ibid, [505]. *Board of Trade v Steel Bros & Co Ltd* [1952] 1 Lloyd's Rep 87 applied; *Peekay Intermark Ltd v Australia and New Zealand Banking Group Ltd* [2006] All ER (D) 70 (Apr) applied.

[95] ibid, [263] and [264].

[96] ibid, [266].

[97] ibid, [267], [371] and [463].

[98] ibid, [482].

[99] ibid, [278].

[100] ibid, [368], [406], [424], [449] and [457].

8. CRSM was contractually estopped from making misrepresentation claims by clauses 5 and 6 of the purchase contracts.[101] However, the claimant was not estopped by clause 6 from the claims in respect of representations made in relation to the restructuring transaction, as any representations made did not cause the claimant to misunderstand the risks of entering the restructuring transaction, but they were rather statements as to the criteria to be applied in carrying out the restructuring.[102]
9. In relation to the arbitrage claim, the term that CRSM alleged was not to be implied into the contract, as such a term was not capable of clear expression, was not necessary to make the contract work, nor was it reasonable as its inclusion would potentially undermine the practices of the banking market, as arbitrage was a common practice. Furthermore, it contradicted the express terms of the contract, and was not what a reasonable person would have understood the contract to mean.[103]

Cassa di Risparmio v Barclays was followed by *Standard Chartered Bank v Ceylon Petroleum Corporation*.[104] In this case, the parties entered into oil derivative transactions, which required SCB to make payments to CPC when oil prices were high while CPC was required to make payments to SCB if the price of oil fell below an agreed floor. When oil prices fell rapidly, CPC became 'out-of-the-money' on its derivative transactions and refused to pay SCB the full sums owing. SCB sued for repayment. CPC contended that because it had no experience in commodity derivative transactions and was engaging in novel and sophisticated transactions, SCB had held itself out to CPC as adviser and encouraged it to enter into transactions that did not hedge its risks, but instead provided the prospect of insignificant upfront fixed profits in return for taking on vast and disproportionate downside risk.

The Court rejected the counterclaim and set out the various tests for establishing duty of care in tort:[105]

1. the assumption of responsibility test, coupled with reliance;
2. the threefold-test (whether the loss was reasonably foreseeable, whether the relationship between the parties was of sufficient proximity and whether in all the circumstances it was fair just and reasonable to impose such a duty); and
3. the incremental test.

[101] ibid, [514] and [525]–[526].

[102] ibid, [525]–[527].

[103] ibid, [544]–[545]. *BP Refinery (Westernport) Pty Ltd v Hastings Shire Council* 52 ALJR 20 applied; *A-G of Belize v Belize Telecom Ltd* [2009] 2 All ER (Comm) 1 applied; *Mediterranean Salvage and Towage Ltd v Seamar Trading and Commerce Inc; The Reborn* [2010] 1 All ER (Comm) 1 applied.

[104] [2011] All ER (D) 113.

[105] ibid, [478]–[480]. *Bankers Trust v PT Dharmala Sakti Sejahtera* (n 42) applied; *Williams v Natural Life Health Foods Ltd* [1998] 1 WLR 830 considered; *JP Morgan Chase Bank v Springwell Navigation Corp* [2007] 1 All ER (Comm) 549 considered.

Further, the Court held that to establish inducement by misrepresentation for the purpose of a claim under section 2 of the 1967 Misrepresentation Act, it was necessary to show that, but for the representation, the claimant would not have entered into the contract.[106]

The *IFE, Cassa di Risparmio* and *Standard Chartered Bank* decisions were cited in *Graiseley Properties Ltd v Barclays Bank Plc*[107] and *Brown v Innovatorone plc.*[108] The Court in *Graiseley Properties Ltd* cited with approval the test for implied representations set out by Toulson J at paragraph 50 in *IFE*:

> In determining whether there has been an express representation, and to what effect, the court has to consider what a reasonable person would have understood from the words used in the context in which they were used. In determining what, if any, implied representation has been made, the court has to perform a similar task, except that it has to consider what a reasonable person would have inferred was being implicitly represented by the representor's words and conduct in their context.[109]

Brown v Innovatorone plc cited with approval the test for implied representations and restated as follows:

> That involves considering whether a reasonable representee in the position and with the known characteristics of the actual representee would reasonably have understood that an implied representation was being made and being made substantially in the terms or to the effect alleged.

The Court in this case also cited with approval the ruling in *IFE* that a disclaimer meant there was no assumption of responsibility and therefore, no duty of care arose.

Based on the above cases, the English courts have taken a narrow view of the duty of care of banks in promoting structured financial products to third party commercial investors who are sold the products by separate legal entities based on contracts that contain express disclaimers that the investors are relying only on representations made in the written contract of sale and not on any representations that the bank may have made—verbal or otherwise—to promote and sell the product. Professional investors have attempted to circumvent these disclaimers by asserting claims in negligence, misrepresentation and/or deceit against the banks that they have engaged in culpable conduct that undermines the integrity of the transaction, and that the banks should be held liable for any false or misleading representations extrinsic to the contract that induced the claimants to purchase the investment product, even though the claimants state in the contract's disclaimer that they have not relied upon an representations extrinsic to the contract. The consistency of the English courts in limiting the bank's duty of care in the sale of structured finance and other wholesale debt investments is well established in

[106] ibid, [552].
[107] [2013] All ER (D) 100 (Nov).
[108] [2012] All ER (D) 273 (May, 2013).
[109] *Graiseley Properties Ltd v Barclays Bank Plc* (n 107) [19].

case law and undoubtedly is part of a broader legal policy to maintain London's preeminent position in the global capital markets for the issuance and trading of these instruments. It would be in line with this reasoning to suggest that the bank's duty of care would be even further restricted had a case arisen where an investor claimed to suffer loss as a result of the actions of a bank they had no binding contract with.

Generally, the legal principles and doctrines of contract, tort and fiduciary duties that determine the content and scope of the bank's duty of care to its customers and third parties are also applicable to other professional service providers, such as the Lloyd's reinsurance network and auditors.[110] Generally, the English courts recognise the principles established in *Hedley Byrne*[111] and *Caparo Industries*[112] that hold that a claimant does not have a legal claim against a third party (ie professional services provider) with whom the claimant does not have a direct relationship (ie privity of contract), unless there are facts to show that the third party has made some representations to, or established some type of direct relationship with, the claimant in respect of its claim. The three tests for establishing a duty of care[113] articulated by Lord Bingham in *Commissioners of Customs and Excise v Barclays Bank plc*[114] are applicable: (1) assumption of responsibility; (2) a threefold test showing whether the loss to the claimant was a reasonably foreseeable consequence of what the defendant did or failed to do; whether the parties' relationship was sufficiently proximate; and whether it was fair, just and reasonable to impose a duty of care; and (3) the incremental test: that the law should develop novel categories of negligence incrementally and by analogy with established categories.[115]

In *Merrett Syndicates Ltd*,[116] the assumption of liability test was set forth by the House of Lords in a case involving Lloyd's names as plaintiffs who were members of syndicates managed by the defendant underwriting agents. The relationship between names, members' agents and managing agents was regulated by the terms of agency agreements which gave the agent 'absolute discretion' in respect

[110] As stated above, banks are not subject to autonomous duties, but rather duties deriving from contract law, tort law, trust law or fiduciary duties, and public law, especially regulatory law under FSMA. See the discussion of public regulatory law in s II.A that derives from s 138D of the Financial Services and Markets Act 2000 (implementing the relevant provisions of the EU Market in Financial Instruments Directive 2004).

[111] *Hedley Byrne & Co Ltd v Heller & Partners Ltd* (n 73).

[112] *Caparo Industries plc v Dickman* (n 45).

[113] In setting forth these tests, Lord Bingham cited the leading cases: *Hedley Byrne & Co Ltd v Heller & Partners Ltd* (n 73), *Ministry of Housing and Local Government v Sharp* [1970] 2 QB 223, *Smith v Eric S Bush* [1989] 2 All ER 514, *Caparo Industries plc v Dickman* (n 45), *Henderson v Merrett Syndicates Ltd* (n 28); *White v Jones* [1995] 1 All ER 691, [1995] 2 AC 207; *Spring v Guardian Assurance plc* [1994] 3 All ER 129, [1995] 2 AC 296; *Williams v Natural Life Health Foods Ltd* (n 105) and *Phelps v Hillingdon London Borough Council* [2000] 4 All ER 504, [2001] 2 AC 619.

[114] *Commissioners of Customs and Excise v Barclays Bank plc* (n 43).

[115] This third condition is addressed in greater detail in *Sutherland Shire Council v Heyman* (n 44).

[116] *Henderson v Merrett Syndicates Ltd* (n 28).

of underwriting business conducted on behalf of the name but *it was accepted that it was an implied term of the agreements that the agents would exercise due care and skill in the exercise of their functions as managing agents* (italics added). The plaintiffs brought proceedings against the defendants alleging that the defendants had been negligent in the conduct and management of the plaintiffs' syndicates, and wished, for limitation purposes, to establish a duty of care in tort in addition to any contractual duty that might be owed by the defendants.

The High Court addressed the following issues:

1. whether members' agents owed a duty of care to direct names notwithstanding the contractual relationship between the parties;
2. whether managing agents appointed as sub-agents by members' agents owed a duty of care to indirect names;
3. whether members' agents were responsible to names for any failure to exercise reasonable skill and care on the part of managing agents to whom underwriting was delegated by the members' agents; and
4. whether the members' agents were required to exercise skill and care only in relation to those activities and functions which members' agents by custom and practice actually performed for the names personally.

The judge found in favour of the plaintiffs on all the issues. The defendants' appeal to the Court of Appeal was dismissed. A further appeal to the House of Lords was dismissed on the following grounds:

1. Where a person *assumed responsibility* to perform professional or quasi-professional services for another who *relied* on those services, the relationship between the parties was itself sufficient, without more, to give rise to a duty on the part of the person providing the services to exercise reasonable skill and care in doing so. Accordingly, managing agents at Lloyd's owed a duty of care to names who were members of syndicates under the agents' management, since the agents by holding themselves out as possessing a special expertise to advise the names on the suitability of risks to be underwritten and on the circumstances in which, and the extent to which, reinsurance should be taken out and claims should be settled, plainly assumed responsibility towards the names in their syndicates. Moreover, names, as the managing agents well knew, placed *implicit reliance* on that expertise, in that they *gave authority* to the managing agents to bind them to contracts of insurance and reinsurance and to the settlement of claims. The fact that the agency and sub-agency agreements gave the agent 'absolute discretion' in respect of underwriting business conducted on behalf of the names did not have the effect of excluding a duty of care, contractual or otherwise. The discretion given to agents merely defined the scope of the agents' authority, not the standard of skill and care required of agents in carrying on underwriting business on behalf of names.
2. An *assumption of responsibility* by a person rendering professional or quasi-professional services coupled with a *concomitant reliance* by the person

for whom the services were rendered could give rise to a tortious duty of care irrespective of whether there was a contractual relationship between the parties. In consequence, unless the contract between the parties precluded him from doing so, a plaintiff who had available to him concurrent remedies in contract and tort was entitled to choose that remedy which appeared to him to be the most advantageous. In the case of direct names their contract with their members' agents did not operate to exclude a tortious duty, since it was an implied term that the agents would exercise due care and skill in the exercise of their functions as managing agents under the agreement and that duty of care was no different from the duty of care owed by them to the names in tort. Accordingly, it was open to direct names to pursue either remedy against the agents. Likewise, indirect names were not prevented by the chain of contracts contained in the agency and sub-agency agreements from suing managing agents in tort. In particular, the fact that the managing agents had, with the consent of the indirect names, assumed responsibility in respect of the relevant activities to another party, ie the members' agents, under a sub-agency agreement did not prevent the managing agents assuming responsibility in respect of the same activities to the indirect names.[117]

B. The Bank's Liability to Pay Compensation/Damages for Breaching the Duty of Care

This section addresses damages that arise in tort for a bank that breaches its duty of care. These damages would also apply in the case of breaches of the duty to investigate and to warn. The general purpose of damages in tort is to put the claimant in the same position as if the tort had not been committed.[118] In order to award damages in tort, a court will consider the following issue heads.

[117] Clause 2(a) of the agency agreement prescribed by Lloyd's Byelaw No 4 of 1984 contained an express undertaking by the underwriting agent to act as the underwriting agent of the name, whether the agent was acting as a members' agent or was a combined agent acting as managing agent in respect of a syndicate of which the name was a member, the only difference being that in the former case the members' agent carried out the underwriting through the agency of a managing agent under the terms of the prescribed form of sub-agency agreement, whereas in the latter case the agent carried out the underwriting itself. It followed that members' agents were responsible to the names for any failure to exercise reasonable skill and care on the part of managing agents to whom underwriting was delegated by the members' agents.

[118] *Livingstone v Rawyards Coal Co* (1880) 5 App Cas 25 at 39, per Lord Blackburn; *Monarch Steamship Co v Karlshamns Oljefarbriker AB* [1949] AC 196 at 221, [1949] 1 All ER 1 at 12–13, HL, per Lord Wright; *Liesbosch Dredger v SS Edison* [1933] AC 449 at 463, HL, per Lord Wright. Exceptionally there may be liability for loss of expectation: *White v Jones* (n 113); *Ross v Caunters* [1980] Ch 297, [1979] 3 All ER 580.

i. Remoteness

The wrongdoer is only responsible for any type of damage which should have been foreseen by a reasonable person[119] as being something of which there was a real risk,[120] even though the risk would actually occur only in very exceptional circumstances, or in the most unusual case,[121] unless the risk was so small that the reasonable person would feel justified in neglecting it[122] or brushing it aside as far-fetched.[123] The magnitude of the risk, namely the likelihood of the occurrence and the gravity of potential results, must be weighed against the expense of eliminating it.[124] The assessment by the courts of remoteness of damages is demonstrated in some recent cases cited below.

In *Rubenstein v HSBC Bank plc*,[125] the Court observed in the context of a negligent investment advice claim:

> If such an investment goes wrong, there will nearly always be other causes (bad management, bad markets, fraud, political change etc): but it will be an exercise in legal judgment to decide whether some change in markets is so extraneous to the validity of the investment advice as to absolve the adviser for failing to carry out his duty or duties on the basis that the result was not within the scope of those duties.

The Court concluded that the plaintiff's loss was not too remote because:

> what went wrong was the investment itself, and for the very reason that it was structured in a way which exposed Mr Rubenstein to the very risk (of loss to his capital by reason of market movements) which he had wanted to avoid by investing, as he was led to believe he had, in a safe investment equivalent to a cash deposit.[126]

[119] *Overseas Tankship (UK) Ltd v Morts Dock and Engineering Co Ltd, The Wagon Mound* [1961] AC 388, [1961] 1 All ER 404, PC; *Overseas Tankship (UK) Ltd v Miller Steamship Co Pty, The Wagon Mound (No 2)* [1967] 1 AC 617 at 640, [1966] 2 All ER 709 at 716, PC. There is no liability for a foreseeable injury when it is not of a type which the defendant was under a duty to guard against: *Banque Bruxelles Lambert SA v Eagle Star Insurance Co Ltd* [1997] AC 191, sub nom *South Australia Asset Management Corpn v York Montague Ltd* [1996] 3 All ER 365, HL (negligent valuer liable only for difference in values immediately after valuation, not for later losses from general collapse of property market).

[120] *Overseas Tankship (UK) Ltd v Miller Steamship Co Pty, The Wagon Mound (No 2)* [1967] 1 AC 617 at 642, [1966] 2 All ER 709 at 718, PC.

[121] *Koufos v C Czarnikow Ltd* [1969] 1 AC 350 at 385, sub nom *Koufos v C Czarnikow Ltd, The Heron II* [1967] 3 All ER 686 at 692, HL, per Lord Reid (see [851] note 1 ante); *Stewart v West African Terminals Ltd* [1964] 2 Lloyd's Rep 371 at 375, CA, per Lord Denning MR; *Sullivan v South Glamorgan County Council* (1985) 84 LGR 415; *Draper v Hodder* [1972] 2 QB 556, [1972] 2 All ER 210, CA; *The Trecarrell* [1973] 1 Lloyd's Rep 402.

[122] *Koufos v C Czarnikow Ltd* [1969] 1 AC 350 at 385–86, sub nom *Koufos v C Czarnikow Ltd, The Heron II* [1967] 3 All ER 686 at 692, HL, per Lord Reid, and see at 411 and 708, per Lord Hodson.

[123] *Koufos v C Czarnikow Ltd* [1969] 1 AC 350 at 422, sub nom *Koufos v C Czarnikow Ltd, The Heron II* [1967] 3 All ER 686 at 715, HL, per Lord Upjohn; and see *Overseas Tankship (UK) Ltd v Miller Steamship Co Pty, The Wagon Mound (No 2)* [1967] 1 AC 617 at 643, [1966] 2 All ER 709 at 719, PC.

[124] *Overseas Tankship (UK) Ltd v Miller Steamship Co Pty, The Wagon Mound (No 2)* 1 AC 617 at 642, [1966] 2 All ER 709 at 718, PC.

[125] [2013] 1 All ER (Comm) 915 at 945.

[126] ibid, 947.

In *Brown v KMR Services Ltd*,[127] Hobhouse LJ stated:

> If it was the duty of the defendants to protect the plaintiff from losses of the kind which he subsequently suffers, how can it be just or appropriate to say that, because those losses are larger than either party anticipated, the plaintiff must bear those losses not the defendants?

In *Camerata Property Inc v Credit Suisse Securities (Europe) Ltd (No 2)*,[128] Flaux J observed that:

> even if Camerata could establish its general wrong advice case and even if it could show that it would not have invested in the Note had it been given the right advice, the claim for damages would still fail because the actual cause of the loss was issuer default as a consequence of the collapse of Lehman Brothers, which was wholly unexpected and unforeseeable.

ii. Measure of Damages

In the context of negligent advice, damages are to place the claimant in the same position as if the misrepresentation had not been made,[129] under both common law[130] and the Misrepresentation Act 1967 for negligent misrepresentation,[131] but damages under the Act in substitution for rescission for innocent misrepresentation attract the contractual measure, placing the plaintiff in the same position as if the misrepresentation had been true.[132]

The first instance judge in *Rubenstein*[133] set out the measure of damages as the sum that will place the claimant in the position he would have been in if the contract with the bank had not been breached, that is, if the bank had succeeded in recommending the most suitable investment, using that investment as a comparator.

iii. Interest

English courts have discretion to award simple interest on the damages in respect of which judgment is given or payment is made before judgment.[134] Interest is at

[127] [1995] 4 All ER 598 at 643.

[128] [2012] EWHC 7 (Comm) at 68.

[129] *Doyle v Olby (Ironmongers) Ltd* CA; *Downs v Chappell* [1997] 1 WLR 426, CA; *Shelley v Paddock* [1980] 1 QB 348 CA; *Archer v Brown* [1985] QB 401, [1984] 2 All ER 267; *McConnel v Wright* [1903] 1 Ch 546, CA; *Twycross v Grant* (1877) 2 CPD 469, CA.

[130] *Esso Petroleum Co Ltd v Mardon* [1976] QB 801, [1976] 2 All ER 5, CA.

[131] *Royscott Trust Ltd v Rogerson* [1991] 2 QB 297, [1991] 3 All ER 294, CA; *Cemp Properties (UK) Ltd v Dentsply Research and Development Corp* [1991] 2 EGLR 197, CA; *Chesneau v Interhome Ltd* (1983) 134 NLJ 341, CA; *Downs v Chappell* [1996] 3 All ER 344, [1997] 1 WLR 426, CA; *Thomas Witter Ltd v TBP Industries Ltd* [1996] 2 All ER 573.

[132] *William Sindall plc v Cambridgeshire County Council* [1994] 3 All ER 932 at 962, [1994] 1 WLR 1016 at 1045, CA, per Evans LJ discussing the Misrepresentation Act 1967, s 2(2).

[133] *Rubenstein v HSBC Bank Plc* [2011] EWHC 2304 (QB) (02 September 2011), per Judge Havelock-Allan at [124]–[127].

[134] Senior Courts Act 1981, s 35A(1) (s 35A added by the Administration of Justice Act 1982, s 15(1), Sch 1, Pt I); the County Courts Act 1984, s 69(1) (amended by the Civil Procedure Act 1997, s 10, Sch 2, para 2(2)).

such rate as the court thinks fit or as rules of court provide on all or any part of the damages for all or any part of the period between the date when the cause of action arose and the date of the judgment or, in the case of any sum paid before judgment, the date of the payment. According to this principle, pre-judgment interest which, in respect of losses, could run only from the respective date of sale of the financial product to the date the investment was sold or cashed-out.

iv. Proving Loss and Damages

Generally, the calculation of damages for the investor's loss is the difference between the purchase price and the value of the asset left with the investor after cashing-out the investment.[135] There is no deduction for coupon payments that were already received by the investors prior to cashing-out. Measuring the difference between what the claimant paid for the asset it acquired and the benefits left in the claimant's hands (eg income received from the asset during the period the claimant owned it, plus the proceeds from its sale or its value as at the trial date) was considered by an Australian court in *HTW Valuers (Central Qld) Pty Ltd v Astonland Pty Ltd.*[136]

There are no set provisions for courts to calculate damages in cases where several claimants have standing to sue. These cases would either be treated as separate claims against the bank or fall under general UK class action rules[137] (with their own legal regime containing principles like 'first come first served' or pro rata distribution within a certain limit). All claimants would obviously separately have to fulfil the same basic requirements regarding privity of contract, misrepresentation and reliance or negligence and duty of care, as well as suffer actual loss to be able to sue for the bank's avoidable behaviour.

IV. Limiting the Bank's Liability—Contributory Negligence

A. Contributory Negligence

Under English law, a claimant should take reasonable steps to mitigate their loss in tort[138] and the defendant must prove that the plaintiff has acted unreasonably.[139]

[135] See *HTW Valuers (Central Old) Pty Ltd v Astonland Pty Ltd.* (2004) 217 CLR 640, [3463].

[136] ibid, [3373].

[137] Civil Procedure Rules, pt 19.6, www.justice.gov.uk/courts/procedure-rules/civil/rules/part19.

[138] *Admiralty Comrs v SS Chekiang* [1926] AC 637 (HL), per Lord Sumner; *Admiralty Comrs v SS Susquehanna, The Susquehanna* [1926] AC 655 at 663, HL, per Lord Sumner; *The Liverpool (No 2)* ER 465 at 474, [1959] 2 Lloyd's Rep 611 at 624 per Lord Merriman P (revsd on other grounds [1960] 3 All ER 307, CA).

[139] *Roper v Johnson* (1873) LR 8 CP 167; *Garnac Grain Co Inc v HMF Faure & Fairclough Ltd* [1968] AC, [1967] 2 All ER 353, HL; *London and South of England Building Society v Stone* [1983] 3 All ER 105,

Where any person suffers damage as the result partly of his own fault and partly of the fault of any other person, their claim for damages is not defeated but will be reduced to such extent as the court thinks just and equitable having regard to the claimant's share in the responsibility for the damage.[140] The apportionment may be expressed by the court determining the percentage by which the plaintiff contributed to the harm that they suffered and then reducing what would otherwise have been the total of the damages by that percentage. Notwithstanding the above, the trial judge in *Rubenstein v HSBC Bank*[141] held that if he had found in favour of the plaintiff on liability, he would not have reduced damages for contributory negligence because the plaintiff had asked the key question about risk of the product and was advised that the risk of investing in it was the same as a cash deposit and therefore he did not need to enquire further about the product.[142]

B. Apportionment of Liability for Multiple Tortfeasors

The bank's exposure to tort liability can be reduced if there are two or more joint tortfeasors liable for the entire damage resulting from the tort.[143] If each of several persons, not acting jointly, commits a tort against another person substantially contemporaneously and causing the same or indivisible damage, each several tortfeasor is liable for the whole damage.[144] If each of several persons commits an independent tort consecutively against the same person, each is liable for the damage caused by his tortious act, assuming the damage proximately caused by each tort to be distinct.[145] Thus, if the second tortfeasor's act caused no further

[1983] 1 WLR 1242, CA; *Gebruder Metelman GmbH & Co KG v NBR (London) Ltd* [1984] 1 Lloyd's Rep 614 at 631, per Sir John Donaldson MR; *Richardson v Redpath Brown & Co Ltd* [1944] AC 62, [1944] 1 All ER 110, HL.

140 See particularly cases where the client had ignored advice from the finance professional: *Spreadex Ltd v Sekhon* [2008] EWHC 1136 (Ch): the plaintiff was found to be 85 per cent at fault; *Bank Leumi (UK) plc v Wachner* [2011] EWHC 656 (Comm): Flaux J would have been prepared to hold Mrs Wachner 75 per cent responsible for her loss if he had found in her favour on liability.

141 *Rubenstein v HSBC Bank Plc* [2011] EWHC 2304 (QB) (02 September 2011), per Judge Havelock-Allan.

142 Reduction of damages for contributory negligence is also available under the Law Reform (Contributory Negligence) Act 1945.

143 *Ferguson v Earl of Kinnoull* (1842) 9 Cl & Fin 251, HL; *Clark v Newsam* (1847) 1 Exch 131; *London Association for Protection of Trade v Greenlands Ltd* [1916] 2 AC 15 at 31; *Fish & Fish Ltd v Sea Shepherd UK* [2013] EWCA Civ 544, [2013] All ER (D) 191 (May).

144 *Devonshire (Owners) v Barge Leslie (Owners)* [1912] AC 634 at 657, HL; *Bank View Mill Ltd v Nelson Corpn and Fryer & Co (Nelson) Ltd* [1942] 2 All ER 477 at 483 per Stable J (revsd on other grounds [1943] 1 KB 337, [1943] 1 All ER 299, CA); *Dingle v Associated Newspapers Ltd* [1961] 2 QB 162 at 189–190, [1961] 1 All ER 897 at 916, CA, per Devlin LJ; *Rahman v Arearose Ltd* [2001] QB 351 at [17], (2000) 62 BMLR 84 at [17], CA, per Laws LJ.

145 *Dingle v Associated Newspapers Ltd* [1961] 2 QB 162 at 188–89, [1961] 1 All ER 897 at 916, CA, per Devlin LJ; *Holtby v Brigham & Cowan (Hull) Ltd* [2000] 3 All ER 421, [2000] ICR 1086, CA; *Rahman v Arearose Ltd* [2001] QB 351, (2000) 62 BMLR 84, CA.

damage or merely duplicated damage caused by the first tort, the second tortfeasor will not be liable;[146] but, if his act aggravated the damage caused by the first tort, each tortfeasor will be liable only in respect of the part of the damage which his tort caused, assuming that it is possible to separate and quantify the aggravation of damage.[147] Where liability is premised on the material contribution of several tortfeasors to the risk of harm, rather than to the harm itself, their liability is attributed according to their relative degree of contribution to the risk.[148] Any person liable in respect of any damage suffered by another person may recover a contribution from any other person liable in respect of the same damage (whether jointly with him or otherwise).[149]

In proceedings for contribution to damages, the amount of the contribution recoverable from any person is such as may be found by the court to be just and equitable having regard to that person's responsibility for the damage;[150] and the court has power to exempt any person from liability to make contribution, or to direct that the contribution is to amount to a complete indemnity.[151] The court must have regard both to causation and to the relative blameworthiness of the parties.[152] Where the damages assessed have been

[146] *Carslogie Steamship Co Ltd v Royal Norwegian Government* [1952] AC 292 at 303, [1952] 1 All ER 20 at 25, HL (explaining *The Haversham Grange* [1905] P 307, CA); *Performance Cars Ltd v Abraham* [1962] 1 QB 33, [1961] 3 All ER 413, CA; cf *Baker v Willoughby* [1970] AC 467, [1969] 3 All ER 1528, HL (effect of second tort on first tortfeasor's liability).

[147] *Holtby v Brigham & Cowan (Hull) Ltd* [2000] 3 All ER 421, [2000] ICR 1086, CA; *Rahman v Arearose Ltd* [2001] QB 351, (2000) 62 BMLR 84, CA. In the absence of evidence to apportion damage between independent tortfeasors where the damage is not indivisible, the law will, it seems, apportion the damage equally: see *Bank View Mill Ltd v Nelson Corpn and Fryer & Co (Nelson) Ltd* [1942] 2 All ER 477 at 483 per Stable J (revsd on other grounds [1943] KB 337, [1943] 1 All ER 299, CA).

[148] *Barker v Corus UK Ltd* [2006] [2006] UKHL 20, [2006] 2 AC 572, [2006] 3 All ER 785.

[149] Civil Liability (Contribution) Act 1978, ss 1(1) and 7(1); *Adams v Associated Newspapers Ltd* [1999] EMLR 26, CA.

[150] Civil Liability (Contribution) Act 1978 s 2(1).

[151] Civil Liability (Contribution) Act 1978 s 2(2); and *Diboll v City of Newcastle* [1993] PIQR P16, CA; *Adams v Associated Newspapers Ltd* [1999] EMLR 26, CA; *Cressman v Coys of Kensington (McDonald, Pt 20 defendant)* [2004] EWCA Civ 47, [2004] 1 WLR 2775, 148 Sol Jo LB 182; *Dubai Aluminium Co Ltd v Salaam (Livingstone, third parties)* [2002] UKHL 48, [2003] 2 AC 366, [2003] 1 All ER 97; *Niru Battery Manufacturing Co v Milestone Trading Ltd (No 2)* [2004] EWCA Civ 487, [2004] 2 Lloyd's Rep 319, [2004] 2 All ER (Comm) 289 at [50], [73] and [78] per Clarke LJ, and at [81] per Sedley LJ; *Charter plc v City Index Ltd (Gawler, Pt 20 defendants)* [2007] EWCA Civ 1382, [2008] Ch 313, [2008] 3 All ER 126.

[152] *Miraflores (Owners) v George Livanos (Owners)* [1967] 1 AC 826 at 845, sub nom *The Miraflores (Owners) and The Abadesa (Owners)* [1967] 1 All ER 672 at 677, HL, per Lord Pearce; *Brown v Thompson* [1968] 2 All ER 708 at 709, [1968] 1 WLR 1003 at 1008, CA, per Winn LJ; *Baker v Willoughby* [1970] AC 467 at 490, [1969] 3 All ER 1528 at 1530, HL, per Lord Reid; *Madden v Quirk* [1989] 1 WLR 702 at 707, [1989] RTR 304 at 309 per Simon Brown J. In apportioning damages, the court may exceptionally have regard to non-causative aspects of a defendant's conduct if there is a close connection between them and the acts or omissions giving rise to liability: *Re-Source America International Ltd v Platt Site Services Ltd (Barkin Construction Ltd, Pt 20 defendant)* [2004] EWCA Civ 665, (2004) 95 Con LR 1; *Brian Warwicker Partnership v HOK International Ltd (HOK International Ltd, Pt 20 defendant)* [2005] EWCA Civ 962, 103 Con LR 112.

apportioned as between defendants, the costs remain entirely within the court's discretion and need not be apportioned between the defendants in the same proportion as the damages.[153]

V. Conclusion

This chapter's goal was to provide an overview of the legal regime surrounding a bank's duty of care under the law in force in England and Wales. While traditionally courts tended to be more lenient towards banks and require alleged victims to prove the existence and the breach of a duty of care, the atmosphere has recently changed owing to the financial crisis and the European Union's legislative reaction. The banks' obligations are no longer limited to explicit misrepresentations in breach of contract, especially in cases where the bargaining power between the parties is unequal. Moreover, customers are increasingly protected by UK regulatory law, including the Financial Ombudsman system. While there remains no general duty of good faith in contracting under English law, repugnant and dishonest behaviour is frowned upon enough to influence the court's deliberations. The establishment of a bank's duty of care and the measure of damages to its client must still satisfy the requirements of common law of tort, but is now supported by binding regulatory instruments supervised by the UK's Financial Conduct Authority as well as the European Securities and Markets Authority adoption of technical implementing standards under MiFID II. It remains to be seen how Brexit will influence the relationship between the UK and the EU in banking regulation, particularly the extent to which regulatory law will continue to influence the scope and content of a bank's duty of care.

[153] *Moy v Pettman Smith (a firm) (No 2)* [2003] EWCA Civ 467, [2003] PNLR 31 (revsd on other grounds: [2005] UKHL 7, [2005] 1 All ER 903, [2005] 1 WLR 581); *Nationwide Building Society v Dunlop Haywards (DHL) Ltd* [2009] EWHC 254 (Comm), [2009] 2 All ER (Comm) 715, [2009] 1 Lloyd's Rep 447. Cf apportionment of cases between claimant and defendant where there is a successful defence of contributory negligence: *William A Jay & Sons v JS Veevers Ltd* [1946] 1 All ER 646; *Howitt v Alexander & Sons* 1948 SC 154, Ct of Sess; *McCarthy v Raylton Productions Ltd* [1951] WN 376, CA (costs following the event). As to the situation where the claimant counterclaims, see *Smith v WH Smith & Sons Ltd* [1952] 1 All ER 528, CA.

10

Ireland

BLANAID CLARKE

I. Introduction

The basis for liability of a financial institution in the common law resides in contract law, tort law and fiduciary law. A breach of a duty of care in tort or contract may give rise to a claim for damages for the injured party and these duties may co-exist.[1] In determining whether any such duties are owed by a financial institution, general principles of private law are applied.[2] Although the special position occupied by banks in society has been acknowledged by the Irish courts,[3] the standard of care to be applied by a bank is the standard to be applied by any professional service provider. This is in contrast to jurisdictions such as the Netherlands, where a bank's civil liability to clients and to third parties is established on the basis of a 'special duty of care' (*bijzondere zorgplicht*) or a 'bank's duty of care' (*bancaire zorgplicht*). That said, as will be seen, the circumstances in which a financial institution interacts with its clients and the nature of its dealings mean that the general rules may apply to them with a particular effect and the standard of behaviour required will be influenced by the applicable codes of conduct.

In addition to common law duties, a number of statutory duties exist. The Markets in Financial Instruments Directive 2004/39/EC[4] (MiFID) was implemented by the European Communities (Markets in Financial Instruments) Regulations 2007 (MiFID Regulations)[5] and applies to credit institutions providing

[1] *Haughey v J&E Davy t/a Davy & Others* [2014] IEHC 206.

[2] In *Allied Irish Bank v O'Brien & Fingleton* [2015] IEHC 260, the High Court rejected an argument that principles of public law are imported into the private contractual banking and day-to-day relationship between a bank, which was almost wholly state owned, and its customers.

[3] *Director of Corporate Enforcement v D'Arcy* [2006] 2 IR 163.

[4] OJ L 145, 30 April 2004, 1.

[5] SI 60/2007. The MiFID Regulations have been amended by the European Communities (Markets in Financial Instruments) (Amendment) Regulations 2007 (SI 663/2007), the European Communities (Markets in Financial Instruments) (Amendment) Regulations (No 2) 2007 (SI 773/2007) and the European Union (Markets in Financial Instruments) (Amendment) Regulations 2012 (SI 299/2012).

investment services as well as to investment firms. From 3 January 2018, the Markets in Financial Instruments Directive 2014/65/EU[6] (MiFID II) and the Markets in Financial Instruments Regulation (MiFIR)[7] will apply. It is likely that MiFID II will be implemented in Ireland by copying across the EU requirements verbatim as was done in the case of MiFID. Under MiFID II, Member States will be required to apply a harmonised approach to breaches of MiFID II and MiFIR through the imposition of standardised administrative sanctions. The Central Bank of Ireland has also introduced a number of codes including the Consumer Protection Code 2012 which applies to the regulated activities of regulated financial services providers in Ireland. This code requires regulated entities to ensure that in its dealings with customers, it acts honestly, fairly and professionally in the best interests of its customers and the integrity of the market. It contains provisions to ensure that a firm does not recklessly, negligently or deliberately mislead a customer as to the real or perceived advantages or disadvantages of any product or service and that it seeks appropriate information from, and provides appropriate information to, its customers.

Section II of the chapter provides a brief examination of the general rules which apply in tort, contract and equity and outlines the duties which may be imposed on financial institutions as a consequence. Sections III and IV consider the manner in which liability may be reduced where exemption clauses have been incorporated and where the parties have contributed in some way to their own loss. Section V examines the duties imposed pursuant to the MiFID Regulations and the Central Bank codes and considers the potential for civil action where these have been breached. Section VI focuses on the significant new right of action for customers for certain breaches of statutory duties set out in the Central Bank (Supervision and Enforcement) Act 2013. Finally, section VII considers the active role played by the Financial Services Ombudsman in resolving complaints against financial services providers.

II. Private Law Duties of Care

An action may be taken in tort where a party breaches a duty of care which it owes to another party. An action may also lie in tort for fraudulent misrepresentation (deceit), negligent misstatement or innocent misrepresentation. In contract law, an action will lie for breach of a duty expressed in a contract between the parties or for breach of a duty implied into such a contract. The question of whether a duty of care exists is frequently litigated before the Irish courts and in the aftermath of the Irish banking crisis, many of these cases involved the responsibilities

[6] OJ L 173, 12 June 2014, 349.
[7] Regulation (EU) No 600/2014, OJ L 173, 12 June 2014, 84.

of financial institutions. The courts will examine the circumstances of the case to determine whether on the facts before it: a duty of care arises; that duty has been breached and; there has been consequent injury or loss. A duty to exercise reasonable care and skill for anyone providing a service, including giving advice, exists in contract, tort and fiduciary law.

In tort law, an award of damages generally addresses the actual loss sustained as a result of the tort. It seeks thus to restore the injured party to the position he or she would have been in had the tort not occurred. By contrast, in contract law the purpose of damages is to put the injured party in the position he or she would have been in had the contract been performed as agreed. This allows them to recover for expectation loss, reliance loss or consequential loss. Generally, only financial loss will be recoverable for breach of contract.

It is the case of course that cases may settle prior to reaching the courts or prior to the handing down of a judgment. In 2013 for example, a settlement was reported of a number of test cases of fraudulent misrepresentation before the Commercial Court.[8] These cases involved customers of a credit institution who had suffered substantial losses after borrowing to invest in tracker bonds marketed by the institution as 'low risk' at a time it was claimed the institution was aware of concerns expressed by the Financial Regulator, actuaries and within the institution itself about such products.

A. Duty of Care in Tort

The nature of the duty of care was explained by Lord Atkin in the seminal English case of *Donoghue v Stevenson* in the following terms:

> You must take reasonable care to avoid acts or omissions which you can reasonably foresee would be likely to injure your neighbour. Who, then, in law is my neighbour? The answer seems to be—persons who are so closely and directly affected by my act that I ought reasonably to have them in contemplation as being so affected when I am directing my mind to the acts or omissions which are called in question.[9]

This principle was accepted by the Irish courts in *Kirby v Burke & Holloway*.[10]

A major milestone in the evolution of the law of negligence was marked by the English case *Hedley Byrne & Co v Heller Byrne*,[11] which allowed liability for pure economic loss. In that case a bank made representations to the effect that a company was financially sound and the appellant, relying on these representations, invested in the company. When the company failed, the appellant took an action against the bank to recover loss suffered. The House of Lords held that

[8] A O'Loughlin, '500 ACC Bond Cases Settled in one Pen Stroke' *Irish Examiner* (9 November 2012).
[9] [1931] AC 562 at 580.
[10] (1944) IR 207.
[11] *Hedley Byrne & Co Ltd v Heller & Partners Ltd* [1964] AC 465.

independent of any contractual or fiduciary relationship, a negligent, though honest, misrepresentation could give rise to an action for damages for the financial loss it had caused. It stated that the law would imply a duty of care when a party seeks information from a party possessed of a special skill, trusting them to exercise due care and in circumstances where that party knows or ought to know that reliance is being placed on their skill and judgment. This principle was accepted in Ireland in *Securities Trust Ltd v Hugh Moore & Alexander Ltd*,[12] where Davitt P in the High Court defined the context in which liability may arise as follows:

> circumstances may create a relationship between two parties in which, if one seeks information from the other and is given it, that other is under a duty to take reasonable care to ensure that the information given is correct.[13]

In determining liability in negligence, the Irish courts adopt an incremental approach similar to that applied by the Australian[14] and English courts.[15] In *Glencar Explorations PLC v Mayo Co Council*,[16] a case which has been described as 'the foundation stone of modern jurisprudence on the tort of negligence',[17] Keane CJ stated:

> There is, in my view, no reason why courts determining whether a duty of care arises should consider themselves obliged to hold that it does in every case where injury or damage to property was reasonably foreseeable and the notoriously difficult and illusive test of 'proximity' or 'neighbourhood' can be said to have been met, unless very powerful public policy considerations dictate otherwise. It seems to me that no injustice will be done if they are required to take the further step of considering whether, in all the circumstances, it is just and reasonable that the law should impose a duty of a given scope on the defendant for the benefit of the plaintiff.[18]

A court is thus required, before imposing a duty of care in negligence, to satisfy itself also that it would be 'just and reasonable' to do so. It has been observed that this more restrictive approach makes it harder to establish a duty of care particularly in the case of previously unlitigated fact-situations.[19]

One of the policy considerations which the courts have taken into account relates to concommitant contractual authority. In a number of cases for example where actions have been taken against banks, the courts have indicated that

[12] [1964] IR 417.

[13] ibid, 421.

[14] *Sutherland Shire Council v Heyman* (1985) 60 ALR 1.

[15] *Caparo plc v Dickman* [1990] 2 AC 605.

[16] [2002] 1 IR 84. This case represented a move away from an earlier 2-step approach to determining liability based on proximity and public policy and set out in *Ward v McMaster* [1988] IR 337 at 349, following *Anns v Merton London Borough Council* [1978] AC 728.

[17] *Whelan, Lynch & Others v Allied Irish Banks plc, Matheson Ormsby Prentice Solicitors, and LK Shields Solicitors* [2014] IEWC 3 at [64].

[18] This was followed by the Supreme Court in *Whelan, Lynch & Others v Allied Irish Banks plc, Matheson Ormsby Prentice Solicitors, and LK Shields Solicitors*, ibid.

[19] W Binchy, 'Recent Developments in the Law of Torts' (2004) 4 *Judicial Studies Institute Journal* 8, 10.

where the parties have ordered their relationship on the basis of detailed, precise and elaborate contractual provisions, the defendant's obligations in tort cannot be more extensive than what the parties have by contract determined should be the position.[20] This was confirmed recently by the Supreme Court in *McCaughey v Anglo Irish Bank Corporation Limited and Mainland Ventures Corp.*[21]

It will be up to the plaintiff to establish that a duty is owed to him or her by a financial institution on the particular facts of each case. In *Tulsk Co-operative Livestock Mart Ltd v Ulster Bank Ltd*,[22] the High Court considered such a duty was proven in a case where a bank was found to have been overly slow in processing cheques and obtaining payment for its customer. The customer in question operated a cattle market buying and selling a large number of cattle every week and a delay of three weeks to clear a cheque received on a sale was deemed unreasonable. O'Hanlon J noted that:

> The nature of the relationship between the Bank and the Mart, the nature of the business of the Mart and its dependence on the services of the Bank, the nature of the financial commitments and the decisions in relation thereto of the Mart, the nature of the Bank's knowledge of and involvement with the Mart's financial commitments and decisions … imposed on the Bank a duty of care to the Mart beyond that of a simple banker and customer relationship. The fact that there was the contractual relationship between the Mart and the Bank of customer and banker does not limit the duty owed to the Mart by the Bank if there are, as in this case manifestly there were, in the general relationship many other factors from which the law will impute a duty of care to avoid harm on what has come to be called 'the neighbour principle'.

To succeed in an action for negligence, in addition to proving a breach, the plaintiff will have to prove both loss or damage and also a causal link between the breach of the duty of care and the loss or damage suffered. The plaintiff will be required to prove that the financial institution's conduct caused its loss as a matter of fact and a matter of law. The latter involves proving that the court ought to hold the institution responsible for the loss. In *Clancy v Dublin Corporation*,[23] the Supreme Court held that it was not enough to provide evidence from which a judge or jury 'could' infer negligence. Instead, the evidence must be such that the judge or jury 'ought' to infer negligence. The court will consider whether the damage caused was a reasonably foreseeable consequence of the bank's negligence or whether its occurrence was causatively remote. The court will consider whether a 'reasonable man' should have foreseen the loss.

A number of recent cases have considered the relevant statutory limitation periods under the Statute of Limitations 1957 for actions based on breaches of the

[20] *Kennedy v AIB* [1998] 2 IR. Reference was made to the UK Court of Appeal in *National Bank of Greece SA v Pinios Shipping Company (No 3)* [1998] 2 Lloyd's Rep 126.

[21] [2013] IESC 17.

[22] Unreported, High Court (Gannon J), 13 May 1983. See also *Towey v Ulster Bank Ltd* [1987] ILRM 142 and *TE Potterton Ltd v Northern Bank Ltd* [1993] 1 IR 413.

[23] Unreported, Supreme Court, 22 November 1988.

duty of care by financial institutions. In *Gallagher v ACC Bank*,[24] the Supreme Court determined that claimants must institute negligence proceedings in respect of financial loss within six years of the date on which the alleged loss occurred.[25] In that case, the plaintiff sued ACC Bank (ACC) more than six years after he contended he was induced by the negligence of ACC to invest €500,000 in 'Solid World Bond', a financial product marketed and financed by ACC Bank. He claimed that the bond was wholly unsuitable for him or any other investor and it was unlikely from the outset that it would sufficiently outperform the market to offset the cost of the loan transaction. He argued that he would not have entered the transaction but for the alleged negligence and misrepresentations of ACC. The Supreme Court held that the damage was suffered in this case by the very fact of entering into the transaction and purchasing the bond and that the cause of action thus accrued on that date. The action was thus time-barred. However, Fennelly J distinguished this from a case where there is only a 'mere possibility' of loss in a case and the action accrues on the date that loss materialises. In *Komady Limited & Michael O'Reilly v Ulster Bank Ireland Limited*,[26] the High Court dismissed a swaps mis-selling claim against Ulster Bank Ireland Limited (UBIL) on the grounds that it too was time-barred. The Court in this case too held any damage would have been suffered when the plaintiffs entered into the swaps in July 2006. A core component of their claim for breach of duty, breach of contract and negligent mis-statement was that the Central Bank's Code of Conduct for Investment Business[27] applied to the swaps and that UBIL had failed to comply with its obligations under the Code: to act honestly and fairly in the best interests of the plaintiffs; to seek from the customer information regarding their financial situations, investment experience and objectives; and to make adequate disclosure of material information. The plaintiffs also argued that had they been informed about MiFID, and had the bank complied with its obligations under the MiFID Regulations, they would have been put in a position to know that the swaps were not suitable for their stated purposes and financial objectives. Peart J opined:

> Much reliance is placed by the plaintiffs on the existence of the fiduciary relationship between the parties at the time these Swaps were entered into. I can agree that such a relationship could impose a greater obligation of disclosure upon the bank. But in my view, even given that relationship for the purpose of this preliminary issue, that fact remains that everything the plaintiffs needed to know in order to get any advice on these swaps was known to them by the 18th July 2006 … Instead, they did nothing until they ran into financial difficulties in 2012 whereupon a financial review was undertaken … The fiduciary relationship does not add anything to those facts. The coming into force of the MiFID in November 2007 adds nothing of relevance to those facts. It did not suddenly reveal to the plaintiffs some vital fact that was not available to them from July 2006 and which was essential to their knowledge that they had a cause of action.

24 [2012] IESC 35.
25 The parties had agreed that the claim in contract was statute-barred.
26 [2014] IEHC 325.
27 Discussed further in section V.2.

The Consumer Credit Act 1995 and European Communities (Consumer Credit Agreements) Regulations 2010[28] rules apply to almost all credit agreements, hire-purchase agreements and consumer-hire agreements to which a consumer is a party.[29] Donnelly in the *Law of Credit and Security* argues that a duty of care may lie on the part of the lender to take reasonable steps to comply with these Regulations and that any loss to the consumer as a result may be recoverable. In addition, as these regulations fall within the scope of section 44 of the Central Bank (Supervision and Enforcement) Act 2013 discussed below, a private right of action will arise in the case of non-compliance with their various obligations.

B. Misstatements and Misrepresentations

In order to take an action for negligent misstatement, a special relationship must exist between the parties and there must be an assumption of responsibility by the party making the representation or providing the information and that party must possess special knowledge or skill. Finally, there must be some reliance on that representation or information.

The courts have recently addressed the issue of whether a claim could arise when the negligent misrepresentation was not made to the plaintiff directly but to another person. In *Wildgust v Bank of Ireland*,[30] the Supreme Court confirmed that a duty of care to avoid negligent misstatements or to avoid causing pure economic loss will arise if there is a special relationship between the parties. It determined, however, that it is not necessary for a plaintiff to show receipt of and reliance on the representation. Kearns J stated that the proximity test in *Hedley Byrne* went further than just the person to whom the negligent misstatement is addressed and includes

> persons in a limited and identifiable class when the maker of the statement can reasonably expect, in the context of a particular inquiry, that reliance will be placed thereon by such person or persons to act or not to act in a particular manner in relation to that transaction.

The Court held that the person who made the statement would have realised that an incorrect answer would potentially damage the plaintiff and this was deemed sufficient to create a 'special relationship' for the purposes of the law of negligence.

An action may lie in the tort of deceit for a fraudulent misrepresentation. This requires proof that the false representation has been made knowingly, or without belief in its truth, or recklessly, without caring whether it is true or

[28] SI 281/2010. These Regulations implement the Consumer Credit Directive 2008/48/EC.

[29] In addition, the European Union (Consumer Mortgage Credit Agreements) Regulations 2016 introduced new rules for mortgage credit and property-related loans in 2016.

[30] [2006] 2 ILRM 28. See also *White v Jones* [1995] 2 AC 207.

false and intending it to be relied on by the recipient, and the recipient acts to his or her detriment in reliance on it.[31] In *Stafford v Keane Mahony Smith*,[32] Doyle J explained that liability for fraudulent misrepresentation would arise where a representation is made to 'a person to whom that information is intended to be conveyed or to whom it might reasonably be expected that the information would be conveyed' where that person acts upon the representation to his detriment. Shanley J in *Forshall v Walsh and Bank of Ireland*[33] emphasised that 'Where fraudulent misrepresentation is alleged it must be established that the representation … was intended to and did induce the agreement in respect of which the claim for damages arises'.[34] A difficulty in basing an action in deceit is the need to prove that the defendant knew that statements prepared by it were false or was reckless as to their veracity. In contrast however to negligent misstatement, there is no need to show a special relationship between the parties. It is also unnecessary to prove that the damage was reasonably foreseeable. It is sufficient to prove that it was a direct consequence of the misrepresentation. In *Beausang v Irish Life and Permanent Plc*,[35] Hogan J noted that it was 'striking that there is little contemporary case-law on the extent to which (if at all) silence on the part of a person who is not a fiduciary can amount to deceit'. In that case too, the High Court refused to rule out the possibility that a credit institution could be made liable for the tortious conduct of its employees. The determining factor would be whether there is any close connection between the role of the employees and the alleged torts.

In *McCaughey v Anglo Irish Bank Corporation Limited and Mainland Ventures Corp*,[36] the plaintiff, a client of a bank's private banking operation, invested in a property fund operated by the bank's US subsidiary. Part of the investment was met by a loan the plaintiff received from the bank. The fund intended to acquire and renovate two hotels and they furnished investors with a brochure describing the investment. This brochure stated that the investment was 'high risk'. The investors were not told however that the bank itself was contractually bound to acquire the hotels if it could not find third party investors. The plaintiff initiated the action as a test case when the fund subsequently failed. He claimed fraudulent misrepresentation, fraudulent concealment, misrepresentation, negligent misstatement, breach of fiduciary duty, intentional interference with the plaintiff's economic interest, unjust enrichment and conspiracy. He alleged that the renovation budgets investors were given were false and unrealistic and that the bank had not

[31] *Fenton v Schofield* (1966) 100 ILTR 69.
[32] [1980] ILRM 53.
[33] Unreported, High Court (Shanley J), 18 June 1997.
[34] ibid, 64.
[35] [2014] IEHC 1.
[36] 2011 IEHC 546. The Supreme Court ([2013] IESC 17) found no evidence to disturb the findings of the High Court.

disclosed information in relation to zoning and sitting tenants. Birmingham J in the High Court stated that in order to prove fraud:

> a simple lack of care will not of itself suffice. The threshold that the plaintiff has to cross is knowledge of or belief in the falsity of the representation or recklessness as to its truth, that is to say not caring whether the representation is true or false … However, in some circumstances evidence of a lack of care may go some distance to providing evidence that a defendant in truth, lacked belief in the truth of what he was saying or did not care whether what he was saying was true.

An interesting observation was also made in relation to the reliance which might be placed on statements or representations by a bank. Birmingham J noted:

> the days when a bank manager was seen as occupying a highly respected position in the local community, a pillar of the local establishment seen as an independent and disinterested advisor, or a confessor type figure are long gone, if indeed that ever represented the reality. Much of the activity of a bank involves selling products or services and those to whom products or services are offered will be wise to realise that few salesmen undersell their wares.

The High Court determined that the plaintiff had failed to establish the evidence and entitlement to succeed on any of the fraud or non-fraud elements of the claim.

Finally, to the extent that an agreement between the bank and its customer is a contract for the supply of services pursuant to the Sale of Goods and Supply of Services Act 1980, an innocent misrepresentation may lead to an action under section 45(1) of that Act where a person enters into the contract after an actionable misrepresentation. However, in practice, the courts are more likely to characterise a pre-contractual statement as a term rather than a mere representation.[37]

C. Duty of Care in Contract

Where parties are in a contractual relationship, one party will be liable for breach of contract in the event of non compliance with the terms of the contract. Contracts may be in writing or oral and their terms may be gleaned on the basis of more than one document or exchange. While it may be unusual to find an express duty of care in a contract between a financial institution and its client, such a term may be implied at common law.

Terms will be implied in order to give effect to the intentions of the parties.[38] Clark has noted that 'if the courts start from the premise that the parties are reasonable persons who wish to act reasonably and facilitate the commercial interests

[37] *Bank of Ireland v Smith* [1966] IR 646. See generally R Clark, *Contract Law in Ireland* (Dublin: Roundhall, 2016) 412–15.

[38] *Butler v McAlpine* [1904] 2 IR 445.

of the other party, a considerable amount can be inserted into the agreement by way of implied terms'.[39] There are two formulations of a test which will determine whether this is the case. The first is the 'officious bystander test' which allows a term to be implied if it is so obvious that it goes without saying that the parties would have intended to include it.[40] The second formulation is the 'business efficacy test' which allows a term to be implied if the court considers it necessary to give business efficacy to the contract to prevent such a failure of consideration as cannot have been within the contemplation of either of the parties.[41] Neither test is easy to overcome however, particularly in the context of a commercial transaction. The courts will not impose a duty of care on a financial institution merely because such a term would have been beneficial to a customer or because the failure to include it has detrimental consequences for them. In *Tradax (Ireland) Ltd v Irish Grain Board Ltd*,[42] O'Higgins CJ said a term could be implied if necessary to 'repair an intrinsic failure of expression' but he emphasised that:

> The courts have no role in acting as contract makers, or as counsellors, to advise or direct which agreement ought to have been made by two people, whether businessmen or not, who chose to enter into contractual relations with each other.[43]

In *Zurich Bank v McConnon*,[44] discussed further below, the officious bystander test was applied by the High Court in finding that a term was not implied into a contract between a bank and a borrower that the bank would comply with the Consumer Protection Code. The borrower contended that the terms of the Code formed an implied term of the contract between the parties, a breach of which created rights for the defendant. The Court stated that the only implied term that would assist the defendant would be a term that the bank was obliged to comply in all respects with the Code and that the consequence of non-compliance was that the borrower was exempted from the liability to repay the loan:

> If one introduces the traditional officious bystander into the equation then it would be seen that such a suggestion has little reality. The notion that a bystander asking whether such a term formed part of the agreement would be hushed by the parties jointly and impatiently snapping 'of course' seems more than improbable. In summary I can see no basis for suggesting that any alleged breach of the Code exempts the borrower from repaying his loan.[45]

[39] Clark, *Contract Law in Ireland* (n 38) 202.

[40] *Shirlaw v Southern Foundries* [1939] 2 KB 206.

[41] *The Moorcock* (1889) 14 PD 64.

[42] [1984] IR 1.

[43] This case was confirmed in *Irish Bank Resolution Corporation Ltd v Morrissey* [2013] IEHC 208, referred to below, where an argument as to the existence of an implied term in a particular contract between a bank and borrower was rejected.

[44] [2011] IEHC 75. See also *Friends First Finance v Cronin* [2013] IEHC 5.

[45] This extract from the judgment was cited with approval by Baker J in *Allied Irish Bank v O'Brien & Fingleton* [2015] IEHC 260. A similar conclusion was reached by the Supreme Court in *Irish Life and Permanent plc v Dunne and Irish Life and Permanent plc v Dunphy* [2015] IESC 46 in relation to the terms of the Code of Conduct on Mortgage Arrears.

Terms may be implied at law where the courts feel it necessary to do so. The cases in which this has been done involved incidents of well recognised legal relationships involving definable categories of contracts.[46] These include contracts between housing authorities and tenants where terms are implied that the houses are fit for human habitation[47] and contracts between employer and employee where a duty is implied to provide a safe work environment.[48] In *Royal Trust Company of Canada (Ireland) Ltd v Kelley*,[49] the issue arose in connection with a financial institution which provided mortgage finance to employees at preferential rates. An express term in the mortgage contract obliged the employee to repay the loan on cessation of employment and in the case at hand the institution terminated all its employees' contracts as it was closing its Irish operation. Its former staff claimed that the mortgage contract was subject to an implied term that cessation of employment should not be the result of the institution's voluntary act and a further implied term that the institution would not do anything to prevent the loan from being fully redeemed and its closure of operations in Ireland breached that term. While the High Court rejected this argument on the basis that the contract of employment itself was terminable at will, Clark has argued that Barron J in the case was moving towards the view that the lender was bound not to act capriciously in the contract in question.[50]

In order to succeed in an action for breach of contractual duty, the plaintiff will have to prove that the loss

> may fairly and reasonably be considered either arising naturally, i.e. according to the usual course of things, from such breach of contract or such as may reasonably be supposed to have been in the contemplation of both parties, at the time they made the contract, as the probable result of the breach of it.[51]

The plaintiff will need to prove that the loss was foreseeable by the financial institution either because the loss is the result of the ordinary course of events or alternatively, when there are special circumstances of which the manager had actual knowledge.[52] In *Valse Holdings SA v Merrill Lynch International Bank Ltd*,[53] Morison J stated that it was not the client's lack of understanding about the objectives of the portfolio that was of importance but rather his 'failure to take advice when it was given and a determination to pursue a course of action which he believed was in the best interests of the portfolio'. He thus concluded that even had there been a breach of duty, it was not causative of any loss as the portfolio was in the shape that the client had wanted and he was a knowing and informed investor.

[46] *Sweeney v Duggan* [1997] 2 ILRM 211.
[47] *Siney v Dublin Corporation* [1980] IR 400.
[48] *McCann v Brinks Allied Ltd* [1997] 1 ILRM 461.
[49] Unreported, High Court, 27 February 1989.
[50] Clark (n 38) 218.
[51] Per Alderson B in *Hadley v Baxendale* (1854) 9 EX 341 at 354–55, applied in *Ireland in Lennon v Talbot Ireland Ltd*, unreported, High Court, 20 December 1985.
[52] *Victoria Laundry (Windsor) Ltd v Newman Industries Ltd* [1949] 2 KB 528.
[53] [2004] EWHC 2471 (Comm).

Finally it should be noted that the normal vitiating factors in contract law—undue influence, duress and unconscionability—may also arise in the contract between a financial institution and its customer. A number of cases taken by banks against borrowers to enforce loan agreements have involved claims that the contract should be voided on these grounds. For example in *Ulster Bank Ireland Limited v Roche & Buttimer*,[54] the High Court considered whether a bank should have responsibility for advising a guarantor of her partner's company of the consequences of a guarantee. It referred to the seminal English case of *Royal Bank of Scotland v Etridge (No 2)*,[55] which established that whenever a wife offered to act as guarantor for the indebtedness of her husband or his business, the bank was put on inquiry and was obliged to take reasonable steps to satisfy itself that she had understood and freely entered into the transaction. Clarke J determined

> that the general principle, which underlies *Etridge*, is to the effect that a bank is placed on inquiry where it is aware of facts which suggest, or ought to suggest, that there may be a non-commercial element to a guarantee.

The Court held that the bank was aware of the personal relationship between the surety and the owner of the company and that the former had no direct interest in the company and it was obliged to take 'at least some measures to seek to ensure that the proposed surety [was] openly and freely agreeing to provide the requested security'. As it had not done so, the surety was entitled to rely on the undue influence which her partner exercised over her.

D. Fiduciary Relationship

A fiduciary relationship exists where a person has been entrusted with powers which he or she must exercise for the benefit of others. In such cases, fiduciary duties arise and are enforceable. Fiduciary relationships have been held to exist between a trustee and beneficiary, a lawyer and client and an agent and principal. The Irish courts have also accepted that the categories of fiduciary relationships are not closed and the existence or not of a fiduciary relationship is primarily a question of fact to be determined by examining the specific facts and circumstances. The courts have cited with approval[56] the following extract from the judgment of Millett LJ in *Bristol and West Building Society v Mothew* as representing the law in this area:[57]

> A fiduciary is someone who has undertaken to act for or on behalf of another in a particular matter in circumstances which give rise to a relationship of trust and confidence.

[54] [2012] IEHC 166. See also *ACC Bank Plc v Connolly & anor* [2015] IEHC 188.

[55] [2002] 2 AC 773.

[56] *Clements and others v Meagher and others*, unreported, 25 July 2008; *Irish Bank Resolution Corporation Ltd v Morrissey* (n 43).

[57] [1998] Ch 1 at 18.

> The distinguishing obligation of a fiduciary is the obligation of loyalty. The principal is entitled to the single-minded loyalty of his fiduciary. This core liability has several facets. A fiduciary must act in good faith; he must not make a profit out of his trust; he must not place himself in a position where his duty and his interest may conflict; he may not act for his own benefit or the benefit of a third person without the informed consent of his principal. This is not intended to be an exhaustive list, but it is sufficient to indicate the nature of fiduciary obligations. They are the defining characteristics of the fiduciary. As Dr. Finn pointed out in his classic work *Fiduciary Obligations* (1977), p. 2, he is not subject to fiduciary obligations because he is a fiduciary; it is because he is subject to them that he is a fiduciary.

While a financial institution will not normally have a fiduciary relationship with a customer, such a relationship may be created depending upon the role of the institution. For example, an asset manager authorised to enter into portfolio transactions with third parties which bind the client will be a contractual agent of the client principal and thus in a fiduciary relationship with the client. Cranston has observed that there are two circumstances in which common law courts have imposed fiduciary duties on banks outside trust and agency. The first arises when a bank has assumed the role of financial adviser as promoter of a particular scheme particularly where it has a financial interest in the investment. The second arises where a bank has led a customer to believe that it will act in that customer's interests in advising it on an investment but the bank is also acting for another party and promoting their interests to the detriment of the customer's interests.[58] He states clearly however that:

> A fiduciary relationship cannot exist if a bank has no reason to believe that the customer is placing trust and confidence in it and relying on it to put the customer's interests above all else. Only in very special circumstances will this occur in the banking context.[59]

In *Irish Life and Permanent plc v Financial Services Ombudsman*,[60] the High Court considered the duties of a bank towards customers who sought advice in relation to a mortgage product. The customers argued that they were poorly advised in switching out of beneficial tracker mortgages. Hogan J opined that:

> There is no doubt that the lender/borrower relationship does not generally impose fiduciary duties on the lender. The whole object of a fiduciary is based upon a recognition that certain categories of persons owe duties to others over and above conventional contractual obligations by virtue of the special nature of their profession, occupation or position, so that … such persons 'are obliged to act in a completely selfless manner': see Delany, *Equity and the Law of Trusts in Ireland* (4th.ed,) (at 213). Trustees, agents, directors and partners are among those normally regarded as fiduciaries. … While the categories of fiduciaries are never closed, there is, I think, a reluctance to extend their boundaries beyond the traditional categories because to do so would effectively impose

[58] R Cranston, *Principles of Banking Law* (Oxford: Oxford University Press, 2002) 190–91.
[59] ibid, 191.
[60] [2012] IEHC 367.

super-added duties of utmost good faith and complete disclosure to persons who never contracted to do so and thus potentially frustrate the ordinary workings of the commercial world.

Hogan J determined that save in the special case where the mortgagee enters into possession of mortgaged property, the mortgagor/mortgagee relationship is not a fiduciary one[61] and there is no general duty on a bank to insist that customers take independent advice in relation to bank dealings.[62] However, he then went on to say that:

> The banking system is, by its nature, a highly regulated one which, is- or, at least, ought to be- based on trust[63] ... The laissez-faire rules which might apply in the case of the borrowing and lending on the international capital markets cannot be applied in exactly the same way in the case of the domestic mortgage market, given that these are matters which gravely affect the long term welfare of most members of the general public.

Referring to *Hedley Byrne*, Hogan J noted that a bank can assume a liability for advice gratuitously given and that the bank with its reference to mortgage advisers and a mortgage advice centre appears to have created 'something of a similar aura and expectation on behalf of customers'. In these circumstances, the Court found that it was reasonable to conclude that the borrowers had contacted the bank for advice as well as for information in relation to their mortgage products and that the bank's response should be judged against that background.

In *Irish Bank Resolution Corporation Ltd v Morrissey*,[64] the High Court acknowledged that it was accepted by both parties that their relationship did not fall within one of the settled categories of fiduciary relationships simply by reason of the existence of a loan arrangement and it set about determining whether a relationship arose upon the particular facts of the case. The plaintiff bank sought to make demands under a loan facility and the borrower argued that his dealings with the bank over a period gave rise to such a relationship. The Court was unable to find that the relationship went beyond that of a contractual relationship. The plaintiff submitted that the existence of a commercial relationship governed by a contract between parties of equal status has been held to be a strong indicator that a fiduciary relationship does not subsist. Counsel referred to the case of *Hospital Products Ltd v United States Surgical Corp*,[65] where Gibbs CJ in the High Court of Australia stated:

> the fact that the arrangement between the parties was of a purely commercial kind and that they had dealt at arm's length and on an equal footing has consistently been regarded by this Court as important, if not decisive, in indicating that no fiduciary duty arose.

[61] Citing *Irish Life and Permanent plc v Financial Services Ombudsman* [2011] IEHC 439.

[62] Citing *Bank of Ireland v Smyth* [1996] I ILRM 241 at 249 and J Breslin, *Banking Law*, 2nd edn (Dublin: Thomson Round Hall, 2007) 125.

[63] Citing Kelly J in *Director of Corporate Enforcement v D'Arcy* [2006] 2 IR 163.

[64] [2013] IEHC 208. See also *Beausang v Irish Life and Permanent Plc* [2014] IEHC 1 on this point.

[65] (1984) 156 CLR 41.

Finlay Geoghegan J found that the evidence indicated that no advice had been sought or offered by the bank and no other steps had been undertaken which took the relationship outside of the normal commercial relationship of a lending bank and borrowing by an experienced entrepreneur or business person. She noted:

> the reason for which each was keen to do such business was that each perceived it to be in their respective commercial interests to do business with the other.

Not every duty that a fiduciary owes will constitute a fiduciary duty.[66] In *Girardet v Crease & Co*,[67] it was determined that simple carelessness in giving advice would not constitute a breach of a fiduciary duty. Breslin has observed that in Irish law the distinction between breach of fiduciary duty and negligence can be blurred.[68] In *Henderson v Merritt Syndicates Ltd*,[69] Browne-Wilkinson L referred to the same problem. He opined that the liability of a fiduciary for the negligent transaction of his duties is not a separate head of liability but 'the paradigm of the general duty to act with care imposed by law on those who take it upon themselves to act for or advise others'. Such a duty, he explained, arises from the circumstances in which the fiduciary is acting, ie their assumption of responsibility and not from their status or description. Thus, the nature of the transaction is crucial in determining the nature and scope of fiduciary obligations.

A breach of fiduciary duty may give rise to an action for damages, an action for an account of profits made from the breach, an application seeking the imposition of a constructive trust over property acquired by the fiduciary in breach of his duties or more generally an action for unjust enrichment.[70] Proof of damage has never been considered to be an essential requirement for such an action for breach of fiduciary duty.[71] However, when suing to recover for loss suffered as a result of a breach of a fiduciary duty, a causal connection will also be required between the breach of duty and the loss.

E. Common Law Duty to Advise or to Warn

As the previous cases suggest, while a financial institution does not ordinarily owe a duty to advise or to explain documentation, such a duty may arise depending on the facts of the case. It should also be noted at the outset that these duties may arise in the context of customers and third parties. Third parties may sue institutions for negligent advice, or less commonly fraudulent advice.

[66] *Bristol and West Building Society v Mothew* [1998] Ch 1.
[67] (1987) 11 BCLR (2d) 361 at 362, cited in *Bristol and West Building Society v Mothew* (n 66).
[68] J Breslin, 'Banks as Fiduciaries' (1998) 5(2) *Commercial Law Practitioner* 47; *O'Brien v Mitchelstown Loan Fund Society* [1903] 1 IR 282.
[69] [1995] 2 AC 145, expressly referred to by the Supreme Court in *Kennedy v AIB plc* (n 20).
[70] Breslin 'Banks as Fiduciaries' (n 68).
[71] *Fyffes Plc v DCC Plc, S & L Investments Limited, James Flavin, Lotus Green Limited* [2005] IEHC 477.

In successful actions for negligent misstatement, the court may find a financial institution liable not for what it said but rather what it failed to state. As Hardiman J opined in the Supreme Court in *McCaughey v Anglo Irish Bank Corporation Limited and Mainland Ventures Corp*,[72] 'it is obvious that to suppress a material fact may give a false impression even though no positive falsehood is spoken or written'. In such a case, the institution must reveal the complete story. A duty of disclosure may also arise where the relationship between the parties is fiduciary in character and the institution wishes to avoid liability for putting its own interests above its duty to its customer.

In addition, if a financial institution offers advice to an individual, it may assume additional duties which may render it liable in the event that the advice is deficient. In *ACC Bank plc v Deacon & anor*,[73] Ryan J quoted with approval the following extract from the *Encyclopaedia of Banking Law* (2013):

> Where a bank assumes the role of financial adviser to its customer, it owes the customer a duty to exercise reasonable care and skill in the execution of that role. However, a bank does not usually assume the role of financial adviser to a customer who merely approaches it for a loan or for some other form of financial accommodation. As Scott LJ said in *Lloyd's Bank plc v Cobb* (18th December 1991):
>
> '… the ordinary relationship of banker and customer does not place on the bank any contractual or tortious duty to advise the customer in the wisdom of commercial projects for the purpose of which the bank is asked to lend money. If the bank is to be placed under such a duty, there must be a request from the customer, accepted by the bank, or some other arrangement between the customer and the bank, under which the advice is to be given'.

In determining whether this is the case, the court will examine all the circumstances, including the bank's communications and promotional material as this may lead it to the conclusion that it has taken on the responsibility of a financial adviser. In *Towey v Ulster Bank Ltd*,[74] the plaintiff initiated an action against a bank of which he was a customer for breach of contract and negligence. He complained that he had sought advice from the bank as to the credit-worthiness of an individual who was paying him by cheque and that the bank failed to advise him of any risk despite being aware of evidence suggesting caution. The High Court accepted that in the circumstances the bank's obligations extended beyond the conventional duty of a collecting banker and that in failing to advise him in a careful manner and in failing in its capacity as collecting banker to take the steps necessary to protect the interest of its customer, the defendant was in breach of the duty it owed to the plaintiff. In *Tulsk Co-Operative Livestock Mart Ltd v Ulster Bank Ltd*,[75] referred to above, the bank was held liable in negligence where it gave advice

[72] [2011] IEHC 546 and [2013] IESC 17.

[73] [2013] IEHC 427.

[74] [1987] ILRM 142. See also *T.E. Potterton Ltd v Northern Bank Ltd* [1993] 1 IR 413 and *David Walsh v Jones Lang Lasalle Ltd* [2007] IEHC 28.

[75] Unreported, High Court (Gannon J), 13 May 1983.

to the plaintiff, a customer, on the credit-worthiness of another customer without warning it about his financial precariousness. It was aware that the plaintiff was relying upon this information in making its business decision and very dependent upon the information being true.[76]

Where the recipients of the information are not sophisticated or are clearly missing important information, there may be a greater responsibility on the bank to give advice. In *Bank of Ireland v Lennon*,[77] the High Court held that in order for a duty of care to arise in tort, it would have to be proven that: the bank had chosen to offer an explanation of the security documents in question to the customer; that the bank was so acting having regard to the interests of the customer rather than exclusively to its own interests; that the customer did not know, nor could it have known, from his or her own knowledge and experience the nature and consequences of the transaction; and finally, and in the alternative, it must be established whether the customer requested any information and whether any information so given was given in a negligent manner. The Court held on the facts that the plaintiff had failed to establish, on the balance of probabilities, that the bank had breached a duty of care in tort to explain the nature of the security. The Court found instead that the customer had chosen to keep information about his real intentions as to the security from the bank. In *Allied Irish Banks Plc v Pierse & Anor*,[78] the High Court rejected an argument that a bank owed a duty to provide advice in relation to a client's agreement to purchase the foreign properties financed by way of a loan facility that they were seeking or in respect of a concluded land sale agreement with one of the bank's other customers, a developer. Keane J did not express a view on what he described as the 'novel argument' that the bank was under a duty to decline a customer's application for finance in respect of any transaction in which another customer is involved if there is any basis for any concern on the part of that bank regarding the financial position of that other customer. He explained that even if it were accepted as a correct statement of the law, there was no evidence before him that the bank knew or ought to have known about the developer's financial position.[79]

In *Whelan, Lynch & Others v Allied Irish Banks plc, Matheson Ormsby Prentice Solicitors, and LK Shields Solicitors*,[80] an allegation of negligence was made against a firm of solicitors advising a client as to the nature of a facility agreement it was completing with its bank. The trial judge had concluded that the firm did not owe

[76] See however *Gayson v AIB*, unreported, High Court (Geoghegan J), 28 January 2000.

[77] Unreported, High Court (Lavan J), 17 February 1998.

[78] [2015] IEHC 136.

[79] The Court also found that in seeking and obtaining loan finance to acquire jointly with her husband two apartment blocks in Corsica, the second named defendant was not concluding that contract for the purpose of satisfying her individual needs in terms of private consumption. The couple were found to be acquiring the properties for profit and engaging in business and thus outside the definition of 'consumer' in the Consumer Credit Act 1995.

[80] [2014] IESC 3.

a duty of care to its client because the imposition of such a duty would not be just and reasonable. This finding was rejected by the Supreme Court which noted that it was well established that it is just and reasonable that a professional adviser should owe a duty of care in such circumstances.[81] O'Donnell J explained thus:

> the law has consistently and correctly held that an advisor such as a solicitor will owe a duty of care when giving advice to a client on an area within his or her expertise and where the request for the advice, and provision of it, is neither in casual circumstances nor entirely separate from the business then being transacted. It is not necessary that a client make very clear that the advice is critical to any decision which he or she might make, or that it be the sole or decisive factor. The obligation of a professional person is to give advice some of which may be unwelcome. Clients may be slow to appreciate advice, which they are paying for, but which warns them against a course of action which they wish to follow. The practice of law and other professions have developed considerably, and in many cases for the better, but there can be strong pressures on lawyers and other advisors to take a 'commercial' view of matters, and to bring only the good news to a client. It remains very important that advisors give independent advice which, in an appropriate case, may counsel caution.[82]

The Court found that certain of the factors considered by the trial judge such as the solicitors' limited retainer, their late involvement in the transaction and the failure of the plaintiff to give any indication of the significance they subsequently claimed to have attached to the question of the recourse of the loans might be more relevant to the question of reliance, causation and contributory negligence than to the legal issue of the duty of care.

F. Reckless Lending as a Separate Tort

An attempt was made in the Irish courts to establish a new tort which would apply to credit institutions which would have the effect of imposing a special duty of care on them in relation to their lending.

In *ICS Building v Grant*,[83] a borrower sought to resist a repossession order arguing that the lender had engaged in reckless lending. He questioned his duty to repay his loan when the banks were being bailed out by the Irish taxpayer. Charleton J noted the reluctance of the courts to interfere with a contract freely entered into and unaffected by duress or undue influence, neither of which was raised in this case. He then stated that:

> the argued for tort of reckless lending does not exist in law as a civil wrong. It is not within the competence of the court to invent such a tort.

[81] He referred to Lord Browne-Wilkinson's observation in *Barrett v Enfield London Borough Council* [2001] 2 AC 550 at 559–60.

[82] *Whelan, Lynch & Others v Allied Irish Banks plc, Matheson Ormsby Prentice Solicitors, and LK Shields Solicitors* [2014] IEWC 3 at [67].

[83] [2010] IEHC 17.

It was acknowledged that it would be open to the legislature to introduce such a civil wrong in statute but he opined that:

> Defining that civil wrong would tend to remove the presumption of arm's length dealing as between borrower and bank and replace it with a new relationship based on a duty of nurture that other common law countries do not see it as their duty to put into the marketplace as any argued-for law as to reckless lending does not appear in the works on tort that I have consulted from other common law jurisdictions.

These views were reiterated in *McConnon v President of Ireland*[84] and *Healy v Stepstone Mortgage Funding Ltd*.[85] In the latter case, a borrower claimed that his mortgage contract was flawed and he sought damages for 'reckless lending procedures' by a lender. The High Court granted an order striking out the claim having confirmed that 'it is absolutely clear that there is no such common law tort of reckless lending'. Hogan J added that:

> there is no known example in the common law of a claim of this kind being judicially recognised as an established tort. Nor could a claim of this kind be said properly to represent an incremental development of the existing common law by the application of established (or even developing) principles to new sets of facts and circumstances.

A related claim which has been considered by the Irish courts in the wake of the Global Financial Crisis is that the money lent to a borrower was 'created … out of thin air on a computer keyboard'. In *McCarthy and Others v Bank of Scotland PLC and Others*.[86] Hogan J noted that the rejection of this theory as 'fanciful' and 'completely devoid of merit' by the courts in British Columbia[87] has not deterred other litigants in this jurisdiction advancing similar arguments and that they were 'equally lacking in merit and which, indeed, lack any relationship to contractual or other legal realities'. Such claims would be likely to be struck out by a court as frivolous.

III. Exemption or Limitation Clauses

A bank may attempt to limit the scope of its common law duties by means of an exemption or limitation clause incorporated in a contract between the parties. Such a clause may be incorporated into a written contract which has been signed by the customer even if the customer has not noticed or read that clause.[88] It may also be incorporated by means of reasonable notice or by a course of dealing.

[84] [2012] IR 449.
[85] [2014] IEHC 134.
[86] [2014] IEHC 340. See also *Freeman and Another v Bank of Scotland Ireland Limited and Others* [2013] IEHC 371; *Kearney v KBC Bank Ireland PLC and Others* [2014] IEHC 260; and *Harrold v Nua Mortgages Limited* [2015] IEHC 15.
[87] *Dempsey v Enviston Credit Union* [2006] BCSC 750. See also *Meads v Meads* [2012] ABQB 571.
[88] *L'Estrange v Graucob* [1934] 2 KB 394.

In *ACC Bank plc v Kelly & Anor*,[89] the defendants argued inter alia that they were unaware that their loan was a demand facility. Clarke J commented:

> By signing a commercial banking arrangement, a borrower agrees to be bound by the terms of that arrangement and if the borrower has not taken the trouble to adequately read the document or be adequately informed as to its meaning then the borrower must accept the consequences of having signed a commercially binding agreement in those circumstances. After all, those are the terms on which the borrower gets the money. The borrower has taken the money. The borrower cannot then turn around and say that the terms were not properly understood unless the relevant financial institution has been guilty of legal wrongdoing in the way in which the contract came to be signed such as by misrepresenting its contents or the like.[90]

It is accepted that a signature will not evidence assent to the contract, including the exemption clauses, if the signature is proven to have been obtained by fraud or misrepresentation.[91] In *AGM Londis Plc v Gorman's Supermarket Ltd*,[92] Barrett J seemed to go a step further in his statement that a 'less than rigorous application of the "signature rule"' might be merited where 'a significant degree of uncertainty has arisen in the dealings between parties and that uncertainty is accentuated by the actions of a stronger party'. The distinguishing feature in such a case would appear to be that the stronger party admits that the understanding of 'a significantly weaker party' was complicated by its own actions.

The High Court in *AIB plc v Galvin Developments*[93] held that the incorporation of the bank's general terms and conditions was done by means of the well-established principle of contract law that terms may be incorporated into a contract by express reference. There was an express reference to the general terms and conditions in the letter of loan sanction and the Court determined that the failure to enclose a copy of the conditions did not preclude their incorporation by express reference. This was followed recently in *Allied Irish Bank v O'Brien & Fingleton*,[94] where the High Court rejected an argument that the absence of the general conditions had the effect that there was no consensus *ad idem* between the Bank and the second defendant, such that the second defendant was not contractually bound, and that there was no contract or that no terms and conditions of lending were agreed.

To be effective, the clause must be clear and unambiguous and cover the event that has occurred. In cases of ambiguity, a contractual clause will be interpreted in favour of the party who did not draft the contract, ie *contra proferentem*. Where a financial institution seeks to avoid liability based on negligence, a three-step test would be used. First, if the clause contains language that expressly exempts

[89] [2011] IEHC 7.
[90] See also *Irish Bank Resolution Corporation Limited v Quinn & Anor* [2011] IEHC 470.
[91] *Curtis v Chemical Cleaning and Dyeing Company* [1951] 1 KB 805.
[92] [2014] IEHC 95.
[93] [2011] IEHC 314.
[94] [2015] IEHC 260.

the institution from the consequences of the negligence, effect will be given to the clause. Secondly, if there is no express reference to negligence and the words are not wide enough, in their ordinary meaning, to cover negligence, the clause will not exempt the institution from liability for negligence. Thirdly, if there is no express reference to negligence but the words used in the clause are general and could potentially cover negligence, the court will consider whether the 'head of damage' may be based on a ground other than negligence. If such other ground is not remote or 'fanciful', the clause will not protect the proferens. If no other ground exists, effect will be given to the clause.

In exempting or limiting liability, the courts have expressed the view that in order to give reasonable notice of a very onerous and wide-ranging clause, the proferens may need to draw it to the attention of the other party. *In McCaughey v Irish Bank Resolution Corp Ltd & anor,*[95] the facts of which are described above, the commitment agreement excluded liability for anything but fraud or fraudulent concealment, and purported to exclude even a duty to take care in the making of any representations. The plaintiff had argued that the clause was 'particularly onerous or unusual' and citing the UK case *Inter-photo Picture Library Limited v Stiletto Visual Programme Limited*[96] should have been 'brought fairly and reasonably to the attention of the other party'. The High Court had distinguished this case on its facts, Bermingham J holding:

> Here, in contrast, the plaintiff called to the defendant's premises specifically for the purpose of executing documentation. The documentation was obviously of a legal character and the plaintiff accepts that he was aware that the document contained legal terms. That a contract would seek to regulate the relationship between plaintiff and defendant is not at all unusual, on the contrary, it is to be expected. Neither is there anything unusual in a pre-printed contract containing provisions seeking to safeguard and strengthen the position of the party that prepared it, indeed quite the contrary. How broad the terms of any exclusions or how specific any recommendations will be, can be expected to vary considerably but that very fact means that it is incumbent on a party who is signing a document that he knows contains contractual terms to satisfy himself that these are appropriate to his situation.[97]

On appeal, Hardiman J in the Supreme Court stated obiter that despite the circumstances in which the plaintiff signed the commitment agreement and the fact that the nature and appearance of the agreement would make anyone aware it contained legal terms, having regard to the principles set out in *Inter-photo Picture Library Limited* and having regard in particular to 'the breathtaking scope of the clauses' he did not necessarily agree that the actual nature and content of the clauses had been fairly brought to the attention of the plaintiff. He continued

[95] [2011] IEHC 546 and [2013] IESC 17.
[96] [1989] 1 QB 433.
[97] At 37.

> It may be, having regard to the scope of the clauses, and to their variance with the nature of the previous relationship between the parties, that such a person's attention should be drawn in absolutely express terms to their enormous scope and to the total exclusion of liability which they attempt.

In *Parsley Properties Limited & Ors v Bank of Scotland plc & Anor*,[98] a dispute arose about interest rate swap arrangements, described by the plaintiffs as an unsuitable 'sophisticated high risk derivative product'. The plaintiffs alleged that the bank mis-sold the interest rate swaps, misstated the position and acted negligently and in breach of fiduciary duty. The High Court reviewed a very broad exclusion clause in an action for mis-selling an interest rate swap. Citing Birmingham J in *McCaughey* above, McGovern J concluded:

> I cannot, on the basis of the evidence before me, envisage any circumstances under which Parsley might avoid the terms of the various instruments entered into by it. Even if it is the case that interest rate swap arrangements were unsuitable for its purposes, it is a corporate entity forming part of a sophisticated structure, being held by a trust and interacting with other corporate vehicles registered in other jurisdictions. Parsley was managed by professional trustees and had available to it the possibility of obtaining any necessary legal or financial advice in relation to the transaction in question. The exclusionary terms were clear and are enforceable, in circumstances where the plaintiffs have not specifically pleaded fraud or fraudulent concealment.[99]

In the case of statutory duties, a financial institution would be unlikely to succeed in an attempt to exempt itself from liability in respect of certain absolute statutory duties. Any exemption clause purporting to do so, particularly in the case of a retail customer where there is no informed consent, may be determined by an Irish Court to be void as being contrary to public policy. In addition, the Consumer Protection Code provides that:

> a regulated entity must not, in any communication or agreement with a consumer (except where permitted by applicable legislation), exclude or restrict, or seek to exclude or restrict:
>
> a) any legal liability or duty of care to a consumer which it has under applicable law or under this Code;
> b) any other duty to act with skill, care and diligence which is owed to a consumer in connection with the provision to that consumer of financial services; or
> c) any liability owed to a consumer for failure to exercise the degree of skill, care and diligence that may reasonably be expected of it in the provision of a financial service.[100]

[98] [2013] IEHC 624.

[99] This was followed by the High Court in *Vieira Limited v Ulster Bank Ireland Limited; European Property Fund plc & anor v Ulster Bank Limited* [2014] IEHC 591.

[100] Consumer Protection Code, para 3.8.

It also provides that regulated entities must ensure that all warning statements required by this Code are prominent.[101]

Finally, customers may be protected by the Sale of Goods and Supply of Services Acts 1893 and 1980 for consumer transactions and by the European Communities (Unfair Terms in Consumer Contracts) Regulations 1995,[102] both of which may limit the ability of the bank to rely on an exemption clause.

IV. Contributory Negligence

A financial institution may successfully avoid or limit the extent of its liability by relying on contributory negligence. Contributory negligence is relevant in Ireland both to actions in contract and tort. Apportionment of liability is provided under the Civil Liability Act 1961 for 'wrongs', which under section 2 include 'a tort, breach of contract or breach of trust'. Section 34(1) of the Act states that if contributory negligence is proven 'the damages recoverable in respect of the said wrong shall be reduced by such amount as the court thinks just and equitable having regard to the degrees of fault of the plaintiff and defendant'. In *Lyons v Thomas*,[103] the purchaser of property sought damages for the deterioration in condition of the property between the date of the agreement and the closing of the sale. Although the vendor was held to be liable, a 10 per cent deduction was made on the basis that the plaintiff was aware of the deterioration but failed to notify the vendor. When it is not possible to establish different degrees of fault, liability will be apportioned equally.

In *KBC Bank v BCM Hanby Wallace*,[104] the Supreme Court upheld an appeal by a firm of solicitors against aspects of the decision of McGovern J in the High Court. McGovern J had held that the firm had been negligent in its actions on behalf of the respondent bank in respect of significant loans to two individuals who had defaulted on their loan obligations. The negligence in question related to the release of loan monies before the security agreed had been provided and to representations made in this respect. McGovern J had also rejected the firm's argument that the bank had been guilty of contributory negligence because it had not made sufficient inquiries into the financial affairs of the borrowers before agreeing to lend them very large sums. The argument put forward had been that, if the bank had properly assessed the borrowers, it would not have agreed to lend to them and therefore the issue of negligence in completing the transaction without proper security being in place would not have arisen. McGovern J had disposed of this

[101] ibid, para 3.9.

[102] SI 27/1995 as amended. These Regulations do not apply where the term in question has been individually negotiated.

[103] [1986] IR 666.

[104] [2013] IESC 32.

argument on causation grounds, finding that '[i]f the decision of the plaintiff to approve the loans was, to some extent, due to its own negligence in assessing the borrowers, this was a causa sine qua non'. The Supreme Court found that while the solicitors' negligence was a proximate cause of the respondent bank's loss, it was not the only effective cause as the actions of the bank were also an effective cause of the loss. Fennelly J stated:

> When a bank reviews a potential loan transaction, it should assess the soundness, financial standing and above all the trustworthiness of the borrower and the viability of the proposed venture … It should have robust and comprehensive credit analysis and approval processes, internal controls to monitor risk and to ensure adequate monitoring of the completion of security.

The Supreme Court did not make a determination as to whether or not the bank's conduct amounted to contributory negligence, remitting the matter back to the High Court to determine whether 'the bank was wanting in care for its own interests in entering into the loan transactions' and whether 'if it had exercised reasonable care, it would have discovered the truth about the borrowers and would not have agreed to lend them any money'. The High Court was asked to determine whether these assumptions were correct and, 'if so, to decide on the relative blameworthiness and causative contribution of the respective faults of the appellant and the bank respectively'.

In *Harrold v Nua Mortgages Limited*,[105] in addition to an unsuccessful claim in the tort of reckless lending, the plaintiff claimed professional negligence and/or contributory negligence relying on the aforementioned *BCM* case. The plaintiff argued a bank was negligent in relation to the financial assessment carried out to establish his ability to service the mortgage and by failing to have regard to warning signs from the US regarding the risks associated with 'lending to people who could not afford the repayments'. It contended that the bank breached its duty of care and negligently increased the risk of injury and damage to the plaintiff. As a result, the plaintiff submitted that he was induced into making a decision he would not otherwise have made. The High Court distinguished *BCM* on the basis that in the case before it, a risk assessment and an Irish Credit Bureau check were carried out by the bank. In addition, the bank did satisfy itself that adequate security was in place, namely, the property itself. In *Allied Irish Bank PLC v Fahey*,[106] the *BCM Hanby Wallace* case was relied upon as allowing a defence of contributory negligence to be raised against a lender in very limited circumstances. The High Court found however that there was no evidence to support any such defence beyond a 'speculative assertion'.

[105] [2015] IEHC 15.
[106] [2016] IEHC 182.

V. Statutory Requirements and Codes of Conduct

The Central Bank is the statutory body responsible for central banking and financial regulation in Ireland.[107] Its functions include the proper and effective regulation of financial institutions and markets and the protection of financial services consumers. It is responsible for the authorisation, regulation and supervision of credit institutions operating in Ireland and also for oversight of liquidity and conduct of business for branches of non-Irish licensed banks operating in Ireland. In 2015, the Central Bank implemented a Mortgage Redress Programme for 1,372 tracker mortgage account holders of a particular financial institution involving repayment of overpayments, compensation payments and additional payments in respect of detriment suffered by customers.[108] The Central Bank subsequently determined that a system-wide review was necessary, to ensure that all lenders are acting in their customers' best interests and, to date, approximately 8,200 impacted accounts have been identified in a number of institutions.[109] The Central Bank is also responsible for authorising and supervising investment firms under the Investment Intermediaries Act 1995[110] and under the MiFID Regulations.

A. MiFID

The MiFID Regulations classify parties as: professional clients; retail clients or eligible counterparties with different levels of regulatory protection attaching to each. A 'professional client' is defined in the Regulations as 'a client who possesses the experience, knowledge and expertise to make its own investment decisions and properly assess the risks that it incurs'[111] and Schedule 2 lists the categories of client who are considered to be professionals. A 'retail client' is simply one who is not a professional client.[112] An 'eligible counterparty' is defined in Regulation 111(1) and includes investment firms, credit institutions, UCITS and pension funds.

Regulation 76 sets out conduct-of-business obligations for firms providing investment services to clients. A firm must 'act honestly, fairly and professionally

107 It was established pursuant to the Central Bank Act 1942 as amended.

108 Central Bank, *Annual Performance Statement (Financial Regulation) 2015–2016*, 44.

109 Central Bank, *Update on Examination of Tracker Mortgages* (19 December 2016) available at: www.centralbank.ie/press-area/press-releases/Pages/UpdateTrackerMortgages.aspx.

110 The Investment Intermediaries Act 1995 remains relevant for investment intermediaries and for investment advisers who fall within an exemption from MiFID (reg 5(3)) and do not intend to passport their services.

111 Sch 2, s 1. Reg 3(1) defines a 'professional client' as a client meeting the criteria laid down in Sch 2 of the Regulations.

112 MiFID Regulations, reg 3(1).

in accordance with the best interests of its clients' and comply, in particular, with the principles set out in Regulation 76(2) to (6) and in Regulation 98.[113] Information communicated by the investment firm to clients or potential clients must be 'fair, clear and not misleading'.[114] It must be provided in a 'comprehensible form' and relate to key issues including 'appropriate guidance on and warnings of the risks associated with investments in those instruments or in respect of particular investment strategies' so that 'the clients or potential clients are reasonably able to understand the nature and risk of the investment service and of the specific type of financial instrument that is being offered and, consequently, to take investment decisions on an informed basis'.[115] MiFID II will also require the aforementioned guidance to indicate 'whether the financial instrument is intended for retail or professional clients, taking account of the identified target market'.[116] Information to be given for the purposes of this paragraph may be provided in a standardised format. MiFID II provides that 'Member States' rather than investment firms may decide that the information will be provided in a standardised format.[117] It is not clear yet whether Ireland will exercise this option.

An investment firm providing investment advice or portfolio management must obtain:

> all of the information about–
>
> (a) the client's or potential client's knowledge and experience in the investment field relevant to the specific type of product or service offered to the client by the investment firm,
> (b) the client's financial situation, and
> (c) the client's investment objectives,
>
> that is necessary for the firm to obtain so the firm is able to recommend to the client or potential client those investment services and financial instruments that are suitable for the client.[118]

When providing investment services other than investment advice or portfolio management the firm must ask for and take into account the information referred to in (a).[119] If no information or insufficient information is provided, the firm must warn the client or potential client that it will not be able to determine the appropriateness of the service or product envisaged for the client.[120] If the information leads the firm to determine that the investment service or product is not

[113] ibid, reg 76(1).
[114] ibid, reg 76(2)(a).
[115] Ibid, reg 76(2)(c).
[116] MiFID II, Art 24(4)(b).
[117] ibid, Art 24(5).
[118] MiFID Regulations, reg 76(3).
[119] ibid, reg 76(4).
[120] ibid, reg 76(6).

appropriate to the client or potential client, it must warn the client or potential client.[121] Both warnings may be provided in a standardised format.

Regulation 80 lists a number of requirements to be met by investment firms providing information to retail clients or potential retail clients. For example, the information must be accurate[122] and must not emphasise any potential benefits of an investment service or financial instrument without also giving a fair and prominent indication of any relevant risks.[123] It must be sufficient for, and be presented in a way likely to be understood by 'the average member of the group to whom the information is directed, or the person likely to receive the information'[124] and it must not 'disguise, diminish or obscure important items, statements or warnings'.[125] Regulation 84 requires the firm to provide all clients or potential clients with a general description of the nature and risks of financial instruments. This should take into account the client's categorisation as either a retail client or a professional client, and explain the nature of the specific instrument and the risks particular to it 'in sufficient detail to enable the client to make informed investment decisions'.[126] The description of the risks should include:

> where relevant to the specific type of instrument concerned and the status and level of knowledge of the client, the following elements:
>
> (a) the risks associated with that type of financial instrument including an explanation of leverage and its effects and the risk of losing the entire investment;
> (b) the volatility of the price of such instruments and any limitations on the available market for such instruments;
> (c) the fact that an investor might assume, as a result of transactions in such instruments, financial commitments and other additional obligations, including contingent liabilities, additional to the cost of acquiring the instruments;
> (d) any margin requirements or similar obligations, applicable to instruments of that type.[127]

The Central Bank is empowered to specify the precise terms, or the contents, of the description of the risks required under this paragraph.

Regulation 94 requires investment firms to obtain from clients or potential clients such information as is necessary for the firm to understand the essential facts about the client, and to have a reasonable basis for believing that the specific transaction to be recommended, or entered into in the course of providing a portfolio management service: meets the investment objectives of the client in question; is such that the client is able financially to bear any related investment

121 ibid, reg 76(5).
122 ibid, reg 80(2)(b).
123 ibid, reg 80(2)(c).
124 ibid, reg 80(2)(d).
125 ibid, reg 80(2)(e).
126 ibid, reg 84(1).
127 ibid, reg 84(2).

risks consistent with their investment objectives; and 'is such that the client has the necessary experience and knowledge in order to understand the risks involved in the transaction or in the management of the client's portfolio'.[128]

MiFID II and MiFIR will introduce inter alia an expanded obligation to act in the best interests of the client. Although firms advising retail clients are currently required to assess suitability of product, there will be a new requirement to provide a suitability statement specifying the advice given and how that advice meets the preferences, objective and other characteristics of the retail client. There will also be an expanded obligation to ensure the suitability of a financial instrument or product to a client in the context of the client's capacity to absorb losses and tolerate risk.

Article 51(1) of MiFID provides in addition to any procedures for the withdrawal of authorisation or to the right of Member States to impose criminal sanctions, that Member States must 'ensure, in conformity with their national law, that the appropriate administrative measures can be taken or administrative sanctions be imposed against the persons responsible' for non-compliance with the directive. These measures must be 'effective, proportionate and dissuasive'. The Central Bank has been engaged in enforcing breaches of the MiFID Regulations using administrative sanctions. It publishes a list of settlement agreements on its website and a perusal of the list indicates a number of agreements relating to breaches of regulated firms' obligations under the MiFID Regulations including for example a breach of a firm's duty to ensure that it had in place and used sound administrative and accounting procedures and internal control mechanisms to ensure compliance with the permitted limits and the reporting obligations set out in the Capital Adequacy Regulations.

MiFID does not deal with the consequences of non-compliance with MiFID obligations on an underlying contract. In such circumstances the European Court of Justice has held that 'it is for the internal legal order of each Member State to determine the contractual consequences of non-compliance with those obligations, subject to observance of the principles of equivalence and effectiviness'.[129] Article 69 of MiFID II provides that

> Member States shall ensure that mechanisms are in place to ensure that compensation may be paid or other remedial action be taken in accordance with national law for any financial loss or damage suffered as a result of an infringement of this Directive or of Regulation (EU) No 600/2014.

Section 44 of the Central Bank (Supervision and Enforcement) Act 2013, discussed in section VI below, now provides a right of action to investors for breach of the MiFID Regulations.

[128] ibid, reg 94(1).

[129] C-604/11 *Genil 48 SL and Comercial Hostelera de Grandes Vinos SL v Bankinter SA and Banco Bilbao Vizcaya Argentaria SA* (ECLI:EU:C:2013:344).

The case of *Quinn and Ors v Irish Bank Resolution Corporation Limited (In Special Liquidation) and Ors*[130] may perhaps be instructive in considering the impact on an underlying contract of a breach of MiFID. One of the allegations made in that case was that a number of loans guaranteed by members of the Quinn family in connection with Seán Quinn's payment obligations under contracts for differences, together with the purchase of shares in Anglo Irish Bank designed to unwind Seán Quinn's interest in Anglo amounted to illegal contracts as they were in breach of the Market Abuse (Directive 2003/6/EC) Regulations 2005 (MAR) and/or section 60 of the Companies Act 1963. One of the arguments put forward by Anglo was that the introduction of unenforceability would introduce chaos into the marketplace and disturb the scheme of regulation which was founded on the market abuse legislation. Neither MAR nor the legislation expressly provided that transactions in breach of their terms were illegal, invalid or void. Anglo also contended that there is no suggestion in the Market Abuse Directive that private civil law actions were 'necessary or desirable' and instead the emphasis is on administrative and public law provisions in order to promote a consistent framework of enforcement and cooperation. While Anglo acknowledged that the Market Abuse Directive permits civil sanctions, it argued that it is 'a fundamental principle of European law that a Member State is not permitted to undermine the provisions or the object and purpose of a directive' and 'a civil remedy which rendered transactions pertaining to the purchase or sale of financial instruments invalid, illegal, or unenforceable would be tantamount to undermining the Directive'.[131] Additionally, Anglo claimed that such a remedy would be inconsistent with the principles of legal certainty and proportionality. The Supreme Court held that the alleged breaches of section 60 or MAR would not render the guarantees invalid. Clarke J opined that:

> Where, however, the relevant legislation is silent as to whether any particular type of contract is to be regarded as void or unenforceable, the court must consider whether the requirements of public policy (which suggest that a court refrain from enforcing a contract tainted by illegality) and the policy of the legislation concerned, gleaned from its terms, are such as to require that, in addition to whatever express consequences are provided for in the relevant legislation, an additional sanction or consequence in the form of treating relevant contracts as being void or unenforceable must be imposed.

In carrying out such an assessment, he opined that appropriate weight should be given to the general undesirability of courts becoming involved in the enforcement of contracts tainted by illegality unless there are significant countervailing factors evident from the language or policy of the particular statute. Factors considered relevant in determining unenforceability included:

> 3(a) Whether the contract in question is designed to carry out the very act which the relevant legislation is designed to prevent …

[130] [2015] IESC 29.
[131] ibid, [5.8].

> 3(b) Whether the wording of the statute itself might be taken to strongly imply that the remedies or consequences specified in the statute are sufficient to meet the statutory end …
>
> 3(c) Whether the policy of the legislation is designed to apply equally or substantially to both parties to a relevant contract or whether that policy is exclusively or principally directed towards one party. Therefore, legislation which is designed to impose burdens on one category of persons for the purposes of protecting another category may be considered differently from legislation which is designed to place a burden of compliance with an appropriate regulatory regime on both participants …
>
> 3(d) Whether the imposition of voidness or unenforceability may be counterproductive to the statutory aim as found in the statute itself …
>
> 4(a) Whether, having regard to the purpose of the statute, the range of adverse consequences for which express provision is made might be considered, in the absence of treating relevant contracts as unenforceable, to be adequate to secure those purposes…
>
> 4(b) Whether the imposition of voidness or unenforceability may be disproportionate to the seriousness of the unlawful conduct in question in the context of the relevant statutory regime in general[132]

In applying these principles, Clarke J observed that the statutory purpose of MAR is principally directed towards protecting the interests of those who are investors, or potential investors and that imposing an additional burden on them by rendering unenforceable contracts which Anglo entered into would not serve the purpose of the statute. He also noted that 'the sort of activity which might be found to be in breach of the MAR and the scale, whether in terms of the financial extent of the wrongdoing or the degree to which such wrongdoing might be regarded as reprehensible, can vary enormously from case to case'[133] and that 'if contracts which are tainted by their association with that wrongdoing are to be treated as unenforceable then the consequences could vary enormously from case to case' and the effect in some cases 'might greatly outweigh or be disproportionate to the scale of the wrongdoing concerned'.[134] He opined however that:

> If the imposition of unenforceability imposes a significant additional deterrence in circumstances where the express statutory consequences of wrongdoing may not be particularly severe, and if the imposition of unenforceability does not do any harm to that statutory purpose, then it may well be easy to infer that the legislation contemplates contracts being unenforceable by reason of illegality connected with the statute. But where unenforceability may actually be counterproductive in the context of protecting the very persons whose interests the statute is designed to protect, the overall assessment may require to be different, particularly where, as here, there are very significant sanctions available in any event.[135]

[132] ibid, [8.55].
[133] ibid, [11.35].
[134] ibid, [11.38].
[135] ibid, [11.39].

This it is submitted provides a well reasoned and useful test to be applied to determine the legal consequences of breaches of statutory duties.

B. Consumer Protection Codes

Section 117 of the Central Bank Act 1989 empowers the Central Bank to draw up codes of practice relating to any persons supervised by it. In drawing up these codes, the Central Bank is required to have regard to: the interest of customers and the general public; and the promotion of fair competition in financial markets in the state. The first code issued pursuant to this power was a one-page Code of Practice for Credit Institutions in 2001, which set down standards of good banking practice to be followed by all credit institutions. Today, a number of codes exist pursuant to section 117 including the Consumer Protection Code and the Code of Conduct on Mortgage Arrears.[136] Of most relevance for this chapter is the Consumer Protection Code,[137] which applies to the regulated activities of regulated financial services providers including banks operating in the state. It deals inter alia with: the provision of information; knowing the customer and suitability; post-sale information requirements; rebates and claims processing; arrears handling; advertising; errors and complaints resolutions; and records and compliance. A number of activities and providers are excluded from the application of the Consumer Protection Code. It does not apply for example to services provided to persons outside the state, to credit union activity or to any service or activity set out in the MiFID Regulations 2007.[138] The Central Bank advises that a firm may use one set of documents to cover MiFID and non-MiFID activities and services provided the documents cover the obligations of both the MiFID Regulations and the Consumer Protection Code for the firm's business.

Chapter 2 of the Consumer Protection Code sets out 12 General Principles which apply to all customers in the state and include requirements to: act honestly, fairly and professionally in the best interests of its customers and the integrity of the market; act with due skill, care and diligence in the best interests of its customers; not recklessly, negligently or deliberately mislead a customer as to the real or perceived advantages or disadvantages of any product or service; seek from

[136] A Code of Conduct for Business Lending to Small and Medium Enterprises was replaced in 2016 by the Central Bank (Supervision And Enforcement) Act 2013 (Section 48) (Lending To Small And Medium-Sized Enterprises) Regulations 2015.

[137] The Code was also issued pursuant to powers under s 117 of the Central Bank Act 1989; ss 23 and 37 of the Investment Intermediaries Act 1995; s 8H of the Consumer Credit Act 1995; and s 61 of the Insurance Act 1989. The current version of the Code came into effect in January 2012 with a new chapter being added for debt management companies effective from January 2015.

[138] In addition for certain regulated entities certain provisions of the Consumer Protection Code do not apply. These include entities providing credit under credit agreements which fall within the scope of the European Communities (Consumer Credit Agreements) Regulations 2010 and entities providing payment services or issuing electric money.

its customers information relevant to the product or service requested; make full disclosure of all relevant material information, including all charges, in a way that seeks to inform the customer; and seek to avoid conflicts of interest. The other chapters in the Consumer Protection Code apply only in respect of customers in the state who fall within the definition of 'consumer' and 'personal consumer'.[139]

If the Codes are breached, the Central Bank may impose administrative sanctions under Part IIIC of the Central Bank Act 1942 as amended.[140] Breaches may also lead to: the prosecution of an offence; the refusal to appoint a proposed director to any pre- approval controlled function where prescribed by the Central Bank pursuant to Part 3 of the Central Bank Reform Act 2010; and/or the suspension, removal or prohibition of an individual from carrying out a controlled function where prescribed by the Central Bank pursuant to Part 3 of the Central Bank Reform Act 2010. In 2011, the Central Bank undertook a themed inspection into compliance by credit institutions with the Consumer Protection Code during the payment protection insurance (PPI) sales process. This led to 11 credit institutions being required to refund approximately 77,000 clients €67.4 million for non-compliance with the Code when selling PPI or an inability to demonstrate compliance with the Code. A breach of the Code may also give rise to a complaint by a customer to the Financial Services Ombudsman.

C. Civil Liability

There are no express provisions under the Central Bank Act 1989 or the section 117 Codes conferring civil law remedies on customers for breaches of the Code. This question has given rise to much judicial deliberation.

In *Zurich Bank v McConnon*,[141] though obiter, Birmingham J rejected the suggestion that the Consumer Protection Code created any justiciable rights at the hands of a consumer. In *Stepstone Mortgage Funding Limited v Fitzell & Anor*[142]

[139] A 'consumer' is defined in ch 12 as '(a) a person or group of persons, but not an incorporated body with an annual turnover in excess of €3 million in the previous financial year (for the avoidance of doubt a group of persons includes partnerships and other unincorporated bodies such as clubs, charities and trusts, not consisting entirely of bodies corporate) or (b) incorporated bodies having an annual turnover of €3 million or less in the previous financial year (provided that such body shall not be a member of a group of companies having a combined turnover greater than the said €3 million)'. A 'personal consumer' is defined in the same chapter as 'a consumer who is a natural person acting outside his or her business, trade or profession'.

[140] eg in 2012, the Central Bank entered into a Settlement Agreement with Irish Mortgage Corporation Limited trading as Moneyzone relating to breaches of the Consumer Protection Code in relation to sub-prime mortgages recommended to their customers. The firm was found to have breached General Principle 1 of the Code in failing to act professionally in the best interests of its customers and other rules including being unable to ensure that the mortgages recommended were suitable to those consumers. It reprimanded the firm and required it to pay a monetary penalty of €65,000.

[141] [2011] IEHC 75. See also *Start Mortgages & Ors v Gunn & Ors* and *EBS Building Society v Gillespie* [2012] IEHC 243 and *Friends First Finance v Cronin* [2013] IEHC 5.

[142] [2012] IEHC 142.

and *Irish Life and Permanent Plc v Duff & Anor*,[143] repossession orders were refused in circumstances where the credit institutions had failed to comply with the Code of Conduct on Mortgage Arrears. In *ACC Bank Plc v Deacon & Anor*,[144] the refusal of relief in *Fitzell* and *Duff* was said to be confined to 'claims for repossession of family homes' and the High Court said that a failure to comply with the Code of Conduct on Business Lending to Small and Medium Enterprises did not extinguish the loan or furnish a defence to the borrower.[145] McGovern J in *Freeman & Anor v Bank of Scotland (Ireland) & ors*[146] opined:

> It is clear, therefore, that non-compliance with a statutory code does not relieve a borrower from his obligations under a loan to repay the lender, nor does it deprive the lender of its rights and powers under the loan agreement. If that is the case so far as statutory codes of conduct are concerned, then, *a fortiori*, the plaintiffs in this action cannot make the case that they are relieved from their obligations under the loan or that the Bank is deprived of its rights under the loan agreements, if there has been a breach by the Bank of what is a voluntary code.

In addition to the implications of a breach on the right of a lender to secure repossession or the right of a borrower to claim the extinguishment of the loan or to defend against an action, the Court also considered whether a breach may give rise to a positive right of a borrower to take an action in tort or contract. In *McGuinness v Allied Irish Banks Plc*,[147] the High Court noted that the *Fitzell* decision involved a case where 'the Code was used as a shield rather than a sword by the borrower in response to a repossession claim brought by the plaintiff'. The plaintiff sought inter alia to enforce alleged breaches of the Code of Conduct on Mortgage Arrears against the lender claiming inter alia breach of contract. Gilligan J refused to grant interlocutory relief stating describing the decisions of the courts in *Duff* and *Fitzell* as 'narrow in nature' and only determining that compliance by a lender with the Code was necessary in order for the making of an order for repossession: 'They are not relevant to the facts at issue in these proceedings and would not have a bearing on the status of the Code in relation to the right of the borrower to use non-compliance with the Code as a cause of action against a lender. This matter has yet to be determined'.

In *Allied Irish Bank v O'Brien & Fingleton*,[148] the second defendant claimed the bank failed to furnish information relating to the interest rates applicable to the facility and that it did not thus meet its obligation under the Consumer Protection Code to make disclosure of relevant information including all charges applicable

[143] [2013] IEHC 43.
[144] [2013] IEHC 427.
[145] This principle was reiterated by Baker J in *Ryan v Danske Bank A/S t/a Danske Bank & anor* [2014] IEHC 236.
[146] [2014] IEHC 284.
[147] [2014] IEHC 191.
[148] [2015] IEHC 260 (27 March 2015).

to the facility.[149] It was argued that the Code's general conditions implied a term into the parties' contract, breach of which created rights for the defendant. Baker J held

> I consider that breach of the general conditions in the Code of Conduct of 2006 … does not afford [Mr Fingleton] an arguable defence to the claim for judgment, and he has identified no breach of the Code which would be actionable even were it to be shown that the Code had become incorporated into his contract with the Bank.

These issues were considered by the Supreme Court recently in *Irish Life and Permanent plc v Dunne and Irish Life and Permanent plc v Dunphy*[150] in the context of the Code of Conduct on Mortgage Arrears. The Court acknowledged that the Code involves a range of measures of greater and lesser importance which are expressed in more or less concrete terms from a moratorium period under which a financial institution is precluded from commencing repossession proceedings to measures on matters such as the obligation to keep a record of all contact with a borrower. The Court considered the extent to which the Code could impact on the legal rights and obligations as and between a regulated lender and a borrower. Clarke J opined that the issues which this argument raises were very similar to those at issue in *Quinn and Ors v Irish Bank Resolution Corporation Limited (In Special Liquidation) and Ors.*[151] Although he noted there was no suggestion in the current case that the underlying contract between the parties was in any way tainted by illegality, the Court had to consider whether the seeking of possession itself may be tainted by illegality if the bank had failed to comply with the Code prior to seeking possession. Applying the test set out by the Supreme Court in *Quinn* and described earlier in this chapter, Clarke J opined:

> For a court to entertain an application for possession which was brought in circumstances of clear breach of the moratorium would be for a court to act in aid of the actions of a financial institution which were clearly unlawful (by being in breach of the Code) and in circumstances where the very act of the financial institution concerned in seeking possession was contrary to the intention or purpose behind the Code itself. In my view a court could not properly act to consider a possession application in those circumstances … [However] it does not seem to me … that the statutory policy of the 1989 Act and the Code-making powers contained therein is such that the same is intended to, as it were, by the backdoor, create a whole new jurisdiction for the courts in which the court would be required to assess in some detail the type of engagement entered into between a financial institution and a borrower who is in sufficient arrears to enable that financial institution, as a matter of law, to seek possession. In such circumstances it seems to me that criterion

[149] The second defendant did not make the argument that he was a consumer for the purposes of the Code, but even were he to have made this argument the relevant provisions of the Code which are applicable to consumers did not come into force until after the drawdown of the loan. He was confined in his argument with regard to the applicability of the Code thus to ch 1 of the Code which is entitled 'General Principles'.

[150] [2015] IESC 46 (15 May 2015, Clarke J).

[151] [2015] IESC 29.

> 3(b) of the test set out in *Quinn v. I.B.R.C.* would lean heavily against implying that the courts have any role in declining possession in cases other than where the breach of the Code alleged is a failure to abide by the moratorium.

The role of the courts is likely thus in practice to be to adjourn a case in order to allow the parties to attempt to reach some accommodation. The Supreme Court did not address the question of whether a customer would be entitled to damages as a result of non-compliance with the Code. However, Breslin and Corcoran make the sound argument that in light of Clarke J's observation that legislative intervention would be needed to give the courts wider jurisdiction in the case of repossession cases, such a case would be unlikely to find favour.[152]

VI. The Central Bank (Supervision and Enforcement) Act 2013

The Central Bank (Supervision and Enforcement) Act 2013 makes a number of significant amendments to the enforcement of financial services legislation in Ireland. It increased the penalties and fines applicable to the administrative sanctions regime. More importantly in the context of this chapter, it has increased the opportunities for individuals to seek redress where financial institutions have breached certain statutory duties of care to them.

Section 43(1) of the Central Bank (Supervision and Enforcement) Act 2013 grants the Central Bank power to direct that redress be afforded to customers of a regulated financial services provider where they have suffered or will suffer a loss as a result of widespread or regular relevant defaults by a regulated financial services provider. These 'relevant defaults' are defined as:

> charging a customer an amount which the regulated financial service provider is not entitled to charge, providing a customer with a financial service which the customer has not agreed to receive, providing a customer with a financial service which was not suitable for the customer at the time when it was provided, providing a customer with inaccurate information which influences the customer in making a decision about any financial service, a failure of any system or controls of the regulated financial service provider, or a prescribed contravention.[153]

A 'prescribed contravention' is

> a breach of: a provision of a designated enactment, including any instrument made thereunder, or a designated statutory instrument; or a code made, or a direction given, under such a provision; or any condition or requirement imposed under a provision

[152] J Breslin and E Corcoran, 'New Private Right of Action for Damages in Financial Services Litigation' (2015) 38 *Dublin University Law Journal* 17, 26–27.

[153] Central Bank (Supervision and Enforcement) Act 2013, s 43(2).

> of a designated enactment, designated statutory instrument, code or direction; or any obligation imposed on any person by Part IIIC of the Central Bank Act 1942 or imposed by the Central Bank pursuant to a power exercised under Part IIIC of the Central Bank Act 1942.[154]

The term 'appropriate redress' is defined as:

> such monetary or other redress as is specified in the direction and (in the case of redress for pecuniary loss) as does not exceed the amount of the loss suffered or anticipated to be suffered, together (where appropriate) with interest at such rate as is so specified.[155]

Of even greater consequence is section 44 of the Central Bank (Supervision and Enforcement) Act 2013, which provides a statutory basis for an action for damages by 'customers' who have suffered loss as a result of any failure by the financial services provider to comply with its obligations under financial services legislation.[156] Section 44 provides as follows:

> A failure by a regulated financial service provider to comply with any obligation under financial services legislation is actionable by any customer of the regulated financial service provider who suffers loss or damage as a result of such failure.

Section 3(1) defines a 'customer' in relation to a regulated financial service provider as

> (a) any person to whom the regulated financial service provider provides or offers financial services, or (b) any person who requests the provision of financial services from the regulated financial service provider, and includes a potential customer and a former customer.

It thus would include non-retail customers such as large corporate customers. Financial services legislation in this context means 'designated enactments', 'designated statutory instruments' listed in Schedule 2 of the Central Bank Act 1942, the Central Bank Acts 1942 to 2013 and statutory instruments made under those Acts.[157] The list of designated enactments and statutory instruments is very extensive and includes the MiFID Regulations. Breslin and Corcoran argue that although the Consumer Protection Codes referred to in section V.B of this chapter, are not expressly listed as designated statutory instruments, as a matter of statutory interpretation they would be included on the basis that they are statutory instruments made under the Central Bank Acts.[158] Section 44 presents

[154] Central Bank Act of 1942, s 33AN.

[155] Central Bank (Supervision and Enforcement) Act 2013, s 43(3).

[156] Interestingly, in *Allied Irish Bank PLC v Fahey* [2016] IEHC 182, a defendant sought to rely on the provisions of s 44 in relation to a bank's failure to comply with its obligations under the Consumer Credit Act 1995 and the Consumer Protection Code. This was rejected on the basis that the defendant had not provided any actual or legal basis upon which such a conclusion could be reached.

[157] s 3.

[158] Breslin and Corcoran, 'New Private Right of Action for Damages in Financial Services Litigation' (n 152) 50. The authors argue as an alternative that a breach of the Consumer Protection Codes would constitute a breach of s 117 and thus be included within the scope of s 44 as a breach of the Central Bank Acts.

a very significant new exposure for banks introducing a private right of action in respect of an extraordinarily wide range of failings. A customer who can prove that the financial institution that has provided some form of financial services to them in the course of which the institution has breached a statutory duty of care has passed the first hurdle. Strict liability applies so that 'where a failure to comply with the relevant provision has been established, it will not be sufficient for the defendant to show that it behaved with due care'.[159] The second hurdle which may not be so easy will be to prove a causal link between the breach and the loss or damage.

On a related point, the Central Bank has expressed the view that compliance with its Corporate Governance Code for Credit Institutions and Insurance Undertakings is a necessary component of an institutions' compliance with requirements under certain financial services legislation to the effect that an institution manages its business on a sound administrative basis.[160] For example, Regulation 16(1) of the European Communities (Licensing and Supervision of Credit Institutions) Regulations 1992[161] provides that:

> Every credit institution authorised by the Bank shall manage its business in accordance with sound administrative and accounting principles and shall put in place and maintain internal control and reporting arrangements and procedures to ensure that the business is so managed.

It has been suggested that a court would treat this conclusion with considerable deference and conclude that a breach of the Code automatically constitutes a breach of Regulation 16.[162] In light of section 44, it might be considered that such a breach of the Code may attract civil liability to any of its customers who had suffered loss or damage as a result of the breach.

A further provision of the Central Bank (Supervision and Enforcement) Act 2013 which merits consideration is section 54. This section empowers the Central Bank to apply to the High Court for a 'restitution order' in cases where a sanction has been imposed on a person pursuant to specified statutory provisions (such as the market abuse regulations) or where the person has been convicted of an offence under financial services legislation and there has been unjust enrichment or loss. The restitution order will require the regulated financial

[159] ibid, 33. This very useful article also explores (38–46) the defences which would exist to a claim under s 44.

[160] Para 3.2 of the Code. The relevant legislation is reg 16 of the European Communities (Licensing and Supervision of Credit Institutions) Regulations 1992 (SI 395/1992); Art 10(3) of the European Communities (Non-Life Insurance) Framework Regulations 1994 (SI 359/1994); Art 10(3) of the European Communities (Life Assurance) Framework Regulations 1994 (SI 360/ 1994); and reg 20 of the European Communities (Reinsurance) Regulations 2006 (SI 380/2006).

[161] SI 395/1992.

[162] N Murphy et al, *Central Bank of Ireland Revised Corporate Governance Code* (Dublin: Maples and Calder, 2014) available at: www.maplesandcalder.com/news/article/central-bank-of-ireland-revised-corporate-governance-code-691/.

service provider concerned to provide to the Central Bank an amount equal to the unjust gain or loss, which the Central Bank would then distribute.

VII. Role of the Financial Services Ombudsman

The Financial Services Ombudsman (Ombudsman) is a statutory officer established by Part VIIB of the Central Bank and Financial Services Authority of Ireland Act 2004. (A decision was taken to amalgamate this office with the Pensions Ombudsman and as soon as the relevant legislation is enacted, the post will become the Financial Services and Pensions Ombudsman.) It offers an informal and independent mechanism for the resolution of complaints. The Central Bank's Consumer Protection Code requires all regulated financial services firms to have a complaints handling procedure in place. Complaints against banks should first be discussed with the bank concerned. At that stage however if the complainant is dissatisfied with the bank's response, a complaint can be made to the Ombudsman.

Once the Ombudsman is satisfied that the complaint is within his jurisdiction, he is obliged to investigate. Section 57BK(4) of the Central Bank Act 1942 as amended provides that the Financial Services Ombudsman is entitled:

> to perform the functions imposed, and exercise the powers conferred, by this Act free from interference by any other person and, when dealing with a particular complaint, is required to act in an informal manner and according to equity, good conscience and the substantial merits of the complaint without regard to technicality or legal form.

Part of the Ombudsman's investigation involves an oral hearing at which the parties are frequently represented by legal or financial advisers. This differs from the adversarial context in which litigation is conducted before the courts. On completing an investigation of a complaint that has not been settled or withdrawn, the Ombudsman makes a finding in writing that the complaint (1) is substantiated, or (2) is not substantiated, or (3) is partly substantiated in one or more specified respects but not in others. Section 57CI(2) of the Central Bank Act 1942 as amended provides that a complaint may be found to be substantiated on one or more of the following grounds:

a. the conduct complained of was contrary to law;
b. the conduct complained of was unreasonable, unjust, oppressive or improperly discriminatory in its application to the complainant;
c. although the conduct complained of was in accordance with a law or an established practice or regulatory standard, the law, practice, or standard is, or may be, unreasonable, unjust, oppressive or improperly discriminatory in its application to the complainant;

d. the conduct complained of was based wholly or partly on an improper motive, an irrelevant ground, or an irrelevant consideration;
e. the conduct complained of was based wholly or partly on a mistake of law or fact;
f. an explanation for the conduct complained of was not given when it should have been given; or
g. the conduct complained of was otherwise improper.

If a complaint is found to be wholly or partly substantiated, the Ombudsman may direct the bank to do one or more of the following:

a. to review, rectify, mitigate, or change the conduct complained of or its consequences;
b. to provide reasons or explanations for that conduct;
c. to change a practice relating to that conduct;
d. to pay an amount of compensation to the complainant for any loss, expense or inconvenience sustained by the complainant as a result of the conduct complained of; or
e. to take any other lawful action.

Importantly, a complaint may be upheld even if the conduct complained of was in accordance with a law or an established practice, if it is unreasonable, unjust or oppressive; if an explanation for the conduct complained of was not given when it should have been given; or when the conduct complained of was otherwise improper.

In *Koczan v Financial Services Ombudsman*,[163] Hohan J commented that:

> The Ombudsman's task, therefore, runs well beyond that of the resolution of contract disputes in the manner traditionally performed by the courts. It is clear from the terms of s. 57BK(4) that the Ombudsman must, utilising his or her specialist skill and expertise, resolve such complaints according to wider conceptions of *et aequo et bono* which go beyond the traditional limitations of the law of contract.

In *De Paor v Financial Services Ombudsman*,[164] McGovern J explained that 'The whole purpose of the legislative scheme is to keep the process—so far as possible—out of the courts'. The Finding of the Ombudsman is legally binding on both parties, subject only to appeal by either party to the High Court.[165] The High Court's role in this regard is limited to considering whether or not the Ombudsman erred in its decision. The appeal is not a *de novo* hearing and 'falls somewhere between a judicial review and full appeal'.[166] The applicable test for

[163] [2010] IEHC 407.
[164] [2011] IEHC 483 at [18].
[165] s 57C(9) of the Central Bank Act 1942 as amended.
[166] *Law & anor v Financial Services Ombudsman* [2015] IEHC 29.

an appeal was set out in *Ulster Bank Investment Funds Ltd v Financial Services Ombudsman & Ors*,[167] where Finnegan P stated:

> To succeed on this appeal the Plaintiff must establish as a matter of probability that, taking the adjudicative process as a whole, the decision reached was vitiated by a serious and significant error or a series of such errors. In applying the test the Court will have regard to the degree of expertise and specialist knowledge of the Defendant.[168]

In *Smartt v Financial Services Ombudsman*,[169] Hedigan J noted that 'It is not for this Court to either agree or disagree with his finding as long as it is one reasonably based upon the evidence before him'. As the decision of the Ombudsman will be binding subject to the aforementioned appeal, once the Ombudsman has adjudicated on a complaint and has ruled that the service provider acted in accordance with the terms of the underlying contract and generally did not act unreasonably or unfairly having regard to the provisions of section 57CI(2), the matter is *res judicata* and cannot generally be re-litigated, for example as a breach of contract action.[170] The decision for an individual at the outset is thus to determine whether to avail of the aforementioned complaint procedure or to opt for the litigation route which affords full access to the courts but which is limited in assessment of the claim to much narrower principles of law and rules of evidence. In early 2016, a dedicated Dispute Resolution Service was introduced with the objective of resolving complaints informally through mediation and, only where necessary, by investigation and adjudication. As a result, 'informal methods including mediation, both by telephone and through meetings, are now the first and preferred options for resolving complaints'.[171]

Section 72 of the Central Bank (Supervision and Enforcement) Act 2013 granted the Ombudsman new powers allowing it to report on those individual regulated financial institutions which have had at least three complaints upheld or partly upheld during a 12-month period. The purpose of this was to encourage better complaint management by the institutions and greater earlier settlement of claims thus obviating the need to resort to the Ombudsman. The Ombudsman's Annual Review 2014 indicated that this strategy was working and complaints decreased 42 per cent between 2013 and 2014.

If redress is needed, the Ombudsman can direct the service provider to: change the conduct complained of or its consequences, explain its conduct, pay

[167] [2006] IEHC 323.

[168] The Court held that the deferential standard was that applied by Keane CJ in *Orange v The Director of Telecommunications Regulation & Anor*. See also *Molloy v Financial Services Ombudsman* (Unreported, High Court, 15 April 2011) and *Ryan v Financial Services Ombudsman and Irish Life & Permanent Plc* (Unreported, High Court, 23 September 2011).

[169] [2013] IEHC 518 at [12]. See also *Millar v The Financial Services Ombudsman* [2015] IECA 126.

[170] See *O'Hara v ACC Bank plc* [2011] IEHC 367 and *Crowley v Zurich Life Assurance Plc & Ors* [2015] IEHC 197.

[171] Financial Services Ombudsman, 'Press Release Financial Services Ombudsman Raising the Bar on Consumer Protection and Complaints Handling' (19 February 2016) available at: www.financialombudsman.ie/documents/FSO%20Raising%20the%20Bar%20on%20Consumer%20Protection%20Press%20Release.pdf.

compensation up to a maximum of €250,000 or a €26,000 annual payment over a period of years, or take any other lawful action. In *Walsh & Ors v The Financial Services Ombudsman*,[172] the High Court rejected a claim that the respondent had awarded insufficient compensation where one of the appellants contended that the bank's conduct had exacerbated an ulcerative condition. The appellants had been awarded damages of €2,500 by the Ombudsman. Hedigan J opined that a comparison to the damages which might be awarded in the High Court for stress or personal injury was invalid.

> I do not think such a comparison is valid. Cases in the High Court involve far more formality. In this case there is a note from the first named applicant's general practitioner which states that the he has suffered a reoccurrence of an ulcer due to business stress. This is a long way from showing that Bank of Ireland is wholly responsible for the ulcer. Such a note would not be sufficient in High Court litigation. The Financial Services Ombudsman is an informal cost free system of resolving disputes. It is not a tribunal for measuring damages. In particular, it is not its role to measure general damages as does the High Court.

The Ombudsman's Annual Review 2015 revealed that 4,872 complaints were received in 2015 and that 65 per cent of the 1,206 complaints that resulted in a formal adjudication and finding were not upheld. However, compensation awarded during 2015 amounted to a total of €1,112,885.

VIII. Conclusion

An examination of Irish law indicates that financial institutions are subject to significant common law duties to their clients and third parties supplemented by a strong consumer protection regime operated by the Central Bank as Financial Regulator and supported by administrative sanctions. Since the Banking Crisis and the subsequent economic downturn, there has been a large increase in the number of cases before the courts alleging breaches of these common law duties and the Central Bank's Codes. These have arisen in the context of loans, mortgages and other investment products to both personal consumers and professional clients. The existence and extent of the duty owed in common law depends very much on the circumstances of the case and the nature of the role being played by the financial institution. At one extreme, a fiduciary relationship may exist involving not only a duty of care but also a duty to advise appropriately and to warn the client of potential dangers. In other cases, the nature of the relationship may be purely commercial and the financial institution will be subject to substantially less onerous duties. Statutory protections are established in the MiFID Regulations and in the Consumer Protection Code. These too prescribe various responsibilities on

[172] [2012] IEHC 258.

service providers depending on the nature of the client. The latter duties are more difficult to avoid through express exemption or limitation clauses. The Irish courts have deliberated at length the consequences of a breach of the statutory duty on an underlying contract and in *Quinn and Ors v Irish Bank Resolution Corporation Limited (In Special Liquidation) and Ors* established a test which focuses on the underlying objective and public policy dimension of the relevant legislation. In Ireland, the Financial Services Ombudsman provides an alternative source of dispute resolution between financial institutions and their customers and is not bound by strict legal rules in reaching a decision on the cases before him.

A noteworthy consequence of the easy availability of finance in the early 2000s was the difficulty of distinguishing between personal consumers and professional clients in Ireland. The question of whether a party to a loan agreement is a 'consumer' is determined by the position of the person entering the loan agreement, having regard to its nature and aims. In *Allied Irish Bank plc v Higgins and Others*,[173] Kelly J considered the decision of the European Court of Justice in *Benincasa v Dentalkit*[174] and concluded:

> The European Court of Justice clearly envisaged that the concept of the consumer was confined to a person acting in a private capacity and not engaged in trade or professional activities. … Only contracts concluded for the purpose of satisfying an individual's needs in terms of private consumption are protected by [Council Directive 87/102/EEC as amended]. There is nothing in the [Consumer Credit] Act suggesting that the legislature here sought to go further than the Directive.

Kelly J determined that the defendants acted as partners in a partnership 'with a view to investing in property and its development for profit' and were not thus consumers. In *Ulster Bank v Healy*,[175] Barrett J held an individual who owed more than half a million euros to a bank was a consumer for the purpose of the Consumer Credit Act 1995 and 'acting outside his business, trade and profession' as he had engaged in 'personal investments … so as to meet the retirement or other future requirements of himself or his family'. He opined that:

> The court does not consider that a consumer who on one or more occasions places saved or borrowed monies in a particular form of investment, such as property, with a view to making a profit therefrom necessarily becomes a person whose business, trade or profession is that of professional investor or property investor and thus no longer a 'consumer' for the purposes of the Consumer Credit Act. Of course there must come a point when a person crosses the Rubicon from consumer to professional. However, it could be contended that a man such as Mr. Healy who has invested not insignificant but not extravagant sums in property in order to provide for his retirement and to benefit his family has not necessarily crossed this line.

[173] [2010] IEHC 219 at [28]. See also *Allied Irish Bank Plc v Fahy* [2014] IEHC 244 at [65].
[174] Case C-269/95 [1997] ECR I-03767.
[175] [2014] IEHC 96.

However in *Stapleford Finance Limited v Lavelle*,[176] Baker J described this statement of Barrett J that there might exist a Rubicon which could determine the characterisation of a consumer contract as obiter and not supported in the authorities. She stated clearly that 'the case law identifies the purpose of the loan as being the defining or identifying characteristic and not the quantum of the loan'. In *Danske Bank v Miley*,[177] Baker J determined that the defendant had not proven that she was a 'consumer' for the purposes of a loan, because the purpose of the loan was to refinance what was itself a commercial loan to her husband to invest in properties in Ireland and abroad. The approach taken by the Irish Courts to the matter of client classification epitomises the very pragmatic and reasoned approach taken to the private law duties and their relationship with regulatory duties.

[176] [2016] IEHC 385.
[177] [2016] IEHC 105.

11

United States of America

GEORGE C HARRIS, HANNIBAL TRAVIS AND SABRINA LARSON

I. Introduction

The banking and financial services industry is one of the largest segments of the US economy and operates in a highly complex regulatory framework at both the national and state level. The result is a dual banking system in which parallel state and federal banking systems coexist. Federal banks operate under federal charters and federal laws, while state banks operate under state charters and state laws.[1] The two systems are, however, interrelated, and most state-chartered banks are subject to certain federal regulations, while federal banks are subject to certain state laws. Commentators note that a benefit of the dual system is that state and national banks can innovate in the interest of customer service in spheres of different sizes, with state banks serving in a way as laboratories for new developments in bank powers, structures and consumer protection.[2] One commentator states:

> When state or national regulatory programs saw customers migrating from one charter to the other, regulators responded with measures enhancing the ability of banks to provide services that customers wanted. That is no small reason why so many innovations in bank services in the last century were developed by U.S. banks.[3]

State law that conflicts with federal law is pre-empted under the US Constitution. Various uniform codes have been promulgated, such as the Uniform Commercial Code (UCC) and the Uniform Trust Code, as guidelines that states may adopt and modify, in an effort to promote consistency in fundamental areas of law. The restatements of law, such as the Restatement of Torts and the Restatement of Trusts, serve this function as well.

US banks also have had a unique history in terms of regulation of their various functions. For most of the twentieth century, banks were limited in their securities

[1] Comptroller of the Currency, *National Banks and The Dual Banking System* (September 2003) www.occ.gov/publications/publications-by-type/other-publications-reports/national-banks-and-the-dual-banking-system.pdf.

[2] ibid, 10.

[3] WA Abernathy, 'Dual Banking System Has Stood Test of Time' *American Banker* (25 February 2013) www.americanbanker.com/bankthink/dual-banking-system-has-stood-test-of-time-1056994-1.html.

activities by the 1933 Glass-Steagall Act (Glass Steagall), which imposed separations between investment and commercial banking functions. Glass-Steagall was partially repealed by the 1999 Gramm-Leach-Biley Act, and US banks and their subsidiaries now offer a broad range of both commercial and securities services.

US banks' duty of care is, therefore, defined across a complex network of federal and state common law, statutory law and regulatory law. This chapter provides an overview of the sources of that duty—from cases about individual bank customers to those arising from nationwide financial crises, and from national standards to minority views—and of the articulation of that duty in various contexts, from the basic mandatory duties of disclosure to the context-dependent duties of fiduciaries.

II. Commercial Banking Functions

A note on terminology: To average Americans, the term 'bank' means the institution where they go to accomplish their everyday banking functions—opening a checking account, opening a savings account and depositing and withdrawing money into and from those accounts. In the United States, more precise terminology developed as a result of legislation that divided banks into those that performed the everyday functions of retail banks, known as commercial banks, and those that acted as investment institutions. A commercial bank can also be distinguished from a retail bank in that the former may be a division of the bank that does business primarily with corporations and businesses, whereas the latter deals directly with individual customers.

A. Depository Functions

i. Duties to Customers

At common law, a bank and its client had the relation of debtor and creditor.[4] The common law created a duty on the part of the bank to pay out cheques only in accordance with the client's instructions.[5]

The foundation of modern commercial banking procedures is found in the UCC, first published in 1952. Article 3 of the UCC governs negotiable instruments—drafts and cheques. Article 4 covers bank deposits and collections. Throughout the country, the UCC, as adopted by each of the states,[6] determines the duty of care that banks owe to their customers.

[4] *Shipman v Bank of State of NY*, 126 NY 318, 27 NE 371 (1891).

[5] ibid. See also *Frederic A Potts & Co v Lafayette Nat'l Bank*, 269 NY 181, 199 NE 50 (1935).

[6] The UCC is not the law itself, but rather a recommendation of the laws that should be adopted in the states with the goal of maintaining uniformity across national commercial transactions. It has been enacted in all 50 states and codified in the states' statutory codes.

A bank owes its primary duty to its depositors. As stated by a New York court in 1935, 'a bank's duty is primarily to its depositors, secondarily to its stockholders, and thirdly to the public'.[7] The customer is the account holder, the person who opens a deposit account such as a savings or checking (current) account. Under the UCC, the bank agrees to collect deposits to the customer's account.[8]

Identifying the customer is not always straightforward. Complications may arise, for example, when an account is held in the name of a corporation. While some courts interpret 'customer' narrowly, such that if the account is in the name of a business entity, only that entity may recover against the bank,[9] others interpret 'customer' more broadly by evaluating the relationship between the individuals and the corporation.[10]

a. The Duty of Ordinary Care under the UCC

A contractual relationship of debtor-creditor is formed when a customer deposits its money into the bank. From this relationship arises the basic duty of banks to make no payments out of a depositor's account except those that are authorised by the customer. Under UCC section 4-401, a bank may charge against a customer's account an 'item that is properly payable. An item is properly payable if it is authorized by the customer and is in accordance with any agreement between the customer and bank'.[11] By allowing third parties to draw upon a bank account or credit line without the customer's authorisation, the bank may breach its contract with the client.[12] Moreover, the Uniform Fiduciaries Act, which has been adopted in some states, makes banks potentially liable for their bad-faith honouring of cheques drawn by fiduciaries in order to misappropriate funds from the principals who own the accounts.[13]

The duty of the bank under this debtor-creditor relationship is one of good faith and ordinary care. Most modern banking relationships will involve a standardised contract presented to the customer. While the UCC permits parties to vary its provisions by agreement, the related duties of good faith and ordinary care cannot be waived:

> [T]he parties to the agreement cannot disclaim a bank's responsibility for its lack of good faith or failure to exercise ordinary care or limit the measure of damages for the

[7] *First Trust & Deposit Co v Potter*, 278 NYS 847, 856 (NY App Div 1935).

[8] UCC § 4-104(a)(5).

[9] See eg *Loucks v Albuquerque Nat'l Bank*, 76 NM 735, 418 P2d 191 (NM 1966).

[10] See eg *Kendall Yacht Corp v United Cal Bank*, 50 Cal App 3d 949, 955, 123 Cal Rptr 848, 852 (Cal Ct App 1975); *Am Nat'l Bank v Stanfill*, 205 Cal App 3d 1089, 1100, 252 Cal Rptr 861, 867 (Cal Ct App 1988).

[11] UCC § 4-401(a). An 'item' is an instrument, or a promise or order to pay money handled by a bank for collection or payment; ibid, § 4-104(a)(9). A cheque is the most common form. See also *Medford Irrigation Dist v W Bank*, 66 Or App 589, 594, 676 P.2d 329, 333 (Or Ct App 1984); *Danning v Bank of Am*, 151 Cal App 3d 961, 969, 199 Cal Rptr 163, 168 (Cal Ct App 1984).

[12] *Geimer v Bank of Am, NA*, 784 F Supp 2d 926, 935–36 (ND Ill 2011).

[13] *Appley v West*, 832 F2d 1021, 1031 (7th Cir 1987) (citing Illinois Annotated Statutes, ch 17, paras 2004–09), *aff'd*, 929 F2d 1176 (7th Cir 1991).

lack or failure. However, the parties may determine by agreement the standards by which the bank's responsibility is to be measured if those standards are not manifestly unreasonable.[14]

Good faith is defined as 'honesty in fact and the observance of reasonable commercial standards of fair dealing'.[15] Ordinary care is defined under UCC, Article 3 as 'observance of reasonable commercial standards, prevailing in the area in which the person is located, with respect to the business in which the person is engaged'.[16] Under UCC, Article 4, ordinary care is further defined as action or non-action that is approved by Article 4, a Federal Reserve regulation, 'clearing-house rules and the like', or 'a general banking usage not disapproved by this Article'.[17]

A corollary of the duty of the bank not to make any payment that is not properly payable is the duty to detect forgery and to determine the genuineness of instruments and their endorsements.

A payment of a client's funds to a third party on a materially altered or fraudulent cheque could result in the bank's liability to the third party without a consequent right for the bank to deduct from the client's deposits for the amount of the transaction.[18] However, New York's doctrine of 'account stated' distinguishes between a situation in which a depositor, by his or her own negligence, fails to complain of account irregularities, thereby relieving the bank of liability, and a situation in which the fraud or error could not be discovered by the depositor through due care, and, therefore, the risk of loss should fall on the bank.[19] New York's highest court, the Court of Appeals, has held that the drawer of a check is not required to frustrate all potential tampering with a cheque, but that if the drawer leaves the cheque so incomplete as to encourage fraudulent alteration, the bank may not be liable.[20]

A bank does not exercise ordinary care if it fails to adopt any system for the detection of forgery of customers' names on cheques. The duty of ordinary care requires banks to ensure that an account is debited only with cheques bearing the authorised signature of the drawer. As the UCC's 2001 amendment makes clear, however, automated systems may now be sufficient to establish that the bank satisfied its duty of care; so specific is the UCC on this point that it includes this note in the definition for ordinary care:

> In the case of a bank that takes an instrument for processing for collection or payment by automated means, reasonable commercial standards do not require the bank to examine the instrument if the failure to examine does not violate the bank's prescribed procedures

14 UCC § 4-103(a).
15 ibid, § 1-201(b)(20).
16 ibid, § 3-103(a)(9).
17 ibid, § 4-103(c).
18 Notes: 'Negotiable Instruments: Payment of Materially Altered Checks' (1954–55) 40(4) *Cornell Law Quarterly* 795–96.
19 *Frederic A Potts & Co* (n 5).
20 *Critten v Chem Nat'l Bank*, 171 NY 219, 63 NE 969 (NY 1902).

> and the bank's procedures do not vary unreasonably from general banking usage not disapproved by this Article or Article 4.[21]

As noted above, the UCC's Article 4 definition of ordinary care includes action or non-action consistent with 'general banking usage' that is not inconsistent with the Code.[22] How to define 'general banking usage' is the subject of disagreement among courts.

It is a general principle of tort law that acting in accordance with custom is not dispositive in assessing whether the duty of care has been met.[23] Courts have applied this principle in the context of banking. For example, an Oregon appeals court found that a bank failed to exercise ordinary care as a matter of law when it improperly paid a forged cheque as part of its procedure to automatically pay all cheques under $5,000 without reviewing them to detect unauthorised signatures.[24] The bank had defended by stating that its practice was consistent with that of most banks of comparable size in the country, and that review of small cheques would cost the bank approximately $200,000 per year, thereby greatly exceeding the benefit of reviewing cheques.[25] The Court reasoned that the fact that a procedure may be common throughout the banking industry does not itself establish that the procedure is reasonable. It held 'that the procedure used must reasonably relate to the detection of unauthorized signatures in order to be considered an exercise of ordinary care or reasonable commercial banking standards'.[26]

Other courts have taken a different view of custom as it relates to ordinary care. For example, the Illinois Supreme Court reversed the lower court's summary judgment in favour of the customer where the bank did not manually verify signatures on cheques of $1,000 or less, but rather relied on an automated system.[27] The Court noted that the UCC does not define 'general banking usage' and provides in commentary that:

> Where the adjective 'general' is used, the intention is to require a usage broader than a mere practice between two or three banks but it is not intended to require anything as broad as a country-wide usage. *A usage followed generally throughout* a state, a substantial portion of a state, a *metropolitan area or the like would certainly be sufficient.*[28]

[21] UCC § 3-103(a)(9).

[22] ibid.

[23] *The TJ Hooper*, 60 F2d 737, 740 (2d Cir 1932) ('[T]here are precautions so imperative that even their universal disregard will not excuse their omission').

[24] *Medford Irrigation Dist v W Bank*, 66 Or App 589, 592, 676 P.2d 329, 331 (Or Ct App 1984). Note that as a result of the UCC 2001 amendment referenced above regarding automated payments, the factual analysis of earlier cases as they relate to automatic payments may no longer be good law; such cases are, however, illustrative of the common law exploration and development of the duty of ordinary care in the banking context.

[25] ibid.

[26] ibid, 593, 332.

[27] *Wilder Binding Co v Oak Park Trust & Sav Bank*, 135 Ill.2d 121, 552 NE2d 782 (Ill 1990).

[28] ibid, 128–29, 786 (emphasis in original) (quoting Ill AnnStat, ch 26, para 4-103, Uniform Commercial Code Comment, 441 (Smith-Hurd, 1963)); *Valley Bank of Ronan v Hughes*, 2006 MT 285, 349, 147 P3d 185 (Mont 2006) (defining banks' duty of ordinary care with respect to the community in which the bank is situated).

The bank submitted an affidavit that two or three banks in the same metropolitan area also used an automated system for cheques less than a certain amount.[29] The Court found this sufficient to create a genuine issue of material fact as to whether the bank exercised ordinary care under the circumstances.[30]

Under tort law, ordinary care or 'due care' does not mean expert care. Requiring an expert level of review may be more than ordinary care.

For example, a New Jersey case analysed the standard of ordinary care versus expert care regarding protection of a customer against forgery.[31] In that case, when the plaintiff opened her account with a bank, she signed a signature card. She testified that the bank told her it would check the signatures on cheques presented for cashing against the plaintiff's signature. After the plaintiff became disabled, she hired a caretaker, and she soon discovered that her caretaker had been forging cheques and withdrawing from her account. The plaintiff alleged that the bank failed to compare her signature with the signature on the forged cheques, and that if it had done so, it would have seen that the plaintiff always signed with the middle initial 'Z', and that none of the forged cheques conformed to that habit. The court analysed the facts under the premise that 'a bank must [use] reasonable and proper methods to detect forgeries, but the tellers and bookkeepers of the bank are not held to a degree of expertness which a handwriting expert possesses'.[32] It held that the bank's practices in this situation were commercially reasonable and sufficient to satisfy its duty of ordinary care.

An unauthorised signature most commonly is a forgery, but an interesting wrinkle is presented by the situation of a signature under duress. A bank's duty of care persists in this situation. For example, in one New York case, the plaintiff was forced at knifepoint by strangers to withdraw money from her account.[33] The bank's practice was to ask for basic biographical information, including date of birth, prior to the transaction. The customer gave an incorrect date of birth in an attempt to alert the teller that she was withdrawing under duress. The teller, however, disregarded the discrepancy and disbursed the funds. The Court found the bank liable under both the UCC and common law negligence for failing to explore the discrepant biographical data.

Deviation from the duty of care sets the measure of damages that a customer may recover from a bank for its breach. Under the UCC, following the common law,

> [t]he measure of damages for failure to exercise ordinary care in handling an item is the amount of the item reduced by an amount that could not have been realized by the exercise of ordinary care.[34]

[29] *Wilder Binding Co* (n 27) at 786.
[30] ibid, 131, 787.
[31] *Estate of Paley v Bank of Am*, 18 A.3d 1033, 1035 (NJ Super Ct App Div 2011).
[32] ibid, 1041 (internal quotations omitted).
[33] *Reynolds v Dime Sav Bank*, 467 N.Y.S.2d 971, 972 (Sup Ct Kings Cnty 1983).
[34] UCC § 4-103.

In the absence of bad faith, the maximum recovery is the amount of the item at issue. Only when bad faith is shown can the plaintiff recover other proximately caused damages. Bad faith is not defined by the UCC, but its 'connotation is the absence of good faith'.[35]

b. Other Statutory Duties

Truth in Savings Act

The Truth in Savings Act (TISA)[36] governs the disclosure requirements of banks regarding deposit accounts held by consumers.[37] The statute requires depositary banks to disclose to consumers[38] the fees and interest rates associated with deposit accounts when consumers apply for or seek information on savings accounts. It also requires banks to send periodic statements to consumers.

Congress amended TISA in 1996 to remove a private right of action for a violation of TISA.[39] Nonetheless, the California Supreme Court, in *Rose v Bank of America*, recently held that a TISA violation can serve as a predicate violation of a federal statute under California's Unfair Competition Law (UCL).[40] The plaintiffs in *Rose* filed a class action against Bank of America, alleging unlawful and unfair business practices based on violations of TISA's disclosure requirements.[41] Bank of America argued that the suit was barred by Congress' removal of TISA's private cause of action. The Court disagreed, noting that Congress left intact TISA's savings clause, which permits enforcement of state laws 'relating to the disclosure of yields payable or terms for accounts … except to the extent that those laws are inconsistent with the provisions of this subtitle'.[42] Because the UCL makes violations of other statutes independently actionable under its terms and because

[35] ibid, cmt 6.

[36] 12 USC §§ 4301 et seq and Regulation DD at 12 CFR §§ 1030 et seq. The Truth in Savings Act is regulated through the Federal Reserve System. The Dodd-Frank Wall Street Reform and Consumer Protection Act of 2010 (Dodd-Frank Act) established the Consumer Financial Protection Bureau (CFPB), which became effective in mid 2011, as an independent entity within the Federal Reserve to regulate the provision of financial products to consumers under the federal consumer financial protection laws.

[37] D Resseguie, *Banking Law, Truth in Savings* (Miamisberg, Ohio: Matthew Bender & Company, 2014) § 151.01, 7-151.

[38] TISA defines a 'consumer' to mean 'a natural person who holds an account primarily for personal, family, or household purposes, to whom such an account is offered'; 12 CFR § 1030.2.

[39] *Rose v Bank of Am, NA*, 57 Cal 4th 390, 393, 304 P.3d 181, 183 (Cal 2013), *cert denied*, 234 S Ct 2870 (2014) (citing Omnibus Consolidated Appropriations Act of 1997, PubL No 104-208, § 2604(a) (30 September 1996) 110 Stat 2009-470).

[40] ibid. California's Unfair Competition Law is found at California Business & Professions Code, ss 17200 et seq. Under the UCL, there are 3 types of business acts that are defined as unfair competition: unlawful acts, unfair acts and fraudulent acts. Included among unlawful business acts are those that violate another federal or state statute. The UCL allows private plaintiffs to recover only injunctive and restitutionary relief; Cal Bus & Prof Code §§ 17200 et seq.

[41] *Rose* (n 39) at 183.

[42] ibid, 395, 184 (citing Cal Bus & Prof Code § 4312).

doing so is not inconsistent with the provisions of TISA, the Court held that the plaintiffs' suit could go forward.[43]

Electronic Fund Transfer Act

The federal Electronic Fund Transfer Act (EFTA)[44] governs transactions occurring through electronic transfer. EFTA sets forth required disclosures, as well as other duties, such as documenting fund transfers and providing periodic statements to customers. A failure to accurately disclose overdraft fees charged even if a consumer has funds available may give rise to a claim for violation of EFTA and a Federal Reserve Board regulation.[45] In addition, a failure to disclose use fees on the screen of an automated teller machine and on the exterior of such a machine may permit individual users to sue for statutory damages of $100 to $1,000.[46]

Recent litigation has raised the issue of whether EFTA and other consumer protection acts provide standing for plaintiffs even when they suffer no direct financial harm as a result of the violation. In *First National Bank of Wahoo & Mutual First Federal Credit Union v Charvat*, the Eighth Circuit held that the plaintiffs had standing to sue despite suffering no direct financial harm as a result of the banks' EFTA violations, rejecting the banks' argument that if the plaintiffs were found to have standing for an EFTA violation resulting in no actual harm, the same could be true under other consumer protection statutes, including the Truth in Lending Act, the Fair Debt Collection Practices Act, the Fair Credit Reporting Act and the Fair and Accurate Credit Transaction Act.[47] The Supreme Court denied review.[48]

c. Federal Regulation

Federal legislation has subjected banks to a series of federal regulatory regimes. First, the National Bank Act of 1864, which conveyed certain powers and imposed certain duties on nationally chartered banks, gives the Office of the Comptroller of the Currency (OCC) the ability to regulate the opening of branches and certain bank mergers. Chartered banks remain subject to certain state law regulatory duties unless the laws are federally pre-empted. Second, the Federal Reserve Act subjects national banks to the money supply and reserve requirement regulations of the Open Market Committee of the Federal Reserve System. Third, the Office of Thrift Supervision (established in 1989), until its functions were divided in

[43] ibid, 399, 187.

[44] 15 USC §§ 1693 et seq.

[45] eg *Gunter v United Fed Credit Union*, No 3:15-cv-00483-MMD-WGC, 2016 WL 3457009 (D Nev 22 June 2016) (citing 15 USC § 1693m; 12 CFR § 1005.17).

[46] eg *Frey v First Nat Bank SW*, 602 F App'x 164 (5th Cir 2015).

[47] Petition for Writ of Certiorari, *First Nat'l Bank of Wahoo v Charvat*, No 13-679, 2013 WL 6354864, at *9-10 (US 2 December 2013).

[48] *First Nat'l Bank of Wahoo v Charvat*, 134 S Ct 1515 (2014). See also A Scurria, 'Justices Again Snub Class Action Standing Question' *Law 360* (10 March 2014) www.law360.com/articles/516786/justices-again-snub-class-action-standing-question.

2011 among the Office of the Comptroller of the Currency, the Federal Deposit Insurance Corporation (FDIC), the Federal Reserve Board of Governors and the Consumer Financial Protection Bureau (CFPB), imposed duties relating to savings and loan associations from their inception to their dissolution. The CFPB and OCC, for example, ordered Discover Bank to pay $200 million in refunds to consumers who may have been deceived by the marketing of credit card services including payment protection and credit-score protection as being free, a trial service, or more generous than they were in fact.[49] The FDIC imposes duties relating to insurance of commercial (as opposed to investment bank or brokerage) accounts.[50] The FDIC obtains settlements and verdicts against financial institutions and their officers or directors, with the recoveries going to depositors, financial creditors and deposit insurance funds.[51] There is some authority indicating that in this capacity the FDIC is not subject to the defences of estoppel, contributory negligence, regulatory negligence, economic difficulties, laches, waiver, or failure to mitigate damages on the part of officers and directors.[52] Fourth, the Federal Trade Commission has promulgated regulations that impose other duties on banks, including regulations of the holders of consumer credit contracts and a general obligation not to use unfair or deceptive acts or practices in interstate commerce. In one notable case, the FTC obtained restitution of more than $100 million in mortgage servicing overcharges levied against consumers by Countrywide Home Loans, Inc, now owned by Bank of America.[53] Fifth, state and local regulatory agencies may impose additional duties, but the National Bank Act or EFTA may pre-empt some of those purported duties. State laws providing remedies for misrepresentations by banks, or for breaches of contractual duties, often are not pre-empted by federal law. Some state usury laws also are not pre-empted.

[49] CFPB, 'Federal Deposit Insurance Corporation and Consumer Financial Protection Bureau Order Discover to Pay $200 Million Consumer Refund for Deceptive Marketing' (24 September 2012) www.consumerfinance.gov/newsroom/discover-consent-order/.

[50] The FDIC is a government corporation that operates as an independent agency and provides deposit insurance. The FDIC is the primary federal regulator of state-chartered banks that do not join the Federal Reserve System. See FDIC, 'Who is the FDIC?' (30 October 2014) https://www.fdic.gov/about/learn/symbol/. It insures deposits in banks and thrift institutions for at least $250,000 per depositor; ibid. The FDIC also provides oversight by examining banks for compliance with consumer protection laws; ibid.

[51] FDIC, 'FDIC Announces Settlement with J.P. Morgan Chase & Co' (19 November 2013) www.fdic.gov/news/news/press/2013/pr13103.html. In 2013, the FDIC arrived at about $40 million in such settlements and verdicts in lawsuits involving the directors or officers of banks. Cornerstone Research, 'Characteristics of FDIC Lawsuits against Directors and Officers of Failed Financial Institutions' (November 2014) www.cornerstone.com/Publications/Reports/Characteristics-of-FDIC-Lawsuits-Feb-2014.

[52] See EF Mannino, *Lender Liability and Banking Litigation* (New York: Law Journal Press: 2006) 11-32–11-33.

[53] See FTC, 'FTC Returns nearly $108 Million to 450,000 Homeowners Overcharged by Countrywide for Loan Servicing Fees' (20 July 2011) www.ftc.gov/news-events/press-releases/2011/07/ftc-returns-nearly-108-million-450000-homeowners-overcharged.

d. Tort

Negligence

A bank's failure to exercise ordinary care in administering its clients' accounts may give rise to a tort action by clients suffering harm.[54]

A plaintiff will often seek to recover for a bank's violation under both UCC, section 4-401 and common law negligence. As the official comments to the UCC state,

> while principles of common law and equity may *supplement* provisions of the Uniform Commercial Code, they may not be used to *supplant* its provisions, or the purposes and policies those provisions reflect.[55]

Courts have found some negligence claims displaced or pre-empted by the UCC.[56]

Fiduciary Duty

A fiduciary relationship is a relationship defined by trust and confidence, and gives rise to a heightened duty of care. A fiduciary duty can arise either by law, such as in the attorney-client or the trustee-beneficiary relationship, or by circumstances. The general rule is that a fiduciary duty does not exist between commercial parties operating at arm's length.[57] Under this general rule, the bank-customer relationship is consistently found to be insufficient to create a fiduciary relationship, absent additional and unique facts.[58] As stated by a California federal court, '[a] bank has limited duties to its customers. The relationship between the two is not fiduciary, but rather is contractual in nature'.[59] As another court stated: 'To establish a fiduciary relationship in banking transactions there must be evidence establishing that the transaction involved more trust and confidence than a typical arm's length transaction'.[60] Special circumstances, however, even in commercial transactions in the banking context, can give rise to fiduciary duties.

[54] *Mut Serv Cas Ins Co v Elizabeth State Bank*, 265 F3d 601, 618 (7th Cir 2001) (citing *Congregation of the Passion, Holy Cross Province v Touche Ross & Co*, 159 Ill2d 137, 636 NE2d 503 (1994)).

[55] UCC § 1-103, cmt 2 (emphasis in original).

[56] See eg *Donovan v Bank of Am*, 574 F Supp 2d 192, 200 (D Me 2008) (where the plaintiff raised several negligence claims, the Court stated: 'To the extent that they relate to the Bank's handling of the checks, the claims are displaced by the UCC').

[57] See eg *Kitsap Bank v Denley*, 177 Wash App 559, 312 P3d 711, 719 (Wash App Ct 2013) (internal quotation and citation omitted) ('As a general rule, participants in a business transaction deal at arm's length and do not enter into a fiduciary relationship'); *Bank of Am, NA v Corporex Realty & Inv., LLC*, 875 F Supp 2d 689, 705 (ED Ky 2012) ('In an arms-length commercial transaction, where each party is assumed to be protecting its own interest, no such duty arises').

[58] AT Schwing, *2 California Affirmative Defences* (Eagan, Minn: Bancroft-Whitney (Thomson West) 2013 edn) § 46:3. See also *Polek v JP Morgan Chase Bank, NA*, 424 Md 333, 366, 36 A.3d 399, 418 (Md 2012) ('The butcher, the baker and the candle-stick maker do not occupy a fiduciary relation toward every customer who has too much faith in human nature or is too busy or too careless (whichever way he may properly be characterized) to count his change') (quoting *Johnson v Bugle Coat, Apron & Linen Serv*, 60 A2d 686, 689 (Md 1948)).

[59] *Simi Mgmt Corp v Bank of Am, NA*, 930 F Supp 2d 1082, 1100 (ND Cal 2013) (internal citations omitted).

[60] *Kitsap Bank*, 177 Wash App at 574, 312 P3d at 719 (internal quotation and citation omitted).

Facts that Give Rise to a Fiduciary Relationship

Most states find existence of a fiduciary duty in the banking context, as in other contexts, to be a question of fact determined on a case-by-case basis.[61] The court looks to the facts of the relationship between the parties and whether one party reposes confidence and trust in the other, who voluntarily accepts that confidence. Factors in making this determination include whether the bank holds itself out as an expert in advising in investment transactions and the extent of a customer's vulnerability.[62] Factors indicating vulnerability may include youth, advanced age, illness, lack of education or lack of capacity.

For example, in *Brown v Wells Fargo Bank, NA*,[63] a California Court of Appeal held that a fiduciary relationship existed between a bank and its customers, an elderly couple for whom the bank provided asset management, investment advice and brokerage services. The claim was for fraud in the execution of the brokerage agreement. The plaintiffs alleged that the bank failed to disclose the inclusion of an arbitration clause and that it had a fiduciary duty to do so. The bank argued that no fiduciary relationship existed prior to entering into the brokerage agreement and, therefore, at the time of signing, it had no duty to disclose the agreement's material terms.[64] The Court explained that

> [t]he essence of a fiduciary or confidential relationship is that the parties do not deal on equal terms, because the person in whom trust and confidence is reposed and who accepts that trust and confidence is in a superior position to exert unique influence over the dependent party.[65]

It found those circumstances present because the Browns were an elderly couple in declining health for whom the bank had provided a 'relationship manager' who visited their home, had access to all of their financial information and provided them with investment advice.[66] The bank thereby voluntarily and knowingly induced the Browns to repose trust and confidence in its employees.[67] The court referred, however, to the 'unique factual circumstances of this case',[68] leaving uncertain the breadth of its holding.

[61] For a review of case-law, see 'Existence of Fiduciary Relationship between Bank and Depositor or Customer so as to Impose Special Duty of Disclosure upon Bank' 70 ALR3d 1344 (originally published in 1976).

[62] *City of Hope Nat'l Med Ctr v Genentech, Inc*, 43 Cal 4th 375, 389, 181 P3d 142, 152 (Cal 2008). See also *AG Capital Funding Partners v State Street Bank & Trust Co*, 11 NY3d 146, 158, 896 NE2d 578 (NY 2008) (fiduciary relationship may exist where trust and confidence in the other, and the other party enjoys influence as a result); *Bldg Educ Corp v Ocean Bank*, 982 So 2d 37, 39–41 (Fla Dist Ct App 2008) (similar); *Hooper v Barnett Bank of West Fla*, 474 So 2d 1253, 1257 (Fla Dist Ct App 1985) (similar).

[63] 168 Cal App 4th 938, 85 Cal Rptr 3d 817 (Cal Ct App 2008).

[64] ibid, 960, 835.

[65] ibid (internal quotation omitted).

[66] ibid.

[67] ibid, 961–62, 835–36.

[68] ibid, 960, 835.

Duties that Arise from a Fiduciary Relationship

A fiduciary is 'duty bound to act with the utmost good faith for the benefit of the other'.[69] As illustrated in *Brown*, one central duty arising from a fiduciary duty is the duty of disclosure. The duty of disclosure requires the fiduciary 'to disclose all material facts that may affect its customer's interests'.[70] A further fiduciary duty recognised in some jurisdictions is to serve as constructive trustee of profits resulting from a breach of fiduciary duty to the principal.[71]

Other Circumstances Giving Rise to a Duty to Disclose

The duty to disclose arising from a fiduciary relationship is a special duty because there is no general duty to disclose. US tort law recognises other circumstances that have been applied to banks and that may also give rise to a duty to disclose.

As set forth in Restatement of Torts (Second) section 551, Liability for Nondisclosure, a party in a business transaction is under a duty to exercise reasonable care to disclose essential information in five circumstances: (1) where the parties are in a fiduciary relationship or a similar relationship of trust and confidence; (2) where a party has made a partial or ambiguous statement that he knows may be misleading and knows additional statements are necessary to prevent the other party from being misled; (3) where he has subsequently acquired information that makes a previous statement untrue, and his further disclosure will correct that untruth; (4) where he learns that the other party is about to act in reliance upon an earlier, false statement he made not expecting it to be acted upon; and (5) if he knows of facts basic to the transaction and knows the other party is about to enter into the transaction under a mistake as to those facts, and the other party would reasonably expect a disclosure of those facts, whether because of the parties' relationship or because of the customs of trade or other objective circumstances.[72] A bank also has a duty to disclose when it has actual knowledge of fraud.

A bank also has a duty *not* to disclose customer confidences, which may come into tension with its duty to disclose to another customer in the above circumstances. For example, in one Florida case, a bank's customer brought an action against the bank to cancel a promissory note on the grounds that the bank failed to reveal to him the financial condition of another customer, the person who arranged the bank loan.[73] The customer claimed that the bank was aware of the

69 *Herbert v Lankershim*, 9 Cal 2d 409, 483, 71 P2d 220, 257 (Cal 1937).

70 See eg *Regions Bank v Schmauch*, 354 SC 648, 671, 582 SE2d 432, 444 (SC Ct App 2003).

71 Restatement (Second) of Torts § 874, cmt b (1979). See also DA DeMott, 'Breach of Fiduciary Duty: On Justifiable Expectations of Loyalty & Their Consequences' (2006) 48 *Arizona Law Review* 925, 928 and note 17 (citing 2 DB Dobbs, *The Law of Remedies: Damages, Equity Restitution*, 2d edn (Eagan, Minn: West Publishing Company, 1993) 670).

72 Restatement (Second) of Torts § 551: Liability for Nondisclosure.

73 *Hooper v Barnett Bank of W Fla* (n 62), *decision approved*, 498 So 2d 923 (Fla 1986).

fraudulent activity of the other customer but failed to disclose this fact and instead made the loan knowing it was a fraud.[74] The bank acknowledged that it knew the lending customer was being investigated by the IRS and that it suspected, but had not confirmed, fraudulent activity.[75] The bank employee who coordinated the loan stated he did not disclose his suspicions to the borrowing customer because of the duty of confidentiality owed to the other customer.[76] The appellate court reversed the trial court's directed verdict for the bank, stating that a jury could have found 'the bank had knowledge of material facts concerning this transaction which it was under a duty to disclose'.[77] Thus, the Court reasoned,

in cases such as this, where a fiduciary duty to disclose may arise under the facts and circumstances, the jury is entitled to weigh this duty to disclose against the bank's duty of confidentiality to its depositors.[78]

ii. Duty to Non-customers

In addition to the common law and contractual duties of retail banks to deliver reasonably prudent services to their depositors, banks have a common law duty in tort to some non-customers. Historically, courts employed the doctrine of 'constructive fraud' as a catch-all for omissions contrary to a legal or equitable duty to act, causing injury to another in circumstances offending 'good conscience'.[79] Although in some states there may be no duty in tort to non-customers to detect and prevent a bank customer's fraudulent conduct, many states do impose criminal and tort liability for aiding and abetting violations of law.

Typically, such liability is triggered by knowing aid to a violation, or reckless disregard of the possibility of a violation, not by mere negligence. Thus, there may be no bank duty to police customer accounts proactively for purposes of protecting non-customers. However, if a bank has actual knowledge of wrongdoing, it may be liable for aiding and abetting a breach of fiduciary duty owed by a customer to a non-customer. It may also be liable on a theory of 'conscious avoidance:

> Conscious avoidance … involves a culpable state of mind whereas constructive knowledge imputes a state of mind on a theory of negligence. Reflecting this analysis, the Second Circuit has held in the criminal context that conscious avoidance may satisfy the knowledge prong of an aiding and abetting charge. Accordingly, the Court sees no reason to spare a putative aider and abettor who consciously avoids confirming facts that, if known, would demonstrate the fraudulent nature of the endeavor he or she substantially furthers.[80]

[74] ibid, 1254.
[75] ibid, 1255.
[76] ibid, 1257.
[77] ibid, 1258.
[78] ibid, 1259.
[79] *Jackson v Jackson*, 47 Ga 100, 109 (1872).
[80] *Fraternity Fund Ltd v Beacon Hill Asset Mgmt, LLC*, 479 F Supp 2d 349, 367–68 (SDNY 2007).

So-called 'red flags' of wrongdoing may be sufficient to hold a bank liable in such a case, even without a definitive adjudication against or criminal conviction of the customer.[81]

B. Lending Functions

A bank's duty to borrowers is triggered by processing loan applications, administering loans, and servicing mortgages. Careless or malicious processing of loan applications, foreclosures, or mortgage documents may give rise to negligence actions. For example, in New York, a cause of action for wrongful foreclosure may exist where a mortgaged property is foreclosed after a defect in the servicing or foreclosure process or after a borrower exercises the right of redemption.[82] In other states, foreclosure in the absence of a borrower's default on the mortgage or in violation of a contractual or statutory duty to the borrower may give rise to a claim for wrongful foreclosure.[83] Other states may not recognise such a claim.[84] When there is a claim, damages may be measured by the value of the property at the time of foreclosure minus the balance on the mortgage.[85]

State laws governing debt collection and deceptive acts in commerce may also impose duties on banks.[86] Under the common law of some states, a bank's negligent misrepresentation that it is entitled to service a mortgage and/or to foreclose on a loan may be tortious.[87] Other generally applicable statutes impose a duty not to make misrepresentations of fact in commerce.[88] In addition, under the common

[81] *Lerner v Fleet Bank, NA*, 459 F3d 273 (2d Cir 2006); *Fraternity Fund Ltd v Beacon Hill Asset Mgmt, LLC* (n 80); *Casey v US Bank Nat'l Ass'n*, 127 Cal App 4th 1138, 26 Cal Rptr 3d 401 (Cal Ct App 2005).

[82] *LFJ Realty Co v Bank of NY*, 929 N.Y.S.2d 200 (2011) (citing, inter alia, *Mooney v Byrne*, 163 NY 86, 89–92 (1900)).

[83] *Cervantes v Countrywide Home Loans, Inc*, 656 F.3d 1034, 1043–44 (9th Cir 2011) (citing *Mechanics Nat'l Bank of Worcester v Killeen*, 377 Mass 100, 384 NE2d 1231, 1236 (Mass 1979); *Fields v Millsap & Singer, PC*, 295 SW3d 567, 571 (Mo Ct App 2009); *Gregorakos v Wells Fargo Nat'l Ass'n*, 285 Ga App 744, 647 SE2d 289, 292 (Ga Ct App 2007); *Collins v Union Fed Sav & Loan Ass'n*, 99 Nev 284, 662 P2d 610, 623 (Nev1983)); *Jolley v Chase Home Fin, LLC*, 213 Cal App 4th 872, 153 Cal Rptr 3d 546 (Cal Ct App 2013); *Bank of NY Mellon v Reyes*, 126 So 3d 304, 308 (Fla Dist Ct App 2013) (citing *Republic Nat'l Life Ins Co v Creative Investors Real Estate, Inc*, 429 So 2d 87 (Fla Dist Ct App 1983)); *Harper v Interstate Brewery Co*, 120 P2d 757, 762–64 (Or 1942); *Farrell v Hunt*, 714 SW2d 298, 299 (Tex 1986).

[84] *Ed Peters Jewelry Co v C & J Jewelry Co*, 124 F3d 252, 262–63 (1st Cir 1997).

[85] *Farrell v Hunt* (n 83).

[86] *Biggers v BAC Home Loans Servicing, LP*, 767 F Supp 2d 725, 729–32 (ND Tex 2011) (citing Tex Fin Code Ann § 392.001; Tex Fin Code Ann. § 392.403–392.404; *Rey v Acosta*, 860 SW2d 654, 659 (Tex App 1993), *no writ*; *Dixon v Brooks*, 604 SW2d 330, 334 (Tex App 1980), *writ ref'd nre* (13 May 1998).

[87] Restatement (Second) of Torts § 552B: Damages for Negligent Misrepresentation (1977); *Biggers* (n 86) at 734–35.

[88] In 2013, citing one such statute, a court stated that 'a lender does owe a duty to a borrower to not make material misrepresentations about the status of an application for a loan modification or about the date, time, or status of a foreclosure sale'; *Lueras v BAC Home Loans Servicing, LP*, 221 Cal App 4th 49, 68, 163 Cal Rptr 3d 804, 821 (Cal Ct App 2013).

law and some statutes, a bank may owe a borrower a duty of good faith and fair dealing when servicing a loan or exercising other discretionary powers.[89]

Online marketplace lending, which began as a small lender to small borrower marketplace, has attracted the interest of larger companies, including banks.[90] Loan origination of this type could exceed $90 billion in a few years' time.[91] The US Department of the Treasury is particularly interested in lending to a consumer with a term of repayment of more than 45 days and an annual percentage rate of less than 36 per cent, or if greater than 36 per cent, where it does not constitute a vehicle title, deposit advance or paycheck (payday) loan, which may soon be regulated by the CFPB.[92] Observers have expressed concern to regulators that disparities in the treatment of online marketplaces versus traditional lenders may undermine consumers' rights.[93] On the other hand, some consumers may enjoy lower rates on online personal loans than on traditional credit cards, home equity loans, lines of credit or student loans.[94] Meanwhile, consumers declined credit elsewhere may find opportunities to borrow in online marketplaces.[95] These marketplaces are likely to attract new efforts at regulation by the Treasury Department, the Federal Deposit Insurance Corporation, the Office of the Comptroller of the Currency and/or the CFPB, potentially focused on anti-usury, due diligence and anti-discrimination objectives.[96]

The CFPB also expresses concern that virtual currencies may be riskier than credit, debit or bank cards. While some virtual currencies like Bitcoin have risen in value dramatically, Bitcoin has also been known to drop in value by as much as 80 per cent in one day.[97] The state of Oregon may have passed the first Bitcoin-related

[89] ibid, 76, 827 (citing, inter alia, *Kendall v Ernest Pestana, Inc*, 40 Cal 3d 488, 500, 709 P2d 837 (Cal 1985)). In 2015, citing such common law and statutory duties, a court held that a lender who offers a borrower a federal Home Affordable Modification Program (HAMP) loan modification may be liable for obligating the borrower to make payments on a modified schedule while breaching the terms of its own reciprocal promises to modify the loan's terms or for committing consumer fraud in the course of such a breach. See *Arias v Elite Mortg Grp, Inc*, 439 NJ Super 273, 108 A3d 21(NJ Super Ct App 2015) (approved for publication).

[90] US Department of the Treasury, 'Opportunities and Challenges in Online Marketplace Lending' (10 May 10, 2016) 5, www.treasury.gov/connect/blog/Documents/Opportunities_and_Challenges_in_Online_Marketplace_Lending_white_paper.pdf.

[91] ibid, 9.

[92] ibid, 3 note 2 (citing CFPB, 'Small Business Advisory Review Panel for Potential Rulemakings for Payday, Vehicle Title, and Similar Loans: Outline of Proposals under Consideration and Alternatives Considered' (26 March 2015) http://files.consumerfinance.gov/f/201503_cfpb_outline-of-the-proposals-from-small-business-review-panel.pdf).

[93] ibid, 23–25, 28.

[94] ibid, 11, 14–15 (citing R Nash and E Beardsley, 'The Future of Finance: The Rise of the New Shadow Bank' Goldman Sachs Equity Research (3 March 2015) https://singaporefintech.com/the-future-of-finance-part-1).

[95] ibid, 1.

[96] See A Nolan, E Dartley and S Goseffi, 'Bridging The Divide Between Banks And Marketplace Lenders' *Law360* (28 July 2016) www.law360.com/articles/822253/bridging-the-divide-between-banks-and-marketplace-lenders.

[97] See CFPB, 'Consumer Advisory: Risks to Consumers Posed by Virtual Currencies' (August 2014) http://files.consumerfinance.gov/f/201408_cfpb_consumer-advisory_virtual-currencies.pdf; O Kharif,

law with an effective date of May 2015. The law calls upon the director of the Department of Consumer and Business Services to license and/or register money transmitters and cheque cashers, including transmitters of valuable currency that is not US legal tender such as Bitcoin, and to renew such licences.[98]

The federal Truth in Lending Act (TILA)[99] imposes disclosure duties on creditors, including financial institutions. It requires disclosure of all critical terms of the credit transaction, including the annual percentage rate. Unlike TISA, TILA allows for civil penalties.

III. Investment Banking Functions

A. Banks' Duties Not To Commit Fraud or Market Manipulation

i. Relationship of Federal and State Law

Banks' investment banking functions are governed by the Federal Reserve Act of 1913, the Securities Act of 1933, the Securities Exchange Act of 1934, the Investment Company Act of 1940, the Commodity Exchange Act of 1936, the Commodity Futures Trading Commission Act of 1974, the Securities Investors Protection Act of 1970, the Sarbanes-Oxley Act of 2002 and the Wall Street Reform and Consumer Protection ('Dodd-Frank') Act of 2010. Banks and other corporations are generally 'creatures of state law', but investors in banks (and through banks as market makers) entrust their funds on the basis that federal law may expressly require certain responsibilities of corporate directors, managers and shareholders.[100]

ii. The Duty not to Commit Fraud or Manipulation under Federal Law

The Securities Act of 1933 created requirements to disclose the risks of an investment in non-exempt securities and to register certain securities issuers.[101] Section 11 makes underwriters of initial public offerings and other securities transactions liable to investors for negligently releasing a registration statement containing an untrue statement of material fact or an omission of material fact whose disclosure is required to make a previous statement not misleading.[102] In late 2013,

'The Final Days of the Bitcoin Foundation?' *Bloomberg News* (20 December 2015) www.bloomberg.com/news/articles/2015-12-30/the-final-days-of-the-bitcoin-foundation.

[98] See H Morton, National Conference of State Legislatures (21 September 2015) www.ncsl.org/blog/2015/09/21/do-you-have-change-for-a-bitcoin-.aspx.

[99] 15 USC §§ 1601 et seq.

[100] *Santa Fe Indus, Inc v Green*, 430 US 462, 479 (1977).

[101] Securities Act of 1933, Pub L No 73-22, 48 Stat 74 (codified as amended at 15 USC §§ 77a–77aa (2014)).

[102] 15 USC § 77k(a).

a federal district court ruled that investors could sue the underwriters of the Facebook, Inc initial public offering for failing to disclose to the public information that Facebook's executives conveyed to them concerning threats to future revenue and profit growth.[103] The financial industry defendants included Morgan Stanley & Co LLC, JP Morgan Securities LLC, Goldman, Sachs & Co, Barclays Capital Inc, Credit Suisse Securities (USA) LLC, E*TRADE Securities LLC, Merrill Lynch, Pierce, Fenner & Smith Incorporated and Wells Fargo Securities, LLC, among others.[104] In 2014, the trial court granted the motion to dismiss one complaint against defendants Morgan Stanley, JP Morgan Securities and Goldman Sachs on the grounds that sections 13 and 16 of the 1934 Act do not require greater disclosure of agreements not to sell Facebook shares under certain conditions (ie lock-up agreements), unless the underwriters form a 'group' or 'combination' for one of a series of 'purposes enumerated by statute and SEC regulations'.[105] While two plaintiffs seek to appeal the failure of class counsel to plead a 1934 Act claim in the consolidated class-action complaint, the NASDAQ OMX Group stock exchange tentatively agreed to settle claims that the design of its market-making systems for the Facebook IPO led to investor losses and that NASDAQ should have disclosed the design weaknesses to investors.[106]

Under section 12(a)(2) of the 1933 Act, offering or selling a security using a prospectus that includes an untrue statement of material fact or an omission of material fact creates liability to the purchaser.[107]

The Securities Exchange Act of 1934 prohibits fraud or manipulation in connection with securities markets, as well as specific deceptive conduct, such as matched orders and wash sales.[108] Buying up a security for purposes of 'inducing' demand is also restricted.[109] For purposes of the expansive anti-fraud provisions of federal securities law, loan participation (or splitting loans among several banks) has been held to be a security on some occasions.[110]

Section 14(a) of the Securities Exchange Act of 1934 renders it unlawful for a bank or any person to use the mails, a national securities exchange, or other avenue

[103] *In re Facebook, Inc, IPO Sec & Derivative Litig*, MDL No 12-2389, 2013 US Dist LEXIS 178154 (SDNY 12 December 2013).

[104] ibid, *2 n 2.

[105] *In re Facebook, Inc, IPO Sec & Deriv Litig*, 43 F Supp 3d 369 (SDNY 2014) (citing SEC Rules 16a-7, 13d-3(d)(4)). See also *In re Facebook, Inc, IPO Sec & Deriv Litig*, 986 F Supp 2d 544 (SDNY 2014) (citing 15 USC §§ 78m(d)(3), 78p(b); 17 C.F.R. §§ 240.13d-5(b)(1), 240.16a-1).

[106] See I Kossov, 'Facebook IPO Investors Move for Class Certification' *Law360* (13 January 2015) www.law360.com/articles/611067/facebook-ipo-investors-move-for-class-certification; Z Zagger, 'Underwriters Blast Plaintiffs' Bid to Exit Facebook-IPO MDL' *Law360* (30 March 2015) www.law360.com/articles/637097/underwriters-blast-plaintiffs-bid-to-exit-facebook-ipo-mdl; Reuters, 'Nasdaq to Settle Facebook IPO Lawsuit for $26.5M', *CNBC* (24 April 2015) www.cnbc.com/2015/04/24/nasdaq-to-settle-facebook-ipo-lawsuit-for-265m.html.

[107] 15 USC § 77-*l*(a)(2).

[108] 15 USC §§ 78a–78m; Securities Exchange Act of 1934, Pub L No 73-291, 48 Stat 881 (2003).

[109] 15 USC § 78i(a)(2).

[110] eg JT Cookson, Note, 'Loan Participation Agreements As Securities: Judicial Interpretations of the Securities Act of 1922 and the Securities Exchange Act of 1934' (1983) 24 *William & Mary Law Review* 295.

of interstate commerce to solicit or be named in connection with the solicitation of a non-exempted security required to be registered with the Securities Exchange Commission (SEC), where such solicitation or use is in violation of 'such rules and regulations as the Commission may prescribe as necessary or appropriate in the public interest or for the protection of investors'.[111] Under this section, the relevant rule states that:

> No solicitation subject to this regulation shall be made by means of any proxy statement … containing any statement which, at the time and in the light of the circumstances under which it is made, is false or misleading with respect to any material fact, or which omits to state any material fact necessary in order to make the statements therein not false or misleading[112]

The Supreme Court has held that, for the shareholders casting such tainted votes to have a private right of action to challenge a merger or other fundamental corporation transaction, there must be a showing that a materially false or misleading solicitation has resulted in a tainted authorisation of the transaction.[113]

Statements other than proxy solicitations are governed by distinct provisions of the US Code, as well as by SEC anti-fraud rules and regulations analogous to Rule 14a-9.[114]

Section 10(b) and SEC Rule 10b-5[115] protect investors from fraud, deception and manipulation in connection with the purchase or sale of a security. A violation requires a material misstatement or omission[116] and the 'intent to deceive, manipulate, or defraud'.[117] The US Supreme Court has not addressed whether reckless behaviour is also sufficient for liability under the Exchange Act, but '[e]very Court of Appeals that has considered the issue has held that a plaintiff may meet the scienter requirement by showing that the defendant acted intentionally or recklessly, though the Circuits differ on the degree of recklessness required'.[118] Rule 10b-5 makes it unlawful, among other things, to make an untrue assertion or to fail to disclose a truthful fact needed to cure the misleading effect of a technically true assertion, while communicating in interstate commerce.[119] It also imposes a duty not to engage in a scheme to defraud, or in any practice or 'course of business which operates or would operate as a fraud or deceit', whether directly or indirectly, on a national securities exchange or other interstate commerce.[120]

[111] 15 USC § 78n(a)(1).

[112] 17 CFR § 240.14a-9 (1990).

[113] *Va Bankshares, Inc v Sandberg*, 501 US 1083, 1087 (1991).

[114] See 15 USC § 78n(c); 17 CFR § 240.14c-6 (1990).

[115] 17 CFR § 240.10b-5 (1988).

[116] *ECA & Local 134 IBEW Joint Pension Trust of Chi v JP Morgan Chase Co*, 553 F3d 187, 197 (2d Cir 2009); *Castellano v Young & Rubicam, Inc*, 257 F3d 171, 180 (2d Cir 2001).

[117] *Ernst & Ernst v Hochfelder*, 425 US 185, 193 (1976).

[118] *Tellabs, Inc v Makor Issues & Rights, Ltd*, 551 U.S. 308, 319 n 3 (2007). See also *Ottmann v Hanger Orthopedic Grp, Inc*, 353 F3d 338, 343 (4th Cir 2003) (collecting cases).

[119] 17 CFR § 240.10b-5.

[120] ibid.

Under the securities laws, an investment bank or other participant in the securities markets has a duty to correct 'statements that are false at the time they were made', at such time as the investment bank or other participant learns that its prior statements were untrue.[121] This 'duty to update applies to a statement made misleading by intervening events, even if the statement was true when made'.[122] Statements of opinion accompanied by statements of fact may be false or misleading for purposes of these laws.[123]

An example of such a deceptive or manipulative scheme is the 'churning' of an investment bank's customer accounts in order to generate excessive broker or banker commissions or fees. As one court stated:

> 'Churning' occurs when a broker, directing the volume and frequency of trades, abuses his customer's confidence for personal gain by initiating transactions that are excessive in view of the character of the account and the customer's objectives as expressed to the broker. Churning cannot occur as to any trade directed by the customer. …
>
> Under the law of this circuit, if an account earned $50,000 but would have earned $100,000 if it was not churned, the customer has sustained actual damages in the amount of $50,000 plus excess commissions paid.[124]

In that case, a brokerage account executive engaged in more than 100 unauthorised trades for a client.[125] The client earned more than $50,000 in profits on more than $2 million in aggregate trading activity, but the Court determined that the client would have earned $50,000 more had her account not been 'churned' and awarded that amount as actual damages.[126]

Forward-looking predictions or promises are governed by the 'bespeaks caution' doctrine, which limits a bank's (or other entity's) duty to disclose when 'cautionary statements' or risk disclosures accompany a prediction or promise and place the reader or listener on notice that the predicted or promised outcome might not materialise.[127] Under more recent case-law, this doctrine may not shield banks that fail to disclose existing financial or business-related travails of a client whose securities they are underwriting.[128]

The Private Securities Litigation Reform Act of 1995 (PSLRA) imposes a heightened pleading standard in order to deter or secure the speedy resolution of claims lacking merit. It states that claims under the Securities Exchange Act must be pleaded with specificity, including each statement alleged to be misleading, why it was misleading, and all facts based on which the claimant believes the

[121] *In re JP Jeanneret Assocs Inc*, 769 F Supp 2d 340, 375 (SDNY 2011).
[122] *In re NovaGold Res Inc Sec Litig*, 629 F Supp 2d 272, 301 (SDNY 2009).
[123] *In re Donald J Trump Casino Sec Litig*, 7 F3d 357, 368 (3d Cir 1993); *In re IBM Corporate Sec Litig*, 163 F3d 102, 107 (2d Cir 1998).
[124] *Davis v Merrill Lynch, Pierce, Fenner & Smith*, 906 F2d 1206, 1211 n 3, 1219 (8th Cir 1990).
[125] ibid, 1216–18.
[126] ibid, 1219.
[127] *See Grossman v Novell, Inc*, 120 F3d 1113, 1119–23 (10th Cir 1997).
[128] *See Iowa Pub Emps' Ret Sys v MF Global, Ltd*, 620 F3d 137, 142 (2d Cir 2010); *In re Facebook, Inc*, 2013 US Dist LEXIS 178134, at *51.

statement to be misleading.[129] This pleading requirement does not apply to registration claims under the 1933 Act.[130] The PSLRA also makes it nearly impossible to sue a bank for mafia-like fraud ('racketeering') in connection with securities purchases or sales.[131]

In the wake of the financial crisis of 2007–12, plaintiffs brought suit under section 10(b) against investment banks, accountants, lawyers and ratings agencies. In one case, a court held that a municipality could sue an international bank for negligent misrepresentation after the bank allegedly unloaded its low-quality mortgage-backed securities into a special investment vehicle, which was then unjustifiably rated safe by ratings agencies.[132] The Court stated that although

> the offering documents contained disclaimers of liability and warnings that investors should conduct their own investigation, … plaintiffs could prove that their reliance was justified given their lack of access to the information upon which the ratings were based.[133]

In another case, the Court held that section 10(b) claims could be pleaded against ratings agencies, assuming that fraud, materiality, reliance and the other elements of such claims existed.[134] Some courts have found parallels between section 10(b) claims and New York state claims for fraud or negligent misrepresentation.[135] Although secondary actors such as law firms and accounting firms are typically not civilly liable for advising their clients to mislead securities investors, the SEC may be able to sue banks who prepare false claims for their clients.[136]

iii. Commodities Trading and Investment Banks' Duties to Non-customers

The Commodity Exchange Act of 1936 provided for the registration of futures commission merchants and commodities brokers and the regulation of fees and charges for commodities trading services. The Commodity Futures Trading Commission Act of 1974 provided for a federal commission to issue comprehensive rules and regulations governing contracts for the 'future delivery' of goods,

[129] 15 USC § 78u-4(b).

[130] *In re Morgan Stanley Info Fund Sec Litig*, 592 F3d 347, 359 (2d Cir 2010); *In re Facebook, Inc* (n 128) at *36.

[131] *MLSMK Inv Co v JP Morgan Chase & Co*, 651 F3d 268 (2d Cir 2011).

[132] *King Cnty v IKB Deutsche Industriebank AG*, 863 F Supp 2d 288 (SDNY 2012).

[133] ibid, 312.

[134] *In re Lehman Bros Mortgage-Backed Sec Litig*, 650 F3d 167, 185 (2d Cir 2011) (citing *In re Morgan Stanley Info Fund Sec Litig* (n 130) 359–60.

[135] *See In re Optimal US Litig*, 837 F Supp 2d 244, 252 (SDNY 2011) (citing *AIG Global Sec Lending Corp v Banc of Am Sec, LLC*, No 01 Civ. 11448, 2005 US Dist LEXIS 21605, at *16 (SDNY 26 September 2005)).

[136] *SEC v Pentagon Capital Mgmt PLC*, 725 F3d 279 (2d Cir 2013), *cert. denied*, 134 S Ct 2896 (2014); S Paradise et al, 'New Decision Creates Split in Southern District of New York Over Janus Decision' *Vinson & Elkins Litigation & Enforcement Update* (24 February 2012) www.mondaq.com/unitedstates/x/166722/securities/New+Decision+Creates+Split+In+New+York+Over+Janus+Decisiont.

services, rights or interests.[137] In 1982, Congress provided private persons and entities with a private federal remedy for violation of certain provisions of the commodities trading laws.[138] Even prior to this, the Supreme Court had held that there is an 'implied' private cause of action under the 1974 amendments.[139] The commodities laws provide for civil remedies against banks for participating in manipulative practices with respect to the commodities markets.[140] Manipulation includes such practices as 'wash sales, matched orders, or rigged prices, that … artificially affect[] market activity'.[141] Churning of commodities accounts may also be remediable by a civil action.[142]

In July 2011, the commission created by the 1974 Act announced Rule 180.1(a), which resembles Rule 10b-5 except that it operates 'in connection with any swap, or contract of sale of any commodity in interstate commerce'. The rule implements amended section 6(c) of the Commodity Exchange Act, which the 2010 Dodd-Frank Act amended to extend protections to investors in the derivatives and swaps markets.[143] The Dodd-Frank Act also amended section 9 of the Securities Exchange Act to prohibit a transaction in, or attempt to induce a transaction in, 'any security-based swap' affected with 'any fraudulent, deceptive, or manipulative act or practice, … any fictitious quotation' or deceptive 'course of business'.[144]

iv. Deceptive Schemes and Banks' Duties to Customers' Investment Clients

Starting sometime in the late 1960s, Bernard Madoff operated a fraudulent investment advisory business based in Manhattan, which promised clients returns of up to 10–12 per cent per year.[145] The global financial services corporation JP Morgan Chase & Co allegedly served as the depository institution for Madoff's firm and developed a derivative product for Madoff's European clients, which

[137] Commodity Futures Trading Commission Act of 1974, as amended, 88 Stat 1389 (1974), codified at 7 USC §§ 1 et seq as The Commodity Exchange Act; 17 CFR §§ 140.1 et seq; *In re Amaranth Natural Gas Commodities Litig*, 730 F3d 170 (2d Cir 2013). The Supreme Court struck down as unconstitutional predecessor legislation known as the Future Trading Act of 1921, because it was not limited to interstate commerce by its terms, and because the Constitution as then interpreted commanded that Congress refrain from regulating intrastate commerce as a domain of the states' police powers; *Hill v Wallace*, 259 US 44, 44–46, 68–70 (1922). The Supreme Court later adopted a more expansive interpretation of the constitutional powers of Congress, paving the way for extensive federal regulation of financial and other services. See *Fla ex rel McCollum v United States Dep't of Health & Human Servs*, 716 F Supp 2d 1120 (ND Fla 2010).

[138] 7 USC § 25.

[139] *Merrill Lynch, Pierce, Fenner & Smith, Inc v Curran*, 456 US 353 (1982).

[140] 7 USC §§ 1a, 2(a)(1)(B), 7, 13, 25; 28 USC §§ 1331, 1332, 1337, 1391.

[141] *Eagletech Commc'ns Inc v Citigroup, Inc*, No 07-60668-CIV-Gold/McAliley, 2008 US Dist LEXIS 49432, at *42 (SD Fla 27 June 2008) (quoting *Santa Fe Indus, Inc v Green*, 430 US 462, 476 (1977)).

[142] 7 USC § 6b.

[143] DH Kaufman et al, 'Fraud, Manipulation and Deception: CFTC/SEC Proposed Rules' *Morrison & Foerster News Bulletin* (13 December 2010) www.mofo.com/files/Uploads/Images/101213-CFTC-and-SEC-Proposed-Rules.pdf.

[144] ibid, 3 (quoting Dodd-Frank Act § 763(g)).

[145] *MLSMK Inv Co* (n 131) at 270.

eventually had assets of more than $7 billion.[146] Some investors in Madoff's scheme alleged that JP Morgan knew in late 2008 that Madoff was committing fraud, and that its agents withdrew JP Morgan's own investment as a result.[147] One of these investors sued JP Morgan for conspiring to commit fraud over interstate commerce using the telecommunications wires, aiding and abetting breach of fiduciary duty, bad faith acts in commerce and negligence under New York law. The Second Circuit held that all claims were properly dismissed—the wire fraud claim due to the PSLRA, and the state law claims for other reasons.[148] Previously, another court had held that banks could not be sued for arranging transactions for Enron, which had engaged in misleading accounting practices, unless the injured parties had been in a fiduciary relationship with the banks at the time.[149] The Court rejected the idea that the banks had a general duty to the public not to engage in a fraudulent scheme.[150] However, Enron's banks such as CIBC settled with Enron's shareholders and other creditors for more than $7 billion,[151] while Enron's accounting and law firms agreed to millions of dollars of settlements in connection with Enron's bankruptcy.[152] Similarly, in the Madoff case, the bankruptcy trustee and federal prosecutors entered into a deferred prosecution agreement with JP Morgan worth $1.7 billion in civil forfeitures, and a $543 million pact settling common law and SIPA claims on behalf of Madoff's investors.[153] In 2015, the Second Circuit ruled in a separate case that certain defendants who allegedly failed to provide auditing, consulting or management services to two funds that invested in Madoff's firm could be held liable for breaching contractual, fiduciary, and/or tort obligations to detect Madoff's frauds.[154]

[146] ibid, 271.

[147] ibid, 271–72.

[148] ibid, 272–73, 278–80.

[149] *See Regents of Univ of Cal v Credit Suisse First Boston (USA), Inc*, 482 F3d 372 (5th Cir 2007).

[150] ibid.

[151] See D Manvin, 'TD, Royal Banks Win Enron Break' *The Financial Post/The National Post (Canada)* (22 January 2008) www.nationalpost.com/news/story.html?id=256017.

[152] J Glater, 'Enron Holders in Pact with Andersen Overseas Firms' *The New York Times* (28 August 2002) www.nytimes.com/2002/08/28/business/enron-holders-in-pact-with-andersen-overseas-firms.html; B James, 'Texas Firm to Settle Enron Claims For $18.5M' *Law360* (23 January 2007) www.law360.com/articles/17039/texas-firm-to-settle-enron-claims-for-18-5m.

[153] See Office of Irving Picard, SIPA Trustee for the Liquidation of Bernard L. Madoff Investment Securities LLC, 'SIPA Trustee Announces Settlement Agreements Reached with JP Morgan' *Business Wire* (7 January 2014) www.businesswire.com/news/home/20140107006710/en/SIPA-Trustee-Announces-Settlement-Agreements-Reached-JPMorgan.

[154] *See In re Kingate Mgmt Ltd Litig*, 784 F3d 128, 132, 136–42 (2d Cir 2015). The Court dismissed the plaintiffs' claims, however, to the extent they were based on making or aiding and abetting misrepresentations and distinguished a prior case in which Madoff-related state-law claims against a feeder fund were 'camouflage[d]' federal securities fraud claims and were therefore dismissed under the Securities Litigation Uniform Standards Act of 1998. See ibid, 133–34, 136–42 (citing *In re Herald*, 753 F3d 110, 117–20 (2d Cir 2014)).

B. Negligent Misrepresentation in Providing Investment Advice

The tort of giving negligent investing advice[155] is a relatively new arrival to the law of torts, having evolved out of the tort of negligent misrepresentation to operate specifically in the financial world. The tort of negligent investment advice in the financial field, just like the general tort of negligent misrepresentation, is at the centre of the doctrinal complexity surrounding the scope of the duty of a supplier of information. The relationship between the customer and the bank or adviser will be covered by contract or statute—but, in the absence of privity of contract, how far and to whom does the supplier of information's duty of care extend?

The tort of negligent misrepresentation in investment advice covers a gap left by federal and state securities statutes, which, as discussed above, prohibit a false statement 'in connection with a purchase or sale of a security'. Those statutory prohibitions do not apply to cases not involving securities and/or not involving a sale.[156]

Restatement section 552 states:

> (1) One who, in the course of his business, profession or employment, or in any other transaction in which he has a pecuniary interest, supplies false information for the guidance of others in their business transactions, is subject to liability for pecuniary loss caused to them by their justifiable reliance upon the information, if he fails to exercise reasonable care or competence in obtaining or communicating the information.
>
> (2) Except as stated in Subsection (3), the liability stated in Subsection (1) is limited to loss suffered
>
> (a) by the person or one of a limited group of persons for whose benefit and guidance he intends to supply the information or knows that the recipient intends to supply it; and
>
> (b) through reliance upon it in a transaction that he intends the information to influence or knows that the recipient so intends or in a substantially similar transaction.

This Restatement section has been adopted or endorsed in nearly all states, with the exception of New York, discussed below.[157]

'Information' under section 552 can include an opinion under certain circumstances. As stated in the Official Comments, the rule applies 'also to an opinion given upon facts equally well known to both the supplier and the recipient'.[158]

[155] SE Lipner and LA Catalano, 'The Tort of Giving Negligent Investment Advice', (2009) 39 *University of Memphis Law Review* 663. Lipner and Catalano coined this term, calling it a 'sub-species' of the tort of negligent misrepresentation.

[156] ibid, 4 (citations omitted).

[157] Restatement (Second) of Torts § 552: Information Negligently Supplied for the Guidance of Others (1977).

[158] ibid, cmt b.

i. Who Can be a Defendant

a. Majority View

The majority view, and that reflected in the Restatement, is that everyone engaged in a financial transaction with another has a duty of care to avoid making false statements of fact. The Restatement identifies the potential defendant in the negligent supply of information as one who acts 'in the course of his business, profession or employment, or in any other transaction in which he has a pecuniary interest'. Therefore, someone providing information for free cannot be liable under this tort.

Whether one is in 'the business of supplying information' is not always clear. As analysed by the Seventh Circuit in *Rankow v First Chicago Corp*,[159] a spectrum exists between those who are squarely in the business of supplying information, such as real estate brokers and termite inspectors, and those who are squarely in the business of supplying tangible products to which the information provided is merely incidental.[160] As the Court stated,

> [f]inancial services such as those provided by banks and stockbrokers present a particularly difficult problem, because there is a very thin line between an exchange of information about finances and actual financial transactions.[161]

In *Rankow*, the Court found that the bank was in the business of supplying information because it offered its stockholders information on pricing dates as part of a reinvestment and stock purchase plan.[162]

b. Minority View

The minority view finds a more limited scope of liability. In Oregon, for example, there can be no liability for negligent misrepresentation in an arm's-length business transaction; such liability is limited to those professional relationships where the law or a fiduciary duty gives rise to a duty to exercise reasonable care on behalf of the other party's interests.[163] Those professionals for whom this

[159] 870 F2d 356 (7th Cir 1989). *Rankow* had interpreted Illinois law to require that the information be supplied to the recipient for use in business relations with third parties. On this point, *Rankow* was subsequently overruled, as recognised by *United National Insurance Co v Aon Ltd*, No 04-539, 2008 US Dist LEXIS 28249, at *10 (ED Pa 7 April, 2008) ('[T]he [Illinois] Supreme Court necessarily overruled *Rankow* on that point, since the Seventh Circuit, powerful as it may be in other respects, has no authority to disagree with the Supreme Court of Illinois on questions of Illinois law'.).

[160] *Rankow*, 870 F2d at 364.

[161] ibid.

[162] ibid.

[163] See eg *Onita Pac Corp v Trs of Bronson*, 315 Or 149, 165, 843 P2d 890, 899 (Or 1992) ('[N]ongratuitous suppliers of information owe a duty to their clients or employers or to intended third-party beneficiaries of their contractual, professional, or employment relationship to exercise reasonable care to avoid misrepresenting facts'—as contrasted to those in an arm's-length commercial transaction, which is an adversarial relationship.).

duty arises in this context are narrowly limited to 'nongratuitous suppliers of information'.[164]

c. New York and the Special Relationship Test

New York is one of the few states that has not adopted the Restatement section 552. New York applies instead a 'special relationship' test.[165] Case-law suggests that 'the advice contemplated by [brokers and investment advisers] creates the 'special relationship' that New York law requires'.[166] Ultimately, the cases analysed by commentators Lipner and Catalano illustrate that the application of the special relationship test to those in the business of offering investment advice has evolved to be co-extensive with that of section 552.[167]

ii. Who Can be a Plaintiff

Subsection 2 of section 552 limits the class of people to whom the defendant can be liable for the negligent supply of information. Those people are at most a 'limited group of people' who must satisfy a two-part test: (1) they must be the people for whose benefit and guidance the speaker intends to supply the information or people to whom the speaker knows his recipient intends to supply it; and (2) they must rely upon it in the type of transaction that the speaker intends the information to influence, or that he knows the recipient in turn intends to influence, or 'a substantially similar transaction'.

iii. The Duty of Care

The duty of care required by a supplier of information varies according to the circumstances. The Restatement points out the distinction between the duty of honesty and the duty of care.[168] The latter duty

> implies an undertaking to observe a relative standard, which may be defined only in terms of the use to which the information will be put, weighed against the magnitude and probability of loss that might attend that use if the information proves to be incorrect.[169]

The duty of reasonable care depends on the circumstances. As the Restatement notes, '[t]he question is one for the jury, unless the facts are so clear as to permit only one conclusion'.[170] Factors bearing on the scope of the duty include whether the speaker speaks in his or her professional capacity and professes expertise and knowledge in the field, as will be the case with banking and investment professionals.

[164] ibid.
[165] Lipner and Catalano, 'The Tort of Giving Negligent Investment Advice' (n 155) 709 (quoting *Kimmell v Schaefer*, 675 NE2d 450, 453 (1996)).
[166] ibid.
[167] ibid, 715.
[168] Restatement (Second) of Torts, § 552 cmt a.
[169] ibid.
[170] ibid, cmt e.

C. Trust and Investment Services to Customers

US banks have traditionally acted in a variety of fiduciary capacities for customers, including as personal trustee, investment adviser, securities broker, managing agent for customer assets, custodial agent and other agency roles. In those capacities, banks have been held to fiduciary standards established by the laws of each state in which they operate, including the prudent investor standard, as well as to federal regulatory standards. The 1933 Glass-Steagall Act, enacted by the Depression-era US Congress, and initial regulatory interpretations of the Act limited banks' securities activities even on behalf of customers. As a result of regulatory erosion of those limitations and ultimate repeal of large portions of Glass-Steagall by the 1999 Gramm-Leach-Bliley Act (GLBA), however, banks and bank affiliates now provide a full range of investment services to customers, including full-scale brokerage services and retail sales of mutual funds. In those capacities, they are subject to requirements that are the same as or parallel to those applied to other investment advisers and securities broker-dealers through regulation and common law.

i. Trust Services and Fiduciary Duties of Loyalty and Prudence

State statutes commonly empower state banks to establish trust departments and to act as trustees, with the approval of the state banking department and in compliance with various provisions of state law, typically including requirements for capitalisation, security and separation of the trust business from other bank business.[171] Under federal law, the Comptroller of the Currency is empowered to grant parallel permits to national banks.[172]

Whether a state or national bank, a bank's duties to trust customers are generally a matter of state statutory and common law. A bank owes its trust customers primary duties of loyalty and prudence.

a. The Duty of Loyalty

A trustee's duty of loyalty in the administration of trust assets is a universal principle of state trust law. It is 'perhaps the most fundamental duty of the trustee'.[173] The trustee owes a duty of undivided loyalty.[174]

[171] GG Bogert and GT Bogert, *The Law of Trusts & Trustees*, 2nd edn, rev (St Paul, Minn: West Publishing, 1984) § 135.

[172] 12 USC § 92a(a) (empowering Comptroller of the Currency to grant permits 'when not in contravention of State or local law, the right to act as trustee, executor, administrator, registrar of stocks and bonds, guardian of estates, assignee, receiver, or in any other fiduciary capacity or in any other fiduciary capacity in which State banks, trust companies, or other corporations which come into competition with national banks are permitted to act under the laws of the State in which the national bank is located'). See also Bogert, *The Law of Trusts & Trustees* (n 171) § 134.

[173] Uniform Trust Code (UTC), cmt to § 802, 'Duty of Loyalty' (2010).

[174] *City Bank Farmers Trust Co v Cannon*, 291 NY 125, 131–32, 51 NE2d 674–76 (NY 1943).

Section 78 of the Third Restatement of the Law of Trusts, 'Duty of Loyalty', provides:

(1) Except as otherwise provided in the terms of the trust, a trustee has a duty to administer the trust solely in the interest of the beneficiaries, or solely in furtherance of its charitable purpose.
(2) Except in discrete circumstances, the trustee is strictly prohibited from engaging in transactions that involve self-dealing or that otherwise involve or create a conflict between the trustee's fiduciary duties and personal interests.
(3) Whether acting in a fiduciary or personal capacity, a trustee has a duty in dealing with a beneficiary to deal fairly and to communicate to the beneficiary all material facts the trustee knows or should know in connection with the matter.[175]

Many states have codified the trustee's duty of loyalty as a matter of statute.[176] The Uniform Trust Code (first promulgated in 2000), which includes the 'Duty of Loyalty' at section 802, has been adopted in some form by a majority of states.[177] Section 802(a) of the Uniform Trust Code provides, similarly to the Restatement, that: 'A trustee shall administer the trust solely in the interests of the beneficiaries'.[178]

State law duties of loyalty generally prohibit or make voidable by the beneficiary transactions between the trust and the trustee or parties related to the trustee, or other transactions in which the trustee has a conflict of interest, unless the transaction is authorised by the terms of the trust, approved by the court or properly consented to by the beneficiary.[179] Federal regulations also prohibit such unauthorised 'self-dealing' by national banks.[180] Good faith on the part of the trustee is not a defence to a claim of disloyalty, and it is not necessary to find that the trustee gained from the transaction to find that it is disloyal.

A corollary of this principle is that the trustee can proceed despite a conflict of interest with proper consent unless the trustee acts in bad faith or abuses its discretion. As articulated by one case:

> This rule [of undivided loyalty] is not, however, without exception. It is well established that a trustee may occupy conflicting positions in handling the trust where the trust instrument contemplates, creates, or sanctions the conflict of interest. The creator of the trust can waive the rule of undivided loyalty by expressly conferring upon the trustee the power to act in a dual capacity, or he can waive the rule by implication where he knowingly places the trustee in a position which might conflict with the interest of the beneficiaries. … Where a conflict of interest is approved or created by the testator, the fiduciary will not be held liable for his conduct unless the fiduciary has acted dishonestly or in bad faith, or has abused his discretion.[181]

[175] The American Law Institute, Restatement (Third) of the Law of Trusts ('Third Restatement of Trusts'), § 78, Duty of Loyalty (2007).

[176] See eg Cal Prob Code § 16002; Ind Code Ann § 30-4-3-5; NY Est Powers & Trusts § 10-10.1.

[177] 7C ULA 229 (Supp).

[178] UTC § 802(a).

[179] See Third Restatement of Trusts, § 78, cmts (b)–(g) (2007); UTC § 802(b)–(h).

[180] See 12 CFR § 9.12 ('Self-dealing and conflicts of interest').

[181] *Dick v Peoples Mid-Ill Corp*, 242 Ill App 3d 297, 303, 609 NE2d 997, 1002 (Ill App Ct 1993).

Thus, 'the trust instrument may waive the general rule and authorize the trustee to engage in transactions that involve self-dealing'.[182] However, '[g]eneral language granting broad powers to the trustee is not sufficient to waive the prohibition; to be effective, the authorization to self-deal must be express and clear'.[183]

b. The Duty of Prudence

Traditionally, the trustee's exercise of discretion in the management of trust assets was governed by the 'prudent person' rule. As articulated by the Supreme Judicial Court of Massachusetts in 1830, a trustee was

> to observe how men of prudence, discretion and intelligence manage their own affairs, not in regard to speculation, but in regard to the permanent disposition of their funds, considering probable income, as well as the probable safety of the capital to be invested.[184]

The Second Restatement of Trusts directed trustees 'to make such investments and only such investments as a prudent man would make of his own property having in view the preservation of the estate and the amount and regularity of the income to be derived'.[185] Some variation of the prudent person rule was adopted by decision or legislation in virtually every US jurisdiction.

As interpreted by the courts, the prudent person rule tended to be applied narrowly with a strong emphasis on avoiding speculation.[186] Categories of investments were classified as speculative and per se imprudent.

This led to replacement of the prudent person rule with the 'prudent investor' rule, which assesses prudence based on the entire trust portfolio rather than on specific investments in isolation, with no categories of investments or investment techniques considered per se imprudent.

The prudent investor rule, as adopted and promulgated in Third Restatement of Trusts in 1990, provides:

> The trustee is under a duty to the beneficiaries to invest and manage the funds of the trust as a prudent investor would, in light of the purposes, terms, distribution requirements, and other circumstances of the trust.
>
> (a) This standard requires the exercise of reasonable care, skill, and caution, and is to be applied to investments not in isolation but in the context of the trust portfolio and as part of an overall investment strategy, which should incorporate risk and return objectives reasonably suitable to the trust.

182 *French v Wachovia Bank, NA*, 722 F3d 1079, 1085–86 (7th Cir 2013) (citing Restatement (Third) of Trusts § 78 cmt c(2)) (finding waiver of prohibition of self-dealing based on trust provision that trustee had power '*to continue as trustee and to deal with any trust hereunder without regard to conflicts of interest*') (emphasis added).

183 ibid.

184 *Harvard Coll v Amory*, 9 Pick 446, 461 (Mass 1830).

185 Restatement (Second) of Trusts § 227: Investments Which A Trust Can Properly Make (1959).

186 See JH Langbein, 'The Uniform Prudent Investor Act and the Future of Trust Investing' (1996) 81 *Iowa Law Review* 641, 643.

(b) In making and implementing investment decisions, the trustee has a duty to diversify the investments of the trust unless, under the circumstances, it is prudent not to do so.[187]

The Restatement articulation of the prudent investor rule also references the trustee's duties of loyalty, impartiality, prudence in the delegation of authority and selection and supervision of agents, and reasonableness in incurring trust costs.[188]

The principles of the prudent investor rule were incorporated in the Uniform Prudent Investor Act (UPIA), which was promulgated by the National Conference of Commissioners on Uniform State Laws in 1994. Virtually every state has now adopted the UPIA with some variations.[189] In addition to articulating the general principle that investment decisions must be evaluated 'in the context of the trust portfolio as a whole and as part of an overall investment strategy', the UPIA gives examples of 'circumstances that a trustee shall consider in investing and managing trust assets', including general economic conditions and tax as well as the assets and life circumstances of the beneficiary.[190] It also provides that '[a] trustee who has special skills or expertise … has a duty to use those special skills or expertise'.[191]

The prudent investor standard of care is a default rule subject to the actual terms of the trust:

> The prudent investor rule, a default rule, may be expanded, restricted or eliminated, or otherwise altered by the provisions of the trust. A trustee is not liable to a beneficiary to the extent that the trustee acted in reasonable reliance on the provisions of the trust.[192]

A recent case applying that principle, *French v Wachovia Bank, NA*,[193] is illustrative. In that case the trust instrument provided that:

> The trustee … shall have … the power: … to retain, invest and reinvest in any property *without regard to whether the same may be authorized by law, regardless of any risk, lack of diversification or unproductivity involved*[194]

The Court held that this 'contractual workaround' 'displace[d] the prudent investor rule'.[195] The Court noted further that '[t]he trustee is always obligated to administer the trust in good faith', but found 'no evidence of bad faith'.[196]

[187] Restatement (Third) of Trusts § 227: General Standard of Prudent Investment (1990).

[188] ibid, § 227(c).

[189] AM Hess et al, *Bogert, Trusts and Estates, Cumulative Supp* (Eagan, Minn: Thomson West Library, 2013) § 613, 25.

[190] UPIA § 2, Standard of Care; Portfolio Strategy; Risk and Return Objectives (1995).

[191] ibid.

[192] ibid, § 1(b). See also Restatement (Third) Trusts § 228(b) (trustee 'has the powers expressly or impliedly granted by the terms of the trust and … has a duty to the beneficiaries to conform to the terms of the trust directing or restricting investments by the trustee').

[193] 722 F3d 1079 (7th Cir 2013).

[194] ibid, 1086–87 (emphasis added).

[195] ibid.

[196] ibid.

Less absolute permissive trust provisions may be more limited in their effect on the trustee's duty of care under the prudent investor rule. For example, in *Donato v BankBoston, NA*,[197] the trust instrument

> authorize[d] investment in 'securities not ordinarily considered appropriate for trust investment' and other investments 'in each case in amounts which normally would be regarded as disproportionately large for the trust investment.'[198]

The Court held that this kind of

> permissive provision does not relieve trustees from scrutiny under a 'prudence' standard for their investment decisions; it means only that a trustee cannot be found to have acted imprudently *per se* for holding a particular type of investment or for holding a disproportionately large amount of one investment.[199]

The Court also held that an 'exculpatory provision' that 'grant[ed] investment discretion "without liability except in cases of negligence or bad faith"' did 'nothing to alter the degree of scrutiny required under the "prudent man" rule'.[200] A more effective, and probably more common, exculpatory provision would limit the trustee's liability to instances of *gross* negligence or bad faith.

ii. Investment Adviser and Brokerage Services

Glass Steagall, enacted in 1933, separated to a degree commercial banking from investment banking and placed limits on US banks' securities activities. But during the latter part of the twentieth century, Federal Reserve Board rulings and Supreme Court decisions took an increasingly flexible approach to banks' provision of securities' services. The 1999 GLBA repealed portions of Glass Steagall and allowed for broad affiliations between commercial banks and securities firms. US bank holding companies and their subsidiaries now provide a wide range of securities services, including portfolio investment advice and brokerage services.[201] Those services are subject to federal regulation and SEC enforcement as well as private rights of action under state statutory and common law.

a. Investment Advice

Before and after Glass Steagall, US banks have provided investment advice to customers through their fiduciary functions as trustees and managing agents of funds subject to standards discussed above (see section III.C.i). As noted by the Supreme

[197] 110 F Supp 2d 42 (DRI 2000).
[198] ibid, 49 (citations omitted).
[199] ibid.
[200] ibid (citations omitted).
[201] See generally DH Carpenter and MM Murphy, *Permissible Securities Activities of Commercial Banks under the Glass-Steagall Act (GSA) and the Gramm-Leach-Bliley Act (GLBA)*, Congressional Research Service, CRS Report for Congress R41181 (12 April 2010).

Court in its 1981 decision in *Board of Governors v Investment Company Institute* (*ICI*):

> The services of an investment adviser are not significantly different from the traditional fiduciary functions of banks. The principal activity of an investment adviser is to manage the investment portfolio of its advisee—to invest and reinvest the funds of the client. Banks have engaged in that sort of activity for decades. As executor, trustee, or managing agent of funds committed to its custody, a bank regularly buys and sells securities for its customers. Bank trust departments manage employee benefits trusts, institutional and corporate agency accounts, and personal trust and agency accounts. Moreover, for over 50 years banks have performed these tasks for trust funds consisting of commingled funds of customers.[202]

In *ICI*, the Court held that regulatory amendments by the Board of Governors of the Federal Reserve System permitting bank holding companies and non-banking subsidiaries of banks to act as investment advisers to closed-end investment companies did not violate Glass Steagall. The Court recognised in *ICI* that Glass Steagall did not prohibit portfolio investment advice:

> The management of a customer's investment portfolio—even when the manager has the power to sell securities owned by the customer—is not the kind of selling activity that Congress contemplated when it enacted § 21 [of Glass Steagall]. If it were, the statute would prohibit banks from continuing to manage investment accounts in a fiduciary capacity or as an agent for an individual.[203]

Current regulations authorise bank holding companies to provide financial advice to 'any person'[204] and to serve as investment advisers to open-end investment companies, ie mutual funds, as well as to closed-end investment companies.[205] A national bank that offers investment advice for a fee or exercises investment discretion on behalf of customers, or has an operating subsidiary that does so, is required to have a licence to exercise fiduciary powers.[206]

Investment advisers are generally subject to regulation by the SEC under the Investment Advisers Act of 1940 (the Advisers Act). Banks and bank holding companies are exempt from the Advisers Act, but their non-bank subsidiaries are not.[207] Investment advisers with less than $100 million of assets under management are exempt from federal registration if they are subject to state regulation and 'act[] solely as an adviser to private funds'.[208]

202 450 US 46, 55 (1981).

203 ibid, 63.

204 12 CFR § 225.28(b)(6).

205 ibid, §§ 225.125, 225.28(b)(6)(i).

206 See 12 CFR § 5.26 ('Fiduciary powers'); § 5.34(e)(5)(i)(A)(2) ('If an operating subsidiary proposes to exercise investment discretion on behalf of customers or provide investment advice for a fee, the national bank must have prior OCC approval to exercise fiduciary powers pursuant to § 5.26'.).

207 See Investment Advisers Act, 15 USC § 80b-2(a)(11)(A)–(G), 15 U.S.C. § 80b-2 (2014) (listing exclusions from definition of investment adviser).

208 ibid, § 80b-3(m).

Section 206(1) of the Advisers Act prohibits the intentional or reckless use of any device, scheme or artifice by an investment adviser to make untrue statements to or otherwise mislead any client or prospective client.[209] Section 206(2) prohibits the negligent, reckless or intentional employment of a transaction, practice or course of business that operates as a fraud or deceit on a client or prospective client.[210]

The SEC has long taken the position that an investment adviser is a fiduciary and is subject to common law fiduciary duties, including the duty to act in the interests of his or her client with undivided loyalty.[211]

The Supreme Court has endorsed this view. In *SEC v Capital Gains Research Bureau* (*Capital Gains*),[212] the Court held that the SEC could obtain an injunction under the Advisers Act compelling a registered investment adviser to disclose to his clients a practice known as 'scalping'—'purchasing shares of a security for his own account shortly before recommending that security for a long-term investment and then immediately selling the shares for a profit following the recommendation'.[213] For purposes of its analysis, the Court started with the premise that the investment adviser owed fiduciary duties to his clients. It characterised the Advisers Act as 'reflect[ing] a congressional recognition "of the delicate fiduciary nature of an investment advisory relationship"',[214] and reasoned that it was not 'necessary in a suit against a fiduciary, which Congress recognized the investment adviser to be, to establish all the elements required in a suit against a party to an arm's-length transaction'.[215] It went on to note that '[c]ourts have imposed on a fiduciary an affirmative duty of "utmost good faith, and full and fair disclosure of all material facts"' as well as an affirmative obligation '"to employ reasonable care to avoid misleading" his clients'.[216]

Capital Gains, the Supreme Court's first interpretation of the Advisers Act more than 50 years ago, 'remains the cornerstone of the regulatory scheme for advisers' and is routinely relied on by the SEC 'in enforcement actions, rulemaking proceedings, and no-action letters issued under the Act'.[217] Subsequent Supreme Court cases have characterised it as holding 'that Congress intended the Investment Advisers Act to establish federal fiduciary standards for investment advisers'.[218]

[209] 15 USC § 80b-6(1).

[210] ibid, § 80b-6(2).

[211] Investment Advisers Act of 1940, SEC Release No 40, 1945 WL 26361 (5 February 1945).

[212] 375 US 180 (1963).

[213] ibid, 181.

[214] ibid, 191 (quoting 2 L Loss, *Securities Regulation*, 2nd edn (New York: Little Brown & Company, 1961)) 1412.

[215] ibid, 194.

[216] ibid (quoting W Prosser, *Law of Torts*, 2nd edn (Eagan, Minn: West Publishing, 1955) 534–35 (citing cases)).

[217] AB Laby, 'Current Issues in Fiduciary Law: SEC v. Capital Gains Research Bureau and the Investment Advisers Act of 1940' (2011) 91 *Boston University Law Review* 1051, 1052.

[218] *Santa Fe Indus v Green*, 430 US 462, 472 (1977); see also *Transamerica Mortg Advisors, Inc v Lewis*, 444 US 11, 17 (1979) ('the Act's legislative history leaves no doubt that Congress intended to impose enforceable fiduciary obligations'); but see Laby, *Current Issues in Fiduciary Law* (n 217) 1069 (arguing that '[n]either the statutory text nor the legislative history [of the Advisers Act] supports the proposition that Congress intended to establish federal fiduciary duties for advisers').

Lower courts have followed *Capital Gains* in applying the Advisers Act in SEC enforcement actions. As summarised by one court, with citation to *Capital Gains* and subsequent Supreme Court precedent interpreting it:

> Section 206 of the Advisers Act establishes a statutory fiduciary duty for investment advisers to act for the benefit of their clients, requiring advisers to exercise the utmost good faith in dealing with clients, to disclose all material facts, and to employ reasonable care to avoid misleading clients.[219]

While holding that the Advisers Act 'establishe[d] "federal fiduciary standards to govern the conduct of investment advisers"',[220] the Supreme Court has also held that 'that there exists [only] a limited private remedy under the [Advisers Act] to void an investment adviser's contract, [and] the Act confers no other private causes of action, legal or equitable'.[221] Thus, litigation to enforce the fiduciary standards established by the Advisers Act is limited to SEC enforcement actions, and private damages claims for breaches of an investment adviser's fiduciary duties or negligence are a matter of state law.[222]

b. Brokerage Services

Federal Regulation

The Advisers Act's definition of 'investment adviser' excludes any broker-dealer 'whose performance of such services is solely incidental to the conduct of his business as a broker or dealer and who receives no special compensation therefor'.[223] Section 15(a) of the 1934 Exchange Act requires securities brokers or dealers to register with the SEC and to become members of a self-regulatory organisation (SRO).[224] For registered broker-dealers that deal with the public this generally means becoming a member of the Financial Industry Regulatory Authority (FINRA), which is the only national securities association registered with the SEC under section 15(a).[225] FINRA helps uncover and remedy fraudulent or illegal practices in the industry, and awarded a record $34 million in restitution to

[219] *SEC v Moran*, 922 F Supp 867, 895–96 (SDNY 1996); *accord SEC v Treadway*, 430 F Supp 2d 293, 338 (SDNY 2006). See also *Fin Planning Ass'n v SEC*, 482 F3d 481, 490 (DC Cir 2007) (Advisers Act 'establish[ed] a federal fiduciary standard to govern the conduct of investment advisers, broadly defined'.).

[220] *Transamerica Mortg Advisors, Inc* (n 218) at 17.

[221] ibid, 24. As amended in 1970, the Advisers Act also 'impose[s] upon investment advisers a "fiduciary duty" with respect to compensation received from a mutual fund, 15 U.S.C. § 80a-35(b), and grant[s] individual investors a private right of action for breach of that duty, *ibid*'; *Jones v Harris Assocs LP*, 130 S Ct 1418, 1423 (2010).

[222] *See Davis v Merrill Lynch, Pierce, Fenner & Smith, Inc*, 906 F2d 1206, 1215 (8th Cir 1990) ('The question of whether a fiduciary relationship exists is a question of state law'.). See also eg *Stokes v Henson*, 217 Cal App 3d 187, 265 Cal Rptr 836 (Cal Ct App 1990) (affirming judgment against investment adviser for breach of fiduciary duty under California law).

[223] 15 USC 80b-2(a)(ii).

[224] 15 USC § 78o(b)(8); 17 CFR § 240.15b9-1. See also 15 USC § 7006 (defining SROs).

[225] See SEC Study on Investment Advisers and Broker-Dealers (January 2011) 47.

consumers in 2012.[226] FINRA may also refer wrongdoing to the SEC, which may seek disgorgement in court or by settlement.[227] In one notable case involving the SEC, a federal court established a claims fund for victims of Prudential Securities, with about $940 million in distributions from the fund.[228]

GLBA repealed banks' exemption from broker-dealer registration but with exceptions, including for trust activities in a fiduciary capacity.[229] Fiduciary capacity is defined to include acting 'as an investment adviser if the bank receives a fee for its investment advice'.[230]

The Exchange Act's 'anti-fraud' provisions—sections 9(a), 10(b), 15(c)(1) and 15(c)(2)—broadly prohibit misleading omissions of material facts as well affirmative misstatements and fraudulent or manipulative acts or practices. The SEC has adopted rules, issued interpretations and brought enforcement actions that define these prohibited practices as they apply to broker-dealers.[231] Important among broker-dealers' defined duties are fair dealing, compliance with suitability requirements and best execution.

Under the anti-fraud provisions, as interpreted by the SEC, broker-dealers owe their customers a duty of fair dealing.

> Under the so-called 'shingle theory', by virtue of engaging in the brokerage profession (e.g., hanging out the broker-dealer's business sign, or 'shingle'), a broker-dealer makes an implicit representation to those persons with whom it transacts business that it will deal fairly with them, consistent with the standards of the profession.[232]

The obligation of fair dealing

> includes having a reasonable basis for recommendations in light of a customer's financial situation to the extent known to the broker (suitability), engaging in fair and

[226] See FINRA, 'FINRA Ordered $68M in Fines, $34M in Restitution, in 2012' (8 January 2013) www.futuresmag.com/2013/01/08/finra-ordered-68m-fines-34m-restitution-2012.

[227] ibid; SEC, 'How Can Investors Get Money Back in a Fraud Case Involving a Violation of the Federal Securities Laws?' (24 February 2009) www.sec.gov/answers/recoverfunds.htm.

[228] See SEC, Report Pursuant to Section 308(c) of the Sarbanes Oxley Act of 2002' (2002) 15, www.sec.gov/news/studies/sox308creport.pdf. At least one estimate of investor losses due to Prudential Securities' deceptive marketing of limited partnerships, churning and other abuses was put at $3 billion; SJ Paltrow, 'Prudential to Pay at Least $371 Million in Fraud Settlement: Securities' *Los Angeles Times* (22 October 1993) http://webcache.googleusercontent.com/search?q=cache:HErN_-CxaMQJ:articles.latimes.com/1993-10-22/business/fi-48551_1_prudential-securities+prudential+sec+investigation+%24330&cd=8&hl=en&ct=clnk&gl=us. More recently, the SEC obtained at least $270 million from Prudential Securities to help compensate investors victimised by a deceptive market-timing scheme. See SEC, 'Prudential to Pay $600 Million in Global Settlement of Fraud Charges in Connection With Deceptive Market Timing of Mutual Funds' (28 August 2006) www.sec.gov/news/press/2006/2006-145.htm.

[229] See 15 USC §§ 80b, 78c(a)(4)(D) (defining 'Trust activities').

[230] 15 USC § 78c(a)(4)(D).

[231] See generally SEC Study (n 225) 51–72; SEC, 'SEC Guide to Broker-Dealer Registration' (April 2008) www.sec.gov/divisions/marketreg/bdguide.htm.

[232] SEC Study (n 225) 51; see also *Charles Hughes & Co v SEC*, 139 F2d 434, 437 (2d Cir 1943) (holding that broker-dealer was under 'special duty, in view of its expert knowledge and proffered advice, not to take advantage of customers' ignorance of market conditions'); *Hanly v SEC*, 415 F2d 589, 596 (2d Cir 1969) ('A securities dealer occupies a special relationship to a buyer of securities in that by his position he implicitly represents he has an adequate basis for the opinions he renders'.).

balanced communications with the public, providing timely and adequate confirmation of transactions, providing account statements, disclosing conflicts of interest, receiving fair compensation both in agency and principal transactions, and giving customers the opportunity for redress of disputes through arbitration.[233]

The suitability requirement is codified in SRO rules. It 'generally requires a broker-dealer to make recommendations that are consistent with the best interests of his customer'.[234] A broker-dealer must have an adequate and reasonable basis to believe that a securities recommendation is 'suitable for its customer light of the customer's financial needs, objectives and circumstances'.[235] It is not relieved of the duty to make suitable recommendations by a client's consent to an unsuitable transaction.[236]

FINRA's suitability rule requires a broker to 'have a reasonable basis to believe that a recommended transaction or investment strategy … is suitable for the customer, based on the information obtained through [the broker's] reasonable diligence' and gives, as non-exclusive examples of profile information, 'the customer's age, other investments, financial situation and needs, tax status, investment objectives, investment experience, investment time horizon, liquidity needs, [and] risk tolerance'.[237] Official commentary to the rule identifies three main components of the suitability obligations: (1) 'reasonable-basis suitability', a reasonable belief based on reasonable diligence that 'the recommendation is suitable for at least *some* investors'; (2) 'customer-specific suitability', which requires that the recommendation be 'suitable for a particular customer based on that customer's investment profile'; and (3) 'quantitative suitability', which requires a reasonable belief that a series of transactions taken as a whole is not 'excessive and unsuitable in light of the customer's investment profile'.[238] Although there is no private cause of action for violation of the SEC's suitability rule, courts 'have held that the suitability rule may set brokers' common law duty of care toward clients'.[239]

Recently, FINRA fined an independent broker-dealer $95,000 for failure to adequately supervise investments. FINRA found that the broker-dealer did not have an adequate system in place to review compliance with state suitability requirements

233 SEC Study (n 225) 52 (citing SRO rules).
234 ibid, 59.
235 ibid, 61.
236 ibid, 62.
237 Financial Industry Regulatory Authority Manual, Suitability, r 2111(a) http://lifemark.com/portals/0/rule%202111.pdf.
238 ibid, cmt 05.
239 *Ives v Ramsden*, 142 Wash App 369, 390, 174 P3d 1231, 1242 (Wash Ct App 2008) (collecting cases); see eg *Scott v Dime Sav Bank of NY, FSB*, 886 F Supp 1073, 1080–81 (SDNY 1995) (upholding negligence claim based on evidence of violation of suitability rule); *cf Merrill Lynch, Pierce, Fenner & Smith, Inc v Chen*, 697 F Supp 1224, 1227 (DDC 1998) (violation of suitability rule 'will not automatically result in [broker] being held liable for negligence' but 'would simply be a factor for consideration by the jury as to whether he acted as a "reasonable" person').

and failed to train its registered representatives appropriately to apply the suitability guidelines.[240]

Under the Exchange Act's anti-fraud provisions and SRO rules, broker-dealers also have a duty of best execution, which requires reasonable diligence in determining the best market for a security such that the price of the purchase or sale is as favourable as possible under the prevailing market conditions. The most important factor in determining compliance with the best execution requirement is price, but the SEC has identified

> six additional factors: (1) the size of the order; (2) the speed of execution available on competing markets; (3) the trading characteristics of the security; (4) the availability of accurate information comparing markets and the technology to process the data; (5) the availability of access to competing markets; and (6) the cost of such access.[241]

Unlike investment advisers, broker-dealers do not have a per se fiduciary duty to customers under federal laws and regulations. Whether they should is a matter of considerable current commentary and debate.[242] The Dodd-Frank Act required the SEC to conduct a study to evaluate the comparative regulatory standards of care for broker-dealers and investment advisers.

A January 2011 SEC staff study recommended adoption of a 'uniform fiduciary standard':

> the standard of conduct for all brokers, dealers, and investment advisers, when providing personalized investment advice about securities to retail customers ..., shall be to act in the best interest of the customer without regard to the financial or other interest of the broker, dealer, or investment adviser providing the advice.[243]

It 'interpret[ed] the uniform fiduciary standard to include at a minimum, the duties of loyalty and care as interpreted and developed under [the Advisers Act]'.[244] Two SEC commissioners dissented from release of the staff study on the grounds that its recommendation was not adequately supported by empirical data regarding costs and benefits.[245]

[240] J Jaeger, 'FINRA Fines Broker-Dealer $95K for Supervisory Lapses, Compliance Week' (28 March 2014) www.complianceweek.com/blogs/enforcement-action/finra-fines-broker-dealer-950k-for-supervisory-lapses#.V-2bHmlTF9A; D Nathan and A-M Ignat, 'FINRA Provides a Detailed Analysis of Broker-Dealer's Failure to Adequately Supervise Alternative Investment Sales' *Morrison & Foerster Client Alert* (27 March 2014) https://media2.mofo.com/documents/140327-finra-provides-a-detailed-analysis.pdf.

[241] SEC Study (n 225) 69.

[242] See eg AB Laby, 'Fiduciary Obligations of Broker-Dealers and Investment Advisers' (2010) 55 *Villanova Law Review* 701, 704 (arguing that 'a fiduciary obligation should be imposed, albeit cautiously, on brokers that provide advice').

[243] SEC Study (n 225) 109.

[244] ibid, 110–11.

[245] K Casey and T Paredes, 'Dissent from SEC Study of Uniform Standards for Investment Advisers and Broker-Dealers' (21 January 2011) http://sec.gov/news/speech/2011/spch012211klctap.htm.

More than two years later, in March 2013, the SEC issued a public release requesting data and economic analysis relating to the benefits and costs from adoption of the proposed uniform fiduciary standard.[246] In November 2013, the SEC's Investment Advisory Committee recommended adoption of rules imposing a fiduciary duty on broker-dealers when they provide personalised investment advice to retail investors.[247] The Committee favoured narrowing the broker-dealer Advisers Act exclusion and providing a safe harbour for brokers who do not engage in or hold themselves out as providing advisory services.[248] As of the time of this publication, the SEC has not yet acted on the Committee's recommendation.

State Common Law

State common law varies greatly with regard to whether and in what regards a broker owes fiduciary duties to its customers.[249] A key factor is whether the brokerage account is discretionary, such that the broker controls purchases and sales, or non-discretionary, such that the customer determines which purchases and sales to make.[250] In the case of a discretionary account, the broker will almost always be held to have fiduciary duties, but courts have taken a variety of approaches in analysing the duties owed in the case of a non-discretionary account. Some courts have found a fiduciary relationship despite a non-discretionary account where the broker exercises de facto control over the account. For example, 'where the agent "for all practical purposes" controls the account … California law imposes fiduciary obligations'.[251]

[246] SEC, 'Duties of Brokers, Dealers, and Investment Advisers' SEC Release No 34-69013; IA-3558; File No 4-606 (March 2013).

[247] SEC, 'Recommendations of the Investor Advisory Committee: Broker-Dealer Fiduciary Duty' (November 2013) www.sec.gov/spotlight/investor-advisory-committee-2012/fiduciary-duty-recommendation-2013.pdf.

[248] ibid, 2, 5.

[249] See eg *Grandon v Merrill Lynch & Co, Inc*, No 95 Civ 10742 (SWK), 2003 US Dist LEXIS 16003, at *30 (SDNY 10 September 2003) ('The fiduciary duties of securities brokers are materially different in each of the fifty states'.).

[250] See eg *Patsos v First Albany Corp*, 433 Mass 323, 332, 741 NE2d 841, 849 (Mass 2001) ('Where the account is "non-discretionary," … the relationship generally does not give rise to general fiduciary duties'.); *Refco, Inc v Troika Inv Ltd*, 702 F Supp 684, 687 (ND Ill 1988) (interpreting Illinois law; '[i]n general only a broker operating a discretionary account is viewed as a fiduciary'); see also Laby, *Fiduciary Obligations of Broker-Dealers and Investment Advisers* (n 242) 723 ('Most courts, looking to state law for guidance, conclude that only brokers for discretionary, as opposed to non-discretionary, accounts are considered fiduciaries'.).

[251] *Leboce, CA v Merrill-Lynch, Pierce, Fenner & Smith, Inc*, 709 F.2d 605, 607 (9th Cir 1983) (citing *Twomey v Mitchum, Jones & Templeton, Inc*, 262 Cal App 2d 690, 69 Cal Rptr 222 (Cal Ct App 1968)); see *Brown*, 168 Cal App 4th at 960, 85 Cal Rptr 3d at 835 ('A stockbroker is a fiduciary'.); see also *Mihara v Dean Witter & Co, Inc*, 619 F2d 814, 821–22 (9th Cir 1980) (finding fiduciary relationship and that, in context of a churning claim, 'the requisite degree of control is met when the client routinely follows the recommendations of the broker' such that there is 'a pattern of de facto control by the broker'); *Hotmar v Lowell H Listrom & Co*, 808 F2d 1384, 1385 (10th Cir 1987) ('even though there be a non-discretionary account, the broker may still exercise control over the account').

As analysed by one federal district court, the approaches of the various states can be categorised as falling in four basic groups:

> The cases … illustrate four methods that courts employ in answering whether a fiduciary relationship exists between a broker and a customer with non-discretionary accounts. Two of these methods involve an absolute rule: either finding no fiduciary relationship because the account is nondiscretionary, *see Refco, Inc. v. Troika Inv. Ltd.*, 702 F. Supp. 684, 687 (N.D. Ill. 1988) [interpreting Illinois law], or finding a fiduciary relationship regardless of whether the account is discretionary, *see Romano v. Merrill, Lynch, Pierce, Fenner & Smith*, 834 F.2d 523, 530 (5th Cir. 1987) [interpreting federal securities law]. Other courts, using a flexible approach, base the existence of a fiduciary relationship, not on the nature of the account, but on the nature of the relationship, and find a fiduciary relationship either if the broker has agreed to manage the account, *see Hotmar v. Listrom & Co.*, 808 F.2d 1384, 1386 (10th Cir. 1987) [interpreting Kansas law], or if the broker exercises de facto control over the account, *see Davis v. Merrill, Lynch, Pierce, Fenner & Smith*, 906 F.2d 1206, 1216-17 (8th Cir. 1990) [interpreting South Dakota law].[252]

Interpreting Utah law, that court, following *Hotmar*, adopted a 'two-part inquiry':

> The first part queries whether the account is discretionary or nondiscretionary. If discretionary, a fiduciary relationship exists; if nondiscretionary, the court proceeds to the second part of the inquiry. In the second part of the analysis, the court queries whether the broker has merely offered advice or whether he has agreed to manage the account. If the broker has agreed to manage the account, a fiduciary relationship exists.[253]

One pair of commentators divides the approaches of the various states

> into three categories: (1) states that unambiguously apply a fiduciary standard to brokers in that state; (2) states that unambiguously apply no fiduciary standard to brokers; and (3) states where there is evidence of a limited fiduciary standard applied to brokers.[254]

They identify only four states—California, Missouri, South Dakota and South Carolina—in the first category of states that unambiguously apply a fiduciary standard.[255] They place 14 states in the second category, which they construe to include states that have expressly stated that a broker owes no fiduciary duty to a client,[256] those that have concluded that brokers do not owe a duty to holders of non-discretionary accounts[257] and those that hold that a broker does not owe a fiduciary duty absent a special agreement.[258] They categorise the remaining 36 'quasi-fiduciary' states as ones that have 'impose[d] either a limited fiduciary standard, or the courts have interpreted state law to impose duties that appear

[252] *Marchese v Nelson*, 809 F Supp 880, 894 (D Utah 1993).

[253] ibid.

[254] M Finke and T Langdon, 'The Impact of the Broker-Dealer Fiduciary Standard on Financial Advice' (2012) 25(7) *The Journal of Financial Planning* 32.

[255] ibid.

[256] ibid. (Arkansas, Hawaii, Massachusetts, Montana and Washington are included in this group.).

[257] ibid. (Arizona, Colorado, Mississippi, New York, North Carolina, North Dakota and Oregon are included in this group.).

[258] ibid. (Minnesota and Wisconsin are included in this category.).

to be fiduciary in nature'.[259] This 'quasi-fiduciary' category includes states like Utah and Kansas, which, as discussed above, take a 'flexible approach', focusing on the nature of the relationship and whether the broker has agreed to manage the account.[260]

Even when a brokerage account is non-discretionary and the relationship is not deemed fiduciary, the broker owes substantial duties to the customer with regard to transactions executed on behalf of the customer. As summarised by the oft-cited opinion *Leib v Merrill Lynch, Pierce, Fenner & Smith*:

> In a non-discretionary account each transaction is viewed singly. In such cases the broker is bound to act in the customer's interest when transacting business for the account; however, all duties to the customer cease when the transaction is closed. Duties associated with a non-discretionary account include: (1) the duty to recommend a stock only after studying it sufficiently to become informed as to its nature, price and financial prognosis; (2) the duty to carry out the customer's orders promptly in a manner best suited to serve the customer's interests; (3) the duty to inform the customer of the risks involved in purchasing or selling a particular security; (4) the duty to refrain from self-dealing or refusing to disclose any personal interest the broker may have in a particular recommended security; (5) the duty not to misrepresent any fact material to the transaction; and (6) the duty to transact business only after receiving prior authorization from the customer.[261]

As articulated by another leading case:

> On a transaction-by-transaction basis, the broker owes duties of diligence and competence in executing the client's trade orders, and is obliged to give honest and complete information when recommending a purchase or sale. The client may enjoy the broker's advice and recommendations with respect to a given trade, but has no legal claim on the broker's ongoing attention.[262]

In *Press v Chemical Investment Services Corp*,[263] the Second Circuit, construing New York law, noted authority both for the proposition that 'in the context of an ordinary broker-client relationship, the broker owes no fiduciary duty to the purchaser of the security' and for the contrary principle that 'the relationship between a stockbroker and a customer is that of principal and agent and is fiduciary in nature'.[264] It found that these two conflicting lines of authority could be reconciled, however, because '[t]he cases that have recognized the fiduciary

[259] ibid.

[260] *Marchese* (n 252) 894.

[261] 461 F Supp. 951, 952–53 (ED Mich 1978) (citations omitted); *accord Patsos*, 433 Mass (n 250) at 332–33, 741 NE2d at 849 and note 15.

[262] *De Kwiatkowski v Bear, Stearns & Co Inc*, 306 F3d 1293, 1302 (2d Cir 2002); ibid, 1305 ('No doubt, a duty of reasonable care applies to the broker's performance of its obligations to customers with nondiscretionary accounts'.).

[263] 166 F3d 529 (2d Cir 1999).

[264] ibid, 536 (quoting *Perl v Smith Barney Inc*, 230 AD2d 664, 666, 646 NYS2d 678, 680 (NY App Div 1996)).

relationship as evolving simply from the broker-client relationship have limited the scope of the fiduciary duty to the narrow task of consummating the transaction requested'.[265]

Courts that have held that there is a fiduciary duty whether or not the account is discretionary have generally concluded, however, 'that the nature of the fiduciary duty owed will vary, depending on the relationship between the broker and the investor'.[266] Determination of the nature of the duty is thus 'necessarily particularly fact-based' and 'requires consideration of the degree of trust placed in the broker and the intelligence and personality of the customer'.[267] 'An inexperienced or naive investor is likely to repose special trust in his stockbroker because he lacks the sophistication to question or criticize the broker's advice or judgment'.[268]

Whatever the conclusion with regard to non-discretionary accounts, the fiduciary duties of a broker with regard to a discretionary account are generally held to be broader. As summarised in the *Leib* opinion:

> Unlike the broker who handles a non-discretionary account, the broker handling a discretionary account becomes the fiduciary of his customer in a broad sense. Such a broker, while not needing prior authorization for each transaction, must (1) manage the account in a manner directly comporting with the needs and objectives of the customer as stated in the authorization papers or as apparent from the customer's investment and trading history; (2) keep informed regarding the changes in the market which affect his customer's interest and act responsively to protect those interests; (3) keep his customer informed as to each completed transaction; and (5) [sic] explain forthrightly the practical impact and potential risks of the course of dealing in which the broker is engaged.[269]

As noted by another court, '[a] fiduciary relationship places on the fiduciary a duty of candor, and concomitantly excuses the principal from having to take the same degree of care that is expected of a participant in an arm's length contractual relationship'.[270]

[265] ibid (citations omitted).

[266] *Romano v Merrill, Lynch, Pierce, Fenner & Smith*, 834 F2d 523, 530 (5th Cir 1987); see also *Carr v CIGNA Fin Advisors, Inc*, 95 F3d 544, 547 (7th Cir 1996) (finding no fiduciary relationship but noting that 'provided that the fiduciary's principal is a competent adult, the fiduciary relationship does not excuse the principal from taking the most elementary precautions against a salesman's pitch, such as the precaution of reading a short and plain statement of what one is buying for one's $450,000').

[267] ibid (quoting *Clayton Brokerage Co v Commodity Futures Trading Comm'n*, 794 F2d 573, 582 (11th Cir 1986)).

[268] *Patsos*, 433 Mass (n 250) at 335, 741 NE2d at 851; *cf Brown*, 168 Cal App 4th at 960–61, 85 Cal Rptr 3d at 835 (finding that the bank had created a fiduciary relationship even before the customers opened a brokerage account because it 'knowingly induced the elderly and increasingly frail couple to rely on it to handle their financial affairs'.).

[269] *Leib*, 461 F Supp at 953 (citations omitted); *accord Trumball Invs, Ltd I v Wachovia Bank*, 436 F3d 443, 446 (4th Cir 2006) ('[T]he broker managing a discretionary account has to make investment decisions that are faithful to the needs and objectives of his client'.); *Patsos*, 433 Mass (n 250) at 334, 741 NE2d at 850 and note 16.

[270] *Carr*, 95 F3d (n 266) at 547.

D. Proprietary Trading and Market Trading

In 2010, the Wall Street Reform and Consumer Protection Act added a new section 13 to the Bank Holding Company Act of 1956. Section 13, or the Volcker Rule, has the effect of restricting any 'banking entity' from engaging in 'proprietary trading', owning a 'hedge fund' or 'private equity fund', or engaging in certain securities and investment transactions with any 'hedge fund' or 'private equity fund' for which it serves as a sponsor, investment manager or investment adviser.[271] It applies to any depository institution insured by the FDIC, any company that controls such an institution, any institution that is treated as a bank holding company under the International Banking Act and any affiliate or subsidiary of any of the foregoing institutions.[272] It does not restrict banks from securitising loans.[273] However, certain loan securitisations that have speculative characteristics, like 'asset-backed commercial paper conduits' and collateralised loan obligations, may be covered by the Volcker Rule.[274] Section 10(c)(8) of the rule excludes from the coverage of the loan securitisation exemption all securities and derivatives, other than loan-related interest rate or foreign exchange derivatives designed to hedge risk.[275] Section 11(b) of the rule permits a bank to 'seed' an investment fund by holding an initial equity interest therein while marketing it to investors, which it must divest (except for 3 per cent of the value of the fund) after 12 months.[276] In late 2014, Congress passed a law exempting certain swaps from the scope of the Volcker Rule.[277]

The Wall Street Reform Act made other changes. New section 15G of the Exchange Act requires issuers of asset-backed securities to retain certain risks rather than dumping the risk on clients.[278] Section 7(d) of the Securities Act raises the due diligence and related disclosure requirements in registered offerings of Exchange Act-regulated asset-backed securities, while section 27B of the Exchange Act governs conflicts of interest in the issuance of certain asset-backed securities[279]

[271] Prohibitions and Restrictions on Proprietary Trading and Certain Interests In, and Relationships with, Hedge Funds and Private Equity Funds (to be codified in 12 and 17 C.F.R.) (10 December 2013) www.sec.gov/rules/final/2013/bhca-1.pdf.

[272] ibid. See also *Proposed Rulemaking Under Section 619 of the Wall Street Reform and Consumer Protection Act of 2010*, 76 Fed Reg 68,846 (7 November 2011).

[273] Financial Stability Oversight Council, 'Study & Recommendations on Prohibitions on Proprietary Trading & Certain Relationships With Hedge Funds and Private Equity Funds' (January 2011).

[274] Skadden, 'The Final Volcker Rule: Impact on Securitizations' *Structured Finance Alert* (2014) www.skadden.com/newsletters/Structured_Finance_Alert_The_Final_Volcker_Rule_Impact_on_Securitization.pdf.

[275] ibid, 4.

[276] ibid, 9.

[277] See Consolidated & Further Continuing Appropriations Act, 2015, tit V, § 630 (2014) www.gpo.gov/fdsys/pkg/BILLS-113hr83enr/pdf/BILLS-113hr83enr.pdf; Sen Elizabeth Warren, 'Warren & Cummings Ask Banks about Swaps Trading Practices After Key Section of Dodd-Frank Gutted' Press Release (29 January 2015) www.warren.senate.gov/?p=press_release&id=715.

[278] 15 USC § 78o-11.

[279] 15 USC § 77z–2a.

and section 15E(s)(4)(A) of the Exchange Act calls upon securities rating agencies, issuers and underwriters to disclose to the public the findings and conclusions of certain due diligence reports prepared by third parties related to an asset-backed security.[280]

IV. Conclusion

The duty of care of US banks is complex and continually evolving. The duty arises in a variety of forms, at the state level and at the national level, from statutes, regulations and common law. The unique history of the United States has given rise to this complex patchwork of regulation, with the dual banking system a result of the nation's early history and the allocation of power between the federal government and the states. The author of a leading treatise on US banking law writes that the industry consists of a 'confusing array of financial institutions, regulatory agencies and statutes'.[281] He notes,

> [t]his system of laws, institutions and regulators is not the result of any preconceived plan or rational design. Rather, it evolved in response to historical accident, to the particular financial needs of different segments of the nation and to the concepts of Federalism basic to the American political system.[282]

The US banking system continues to evolve, most recently in the Dodd-Frank Act in response to the 2007–09 financial crises. A bank's duty of care in various circumstances has evolved throughout this history, at all levels of the dual banking industry and in all sources of US law.

280 15 USC § 78o-7(s).
281 Resseguie, *Banking Law* (n 37) § 1.02, 1-1.
282 ibid.

Part V

Comparative Conclusions

12

A Bank's Duty of Care: Perspectives from European and Comparative Law

DANNY BUSCH AND CEES VAN DAM

I. Introduction

The financial crisis of 2007–12 sparked a flood of litigation across Europe and the United States. This may be gleaned from the previous chapters, which all provide an overview of the major cases and affairs in which banks have been subject to litigation and in a number of cases have been held civilly liable to investors for mis-selling financial products, poor financial advice, insufficient disclosure of and warning for financial risks. Many of these disputes and scandals were triggered by the crisis. The chapters mention litigation and affairs on a vast array of financial products and services, including interest rate swaps, futures, options, short sales, structured finance products, payment protection insurances (PPIs), shares, bonds, mutual funds, loan contracts and mortgage lending. Many of these cases are somehow linked to the fall of Lehman Brothers, the US housing crisis and the fraudulent Madoff scheme.

The previous chapters offer a treatment of a bank's duty of care from the viewpoint of national jurisdictions. In this chapter we place a bank's duty of care in a European and comparative law perspective. Looking at the national reports from this angle, the first thing that strikes is that courts throughout the jurisdictions approach the questions with respect to the bank's duty of care in a pragmatic way. They do not seem to feel strongly bound or hindered by dogmatic or theoretical distinctions. For example, the courts do not generally distinguish between consumers and professionals but focus on the circumstances of the case and assess whether the client had sufficient knowledge to understand the financial product that was provided. The more knowledge and experience, the less protection he needs. And vice versa, the less knowledge and experience, the more protection he needs. From this balancing act, the courts find and shape the tools in their national legal system to achieve the outcome they deem to be fair, just and reasonable.

However, even though the courts are similarly pragmatic in their use of legal tools to decide cases, they clearly do not strike the balance in the same way. In particular, they are not equally protective for investors. This does not come as a surprise, as the question what amounts to a fair and just decision very much depends on the legal-cultural and legal-social make-up of the country in which the courts hand down their decision. Hence, courts are pragmatic in choosing the road to their decision and to embed their decision into the legal system but the substance of these decisions differs between the legal systems.[1]

For this chapter, we have chosen five topics which are hotly debated in theory and practice. The first topic is the scope and intensity of the essential duties which typically flow from a bank's duty of care: duties to investigate, duties to disclose or warn, and—in exceptional cases—outright duties to refuse to render financial services or products (section II). In some jurisdictions, financial disputes between investors and banks are not so much resolved by reference to a bank's duty of care, but by reference to the traditional doctrine of error or mistake, and fraud. That is the second topic we discuss in this chapter (section III). The third topic is the impact of the European Markets in Financial Instruments Directive (MiFID) on a banks' duty of care (section IV). The fourth topic focuses on the role of the financial regulator in settling disputes between banks and clients (section V). We conclude this chapter with the bigger picture and relevant reform perspectives (section VI).

II. Scope, Content and Intensity of a Bank's Duty of Care

A. General

i. The Imposed Duties

The picture that emerges from the previous chapters is that the courts typically resolve financial disputes between investors and banks by reference to duties to investigate (also known as Know your Customer or KYC rules) and duties to disclose or warn, often stemming from a duty of care, good faith, fiduciary law or statutory law. As for the Netherlands, the Dutch Supreme Court (Hoge Raad or HR) has many times stated that the position of banks in society brings with it a 'special' duty of care towards consumer clients. According to the Dutch Supreme Court, a bank's special duty of care is also based on the fact that banks are professional service providers which must be deemed to have the necessary expertise.

[1] See eg C van Dam, 'Who is Afraid of Diversity? Cultural Diversity, European Co-operation, and European Tort Law' (2009) 20 *King's Law Journal* 281–308.

The scope of this duty of care depends on the circumstances of the case. These circumstances may include the client's expertise, if any, its financial position, the complexity of the financial product involved and the regulatory rules to which the bank is subject.[2] The French duty to warn seems not so much based on the role of the bank in society and its expertise knowledge, but, as one French commentator puts it, on the idea of risk.[3]

Whatever the exact rationale of the relevant concepts, in France, Germany, Italy and the Netherlands there is a steady flow of case-law in which the courts submit banks to duties to investigate and disclose or warn by reference to a duty of care or by reference to a general notion of good faith—always subject to the caveat that in the end the facts of the individual case are decisive.[4] On at least a theoretical level the approach is similar in Spain, but as a practical matter disputes with banks are often resolved by reference to a defect of consent, in particular the doctrine of error or mistake.[5] This is also the case in Austria, but perhaps to a lesser extent.[6] Although the Dutch courts normally resolve disputes by reference to breach of duty of care, it is noteworthy that the Amsterdam Court of Appeal recently revived the doctrine of mistake with respect to banks advising SMEs on interest rate swaps.[7] And it is needless to say that information duties are also of paramount importance in the context of mistake. We will return to this in more detail in section III below. The civil law jurisdictions included in this book generally tend to protect investors, not only consumers, but also less experienced commercial parties.

In the common law jurisdiction of England and Wales, breach of duty of care is the most frequently invoked issue in financial litigation regarding the bank's rendering of advice, or failing to give advice, and the same is true for Ireland. But the success rate is rather small, both in England and Wales and in Ireland.

[2] See Dutch Chapter, s III.

[3] See French Chapter, s IV.A.

[4] French Chapter, ss I–IV; German Chapter, s III.D; Italian Chapter, s II.A–II.C; Dutch Chapter, ss II and III. Although arguably less so in French law. The author of the French chapter puts it as follows: 'For a French lawyer, the main cases are less connected to the facts or circumstances of the case than to the rules or principles mentioned by the French Supreme Court in its decisions' (French Chapter, s I).

[5] See Spanish Chapter, s III, *in fine* (in a general sense), s II (examples from case-law). However, based on SR Bachs and ED Ruiz, 'Chapter 9—Spain' in D Busch and DA DeMott (eds), *Liability of Asset Managers* (Oxford: Oxford University Press, 2012) and the Spanish case-law they mention, this appears to be different in the context of banks (and other financial institutions) providing asset management services, where damages *are* awarded on the basis of breach of contract or tort law. See ss 9.59–9.80.

[6] See Austrian Chapter, ss I.C and I.F. See for a case where the defect of consent of fraud was successfully invoked, Austrian Chapter, s I.G, *in fine*. In Italy, some lower courts previously resolved disputes between banks and their customers by applying the doctrines of mistake and fraud, but after a clear ruling by the United Chambers of the Italian Supreme Court this is no longer the case. See Italian Chapter, ss III.A and III.B.i. See for more detail s III below.

[7] See Amsterdam Court of Appeal 15 September 2015, ECLI:NL:GHAMS:2015:3842, *Ondernemingsrecht* 2016/37 with annotation by Arons, *JOR* 2015/334 with annotation by Atema & Hopman (*X/ING BANK NV*); Amsterdam Court of Appeal 11 November 2015, ECLI:NL:GHAMS:2015:4647, *JOR* 2016/37 with annotation Van der Wiel & Wijnberg; Court of Appeal Amsterdam 11 October 2016, case number 200.153.823/01 (*X Vastgoed BV/ABN AMRO NV*). See on these cases Dutch Chapter, ss II.E and VII.C.

The liability rules of England and Wales, and Ireland, tend to favour banks and impose a heavy burden on clients to prove breach of any statutory, common law or fiduciary duties. A major hurdle for a client to overcome is to show that the bank owed it a duty of care in the sale of a product or the rendering of advice regarding the risks associated with the bank's products and investments. In principle, all banks that sell financial products and services to clients in England and Wales are subject to a duty of care in the sale of these products and services. But this duty of care is subject to limitations imposed by the principle of freedom of contract and the contractual estoppel doctrine. Moreover, the absence of any principle of good faith or unconscionability in English law further safeguards banks from a high volume of successful claims. English common law generally allows a bank and its customer to contract out of the duty of care, resulting in an arm's length relationship between the bank and the customer in which the bank has no obligation to inform or advise its client, nor to reveal any of the risks associated with its product or to assess the suitability of its customer for the products it sells. A bank does have a duty of care not carelessly to misstate facts—which is breached to the extent that its representations or statements are inaccurate or false. But as Mance J once put it, a duty of care to advise clients of the risks or on the suitability of a product, 'should not be readily inferred in a commercial relationship'.[8,9]

However, in England and Wales it explicitly follows from section 138D (previously 150) of the Financial Services and Markets Act 2000 (FSMA) that a breach of the FCA's (previously FSA's) organisational or conduct-of-business rules under Part X, Chapter I of FSMA (which includes the implementation of organisational or conduct-of-business rules pursuant to MiFID) is directly actionable at the suit of a 'private person' (ie a non-professional, or private, investor), subject to the defences and other incidents applicable to breach of statutory duty. Section 44 of the Central Bank (Supervision and Enforcement) Act 2013 contains a similar provision, subject to two important differences. First, it provides a statutory basis for an action for damages by customers in general, including commercial parties. Second, it applies to customers who have suffered loss as a result of *any* failure by the financial services provider to comply with its obligations under financial services legislation, and not merely the conduct-of-business rules it contains.[10]

Turning to the US, it is first of all important to note that the 1933 Glass Steagall Act separated to a degree commercial banking from investment banking and placed limits on US banks' securities activities. But during the latter part of the twentieth century, Federal Reserve Board rulings and Supreme Court decisions

[8] See *Bankers Trust International plc v PT Dharmala Sakti Sejahtera* [1996] CL.C 531, per Mance J (on which see Chapter England and Wales, s I.B).

[9] See England and Wales Chapter, s I. See for Ireland, Irish Chapter, s II.A (duty of care in tort), s II.C (duty of care in contract). In the context of a duty of care in contract, the author of the Irish chapter remarks that '[t]he Courts will not impose a duty of care on a financial institution merely because such a term would have been beneficial to a customer or because the failure to include it has detrimental consequences for them' (s II.C).

[10] See also ss III.B.ii, II.C, II.D, IV.B and IV.E.i.

took an increasingly flexible approach to banks' provision of securities' services. The 1999 Gramm-Leach-Bliley Act repealed portions of Glass Steagall and allowed for broad affiliations between commercial banks and securities firms. US bank holding companies and their subsidiaries now provide a wide-range of securities services, including investment management, investment advice and execution-only services. Those services are subject to federal regulation and SEC enforcement as well as private rights of action under state statutory and common law.[11]

For US law purposes, a distinction must be drawn between investment advisers (including asset managers and investment advisers) and broker-dealers (including providers of execution-only services). *Investment advisers* are subject to the Investment Advisers Act of 1940. Section 206 of this Act establishes a statutory fiduciary duty for investment advisers to act for the benefit of their clients, submitting advisers to duties to investigate (known as the suitability test) and duties to disclose all material facts, and to employ reasonable care to avoid misleading clients.[12] While holding that the Advisers Act 'establishe[d] 'federal fiduciary standards to govern the conduct of investment advisers',[13] the Supreme Court has also held that 'that there exists [only] a limited private remedy under the [Advisers Act] to void an investment adviser's contract, [and] the Act confers no other private causes of action, legal or equitable'.[14] Thus, litigation to enforce the fiduciary standards established by the Advisers Act is limited to SEC enforcement actions, and private damages claims for breaches of an investment adviser's fiduciary duties or negligence are a matter of state law.[15]

Broker-dealers are subject to the anti-fraud provisions of the Securities Exchange Act of 1934, broadly prohibiting misleading omissions of material facts as well as affirmative statements and fraudulent or manipulative acts or practices. The SEC has adopted rules, issued interpretations and brought enforcement actions that define these prohibited practices that apply to broker-dealers. Important among broker-dealers are duties of fair dealing, duties of disclosure and compliance with suitability requirements. For broker-dealers, the suitability requirement is codified in self-regulatory organisation (SRO) rules.[16] But according to the SEC, the suitability doctrine is not limited to broker-dealers. The doctrine is applicable to investment advisers and has been enforced against advisers under section 206 of

[11] See US Chapter, s III.B.iii.

[12] See US Chapter, s III.C.ii.a.

[13] *Transamerica Mortg Advisors, Inc*, 444 U.S. at 17. See US Chapter, s III.C.ii.a.

[14] ibid, 24. See U.S. Chapter, s III.C.ii.a. As amended in 1970, the Advisers Act also 'impose[s] upon investment advisers a "fiduciary duty" with respect to compensation received from a mutual fund, 15 U.S.C. § 80a-35(b), and grant[s] individual investors a private right of action for breach of that duty, *ibid*'; *Jones v Harris Assocs LP*, 130 S. Ct. 1418, 1423 (2010). See US Chapter, s III.C.ii.a, n 221.

[15] See US Chapter, s III.C.ii.a. See *Davis v Merrill Lynch, Pierce, Fenner & Smith, Inc*, 906 F2d 1206, 1215 (8th Cir 1990) ('The question of whether a fiduciary relationship exists is a question of state law'.). See also eg *Stokes v Henson*, 217 Cal App 3d 187, 265 Cal Rptr 836 (Cal Ct App 1990) (affirming judgment against investment adviser for breach of fiduciary duty under California law). See US Chapter, s III.C.ii.a, n 222.

[16] See US Chapter, s III.C.ii.b.

the Advisers Act.[17] Although there is no private cause of action for violation of the SEC's suitability rule, courts 'have held that the suitability rule may set brokers' common law duty of care toward clients'.[18]

ii. Sources for the Imposed Duties

Sources for the bank's duties to investigate, to disclose or to warn vary strongly throughout the legal systems: they are found in tort law, contract law, fiduciary law and statutory law (section II.A.i).

In the continental European jurisdictions, the courts have developed these duties mostly within the framework of contract and in tort law on the basis of unwritten (uncodified) law but with distinct accents. Spain very much focuses on general rules of contract law (error/mistake). Also in France, Germany and Italy duties to investigate, disclose and warn have been developed in general contract law without reference to statutory developments. Italy and the Netherlands show a more mixed picture with developments in general contract law, with references to statutory (MiFID) developments as a confirmation or justification when applying general contract law, at the same time ensuring that they are not a follower of the statutory fashion but keep developing contract law independently.

In general, investors may claim both on the basis of general contract law and on the basis of breach of a statutory duty. What is crucial, however, is that in continental Europe, the former is developed independently from the latter and often sets higher requirements for banks to comply with than follows from legislation. It shows how courts are able and, apparently, keen to provide protection to investors, particularly private investors and small commercial investors, regardless of the rules set by the legislator.

This does not exclude, however, that in continental European jurisdictions the violation of a regulatory rule may indirectly influence the extent of the bank's contractual duty. In Austria and Germany this is called a 'radiating' or a 'concretising' effect of regulatory duties. In the Netherlands, a violation of MiFID duties may not only amount to a tort but also to a failure in the performance of a contractual obligation. The same goes for Spain where it is accepted that non-compliance with MiFID duties may have a bearing on a claim based on the contractual tenet of mistake (section IV.J).

[17] See DA DeMott and AB Laby, 'Chapter 13—United States of America' in Busch and DeMott (eds), *Liability of Asset Managers* (n 5) § 13.67, in fn 83 referring to Advisers Act Release, No 1406.

[18] See US Chapter, s III.C.ii.b. *Ives v Ramsden*, 142 Wash App 369, 390, 174 P3d 1231, 1242 (Wash Ct App 2008) (collecting cases); see eg *Scott v Dime Sav Bank of NY, FSB*, 886 F Supp 1073, 1080–81 (SDNY 1995) (upholding negligence claim based on evidence of violation of suitability rule); *cf Merrill Lynch, Pierce, Fenner & Smith, Inc v Chen*, 697 F Supp 1224, 1227 (DDC 1998) (violation of suitability rule 'will not automatically result in [broker] being held liable for negligence' but 'would simply be a factor for consideration by the jury as to whether he acted as a "reasonable" person'). See US Chapter, s III.c.ii.b, n 239.

The breach of a contractual duty to investigate, disclose or warn usually gives rise to damages. However, if these duties are considered in the framework of the contractual doctrines of error or mistake, the breach of such a duty will make the contract null and void or voidable, giving rise to restitution obligations for banks. These can be more onerous for banks, also because, unlike in the case of damages, contributory negligence of the investor is not a defence.

In the common law systems, particularly in England and Wales and Ireland, the emphasis is less on contract law and tort law and more on statutory law. Here, the distinction between common law and statutory is rather strict; they clearly do not mix. Although investors also bring claims against banks based on common law, they are generally less successful than in other jurisdictions. As mentioned above, in England and Wales and Ireland, courts are reluctant to accept contractual duties for banks to investigate, to disclose and to warn their clients regarding the risks associated with the bank's products and investments, even when the investor is a consumer. This reluctant approach by the courts is not owing to any systematic limitation of the common law but to the stronger endorsement of the principle of the freedom of contract, as expressed, inter alia, in the contractual estoppel doctrine (in case of a written contract, neither party can subsequently deny the existence of the facts and matters upon which they have agreed). Moreover, considerations of reasonableness or unconscionability are unknown in common law. Therefore it does not come as a surprise that investors rely more heavily on the bank's statutory duties, inter alia following the implemented MiFID legislation.

In the United States, the picture is different from other common law jurisdictions (section II.A.i). Federal tort law does not allow claims against investment advisers. Private damages claims for breaches of an investment adviser's fiduciary duties or negligence are a matter of state law. Under state law, common law contractual duties are imposed on retail banks to deliver reasonably prudent services to their depositors (section II.C.iv). Under federal law, broker-dealers are subject to statutory rules such as the so-called suitability rule but violation of these rules is not privately enforceable: they are enforced by the SEC. However, state courts have held that the suitability rule may set brokers' common law duty of care towards clients. This cross-over from statutory law to common law is more common in the US, where the tort of negligence and breach of statutory duty are interconnected, whereas in English law they are two distinct torts with limited intertwinement.[19]

[19] C van Dam, *European Tort Law* (Oxford: Oxford University Press, 2013) s 902-1; WHV Rogers (ed), *Winfield and Jolowicz on Tort*, 18th edn (London: Sweet & Maxwell, 2010) para 7.1, points out that other common law countries and the majority of jurisdictions in the United States generally consider the statute to 'concretise' the common law duty under the tort of negligence, which resembles more the German and French approach: Van Dam, *European Tort Law* (n 19) ss 903 and 904. See, however, also A Burrows, 'The Relationship between Common Law and Statute in the Law of Obligations' (2012) 128 *Law Quarterly Review* 232–59.

B. Scope

i. General

In this subsection, we analyse and discuss the scope of duties to investigate and duties to disclose or warn. First, do these duties only apply in relation to consumers or do they also apply in relation to commercial parties? Second, do duties to investigate and duties to disclose or warn only apply within the context of investment management, investment advice and execution-only services, or also beyond the scope of investment services? Third, are duties to investigate or warn also accepted in relation to third parties, and if so in which circumstances?

ii. Consumers and Commercial Parties

As regards the first aspect, duties to investigate and duties to warn or disclose are widely accepted with respect to consumers in the jurisdictions covered in this book. Owing to their lack of knowledge and experience when it comes to financial products and services, they are considered most worthy of protection.

In the Netherlands, the question whether banks also owe a special duty of care to SMEs and other commercial clients is hotly debated, largely triggered by the massive mis-selling of interest rate swaps to SMEs. There is some lower court case-law on interest rate swaps which accepts that banks are also subject to a special duty of care towards SMEs, resulting in the usual duties to investigate and warn. However, the Dutch Supreme Court has not yet had the chance to confirm or reject this view.[20]

In France there is more clarity. A duty to warn of the risks of speculative financial operations exists in all cases in which the client is ignorant of the risks involved in the transaction. It does not matter whether the client is a consumer or not, only his lack of knowledge is relevant. So in France the distinction between retail and commercial clients is not in itself decisive.[21]

In Germany, in the context of investment advice, the differentiation between retail and commercial clients is likewise not relevant for determining the scope and intensity of the duty of care, as each provision of advice has to be tailored to the facts of the specific case. In a much discussed 2011 decision rendered by the Federal Supreme Court (Bundesgerichtshof or BGH), a bank was held liable in

[20] See Dutch Chapter, s II.E. See esp Court of Appeal Den Bosch, 15 April 2014, *JOR* 2014/168, with annotation Van der Wiel & Wijnberg; *Ondernemingsrecht* 2014/92, with annotation Arons (*Holding Westkant BV, in liquidatie/ABN AMRO Bank NV*), mentioned in s II.E, n 12. Please also note that the open norms in the Dutch Civil Code could in any even facilitate the development of any such special duty of care towards commercial parties. See Dutch Civil Code, Arts 6:2, 6:248 and 7:401. See s II.E, n 12. See on these provisions Dutch Chapter, ss III and VII.B.

[21] See French Chapter, s IV.A.

damages for breach of its duty of care after having sold a highly complex interest rate swap—a spread ladder swap—to a corporate client.[22]

In England and Wales and Ireland, the distinction between retail and commercial clients is not in itself decisive for determining the existence, scope and intensity of the duty of care, as the assessment much depends on the specific facts of the relevant case.[23] The same is true for the US, where this likewise depends on the circumstances.[24] However, the distinction between private and commercial clients *is* in itself decisive in England and Wales in the case of a claim for damages based on section 138D (previously section 150) of FSMA. This claim for breach of regulatory requirement for the provision of suitable and adequate advice in the sale of financial products or investments provides a statutory right of action where breach of these regulatory requirements cause loss to a 'private person'. Generally, the claimant must therefore be an individual. Corporate clients may only use this provision if they were not 'conducting business of any kind'. In *Titan Steel Wheels Ltd v Royal Bank of Scotland plc*,[25] the Court gave a narrow interpretation to the concept of a private person. A steel manufacturer who had been sold inappropriate swaps by a bank was not able to use section 138D. It was held to be conducting business, even though it was not experienced in financial markets.[26] Irish law is different in this respect. Section 44 of the Central Bank (Supervision and Enforcement) Act 2013 also contains a statutory claim, but with a much wider scope. First, it provides a statutory basis for an action for damages by 'customers' in general, including commercial parties. Second, it includes customers who have

[22] BGH 22 March 2011—XI ZR 33/10, reported in BGHZ 189, 13, on which see German Chapter, s III.B.i.

[23] See Chapter on England and Wales, s II.A, stating that '[d]espite the limitations in establishing a duty of care between a bank *and* commercial or individual clients, the duty of care issue is the most frequently invoked issue in financial litigation regarding the bank's rendering of advice, or failing to give advice'. See for Ireland, Irish Chapter, s II.E, stating that 'while a financial institution does not ordinarily owe a duty of to advise or to explain documentation, such a duty may arise depending on the facts of the case'. See also on commercial and consumer clients, Chapter on England and Wales, s II.A and see s III for several examples of claims by third parties against banks (referred to in the chapter on England and Wales as 'third party banks'; see further on liability against third parties s II.B.iv). In the Irish Chapter it is also stated that '[w]here the recipients of the information are not sophisticated or are clearly missing important information, there may be a greater responsibility on the Bank to give advice' (s II.E).

[24] The US Chapter remarks that '[t]he general rule is that a fiduciary duty does not exist between commercial parties operating at arm's length. [...] Special circumstances, however, even in commercial transactions in the banking context, can give rise to fiduciary duties'. (s II.A.i.d). See also the statement (s II.A.i.d) that '[m]ost states find existence of fiduciary duty in the banking context, as in other contexts, to be a question of fact to be determined on a case-by-case basis'.

[25] [2010] EWHC 211.

[26] See the UK Law Commission (LAW Com No 350), *Fiduciary Duties of Investment Intermediaries* (2014) § 11.12. In this paper, the Law Commission considered an extension of Art 138D. The Law Commission concluded that there are arguments to be made both for and against an extension of s 138D. Given the controversy involved the Law Commission concluded that the issue is one for government. If the government were sympathetic to this change, the Law Commission thinks that the issue would merit further research and debate. See § 11.33–11.35.

suffered loss as a result of *any* failure by the financial services provider to comply with its obligations under financial services legislation, and not merely some of the conduct-of-business rules it contains.[27]

In Italy, it seems that the distinction between consumers and commercial clients is not in itself decisive either. Nevertheless, there is empirical evidence which confirms that a claim brought by an unsophisticated investor has more probability of being upheld: the probability of having such a claim upheld equals to 94.3 per cent, while the probability for a claim by an expert investor to be rejected is 77.8 per cent.[28]

Finally, in Spain, the parties and the civil courts do not normally resort to breach of duty of care to resolve civil disputes between banks and customers. It is much more common to argue that there is a lack of consent, principally on the basis of mistake or even fraud. But, as may be evidenced by recent Spanish interest rate swap litigation, in the context of mistake, it is not so much the status of the client that is relevant (consumer or commercial), but rather his knowledge and expertise as regards the financial product or service concerned.[29]

In conclusion it can be said that the courts generally do not distinguish between consumers and professionals but focus on the circumstances of the case and assess whether the client had sufficient knowledge to understand the financial product that was provided.

iii. Extensions beyond the Scope of Provision of Investment Services

a. Bank Loans

Turning to the second aspect, the scope of the French duty of care is not confined to investment services. Duties to investigate and warn may also exist in the context of a simple loan agreement between the bank and its contractual counterparty. The French chapter indicates that in the case of loans the bank has a duty to investigate the financial situation of the client and warn him, if the loan is disproportionate in view of his financial situation. So debtors must be warned only if there is excessive risk, unless he knows of the risk.[30]

As for Austrian law, it is noteworthy that in 2013, the Austrian Supreme Court (Oberster Gerichtshof or OGH) assumed a breach of duties to investigate and warn in a case beyond the scope of the provision of investment services, ie in a case

[27] See Irish Chapter, s VI. See also IV.B below.

[28] See Italian Chapter, s I.

[29] Spanish Chapter, ss II.B, II.C, II.D and III. Finally, the Austrian chapter does not explicitly address the question of whether a bank's duty of care cannot extend beyond consumers. At the same time, the chapter does not contain any indications that this should not be possible. On the contrary, the open norms contained in § 1299 and § 1300 ABGB would appear to be able to facilitate any such development. See on these provisions, Austrian Chapter, s IV, *in fine.*

[30] French Chapter, s IV.B.

in which a bank must have noticed that a foreign currency loan was not suitable for its customer, but failed to warn accordingly.[31] Of course, a foreign currency loan is far more risky than a simple loan agreement, as the actual payments on the loan by the debtor are subject to the exchange rate between the currency in which the debtor actually pays his debt and the relevant foreign currency. A sharp change in the exchange rate may cause severe financial problems for the debtor. To take a recent example, on 15 January 2015, the Swiss National Bank (SNB) discontinued the minimum exchange rate of CHF 1.20 per euro.[32] The result was a sharp change in the exchange rate of the CHF in comparison with the euro, making foreign currency loans denominated in CHF much more expensive for debtors who ultimately pay in euros. Private households in Central and Eastern Europe were hit hard by the unexpected decision of the SNB to end the peg to the euro, notably in Poland, Hungary and Croatia.[33]

The French and Austrian approach may be contrasted with the German and Irish approach. In Germany the courts have generally been very reluctant to recognise duties to investigate, inform or warn in the context of a bank loan, holding borrowers fully responsible for both the decision to take out a loan and for the decision how to invest it.[34] In Ireland the approach is similarly reluctant. This may be gleaned from the Irish case *ACC Bank plc v Deacon & anor*,[35] where Ryan J quoted with approval the following extract from the *Encyclopaedia of Banking Law* (2013):

> Where a bank assumes the role of financial adviser to its customer, it owes the customer a duty to exercise reasonable care and skill in the execution of that role. However, a bank does not usually assume the role of financial adviser to a customer who merely approaches it for a loan or for some other form of financial accommodation.

It is notable that an attempt was made in the Irish courts to establish a new tort of reckless lending which would apply to banks and which would have the effect of imposing a special duty of care on them in relation to their lending. So far, the Irish courts have refused to recognise the existence of a tort of reckless lending.[36]

b. Guarantees

Another recurring case in which duties to warn and investigate are accepted by the courts beyond the scope of investment services, is the situation where a consumer acts as the guarantor of a debtor of a bank loan. In both the Netherlands

[31] 8 Ob 66/12g, EvBl 2013, 922 (*Cach*). See Austrian Chapter, ss I.J and II.B, *in fine*.

[32] See Press release SNB dated 15 January 2015, available at: www.snb.ch/en/mmr/reference/pre_20150115/source/pre_20150115.en.pdf.

[33] See http://bruegel.org/2015/10/foreign-loan-hangovers-and-macro-prudential-measures-in-central-eastern-europe/.

[34] German Chapter, s II.

[35] [2013] IEHC 427. See Irish Chapter, s II.B.iii.a.

[36] See Irish Chapter, s II.F. The Chapter on England and Wales does not provide leads in this respect.

and France the bank has a duty to warn such guarantor for the risks involved.[37] See for Austria § 25 KschG, which applies whenever a consumer guarantees (or provides other personal securities) for someone else's loan granted by a bank or other financial institute.[38] In such cases, the creditor must warn this third party accordingly, if it knows, or ought to know, that its customer, the credit recipient, may not be able to pay back the loan. If the bank or other financial institution fails to do so, the third party is not obliged to pay back the loan despite the given guarantee.[39]

Also in Ireland and England and Wales, consumers acting as the guarantor of a debtor of a bank loan are considered special cases, although in such cases the courts have applied the doctrine of undue influence rather than a breach of duty of care or breach of a fiduciary or statutory duty. See for example *Ulster Bank Ireland Limited v Roche & Buttimer*,[40] where the High Court considered whether a bank should have responsibility for advising a guarantor of her partner's company of the consequences of a guarantee. It referred to the seminal English case of *Royal Bank of Scotland v Etridge (No 2)*,[41] which established that whenever a wife offered to act as guarantee for the indebtedness of her husband or his business, the bank was put on inquiry and was obliged to take reasonable steps to satisfy itself that she had understood and freely entered into the transaction. Clarke J determined

> that the general principle, which underlies *Etridge*, is to the effect that a bank is placed on inquiry where it is aware of facts which suggest, or ought to suggest, that there may be a non-commercial element to a guarantee.

The Court held that the bank was aware of the personal relationship between the surety and the owner of the company and that the former had no direct interest in the company and it was obliged to take 'at least some measures to seek to ensure that the proposed surety was openly and freely agreeing to provide the requested security'. As it had not done so, the surety was entitled to rely on the undue influence which her partner exercised over her.[42]

c. Sale of Risky Products to Consumers

Finally, in a case involving the mere selling of risky and complex financial products to consumers (ie without rendering advice or any other type of investment

[37] See HR 1 April 2016, ECLI:NL:HR:2016:543, *NJ* 2016/190 (*Aruba Bank c.s./Hardeveld*), consideration 3.4.1. See for similar reasoning in the context of avoidance of the guarantee on the basis of error (*dwaling*): HR 1 June 1990, *NJ* 1991/759 with annotation Brunner (*Van Lanschot/Bink*). See Dutch Chapter, s II.F. See for France the French Chapter, s II.B.iii.

[38] Of course, the guarantor for the loan does have a contractual relationship with the bank and, therefore, is not a 'third party' of the bank in a strict sense. See Austrian Chapter, s II.E, n 91.

[39] Unless the creditor proves that the third party would have guaranteed for its customer anyway; see S Perner, M Spitzer and GE Kodek, *Bürgerliches Recht*, 3rd edn 630. See Austrian Chapter, s II.E and n 92.

[40] [2012] IEHC 166. See also *ACC Bank Plc v Connolly & anor* [2015] IEHC 188.

[41] [2002] 2 AC 773.

[42] Irish Chapter, s II.C, *in fine*.

services), the Dutch Supreme Court held that it followed from the special duty of care that there was a duty to warn consumers for the risks involved and a duty to comply with KYC rules, even though the bank was only acting as contractual counterparty (seller) and not as a financial services provider. In such a case the MiFID KYC rules would not apply as their application is confined to cases in which the bank provides investment services.[43]

iv. Third Parties

The main part of our questionnaire (and, hence, the country reports) focused on duties banks owe to their customers. However, in a number of countries the case-law has fairly recently also developed duties banks owe to third parties. Obviously, these duties are not based on contract but on tort (liability law). From a quantitative point of view this may not yet be a major development and courts enter this area with caution but it shows that they look beyond the regulatory focus on customers. It also shows that banks do need to broaden their risk perspectives and assessments and look beyond their traditional circle of customers. During the financial crisis it became apparent that the impact banks have on society at large is huge. For this reason, it cannot come as a surprise that courts also see a role for banks to protect third parties against harm and develop duties accordingly.

From a legal-systematic (or dogmatic) point of view, liability to third parties for pure economic loss is a rather underdeveloped area in most jurisdictions, as courts are generally reluctant to adopt duties to protect third parties against pure economic loss. Compensation of pure economic loss is complicated both from a technical and a policy point of view. The policy issue regards the fact that it is thought that compensating pure economic loss on a general basis would open the floodgates to claims. It has been argued that awarding such claims on a general basis would put such a heavy burden on the tortfeasor and the courts that it would be preferable to let the loss lie where it falls.[44]

It is hard to say whether this scenario is a nightmare or reality. The best to be said is that it is the product of a political view. There is no evidence whatsoever that compensating pure economic loss on a more general basis would lead to apocalyptic events. Moreover, in personal injury cases the financial consequences can be extensive too.[45] Moreover, as William Prosser said in the 1930s: 'It is a pitiful confession of incompetence on the part of any court of justice to deny relief upon the ground that it will give the courts too much work to do'.[46]

43 See HR 5 June 2009, *JOR* 2009/199, annotated by Lieverse (*Treek v Dexia Bank Nederland*), consideration 5.2.1. See Dutch Chapter, s II.B; Chapter 2, s III, *in fine*; this chapter, s VI.C, *in fine*.

44 See eg J Spier (ed), *The Limits of Expanding Liability* (The Hague: Kluwer International, 1998).

45 M Bussani and VV Palmer, 'The Notion of Pure Economic Loss and its Setting' in M Bussani and VV Palmer (eds), *Pure Economic Loss in Europe* (Cambridge: Cambridge University Press, 2003) 16–21. See also H Bernstein, 'Civil Liability for Economic Loss' (1998) 46 *American Journal of Comparative Law* 111, 126–28.

46 W Prosser, 'Intentional Infliction of Mental Suffering: A New Tort' (1939) 37 *Michigan Law Review* 877.

Over the past decades, the importance of protection against pure economic loss has become more apparent. The ongoing financial crisis has made clear that the consequences of financial losses can be considerable, particularly when they affect savings, pensions and company assets. In such cases, economic loss is not the loss of some type of luxury or some commercial risk but it may affect a person's essential income and livelihood. The distinction made in tort law between tangible damage on the one hand (personal injury, property loss) and intangible damage on the other (pure economic loss) is artificial and conceals the real value of the damage suffered.

The ways in which the legal systems have translated these policy considerations into legal rules differ considerably. French law has the most open approach, seemingly awarding compensation for pure economic loss on a general basis. However, the control mechanisms can be found in the way the requirements for liability (*faute*, causation and damage) are applied; in particular, the limits provided by the requirements of causation and damage should not be underestimated. The English and German tort law systems both contain high hurdles for compensation of pure economic loss but the judiciaries in both countries have found ways to lower them in certain circumstances. Therefore, the differences between the legal systems are less black and white than the systems suggest, although English judges probably remain the most reluctant when it comes to protecting someone who has suffered pure economic loss.[47]

As the *French-based legal systems* (represented in this book by France, Italy, Spain, and the Netherlands) do not know formal hurdles when it comes to liability for pure economic loss to third parties, one would expect the strongest developments with respect to a bank's duty of care to third parties in these legal systems. In France and Spain the courts have not yet been asked to rule on such a duty but if this would happen, they would not be hindered by any legal-systematic limitations.[48]

The main examples of third party liability of banks come from Italy and the Netherlands. These jurisdictions have accepted such duties but under fairly strict conditions.

In Italy, a duty of care of banks is accepted in the rather specific area of tied agents. According to Italian case-law, the scope of application of such duty of care encompasses also cases of scams committed by a bank's tied agents, even when it is clear that the latter acted in the absence—or beyond the limits—of a proxy to represent the banks. The most common case is that of the tied agent unduly receiving money from the clients and diverting it to its own personal accounts. Indeed, in such cases banks could not be deemed to be providing any service at all to clients, but the mere fact that the tied agent received a mandate by the bank to act in

[47] van Dam (n 19) s 710-1.

[48] French Chapter, s I. In the Spanish Chapter it is not even mentioned as a theoretical possibility. Ruiz and Bachs seem to consider it in theory possible, at least in the context of asset management. See Bachs and Ruiz, 'Chapter 9—Spain' (n 5) § 9.73.

its interest is deemed sufficient to ground a vicarious liability on the bank itself pursuant to Article 2049 of the Italian Civil Code (establishing the liability of the employer for damages caused by its employees to third parties).[49] The main consequence of this trend in the case-law is that the sole effective defence for a bank in these cases is related to a possible contributory negligence by clients, considering that usually tied agents are not entitled at all to directly receive money from clients.

In the Netherlands, the case-law has accepted various scenarios of third party liability of banks. The Dutch Supreme Court justified this 'special duty of care' on the role banks play in society, implying that they also have to take interests of certain third parties into account on the basis of the requirements of unwritten law.

In 1998, in *Mees Pierson/Ten Bos*, the Dutch Supreme Court held that the role that banks have within society causes banks to have a special duty of care, not only towards clients on the basis of contractual relationships, but also towards third parties whose interests the bank has to take into account on the basis of the requirements of unwritten law. The scope of this duty of care depends on the circumstances of the case.[50] The cases *Fortis/Stichting Volendam* and *ABN AMRO/SBGB* concerned fraudulent investment services; the banks' only involvement in these matters was that the fraudulent 'investment services provider' used bank accounts held with these banks. In both cases, the Dutch Supreme Court upheld the Court of Appeal's finding that the banks are liable for the investors' losses (in *ABN AMRO* this was only a conditional finding).[51] In the *Fortis* matter, the bank's liability was grounded on the fact that at some point in time the bank had observed that the services were possibly being provided without the required regulatory licence, but had failed to investigate this further.[52] In the *ABN AMRO* case, the (presumed) liability of the bank was based on the fact that the payments to and from the fraudster's private bank account were unusual in quantity and nature, which should have prompted the bank to further investigate these transactions.[53] In *ABN AMRO*, the Dutch Supreme Court held that the special duty of care towards third parties also aims to protect these third parties against their own rashness or lack of insight.[54]

A final important judgment on a bank's liability towards third parties concerns World Online's IPO.[55] The Hoge Raad held as being relevant aspects for ABN AMRO and Goldman Sachs' duty of care towards investors in World Online, the fact that these banks were the (joint) global coordinators, lead managers and bookrunners to the IPO. According to the Hoge Raad, this meant that they had

[49] See eg Supreme Court, decision no 6091 of 20 March 2006; Supreme Court decision no 19166 of 29 September 2005. See Italian Chapter, s II.F and n 42.

[50] HR 9 January 1998, *NJ* 1999/285 (*Mees Pierson/Ten Bos*).

[51] The Court of Appeal allowed the bank to rebut the assumption of its knowledge of unusual payment transactions.

[52] HR 23 December 2005, *NJ* 2006/289 (*Fortis/Stichting Volendam*).

[53] HR 27 November 2015, ECLI:NL:HR:2015:3399 (*ABN AMRO/SBGB*).

[54] See Dutch Chapter, s II.D.

[55] HR 27 November 2009, *NJ* 2014/201 (*VEB c.s./World Online c.s.*).

been engaged by World Online as issuer to lead the syndicate of banks involved in the IPO and that they were responsible for the determination of the price, for the due diligence investigation and for drafting and distributing the prospectus. As a syndicate leader, a bank has the responsibility to prevent potential investors getting a wrong impression of the issuer, as far as is possible within the syndicate leader's sphere of influence—for example within the scope of the due diligence investigation and when drafting the prospectus.[56]

In common law countries like England and Wales, a duty to third parties is in principle conceivable, also in case of pure economic loss. Such a duty may be based on the *Caparo* case-law but a potentially more successful basis is 'assumption of responsibility', also known as the *Hedley Byrne* rule as part of the tort of negligence.[57] This latter rule implies that a duty of care exists if someone reasonably relies on another person's special skills and knowledge, the main categories being the provision of information and of services. Examples include an inaccurate statement by a bank regarding the solvency of a client, negligent underwriting by managing agents of an insurance syndicate, a negligently conducted survey of a house, and the failure by a solicitor to draw up a will on time.[58] However, in the framework of a bank's duty of care such duties are in practice not or hardly accepted, as banks do not make representations to individualised third parties and therefore do not assume responsibility for third party's interests, let alone that the latter may reasonably rely on it.

Following the financial crisis of 2007–08, a growing number of legal claims have been filed by professional and other sophisticated third party investors against banks[59] who acted as arrangers or managers in the sale of structured finance and other complex financial products. For example, a professional investor holding a structured debt instrument issued as part of a securitisation who suffered losses as a result of negligent statements or misrepresentations in the sale of that product might look for redress to those parties who made the statements and promoted the products (the 'managers') or to those parties who structured the investment (the 'arrangers'). A preliminary issue would be whether the managers/arrangers acted *reasonably* and, if they did not, whether they are *liable* in negligence for making a false statement about the product or rendering negligent advice to its customer in deciding whether to purchase the product. If they did not act reasonably or acted deceitfully, to prove liability the investor must first show whether the bank—as a manager or arranger of the product—owed a duty of care to the investor.[60]

[56] See Dutch Chapter, s II.D.

[57] *Hedley Byrne & Co Ltd v Heller & Partners Ltd* ([1963] 2 All ER 575, [1964] AC 465); *Caparo Industries plc v Dickman* ([1990] 1 All ER 568, [1990] 2 AC 605).

[58] van Dam (n 19) ss 503-4 and 710-4.

[59] Referred to as 'third party banks' in the chapter on England and Wales, s III, but this is just a matter of perspective. What is decisive is that there is no contractual relationship between the investor and the bank in question.

[60] Chapter on England and Wales, s III.

In these cases, the author of the chapter on England and Wales concludes, the English courts have generally resisted expanding the scope of liability to third party banks because, as arrangers or managers of the sale of the complex financial product—they were not the issuers or the sellers of the product or securities in question. Instead, a special purpose vehicle that was a separate legal entity was the seller or the issuer. Therefore, the banks were not parties to the contract with the claimant investors who purchased the investment products. Moreover, the investment contract entered into by the investors with the SPV expressly stated that the investors did not rely on any representations that were not stated in writing in the contract. In other words, any marketing statements or promotions provided by the bank as arranger or manager had no legal effect with respect to liability in the issuance or sale of the investment product.[61]

In the United States, liability of a bank to non-customers is possible in state law but the threshold is high. In addition to the common law and contractual duties of retail banks to deliver reasonably prudent services to their depositors, banks have a common law duty in tort to some non-customers. Historically, courts employed the doctrine of 'constructive fraud' as a catch-all for omissions contrary to a legal or equitable duty to act, causing injury to another in circumstances offending 'good conscience'.[62] Although in some states there may be no duty in tort to non-customers to detect and prevent a bank customer's fraudulent conduct, many states do impose criminal and tort liability for aiding and abetting violations of law. Typically, such liability is triggered by knowing aid to a violation, or reckless disregard of the possibility of a violation, not by mere negligence. Thus, there may be no bank duty to police customer accounts proactively for purposes of protecting non-customers. However, if a bank has actual knowledge of wrongdoing, it may be liable for aiding and abetting a breach of fiduciary duty owed by a customer to a non-customer. It may also be liable on a theory of 'conscious avoidance':

> Conscious avoidance … involves a culpable state of mind whereas constructive knowledge imputes a state of mind on a theory of negligence. Reflecting this analysis, the Second Circuit has held in the criminal context that conscious avoidance may satisfy the knowledge prong of an aiding and abetting charge. Accordingly, the Court sees no reason to spare a putative aider and abettor who consciously avoids confirming facts that, if known, would demonstrate the fraudulent nature of the endeavor he or she substantially furthers.[63]

[61] Chapter on England and Wales, s III. The Irish Chapter does not explicitly address the case of liability of banks towards third parties, but it does refer to the *Hedley Byrne* case, which is good law in Ireland as well. See Irish Chapter, ss II.A, II.B, II.D. So a similar approach as in England and Wales seems feasible in Ireland, at least in theory.

[62] See US Chapter, s II.A.ii and see *Jackson v Jackson*, 47 Ga 100, 109 (1872), mentioned in US Chapter, s II.A.ii, n 79.

[63] See US Chapter, s II.A.ii and see *Fraternity Fund Ltd v Beacon Hill Asset Mgmt, LLC*, 479 F Supp 2d 349, 367–68 (SDNY 2007), mentioned in US Chapter, s II.A.ii, n 80.

So-called 'red flags' of wrongdoing may be sufficient to hold a bank liable in such a case, even without a definitive adjudication against or criminal conviction of the customer.[64]

The Germanic legal systems (Germany and Austria) maintain a strict distinction between tort and contract and at the same time impose strong formal limitations when it comes to compensation for pure economic loss. German tort law has three general rules. Paragraph 823(1) is the most important one but it does not apply to pure economic loss. Paragraph 823(2) establishes liability for breach of a statutory duty and paragraph 826 liability for intentionally caused harm, including pure economic loss; however, it is generally hard to prove intention even though the courts have somewhat relaxed this requirement.

To some extent, this gap is filled by the tenet of the so-called contract with protective effect for third parties (*Vertrag mit Schutzwirkung für Dritte*), which at the same time provides an exception to the otherwise strongly held distinction between contract and tort. The tenet has not only been applied in the area of liability of auditors and attorneys,[65] but also in the area of a bank's duties of care.

In Germany, while liability would normally be restricted to the bank's counterparty, in exceptional circumstances the bank may also be held liable for losses incurred by third parties who do not themselves become party to the contract. Under general principles of contract law, this may be the case where a client informs the bank that its advice will be relied upon by that third party, and where the bank consents to it.[66]

In Austria, this doctrine of *Vertrag mit Schutzwirkung zugunsten Dritter* allows a third party to claim damages resulting from a breach of contractual duties between two other parties. An example is the liability of a bank working as intermediary between the customers and another financial institution as laid down in § 11 KMG. Even though the contract of sale over the investment products is concluded between the customer and the other financial institution, the bank may be held liable for damages caused by wrong information in the product's prospectus, if the bank has acted at least grossly negligently. If both financial institutions violate § 11 KMG, they can be held liable jointly and severally (§ 11(3) KMG).[67]

C. Duties to Investigate

In Italy it is settled case-law that the bank has a duty to investigate, mostly with explicit reference to, and in line with, the regulatory KYC requirements.[68]

[64] See US Chapter, s II.A.ii and see *Lerner v Fleet Bank, NA*, 459 F3d 273 (2d Cir 2006); *Fraternity Fund Ltd v Beacon Hill Asset Mgmt, LLC*, 479 F Supp 2d 349 (SDNY 2007); *Casey v US Bank Nat'l Ass'n*, 127 Cal App 4th 1138, 26 Cal Rptr 3d 401 (Cal Ct App 2005), mentioned in US Chapter, n 81.

[65] van Dam (n 19) s 710-3.

[66] See German Chapter, s IV.B.

[67] See Austrian Chapter, s II.E.

[68] See Italian Chapter, s II.B.

In Germany, in the case of investment advice, there is likewise a duty to investigate, but not so much with explicit reference to regulatory law. The duty to investigate was first established in the *Bond* case, a 1993 landmark decision rendered by the Federal Supreme Court. According to that decision, a provider of investment advice has to investigate the individual client's expertise and past investment experience, as well as his individual risk preferences prior to offering specific advice—and of course the proposed investment must itself be adequate in view of the circumstances. German case-law indicates that the bank may rely on the client's information and, if provided with information requested by the client, is required to pursue further exploration only if and to the extent that it has reason to doubt the correctness. However, if the client, upon request by the bank, responds in an ambiguous way, the bank will need to explore this further and may not simply proceed on the basis of the given response.[69]

According to consistent case-law from the Dutch Supreme Court, the bank must comply with its duty to investigate, and verify the consumer's knowledge and expertise, as well as his financial position, very much in line with, and often even with explicit reference to, the regulatory KYC rules.[70] After having investigated the personal situation of the potential client, it is sometimes even necessary to advise the client not to conclude the relevant financial transaction in case the investigation reveals that the financial means are insufficient to deal with the financial risks which may result from the financial product or service.[71] Admittedly, there is a thin line between a duty to advise the client not to enter into the transaction and a duty to warn the client for the risks involved (on which see section II.D below). This is also apparent from the French chapter, which indicates that initially the French Supreme Court (Cour de Cassation) referred to a duty of advice rather than a duty to warn.[72]

As for KYC requirements, the French Supreme Court has many times decided that whatever the contractual relationship between the client and the bank, the financial institution has the duty to assess the financial situation of the client.[73]

As already indicated in section II.A above, despite the limitations in establishing a duty of care, most claims in England and Wales and Ireland in financial litigation are based on a breach of the bank's duty of care, albeit often unsuccessfully. Be that as it may, depending on the financial product or investment sold, the duty of care could entail a duty to investigate the suitability of the products sold to customers.[74] In England and Wales, as previously mentioned, *private*

[69] See German Chapter, s III.B.ii.

[70] But see s II.B.iii.c, above.

[71] See HR 5 June 2009, *JOR* 2009/199, annotated by Lieverse (*Treek v Dexia Bank Nederland*), consideration 5.2.1. See Dutch Chapter, s II.B.

[72] French Chapter, s IV.B.

[73] French Chapter, s II.A.ii, V.A.

[74] At least in England and Wales, see Chapter England and Wales, s I.C, *in fine*. In the Irish Chapter this is not explicitly mentioned.

(not commercial) investors who claim that there has been a breach of a common law duty of care may also invoke their statutory right of action under section 138D (previously section 150) of FSMA for breach of regulatory requirements, including a breach of the regulatory KYC rules. Also in Ireland, as previously mentioned, a statutory right of action exists. Section 44 of the Central Bank (Supervision and Enforcement) Act 2013 contains a similar provision, subject to two important differences. First, it provides a statutory basis for an action for damages by customers in general, including commercial parties. Second, it applies to customers who have suffered loss as a result of *any* failure by the financial services provider to comply with its obligations under financial services legislation, and not merely KYC rules and other conduct-of-business rules it contains.[75]

In the US, both investment advisers and broker-dealers providing advice have a strict duty to take into consideration a client's circumstances. As already indicated in section II.A above, this obligation is known as a duty of suitability.[76] The duty requires the adviser or broker to evaluate a client's investment objectives, identify an appropriate level of investment risk and tailor investment recommendations to the risk a client can bear.[77] In respect of broker-dealers the suitability requirement is codified in SRO rules. It 'generally requires a broker-dealer to make recommendations that are consistent with the best interests of his customer'.[78] A broker-dealer must have an adequate and reasonable basis to believe that a securities recommendation is 'suitable for its customer light of the customer's financial needs, objectives and circumstances'.[79] It is not relieved of the duty to make suitable recommendations by a client's consent to an unsuitable transaction.[80] At least as for broker-dealers, there is no private cause of action for violation of the SEC's suitability rule, but courts 'have held that the suitability rule may set brokers' common law duty of care toward clients'.[81]

[75] Irish Chapter, s VI.

[76] See DeMott and Laby, 'Chapter 13—United States of America' (n 17) § 13.66, at fn 80 referring to NASD, r 2310 (1996), which, effective 9 July 2012, has become FINRA, r 2111; Suitability of Investment Advice Provided by Investment Advisers; Custodial Account Statements for Certain Advisory Clients, Advisers Act Release, No 1406, 1994 WL 84902 (16 March 1994).

[77] See DeMott and Laby (n 17) 13.66.

[78] See US Chapter, s III.C.ii.b, n 234 to an SEC Study (citing SRO rules) at 59.

[79] See US Chapter, s III.C.ii.b, n 235 to an SEC Study (citing SRO rules) at 61.

[80] See US Chapter, s III.C.ii.b, n 236 to an SEC Study (citing SRO rules) at 62. See US Chapter, s III.C.ii.b. See also on suitability DeMott and Laby (n 17) § 13.66–13.69. For the sake of clarity, in the chapters on Austria and Spain no civil litigation is mentioned on breach of KYC requirements.

[81] See US Chapter, s III.C.ii.b, n 239 referring to *Ives v Ramsden*, 142 Wash App 369, 390, 174 P3d 1231, 1242 (Wash Ct App 2008) (collecting cases); see eg *Scott v Dime Sav Bank of NY, FSB*, 886 F Supp 1073, 1080–81 (SDNY 1995) (upholding negligence claim based on evidence of violation of suitability rule); *cf Merrill Lynch, Pierce, Fenner & Smith, Inc v Chen*, 697 F Supp 1224, 1227 (DDC 1998) (violation of suitability rule 'will not automatically result in [broker] being held liable for negligence' but 'would simply be a factor for consideration by the jury as to whether he acted as a "reasonable" person').

D. Duties to Disclose or Warn

In French law it is settled case-law that banks have a duty to warn their clients of the risks involved in a financial transaction, unless the client knows the risks.[82] In Germany, it follows from the *Bond* judgment[83] that in the case of investment advice, banks are generally also subject to a duty to warn clients. Generally they are required to warn clients if, on the basis of the necessary exploration of their individual expertise and risk profile, they perceive the client to be unaware of specific risks arising in the context of a proposed investment. Likewise, a bank has been held to be under an obligation to warn the client against the risk that potential losses from a certain (credit-funded) investment may exhaust the client's financial resources. This is also consistent with the general principle that investment advice will not be considered to be commensurate with the client's profile if it does not properly take into account his financial means. If the bank is aware of financial irregularities or criminal conduct on the part of the issuer or sponsor of financial products, it must also warn the client accordingly. By contrast, no duty to warn clients has been held to exist if, as a rule, the bank recommends only its own financial products. No duty to warn exists once the advice has been given and the client has placed an order accordingly. While this would be arguable in special circumstances under general principles of contract law, the courts have so far denied that such duties exist in cases where the market price of a proposed investment deteriorated later and held that the bank was under no obligation to continually monitor market developments with regard to recommended securities after the advice was given.[84]

In more general terms, under German law, again as part of their duties as spelled out in the *Bond* case, banks engaging in contracts for investment advice have a duty to inform their clients of all aspects that are material for their investment decision. All information given has to be accurate, prompt and prior to the execution of the client's order, complete and comprehensible given the individual client's profile. In providing the advice, the bank may rely on information provided by issuers of securities, but its duty to inform typically requires more than merely passing on information material provided by the issuer. So if the bank is aware of adverse information concerning the respective issuer or the investment itself, it must not conceal it. It follows from a steady flow of German case-law that the nature and content of information will be deemed to be dependent on the client's expertise and needs in each particular case, so that it is almost impossible to define general standards in this context. Nevertheless, as a rule banks are required to inform the client both of the general risks associated with any type

82 See French Chapter, s II.A.i, s III.B, s IV.
83 BGH 6 July 1993—XI ZR 12/93, reported in BGHZ 123, 126.
84 See German Chapter, s III.B.v.

of investment in given market circumstances and specific types of risk associated with the proposed investment. The more complex the structure of the recommended investment is, the higher the required standard of information will be in this context. Likewise, banks will generally be required to inform their client if the proposed investment entails the risk of full loss of the invested capital. It follows from German case-law that, as a rule, clients must be made aware of the speculative nature of an investment. Also, the bank must inform their clients of conflicts of interest that may affect their advice and have a bearing on the clients' return on investment. A conflict of interest does not exist merely because of the bank's profit or trade margins, as it would be entirely unrealistic and inappropriate for the client to assume that the bank's services are offered pro bono. But the bank does have to inform the client if it has structured the recommended product in such a manner that it facilitates a hidden profit to itself, which the client has no reason to suspect ex ante. In particular, banks are required to disclose kick-back fees even if these are mentioned in the prospectus on the recommended investment, except where the prospectus itself also specifies the size of the kick-back that will be payable to the bank.[85]

In Italy, the duties to inform and warn again closely follow the MiFID rules. But not entirely, so it seems. Article 31 of Consob Regulation 16190 (Information on financial instruments) provides that intermediaries shall provide customers or potential customers with 'a general description of the nature of risks involved with the financial instruments concerned'. Such description, in practice, is provided through a standard form delivered to clients. Nevertheless, according to some Italian case-law the delivery of such document is per se insufficient and the bank would be in default of its duty to inform.[86] So, it seems that a standardised warning for the risks is insufficient, although this is permitted under Article 19(3) of MiFID as implemented in Article 31 of Consob Regulation 16190. Also in Austria claims for damages for breach of duties to warn or inform are filed against banks, although a claim based on mistake or fraud is more common; see section III below.[87]

In the Netherlands, the special duty of care towards consumers typically results in duties to warn explicitly and unequivocally for the specific risks involved in a financial transaction, even alongside a duty to advise the client not to enter into the transaction after having investigated the personal situation of the potential client (on which see section II.C above). More recent Dutch Supreme Court case-law indicates that warning explicitly and unequivocally of the specific risks involved in a financial transaction is in itself not even sufficient: the bank has to verify that the consumer actually understands the warning given by the bank (verification duty). This means that the bank may be obliged to ask control questions so as to make sure the retail client genuinely understands the risks. The verification duty seems

[85] See German Chapter, s III.B.iii.
[86] See Italian Chapter, s II.C.
[87] See Austrian Chapter, ss II.C and II.D.

to imply that the bank should meet the client in person or at least that there is a more or less elaborate telephone conversation with the client to discuss the investment proposition.[88]

As already indicated in section II.A above, despite the limitations in establishing a duty of care, most claims in England and Wales and Ireland in financial litigation are based on a breach of the bank's duty of care, albeit often unsuccessfully. Be that as it may, depending on the financial product or investment sold, the duty of care could entail a duty to warn customers of the risks of investing in products sold to customers.[89] *Private* (not: commercial) investors who claim that there has been a breach of the duty of care at common law may also additionally invoke their statutory right of action of Section 138D (previously section 150) of FSMA for breach of regulatory requirements, including a breach of the regulatory information duties. Ireland also knows a statutory right of action. Section 44 of the Central Bank (Supervision and Enforcement) Act 2013 contains a similar provision, subject to two important differences. First, it provides a statutory basis for an action for damages by 'customers' in general, including commercial parties. Second, it includes customers who have suffered loss as a result of *any* failure by the financial services provider to comply with its obligations under financial services legislation, and not merely regulatory information duties and other conduct-of-business rules it contains.[90]

As for the US, as already indicated in section II.A above, Section 206 of the Investment Advisers Act of 1940 establishes a statutory fiduciary duty for investment advisers to act for the benefit of their clients, including duties to disclose all material facts, and to employ reasonable care to avoid misleading clients.[91] While holding that the Advisers Act 'establishe[d] 'federal fiduciary standards to govern the conduct of investment advisers',[92] the Supreme Court has also held that 'that there exists [only] a limited private remedy under the [Advisers Act] to void an investment adviser's contract, [and] the Act confers no other private causes of action, legal or equitable'.[93] Thus, litigation to enforce the fiduciary standards established by the Advisers Act is limited to SEC enforcement actions, and

[88] HR 24 December 2010, *NJ* 2011/251 (*Fortis/Bourgonje*); HR 2 February 2012, *NJ* 2012/95 (*Rabobank/X.*); HR 14 August 2015, *NJ* 2016/107 (*Brouwer/ABN AMRO*). See Dutch Chapter, ss II.C, IV.C and V.B.

[89] See Chapter England and Wales, s I.C, *in fine*.

[90] See Irish Chapter, s VI.

[91] See US Chapter, s III.C.ii.a and esp where reference is made to the seminal *Capital Gains* case (375 US 180 (1963)).

[92] See US Chapter, s III.C.ii.a and see n 220 where reference is made to *Transamerica Mortg Advisors, Inc*, 444 US at 17.

[93] See US Chapter, s III.C.ii.a and see n 221 where reference is made to *Transamerica Mortg Advisors, Inc*, 444 US at 24. n 224 also mentions that as amended in 1970, the Advisers Act also 'impose[s] upon investment advisers a "fiduciary duty" with respect to compensation received from a mutual fund, 15 U.S.C. § 80a-35(b), and grant[s] individual investors a private right of action for breach of that duty, *ibid*'; *Jones v Harris Assocs LP*, 130 S Ct 1418, 1423 (2010).

private damages claims for breaches of an investment adviser's fiduciary duties or negligence are a matter of state law.[94]

Broker-dealers are subject to the anti-fraud provisions of the Securities Exchange Act of 1934, broadly prohibiting misleading omissions of material facts as well as affirmative statements and fraudulent or manipulative acts or practices.[95]

E. Duty to Refuse?

An outright duty to refuse to transact or advise a client is considered a bridge too far in most of the jurisdictions covered in this book—the principle of freedom of contract is often still paramount in this context.

In Austria, the predominant view in legal doctrine is that a bank is subject to a duty to warn if a product is not suitable or appropriate for the customer, but there is no prohibition against selling these products, if a customer insists on buying such despite any warnings.[96] German law is no different in this respect.[97] Irish law is also similar. In the case of *Allied Irish Banks Plc v Pierse & Anor*,[98] the High Court rejected an argument that a bank owed a duty to provide advice in relation to a client's agreement to purchase the foreign properties financed by way of a loan facility that they were seeking in respect of a concluded land sale agreement with one of the bank's other customers, a developer. Keane J did not express a view on what he described as the 'novel argument' that the bank was under a duty to decline a customer's application for finance in respect of any transaction in which another customer is involved if there is any basis for concern on the part of that bank regarding the financial position of that other customer. He explained that even if it were accepted as a correct statement of the law, there was no evidence before him that the bank knew or ought to have known about the developer's financial position.[99] In the chapters on England and Wales and the US the possibility of a duty to refuse is not even mentioned as a theoretical option.

[94] See US Chapter, s III.C.ii.a and see n 222 where reference is made to *Davis v Merrill Lynch, Pierce, Fenner & Smith, Inc*, 906 F2d 1206, 1215 (8th Cir 1990) ('The question of whether a fiduciary relationship exists is a question of state law'.) and *Stokes v Henson*, 217 Cal App 3d 187, 265 Cal Rptr 836 (Cal Ct App. 1990) (affirming judgment against investment adviser for breach of fiduciary duty under California law).

[95] See US Chapter, s III.C.ii.b.

[96] See Austrian Chapter, s III.C. Although one Austrian author has argued that in a very specific case the bank is obliged to refuse to carry out the customer's instructions. See Austrian Chapter, s III.C.

[97] See German Chapter, s III.B.i. In Germany there is case-law indicating that if the client requests specific information on an investment for which the bank does not have significant experience, it *may* (not: must) refuse to provide the requested advice on these grounds and will not be held liable if the client nonetheless engages in the relevant transaction. See German Chapter, s III.B.i, referring in n 58 to BGH 11 November 2003—XI ZR 21/03, reported in BKR—*Zeitschrift für Bank- und Kapitalmarktrecht* 2004, 124, 126.

[98] [2015] IEHC 136.

[99] See Irish Chapter, s II.E.

In Dutch case-law an outright duty to refuse has explicitly been accepted, albeit in one specific instance. The Dutch Supreme Court has explicitly accepted that in case a consumer-client is not prepared or able to provide sufficient margin for options transactions he wants to execute, the bank violates its special duty of care as soon as the bank executes the options transaction notwithstanding that the client furnished no or insufficient margin. As a consequence, if the option transaction turns out to be a loss, the bank will be liable to pay damages. It should however be noted that the amount payable in these cases is often reduced owing to the client's contributory negligence, for example if the consumer-client ignored warnings on the part of the bank. In this context it is worth mentioning that the Dutch Supreme Court has held several times that negligence of the retail client resulting from his/her frivolity of lack of understanding in principle weighs less heavily than negligence of the bank.[100]

Furthermore, the Italian and French chapter both note the national implementation of Article 35(5) of the MiFID I Implementing Directive, which provides that when advisers and asset managers are unable to obtain the information concerning the client's financial position and investments objectives, they must refuse to provide such services.[101]

Finally, it is noteworthy that in Spain the civil law notary plays an important role in the provision of consumer loans. When granting the notarial instruments that formalise a consumer loan, the notary should not only inform and warn the customers of the most relevant points of the contract, but also check as to what extent the credit institution has respected its duties to warn. What is more, the notary should refuse the authorisation of the loan when he considers that the credit institution has not respected these duties (Article 30.3 of Order EHA/2899/2011).[102]

III. Applications of the Doctrine of Mistake and Fraud

In Spain, the parties often resort to the doctrines of mistake and fraud to resolve disputes between banks and customers. As the authors of the Spanish chapter

[100] See HR 23 May 1997, *NJ* 1998/192 (*Rabobank/Everaars*); HR 11 July 2003, *NJ* 2005/103 (*Kouwenberg/Rabobank*); HR 26 June 1998, *NJ* 1998/660 (*Van de Klundert/Rabobank*); HR 23 March 2007 *NJ* 2007/333 (*ABN AMRO/Van Velzen*) and HR 4 December 2009, *NJ* 2010/67 (*Nabbe/Staalbankiers*), on which see Dutch Chapter, ss II.A, IV.D and VI.F.i. Please note that under Dutch law a duty to refuse to enter into an agreement may also arise with respect to credit agreements between banks and consumers, when a bank concludes that a particular consumer is insufficiently creditworthy. This obligation is in line with Wft, Art 4:34, s 2. See Dutch Chapter, s IV.D.

[101] Italian Chapter, s II.B; French Chapter, s V.A, *in fine*. See on Art 35(5) of the MiFID I Implementing Directive/Article 54(8) of the Draft Commission Delegated Regulation MiFID II, C(2016) 2398 final, 25 April 2016, Ch 2, s VIII.B, *in fine*. See extensively on the private law effect of MiFID I and II, s IV below.

[102] Spanish Chapter, s IV.

indicate, it is perfectly possible to base a duty of loyalty and cooperation on the principle of good faith (Article 1258 of the Spanish Civil Code). At the same time the authors explain that any specification in a given situation of the scope of good faith and the consequent duty of loyalty is not simple or exempt from uncertainties. Consequently, according to the Spanish authors, this principle does not represent a secure foundation and shall always be a last resort option. In recent times, the Spanish Supreme Court (Tribunal Supremo de España) has consistently applied the traditional doctrine of error in cases involving interest rate swaps concluded between banks and their clients. In these cases, the alleged error was basically caused by a lack of information. A much-cited decision of 20 January 2014 was the first to accept that non-compliance with the MiFID duties of information and the MiFID KYC rules may perhaps not be the cause of the error, but makes a mistake on the side of the customer a presumable option.[103]

In Austria, the focal point of financial litigation also appears to be the avoidance of the contract for mistake or fraud, although perhaps less than in Spain, and sometimes successful and sometimes not.[104] In a successful claim against Constantia based on avoidance for mistake the OGH found that there was a violation of duties to inform arising from regulatory provisions applicable to the relevant financial contract. Therefore Constantia had caused a relevant mistake and the claimant was entitled to avoid the contract and the price of the investment was to be paid back.[105] So like in Spain, the test revolves around duties of information. In 2014, the OGH decided over a case against Meinl Bank (MEL). Here, a customer inter alia claimed that he had been purposely misled (*List*), a line of argument that also leads to the long period of limitation of 30 years. The OGH granted the claim, which leads the authors of the Austrian chapter to the assumption that MEL will continue to be subject of a vast number of disputes in the future.[106]

As indicated above, duties to warn are a prominent feature of the bank's duty of care in the Netherlands. But recently the Amsterdam Court of Appeal revived the doctrine of mistake in connection with interest rate swaps.[107] At the time of writing it is not clear whether the Dutch Supreme Court agrees with this approach. In another prominent case regarding the bank's duty of care, the argument of

[103] See Spanish Chapter, ss II and III, *in fine*. Based on Bachs and Ruiz (n 5) and the Spanish case-law they mention, this appears to be different in the context of banks (and other financial institutions) providing asset management services, where damages are awarded on the basis of breach of contract or tort law. See § 9.59–9.80.

[104] See Austrian Chapter, ss I.B, I.C and I.F.

[105] 6 Ob 116/11v., on which Austrian Chapter s I.C.

[106] 6 Ob 203/13s., on which Austrian Chapter, s I.G.

[107] See Amsterdam Court of Appeal 15 September 2015, ECLI:NL:GHAMS:2015:3842, *Ondernemingsrecht* 2016/37 with annotation by Arons, *JOR* 2015/334 with annotation by Atema & Hopman (*X/ING BANK NV*); Amsterdam Court of Appeal 11 November 2015, ECLI:NL:GHAMS:2015:4647, *JOR* 2016/37 with annotation Van der Wiel & Wijnberg; Court of Appeal Amsterdam 11 October 2016, case number 200.153.823/01 (*X Vastgoed B.V./ABN AMRO NV*). See on these cases Dutch Chapter, ss II.E and VII.C.

mistake was rejected and the Dutch Supreme Court resorted to a breach of duty of care for not warning the client explicitly enough for the special risks involved.[108]

Finally it should be noted that in Italy, some lower courts previously held that a financial contract entered into by the customer on the basis of false or erroneous information provided by the bank can be annulled, under the doctrine of mistake or fraud. However, since the decision rendered by the United Chambers of the Italian Supreme Court in the leading case n 26724 on 19 December 2007, this should no longer be the case. With reference to the nature of the liability of intermediaries for having breached the duty of care towards their investors, the United Chambers of the Italian Supreme Court excluded that it leads to the invalidity of the investment contract.[109]

IV. The Impact of MiFID I and II on a Bank's Duty of Care

A. General

Banks providing asset management services, investment advice or execution-only services have been subject to the Markets in Financial Instruments Directive (MiFID I) since 1 November 2007.[110] On 3 January 2018—some 10 years later—the MiFID I regime will be replaced by MiFID II (in the remainder of this chapter, MiFID I and II are collectively referred to as MiFID).[111] MiFID contains a general duty of loyalty, which has to some extent been defined in more specific conduct-of business-rules for banks that provide investment services, including detailed

[108] HR 5 June 2009, *JA* 2009/116 (*Levob Bank/Bolle*) considerations 4.5.6–4.5.7; HR 5 June 2009, *JOR* 2009/199 with annotation by Lieverse; *JA* 2009/117 (*Treek/Dexia Bank Nederland*) considerations 4.10.1–4.10.4; HR 5 June 2009, *JOR* 2009/200; *JA* 2009/118 with annotation by Van Boom (*Stichting Gedupeerden Spaarconstructie/Aegon Bank*) considerations 4.6.4–4.6.13. See on these cases Dutch Chapter, ss II.B and VII.C.

[109] See Italian Chapter, ss III.A and III.B.i.

[110] The MiFID I regime at level 1 and 2 is composed of 3 measures: (1) Directive 2004/39/EC [2004] OJ L145/1; (2) Commission Regulation (EC) No 1287/2006 [2006] OJ L241/1; (3) Commission Directive 2006/73/EC [2006] OJ L241/26. It should be noted that not all Member States of the European Union and countries forming part of the European Economic Area succeeded in implementing the MiFID regime as of 1 November 2007.

[111] The MiFID II regime at level 1 and 2 is composed of the following measures: (1) Directive 2014/65/EU [2014] OJ L 173/349 (MiFID II); (2) Regulation (EU) No 600/2014 [2014] OJ L 173/84 (MiFIR); (3) a truly impressive number of implementing measures. Initially, MiFID II/MiFIR stipulated that the bulk of the new legislation would become binding on the financial sector as per 3 January 2017, but this has been postponed until 3 January 2018 by means of a directive and a regulation published in the OJ on 23 June 2016, see (1) Directive 2016/1034/EU [2016] OJ L 175/8; (2) Regulation (EU) No 2016/1033 [2016] OJ L 175/1.

duties to investigate (KYC rules) and duties to inform.[112] As may be gleaned from the chapters on the EU jurisdictions included in this book, it is now commonly accepted that these regulatory rules, especially the conduct-of-business rules, help to define the pre-contractual and contractual duty of care of banks under private law. Moreover, in many jurisdictions, an infringement of national implementing provisions can constitute not only a breach of the civil duty of care but also a tort (unlawful act) for breach of a statutory duty. It should also be noted that duties of care under public law and other regulatory provisions are regularly explicitly incorporated into the contract, with all the contractual consequences that this entails.

However, the chapters on the EU jurisdictions contained in this book also show that the exact impact of MiFID on a bank's duty of care is largely unsettled. As will be shown below, there are considerable differences among the Member States regarding MiFID's impact on a bank's duty of care and, more broadly, its civil liability. Moreover, in many cases, national private law provides little clarity either. Below, we will explore MiFID's influence in the EU jurisdictions covered by this book on (1) a bank's private law duties, including the bank's duty of care; (2) the requirement of proximity or relativity in the Members States where this is a requirement for liability in tort; (3) proof of causation; and (4) the validity of limitation and exclusion clauses in contracts between banks and their customers. For each of the above topics, we will first provide a comparative overview of the impact on the relevant element of the bank's duty of care or its civil liability as perceived in the EU jurisdictions in this book. Subsequently, we will, again for each of the above topics, examine to what extent the civil courts are bound by MiFID under EU law.

B. Breach of MiFID Duties

This section particularly applies to the EU jurisdictions covered in this book. In all of these jurisdictions, a violation of a financial regulatory rule (such as implemented following MiFID) may lead to the conclusion that the bank is in breach of its private law duties.

The rules for liability based on the violation of a statutory rule differ substantially throughout the legal systems.[113] First, as was already mentioned, the relationship between the violation of a statutory rule and the general liability rules differ. In France, violation of a statutory duty is just another way of establishing a *faute*, in addition to the violation of unwritten law. In Germany, the violation of a statutory rule (§ 823 II BGB) is intended to supplement the possibilities for liability under

[112] MiFID I, Art 19(1); MiFID II, Art 24(1). See for more detail on the MiFID conduct-of-business rules ch 2 of this book.

[113] van Dam (n 19) s 906-1.

§ 823 I BGB (infringement of a right), whereas in England, breach of statutory duty is distinct from the tort of negligence and does not supplement it.

Second, for a breach of statutory duty to be successful in English law, it is required that the legislator, when issuing the statutory rule, intended to provide claimants with an action for damages in tort. This is called the private right of action. Continental European jurisdictions do not know such a requirement but the Germanic legal systems, including the Dutch legal system, require somewhat similarly that the statutory rule aims to protect the victim against the damage he has suffered. This is known as the relativity requirements. However, these differences should not be exaggerated. It can be argued that the requirement of the private right of action is an aspect of the scope of the statutory rule. If a statutory rule does not confer rights on individuals, not one individual is protected; in such a case, the statutory duty is to be fulfilled in the public interest only. Nevertheless, if a rule does confer rights on individuals, the scope issue refers to the question whether the claimant belongs to the class of protected individuals.

Third, even though in French legal systems the scope of a statutory rule is not relevant for establishing a *faute*, it requires a direct and certain causal connection between the harm suffered and the breach of the statutory duty.[114] Hence, in a number of cases one could argue that, if the statutory provision does not in fact aim to protect the victim against the damage suffered, it is likely that the requirement of causation is not fulfilled.

How does this general picture translate into liability for violating financial regulatory rules? In France, a violation of a regulatory duty constitutes a fault, be it in contract or in tort. This means a client may directly invoke a breach of conduct-of-business rules before a civil court and claim damages on that basis. This is easily achieved because no clear distinction between private and public law is drawn in France in this area.[115] In Italy, regulatory duties have a dual nature because they are considered both public and private law duties that a bank owes its clients. Thus, in Italy, a breach of regulatory duties directly triggers private law liability under general rules of civil liability.[116] Also in the Netherlands, the bank's violation of

[114] ibid, ss 904 and 1105.

[115] See explicitly A Couret, P Goutay and B Zabala, 'Chapter 3—France' in Busch and DeMott (n 5) § 3.46.

[116] See explicitly P Giudici and M Bet, 'Chapter 5—Italy' in Busch and DeMott (n 5) § 5.42, 5.62. Cp also Italian Chapter, s I, s II. However, one special rule applies. Art 23(6) of the Consolidated Law on Finance and Intermediaries (CLFI) imposes a special rule regarding the burden of proof. In actions for damages caused to investors in the performance of investment services, the burden of proof concerning diligence always lies on the intermediaries' shoulders. Therefore, the client must show the existence of a pre-contractual or contractual relationship, loss and a causal relation between the loss and the bank's failure in performance or breach of contract. The client can simply allege the occurrence of a failure in performance or a breach of contract, while the bank must offer evidence establishing its compliance with its legal and contractual duties. See Italian Chapter, s III.B.ii; Giudici and Bet, 'Chapter 5—Italy' (n 116) § 5.66.

regulatory duties is tortious on the ground that it constitutes a breach of statutory duty (Article 6:162 DCC).[117]

In England and Wales and Ireland, a client's claim for damages can be based directly on the manager's violation of MiFID duties, particularly the conduct-of-business rules. In England and Wales, it explicitly follows from section 138D (previously 150) of FSMA that a breach of the FCA's (previously FSA's) conduct-of-business rules under Part X, Chapter I of FSMA (which includes the implementation of organisational or conduct-of-business rules pursuant to MiFID) is directly actionable at the suit of a 'private person' (ie a non-professional, or private, investor), subject to the defences and other incidents applicable to breach of statutory duty.[118] Section 44 of the Central Bank (Supervision and Enforcement) Act 2013 contains a similar provision, subject to two important differences. First, it provides a statutory basis for an action for damages by 'customers'[119] in general, including commercial parties. Second, it includes customers who have suffered loss as a result of *any* failure by the financial services provider to comply with its obligations under financial services legislation, and not merely the conduct-of-business rules it contains.[120]

In Austria and Germany, a client can also achieve a direct impact of a violation of MiFID duties on the bank's private law liability. In these jurisdictions, a breach of (in particular) the conduct-of-business rules directly constitutes a breach of a private law duty, even in the absence of an explicit provision such as section 138D FSMA or section 44 of the Central Bank (Supervision and Enforcement) Act 2013 (see above) and even though the regulatory duties are not normally considered to have a private law nature. In Austria and Germany, the courts are reluctant to accept that regulatory rules aim to protect a claimant's patrimonial interests.[121]

A bank's breach of MiFID duties may also have an indirect effect on the bank's private law liability. In Austria and Germany, a violation of regulatory rules may indirectly affect the bank's contractual liability. In Germany, academics increasingly ascribe either a 'radiating' or a 'concretising' effect to regulatory duties in relation to the law of contract. All versions of these theories assume that regulatory duties influence the construction of the bank's contractual duties. This is possible because the private law duties are often 'open norms' that are expressed

[117] See Dutch Chapter, s V.A; D Busch and LJ Silverentand, 'Chapter 7—The Netherlands' in Busch and DeMott (n 5) § 7.90–7.92. Special tort provisions may also apply in this context. See Dutch Chapter, ss V.A, VI.B.v and VI.B.vi; Busch and Silverentand (n 117) § 7.121–7.128.

[118] See Chapter on England and Wales, s II.A, *in fine*. See also LD van Setten and T Plews, 'Chapter 11—England and Wales' in Busch and DeMott (n 5) § 11.67–11.68.

[119] s 3(1) of the Act defines a 'customer' in relation to a regulated financial service provider as '(a) any person to whom the regulated financial service provider provides or offers financial services, or (b) any person who requests the provision of financial services from the regulated financial service provider, and includes a potential customer and a former customer'.

[120] See Irish Chapter, s VI. For a discussion on breach of regulatory duties prior to the enactment of s 44 of the Central Bank (Supervision and Enforcement) Act 2013, see A Bates and B Clarke, 'Chapter 12—Ireland' in Busch and DeMott (n 5) § 12.100–12.103.

[121] See Austrian Chapter, s II.D; German Chapter, s III.A.iii; M Casper and C Altgen, 'Chapter 4—Germany' in Busch and DeMott (n 5) § 4.97–4.99.

in indeterminate legal terms. Therefore, regulatory duties derived from MiFID may serve as a model for interpreting private law duties, such as the standard of care. The contract or a pre-contractual relationship remains the link for liability, although a bank's duties and standard of care are also determined by public law duties.[122]

Likewise, in addition to the direct impact discussed above, a violation of MiFID duties has an indirect effect in the Netherlands. Under Dutch law, the courts frequently specify this duty of care by referring to regulatory duties imposed on the bank, particularly the conduct-of-business rules which apply prior to and during the term of the contract.[123] The breach of regulatory duties that apply prior to the conclusion of the contract in principle amounts to a violation of the pre-contractual duty of care. Such a violation is a tort because it constitutes an act or omission breaching a rule of unwritten law that pertains to proper social conduct.[124] The bank's breach of the regulatory duties applying during the term of the contract in principle amounts to a violation of the duty of care during the contractual term. Such a violation can amount to a tort or to a failure in the performance of a contractual obligation.[125]

Similarly, in Spain, England and Wales and Ireland, the MiFID duties, particularly the conduct-of-business rules, may specify a baseline for the private law standard of care expected from banks. Thus, a breach of regulatory duties may result in a breach of contract, a tort, or a breach of fiduciary duty.[126]

Finally, at least in Italy, the Netherlands and Ireland, and at least asset management agreements, especially those concluded with institutional clients (such as pension funds and insurance companies), may expressly incorporate regulatory duties. Regulatory duties thereby become normal contractual duties carrying all the usual consequences in case of a breach.[127]

One of the main obstacles for concluding that breach of a statutory duty constitutes the breach of a private law duty is the requirement of proximity or relativity or, in common law, the private right of action. In contrast to Austria, Germany

[122] See Austrian Chapter, s II.B; German Chapter, s III.A.iii; Casper and Altgen, 'Chapter 4—Germany' (n 121) § 4.39.

[123] See Dutch Chapter, s V.A; Busch and Silverentand (n 117) § 7.58.

[124] See DCC, Art 6:162(2).

[125] See Dutch Chapter, ss V.A, VI.B.ii, VI.B.v, VI.B.vi and VI.C.ii; Busch and Silverentand (n 117) 7.91–7.92, 7.104–7.105. Please note that a tort claim can also be based directly on a violation of such regulatory rules, in which case the violation of regulatory duties can amount to a tort on the ground that it constitutes an act or omission breaching a statutory duty. See main text above.

[126] See explicitly for Spain: Bachs and Ruiz (n 5) § 9.29–9.33, 9.63–9.67; see explicitly for England and Wales: van Setten and Plews, 'Chapter 11—England and Wales' (n 118) § 11.24–11.25; see explicitly for Ireland: Bates and Clarke, 'Chapter 12—Ireland' (n 120) § 12.79, 12.84, 12.87, 12.95. Please note that, in the case of England and Wales, and Ireland, a direct impact of regulatory law on the bank's private law liability is also possible, see FSMA, s 138D (previously s 150) (England and Wales) and the Central Bank (Supervision and Enforcement) Act 2013, s 44 (Ireland), discussed in the main text above.

[127] See Giudici and Bet (n 116) § 5.42; Dutch Chapter, s V.A; Busch and Silverentand (n 117) § 7.58; Bates and Clarke (n 120) § 12.68–12.74, 12.79.

the Netherlands and England and Wales, no relativity requirement is imposed in France.[128]

In the Netherlands, a tort claim cannot succeed in the absence of 'proximity' or 'relativity' (*relativiteit*) (Article 6:163 DCC). In the present context, this means that a regulatory duty must aim to protect the claimant's patrimonial interests. In the Netherlands, the legislator has explicitly stated that regulatory law rules, including the conduct-of-business rules, are intended to protect a claimant's patrimonial interests.[129]

In Austria and Germany, however, the courts are reluctant to accept that regulatory rules aim to protect a claimant's patrimonial interests. There is considerable academic debate in Germany as to whether regulatory rules aim to protect not only the public interest but also specific individual interests. According to the majority view, at least some regulatory duties can be considered as being imposed by protective statutes, depending on the characteristics of each duty. The courts are taking a similarly nuanced approach.[130]

In Austria, for a statute to qualify as a protective statute, it must be the law's intent to protect a victim against damages typically caused by the forbidden behaviour. So far, the highest Austrian court has not held that any of the financial regulatory rules are to be considered protective statutes.[131]

England and Wales also, at least in a functional sense, requires 'proximity', because section 138D FSMA (discussed above) makes it explicit that only the FCA's organisational or conduct-of-business rules under Part X, Chapter I of FSMA are directly actionable, and only at the suit of a 'private person' (ie a non-professional, or private, investor), not professional investors. This means that only private investors have a private right of action to sue financial institutions on the basis of the violation of regulatory rules. Hence, professional investors are not directly protected by the regulatory rules, in contrast to Ireland which does allow professional investors a statutory right of action.[132]

In conclusion, although in all legal systems breach of statutory duty is a possible avenue for the bank's liability, considerable formal limitations apply in Germany and Austria on the basis of 'relativity' and in England and Wales on the basis of the lack of a private right of action. This once again calls into question the level playing field throughout Europe when it comes to privately enforcing MiFID rules.

Another problem with the harmonising aims of MiFiD occurs if one asks the question: to what extent exactly does MiFID influence the breach of private law duties?

[128] See V Colaert, 'De rechtsverhouding financiële dienstverlener—belegger' (PhD Leuven, 2011) 145; M Tison, 'The Civil Law Effects of MiFID in a Comparative Perspective' in S Grundmann et al (eds), *Festschrift für Klaus J. Hopt zum 70. Geburtstag am 24. August 2010, Unternehmen, Markt und Verantwortung. Band 2* (Berlin: De Gruyter, 2010) 2621–3269, 2631.

[129] See DCC, Art 6:163, on which see Dutch Chapter, s VI.B.iv; Busch and Silverentand (n 117) § 7.99.

[130] See Austrian Chapter, s II.D; German Chapter, s III.A.iii; Casper and Altgen (n 121) § 4.97–4.99.

[131] See Austrian Chapter, § II.D.

[132] See Irish Chapter, s VI.

C. May Civil Courts be Stricter than MiFID?

i. Comparative Law

Are civil courts allowed to be stricter or more demanding than MiFID? In Italy, Spain, Ireland and England and Wales, this seems to be the case: the civil courts appear to subject banks to private law duties that are stricter or more demanding than the MiFID duties.[133]

The situation in France is unclear. Some French authors are of the view that the civil courts in France are not allowed to subject banks to duties that are stricter or more demanding than the applicable regulatory duties, and they explain this result by reference to the principle of strict interpretation of financial rules, on the basis of which *contra legem* decisions (eg decisions that are stricter than the law) are not permitted.[134] Other authors still see some room for private law duties which are stricter than the MiFID duties.[135]

The situation is much debated in Germany, but is likewise unclear. Some authors assume that the civil courts may not be stricter than MiFID, because MiFID was intended to achieve maximum harmonisation. Thus, public law binds private law courts. Others argue that harmonising public law regulation of banks does not (necessarily) preclude stricter private law duties.[136]

Finally, the situation in the Netherlands is also unclear. In 2009, in the *Dexia* case and in two other decisions handed down on the same date, the Dutch Supreme Court ruled that, in the circumstances of the case, the private law duty of care could be stricter than the public law duties of care contained in the conduct-of-business rules.[137] However, these decisions did not concern the conduct-of-business rules implementing the *maximum* harmonisation regime of MiFID, but rather the conduct-of-business rules implementing the *minimum* harmonisation regime of its predecessor, the Investment Services Directive (ISD). It should be noted that the conduct-of-business rules pursuant to ISD were very basic. Only one provision, Article 11, dealt with conduct-of-business rules. In view of this, it is an open question in the Netherlands whether the civil courts can impose a private law duty of care that is stricter than the regulatory rules implementing the current MiFID regime.

The Dutch legal literature is divided on this issue. Some Dutch authors argue that for the sake of legal certainty, and in view of MiFID's purpose a European

[133] See explicitly Giudici and Bet (n 116) § 5.43–5.44; Bachs and Ruiz (n 5) § 9.30, 9.63 (Spain); Spanish Chapter, s III; Bates and Clarke (n 120) § 12.86; van Setten and Plews (n 118) § 11.27.

[134] See Couret, Goutay and Zabala, 'Chapter 3—France' (n 115) § 3.46.

[135] See French Chapter, s IV.A.

[136] See for an overview of the discussion in Germany, Casper and Altgen (n 121) § 4.38. See also German Chapter, s III.A.iii.

[137] HR 5 June 2009, *NJ* 2012/182; *JOR* 2009/199 with annotation by Lieverse (*De Treek/Dexia Bank Nederland*) consideration 4.11.5; HR 5 June 2009, *NJ* 2012/183; *JA* 2009/116 (*Levob Bank/Bolle*) consideration 4.5.8; HR 5 June 2009, *NJ* 2012/184 with annotation by Vranken; *JOR* 2009/200 (*Stichting Gedupeerden Spaarconstructie/Aegon Bank*) consideration 4.6.10.

level playing field and the idea of maximum harmonisation, it should not be possible for civil courts to impose a higher or stricter standard than the conduct-of-business rules contained in MiFID.[138] Other Dutch authors argue that the civil courts can impose a higher or stricter standard, based on an alleged autonomy of private law. After all, these authors argue, MiFID only harmonises regulatory law, not private law. This autonomous position of private law is important, they argue, because the ex ante application of regulatory law may lead to ex post solutions that are unacceptable in the circumstances of a specific case. According to these authors, the *Dexia* case would provide an excellent illustration.[139] The argument that the European civil courts cannot render justice in individual cases because the MiFID duties are inflexible has been rejected as unconvincing by some authors, because important MiFID duties are principles-based. A well-known example is Article 19, providing that a bank must act honestly, fairly and professionally in accordance with the best interests of its clients. It is argued in the legal literature that this and other principles-based provisions give the civil courts sufficient latitude to render justice in individual cases, although, these authors claim, for the sake of legal certainty, the principles-based duties under MiFID should be used with caution.[140]

As for German case-law, it is notable that in 2010 the German Higher Regional Court in Düsseldorf explicitly rejected the view that the civil courts may not impose stricter duties than MiFID.[141] The court ruled that the famous *Bond* judgment (which is stricter than MiFID)[142] is still valid law under MiFID. As regards Dutch law, one cannot rule out that the civil courts would likewise feel free to subject banks to private law duties which are stricter or more demanding than the MiFID duties. This can be illustrated by the *Fortis Bank/Bourgonje* judgment rendered by the Dutch Supreme Court in 2010. In this judgment it was held that Fortis was subject to a special duty of care towards its non-professional client Bourgonje. This special duty of care was based on the fact that Fortis was a professional provider of asset management services with the necessary expertise par excellence. According to the Dutch Supreme Court, this special duty may

[138] Lieverse in her annotation No 12 under HR 5 June, *JOR* 2009/199 (*Treek/Dexia Bank Nederland*); in a similar vein, SB van Baalen, 'Aansprakelijkheid als gevolg van een schending van de Wft-regels' in D Busch et al, *Onderneming en financieel toezicht* (Serie Onderneming en Recht deel 57), 2nd edn (Deventer: Kluwer, 2010) 1013–38, 1024.

[139] See esp OO Cherednychenko, 'European Securities Regulation, Private Law and the Firm-Client Relationship' (2009) *European Review of Private Law* 925–52, 945–46; OO Cherednychenko, 'De bijzondere zorgplicht van de bank in het spanningsveld tussen publiek- en privaatrecht' (2010) *NTBR* 66–77, 74.

[140] See D Busch, 'Why MiFID Matters to Private Law—the Example of MiFID's Impact on an Asset Manager's Civil Liability' (2012) *Capital Markets Law Journal* 386–413, 395–96. See also Dutch Chapter, s V.2.

[141] Higher Regional Court Düsseldorf 16 December 2010, *WM* 2011, 399, 400, explicitly rejecting the view of P Mülbert, *Anlegerschutz bei Zertifikaten* (2007) 1155–57.

[142] BGH 7 July 1993, BGHZ 123, 126. See on the relationship between the *Bond* judgment and MiFID esp Mülbert, *Anlegerschutz bei Zertifikaten* (n 141) 1155–57; P Mülbert, 'The Eclipse of Contract Law' (2006) 317–19.

encompass a duty to explicitly and unequivocally warn the client of the risk of considerable financial loss posed by the composition of the portfolio (excessive concentration of the portfolio in a particular asset). Whether and to what extent such duty to warn exists, and whether it is breached, depends on the relevant circumstances of the case.[143]

The *Fortis Bank/Bourgonje* case came before the Court prior to the implementation of MiFID I. Would the Dutch Supreme Court have rendered the same decision under MiFID I? This cannot be ruled out. In any event, to the extent relevant here, Article 19(3) of MiFID I states the following:

> Appropriate information shall be provided in a comprehensible form to clients or potential clients about:
>
> — (...)
> — financial instruments and proposed investment strategies; this should include appropriate guidance on and warnings of the risk associated with investments in those instruments or in respect of particular investment strategies;
> — (...)
> — (...)
>
> so that they are reasonably able to understand the nature and risks of the investment service and of the specific type of financial instrument that is being offered and, consequently, to take investment decisions on an informed basis. This information may be provided in a standardized format.

In short, the Dutch Supreme Court assumes a duty to warn the non-professional client explicitly and unequivocally of the risk of considerable financial loss posed by the composition of the portfolio (excessive concentration of the portfolio in a particular asset), which depends on the relevant circumstances of the case. Those circumstances may result in a duty to warn that is more or less intense. The circumstances may even lead to the conclusion that there is no duty to warn at all.

Article 19(3), third dash of MiFID I follows a different approach towards non-professional and professional clients. The bank must provide 'appropriate' warnings of the risks associated with particular investment strategies. Now that the composition of a portfolio is based on an investment strategy, we may safely assume that a duty to warn of the risks associated with a particular investment strategy is materially the same as a duty to warn the client of the risk of considerable financial loss posed by the portfolio's composition. 'Appropriate' could be interpreted to mean that a warning should be tailored to the specific circumstances of an individual client. This is of course permitted under MiFID I, but there is no duty to do so. After all, Article 19(3), *in fine*, of MiFID I provides that the warning should be such that the client is reasonably able to understand the risks and take informed decisions, but the warning may be provided in a standardised format.

[143] HR 24 December 2010, *NJ* 2011/251 with annotation by Tjong Tjin Tai; *JOR* 2011/54 with annotation by Pijls (*Fortis Bank/Bourgonje*) consideration 3.4.

Of course, the use of a standardised format does not preclude the possibility of using different standard texts in relation to non-professional and professional clients.[144]

In view of the above, it is submitted that a duty to warn explicitly and unequivocally based on the circumstances of the case goes further than to warn appropriately in a standardised format. Also it should be borne in mind that more recent case-law from the Dutch Supreme Court even requires that the bank should verify whether the consumer actually understood the warning.[145]

It may be concluded from the above survey that the answer to the question whether the civil courts may be stricter than MiFID differs across Europe. In addition, in many jurisdictions the answer is simply not clear.

ii. EU Law

a. General

What does EU law have to say on this issue? In *Genil 48 SL and Others v Bankinter SA and Others*, the EU Court of Justice does not seem to provide a definitive answer to the vexed question of whether civil courts may impose *stricter* duties of care under private law than those resulting from MiFID.[146] If a civil court holds, for example, that although a bank is admittedly not obliged to comply with KYC rules under MiFID (or indeed with other MiFID rules), it is nonetheless obliged to do so in the particular circumstances of the case because of its civil duty of care, the aggrieved client is not denied a claim on account of non-compliance with MiFID rules. If a civil court is stricter than MiFID, there would not appear to be any conflict with the principle of effectiveness as formulated by the Court of Justice in *Genil*. It should be noted, however, that the question whether civil courts may be stricter than MiFID was not at issue in *Genil* and was therefore not explicitly

[144] Please note that the provision of information in a standardised format becomes a Member State option under MIFID II: the Member States *may* allow the information to be provided in a standardised format (see MIFID II, Art 24(5), last sentence). In short, if a Member State does not allow this, it seems as though the information must always be provided in a personalised format. In the Netherlands this Member State option is exercised (implicitly). The relevant Dutch implementing provision (Wft, Art 4:20(6)) is not altered in the Draft Bill to implement MiFID II, and the accompanying Explanatory Memorandum is also silent on this point. See *Dutch Parliamentary Papers II*, 2016/2017, 34 583, no 2 (Draft Bill) and no 3 (Explanatory Memorandum). It will therefore remain possible in the Netherlands to provide information in standardised format. The situation will undoubtedly be different in at least a few other Member States. If the Member States had unanimously considered that information could be provided in standardised format, a compromise in the form of a Member State option would have been unnecessary. In the Italian Chapter, s II.C, it is explicitly reported that at the time of writing the Italian chapter, it was not possible to predict how the Italian legislator would exercise such option. In a similar vein, Spanish Chapter, n 17; Irish Chapter, s V.A. Cf also Austrian Chapter, n 54.

[145] See HR 3 February 2012, *NJ* 2012/95; *Ars Aequi* (2012) 752, with note by Busch; *JOR* 2012/116, with note by Van Baalen (*Coöperatieve Rabobank Vaart en Vecht UA v X*); HR 14 August 2015, *NJ* 2016/107 (*Brouwer/ABN AMRO*). See on these cases Dutch Chapter, ss II.C and IV.C.

[146] ECJ 30 May 2013, C-604/11, *Ars Aequi* (2013) 663, with note by Busch; *JOR* 2013/274, with note by Busch (*Genil 48 SL and Others v Bankinter SA and Others*).

addressed. *Genil* dealt only with the question of the private law consequences of non-compliance with MiFID rules.[147] However, this does not exclude the possibility that an argument could be made on the basis of other principles of EU law that civil courts may not be stricter than MiFID. The recent judgment of the EU Court of Justice in the case of *Nationale-Nederlanden v Van Leeuwen*[148] concerning the sale of insurance policies with exorbitant management charges (*woekerpolissen*) provides some leads in this respect. So this is sufficient reason to pause and consider this judgment at greater length, although it should be noted that it relates to the Third Life Assurance Directive and not to MiFID.

b. *Nationale-Nederlanden v Van Leeuwen*

Facts

In 1999, Mr Van Leeuwen concluded a life assurance contract with Nationale-Nederlanden Assurance forming part of an investment known as 'flexibly insured investing'. It is evident from the policy dated 29 February 2000 that Nationale-Nederlanden insures a benefit of NLG 255,000, or the value of participations in investment funds taken out for Van Leeuwen (plus 10 per cent thereof). Under this contract Mr Van Leeuwen was both the policyholder and the insured.

If Mr Van Leeuwen died before 1 December 2033 the contract offered two options. Benefit A was a guaranteed and fixed amount of NLG 255,000. Benefit B was the (variable) sum of the value of his participations in investment funds (based on the value of those participations) as of the date of his death, plus 10 per cent thereof. If, at the time of his death, benefit B was greater than benefit A, then the higher sum was to be paid to the beneficiaries of his life assurance. Thus, benefit A set a minimum level for the benefit to be paid out in case of death prior to 1 December 2033.[149]

The 'gross premium' consisted of a single payment of NLG 8,800 at the start of the contract and then monthly payments of NLG 200 from the inception date of 1 May 1999. This gross premium was invested in investment funds chosen by the policyholder. Costs such as premiums for the death cover were periodically deducted from the value accrued in this way. These premiums were therefore not charged separately, but—like these costs—formed an integral part of the gross premium.

Before Mr Van Leeuwen concluded this insurance contract with Nationale-Nederlanden, he was supplied with a 'Proposal for flexibly insured investing'. This proposal contained three scenarios based on different returns and management

[147] In the same sense, see C Herresthal, 'Zu den Auswirkungen der MiFID auf das nationale Vertragsrecht' (2013) *ZIP* (2013) 1420–22, 1421; J Lieder, 'EuGH: Anlageberatung bei Zinsswaps' (2013) *LMK* 349404.

[148] ECJ, 29 April 2015, C-51/13, *Ars Aequi* (2015) 696, with annotation by Busch and Arons (*Nationale-Nederlanden Levensverzekering Mij NV/Hubertus Wilhelminus van Leeuwen*).

[149] See Opinion of AG Sharpston, 12 June 2014, Case C-51/13, ECLI:EU:C:2014:1921, [15].

costs of 0.3 per cent. The text under the heading 'product return' contained the following sentence:

> The difference between the fund return and the product yield is dependent on the risks insured, the costs payable as well as any additional coverage.

Legal Framework

Article 31 of the Third Life Assurance Directive[150] (which has now been repealed and replaced by a more recent version)[151] plays a crucial role in this respect and reads as follows:

> 1. Before the assurance contract is concluded, at least the information listed in Annex II(A) shall be communicated to the policyholder.
> 2. The policyholder shall be kept informed throughout the term of the contract of any change concerning the information listed in Annex II(B).
> 3. The Member State of the commitment may require assurance undertakings to furnish information in addition to that listed in Annex II only if it is necessary for a proper understanding by the policyholder of the essential elements of the commitment.
> 4. The detailed rules for implementing this Article and Annex II shall be laid down by the Member State of the commitment.

The obligation to furnish the information specified in Annex II to the Third Life Assurance Directive was transposed into Dutch law at that time in Article 2 of the 1998 Regulation regarding the provision of information to policyholders (*Regeling informatieverstrekking aan verzekeringnemers 1998*). In view of the text of the 1998 Regulation, the Netherlands did not at that time make use of the possibility of imposing a duty to furnish additional information under Article 31(3) of the Third Life Assurance Directive.

It was established that Nationale-Nederlanden, in compliance with Article 2(2)(q) and (r) of the 1998 Regulation, furnished the policyholder with information about the effect of the costs and the risk premiums on the return. However, the policyholder did not receive a summary or full overview of the actual and/or absolute costs and their composition. Nor was this obligatory under the 1998 Regulation. In short, it was established that Nationale-Nederlanden furnished the policyholder with all information which it was bound to supply under the 1998 Regulation.

Nonetheless, in its interim judgment Rotterdam District Court held as follows about the fact that Nationale-Nederlanden had not sent the policyholder a summary or full overview of the actual and/or absolute costs and their composition:

> Although Nationale-Nederlanden fulfilled the requirements referred to in Article 2(2)(q) and (r) of the 1998 Regulation regarding the provision of information to policyholders,

[150] Directive 92/96/EEC, OJ L 360, 1–27.
[151] See the present judgment, [3].

> it nonetheless infringed the open rules (including, in this legal action, the general and/or special duty of care owed by Nationale-Nederlanden to Van Leeuwen in the context of their contractual relations, pre-contractual good faith and/or requirements of reasonableness and fairness) by confining the information it furnished to information about the effect of costs and risk premiums on the return.[152]

Nationale-Nederlanden argued that it could not be required to furnish additional information on the basis of open and/or unwritten rules.

Questions Referred for a Preliminary Ruling

The District Court referred the following two questions to the Court of Justice for a preliminary ruling:

(1) Does EU law, and in particular Article 31(3) of the Third Life Assurance Directive, preclude an obligation on the part of a life assurance provider on the basis of the open and/or unwritten rules of Dutch law—such as the reasonableness and fairness[153] which govern the contractual and pre-contractual relationship between a life assurance provider and a prospective policyholder, and/or a general and/or specific duty of care—to provide policyholders with more information on costs and risk premiums of the insurance than was prescribed in 1999 by the provisions of Dutch law by which the Third Life Assurance Directive was implemented (in particular, Article 2(2)(q) and (r) of the 1998 Regulation)?

(2) Are the consequences, or possible consequences, under Dutch law of a failure to provide that information relevant for the purposes of answering question 1?

Duties to Furnish Additional Information on the Basis of Reasonableness and Fairness?

The first question referred for preliminary ruling is answered negatively. In short, the civil courts may, by reference to the dictates of reasonableness and fairness under Article 6:2 of the Dutch Civil Code (*Burgerlijk Wetboek*, DCC) and Article 6:248 DCC,[154] impose duties to furnish information additional to that required under

[152] Rotterdam District Court 28 November 2012, ECLI:NL:RBROT:2012:BY5159, consideration 2.9.

[153] In Dutch: *redelijkheid en billijkheid.*

[154] DCC, Art 6:2 read as follows: '(1) A creditor and debtor must, as between themselves, act in accordance with the requirements of reasonableness and fairness. (2) A rule binding upon them by virtue of law, usage or legal act does not apply to the extent that in the given circumstances, this would be unacceptable according to criteria of reasonableness and fairness'. See also DCC, Art 6:248: 'A contract has not only the legal effects agreed to by the parties, but also those which, according to the nature of the contract, result from the law, usage or the requirements of reasonableness and fairness. (2) A rule binding upon the parties as a result of the contract does not apply to the extent that, in the given circumstances, this would be unacceptable according to the criteria of reasonableness and fairness'.

the 1998 Regulation, provided that three *cumulative* conditions are fulfilled (this is a matter for the referring court to decide):

1. the information required must be clear and accurate;
2. the information required must be necessary to enable the policyholder to understand the essential elements of the commitment; and
3. legal certainty for the insurer is sufficiently safeguarded (paragraphs 21, 29–31 and 33).

The first two conditions follow from the express wording of Article 31(3) of the Third Life Assurance Directive, Annex II and Recital (23) in the preamble to the Third Life Assurance Directive (paragraph 21). The third condition expresses the principle of legal certainty under EU law. The EU Court of Justice held that the legal basis for the use by the Member State concerned of the possibility provided for in Article 31(3) of the Third Life Assurance Directive must be such that, in accordance with the principle of legal certainty, it enables insurance companies to identify with sufficient foreseeability what additional information they must provide and which the policyholder may expect (paragraph 29). An additional duty to provide information based on the requirements of reasonableness and fairness under Article 6:2 DCC or Article 6:248 DCC would not seem at first sight to fulfil this requirement since this rule is extremely vague and has little if any predictive value. So that seemed to be good news for Nationale-Nederlanden.

But the EU Court of Justice then went on to formulate two arguments that were favourable to the policyholder and unfavourable to Nationale-Nederlanden. It held that when deciding whether the legal certainty principle has been fulfilled the national court *may* (not 'must') take into consideration the fact that it is for the insurer to determine the type and characteristics of the insurance products which it offers, so that, in principle, it should be able to identify the characteristics which its products offer and which are likely to justify a need to provide additional information to policyholders (paragraph 30). In short, the ball is played back into the insurer's court. It knows best what information it should furnish to its clients in order to ensure that they understand the insurance product. What perhaps played a role in this connection is that, according to the EU Court of Justice, the fact that the policyholder should receive a summary or full overview of the actual and/or absolute costs and their composition to be able to understand the operation of the product is so apparent that the insurer itself should have realised it was necessary to furnish this information to the policyholder. The Court of Justice added in this connection that, in accordance with the description of the grounds of the 1998 Regulation, its application is governed, in particular, by the national private law in force, 'including the requirements of reasonableness and fairness' set out in Article 6:2 DCC and Article 6:248 DCC (paragraph 31). In short, the EU Court of Justice clearly considers that Nationale-Nederlanden could and should have known that its responsibility did not begin and end with literal compliance with the 1998 Regulation.

c. May Civil Courts thus be Stricter than MiFID?

It seems to follow from the *Nationale-Nederlanden* judgment that EU law is blind to the distinction between public and private law when it comes to implementing rules of EU law (paragraph 28). After all, the EU Court of Justice had no problem with the fact that directives are transposed into national law by a combination of public and private law. Annex II to the Third Life Assurance Directive has been transposed into Dutch law by the 1998 Regulation (public law), whereas the Member State option to furnish additional information may be implemented by means of the requirement of reasonableness and fairness under Article 6:2 DCC (private law), provided that three conditions are fulfilled (see paragraph IV.B.ii.d above).

If it is indeed true that EU law is blind to the distinction between public and private law, this also has an important bearing on whether civil courts may impose stricter standards than the rules under MiFID. For the most part, MiFID provides for maximum harmonisation. If EU law is truly blind to the distinction between public and private law when it comes to the transposition of EU legal rules, it may be argued that the maximum harmonisation standard also applies to the civil courts. If that is correct, they may not impose stricter duties of care than those that apply under the rules resulting from MiFID. In the abovementioned *Genil* judgment about the private law impact of MiFID, the EU Court of Justice admittedly notes that in the absence of EU legislation it is for the Member States themselves to determine what effect non-compliance with MiFID has under private law (provided that it is not practically impossible to recover compensation for the loss or damage suffered), but this refers to the sanction and not to the substantive rule.[155] If this line of reasoning is rejected because it is considered that the civil courts may be stricter than MiFID, the present judgment in any event shows that legal certainty is an important factor that the civil courts must take into consideration in deciding whether they may impose stricter duties of care than apply under MiFID (see section IV.C.ii.b under 'Duties to Furnish Additional Information on the Basis of Reasonableness and Fairness?' above).

What has been said above can be qualified as follows. MiFID itself also contains open rules. One important rule of this kind is that banks must act honestly, fairly and professionally in accordance with the best interests of their clients (below: duty of honesty).[156] This obligation is admittedly translated into more specific rules in MiFID (including KYC rules and duties to furnish information), but the general rule does not coincide with the more detailed provisions. The general duty of honesty therefore leaves some scope for additional duties of care. This scope could be used by the civil courts. By doing so, they would not, strictly speaking, be applying stricter standards than MiFID since they would be using the space

[155] ECJ, 30 May 2013, C-604/11, *Ars Aequi* (2013) 663, with note by Busch; *JOR* 2013/274, with note by Busch (*Genil 48 SL and Others v Bankinter SA and Others*).

[156] MIFID I, Art 19(1); MIFID II, Art 24(1).

provided by MiFID itself. The only question is how much space exactly is left by the open rule, bearing in mind the EU principle of legal certainty.

Let us take an example. Under MiFID, warnings may be provided in a standardised format.[157] An approach in which the civil courts hold that the special duty of care means that banks are obliged to provide express investment risk warnings in terms that are not misleading, and that the banks must subsequently check to ensure that the private investor is actually aware of these risks seems to go further than a standard warning,[158] although a standard warning too must naturally be sufficiently clear. Would a civil court then be justified in adopting the following reasoning?

> The bank has discharged its duty to provide a warning in standardised format of the risks of the product and has thus complied with its specific duty to provide information under MiFID. However, in view of the general duty of honesty, the bank should nonetheless have given an express warning in not misleading terms, and should have subsequently checked to ensure that the private investor was actually aware of these risks. Consequently, the bank has breached the general duty of honesty under MiFID and must pay damages to the investor.

Reservations based on the EU principle of legal certainty could be expressed about this argument. Nonetheless, the *Nationale-Nederlanden* judgment shows that the EU Court of Justice is prepared to adopt a flexible approach to the principle of legal certainty and does not shun acrobatic reasoning in its efforts to achieve a just result.

It remains to be seen, therefore, whether the EU Court of Justice will actually bar civil courts of the Member States from using the argument that banks have a general duty of honesty under MiFID as a ground for requiring them to issue personalised rather than standardised risk warnings on the risk.

[157] Please note that the provision of information in a standardised format becomes a Member State option under MIFID II: the Member States *may* allow the information to be provided in a standardised format (see MIFID II, Art 24(5), last sentence). In short, if a Member State does not allow this, it seems as though the information must always be provided in a personalised format. In the Netherlands this Member State option is exercised (implicitly). The relevant Dutch implementing provision (Wft, Art 4:20(6)) is not altered in the Draft Bill to implement MiFID II, and the accompanying Explanatory Memorandum is also silent on this point. See *Dutch Parliamentary Papers II*, 2016/2017, 34 583, no 2 (Draft Bill) and no 3 (Explanatory Memorandum). It will therefore remain possible in the Netherlands to provide information in standardised format. The situation will undoubtedly be different in at least a few other Member States. If the Member States had unanimously considered that information could be provided in standardised format, a compromise in the form of a Member State option would have been unnecessary. In the Italian Chapter, s II.C, it is explicitly reported that at the time of writing the Italian Chapter, it was not possible to predict how the Italian legislator would exercise such option. In a similar vein, Spanish Chapter, n 17; Irish Chapter, s V.A. *Cf* also Austrian Chapter, n 54.

[158] For this approach in relation to private investors, see HR 3 February 2012, *NJ* 2012/95; *Ars Aequi* (2012) 752, with note by Busch; *JOR* 2012/116, with note by Van Baalen (*Coöperatieve Rabobank Vaart en Vecht UA v X*) (duty of care in relation to the provision of investment advice) consideration 3.6.2. It should be noted that these (and other) judgments of the Dutch Supreme Court about the duty to provide warnings relate, without exception, to the pre-MiFID era. Whether the Supreme Court will continue this line of reasoning under MiFID remains to be seen.

D. May Civil Courts be less Strict than MiFID?

i. Comparative Law

May the civil courts be less demanding than MiFID? One may argue that the question is largely academic and not very relevant to legal practice. In most European jurisdictions, civil courts favour the interests of the investor, particularly non-professional investors. In view of this, it may be argued that civil courts across Europe are in all probability not inclined to impose private law duties on a bank that are less demanding than the MiFID duties to which it is subject.

Let us return to the Dutch Supreme Court case *Fortis/Bourgonje*. What if the private law duty to warn explicitly and unequivocally, accepted in this judgment, does not apply in the circumstances of the case? This is certainly conceivable. The Dutch Supreme Court quashed the decision of the Amsterdam Court of Appeal, in part because the appeal court failed to take into account the client's level of expertise and relevant experience. In *Fortis/Bourgonje* this was very important, because Fortis argued that its non-professional client Bourgonje (1) had more knowledge than Fortis about the value of the ICT shares in which Bourgonje had invested disproportionally; (2) had insider knowledge with respect to the ICT company; and (3) was an experienced businessman and investor in the ICT sector.[159] If the Court of Appeal to which the Supreme Court referred the case were to rule that in the circumstances of the case the bank owed the non-professional client no duty to warn him explicitly and unequivocally, this is clearly less demanding than Article 19(3) of MiFID. After all, according to this provision, the warning must at least be provided in a standardised format.

So may the courts be less demanding than MiFID? This question has hardly been addressed in the legal literature across Europe, let alone in case-law. Nevertheless, there is some discussion of this question in Germany, where some authors advance the view that the civil courts are allowed to be less demanding in the circumstances of a specific case.[160] Other German authors submit that the civil courts are not so permitted, because in their view MiFID provides minimum standards in civil law.[161]

It may well be argued that in many Member States this question is indeed academic after all. In at least England and Wales, Ireland, France, Italy and the Netherlands, a breach of a MiFID duty may directly trigger civil liability for breach of statutory duty, quite apart from any (special) duty of care.[162]

[159] HR 24 December 201, *NJ* 2011/251 with annotation by Tjong Tjin Tai; *JOR* 2011/54 with annotation by Pijls (*Fortis Bank/Bourgonje*) consideration 3.5.

[160] A Fuchs in A Fuchs (ed), *Wertpapierhandelsgesetz* (Munich: C H Beck, 2009) Vor §§ 31 et seq, para 61.

[161] See E Schwark in E Schwark and S Zimmer (eds), *Kapitalmarktrechts-Kommentar*, 4th edn (Munich: C H Beck, 2010) Vor §§ 31 ff WpHG para 16. See for a similar stance, Italian Chapter, s III.B.iii, *in fine*.

[162] See s IV.B above.

ii. EU Law

It seems to follow from the *Genil* case that the EU principle of effectiveness (*effet utile*) prevents the civil courts from imposing private law duties on banks that are less strict than that to which they are subject under the MiFID rules. In *Genil*, the EU Court of Justice held that in the absence of EU legislation it is for the Member States themselves to determine the contractual consequences of non-compliance with the Know your Customer (KYC) rules under MiFID I, but that the principles of equivalence and effectiveness must be observed (paragraph 57).[163] The EU Court of Justice referred in this connection to paragraph 27 of a judgment of 19 July 2012 concerning a tax matter (*Littlewoods Retail and Others*, Case C-591/10) and the case-law cited there. This paragraph reads as follows:

> In the absence of EU legislation, it is for the internal legal order of each Member State to lay down the conditions in which such interest must be paid, particularly the rate of that interest and its method of calculation (simple or 'compound' interest). Those conditions must comply with the principles of equivalence and effectiveness; that is to say that they must not be less favourable than those concerning similar claims based on provisions of national law *or arranged in such a way as to make the exercise of rights conferred by the EU legal order practically impossible* (see, to that effect, *San Giorgio*, paragraph 12; *Weber's Wine World*, paragraph 103; and Case C-291/03 *MyTravel* [2005] ECR I-8477, paragraph 17).

In the MiFID I context, the principle of effectiveness therefore appears to mean that the conditions which an investor must fulfil in order to bring a civil action against a bank may not be such that success is practically impossible. The judgment appears to mean, among other things, that civil courts may not be less strict than MiFID I. Where, according to MiFID I, there is non-compliance with KYC rules in a specific case and the aggrieved investor brings a civil action for damages, the civil courts may not dismiss this claim by arguing that in the particular circumstances it was not necessary to comply with the KYC rules. This would seem, after all, to be at odds with the principle of effectiveness.[164] This approach can be extended to claims for damages for non-compliance with other MiFID I provisions, particularly infringements of other conduct-of-business rules. And the approach can also be extended to MIFID II, especially as under MiFID II the operation of the principle of effectiveness has been explicitly codified in Article 69(2), last paragraph of MIFID II:

> Member States shall ensure that mechanisms are in place to ensure that compensation may be paid or other remedial action be taken in accordance with national law for any

[163] ECJ 30 May 2013, C-604/11, *Ars Aequi* (2013) 663, with note by Busch; *JOR* 2013/274, with note by Busch (*Genil 48 SL and Other v Bankinter SA and Others*).

[164] As regards the question of how the principle of effectiveness affects the impact of EU law on private law in a general sense, see eg AS Hartkamp, *European Law and National Private Law. Effect of EU Law and European Human Rights Law on Legal Relationships between Individuals*, 2nd edn (Cambridge: Intersentia, 2016) 98–116; T Tridimas, *The General Principles of EU Law* (Oxford: Oxford University Press, 2006) 418–76; W van Gerven, 'Of Rights, Remedies and Procedures' (2000) 37 *Common Market Law Review* 501–36.

> financial loss or damage suffered as a result of an infringement of this Directive or of [MiFIR].[165]

In the Italian chapter, it is noted that the Italian legal system seems already in line with *Genil* and Article 69(2), last paragraph of MiFID II, as in Italy the MiFID conduct-of-business rules are deemed a specification of the general principle of good faith established by the Italian Civil Code.[166] The situation in Germany is different. In the German chapter it is noted that so far, courts and leading German commentaries have refused to interpret *Genil* to the effect that EU law requires private law implications, and it is doubtful that this position will change as a consequence of the transposition of MiFID II into German law. It is very likely, the author of the German chapter concludes, that only a further clarification by the EU Court of Justice can eventually accomplish a review of the present position.[167]

E. May the Contracting Parties be less Strict than MiFID?

i. Comparative Law

May the contracting parties themselves be less demanding than MiFID? In other words, are contractual clauses that set lower standards than those following from MiFID effective?

For England and Wales, the FCA's Conduct of Business Sourcebook (COBS, part of the FCA Handbook) provides a clear rule in COBS 2.1.2R, which applies inter alia to banks regulated by the FCA. To the extent relevant here, the provision provides that

> [a] firm must not, in any communication relating to designated investment business seek to (1) exclude or restrict or (2) rely on any exclusion or restriction of, any duty [...] it may have to a client under the regulatory system.[168]

[165] For a different view, see O Eloot and H Tilley, 'Beleggersbescherming in MiFID II en MiFIR' (2014) *Droit Bancaire et Financier* 179–201, 200.

[166] See Italian Chapter, s III.B.iii, *in fine*

[167] See German Chapter, s III.A.iii.

[168] It should be noted that the FSA is of the view that the general regulatory duty to act in the client's best interest (MiFID, Art 19(1) as implemented through 2.1.1R), combined with the general legal principles of the Unfair Terms in Consumer Contracts Regulations 1999 (UTCCR) and the Unfair Contract Terms Act 1977 and its subsidiary legislation (UCTA), already prevent a regulated firm (such as a bank) from contractually restricting or excluding duties (or liabilities) it has to its clients under the regulatory framework (including MiFID). However, the FSA also observed that having the specific duty of COBS 2.1.2R might serve as a further deterrent. See FSA, *Reforming Conduct of Business Regulation* (Policy Statement 07/6, May 2007), para 6.7. The view of the FSA as expressed in the Policy Statement corresponds with the guidance provided in the FSA Handbook with respect to COBS 2.1.1R (the client's best interests rule) and COBS 2.1.2R (exclusion of liability) in COBS 2.1.3G, which to the extent relevant here states that '(1) [i]n order to comply with the client's best interest rule, a firm should not, in any communication to a retail client relating to designated investment business, [...] seek to exclude or restrict; or [...] rely on any exclusion or restriction of, any duty [...] it may have to a client other than under the regulatory system, unless it is honest, fair and professional for it to do so. (2) The general law, including the Unfair Terms Regulations, also limits the scope for a firm to exclude or restrict any duty [...] to a consumer'. See also van Setten and Plews (n 118) 11.60–11.62.

Paragraph 3.8 of the Irish Consumer Protection Code contains a similar provision, albeit that it only applies in relation to consumers.[169]

In France, now that the MiFID implementation rules qualify as mandatory law, provisions setting lower contractual standards than MiFID are likewise ineffective.[170]

In Italy, contractual clauses setting lower standards than MiFID are normally ineffective as well. It has been argued in the Italian legal literature that the validity of contractual clauses setting lower standards than MiFID depends on MiFID's wording. When MiFID uses the expression 'where relevant', regulatory duties are not mandatory, and therefore it is up to the bank to choose whether to comply with the relevant MiFID provision. The wording 'where relevant' can be found, for instance, in MiFID I Implementing Directive, Article 30(1), 31(2), 34(3), (4), 41(2) and 40(4). This wording is also used in corresponding Consob Regulation rules. When MiFID provisions do not use the expression 'where relevant', they are compulsory. The view that the regulatory provisions of the Consob Regulation should be qualified as mandatory private law rules was endorsed by the United Sections of the Cassation Court in two important cases decided in 2007.[171] When a contract does not comply with any mandatory provision, general rules of contract or clause nullity apply (Article 1419 et seq of the Italian Civil Code, ICC).[172]

In Spain, the status of contractual clauses setting lower standards than MiFID is slightly less straightforward. The regulatory laws implementing MiFID in Spain are by their nature mandatory rules from which the contracting parties cannot derogate. With respect to contracts with consumers, any clause which derogates or waives a duty of the bank towards the consumer will be held to be abusive and, as a result, null and void according to Article 83 of the Consolidated text on the Law for the defence of consumers and users. In regard to non-consumers, when the public duties apply, the conclusion may not be so clear, in particular when the relevant rule is prescribed by a lower-rank item of regulation.[173]

In the Netherlands, contractual clauses setting lower standards than the applicable mandatory public law duties are invalid unless the relevant public law legislation states otherwise (Article 3:40 (2) and (3) DCC). In the Netherlands, MiFID

[169] See Irish Chapter, s III. It should be noted that also in Ireland there are other routes available. First, in the case of statutory duties, a financial institution would be unlikely to succeed in an attempt to exempt itself from liability in respect of certain absolute statutory duties. Any exemption clause purporting to do so would be likely to be determined by an Irish Court to be void as being contrary to public policy. Second, consumers may be protected by the Sale of Goods and Supply of Services Acts 1893 and 1980 for consumer transactions and by the European Communities (Unfair Terms in Consumer Contracts) Regulations 1995 both of which may limit the ability of the bank to rely on an exemption clause. See Irish Chapter, s III.

[170] See Couret, Goutay and Zabala (n 115) § 3.57.

[171] See Court of Cassation, No 26724, 19 December 2007, Foro italiano, 2008, I, 784 et seq; Court of Cassation, No 26725, 19 December 2007, Giurisprudenza italiana, 2008, I, 350 et seq, referred to by Giudici and Bet (n 116) § 5.59 in fn 55.

[172] See Giudici and Bet (n 116) § 5.58–5.59.

[173] See Bachs and Ruiz (n 5) § 9.57. *Cf* Spanish Chapter, s V.A.

has been implemented in the Dutch central rulebook for the financial markets, the *Wet op het financieel toezicht* or Wft and lower legislation. The Wft and the lower legislation pursuant to the Wft qualify as mandatory public law. However, Article 1:23 Wft explicitly provides that a juridical act (*rechtshandeling*, eg the conclusion of an asset management agreement) is not invalid solely because it has been performed in violation of a rule laid down by or pursuant to the Wft (except where otherwise provided by the Wft, but this exception does not apply to any of the MiFID duties it implements). In view of this, contractual clauses setting lower standards than the applicable public law duties cannot be void or voidable on the basis that they are contrary to mandatory law (Article 3:40 (2) and (3) DCC). In theory, such clauses may still be null and void on the basis that they are contrary to public morals (*goede zeden*) or public policy (*openbare orde*) (Article 3:40 (1) DCC), but it seems highly unlikely that a civil court would render such clauses null and void. However, this does not mean that contractual clauses subjecting banks to lower standards than MiFID are always effective under Dutch law. Depending on the circumstances of the case, such clauses may be contrary to reasonableness and fairness and therefore inapplicable.[174] In addition, if this type of clause is included in standard terms, it may be unreasonably onerous and therefore voidable, especially if the client is a consumer.[175] The special duty of care to which banks are subject in respect of non-professional clients will probably only reinforce this approach. Nevertheless, in the absence of case-law it is unclear how much weight should be attached to the mandatory public law duties implementing MiFID in assessing whether this type of clause is contrary to reasonableness and fairness and/or unreasonably onerous.

In Germany the position is unclear. Whether or not a contractual duty setting a lower standard than MiFID is possible depends on the interaction between private and public law duties. According to the view that MiFID-derived duties bind private law courts, such a contractual derogation from MiFID duties is not possible. The same is true if one follows the view that MiFID duties have a dual nature and qualify as both private and public law duties. According to the theory of a radiating or a concretising effect, a lower standard would be possible. In such a case, the regulatory duties, particularly the conduct-of-business rules, cannot influence the private law duties if the agreement in question leaves no room for interpretation.

[174] DCC, Art 6:248 (2).

[175] See DCC, Art 6:233, opening words and under (a), stating that '[a] stipulation in general terms and conditions may be avoided [...] if it is unreasonably onerous to the other party [the client], taking into consideration the nature and the further content of the contract, the manner in which the terms and conditions were established, the mutually apparent interests of the parties and the other circumstances of the case'. See also DCC, Art 6:237, opening words and under (b), stating that '[i]n a contract between a user [the bank] and the other party [the client], who is an individual not acting in the conduct of a business or profession, the following stipulations contained in general terms and conditions are presumed to be unreasonably onerous. A stipulation which [...] materially limits the scope of the obligations of the user [the bank] with respect to what the other party [the client] could reasonably expect without such stipulation, taking into account the rules of law which pertain to the contract'.

As a consequence, it would be possible by contract to exclude private law duties, even when they are similar to the conduct-of-business rules following from MiFID.[176]

It may be concluded from the above survey that most jurisdictions tend towards ineffectiveness in one way or another of contractual clauses setting lower standards than those following from MiFID. Nevertheless, in at least Spain, the Netherlands and Germany, the answer is open to doubt.[177]

ii. EU Law

In *Genil*, it was held that although in the absence of European legislation it is admittedly for the Member States themselves to determine the contractual consequences of non-compliance with the MiFID rules, one of the principles that must be observed is the principle of effectiveness. As noted above, the principle of effectiveness has been explicitly codified in Article 69(2), last paragraph of MiFID II. The principle of effectiveness means in this connection that the conditions on which an investor can bring a civil claim against a bank may not be such that successful legal actions are practically impossible. Naturally, however, the argument is less strong in cases where the civil courts, regardless of the contractual provisions, wish to be less strict than MiFID (see section IV.D above)—the investor has, after all, himself agreed to the contract. On the other hand, private investors in particular often have little influence over the contractual conditions. The effectiveness principle could therefore be cited in support of the argument that the civil courts are obliged to hold that the relevant contractual provision is unacceptable, for example (depending on the applicable private law) according to the criteria of reasonableness and fairness or, if included in general terms and conditions, constitutes an unreasonably onerous provision. This goes further, by the way, than an assessment by the courts of their own motion since in the above approach the result of the assessment is also predetermined. The subject of assessments by the court of their own motion is dealt with in section IV.K below.

F. May the Contracting Parties be Stricter than MiFID?

i. Comparative Law

The question whether the contracting parties may be stricter than MiFID has not been much addressed in the legal literature across Europe, let alone in case-law. Nevertheless, in Germany there are some authors who have addressed this question explicitly. In Germany, some authors have advanced the view that it follows

[176] See Casper and Altgen (n 121) § 4.63, 4.38–4.40.

[177] The Austrian Chapter does not provide any leads in this respect.

from the principle of freedom of contract that contractual clauses setting higher standards than those following from MiFID are as a general rule effective.[178]

ii. EU Law

At first sight, it would seem that there could be little objection to contractual provisions that are stricter than MiFID since they can only benefit investor protection. Moreover, unlike the situation where civil courts, regardless of the contract, impose stricter duties of care than apply under the MiFID rules (see section IV.C), legal certainty is not at issue here. After all, the bank voluntarily submits to stricter duties of care. Nonetheless, if banks in a particular Member State were to voluntarily submit on a large scale to stricter duties of care, for example pursuant to local market usage, this might jeopardise the European level playing field. We should add, however, that in our view this is a rather theoretical argument.

Just as in connection with the question of whether civil courts may be stricter than MiFID, *Genil* does not seem to provide a definitive answer to whether contractual provisions that are stricter than MiFID actually produce an effect. In such a case, a client's claim is in any event not rejected on the grounds of non-compliance with MiFID rules. If contracting parties themselves are stricter than MiFID, there would not seem to be any conflict with the principle of effectiveness, as formulated by the Court of Justice in *Genil*.

Could it perhaps be reasoned on the basis of the *Nationale-Nederlanden* case that the civil courts are bound to hold that where a contractual provision is stricter than MiFID it is to this extent unacceptable according to, for example (depending on the applicable private law) the criteria of reasonableness and fairness or, if included in general terms and conditions, that it constitutes an unreasonably onerous provision? Although it may be possible to draw such a conclusion from a strictly logical approach, there are several reasons why we think this is not tenable.

To start with, one of the key objectives of MiFID is to offer investors a high level of protection.[179] If a bank voluntarily submits to stricter contractual rules than apply under MiFID, there could surely be little objection to this.

Moreover, offering contractual conditions that go further than MiFID is one of the ways in which a bank can compete with its rivals. To this extent the question goes to the root of free enterprise. If an entrepreneur wishes to do more than he is obliged to do by law, this must be possible. Another factor here is that the freedom to conduct a business is included in the Charter of Fundamental Rights of

[178] See I Koller in HD Assmann and UH Schneider (eds), *Wertpapierhandelsgesetz*, 5th edn (Cologne: Schmidt, 2009) Vor § 31 para 5; D Einsele, 'Anlegerschutz durch Information und Beratung—Verhaltens- und Schadensersatzpflichten der Wertpapierdienstleistungsunternehmen nach Umsetzung der Finanzmarktrichtlinie (MiFID)' (2008) *Juristenzeitung* 477, 481.

[179] See MiFID I, Recital (2); MiFID II, Recital (70).

the European Union and is therefore a principle that forms part of the European legal order.[180]

Finally, a client may have valid reasons for requesting a bank to submit contractually to rules that are stricter than those applying under MiFID. For example, under the Dutch supervision rules contained in the Pensions Act (*Pensioenwet*) and the Occupational Pension Scheme (Obligatory Membership) Act (*Wet verplichte beroepspensioenregeling*), pension funds are permitted to outsource their portfolio management to one or more external asset managers, but in doing so are required to ensure that the external portfolio manager complies with the rules applicable to them.[181] Insofar as relevant here, these rules mean that outsourcing to an external portfolio manager is permitted only if the contract regulating the outsourcing or portfolio management meets certain requirements, for example that the external portfolio manager enables the pension fund at all times to comply with the provisions laid down by or pursuant to the Pensions Act or the Occupational Pension Scheme (Obligatory Membership) Act.[182] Naturally, any such contractual obligation to which the external portfolio manager concerned is subject does not result from MiFID and may to this extent be stricter than the obligations to which it is subject under MiFID.[183]

G. Influence of MiFID on the Principle of Relativity

i. Comparative Law

In some European jurisdictions a tort claim based on breach of statutory duty cannot succeed in the absence of 'relativity', which means that the relevant duty must not only serve the general interest, but also the claimant's patrimonial interests. In the jurisdictions imposing a relativity requirement the question therefore arises whether the relativity requirement is met in case of a breach of MiFID duties.

[180] EU Charter, Art 16: 'The freedom to conduct a business in accordance with Union law and national laws and practices is recognized'. As to the significance of the EU Charter for financial supervision law, see E Dieben, 'Vijf jaar bindend EU-Handvest en het financieel toezichtrecht' in J Gerards, H de Waele and K Zwaan (eds), *Vijf jaar bindend EU Grondrechtenhandvest* (Deventer: Wolters Kluwer 2015) 277–350.

[181] See Pensions Act, s 34(1) and Occupational Pension Scheme (Obligatory Membership) Act, s 43(1). These provisions are elaborated in ch 4 of the Decree implementing the Pensions Act and the Occupational Pension Scheme (Obligatory Membership) Act.

[182] Decree implementing the Pensions Act and the Occupational Pension Scheme (Obligatory Membership) Act, Art 13(2)(e).

[183] As regards outsourcing by pension funds under Dutch law, see eg PL Laaper, *Uitbesteding in de financiële sector, in het bijzonder van vermogensbeheer door pensioenfondsen*, Onderneming en Recht no 88 (Deventer: Kluwer, 2015); JAMI Hoens, 'Uitbesteding: een achilleshiel in de Pensioenwet?' (2009) *Pensioen & Praktijk* 16–22; RH Maatman and JW van Miltenburg, 'Pensioenfondsen' in D Busch, DR Doorenbos, CM Grundmann-van de Krol, RH Maatman and MP Nieuwe Weme/WAK Rank (eds), *Onderneming en financieel toezicht* (Onderneming en Recht no 57), 2nd edn (Deventer: Kluwer, 2010) 323–59, 339–42.

In the Netherlands, Article 6:163 DCC imposes a relativity requirement (*relativiteitsvereiste*). According to the legislative history of the Dutch central rulebook for the financial markets, the *Wet op het financieel toezicht* or Wft, the relativity requirement of Art. 6:163 DCC is met when a financial institution's client suffers loss as a consequence of a violation of the Wft or lower regulations pursuant to the Wft. This is so because the prudential rules as well as the conduct-of-business rules under or pursuant to the Wft, according to the legislative history, serve clients' individual interests as well as the general interest.[184] In view of the fact that MiFID is implemented in the Wft and subordinate regulations pursuant thereto, it can be concluded that according to the legislative history the relativity requirement is met in the case that a client suffers loss as a consequence of a violation of duties implementing MiFID. Nevertheless, some Dutch authors doubt whether this is the correct approach, arguing that only some conduct-of-business rules are drafted to protect the interests of individual clients and, in particular, prudential rules are not so drafted.[185]

Another jurisdiction where a tort claim cannot succeed in the absence of relativity is Germany. According to German law, a person who breaches a so-called 'protective statute' (*Schutznorm*) is liable to pay compensation for the damage arising from the breach (section 823(2) sentence 1 of the German Civil Code). Protective statutes aim to protect not only the public interest but also specific individual interests. There is considerable academic debate in Germany as to whether regulatory duties qualify as such. Only a minority in the legal literature suggest that regulatory duties are not protective of the bank's clients. According to the majority view, at least some regulatory duties can be considered as being imposed by protective statutes. Whether or not a statutory provision can be considered protective depends on the characteristics of each duty. For some MiFID-derived duties it is clear that the statutory provisions do not protect private interests. The record-keeping and retention obligations, for instance, explicitly exist to enable the German financial regulator to monitor managers' compliance with regulation. Moreover, it seems unlikely that the German civil courts would hold that other organisational duties are protective in favour of the client.[186] In addition, the Federal Supreme Court recently pointed out that not every rule of conduct is protective.[187] Recently, the Federal Supreme Court even concluded that sections 31 et seq WpHG

[184] *Dutch Parliamentary Papers II*, 2003/04, 29 708, No 3, 28–29; *Dutch Parliamentary Papers II*, 2005/06, 29 708, No 19, 393. This view accords with HR 13 October 2006, *NJ* 2008, 529 with annotation by Van Dam; *JOR* 2006/295 with annotation by Busch (*DNB/Stichting Vie d'Or*) consideration 4.2.2, where it was held that the patrimonial interests of policyholders are protected by the prudential rules to which life insurance companies were subject pursuant to the *Wet toezicht verzekeringsbedrijf* (Wtv), one of the predecessors of the Wft. See Dutch Chapter, s VI.B.iv.

[185] See eg Van Baalen, 'Aansprakelijkheid als gevolg van een schending van de Wft-regels' (n 138) 1013–38, 1014–21. See Dutch Chapter, s VI.B.iv.

[186] See eg BGH 22 June 2010, WM 2010, 1393, concluding that WpHG, s 34a (segregation of assets) is not protective.

[187] See BGH 19 February 2008, BGHZ 175, 276, 280 et seq (concerning a version of the WpHG before the implementation of MiFID).

cannot be construed as a statutory duty intended to protect investors within the meaning of section 823(2) German Civil Code.[188]

Austrian law is similar as German law. In order for a statute to qualify as a protective statute, it must be the law's intent to protect a victim against damages typically caused by the forbidden behaviour. The OGH has generally denied that § 15 of the WAG 1997, which explicitly stated that a violation of the respective duties to inform which causes liability, constitutes such a protective law.[189] The Court argued that this rule laid down (pre-)contractual duties. So far, the OGH has not held that any rules of good conduct of the WAG 2007 are to be considered protective statutes.[190]

So all in all, in Austria and Germany the courts are reluctant to accept that regulatory rules generally aim to protect a claimant's patrimonial interests.[191]

England and Wales also, at least in a functional sense, requires 'proximity', because section 138D FSMA makes it explicit that only the FCA's organisational or conduct-of-business rules under Part X, Chapter I of FSMA are directly actionable, but that such a private right of action is only conferred on a 'private person' (ie a non-professional, or private, investor), not on professional investors.[192]

From the above survey it follows that views differ across Europe and even in individual jurisdictions as to whether, and if so, which MiFID duties aim to protect the claimant's patrimonial interests. In addition, in England and Wales only non-professional investors can base their claim for breach of MiFID conduct-of-business duties on section 138D of FSMA.

ii. EU Law

Does the *Genil* case provide any leads in this respect? It is apparent from *Genil* that in the absence of EU legislation it is admittedly for the Member States themselves to determine the contractual consequences of non-compliance with MiFID rules, but one of the principles that must be observed is the principle of effectiveness. According to this principle, the conditions to be fulfilled by an investor in bringing a civil action against a bank may not be such as to virtually exclude

[188] BGH 19 December 2013—XI ZR 332/12, reported in BKR—*Zeitschrift für Bank– und Kapitalmarktrecht* 2014, 32, 34. In this regard, see also (referring to earlier versions of WpHG, ss 31 et seq) BGH 19 December 2006—XI ZR 56/05, reported in BGHZ 170, 226, 232. See for a review of the German discussion of protective statutes and MiFID-derived obligations German Chapter, s III.A.iii; Casper and Altgen (n 121) § 4.97–4.99.

[189] See RIS-Justiz RS0120998, mentioned in the Austrian Chapter, s II.D, n 84.

[190] See Austrian Chapter, s II.D. However, the Court stated that § 48a (1) No 2 lit c BörseG, which prohibits market manipulation through communication of wrong information, is to be seen as a protective law. But this provision is the Austrian transposition of the former Market Abuse Directive (MAD) (now replaced by the Market Abuse Regulation (MAR))—not MiFID. See on the private law effect of MAR, D Busch, 'Private Enforcement of MAR in European Law' in M Ventoruzzo and S Mock (eds), *Market Abuse Regulation—Commentary and Annotated Guide* (Oxford: Oxford University Press, 2017).

[191] See Austrian Chapter, s II.D; German Chapter, s III.A.iii; Casper and Altgen (n 121) § 4.97–4.99.

[192] See Chapter on England and Wales, s II.A; van Setten and Plews (n 118) § 11.67–11.68.

the possibility of success. As noted above, the principle of effectiveness has been explicitly codified in Article 69(2), last paragraph of MIFID II. It is arguable that *Genil* and Article 69(2), last paragraph of MIFID II mean that in view of the principle of effectiveness a claim for damages on account of an infringement of MiFID rules, in particular the conduct-of-business rules, must not fail by virtue of the requirement of relativity.

H. MiFID's Impact on Proof of Causation

i. Comparative Law

It is a universal requirement that a causal connection must be established between the bank's breach of duty (be it in tort, contract or otherwise) and the loss suffered by the client.[193] As a rule, the client claiming damages has the burden of proof with respect to this requirement. However, especially in the case of duties to furnish information or duties to warn, which may or may not be MiFID-derived, proof of this requirement is often problematic. After all, a bank may argue that there is no causal connection between the breach and the loss suffered because the client would have made the same investment decision had the manager complied with its duties to provide information and its duties to warn. In at least the following jurisdictions special rules apply in such cases to remedy the uncertainty in the causal link.

In France, to remedy the uncertainty in the causal link in case of a violation of duties of information or duties to warn, investors almost systematically use the theory of loss of chance. There are many examples in French case-law, including loss of chance to avoid incurring a loss,[194] loss of chance to realise a profit[195] and loss of chance to opt for a more cautious style of asset management.[196] In view of this it seems probable that in France the same approach would be followed in the

[193] See first and foremost the all-time classic of HLA Hart and T Honoré, *Causation in the Law*, 2nd edn (Oxford: Clarendon Press, 1985). See, more recently, MS Moore, *Causation and Responsibility—An Essay in Law, Morals, and Metaphysics* (Oxford: Oxford University Press, 2009). See for the jurisdictions covered by this book: (1) Austrian Chapter, s V.B; (2) French Chapter, s VI.A; Couret, Goutay and Zabala (n 115) § 3.109–3.117; (3) German Chapter, § IV.1; Casper and Altgen (n 121) § 4.116–4.120; (4) Italian Chapter, s III.B.ii; Giudici and Bet (n 116) § 5.86–5.90; (5) Dutch Chapter, s VI.D; (6) Spanish Chapter, s V; Bachs and Ruiz (n 5) § 9.76–9.77; (7) England and Wales Chapter, p. 10-11; van Setten and Plews (n 118) § 11.87–11.101; (8) Irish Chapter, p. 21, 25; Bates and Clarke (n 120) § 12.111–12.114; (9) DeMott and Laby (n 17) § 13.134.

[194] Cass Com, 10 December 1996; Joly Bourse 206 (1997), note H De Vauplane, referred to in Couret, Goutay and Zabala (n 115) § 3.116, fn 82.

[195] CA Paris, 25 June 1993; Juris-Data No 1993-023022, referred to in Couret, Goutay and Zabala (n 115) § 3.116, fn 83.

[196] CA Versailles, 15 December 2005; Joly Bourse 53 para 5 (2006), note L Ruet, referred to in Couret, Goutay and Zabala (n 115) § 3.116, fn 84. See on the theory of loss of chance in connection with a breach of an asset manager's duties of information and to warn referred to in Couret, Goutay and Zabala (n 115) § 3.116; see also French Chapter, s VI.A.

case of a breach of MiFID duties of information and duties to warn, with the effect that only the percentage of the damages which corresponds to the lost chance can be recovered.

A different approach is followed in Germany. In the case of a breach of the bank's duties to furnish information, the client must prove his (hypothetical) reaction to the respective information. However, to reduce this hardship the courts have established the rebuttable presumption that the client would have followed the advice (*Vermuting aufklärungsrichtigen Verhaltens*). The burden of proof shifts when a specific course of action would have been the only reasonable reaction to the information. The doctrine also applies if there are several possible courses of action but none of the alternatives would have caused any damage, for example because every other investment would have resulted in increased profits.[197] In view of this it seems probable that German law would follow the same approach in case of a breach of MiFID duties of information and duties to warn.

ii. EU Law

What is the impact of EU law on proof of causation of breach of MiFID duties of information? In this respect the Dutch *World Online* judgment on prospectus liability is noteworthy. This Supreme Court decision provides a special rule with respect to uncertainty in the causal link based on the EU principle of effectiveness. The case involved loss allegedly suffered by investors, inter alia due to a misleading prospectus issued on the occasion of an initial public offering of shares in a Dutch listed internet company named World Online. The Dutch Supreme Court ruled in summary as follows.

In prospectus liability cases it is often difficult to prove a causal (*condicio sine qua non*) connection between the loss suffered by an investor and the misleading prospectus, with the effect that the European Prospectus Directive's goal of investor protection may in practice become illusory.[198] The European Prospectus Directive provides detailed rules with respect to the content and layout of a prospectus but does not harmonise national regimes on prospectus liability. However, the European Prospectus Directive does provide that Member States shall ensure that their laws, regulations and administrative provisions on civil liability apply to those persons responsible for the information given in a prospectus (Article 6(2), first subparagraph).[199] In view of this, effective legal protection must be provided

[197] See German Chapter, s IV.A; Casper and Altgen (n 121) § 4.118.

[198] Now Directive 2003/71/EC [2003] OJ L345/64, as amended by Directive 2010/73/EU [2010] OJ L327/1, previously Directive 80/390/EEC [1980] OJ L100/1. The amendments following from Directive 2010/73/EU must have been implemented in national law by 1 July 2012 the latest (Directive 2010/73/EU, Art 3).

[199] Directive 2010/73/EU [2010] OJ L327/1 does not amend Art 6(2), first subpara of Directive 2003/71/EC [2003] OJ L345/64. It does, however, supplement the text of Art 6(2), second subpara. Hereinafter, the part in italics highlights the text supplemented by Directive 2010/73/EU: 'However, Member States shall ensure that no civil liability shall attach to any person solely on the basis of the summary, including any translation thereof, unless it is misleading, inaccurate or inconsistent, when

according to the rules of national law. With a view to effective legal protection and in view of the European Prospectus Directive's goal of protection of (potential) investors, it may serve as a 'point of departure' that the causal connection between the misleading statement and the investment decision is present. In principle it must be assumed that, but for the misleading statement, the investor would not have purchased the securities; or, in a secondary-market transaction, would not have purchased them on the same terms. However, taking into account the nature of the misleading information and the other available information, a court might instead arrive at the conclusion that this point of departure should be displaced; for example, in the case of a professional investor, who in view of its experience and knowledge may not have been influenced by the misleading prospectus in making its decision to invest.[200]

It is submitted that this reasoning in *World Online* could also be applied, with appropriate amendments, to a bank which violates duties to furnish information or to warn pursuant to MiFID. One of MiFID's stated aims is investor protection.[201] Although MiFID does not include a provision similar to Article 6(2) of the European Prospectus Directive, it seems fair to assume that the European legislator intended the Member States to provide effective legal protection in relation to MiFID as well. After all, the principle of effectiveness (*effet utile*) is a fundamental principle of European Union law.[202] *Genil* and Article 69(2), last paragraph of MiFID II provide support for this notion. It is apparent from the judgment, after all, that in the absence of EU legislation it is admittedly for the Member States themselves to determine the contractual consequences of non-compliance with MiFID obligations, but that one of the principles to be observed is the principle of effectiveness (paragraph 57). As noted previously, the principle of effectiveness has been explicitly codified in Article 69(2), last paragraph of MiFID II. The principle of effectiveness means in this connection that the conditions on which an investor can bring a civil claim against a bank may not be such as to virtually exclude the possibility of bringing a successful legal action.

read together with the other parts of the prospectus, *or it does not provide, when read together with the other parts of the prospectus, key information in order to aid investors when considering whether to invest in such securities. The summary shall contain a clear warning to that effect*'. Please note that on 30 November 2015 the European Commission published a draft of the Prospectus Regulation which will replace the current Prospectus Directive. See for the proposal and further information: http://ec.europa.eu/finance/securities/prospectus/index_en.htm. The text of Art 6(2), first and second subpara of the Prospectus Directive, remain unchanged in the draft Prospectus Regulation, but the text is moved to Art 11(2), first and second para.

[200] HR 27 November 2009, *JOR* 2010/43 with annotation by Frielink (*Vereniging van Effectenbezitters c.s./World Online International NV*) considerations 4.11.1 and 4.11.2.

[201] MiFID I, consideration (2); MiFID II, consideration (70).

[202] On the principle of effectiveness in European Union law, see eg Hartkamp, *European Law and National Private Law. Effect of EU Law and European Human Rights Law on Legal Relationships between Individuals* (n 164) 98–116; Tridimas, The General Principles of EU Law (n 164) 418–76; van Gerven, *Of Rights, Remedies and Procedures* (n 164).

In keeping with the *World Online* judgment, an exception could be made in the case of professional investors since it could be concluded on the basis of their knowledge and experience that they are not actually misled by the incorrect information into making their investment decision. However, this exception may be less appropriate in the event of non-compliance with duties to provide information and warnings under MiFID.[203] After all, the provisions of MiFID on banks make a clear distinction between duties to provide information and warnings to retail clients on the one hand and professional clients on the other.

The duties under MiFID to provide information and warnings to professional investors are geared to their specific information needs. In the event of non-compliance with one or more of these duties, it is reasonable to suppose that the investment decision of the professional client may have been influenced by this. It therefore seems legitimate to argue that even where a bank infringes its duty under MiFID to provide information or warnings to professional clients, the basic principle must be that a causal connection exists between the infringement and the loss. However, whether this approach would be followed by the civil courts across the EU is at present unclear. Naturally, other approaches which help the client to prove a causal connection may also be in keeping with the principle of effectiveness.[204]

I. MiFID's Impact on Limitation and Exclusion Clauses

i. Comparative Law

Is a contractual exclusion or limitation of liability for breach of MiFID duties valid? In England and Wales, the FCA's Conduct of Business Sourcebook (COBS, part of the FCA Handbook) provides a clear answer to this question in COBS 2.1.2R, which applies inter alia to banks providing investment services regulated by the FCA. To the extent relevant here, the provision provides that '[a] firm must not, in any communication relating to designated investment business seek to (1) exclude or restrict or (2) rely on any exclusion or restriction of, any [...] liability it may have to a client under the regulatory system'.[205] Paragraph 3.8 of

[203] See also Busch, 'Why MiFID Matters to Private Law—the Example of MiFID's Impact on an Asset Manager's Civil Liability (n 140) 408–09.

[204] On this last point, see CJM Klaassen, 'Bewijs van causaal verband tussen beweerdelijk geleden beleggingsschade en schending van een informatie- of waarschuwingsplicht' in D Busch, CJM Klaassen and TMC Arons (eds), *Aansprakelijkheid in de financiële sector* (Onderneming en Recht no 78) (Deventer: Kluwer, 2013) 127–74, 151.

[205] It should be noted that the FSA (the FCA's predecessor) is of the view that the general regulatory duty to act in the client's best interest (MiFID, Art.19(1) as implemented through 2.1.1R), combined with the general legal principles of the Unfair Terms in Consumer Contracts Regulations 1999 (UTCCR) and the Unfair Contract Terms Act 1977 and its subsidiary legislation (UCTA), already prevent a regulated firm (such as banks providing investment services) from contractually restricting or excluding liabilities (or duties) it has to its clients under the regulatory framework (including MiFID).

the Irish Consumer Protection Code contains a similar provision, albeit that it only applies in relation to consumers.[206]

In many other jurisdictions, the question as to the validity of contractual clauses limiting or excluding liability for breach of MiFID duties has not yet been squarely faced, or, if the question has been faced, the answer seems less clear-cut than in England and Wales and Ireland.[207] A jurisdiction in the latter category is the Netherlands. According to the general rules of Dutch private law, a limitation or exclusion of liability for damage caused by wilful default (*opzet*) or gross negligence (*grove schuld*) of the bank or its executives (*leidinggevenden*) is in principle contrary to public morals in the sense of Article 3:40(1) DCC and is thus null and void. A contractual clause limiting or excluding liability for breach of MiFID duties as implemented under or pursuant to the Wft can be regarded as a juridical act in violation of regulatory mandatory law. Such a clause will in any event not be void or voidable on the basis that such clause is contrary to mandatory law in the sense of Article 3:40(2) and (3) DCC. After all, Article 1:23 Wft explicitly provides that a juridical act is not invalid solely because it has been performed in violation of a rule laid down by or pursuant to the Wft (except where otherwise provided by the Wft), which includes the rules implementing MiFID. In theory, such clauses may be null and void on the basis that they are contrary to public morals or public policy (Article 3:40(1) DCC). However, it seems highly unlikely that a court would render such a clause null and void, except of course to the extent that it concerns a violation by bank or its executives caused by wilful default or gross negligence (see above). However, this does not mean that under Dutch law liability for breach of MiFID duties may always be effectively limited or excluded, except to the extent

However, the FSA also observed that having the specific duty of COBS 2.1.2R might serve as a further deterrent. See FSA, *Reforming Conduct of Business Regulation* (Policy Statement 07/6, May 2007) para 6.7. The view of the FSA as expressed in the Policy Statement corresponds with the guidance provided in the FCA (previously FSA) Handbook with respect to COBS 2.1.1R (the client's best interests rule) and COBS 2.1.2R (exclusion of liability) in COBS 2.1.3G, which to the extent relevant here states that '(1) [i]n order to comply with the client's best interest rule, a firm should not, in any communication to a retail client relating to designated investment business, […] seek to exclude or restrict; or […] rely on any exclusion or restriction of, any […] liability it may have to a client other than under the regulatory system, unless it is honest, fair and professional for it to do so. (2) The general law, including the Unfair Terms Regulations, also limits the scope for a firm to exclude or restrict any […] liability to a consumer'. See van Setten and Plews (n 118) § 11.60–11.62.

[206] See Irish Chapter, s III. It should be noted that also in Ireland there are other routes available. First, in the case of statutory duties, a financial institution would be unlikely to succeed in an attempt to exempt itself from liability in respect of certain absolute statutory duties. Any exemption clause purporting to do so would be likely to be determined by an Irish Court to be void as being contrary to public policy. Second, consumers may be protected by the Sale of Goods and Supply of Services Acts 1893 and 1980 for consumer transactions and by the European Communities (Unfair Terms in Consumer Contracts) Regulations 1995 both of which may limit the ability of the bank to rely on an exemption clause. See Irish Chapter, s III.

[207] See (1) French Chapter, s VI.D; Couret, Goutay and Zabala (n 115) § 3.132–136; (2) Casper and Altgen (n 121) § 4.37–4.40, 4.62–4.67, 4.140–4.143 (Germany); (3) Giudici and Bet (n 116) § 5.106–5.110; (4) Dutch Chapter, s VI.7; Busch and Silverentand (n 117) § 7.169–7.182; (5) Spanish Chapter, s VI.2; Bachs and Ruiz (n 5) § 9.84. The Austrian Chapter provides no leads in this respect.

that wilful default or gross negligence is concerned. Similar to the Dutch position with respect to the effectiveness of contractual clauses setting lower standards than following from MiFID,[208] depending on the circumstances of the case such clauses may be contrary to reasonableness and fairness and therefore inapplicable.[209] In addition, if this type of clause is included in standard terms, it may be unreasonably onerous and therefore voidable, especially if the client is a consumer.[210] The special duty of care to which banks are subject in respect of non-professional clients will here also probably only reinforce this approach. Nevertheless, in the absence of case-law, it is unclear how much weight should be attached to the mandatory public law duties implementing MiFID in assessing whether this type of clause is contrary to reasonableness and fairness and/or unreasonably onerous.[211]

ii. EU Law

The principle of effectiveness as formulated in *Genil* and in Article 69(2), last paragraph of MiFID II could be used to argue that in relation to consumers and small businesses the civil courts are obliged to hold that a contractual clause excluding or limiting liability for an infringement of MiFID rules constitutes an unreasonably onerous provision if included in the general terms and conditions, and that the contractual clause does not therefore prevent a claim for damages on account of non-compliance with the MiFID rules. Likewise, it could be argued that the civil courts are obliged to hold that a contractual clause that seeks to exclude or limit liability for infringement of the MiFID rules is unacceptable according to (depending on the applicable private law) the requirements of reasonableness and fairness that the contractual clause does not therefore prevent a claim for damages on account of non-compliance with the MiFID rules (even in relation to clients *other* than consumers and small businesses).

[208] See s IV.E.i above.

[209] DCC, Art 6:248 (2).

[210] See DCC, Art 6:233, opening words and under (a), stating that '[a] stipulation in general terms and conditions may be avoided [...] if it is unreasonably onerous to the other party [the client], taking into consideration the nature and the further content of the contract, the manner in which the terms and conditions were established, the mutually apparent interests of the parties and the other circumstances of the case'. See also DCC, Art 6:237, opening words and under (f), stating that '[i]n a contract between a user [the bank] and the other party [the client], who is an individual not acting in the conduct of a business or profession, the following stipulations contained in general terms and conditions are presumed to be unreasonably onerous. A stipulation which [...] releases the user [the bank]or a third person in whole or in part from a legal obligation to repair damage'. See perhaps also DCC, Art 6:237, opening words and under (b), stating that '[i]n a contract between a user [the bank] and the other party [the client], who is an individual not acting in the conduct of a business or profession, the following stipulations contained in general terms and conditions are presumed to be unreasonably onerous. A stipulation which [...] materially limits the scope of the obligations of the user [the bank] with respect to what the other party [the client] could reasonably expect without such stipulation, taking into account the rules of law which pertain to the contract'.

[211] See Dutch Chapter, s VI.G.

The principle of effectiveness as formulated in *Genil* and in Article 69(2), last paragraph, MiFID II means, after all, that the national conditions which an investor must fulfil in order to bring a civil action against a bank for infringement of MiFID obligations may not be such that success is practically impossible. It could be argued that this also means that contractual clauses that seek to exclude or limit liability for infringement of MiFID rules are contrary to the principle of effectiveness. Naturally, however, the argument is less strong in cases where the civil courts, regardless of the contractual provisions, are less strict than MiFID. After all, the client has himself agreed to the contractual clause. On the other hand, retail clients in particular often have little influence over the contractual conditions. Arguments that also carry weight are, naturally, that clauses of this kind jeopardise the high level of investor protection which MiFID intends to provide and also detract from the level playing field envisaged by MiFID.

An example may help to clarify this. Article 14(1) of the MiFID I Implementing Directive provides that:

> Member States shall ensure that, when investment firms outsource critical or important operational functions or any investment services or activities, the firms remain *fully responsible* [italics added, *DB*] for discharging all of their obligations under [MiFID I].[212]

It follows, for example, that where a portfolio manager outsources part of the management to a third party (eg a more specialised portfolio manager), it remains *fully responsible* (despite the outsourcing) for observance of the regulatory provisions applicable to the outsourced activities under MiFID. In short, if the third party infringes conduct-of-business rules under MiFID during these activities and the portfolio manager's client suffers loss as a result, it can be argued that, according to the principle of effectiveness, the civil courts are obliged in relation to consumers and small businesses to hold that a contractual provision limiting the liability of the portfolio manager to carefully selecting third parties (including independent agents to whom activities have been outsourced) and excluding his liability for infringements of MiFID rules by a third party to whom aspects of the portfolio management have been outsourced constitutes an unreasonably onerous condition if included in general terms and conditions. Likewise (depending on the applicable private law), it can be argued that the civil courts are obliged here to hold that the contractual clause is unacceptable in the light of the requirements of reasonableness and fairness and is not therefore a bar to a claim for damages for infringement of the MiFID rules. This goes further, by the way, than an assessment by the courts of their own motion since in the above approach the result of the assessment is also predetermined. The subject of assessments by the court of their own motion is dealt with in section IV.K below.

[212] See also Draft Commission Delegated Regulation, C(2016) 2398 final, 25 April 2016, Art 31(1), first sentence.

J. MiFID's Impact on the Doctrine of Mistake and on other Restitutionary Claims

In the context of MiFID's impact on the doctrine of mistake a Spanish Supreme Court of 20 January 2014 is noteworthy. It was the first Spanish decision expressly accepting that non-compliance with the MiFID duties of information and the MiFID KYC may have a bearing on a claim based on mistake, in the sense that it made a mistake on the side of the SME a presumable option. The decision explicitly referred to the *Genil* case.[213]

For the sake of clarity it should be noted that the principle of effectiveness as referred to in *Genil* and Article 69(1) of MiFID II is neutral as to which route national private law chooses to provide the client with compensation for a bank's breach of MiFID duties, as long as obtaining compensation is not impossible or very cumbersome under national private law. In view of this, compensation may be provided by way of a damages claim based on tort, contract, fiduciary law, statute law or by way of a restitutionary claim based on a defect of consent such as fraud or mistake. Also, the principle of effectiveness is neutral as to whether rendering investment services without a licence turns the relevant contract into a void or voidable contract. This means, that the Dutch approach that such contract is simply valid is compatible with the EU principle of effectiveness, as long as the client has a real possibility to claim compensation through another route, such as by means of instituting a damages claim. But the converse is also true. In England and Wales, section 26(1) of FSMA explicitly provides that agreements made by persons who carry on a regulated activity if they are neither authorised nor exempt, are unenforceable against the other person. Section 26(2) provides that the other person, ie the bank's client, is entitled to recover any money or other property paid or transferred by that person to the offender and to recover compensation for any loss sustained by him as a result of having parted with it. However, section 28(3) provides that if the court is satisfied that it is just and equitable in the circumstances of the case, it may allow the agreement to be enforced and property paid or transferred under the agreement to be retained.[214] All this is fine from the perspective of the European principle of effectiveness as long as the customer has a real possibility to obtain compensation.

K. MiFID Assessments by the Courts of their own Motion in Relation to Private Investors?

This brings us, finally, to what we regard as an intriguing question that has a bearing on the intensity with which MiFID impacts private law. At present, the

[213] See Spanish Chapter, s II.B, *in fine*, s III, n 54. The decision was followed in subsequent decisions.

[214] See van Setten and Plews (n 118) § 11.111–11.113; Tison, 'The Civil Law Effects of MiFID in a Comparative Perspective' (n 128) 2621–3269, 2626.

parties to a legal action are often unaware that they could invoke an infringement of MiFID (conduct-of-business) rules. Are the civil courts obliged in such cases to determine of their own motion whether the MiFID (conduct-of-business) rules have been infringed? We would certainly not exclude this possibility.

It is apparent from the settled case-law of the Court of Justice that the national courts must determine of their own motion whether, on the basis of the European principle of effectiveness, unreasonably onerous clauses in contracts between businesses and consumers are 'unfair' within the meaning of Directive 93/13/EEC.[215] The Court of Justice may also direct the civil courts to determine of their own motion whether the legislation is applicable.[216]

Indeed, it would seem to be extending the protection to the entire field of consumer protection directives. Recently, the Court of Justice gave such a direction in the case of the Consumer Purchases Directive.[217] In any event, the MiFID conduct-of-business rules can, in our view, be treated as consumer protection provisions insofar as they must be observed in relation to private investors.[218] National civil courts should in that case determine of their own motion whether there has been an infringement of MiFID conduct-of-business rules in disputes between investment firms and private investors.

V. The Role of Financial Regulators in Settling Disputes

In the majority of the jurisdictions covered by this book, the competent financial regulators seem to play an active role in settling disputes between banks and clients, either formally or informally.

This is first and foremost the case in the US. The seminal case *SEC v Capital Gains Research Burea*,[219] is illustrative in this regard. The Court held that the SEC could obtain an injunction under the Advisers Act compelling a registered investment adviser to disclose to his clients a practice known as 'scalping'—'purchasing shares of a security for his own account shortly before recommending

[215] OJ L 95/29, 21 April 1993.

[216] See ECJ 26 October 2006, C-168/05, *NJ* 2007/201, with note by Mok (*Mostaza Claro*); ECJ 4 June 2009, C-243/08, *NJ* 2009/395, with note by Mok (*Pannon*); ECJ 6 October 2009, C-40/08, *NJ* 2010/11 (*Asturcom*); ECJ 30 May 2013, *NJ* 2013/487, with note by Mok (*Asbeek Brusse and De Man Garabito*); ECJ 28 July 2016, C-168/15, *AA* 2016/658, with note by Hartkamp (*Milena Tomášová v Ministerstvo spravodlivosti SR ea*); ECJ 21 December 2016, C-154/15, C-307/15 and C-308/15 (floor clauses).

[217] Directive 1999/44/EC, OJ L 171/12, 07 July 1999. See ECJ 3 October 2013, C-32/12, *AA* 2015/222, with note by Hartkamp (*Soledad Duarte Hueros v Autociba*); ECJ 4 June 2014, C-497/13, *Ars Aequi* 2015/816, with note by Hartkamp (*Froukje Faber v Autobedrijf Hazet Ochten BV*). See also A Ancery and B Krans, 'Ambsthalve toepassing van consumentenrecht: grensbepaling en praktische kwesties' (2016) *Ars Aequi* 2016, 825–30.

[218] One of the key objectives of MIFID is to offer a high level of investor protection. See Recital (2) to MiFID I and Recital (70) to MiFID II.

[219] 375 U.S. 180 (1963).

that security for a long-term investment and then immediately selling the shares for a profit following the recommendation'.[220] It is noteworthy that FINRA, the self-regulatory organisation (SRO) for registered US broker-dealers, also helps uncover and remedy fraudulent or illegal practices in the industry, and awarded a record $34 million in restitution to consumers in 2012. FINRA may also refer wrongdoing to the SEC, which may seek disgorgement in court or by settlement. In one notable case involving the SEC, a federal court established a claims fund for victims of Prudential Securities, with about $940 million in distributions from the fund.[221] The active role of the SEC over the last 50 years or so may perhaps be explained by the fact 'that there exists [only] a limited private remedy under the [Advisers Act] to void an investment adviser's contract, [and] the Act confers no other private causes of action, legal or equitable'.[222] Thus, litigation to enforce the fiduciary standards established by the Advisers Act is limited to SEC enforcement actions, and private damages claims for breaches of an investment adviser's fiduciary duties or negligence are a matter of state law.[223]

The UK Financial Conduct Authority (FCA) (formerly the UK Financial Services Authority (FSA)) has similar powers to the SEC. Pursuant to Part XXV of FSMA the FCA may apply for injunctions and restitution orders.[224] It is also notable that the FCA and the former FSA both played an active role in utilising the Financial Ombudsman Service (FOS) to settle disputes between banks and retail clients and small business customers. Part XVI of FSMA established the FOS, which provides a scheme to allow customer complaints to be adjudicated against financial services firms in cases involving general insurance, banking and credit, and investment. The Ombudsman regime has been extensively utilised to file millions of claims against banks for mis-selling financial products, including payment protection insurance (PPI) and derivative products such as interest rate swaps.[225]

In Ireland, section 43(1) of the Central Bank (Supervision and Enforcement) Act 2013 grants the Central Bank power to direct that redress be afforded to customers of a regulated financial services provider where they have suffered or

[220] ibid, 181. See US Chapter, s III.C.ii.a.

[221] See US Chapter, s III.C.ii.b.

[222] *Transamerica Mortg Advisors, Inc*, 444 U.S. at 24, see US Chapter, s III.C.ii.a and n 221. As amended in 1970, the Advisers Act also 'impose[s] upon investment advisers a "fiduciary duty" with respect to compensation received from a mutual fund, 15 U.S.C. § 80a-35(b), and grant[s] individual investors a private right of action for breach of that duty, *ibid*'; *Jones v Harris Assocs LP*, 130 S Ct 1418, 1423 (2010). See US Chapter, s III.C.ii.a, n 221.

[223] See US Chapter, s III.C.ii.a. See *Davis v Merrill Lynch, Pierce, Fenner & Smith, Inc*, 906 F.2d 1206, 1215 (8th Cir 1990) ('The question of whether a fiduciary relationship exists is a question of state law'.); *Stokes v Henson*, 217 Cal App 3d 187, 265 Cal Rptr 836 (Cal Ct App 1990) (affirming judgment against investment adviser for breach of fiduciary duty under California law), referred to in US Chapter, s III.C.ii.a, n 222.

[224] See extensively G McMeel and J Virgo, *McMeel and Virgo on Financial Advice and Financial Products*, 3rd edn (Oxford: Oxford University Press, 2014) § 18.228–§ 18.292.

[225] See Chapter on England and Wales, s I.C. See for an in-depth analysis McMeel and Virgo, *McMeel and Virgo on Financial Advice and Financial Products* (n 224) § 19.22–§ 19.113.

will suffer a loss as a result of widespread or regular relevant defaults by a regulated financial services provider.[226] Furthermore, section 54 the Central Bank (Supervision and Enforcement) Act 2013 empowers the Central Bank to apply to the High Court for a 'restitution order' in cases where a sanction has been imposed on a person pursuant to specified statutory provisions or where the person has been convicted of an offence under financial services legislation and there has been unjust enrichment or loss. The restitution order will require the regulated financial service provider concerned to provide to the Central Bank an amount equal to the unjust gain or loss, which the Central Bank would then distribute.[227]

The French financial regulator—formerly the Commission des opérations de bourse, now the Autorité des marchés financiers—has also played an active role in settling disputes between financial institutions and clients since 1991. However, it was only in 2003[228] that the French lawmaker passed a law that has given it a legal basis. According to Article L 621-19, Monetary and Financial Code,

> The Autorité des Marchés Financiers is authorised to deal with claims from any interested party relating to matters within its competence and to resolve them appropriately. Where the conditions so permit, it proposes a friendly settlement of the disputes submitted to it, via arbitration or mediation.[229]

In Spain, the so-called Claims Service of the Bank of Spain draws up an annual report which includes a description of the claims received and a determination of what it considers as reasonable banking practices. The annual report is not formally binding on the banks it concerns, but the report has some persuasive authority. It is also worth mentioning Real Decreto-ley 6/2013, of 22 March, specifically designed to resolve disputes on claims concerning the sale of preferred stock and subordinated debt issued by banks being the subject of a state-controlled restructuring process.[230] Real Decreto-ley 6/2013 created a special arbitration process and constituted the so-called 'Commission for Monitoring Hybrid Capital and Subordinated Debt Instruments' (CMHC). CMHC determined the basic criteria to give the investor guidance as to whether his claim will be upheld by the arbitrators. It should however be noted that the CMHC criteria were not formally binding on the arbitrators. The arbitrations took place under private law conducted by private arbitrators. The arbitration procedures did not formally constitute dispute settlement by financial regulators, but the proceedings were established by law and to some extent controlled by the framework set up by CMHC.[231]

[226] See Irish Chapter, s VI.

[227] See Irish Chapter, s VI.

[228] Law n° 2003-707, 1er August 2003, *de sécurité financière*. Referred to in the French Chapter, s VIII, n 101.

[229] See French Chapter, s VIII.

[230] The public body in charge of the restructuring process is the Fund for Orderly Bank Restructuring (FROB), regulated by Act 9/2012, of 14 November 2012, the Act on restructuring and resolution of banks. See Spanish Chapter, s VI.

[231] See Spanish Chapter, s VI.

In the Italian chapter, mention is made of (1) the Banking-Financial Arbitrator (Arbitro Bancario Finanziario, ABF), which is part of the Bank of Italy, and (2) the Conciliation and Arbitration Chamber (Camera di Conciliazione e Arbitrato, CCA), replaced as of 9 January 2017 by the Financial Disputes Arbitrator (Arbitro per le Controversie Finanziarie, ACF), which are both part of financial markets regulator Consob. Both the ABF and the CCA were established in 2005 by Law no 262, enacted as a reaction to certain corporate scandals. ACF was instead established in 2016 in light of the modest success of CCA. While ABF is however not competent for dispute settlement on investment services and investment activities, CCA and ACF are competent to deal with such disputes, but only with respect to retail investors. In 2010, a few years after the introduction of ABF and CCA, the Italian legislator took a further initiative affecting ADRs (also) in financial law matters, by enacting Legislative Decree 4 March 2010, no 28. For many years Italian courts have been experiencing great workloads, whose main effect is that, on average, first instance civil proceedings take not less than three years, so the legislator decided to introduce a mandatory regulation of mediation in civil and commercial matters. Indeed, failure to proceed with this attempt shall result in the preclusion of the claim before ordinary courts. 'Insurance, banking and financial agreements' are included in the list of matters to which such obligation is imposed. It is further provided that the attempt for conciliation under Legislative Decree no 28/2010 shall take place before a body entered in the register kept by the Ministry of Justice. As regards disputes concerning 'Insurance, banking and financial agreements', it has been established that this condition could be satisfied also by using proceedings before the ABF or before the CCA/ACF.[232]

Finally, in the Netherlands, neither the conduct of business regulator AFM, nor prudential regulator DNB, have formal powers to settle disputes between banks and their clients. The same is true for the Dutch Ministry of Finance. Nevertheless, both the AFM and the Ministry of Finance played an active role in settling the massive mis-selling of interest rate swaps to SMEs. In a first stage, the AFM investigated individual interest rate swap contracts with SMEs and concluded that in many cases the MiFID rules pertaining to interest rate swaps had not been complied with. In many cases the client had been insufficiently informed about the mechanics of interest rate swaps in general, and the benefits and risk of any such product for their individual situation. The AFM requested the banks concerned to re-evaluate individual interest rate swap contracts and to the extent necessary compensate their clients. However, the process was badly managed by the AFM and the banks did not fully cooperate. As a result, under pressure from the Dutch Minister of Finance, and in line with the advice of the AFM, the Ministry of Finance appointed a Derivatives Committee (Derivatencommissie), consisting of

[232] See Italian Chapter, s IV.

three independent experts to draw up a uniform settlement framework for derivatives with SMEs (*Uniform Herstelkader Rentederivaten MKB*). On 5 July 2016, the committee published the framework. Under considerable pressure from the Ministry of Finance, the relevant banks in the end accepted the framework.[233] In the view of many commentators, the whole process was far too lengthy. In view of this, some commentators propose a law reform to the effect that the AFM obtains true powers to settle disputes between banks and clients, very much like the UK FCA.[234] The Dutch Ministry of Finance recently solicited stakeholder views on whether the AFM should have formal powers to settle disputes between banks and their clients.[235]

So, all in all, the picture that emerges is that the traditional distinction between public and private law is increasingly blurred. Whether or not this is a good development remains to be seen. In any event, Andrew Bailey, CEO of the FCA since July 2016, accepted that its administrative ad hoc mass redress schemes have not been successful, in particular not for swaps. According to Bailey, the FCA should empower an independent entity to resolve disputes between banks and consumers and should not seek to involve itself in their determination. On 15 December 2016, Members of Parliament debated a motion that the FCA should set up a permanent Financial Services Tribunal modelled on the Employment Tribunals. The motion was carried.[236]

It may gleaned from the foregoing that when it comes to damages claims from investors, courts in continental Europe are generally more investor friendly than courts in the common law countries. Courts impose duties of care on banks in a more extensive way and it also looks like the threshold for breaching such a duty is more easily reached than in common law countries. The same goes for the breach of a statutory duty. Under United States federal law, the breach of a statutory rule is not even privately enforceable.

However, this does not necessarily mean that private investors in continental European jurisdictions are better off than in common law countries. In the latter countries, regulatory authorities generally play a more active role than their continental European counterparts. In the United States, the SEC enforces statutory duties that apply to broker-dealers and in the United Kingdom, the Financial Conduct Authority has similar legal powers (and uses these powers) to apply for

[233] See for further information: www.derivatencommissie.nl/.

[234] See *Financieele Dagblad*, 'Juridisch gat bij swaps moet dicht' (6 July 2016) 2.

[235] See p 12 of the consultation document mentioned in § II.5, last para: Ministerie van Financiën, *Consultatiedocument—Effectiviteit en gewenste mate van bescherming voor zzp-ers en mkb-ers bij financiële diensten en producten* (1 September 2016) (available at: www.internetconsultatie.nl/consultatiebeschermingkleinzakelijk). See Dutch Chapter, s XI.

[236] See Richard Samuel, Tools for Culture Change: FCA, now you are listening! Time to build an independent, low cost forum for conduct dispute resolution, *CMLJ* 2017/2. See also Richard Samuel, Tools for changing banking culture: FCA are you listening?, *CMLJ* 2016/2.

injunctions and restitution orders, hence pushing banks to deal with claims of investors for mis-sold services and products and to provide them with fair compensation. This effect is also facilitated by the role of the Financial Ombudsman Service. Particularly when it comes to claims regarding similar financial products and services, it may very well be that private investors are better off in common law jurisdictions, as they do not need to go to court (individually or as a group), saving time and money in litigation. In individual cases this may mean that an investor is less well off than if he had gone to court but overall the protection for investors may be stronger.

In continental European jurisdictions, regulators do not have the same legal powers as a private claims enforcer or they do not use their powers as forcefully as the UK and the US regulators. In France, where conditions permit, the 'Autorité des Marchés Financiers' proposes friendly settlements of the disputes submitted to it, via arbitration or mediation. The annual report of the Claims Service of the Bank of Spain lists the claims received and a determination of what it considers as reasonable banking practices but these determinations are not formally binding on the banks it concerns. In the Netherlands, the financial regulators do not have legal powers to settle disputes between banks and their clients. An attempt to informally nudge banks to provide redress to buyers of mis-sold products went awry and induced calls to provide the regulators with effective legal powers. In some countries, like in Spain and Italy, regulators only recently obtained new powers and it is not yet clear how effective these powers are or how effectively they are and will be used.

The lack of legal powers of continental regulators makes private litigation by individual investors or by group actions the only effective avenue to obtain redress. As this litigation is costly and lengthy many investors will refrain from it and bear their losses. This increases the social costs of mis-sold financial products and exacerbates the externalising effect of the banks' wrongful conduct.

To a considerable extent, group actions may make up for this negative effect but most jurisdictions do not allow such actions or make them very cumbersome. Remarkably, bar the Netherlands, the strongest limitations on group actions are again in continental European jurisdictions. In countries where both the regulators have limited powers to settle disputes and force banks to provide redress to customers and group actions are not or only very limitedly possible, it is likely that there is a large enforcement deficit when it comes to compliance with the banks' statutory duties of care.

This picture coincides with the generally more active and repressive approach of Anglo-American regulators and prosecutors when it comes to violating the rules of the free market. When it comes to criminal prosecution, the number of convictions in the framework of the financial industry with respect to mis-sold financial products and rigged interest rates is relatively low in the United States and the United Kingdom, but they are still considerably higher than the number of convictions in continental Europe. The same goes for the regulatory fines imposed on financial institutions.

Although links between governments and the corporate world are generally close,[237] it seems that these links work out differently in the Anglo-American world than in continental Europe. Whilst the political influence of big money seems to be bigger in the Anglo-American world, this love affair usually comes to an end where fundamental principles of the free market are violated. In continental Europe, the criminal and administrative response is weaker. This calls into question the independence of continental European prosecutors with respect to crimes related to national corporate interests.

One explanation for this may be that the inherent support for the principle of the free market is weaker and, perhaps for that reason, violation of this principle is considered to be less severe and serious and therefore less eligible for punishment. This difference in approach may also be linked to a generally more consensual approach in politics and society in continental Europe, and a more adversarial approach in the Anglo-American world.

VI. The Bigger Picture and Reform Perspectives

A. General

This book has been concerned with a bank's duty of care, a private law device geared to investor protection. But as we have seen, in not all the jurisdictions covered by the book is this the term of art. Especially in common law jurisdictions the term 'duty of care' is bound to cause confusion. Therefore, we also included discussion on more or less functionally similar concepts, such as fiduciary duties and all kinds of statutory duties. Also, it was not the legal concepts as such that we focused on, but rather the essential duties which typically flow from these concepts, ie duties to investigate, duties to disclose or warn, and—in exceptional cases—outright duties to refuse to render financial services or products. In the remainder of this section we will nevertheless use the term 'duty of care' as a convenient shorthand.

Of course, the bank's duty of care does not operate in a vacuum. A bank's duty of care should also be viewed against the backdrop of the bigger picture. Section IV on the private law effect of MiFID already made this clear and the same is true for the previous paragraph on financial regulators settling disputes between banks and their customers. In this final section, we would like to highlight some recent reform proposals which enable us to put the bank's duty of care into a larger perspective.

[237] eg in 2016, the OECD concluded that many economically advanced countries are failing to fully enforce regulations on political party funding and campaign donations or are leaving loopholes that can be exploited by powerful private interest groups, in particular big corporations and their lobbyists: *Funding Democracy: Funding of Political Parties and Election Campaigns and the Risk of Policy Capture* (Paris: OECD, 2016) www.oecd.org/governance/financing-democracy-9789264249455-en.htm.

B. Product Governance and Product Intervention

First of all, the case-law mentioned in this book clearly shows that some of the financial products sold in recent years have not been in the interests of the client, such as interest rate swaps sold to SMEs in many European countries. This is why consideration has been given to ways of nipping this problem in the bud, in other words by preventing harmful products from even reaching the market. Under MiFID II this has taken the form of a mandatory product approval process.[238] But, as usual, firms will look for ways around these requirements. It would be naive to think that product approval schemes could in practice guarantee that harmful products are no longer marketed. This is why the existence of safety nets continues to be of paramount importance. The bank's duty of care is one of those safety nets and will therefore continue to play its part. MiFID II also introduces another safety net, taking the form of a power for the national competent authorities (NCAs) and also for the European Securities and Markets Authority (ESMA) and European Banking Authority (EBA) to remove harmful products from the market—a system known as product intervention.[239]

The following is also noteworthy. As we have seen, the bank's duty of care very much revolves around duties of disclosure and duties to warn so as to enable the investor to make an informed investment decision. In other words, an essential aim of the bank's duty of care is to safeguard that the investor understands the characteristics and the risks of the product or service involved. In addition, KYC rules—the other essential ingredient of a bank's duty of care—aim to make sure that a product or service meets the investor's needs and is also otherwise appropriate for him. To effectively meet the bank's duty of care, the relevant bank staff must have the necessary expertise. This should go without saying, but the financial crisis revealed that in many cases bank staff did not fully understand the bank's products and services, and the same was true for the needs of the investors concerned. In view of this, the new product governance rules explicitly stipulate that manufacturers of financial products must ensure that relevant staff involved in the manufacturing of products possess the necessary expertise to understand the characteristics and risks of the products they intend to manufacture.[240] Distributors

[238] MiFID II, Art 9(3)(b), 16(3), second to seventh subparas, 24(2). See also the Draft Commission Delegated Directive, C(2016) 2031 final, 7 April 2016, Arts 9 and 10.

[239] MiFIR, Arts 39–43. See also of the Draft Commission Delegated Regulation C(2016) 2860 final, 18 May 2016, Arts 19–21. See also MiFID II, Art 69(2)(s) and (t). See for more detail on product governance and product intervention: D Busch, 'Product Governance and Product Intervention under MiFID II/MiFIR' in D Busch and G Ferrarini, 'Regulation of the EU Financial Markets: MiFID II and MiFIR' (Oxford: Oxford University Press, 2017) 123–46.

[240] Draft Commission Delegated Directive, C(2016) 2031 final, 7 April 2016, Art 9(5) (financial instruments), in conjunction with Art 1(2) (structured deposits). See also ESMA/2014/1569, *Final Report—ESMA's Technical Advice to the Commission on MiFID II and MiFIR* (19 December 2014) 56 (no 6). *Cf* also the corporate governance requirement that the management body should approve the internal organisation of the firm, including criteria for the selection, training, knowledge, skills and experience of the staff. See MiFID II, Art 9(3)(a) (financial instruments) in conjunction with Art 1(4), opening words and (a) (structured deposits); see also Recital (54) to MiFID II.

have a comparable obligation. However, they must ensure not only that relevant staff understand the characteristics and risk of the products they are distributing, but also the needs, characteristics and objectives of the identified target market.[241] This duty ties in with developments reported in some of the previous chapters. In Germany, banks may only recommend investments whose characteristics and risk they understand, whereas in the Italian chapter the Know your Merchandise rule is alluded to.[242]

C. Reclassification of Dealing on own Account to Dealing on Behalf of the Client

Another important innovation of MiFID II clearly geared to better investor protection is the following. MiFID II reclassifies certain cases of dealing on own account (an investment activity) as dealing on behalf of the client (an investment service). In consequence, all kinds of MiFID conduct-of-business rules will become applicable to cases of dealing on own account that are reclassified as dealing on behalf of the client. This reclassification has important consequences for investor protection. If a bank deals wholly or partly on behalf of the investor (as intermediary or representative), it is subjected to all kinds of conduct-of-business rules. If, on the other hand, a bank enters into a transaction with an investor solely as a contractual counterparty, it owes few if any conduct-of-business rules pursuant to MiFID. Once it has been established that the firm is acting on behalf of the client, the level of protection depends next on the classification of the client and the exact framework in which the transactions are carried out (ie whether the transactions involve execution-only, investment advice or portfolio management services). In any event, this reclassification concerns the following two situations.

First, the definition of 'execution of orders on behalf of clients' has been modified to such an extent that some instances of dealing on own account have been reclassified and brought within its ambit, with the result that the definition of 'dealing on own account' is now much narrower. Likewise, under MiFID II the phrase 'the conclusion of agreements to sell financial instruments issued by an investment firm or credit institution at the moment of their issuance' comes within the definition of 'execution of orders on behalf of clients'.[243] What is the exact scope of this change? Some examples may help to clarify this. If a bank sells

[241] Draft Commission Delegated Directive, C(2016) 2031 final, 7 April 2016, Art 10(7), (financial instruments), in conjunction with Art 1(2) (structured deposits). See also ESMA/2014/1569, *Final Report—ESMA's Technical Advice to the Commission on MiFID II and MiFIR* (19 December 2014) 60 (no 27). See also MiFID II, Art 24(2), second para, (financial instruments) in conjunction with Art 1(4), opening words and (b) (structured deposits), which provides that 'an investment firm shall understand the financial instruments they offer or recommend'.

[242] See German Chapter, s III.B.iv; Italian Chapter, s II.B, where reference is made to the 'know your merchandise rule'.

[243] MIFID II, Art 4 lid 1 sub (5).

an investor shares in its own capital at the time of issuance and the sale does not involve the provision of any form of investment service, the bank acts solely as the investor's contractual counterparty. Under MiFID this is an instance of dealing on own account. Under MiFID II, however, it is reclassified as acting on behalf of the client and is suddenly treated as a form of investment service. Issuance is usually taken to mean the issuance of marketable shares and bonds, but in MiFID II it has a broader meaning. In the terminology of MiFID II the concept of issuance is linked to financial instruments. This means that where a bank acts as contractual counterparty in an interest rate swap this too is treated as the conclusion of an agreement for the sale, at the time of issuance, of a financial instrument issued by a bank. After all, an interest rate swap is a financial instrument, like many other derivatives. This interpretation also benefits investor protection, which is one of the key objectives of MiFID and MiFID II. Recital (45) in the preamble to MiFID II explicitly states that this reclassification is intended 'to eliminate uncertainty and strengthen investor protection'.

Second, although this is not apparent from the broadening of the definition of 'execution of orders on behalf of clients' but from Recital (24) in the preamble to MiFID II, matched principal trading (back-to-back trading) is regarded, inter alia, as execution of orders on behalf of the client, although under MiFID it was treated solely as dealing on own account. In Article 4(1), point (38), of MiFID II matched principal trading is defined as

> a transaction where the facilitator interposes itself between the buyer and the seller to the transaction in such a way that it is never exposed to market risk throughout the execution of the transaction, with both sides executed simultaneously, and where the transaction is concluded at a price where the facilitator makes no profit or loss, other than a previously disclosed commission, fee or charge for the transaction.

In terms of economic result, matched principal trading resembles the position in which the firm acts on both sides of a transaction for the client, ie matching opposite client orders (agency crosses).[244]

These two instances of reclassification enhance investor protection, but in our view this is not sufficient. If a bank sells a financial instrument that it has not issued itself, we cannot see any reason why the investor should not enjoy the protection of the MiFID conduct-of-business rules that apply to execution-only services. This approach is also in keeping with the reasonable expectations of

[244] More precisely, Recital (24) in the preamble to MiFID II provides that 'dealing on own account when executing client orders [ie (systematic) internalisation] should include firms executing orders from different clients by matching them on a matched principal basis (back-to-back trading), which should be regarded as acting as principal and should be subject to the provisions of this Directive covering both the execution of orders on behalf of clients and dealing on own account'. Equating matched principal trading with (systematic) internalisation is in fact based on a fallacy. In economic terms, matched principal trading much more closely resembles agency crosses, as opposite client orders are in fact matched with one another.

the investor, certainly in the case of a retail investor. An investor may reasonably expect the bank used by him to look after his interests adequately and thus to observe certain conduct-of-business rules towards him. The bank is, after all, ideally placed to use its expertise. Its fund of knowledge is bound to be superior to that of an investor, particularly a retail investor.[245] Nor is this any different where the bank acts purely as the investor's contractual counterparty. In such cases, the investor is reasonably entitled to expect the bank to observe the same conduct-of-business rules that would apply if it were providing an execution-only service. Moreover, the distinction between dealing on own account (principal dealing) on the one hand and trading on behalf of the client (and other forms of investment service) on the other is tenuous, arbitrary and easy to manipulate. This is all the more so where a contractual clause providing that a bank acts solely as contractual counterparty is claimed to apply even where an employee of the bank advises the investor, contrary to the terms of the agreement.[246] Clearly, MiFID II also provides no practicable criterion. Indeed, to achieve an adequate level of investor protection MiFID II resorts to the artifice of reclassifying certain types of dealing on own account as acting on behalf of the client. Moreover, as already became clear in the Dutch chapter and in this chapter, the Dutch Supreme Court has already extended the special civil duty of care to dealing on own account. In a case involving the offering of risky and complex financial products to retail investors, it held that it followed from the special civil duty of care that there was a duty to warn investors of the risks involved and a duty to comply with KYC rules, even though the bank was only acting as contractual counterparty.[247] Finally, the UK government

[245] In fact, the European Commission acknowledges in its letter to the Committee of European Securities Regulators (CESR) of 19 March 2007 that the investor's reasonable expectations play an important role in answering the question of whether in a given case the bank transacts as agent or solely as principal. That is understandable, since whether or not the bank transacts as agent or solely as principal is a matter of interpretation of the legal relationship. But this approach has its limits. If it is absolutely clear on the facts that the bank transacted solely as principal, it is not possible to argue that the bank in fact transacted as agent. Preferably, therefore, the distinction between acting as agent and acting as principal should simply no longer be treated as relevant in determining the degree of investor protection. For the European Commission's letter, see: Working Document ESC- 07- 2007, Commission answers to CESR scope issues under MiFID and implementing directive (Appendix to CESR, Best Execution under MiFID, Questions & Answers, May 2007, CESR/ 07- 320.

[246] This may be illustrated by the Scottish case *Grant Estates Ltd v The Royal Bank of Scotland plc*, Court of Session 21 August 2012 [2012] CSOH 133. In this case Lord Hodge (now one of the Justices in the UK Supreme Court) held that a clause providing that the bank acted solely as contractual counterparty was valid, despite the fact that an employee had advised the investor. See extensively on this case: D Busch, 'Agency and Principal Dealing under MiFID I and MiFID II' in Busch and Ferrarini, *Regulation of the EU Financial Markets* (n 239) 227–49; D Busch, 'Agency and Principal Dealing under the Markets in Financial Instruments Directive' in D Busch, L Macgregor and P Watts (eds), *Agency Law in Commercial Practice* (Oxford: Oxford University Press, 2016) 141–75. See for similar cases in England & Wales: *Green & Rawley v RBS* [2013] EWCA Civ 1197; *Thornbridge v Barclays* [2015] EWHC 3430 (QB).

[247] See HR 5 June 2009, *JOR* 2009/199, annotated by Lieverse (*Treek v Dexia Bank Nederland*), consideration 5.2.1. See Dutch Chapter, s II.B; ch 2, s III, *in fine*; this chapter, s II.B.iii.c.

(in response to the Kay Review) takes the view that duties of care must also apply where a bank acts solely as an investor's contractual counterparty.[248] Under a future MiFID III, a bank which acts solely as contractual counterparty should be required to observe the same conduct-of-business rules as apply in the case of an execution-only service.[249]

D. Plain Language

Information provided in plain language is essential for consumers and other inexperienced investors. The reality is very different. Information on the characteristics and risks of financial products and services normally takes the shape of very detailed information, expressed in complex language containing highly complex legal and financial terms. MiFID I does not remedy this and the same is true for MiFID II. Under MiFID II, the information paradigm is still predominant. Investor protection is therefore still about providing investors with the information that will enable them to make an informed investment decision. Under MiFID II the amount of information that must be provided to investors is set to increase rather than decrease and the information will also have to be more detailed. This is despite the fact that many people doubt whether the huge volume of information provided really helps investors to make informed and well-considered decisions.[250]

But there is hope. On a national level, it is notable that the Italian Supreme Court emphasises that information should be provided in plain language and that contractual documents should be written in plain language.[251] The Bank of Spain follows a similar path. The Bank of Spain has developed and systematised in detail the issues which contracts should explicitly and clearly explain (sixth standard of Circular 5/2012, 27 June). This standard specifies that contracts should be drafted in clear and understandable language. Banks should avoid using technical jargon, and when its use is inevitable, they must properly explain the meaning.[252]

On a European level, we refer to the Commission draft of the Prospectus Regulation published on 30 November 2015 which will replace the current Prospectus

[248] BIS, *Ensuring Equity Markets support Long-term Growth.* The Government response to the Kay review (November 2012) para 2.8.

[249] For an in-depth analysis of this issue see Busch, 'Agency and Principal Dealing under MiFID I and MiFID II' (n 246) 227–49; Busch, 'Agency and Principal Dealing under the Markets in Financial Instruments Directive' (n 246) 141–75.

[250] See eg N Moloney, *How to Protect Investors—Lessons from the EC and the UK* (Cambridge: Cambridge University Press 2010) 288 et seq; L Enriques and S Gilotta, 'Disclosure & Financial Markets Regulation' in N Moloney, E Ferran and J Payne, *The Oxford Handbook of Financial Regulation* (Oxford: Oxford University Press, 2015) 511–36; V Colaert, 'Building Blocks of Investor Protection—All-embracing Regulation Tightens its Grip (draft paper, to be published); K Broekhuizen, 'Klantbelang, belangenconflict en zorgplicht' (The Hague: Boom juridische uitgevers, 2017).

[251] Italian Chapter, s II.C.

[252] Spanish Chapter, s IV.

Directive. Consideration (23) of the Draft Commission Prospectus Regulation states the following:

> The summary of the prospectus should be short, simple, clear and easy for investors to understand. It should be drafted in plain, non-technical language, presenting the information in an easily accessible way. It should not be a mere compilation of excerpts from the prospectus. It is appropriate to set a maximum length for the summary in order to ensure that investors are not deterred from reading it and to encourage issuers to select the information which is essential for investors.[253]

E. Financial Literacy and Financial Education

Finally, there is the importance of financial literacy and financial education. Their importance in enhancing investor protection is widely accepted by the stakeholders in this discussion.[254] The Organisation for Economic Cooperation and Development (OECD) is especially active in this field. OECD, with the guidance of the International Network on Financial Education, and in consultation with a wide range of stakeholders, develops best practices and principles to help increase financial literacy and raise awareness.[255] The European Commission and the European Parliament also have a keen interest in this topic, but according to Article 165 of the Treaty on the Functioning of the European Union, EU Member States are responsible for legislation on education. Therefore, actions in the field of financial education at EU level can only take the shape of incentive measures.[256] In 2015 the European Banking Federation published a useful report listing national good practices in 32 European countries.[257]

[253] See for the proposal and further information: http://ec.europa.eu/finance/securities/prospectus/index_en.htm.

[254] See for an overview EP briefing May 2015, 'Improving the Financial Literacy of European Consumers' available at www.europarl.europa.eu. See extensively on investor education: Moloney, *How to Protect Investors—Lessons from the EC and the UK* (n 250) 374 et seq.

[255] See www.financial-education.org/standards.html.

[256] See for an overview of these measures EP briefing, 'Improving the Financial Literacy of European Consumers' (n 254).

[257] See the document 'Financial Education—National Strategies in Europe—Good Practices Report', European Banking Federation (March 2015) available at: www.ebf-fbe.eu.

INDEX